(Continued on back endsheets)

American Short-Story Writers Since World War II

Dictionary of Literary Biography® • Volume One Hundred Thirty

American Short-Story Writers Since World War II

Edited by
Patrick Meanor
State University of New York College at Oneonta

A Bruccoli Clark Layman Book
Gale Research Inc.
Detroit, Washington, D.C., London

Printed in the United States of America

Published simultaneously in the United Kingdom
by Gale Research International Limited
(An affiliated company of Gale Research Inc.)

The paper used in this publication meets the minimum requirements
of American National Standard for Information Sciences–Permanence
Paper for Printed Library Materials, ANSI Z39.48-1984. ∞ ™

Library of Congress Catalog Card Number 93-078551
ISBN 0–8103–5389-X

I(T)P™

The trademark ITP is used under license.
10 9 8 7 6 5 4 3 2 1

Contents

Plan of the Series

The advisory board, the editors, and the publisher of the *Dictionary of Literary Biography* are joined in endorsing Mark Twain's declaration. The literature of a nation provides an inexhaustible resource of permanent worth. We intend to make literature and its creators better understood and more accessible to students and the reading public, while satisfying the standards of teachers and scholars.

To meet these requirements, *literary biography* has been construed in terms of the author's achievement. The most important thing about a writer is his writing. Accordingly, the entries in *DLB* are career biographies, tracing the development of the author's canon and the evolution of his reputation.

The purpose of *DLB* is not only to provide reliable information in a convenient format but also to place the figures in the larger perspective of literary history and to offer appraisals of their accomplishments by qualified scholars.

The publication plan for *DLB* resulted from two years of preparation. The project was proposed to Bruccoli Clark by Frederick C. Ruffner, president of the Gale Research Company, in November 1975. After specimen entries were prepared and typeset, an advisory board was formed to refine the entry format and develop the series rationale. In meetings held during 1976, the publisher, series editors, and advisory board approved the scheme for a comprehensive biographical dictionary of persons who contributed to North American literature. Editorial work on the first volume began in January 1977, and it was published in 1978. In order to make *DLB* more than a reference tool and to compile volumes that individually have claim to status as literary history, it was decided to organize volumes by topic, period, or genre. Each of these freestanding volumes provides a biographical-bibliographical guide and overview for a particular area of literature. We are convinced that this organization — as opposed to a single alphabet method — constitutes a valuable innovation in the presentation of reference material. The volume plan necessarily requires many decisions for the placement and treatment of authors who might properly be included in two or three volumes. In some instances a major figure will be included in separate volumes, but with different entries emphasizing the aspect of his career appropriate to each volume. Ernest Hemingway, for example, is represented in *American Writers in Paris, 1920–1939* by an entry focusing on his expatriate apprenticeship; he is also in *American Novelists, 1910–1945* with an entry surveying his entire career. Each volume includes a cumulative index of the subject authors and articles. Comprehensive indexes to the entire series are planned.

With volume ten in 1982 it was decided to enlarge the scope of *DLB*. By the end of 1986 twenty-one volumes treating British literature had been published, and volumes for Commonwealth and Modern European literature were in progress. The series has been further augmented by the *DLB Yearbooks* (since 1981) which update published entries and add new entries to keep the *DLB* current with contemporary activity. There have also been *DLB Documentary Series* volumes which provide biographical and critical source materials for figures whose work is judged to have particular interest for students. One of these companion volumes is entirely devoted to Tennessee Williams.

We define literature as the *intellectual commerce of a nation:* not merely as belles lettres but as that ample and complex process by which ideas are generated, shaped, and transmitted. *DLB* entries are not limited to "creative writers" but extend to other figures who in their time and in their way influenced the mind of a people. Thus the series encompasses historians, journalists, publishers, and screenwriters. By this means readers of *DLB* may be aided to perceive literature not as cult scripture in the keeping of intellectual high priests but firmly positioned at the center of a nation's life.

DLB includes the major writers appropriate to each volume and those standing in the ranks immediately behind them. Scholarly and critical counsel has been sought in deciding which minor figures to include and how full their entries should be. Wherever possible, useful references are made to figures who do not warrant separate entries.

Each *DLB* volume has a volume editor responsible for planning the volume, selecting the figures for inclusion, and assigning the entries. Volume editors are also responsible for preparing, where appropriate, appendices surveying the major periodicals and literary and intellectual movements for their volumes, as well as lists of further readings. Work on the series as a whole is coordinated at the Bruccoli Clark Layman editorial center in Columbia, South Carolina, where the editorial staff is responsible for accuracy of the published volumes.

One feature that distinguishes *DLB* is the illustration policy – its concern with the iconography of literature. Just as an author is influenced by his surroundings, so is the reader's understanding of the author enhanced by a knowledge of his environment. Therefore *DLB* volumes include not only drawings, paintings, and photographs of authors, often depicting them at various stages in their careers, but also illustrations of their families and places where they lived. Title pages are regularly reproduced in facsimile along with dust jackets for modern authors. The dust jackets are a special feature of *DLB* because they often document better than anything else the way in which an author's work was perceived in its own time. Specimens of the writers' manuscripts are included when feasible.

Samuel Johnson rightly decreed that "The chief glory of every people arises from its authors." The purpose of the *Dictionary of Literary Biography* is to compile literary history in the surest way available to us – by accurate and comprehensive treatment of the lives and work of those who contributed to it.

The *DLB* Advisory Board

Introduction

During the 1920s, 1930s, and 1940s, authors could make a living by writing short stories for the large-circulation magazines. After World War II, however, weekly magazines such as the *Saturday Evening Post* and *Collier's* declined and eventually ceased publication. There is little doubt that, starting in the 1950s, the massive presence of television began to undermine the reading habits of the American public. Widespread television viewing ushered in what George Garrett has called "the new illiteracy." Today, because the popular market for short stories has shrunk, most American short fiction is published by literary journals and university presses. Though there are recent signs that the short-story form is gaining ground with readers and publishers, no more than a dozen magazines currently pay four-figure amounts for a story.

Volumes of stories do not sell well. A market-driven publishing world has made it difficult for more-experimental writers to get their novels published, as well. Many of the remaining magazines that had previously published short fiction began to feature memoirs, which frequently replaced short stories. One of the effects of Truman Capote's non-fiction novel *In Cold Blood* (1965) was to blur distinctions between fiction and nonfiction, and writers such as Edward Abbey, Joan Didion, Annie Dillard, John McPhee, and Gay Talese began to publish personal essays that had the appearance of first-person short stories.

An additional influence appeared during these same years: European formalism with its emphasis on avant-garde, experimental literary techniques. Many young writers in the 1960s were no longer getting their start in New York City but in the universities where European influences were taking hold. Many writer/professors, whose literary heroes were likely to be Samuel Beckett, Franz Kafka, Hermann Hesse, and André Breton rather than Ernest Hemingway, William Faulkner, F. Scott Fitzgerald, and Sherwood Anderson, offered their students radically different models that underscored experimental innovations in form and technique. Creative-writing schools also emerged at universities, beginning with the University of Iowa Writers' Workshop, which stressed originality of method rather than content and thus encouraged a variety of new forms that had already begun to appear in the work of younger experimental authors such as Donald Barthelme, John Barth, and Thomas Pynchon — writers additionally influenced by South Americans such as Jorge Luis Borges and the so-called literary outlaws, including William Burroughs.

Because short-fiction writers could no longer make a living in New York, they began accepting jobs throughout the university systems as writer/professors. Tenured positions in English departments enabled them to support their families and continue writing. The University of Iowa, in the late 1940s, began training students in creative writing and then sending out graduates, certified with their Master of Fine Arts degrees, to initiate new creative-writing programs throughout the country.

While the universities became protective environments for many fiction writers, certain risks arose in their sometimes-insular atmospheres. Hortense Calisher, one of America's most respected fiction writers, suggests that "the university has willy-nilly become the café." Writers, who often need a variety of experiences to spark their imaginations, spend a large portion of their academic lives enclosed within the walls of graduate school. Calisher also warns that artists must be careful in talking about their gifts too much: "If one teaches and writes there as well, the effect of immersion in talk about 'techniques' may also enter in. Subtlest of all influences or hazards for the silent persona of a writer may be the constant verbalization of energies and meditations better saved for the page." She points out the appearance in the 1970s and 1980s of more stories set in academia. John Updike, concurring with Calisher regarding the possible negative repercussions of the creative-writing industry, puts it another way:

> Now [speaking in 1984], for the bright young graduates that pour out of the Iowa Writers' Workshop and its sister institutions, publishing short stories is a kind of accreditation, a certificate of worthiness to teach the so-called art of fiction. The Popular market for fiction has shriveled while the academic importance of "creative writing" has swelled; academic quarterlies, operating under one form of subsidy or another, absorb some of the excess. The suspicion persists that short fiction, like

poetry since Kipling and Bridges, has gone from being a popular to a fine art, an art preserved in a kind of floating museum made up of many little superfluous magazines.

Though Calisher and Updike warn against some of the hazards of creative-writing schools, the fact remains that academic quarterlies have become, since the 1950s, a major venue in publishing short fiction in America. The few national magazines that still publish short stories have, however, established much higher literary standards than many of the magazines that folded in the 1950s. Until recently many New York trade publishing houses did not publish or promote short-story collections, and, as a result, university presses have become the most important vehicles in publishing short fiction for most of the writers in this *DLB* volume. Frank Conroy, head of the Iowa Writers' Workshop, claims that the success of the university presses in promoting short fiction has, ironically, "contributed significantly to the forces responsible for the current resurgence of interest of the big houses in serious short fiction."

Whatever long-term effects that creative-writing programs may have had on fiction writing since 1945, they play an important role in this *DLB* because twenty-four out of the forty writers included have either graduated from creative-writing programs, have worked, or are presently working in creative-writing programs as professors in various universities. Eight of the forty have earned Ph.D.'s in academic disciplines.

Besides the flight of writers to universities and the emergence of academic literary quarterlies, the lack of major publishers' interest in short fiction gave rise to independent associations of writers, who established their own little magazines. They sought no direct connections with either the commercialized New York literary scene or the academic world. Just as the writing programs became new "centers," so, too, did the little magazines create their own independent centers, where they were free to create their own aesthetic communities. Many of the editors and contributors of these magazines strongly objected to the homogenized eclecticism coming out of the more conservative writing programs and academic journals such as the *Kenyon Review, Sewanee Review,* and *Southern Review;* or the more trendy liberal journals such as the *Partisan Review* and *Paris Review.* The more radical founders of magazines such as *Big Table, Kulchur,* the *Black Mountain Review, Io, Lillabulero, Caterpillar,* the *Evergreen Review,* the *Chelsea Review,* and many other maverick

publications claimed that the M.F.A. workshops' emphasis on craft and technique had inadvertently replaced viable aesthetic and cultural traditions that had previously activated innovative fiction writing.

The *Black Mountain Review,* on the other hand, published work by students and teachers at Black Mountain College who had come out of a tradition that revered Ezra Pound, William Carlos Williams, and other objectivist writers, such as Charles Olson and Louis Zukofsky, along with the additional influences of both European and American avant-garde artists such as Gaudier Brzeska, Paul Klee, Pablo Picasso, Clyfford Still, Jackson Pollock, and Franz Kline. Students at Black Mountain College were steeped in European traditions in literature, art, and music through artist/scholars such as Josef Albers and Buckminster Fuller and musical performers and composers Lou Harrison, Stefan Wolpe, John Cage, and Merce Cunningham. Craft, as such, was discussed only in relation to a specific tradition and never became the major focus that it assumed in the workshop approach at Iowa and like-minded schools. In short, these alternative little magazines refused to replace literary tradition with mere training in craft and technique. As Michael Anania puts it in his comprehensive study of the history of little magazines: "In the almost totally decentralized literature of the late Sixties and early Seventies, these associations are measures of what was once called influence" (*TriQuarterly,* Fall 1978).

The forty writers presented in *DLB 130* demonstrate an expanding diversity of writings, which can be divided into three major categories. These categories overlap in such a way that one writer may fit in more than one group: realists or neorealists (which includes the subgroup the minimalists); postmodernists or metafictionists; and outsiders. These groups are derived primarily from the prevailing literary approach with which the writers treat their subject matter and thematic concerns, and the geographic location or social class of their characters.

The second group of writers, roughly a third of the authors in *DLB 130,* are postmodernists or metafictionists. Though these terms are difficult to define, they refer to the kind of fiction whose self-reflexive tendency shows a consciousness of itself as an artificial creation. Critic Raymond Federman, though suggesting that all works of fiction are ultimately about themselves, claims that self-reflexive fiction "continually turns back on itself and draws the reader into itself as a text, as an ongoing narration, and before the reader knows what is happening, the text is telling him about itself " (*Columbia*

Literary History of the United States, 1988). Language is no longer employed merely to formulate a narrative but can be analyzed in the process of creating itself as a text. Walter Abish, for example, could be termed a postmodern experimentalist because of the way his language takes on a syntactical/grammatical life of its own. Robert Kelly's and Guy Davenport's stories are frequently presented as self-conscious fictions rather than as realism. Because they practice these techniques, their stories are considered metafiction.

The third category of writers are outsiders because they do not participate markedly in any particular literary tradition in terms of form and content or are not consistently experimental enough to be considered postmodernists or metafictionists, though some, like Fielding Dawson, are both non-aligned and experimental. Paul Goodman, Lucia Berlin, and Charles Bukowski are outsiders because they write about outsiders — lost souls, alcoholics, drug addicts, homosexuals before gay liberation, and other marginalized, tormented victims involved in habitual self-destructive behaviors. Though Alfred Chester, the archetypal self-destructive homosexual of the 1960s, qualifies as an outsider in his subject matter, he also used some metafictional techniques in his later work that would include him with the postmodernist group.

However, the largest group of writers in *DLB 130* belong to the realist or neorealist category of short-fiction writers. Tom Wolfe, in 1973, seemed to think that the pervasive influences of Kafka and Beckett had pretty much replaced realistic writing. But there is little question that, with the appearance of the powerful voice of Raymond Carver, realism was back. American writing has also never been able to flourish without a strong attachment to geography. Place, a specific landscape — named or not — is an integral part of the work of most of the writers considered in this volume. Carver, Russell Banks, and Andre Dubus are sometimes called "Dirty Realists," a term that colorfully suggests the working-class victims who are the principal characters of their fiction. Another epithet used to characterize their work is "Trailer-Park Fiction," because many of the protagonists have lives that are rootless, poverty-ridden, and empty. Early marriages end in divorce and are riddled with alcoholism, adultery, abuse, and other self-destructive behaviors. The men drink, and the women and children suffer. The alienation and brutality that these writers portray are sometimes more disturbing than the generalized cosmic dread and nihilism of Kafka and Beckett — because the down-trodden characters live in

"Edenic" America. Though the settings of Richard Bausch's stories are usually not locatable in a particular place, his ability to evoke a sense of loss and to show characters in conflict with haunted pasts, vaguely tied to an unnamed but ominous location, have become hallmarks of his fiction.

Most of the neorealist writers in this volume create stories about working-class families in specific locales. Dubus chronicles the disintegration of the industrial Northeast, usually in small New England mill towns that have lost their mills. Breece D'J Pancake details the trapped lives of desperately poor West Virginia coal miners, contrasted with the beauty of the local geography to underscore the ugliness of the lives that are lived there. Both Berlin and Wanda Coleman document the bleak lives of poor working-class women. Coleman often chronicles the plight of African-American welfare mothers in Los Angeles who are victimized by urban violence, drug addiction, and homelessness. Many of Berlin's women are also victims of the brutality of their drug-addicted lovers and suffer even more grimly from their own alcoholic self-destructive habits. Her stories are detailed case histories of every facet of the practicing addict. John Fante (a major influence on Bukowski who, in turn, influenced Coleman) occasionally documented the lives of frustrated young poets. Stuart Dybek's working-class ethnic neighborhoods in Chicago show the traditions of the past clashing with the present, especially in his initiation or coming-of-age stories. Although Dybek is considered a neorealist writer, his work sometimes combines the realistic with the fantastic. Gordon Weaver writes stories that also treat the agony of the working class, many of whom use alcohol to relieve their desperate ennui. Though his early stories are primarily realistic pieces, his later work has recently moved toward more-experimental metafictional modes.

The figurative father of this group of working-class writers is Carver, whose rise during the late 1960s and 1970s (with the consistent support of Gordon Lish, fiction editor at *Esquire* at that time) led also to what some critics have labeled minimalism. Carver distinctively voiced the agony of the inarticulate masses in America. His stories detail the failed lives of working-class alcoholics and the self-loathing destructiveness that became the center of their lives. Though much of Joyce Carol Oates's earlier work deals with similar subject matter, she has refined her later work into analyses of more-generalized obstacles that prohibit human connection.

Other realists deal with characters in the middle class rather than the working class. Grinding poverty is not a problem for most of their characters. Ellen Gilchrist, George Garrett, and Lee K. Abbott are usually associated with a particular geographic area of America. Gilchrist's short fictions often spoof the stereotypical southern family frozen in the old order, and she writes as a native southerner. Garrett, also a southerner, often creates stories set in the South in which characters suffer the agony of leaving the old order and the tension that arises as an alien contemporary world brutally overruns valued traditions. His work charts the breakdown of those traditions. Abbott's stories usually take place in southwestern settings, where psychologically wounded young men, sometimes Vietnam War veterans, seek relief from their tormented memories by taking illicit drugs, drinking too much alcohol, and engaging in other self-destructive activities. Tobias Wolff's stories usually take place in the Northwest and document the disorder of family life. Though Leonard Michaels is not usually thought of as belonging to any specific geographic location, most of his stories take place either in New York City or the Bay Area of San Francisco. Michaels's stories are openly autobiographical fictions in which he records the disillusionments and frustrations of romantic love. Another Bay Area writer is Gina Berriault, whose stories usually take place in areas of northern California but whose universal themes about ordinary people in crisis could be set anywhere in America.

Three other writers, though by no means thought of as regional writers, compose stories that are usually located in the Midwest. Charles Baxter's stories carefully record a world of middle-class constraints in midwestern communities. Both Bette Pesetsky and Mary Robison are from the Midwest and detail the loneliness and despair of middle-class family life through the eyes of bored women. Elizabeth Tallent and David Leavitt record lives of quiet desperation within middle- and upper-middle-class families usually in New York or California. Tallent's narratives delineate the complexities of male-female relationships, while Leavitt's record the fears and frustrations of young gay men attempting to live so-called normal lives. Both Barry Targan and David Huddle write of the Northeast and share an interest in the lives of professors and their delicate relationships with students. Targan also deals with middle-class and middle-age endurance in the face of loss and dwindling powers, while Huddle explores a range of intimate experiences, sometimes of poets and writers who also teach on quiet New England campuses. James Salter and J. F. Powers not only are older than most of the other writers but write with an uncompromising sophistication that has distinguished them as two of the most accomplished writers in America. Few writers delineate so subtly the lives of Roman Catholic priests as Powers does, nor has any American writer treated them with such wit and humanity. Salter's style possesses a lyricism that few American writers can equal, and his directness permits him to speak unsentimentally of the shortness of life and the brutality of lost love.

Jerome Klinkowitz calls Stephen Dixon a "postmodern experimental realist" because Dixon's fiction demonstrates the way language can take on a life of its own and control the speaker. Abish deals with essentially the same linguistic dilemmas by elaborating self-reflexive verbal games in stories influenced by Borges, Beckett, and the French "new novelists" Alain Robbe-Grillet and Nathalie Sarraute. Lydia Davis, though not as inclined toward experimental techniques as Abish, also shows clear evidence of French models, especially the works of Maurice Blanchot and Michel Butor. She examines characters haunted by an estrangement from their own language – an estrangement that alienates them from reality. Though Kelly and Davenport are considered experimental metafictionists, some of their work might be more properly considered "irrealism" (a refinement of metafiction), which applies to stories that show loosened versions of reality for the purpose of exploring the reality of illusions. Coleman Dowell's *The Silver Swanne* (a story separately published in 1983) explores the interweaving strands of different time periods to show the precarious position of authorial voices vying for control. The Proustian lyrical studies of Eve Shelnutt are never focused on traditional plot structure but, rather, on a musical counterpointing of remembered voices that creates, aesthetically, a comforting reality. Max Apple's artful combination of fact and fantasy in "The Oranging of America" (in the 1976 book of that name) produces fictions that may seem "truer" than objective reality, enabling readers to understand social and economic patterns that literal discourse could never express. Lish is another realist who experiments. Few writers have so vividly portrayed hysterical lives in permanent existential crises as Lish does in his passionately surreal monologues.

Though the stories of Harold Brodkey have definite plots, his style is so densely textured that the term realism simply does not apply. Mythic, biblical, and literary allusions and subtexts permeate his work to such a degree that multiple critical approaches must be employed for a thorough analysis.

The open-form vignettes of Dawson are even more difficult to pin down. Dawson has been a literary maverick from his earliest work and has studiously avoided what he calls "the tyranny of the obvious." Most of his stories are detailed variations on his persistent theme of "the artist in crisis." Both Bukowski and Chester are outsiders to such a degree that their work is sometimes categorized in the outlaw genre. Bukowski resolutely refuses to participate in any established literary group and prides himself on his outsider status. His autobiographical fiction, like that of Dawson, frequently shows a poet desperately trying to create some kind of meaning out of the drunken chaos of literary fame. The quirky fictions of Chester explore, in *Head of a Sad Angel* (1990), a homosexual underground inhabited by a doomed, self-destructive genius in Paris. And, finally, the impressionistic, confessional stories of Goodman show sexual politics more reminiscent of Nathaniel Hawthorne and Virginia Woolf than of recent European avant-garde models.

Though there has been since the 1950s a drastic reduction in the number of magazines that actually publish short fiction, a certain few still maintain their respected positions at the very top echelons of the publishing world. *Esquire* has always been one of the most desirable places to publish because it pays well and its readership is literate and sophisticated. Rust Hills is the present fiction editor at *Esquire,* but former editor Lish, particularly during the late 1960s and early 1970s, published many younger writers who eventually attained major careers: Carver, Robison, Huddle, Dubus, Salter, Banks, Richard Ford, and Barry Hannah. *Playboy,* since its inception in the late 1950s, has regularly published the best of the more established writers and paid them handsomely. Under the editorship of Alice K. Turner, *Playboy* has continued to feature the most distinguished short-story writers. The only weekly mainstream magazine to publish short fiction, though, is the *New Yorker. Harper's,* edited by Lewis Lapham, and the *Atlantic Monthly,* under fiction editor C. Michael Curtis, continue to publish one story a month. *Redbook,* under its fiction editor, Deborah Purcell, actively seeks out new short-story writers while continuing to publish short stories monthly. Almost half of the writers in this volume of the *DLB* have published in one or more of these high-paying established magazines.

More than half of the remaining writers in this volume, however, established their literary reputations without having appeared in the *New Yorker* or any of the other magazines just mentioned. Important academically connected journals in which most of these writers have appeared include, among others: the *Georgia Review, Kenyon Review, Iowa Review, Carolina Quarterly, Antaeus, Conjunctions, Paris Review, Hudson Review, Chicago Review, Cimarron Review, TriQuarterly, Missouri Review, Southern Review, Sewanee Review,* and *Southwest Review.*

Connected to these academic journals are editors whose aesthetic and political tastes established new literary centers which fostered and promoted writers whose work seemed to express their own viewpoints. Certainly editor Frederick Morgan's conservative tastes helped determine the kinds of stories that the *Hudson Review* would be more likely to accept, just as the liberal political sympathies of the *Partisan Review* editor, William Phillips, might decide the kind of work that would appear there. Other powerful editors include William Sessions of *Carolina Quarterly,* Daniel Halpern of *Antaeus,* George Plimpton of the *Paris Review,* and Elliott Anderson and Reginald Gibbons of *TriQuarterly.* Academic journals based in the South that have traditionally published superb fiction are the *Southern Review,* James Olney, editor; the *Sewanee Review,* George Core, editor; and the *Virginia Quarterly Review,* edited by Staige Blackford. For many years, Frederick Turner directed and edited the conservative *Kenyon Review,* later edited by George Lanning and Marilyn Hacker. There is little doubt that Theodore Solotaroff's *New American Review,* especially in the 1960s and 1970s, was responsible for the promotion of major careers such as Philip Roth, Stanley Elkin, and many more. Solotaroff also edited, while at Harper and Row, the work of Apple, along with many other young writers. Other journals located in different parts of the country in the decentralized world of the American short story are the *Georgia Review,* edited by Stanley Lindberg; *Southwest Review,* edited by Willard Spiegelman; *Missouri Review,* edited by Speer Morgan and Greg Michaelson; and DeWitt Henry's *Ploughshares.* The *North American Review* from the University of Northern Iowa, edited by Robley Wilson, has been particularly sympathetic to more experimental fiction writers, as has the *Chicago Review* under the editorship of David Nicholls. And certainly the *Iowa Review,* edited by David Hamilton, has maintained its influence as the journal connected to the mother of all creative-writing programs, the Iowa Writers' Workshop. Editor, short-story writer, and novelist Gordon Weaver edits the excellent *Cimarron Review.*

There are other highly influential journals, though, not connected to any particular university or school of writing. Their literary venue is usually built around the reputation of a practicing writer-editor who publishes only those writers whom he or she holds in high esteem. Bradford Morrow's journal, *Conjunctions,* which has not been connected to any school until its recent affiliation with Bard College, has been publishing writers with a heavily international-multicultural emphasis and a postmodernist perspective. Editor Bill Buford's *Granta,* as intellectually challenging as *Conjunctions,* focuses on international writers, few of whom are connected to any university writing program. The recently published *Granta Book of the American Short Story,* edited by Richard Ford, is certainly one of the most eclectic collections of stories ever published. Eleven of the stories in the anthology were written by authors featured in this *DLB* volume. Another highly respected journal not affiliated with any academic institution is *Witness,* a literary journal in which the topics change with each issue; Peter Stine is the editor, and the journal has featured "Writings from Prison," "The Holocaust," and "Evangelism and American Politics."

There is, however, life outside the walls of the writing schools and the academic quarterlies. Several of the writers in this volume have rarely, or never, taught in university writing programs, published their works with university presses, or appeared in university-related scholarly journals. Though Bukowski, the archetypal "outsider-outlaw" writer, is now publishing in such distinguished intellectual journals as *Antaeus,* his earlier work could be found only in the smallest of the little magazines such as *Matrix, Simbolica,* and the *Anagogic & Paudeumic Review.* Other little magazines, some of them long gone, in which Bukowski, Berlin, Dawson, and Kelly appeared are: the *Falcon;* Kelly's *Chelsea Review;* the *Evergreen Review,* edited by Barney Rosset and Donald Allen; and *Caterpillar,* published in the 1960s and 1970s by Clayton Eshleman. A selection of distinguished little magazines would include Richard Grossinger's *Io;* Irving Rosenthal's *Big Table;* Robert Bertholf's *Credences;* Russell Banks's *Lillabulero; Kulchur,* alternately edited by Gilbert Sorrentino, Joel Oppenheimer, and LeRoi Jones; and *Neon,* edited by Sorrentino and Hubert Selby. Other long defunct magazines of note are the *Floating Bear, Yugen, Wild Dog,* and *Measure.*

So-called small presses have had about the same life expectancy as the little magazines, but several of the survivors have maintained the integrity of their single-minded vision in the face of overwhelming pressures. One of the defining characteristics of *DLB 130* is that one-fourth of the writers presented have published with two of the most distinguished small presses in America. John Martin's

Black Sparrow Press in Santa Rosa, California, is responsible, to a great extent, for the literary careers of Bukowski, Kelly, Dawson, Coleman, Shelnutt, Berlin, Goodman (the short stories), and Chester. And some of Oates's early work also came out of Black Sparrow. Though William D. Turnbull's North Point Press of San Francisco has recently gone out of business, it published many of the most respected writers in America, including Davenport, Salter, Berriault, and Dixon, perhaps the most prolific fiction writer in America today.

The most notable surprise is, however, that small presses and university presses have been responsible for the literary careers of all but about ten writers featured in this volume, a fact that dramatically demonstrates, until recently, the generally uncommitted and indifferent attitudes of many of the large New York publishing houses, with the exception of Knopf; Norton; Putnam; Little, Brown; and a few others, in reaping the richest harvest of short-fiction writers that this country has yet produced. The level of writing of these artists is, most of the time, rarely less than spectacularly accomplished.

Other important factors that contribute to the complex world of the contemporary American short story, and substantially promote a writer's career, are the prizes that various organizations award each year and, in most cases, the influential anthologies in which these prizewinning stories appear. And there can be little doubt that Shannon Ravenel, whom Updike called "that St. Louis saint of scrutiny," is probably the most influential editor of short stories in America today. Though a senior editor with Louis D. Rubin, Jr.'s Algonquin Books of Chapel Hill, she has served as the coeditor of the anthology *Best American Short Stories* for the past twenty years. She is the reader who sifts through between 1,500 and 2,000 short stories yearly and sends 100 to her coeditor for the final awarding of the prizes. Some of her coeditors have been Updike, Calisher, Oates, Carver, John Gardner, Ann Beattie, and other first-rate short-story writers in America. Not only are the prizewinners given national recognition and a substantial sum of money, but their stories appear in an annual collection along with other winners. Most of the writers in this volume have been recipients of one or more of these awards, an achievement that substantially advanced their careers. Besides *Best American Short Stories,* the major awards honoring short-story writers are the O. Henry Prize, the Iowa Short Fiction Award, the P.E.N./Hemingway Award, the Pushcart Prize series, and the John Simmons Short Fiction Award. Publishers often look to the award winners first when scouting around for fresh talent. A common pattern with prizewinning writers is that such an award or two leads to more public recognition which, in turn, leads to offers of academic positions that allow them to support a family and have the time to devote to new work.

As important to the promotion of the publication of short fiction as the O. Henry Prize and *Best American Short Stories* is the very active role that university presses have played during the 1980s in awarding prizes and publishing series of annual short-story collections. In 1980 the University of Pittsburgh Press Drue Heinz Literature Prize was specifically created to recognize and encourage the writing of short fiction and to address the neglect of short fiction by the national publishing community. The University of Pittsburgh Press awards five thousand dollars annually to an outstanding young short-fiction writer and publishes his or her first collection. The press also began to publish short-story collections which have come to be known as the "University of Pittsburgh Short-Story Series." The University of Missouri also initiated a short-fiction series of publications known as "The University of Missouri Press Breakthrough Series." The University of Illinois and the University of Georgia also award prizes for short stories. The Flannery O'Connor Award for Short Fiction has been sponsored by the University of Georgia Press for many years while the Iowa Short Fiction Award has been given by the University of Iowa. The University of Illinois Press has published over sixty volumes in its "Illinois Short Fiction Series." Some literary journals also award prizes for short fiction such as the William Goyen Prize for Short Fiction from *TriQuarterly.*

Alone in the field of journals devoted exclusively to short fiction is *Studies in Short Fiction,* now edited by Michael O'Shea, which is a virtual clearinghouse for all activities surrounding the short-story industry. No serious scholar of the short story could do without the accurate bibliographies and high-quality essays supplied by the editors and contributors of this journal.

Though the world of short fiction is a relatively peaceful one compared to the endless bickering that goes on among contemporary American poets, there are a few ongoing skirmishes between some of the more conservative critics and certain writers, particularly regarding the relationship of style and content. In 1986 Madison Smartt Bell mounted a stinging attack in an essay in *Harper's,* "Less is Less: The Dwindling American Short Story." The object of his barbs was a group of

young, highly successful writers that includes Beattie, Leavitt, Amy Hempel, Bobbie Ann Mason, and several others. Bell took issue not only with their philosophical stance toward life, which he characterized as "nihilistic" and "deterministic," but further criticized the movement of their stories as "reductive rather than expansive." Blaming Carver, Beattie, and Robison's minimalist style for these younger artists' "facelessly uniform" stories, "impoverished language," and "starved eloquence," Bell charged the young writers with the inability to transform the "trivial into something other than trivial" and questioned their ability to reconstitute "dreariness into an epiphany." He attacked what he saw as their minimalist style derived from Carver's flat, present-tense, first-person, declarative sentences.

Sven Birkerts and Bruce Bawer decry the state of the contemporary American short story for the same reasons. However, they hurl their criticism directly at Lish, the object of their indignation. Birkerts's essay is titled "The School of Gordon Lish," in his *An Artificial Wilderness,* (1987), and Bawer's is "The Literary Brat Pack," in his *Diminishing Fictions* (1988). Beneath their bitter attacks lies a deep revulsion over the effects of the media, especially television, on the language of the writers who include Tallent, Pesetsky, Robison, and Leavitt, among others. Birkerts sees these writers as belonging to "Lish's squadron" and the "Knopf corral." Carver's minimalist style is again blamed, because Lish was responsible for promoting Carver's early career. Lish, now an editor at Knopf, has energetically championed and promoted many authors who have become some of the most important short-story writers: Robison, Pesetsky, Hempel, Hannah, Michael Martone, Leon Rooke, and many others. Birkerts unfairly compares the accomplishments of these writers to those of European authors such as Woolf, Kafka, James Joyce, and Hermann Broch and finds the younger ones wanting, a charge that is inappropriate.

In spite of the perennial battles between the "ancients" and the "moderns," the contemporary American short story, as documented in this volume, is undergoing a renaissance during difficult political and economic times. Though the short story suffered through a major decentralizing process — viewed as a disaster at the time — it began, happily, to reconstitute itself during the 1980s. The combined efforts of the academic quarterlies and presses, the flourishing writing programs that nourish and promote new talent, and the spirit of innovation preserved in the small presses have successfully sparked renewed interest among the big New York houses in publishing serious short fiction.

– *Patrick Meanor*

ACKNOWLEDGMENTS

This book was produced by Bruccoli Clark Layman, Inc. Karen L. Rood is senior editor for the *Dictionary of Literary Biography* series. Jack Turner was the in-house editor.

Photography editors are Edward Scott and Timothy C. Lundy. Layout and graphics supervisor is Penney L. Haughton. Copyediting supervisor is Bill Adams. Typesetting supervisor is Kathleen M. Flanagan. Samuel Bruce is editorial associate. Systems manager is George F. Dodge. The production staff includes Rowena Betts, Steve Borsanyi, Barbara Brannon, Patricia Coate, Rebecca Crawford, Margaret McGinty Cureton, Denise Edwards, Sarah A. Estes, Joyce Fowler, Robert Fowler, Bonita Graham, Jolyon M. Helterman, Tanya D. Locklair, Ellen McCracken, Kathy Lawler Merlette, John Myrick, Pamela D. Norton, Thomas J. Pickett, Patricia Salisbury, Maxine K. Smalls, Deborah P. Stokes, and Wilma Weant.

Walter W. Ross, Suzanne Burry, and Brenda Gross did library research. They were assisted by the following librarians at the Thomas Cooper Library of the University of South Carolina: Linda Holderfield and the interlibrary-loan staff; reference librarians Gwen Baxter, Daniel Boice, Faye Chadwell, Cathy Eckman, Gary Geer, Qun "Gerry" Jiao, Jean Rhyne, Carol Tobin, Carolyn Tyler, Virginia Weathers, Elizabeth Whisnant, and Connie Widney; circulation-department head Thomas Marcil; and acquisitions-searching supervisor David Haggard.

Dictionary of Literary Biography® • Volume One Hundred Thirty

American Short-Story Writers Since World War II

Dictionary of Literary Biography

Lee K. Abbott

(17 October 1947 –   )

Andy Solomon
University of Tampa

BOOKS: *The Heart Never Fits Its Wanting* (Cedar
Falls, Iowa: North American Review, 1980);
Love Is the Crooked Thing (Chapel Hill, N.C.: Algon-
quin, 1986);
Strangers in Paradise (New York: Putnam, 1986);
Dreams of Distant Lives (New York: Putnam, 1989);
Living After Midnight (New York: Putnam, 1991).

Lee K. Abbott is best known as a short-story
writer who addresses the themes of lost love and
family grief with an inventive voice and a deeply
felt compassion for his naive, self-destructive characters. Abbott's stories tend to be comic, satiric, and
earthy. Since the publication of his first collection of
short stories, *The Heart Never Fits Its Wanting,* in the
fall of 1980, Abbott has become an award-winning,
highly respected writer.

Contemporary writers such as Richard
Bausch who keep their own personalities and values
invisible in their work may be influenced by the
works of Jane Austen, Henry James, and Gustave
Flaubert; Abbott is at the other end of the spectrum,
because his narrative voice becomes a key element
of his fiction, as in the narratives of Henry Fielding.
Abbott's grand, maximalist style is sometimes compared to that of William Styron or John Barth. For
his sensitivity to the perils of living by the dangerous guidelines of middle-class American male behavior, Abbott has also been compared to John
Cheever, to whom he has paid tribute in at least one
story, "The World of Apples" (*Strangers in Paradise,*
1986), in which a character refers to the work of
Cheever's fictional poet Asa Bascomb as "poetry
that puts you in mind of weal, plus what it's like to
live free." This praise resembles what critics have
been saying about Abbott himself for a dozen years.

He embodies the antithesis of the modern minimalist movement. His risk-taking narrative voice

*Lee K. Abbott, circa 1991 (photograph by Andrea
Kochman Schnall)*

and richly textured characters issue a challenge to
the restrained, almost apologetic style of minimalism. Abbott makes no apologies. In a loud, loopy
voice he casts everything out before the reader, presenting characters with full histories and the willingness to tell the reader what they believe to be the
whole story. Abbott says he believes in "the old-
fashioned, but perdurable fundament that it is my
responsibility to take hold of you at the wrist, or at
the neck, and tell you what happened to me when I

was, for twenty pages or so, a bowler named Archie T. Felts or a hostess named Candy Kane; anything less, in this truth-telling trade, is a lie."

Although Abbott is loath to call himself a regional writer, he admits that he draws on what he knows best, the Southwest (which he defines as extending from El Paso to about forty miles east of Los Angeles) and its people. He describes himself as the product of a WASP family that once sent its children to Eastern prep schools, but "by the time my branch of it washed up on the sands of Las Cruces, New Mexico (courtesy of the U.S. Army), we had all the bloodlines and none of the moola."

Abbott was born on 17 October 1947 in the Panama Canal Zone to Lee and Elaine Kelly Abbott. Abbott sums up his childhood by saying, "I had a drunk for a mother, a general for a father, and sucked my thumb until I was six." The influence of the "general" and the "drunk" can be seen in stories such as "Time and Fear and Somehow Love" and "The End of Grief" (both in *Strangers in Paradise*). In "Time and Fear and Somehow Love" an alcoholic mother writes a letter to her son attempting to explain her life and her drinking and says, "I am drunk now. . . . I shall be drunk tomorrow, too, and drunk always until I die, for it is by booze that I know myself best." It is one of Abbott's most powerful stories, leaving the reader stunned with a truth that rings of personal experience. The military influence on Abbott's work is also frequently obvious. In "The End of Grief" a father forces his son to memorize every detail of the Bataan death march, in which the father's brother was killed.

Abbott married bookstore manager Pamela Jo Dennis on 20 December 1969, and they have two sons, Noel and Kelly. In 1970 Abbott received a B.A. in English from New Mexico State University. He spent time in New York City at Columbia University in 1970 but returned to New Mexico State University for an M.A. in English, which he received in 1973. In 1975, having already published several short stories in literary magazines, he began work on an M.F.A. at the University of Arkansas. He published a few more stories in literary magazines before receiving his M.F.A. in 1977.

Abbott's only attempts at novel-length work are "The Villa Narratives," an unpublished novel that was his M.F.A. thesis at Arkansas, and a pornographic novel called "Bang, Bang" (also unpublished), which he wrote in college for "therapeutic reasons. I was a prude. The worst I could get my characters to say on the page was 'hell' and 'damn.' I knew that one day my characters would have to

speak more forthrightly" (*Short Story Review,* Winter 1986–1987). Abbott says he lacks the courage and stamina for a novel and sticks instead to the model of Eudora Welty's *Golden Apples* (1949) and other books of related stories. True to this integrated form, Abbott's characters often return under new names or mention characters from other stories, enhancing the impression that they all inhabit the same fictional world. "Billy Jack Eddie's Stories from Behind the Hits" (*The Heart Never Fits Its Wanting*) is a good example. It is a retelling of the title story, in which Rae Nell Tipton, a recurring character in much of Abbott's work, leaves the narrator for a country-music singer, Billy Jack Eddie, who is the narrator of the second story. In "Billy Jack Eddie's Stories from Behind the Hits" Rae Nell is an author of short stories, one of which is "The Heart Never Fits Its Wanting."

When Abbott published *The Heart Never Fits Its Wanting* he was an assistant professor of English at Case Western Reserve University and had already won the Baucom-Fulkerson Award for Fiction. Several of the ten stories in the collection had already been published, including the title story (in the *Ohio Review*) and "What Jesus Says," perhaps the finest story in the collection (in the *North American Review*). The collection, although somewhat rough, lets readers know just what can be expected of Abbott.

The stories introduce the powerful energy and eccentric, yet all-too-human, people who characterize Abbott's fiction. Rae Nell, a great seductress and ruiner of men, makes her debut in the first story, "Near the Heart-Place of Grue," the tale of a "bona fide numero uno furtivo-creepy . . . loser" named Scooter E. Watts. He is a habitual liar who hitchhikes his way across the country until he comes upon Goree, Texas; Lamar Thobodeaux; and the golf course that becomes Watts's home. He takes a job watering the course at night and hunting gophers with a .22-caliber automatic pistol. With his first paycheck he buys an old set of clubs and practices furiously, telling his left arm, "You stay stiff or be abused," until he becomes the course celebrity. But then Rae Nell arrives with her own golf prodigy, a former football player named Fleece Dee Monroe. Watts is soon destroyed, as much by his night with Rae Nell as by his golf defeat at the hands of Monroe. The story is laced with the fresh descriptive energy that Abbott brings to his fiction. The moon becomes a "fat juicy piece of depraved fruit," and a poor golfer has "a Puritan swing, all kneecaps and elbows, proto-bad and reactionary, his follow-through as novel as war, his weak Vardon grip a violation of things beautiful." As unlikely a place for human revelation as a golf course may seem, Abbott's use of it as a proving ground for his odd breed of men is made to seem perfectly logical because Abbott never stops to explain it. His confidence in his material leaves no gap for a reader to question it.

This confidence also allows Abbott, who has never been in the military, to write convincing Vietnam War stories. While Abbott's stories sidestep vivid warfare realism, they provide a feel for the bizarre, and at times insane, atmosphere that pervaded the conflict. Unlike Tim O'Brien's narrator in *Going After Cacciato* (1978) – who wanders through Asia and into Europe after an AWOL soldier – Abbott's narrator Pfc Leon Busby and his friend Donnie T. Bobo, in "The Viet Cong Love of Sgt. Donnie T. Bobo," don Bermuda shorts and polo shirts and toss into Vietcong tunnels some "proven items of VC lure like dirty pictures of Idaho girls with remarkable bosoms, and PX goodies like tape decks and Otis Redding records." Busby plays Robin to Donnie T.'s Batman, the two having been friends since elementary school. But Donnie T. falls for an eighteen-year-old Vietcong girl with "a body like a poem" and deserts Busby and the army for Paris. Busby returns to America to search for a love of his own, finally realizing that "some of us take a long time to learn something. Others a short time. Donnie T. knew that. I know it now." While the story fails to strike the mark as convincingly as Abbott's later work, it hints at the direction he was to take, and, in the pairing of young men uneasily sharing dangerous adventures, it anticipates Abbott's novella "Living After Midnight" (in the 1991 book of that name).

The most intriguing and beautiful story in Abbott's first collection is "What Jesus Says," a period piece detailing the capture of a member of Gen. John Joseph Pershing's expeditionary force sent to hunt Pancho Villa in 1917. Abbott again uses skillful wordplay and an oddly angled worldview to bring fresh vitality to his subject matter. The young soldier nicknamed "Tump" is full of enthusiasm for Black Jack Pershing and his "splendidly unscientific undertaking." The general has his rowdy soldiers quoting Jesus and rampaging through the Mexican countryside on horses accompanied by a 1914 Buick touring car. Tump is captured by Villa and held until the expeditionary force is dissolved and Pershing is called to Europe. Thirty-one years later Tump attends a Veterans of Foreign Wars convention at which Pershing is a speaker. By story's end Tump is disillusioned and disappointed in his former leader. The last two paragraphs of "What Jesus

Says" contain perhaps the most spiritually polemical writing in the collection.

The Heart Never Fits Its Wanting won the 1981 St. Lawrence Award for Fiction. The book was favorably reviewed around the country. Susan Quist, in the *American Book Review* (March–April 1981), said, "These stories can be swallowed whole and absorbed directly into the bloodstream, where they will warm to your cellular memories of your wasted youth and loonies you have loved and lost." The final story in *The Heart Never Fits Its Wanting*, "Living Alone in Iota," won an O. Henry Award for Fiction in 1984 and was nominated for the Pushcart Prize. It was later reprinted in *Strangers in Paradise*.

In March 1986 Abbott published his second collection, *Love is the Crooked Thing*. Although it received only heavily qualified enthusiasm in the *New York Times Book Review* from Amy Hempel – a short-story writer whose minimalist aesthetic could hardly be expected to embrace Abbott's style – widespread praise from other sources seemed to throw the balance of critical opinion in Abbott's favor. "The Final Proof of Fate and Circumstance" was reprinted in *Best American Short Stories 1984* and nominated for the Pushcart Prize, and four other stories in the collection were listed in "100 Other Distinctive Stories" in *Best American Short Stories* four years in a row: "Stand in a Row and Learn" (1983), "When Our Dream World Finds Us and These Hard Times Are Gone" (1984), "The Unfinished Business of Childhood" (1985), and "Having the Human Thing of Joy" (1986).

"Having the Human Thing of Joy" displays evidence of the ways Abbott has evolved since the publication of *The Heart Never Fits Its Wanting*. His narrative voice, while retaining the freshness and inventiveness of description, has calmed and matured, and he places less emphasis on hairpin plot turns. The same elements of manhood that coalesced in Scooter E. Watts and Tump have been distilled into a middle-aged car dealer named Lamar T. Hoyte with a wife and two sons. He is drawn more directly from Abbott's day-to-day world than any of the characters in *The Heart Never Fits Its Wanting*, and the closeness shows. Abbott seems to be writing closer to what he has actually observed, writing with more unblinking authority, and mastering a technique he employs frequently: bringing together seemingly disparate incidents to reflect on and illuminate each other. Hoyte, while cleaning out a box of his mother's photographs after her death, discovers a nude picture of her taken by his father. Years later, when he discovers his wife's affair with a friend, Hoyte recalls the photograph and

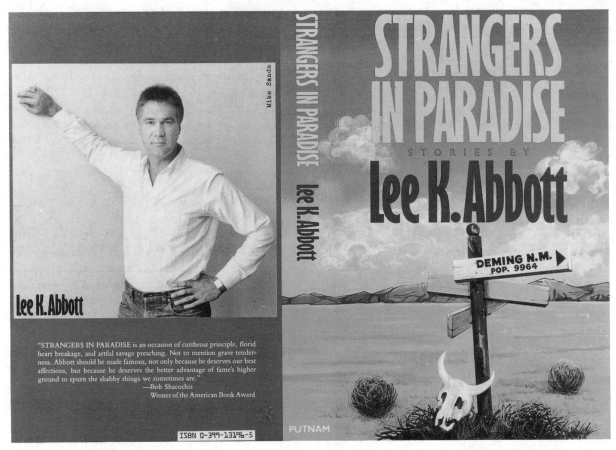

Dust jacket for the 1986 collection of Abbott's stories that novelist Stanley Elkin praised for their "lyrical and generous maximalist's prose"

the feelings it brought out in him, the way it said to him "in effect, 'Welcome into the dark world of grown-up animals.' "

"The Final Proof of Fate and Circumstance," the concluding story in *Love Is the Crooked Thing,* is a raw and intense tale about a father who reveals to his son a second life – including a previous wife, who has died. The father and the son, the narrator, sit drinking on the father's back porch, overlooking the fourteenth fairway of a golf course. As the rum and hours erode the father's inhibitions, he begins to tell his son more and more consequential stories from his youth. After hours of this storytelling, the father finally begins to reveal this past life, relating it as the story of "X" and his French wife, Annette. The narrator later tells the story to his own wife, realizing as he does so that he has left out the most important part (much as his father had by keeping his past life hidden) and vowing to the reader that he will tell his wife in the morning. Even Hempel admitted the story's power. It is a tale of love between father and son, between husband and wife, and between the past

and the present. As the narrator says, it is about "that cozy place few get to these days, that place where your father . . . admits to being a whole hell of a lot like you, which is sometimes confused and often weak."

Strangers in Paradise, Abbott's third collection, was published after he had been promoted to associate professor at Case Western Reserve, and it marked his emergence into major national attention. Published by Putnam, the book received strongly positive reviews and few negative ones. Randall Short (*Newsday,* 15 February 1987) suggested that "the author has caught, through indirection, a kind of visceral, hopeful happiness that only the highest art attains." Of the fourteen stories, ten won individual distinctions. For example, "Youth on Mars" won the *StoryQuarterly* Prize for Fiction, and "The World of Apples" and "The World is Almost Rotten" were both nominated for Pushcart Prizes. "Time and Fear and Somehow Love" won the National Magazine Award for Fiction from the American Society of Magazine Editors, and "X" won a 1986 Pushcart Prize.

"X" is a story in two parts, showing Abbott again exploring the father-son relationship. In the first part the narrator describes how his father, notorious for his temper, struck a man on a golf course and then calmly destroyed the country-club locker room for no obvious reason, all the while muttering in an untranslatable language of the soul, which the narrator, a high-school math teacher, dubs "X." He calls it "funny-pages gobbledygook, those dashes and stars you see in newspapers when the victim of rage empties his mind." He goes on to explain in the story's second part, however, how he found himself speaking that language with his own son some twenty-five years later. The story deals deftly with those moments when father and son mirror each other's nature and share the knowledge that they are "the same: two creatures made blind by the same light and deafened by the same noise." While its theme is not far removed from that of "The Final Proof of Fate and Circumstance," it is no mere echo. The later story provides a gauge of how Abbott's psychological insight has deepened and his storytelling craft has grown more sophisticated.

Reprinted from *The Heart Never Fits Its Wanting,* the O. Henry Award–winning "Living Alone in Iota" deals with, but only flirtingly, the kinds of self-designed heartbreak Abbott was beginning to mine more deeply. It is, however, a virtuoso exercise in Abbott's wedding of voice and incident, so thick with the Abbott trademarks that it might seem like self-parody. Reese – whose girlfriend, Billy Jean LaTook, has left him for a man she calls King Daddy "on account of his smile and many muscles" – flounders through the tale, trying to find a "path out of the pain." He is "love-sawed" by Billy Jean, who "has a body like stolen money," and he goes to buffoonish lengths to get her back or out of his heart. Abbott makes little attempt to address the movement toward epiphany that drives his more powerful work, but rather he spews forth a delightful story told in entertaining prose. The humor is affecting and intense, and the careening language is as amusing to follow as Reese's mad love-run across the desert.

"Time and Fear and Somehow Love" is perhaps the most powerful story in the collection. Abbott has written what he knows best, sticking close to his own background: the military father, the alcoholic mother, and the New Mexico desert setting. About the autobiographical nature of the story Abbott says, "I do worry about offending people. I'm not sure what my mother would make of 'Time and Fear and Somehow Love' if she were to read it. And I suspect she will read it. . . . I don't know what to say. I worry about it, but I don't know a way around it." Such is the spirit of integrity with which Abbott writes.

Not every story in *Strangers in Paradise* proves so successful. "The World of Apples," which displays neither the emotional exploration of stories such as "X" nor the linguistic pageantry of "Living Alone in Iota," is one of the least effective in the collection. The narrator, another Scooter, wanders from page to page, dancing in the supermarket aisle with a high-school teammate's wife, or tearing up a Democratic party meeting by replaying a youthful basketball game and vaulting over chairs and their occupants. He seems neither to know quite where he is going nor to particularly care. His only object is Jane Clute, his Piggly Wiggly dance partner, and his search falls flatly on the ears of readers who expect more. It is a weak choice to be the last story in *Strangers in Paradise.*

In spite of a few misfires, the book is an eminent collection. With *Strangers in Paradise,* it became clear that Abbott was a significant literary talent with a collective vision and a prismatic approach, forming views through separate facets of the same gem.

In April 1989 Putnam published Abbott's fourth collection, *Dreams of Distant Lives.* This collection took as great a leap beyond *Strangers in Paradise* as that collection took beyond *Love Is the Crooked Thing.* Abbott had found a territory few could explore with more truth and none could explore in remotely the same way: the experience of love in motion, either finding itself for the first time or slipping away. As early as in *Love Is the Crooked Thing* Abbott, with stories such as "Having the Human Thing of Joy," inspired assessments that he wrote fiction as powerful as any appearing in the 1980s, and *Strangers in Paradise* encouraged the belief that he could do it freshly and almost at will. Even when he was pulling tricks, as in "Living Alone in Iota," he could construct out of them a thoroughly entertaining story. With *Dreams of Distant Lives,* however, Abbott shows a clear determination to put tricks aside. When the title story of the collection appeared in *Harper's* almost three years before the book was published, Abbott seemed to be serving notice that he was going to focus his eye on the deepest truths he knew. These truths were to let him, as he writes in the story, "make clear the hole the inner life pokes in the outer." In most of the stories in this collection, he does just that. Five of them had already received national acclaim. The title story was included in *Best American Short Stories 1987,* while "Revolutionaries" and "Once Upon a Time" were listed among "100 Other Distinguished Stories of the Year 1987"; "The Era of Great Numbers" was collected in *The Pushcart Prize, XIII,* and "1963" was nominated for *The Pushcart Prize, XIV.*

In *Dreams of Distant Lives* time is not linear but spatial, a canvas of memory on which vulnerable eyes learn to piece the jagged parts into a coherent pattern. Abbott's characters, through their own human frailty, place themselves in transitional moments when the ground shifts underneath them while they totter, trying to stand squarely on a new surface. Time does not move forward, the narrator of "Here in Time and Not" realizes, "but round and round and round until, when the heart is involved, there is no now or then; there is only turmoil with you in the center of it, like a stick." Sometimes Abbott shows love coming, as it does in a turbid way for the adolescent Chappy in "1963": "After she closed the door, he held an inventory of himself: a wild pulse beating in his eyes, breath whooshing in and out of him like a wet wind, and one thought he had no English for." Usually Abbott shows love going – the feeling Bobby Joe in "Once Upon a Time" expresses when he looks across a tennis net at his wife and realizes she does not love him anymore: "I had shut down inside, gone still as a ghost town; there was nothing in the flesh of me but wind and dry cracked organs."

"Dreams of Distant Lives" is a breathtaking mix of anguish and affirmation told by a man whose life reflects his fragmentation at the loss of his marriage. Gradually, however, he rebuilds his world into one with sufficient beauty to enable him to go on, as his final dream reflects his future self, wise enough to nurture and heal the wounded man dreaming.

As before, Abbott's language remains an adventure in the poetry of aural prose. Bill Christophersen (*Newsweek,* 15 May 1989) called it "maximalist with a minimalist's eye for craft . . . spry with metaphor and ironic asides." Abbott creates a narrative voice that evokes the contours of the open-spaced Southwest.

The critical reception to *Dreams of Distant Lives,* despite the complaint by Janet Burroway in the *New York Times Book Review* (23 April 1989) that many stories were too similar, was overwhelmingly positive, most reviewers adopting a tone that suggested they were appraising the work of an acknowledged master. Ilene Barth (*Newsday,* 27 April 1989) said that *Dreams of Distant Lives* "shows how wondrously far Abbott has come."

With his fifth story collection Abbott reaffirmed that he was not only a master but a gambler.

His freewheeling style itself had always set syntax and diction at hazard, and in *Living After Midnight* he risks leaving the territory he had made his trademark. Until then an Abbott story usually focused on father-and-son relationships or, most often, on men who have wives they prize but undervalue, on husbands who are left holding only the wrapping while they throw the gift away.

While the underlying emotional experience does not change radically, the five stories and the title novella in *Living After Midnight* explore how life has too many warps, nooks, dips, and sharp edges to offer a secure pattern. The collection shows that, with flesh and emotion, the whole seldom equals the sum of its parts. This unsettling imbalance appears in each story.

Three stories – "Getting Even," "Freedom, A Theory Of," and "The Who, the What and the Why" – share a Byronic torment based on early memories that become obsessions. Remembrance shapes future behavior, fragments the personality, and leads to self-destruction. While none of these three stories quite reaches the level that had made Abbott's name perpetually listed in annual best-story collections, they seem to be studies for the title novella.

More a long story than a true novella, "Living After Midnight" marks Abbott's first venture into that long form between story and novel. Such a form may, however, prove to be the structural direction Abbott is taking, as his stories are growing beyond the word limits with which commercial magazines feel comfortable and are finding their homes once again in literary magazines. In "Living After Midnight" Abbott weaves a dark tale about college friends inextricably bound. Reed, from a conventional background, leads a drab, directionless life. His cohort, H-man, is a nihilistic rogue who introduces Reed to cocaine, guns, and convenience-store holdups. Reed follows H-man because only with H-man does he feel alive. Abbott had earlier insisted he could not sustain his exhausting style over novel length. But in "Living After Midnight" it is sustained.

The two most successful stories in the collection, "Sweet Cheeks" and "How Love Is Lived in Paradise," dazzle with their synthesis of recognition and lyricism.

"Sweet Cheeks," originally published in *Harper's,* shows how a romance with a lawyer grows into a woman's bittersweet, crippling fixation. The lawyer is an odd choice for her to adore, "the sort who watched his language and used his turn signals and was at pains to say excuse me every time he went to the gents,' " but his quirks enthrall her, how "he'd be at her ear saying good night, Cheeks. Or Babycakes. Or Sweet Chips. Crapola that there ought to be a law against using with an honest-to-goodness grown-up." When he told her he was leaving, "they made love that night, their last. They mumbled 'excuse me' a lot. And 'pardon me.' And damn near tried to keep their give-and-take free of any chitchat that had an L or an O or a V or an E – trying, it seemed already, to reach each other across time and distance, plus whatever other dimension heartache could be measured by." Sweet Cheeks bears his gifts and memory into subsequent relationships as a wall between her and any other man, a searing portrait of our inability to get out of our own way on the path to love.

Beneath a surface bubbling with humor, "How Love Is Lived in Paradise" has power and depth, as college-football coach Bubba Toomer learns of love, heroism, and transcendence from an English tutor and "nearly one thousand yards of Super-8 movie." Bubba has been just another overweight coach yelling at large teenagers, boys "named Ickey and Tongue and Herkie – nearly a hundred who thought nothing of mud and hurly-burly as the medium to be distinguished in," until film of a runty tailback shows him what valor looks like. "Clearly," Bubba thinks as he watches the boy's gridiron heroism, "this was beauty, which is composed of all you love and cannot survive without. . . . It was the creature in him, and me, I was attending to – the thing that in flight looks smooth and intent and imperturbable. The meat of us that turns toward light and sound and shrinks from an unfriendly touch." When, years later, Bubba meets English tutor Mary Louise Tipton, with "a smile that involved the whole of her face," he discovers his own capacity for transcendence, a love that has "eight syllables and half the color wheel."

In *Living After Midnight* Abbott's signature remains the poetic, even acrobatic, southwestern voice that tells his stories. In the Joycean line of writers tenaciously keeping the language fresh, his aesthetic comes from another era, one in which baroque cathedrals were built, when more was more. Abbott's prose does not merely roll gracefully but does backflips on the balance beam, where failure would be humiliating and glaring, as sometimes it is, yet never enough to discourage his next leap. He launches sentences like far-flung nets and usually draws them back full of suprises. A bruised man feels "compelled to speak about my personal life – the hollow it had lately been, its sockets and hinges, the quakes and boom-boom-boom it sometimes was." A college student recalls a lecture, "the way the words had gone in like fishhooks, barbed and bent enough to rip coming out." Teenagers on nitrous oxide discuss "what pleasures might be discovered at the intersection of the raunchy and the lurid."

Living After Midnight received more divergent reviews than *Dreams of Distant Lives*, many that sounded almost delirious in their praise but some that seemed puzzled by Abbott's evolving subject matter. It seems likely, though, that with *Dreams of Distant Lives* Abbott has told his story of love being born or dying as completely and with as sufficient a number of variations as he can. Rather than try to find a new way to tell the story, he found a new story, which makes comparison between *Living After Midnight* and his previous collections inappropriate if not invalid.

In 1990 Abbott moved to Ohio State University, where he is a professor of English. He has held brief adjunct and visiting-writer-in-residence posts with Wichita State University, Southwest Texas State University, and Yale University. He continues to publish short stories in various literary magazines and to write at his home in Worthington, Ohio.

Interview:
Living Church, 203 (13 October 1991): 12–13.

Walter Abish

(24 December 1931 –   )

Maarten van Delden
New York University

BOOKS: *Duel Site* (New York: Tibor de Nagy, 1970);

Alphabetical Africa (New York: New Directions, 1974);

Minds Meet (New York: New Directions, 1975);

In the Future Perfect (New York: New Directions, 1977; London: Faber & Faber, 1984);

How German Is It (New York: New Directions, 1980; Manchester, U.K.: Carcanet New Press, 1982);

99: The New Meaning (Providence, R.I.: Burning Deck, 1990);

Eclipse Fever (New York: Knopf, 1993; London: Faber & Faber, 1993).

OTHER: "Self-Portrait," in *Individuals: Post-Movement Art in America,* edited by Alan Sondheim (New York: Dutton, 1977), pp. 1–25;

"The Shape of Absence," in *Firsthand,* by Cecile Abish (Dayton, Ohio: Fine Arts Gallery, Wright State University, 1978);

"Auctioning Australia," in *Text-Sound-Text,* edited by Richard Kostelanetz (New York: Morrow, 1980), pp. 27–30;

"The Idea of Switzerland," in *The Best American Short Stories 1981,* edited by Hortense Calisher (Boston: Houghton Mifflin, 1981), pp. 1–28;

"Is this really you?," in *Facing Texts: Encounters Between Contemporary Writers and Critics,* edited by Heide Ziegler (Durham, N.C.: Duke University Press, 1988), pp. 153–167.

SELECTED PERIODICAL PUBLICATIONS –
UNCOLLECTED: "The Writer-To-Be: An Impression of Living," *Sub-Stance,* 27 (1980): 101–114;

"Alphabet of Revelations," *New Directions,* 41 (Fall 1980): 66–78;

"Family," *Antaeus,* 52 (Spring 1984): 149–169;

"Happiness," *New Directions,* 50 (Spring 1985): 101–107;

"Just When We Believe That Everything Has Changed," *Conjunctions,* 8 (1985): 25–31;

"The Fall of Summer," *Conjunctions,* 8 (1985): 110–141;

"I Am the Dust Under Your Feet," *Conjunctions,* 10 (1987): 7–33;

"Furniture of Desire," *Granta,* 28 (Autumn 1989): 131–145;

"The Coming Ice Age," *Salmagundi,* 85–86 (Winter-Spring 1990): 152–171;

"House on Fire," *Antaeus,* 64–65 (Spring-Autumn 1990): 146–160.

Walter Abish has been an important presence in contemporary fiction since the publication of his first novel, the playfully experimental *Alphabetical Africa* (1974). The appearance of two volumes of short stories, *Minds Meet* (1975) and *In the Future Perfect* (1977), confirmed his reputation as a master of nonconventional form, as did the publication of *99: The New Meaning* (1990). However, his second novel, *How German Is It* (1980), winner of the first P.E.N./Faulkner Award for Fiction, has to date reached the widest readership and obtained the most critical attention, both in the United States and abroad. *How German Is It* helped Abish's readers see that his work has never confined itself to the elaboration of self-reflexive games. The judges of the P.E.N./Faulkner Award noted in their citation for *How German Is It* that the novel's "very contemporary narrative devices transcend technique until they are no more devices than our eyes are," and Christopher Butler (in *Facing Texts,* 1988) has written in a similar vein that underlying the "experimental technique" of all of Abish's texts there is a "sense of engagement" with significant moral issues. This productive tension between realism and self-reflexiveness goes some way toward explaining the power of Abish's work.

Abish was born in Vienna, Austria, on 24 December 1931 to Adolph and Frieda Rubin Abish, a middle-class Jewish couple. In "Family" (*Antaeus,*

Walter Abish in Key West, 1986 (photograph © Cecile Abish)

Spring 1984), one of several autobiographical essays Abish has published over the years, he writes of being "at once thrust into an orderly life," a life defined by his "efficiently cool and remote mother" and his "energetic businessman father." Against this background of strict bourgeois normality, Abish's literary vocation began to take shape. Abish speculates that his rebellion against the monotonous routines of his childhood existence, his rage at "everything that impeded my freedom," might have constituted a "pre-writerly criticism of the then prevailing bourgeois values." The tendency to question and disrupt the established order of things links the rebellious child to the mature writer.

After Adolf Hitler's annexation of Austria in 1938, the family fled to Nice, and in 1940, just ten days before Germany invaded France, the Abishes departed by boat for Shanghai. They remained there until 1949, when they moved to Israel. There Abish served in the army; at the same time, he developed two strong interests: architecture and writing. He began to write poetry – in English – and, after leaving the army, he studied architecture, which led to a job with a firm that designed small

communities. In 1956 he met an American woman, Cecile Gelb, who was working in city planning in Israel and who was eventually to become a highly respected sculptor and photographer. They married, and, after living in England for a while, they came to New York in late 1957. Walter Abish became a U.S. citizen in 1960.

He worked principally in urban planning over the years to come and also began to establish himself as a writer. It was not until 1970, however, that he published his first book: *Duel Site,* a collection of poems. By this time he had also written several novels, but had been unable to find a publisher for them. When the editors at New Directions turned down one of his novels, they suggested to him that he might want to submit a shorter work of fiction for publication in one of the anthologies of short stories New Directions regularly published. Abish's interest in the short story had been sparked by his reading of the work of Jorge Luis Borges, whose stories had revealed to Abish unsuspected possibilities in what he had until then regarded as a mediocre form.

Abish did most of his work in the genre of the short story in the early to mid 1970s. In 1975 his first collection of stories, *Minds Meet,* was published. The title story is typical of Abish's short fiction for the way it lacks the conventional props of plot and character. The narrative wanders among different, often highly charged subjects, including sex and violence, in an understated, almost insouciant manner. Occasionally the narrator interjects a general statement that appears from its tone and structure to propose a way of gluing the fragments of the narrative together. In fact, observations such as "The above is chiefly referred to by people who are familiar with the below," and instructions such as "To map the abhorrent simply follow the shrieks for help," offer a mockery of the kind of useful knowledge they appear to be purveying. Rather than guiding the reader through the fiction, they throw him even further off track.

Many of Abish's stories are divided into relatively short sections, often less than a page in length. Sometimes the sections are numbered; sometimes they bear titles. The titles of the individual sections of "Minds Meet" offer important clues to the interpretation of the story. After an initial section titled "A History" which offers a sort of history of the semaphore, readers encounter a section titled "A Message." Each of the remaining sections, concerned with the random activities of a group of men and women, bears the word *message* or, in one instance, the cognate *messenger* in its title. In each case *message* is tied to a word beginning with *a*. This device, the apparently arbitrary imposition of some type of formal constraint upon the material of the text, is characteristic of Abish's work. It signals his interest in emphasizing the artifice that goes into the making of any work of art. Yet, in the case of "Minds Meet," the pattern also bears a clear semantic charge, for Abish has selected not just any word beginning with *a* but words that refer to some form of loss, diminution, or deviation from the norm, as in "The Abandoned Message," "Abased by the Message," "The Abbreviated Message," "The Aberrant Messenger," "The Message Is Absent," "The Message Comes Apart." These titles reveal that in this story, as in much of Abish's fiction, minds do not meet.

Abish connects the problems of reading and writing — characteristic concerns of postmodern fiction — to the larger issue of how human beings apprehend the world and try to make it their own. In *Minds Meet* the theme of the familiar is explored most directly in "This Is Not a Film This Is a Precise Act of Disbelief," which opens with the statement "This is a familiar world" and then proceeds to introduce readers to Mrs. Ite, who, as the well-to-do wife of an architect, moves comfortably, "impelled by familiar needs," through the small world of a suburban American community. The opening paragraph of the story focuses on Mrs. Ite's house and garden. In examining the relationship between people and the objects that surround them, Abish suggests, on the one hand, that the material world shapes human behavior — that, for example, "the objects in the familiar interior" of Mrs. Ite's house "channel the needs" of the people who move through it — while, on the other hand, he gives the sense that human needs, which "change from moment to moment," constantly break through and disrupt the frame of the familiar.

As Jerry Varsava has observed, "The 'familiar' can only be effectively depicted through a representational mode that denudes it of its familiarity, making of it something foreign, something unsettling." In "This Is Not a Film" Abish achieves an effect of defamiliarization by focusing relentlessly on the commonplace, surface features of the world of the story, while persistently evoking an unsettling sense of the unmentionable, especially through the references to the sudden disappearance of the architect, Cas Ite. The narrative traces the enigmatic dance of attractions and repulsions among a group of people in the small town of South Tug. The character Michel Bontemps, a trendy French filmmaker, is in South Tug "to make a film exploring America's needs." The unnamed narrator, a member of Bontemps's entourage, fades in and out of the story, adding to the overall effect of diffuseness and fragmentation. Nevertheless, compared to many of Abish's other stories, "This Is Not a Film" has a more concentrated sense of plot: at least part of the reader's interest in the story is made to focus on the mystery of Cas Ite's disappearance. Because the story concludes with the discovery three years later of the missing man's body, it further appears to offer a conventional resolution to the central enigma. Yet, the ending — when it is revealed that Cas Ite's body has been decomposing in his own house for all this time — raises more questions than answers, and it suggests the absurd and frightened unreliability of one's grasp of the world.

Abish was to take up the theme of the familiar again in "The English Garden," the opening story of his second collection, *In the Future Perfect.* "The English Garden" is an important story in the development of Abish's career. It marks his discovery of a subject — contemporary Germany's relationship to its past — that he made his own even though he had never actually been to Germany, a subject to which he was to return in *How German Is It.* The topic

Dust jacket for Abish's 1977 collection, which includes "The English Garden," his first examination of the relationship of contemporary Germany to its past, the subject of his award-winning 1980 novel, How German Is It

seemed uncannily well suited to the specific qualities of his narrative art.

The narrator of "The English Garden" is a nameless American writer who comes to Germany to visit the new town of Brumholdstein, named after a distinguished philosopher. He meets various important people, makes some observations about life in the new Germany, and has a brief affair with Ingeborg Platt, the town librarian. At the end of the story the librarian mysteriously disappears, and the writer leaves Germany. There is a suggestion that he may have been an inmate in the concentration camp that formerly occupied the site on which Brumholdstein has arisen, but there is much of which one cannot be sure. A device Abish uses to create a sense of unity within the story is to intersperse the narrative with descriptions of the illustrations in a coloring book the narrator purchases on his arrival in Germany. The coloring book is a metaphor for the flat, familiar world of the new Germany. In the coloring book, "people, every-

day sort of people, go about their everyday sort of life"; the book acts as "an indicator and recorder of all things that are possible." It registers and propagates a sense of tranquil normality. This sense of the normal is what Abish wishes to explode, for it is tied to the suppression of Germany's past. The story possesses an element of relentlessness — evident, for example, in the narrator's fiercely interrogative mode — that is a highly appropriate vehicle for the expression of an intense but subdued sense of outrage, while, at the same time, the narrator's indirection and reticence prevents the text from undergoing the easy slide into the banal and predictable.

At one point the narrator looks up the German words for *missing* and *disappear;* afterward he discovers that Ingeborg Platt has disappeared from Brumholdstein without leaving a trace. Near the beginning of "Crossing the Great Void," the last story of *In the Future Perfect,* the protagonist, a childlike, hearing-impaired, twenty-four-year-old automobile mechanic named Zachary, plays with his toy automobiles, to one of which, a black passenger car, he has attached a firecracker. Later in the story a black Cadillac, driven by Zachary's uncle, explodes on the Cross Bronx Expressway. These incidents reflect Abish's interest in exploring the connections between word and event, and play and reality, and they also show his desire to question the reader's sense of the hierarchies that regulate these oppositions. Another element that binds the two stories together is the motif of disappearance, for Zachary is obsessed with his father, an officer in the Italian army who disappeared in the North African desert while on a mission behind enemy lines in 1941. Quite a few of Abish's stories are structured around some form of absence. "Crossing the Great Void" is especially significant for the way in which the question of absence is connected to an exploration of familial and sexual relations, as well as for the rich sense of irony with which these issues are handled.

By the late 1970s Abish had established a small but substantial reputation as the creator of an unusual and complex kind of fiction. With the publication of *How German Is It* in 1980, however, Abish obtained recognition as a major figure in contemporary American fiction. The novel is in its eleventh printing and has been translated into ten languages. It offended some readers and critics – surely to Abish's satisfaction – but its reputation as one of the most important novels of the last few decades has been confirmed by the laudatory discussions it has received in important critical surveys of the American novel, such as Frederick Karl's *American Fictions: 1940–1980* (1983) and *The Columbia History of the American Novel* (1991). Although Abish had already been the recipient of several important awards in the 1970s, *How German Is It* helped him win a Guggenheim Fellowship in 1985; a fellowship from the D.A.D.D., a German academic exchange program, which allowed him to spend half a year in Berlin in 1987; a MacArthur Fellowship in 1987; the Award of Merit Medal for the Novel from the American Academy and Institute of Arts and Letters in 1991; and the Lila Wallace–Reader's Digest Award in 1992. The MacArthur Fellowship freed Abish to write full time; he no longer needed to supplement his income by teaching creative writing, something he had been doing at various universities, including Columbia, Yale, and Brown, since the mid 1970s.

During the 1980s Abish published frequently in a variety of journals, including *Conjunctions,* of which he is a contributing editor. He published several pieces of nonfiction, including "Family"; excerpts from a work in progress he has described as a sequel to *How German Is It;* a couple of short stories; and a series of texts constructed out of the juxtaposition of selected passages from works by others. These assemblages were eventually collected under the title *99: The New Meaning.* A new novel, *Eclipse Fever,* set largely in Mexico, was published in 1993.

What is perhaps most striking about Abish's recent publications is that he appears to be moving in two directions at once. *99: The New Meaning* is a rigorous and uncompromising piece of literary experimentation: *Eclipse Fever,* on the other hand, is far more accessible. It has the same controlled energy as *How German Is It* and is just as likely to reach a wide readership.

Although Abish's work has frequently been associated with the postmodernist experiments of his American contemporaries Donald Barthelme, John Barth, Robert Coover, and Thomas Pynchon, the English critic Malcolm Bradbury has rightly pointed out that "It may well be misleading to locate Abish as an American writer at all." The economy, seriousness, and intensity of his work, combined with an oblique, sly sense of humor, set Abish's work apart from what Bradbury describes as the "often hyper-ebullient, agglutinative mode" popular with the American postmodernists. Abish's affinities are with European writers such as Samuel Beckett, Peter Handke, and the French writers of the *nouveau roman* (new novel). In its international orientation, Abish's work offers an interesting challenge to the habit of looking at works of literature as though they belonged to a single national tradition.

Interviews:

Jerome Klinkowitz, *Fiction International,* 4–5 (1975): 93–100;

Sylvere Lotringer, "Wie Deutsche Ist Es," *Semiotext(e),* 4 (Spring 1982): 160–178;

Larry McCaffery and Linda Gregory, *Alive and Writing: Interviews with American Authors* (Urbana: University of Illinois Press, 1987), pp. 7–25.

References:

Alain Arias-Mission, "The New Novel and Television Culture: Reflections on Walter Abish's *How German Is It,*" *Fiction International,* 17, no. 1 (1986): 152–164;

Arias-Misson, "The Puzzle of Walter Abish: In the Future Perfect," *Sub-Stance,* 27 (1980): 115–124;

tentatively was exploring a new version of the genocide. Revisionism as a
new inspiration. Why not? Edgar toyed with the figure of a million or less
dead... No one likes to toy with numbers. Especially of bodies. In a sense,
it has become theoretical. To make history acceptable one must strive for
organizational skill and a means of sustaining the dignity of the participants.

When push comes to shove, Edgar had reported on his return one day from Washington, Moscow may be willing to trade the ashes and teeth of Hitler as well as
a number of medical reports and letters to and from Hitler in return for a
reappraisal, shall we say, of the Katyn forest massacre. We're talking July 43.
he said. Do we have any new numbers, asked Paul. I can't deal with minor
details. Research will have to come up with a plausable version. We're thinking
that the dead died of lead poisoning. Very good, said Paul, not concealing
his contempt. Do you mean, lead water pipes, asked Margarette. Very good,
said Edgar, addressing her as one would a student in grade school. Our Eunuch's
pretty feisty, said PAUL: Had he forgotten that the Eunuchs had once virtually
ruled China. At the end of the meeting Edgar had complacently remarked that
the Poles had proved pretty reasonable. What Poles, asked Paul. Who's a Pole?
What are we dismembering now? I am referring to the gentlemen in Warsaw who
have read the report on Katyn... Are you going to let the Vatican have a peep
at it as well? This from Paul. Edgar, blandly, ignoring this assault on his
authority: If you hear me out. I am referring to the Poles, period. Good guys
and bad guys alike. After all, it's their soup? What's on the menu today, ased
Paul. Just understand this, Edgar responded. Everytime we have the good fortune
to elect a Republican half the Polish population runs to the church to give
thanks. So? Asked Paul. Just this, said Edgar. History aside. I'll keep
voting for Republicans simply to encourage prayer in Poland. Margarette clapped
her hands. Then, embarrased, turned to me: Do you happen to know the German
word for Kerbstone broker?
What#s that?
A commercial broker dealing in unlisted securities.
I thought its a floor trader.
Delete from minutes, said Edgar to Fawn.

Page from the revised typescript for Abish's 1990 story "The Coming Ice Age" (by permission of Walter Abish)

Malcolm Bradbury, Introduction to Abish's *In the Future Perfect* (London: Faber & Faber, 1984), pp. ix–xiii;

Christopher Butler, "Scepticism and Experimental Fiction," *Essays in Criticism,* 36 (January 1986): 47–67;

Butler, "Walter Abish and the Questioning of the Reader," in *Facing Texts: Encounters Between Contemporary Writers and Critics,* edited by Heide Ziegler (Durham, N.C.: Duke University Press, 1988), pp. 168–185;

Maarten van Delden, "Walter Abish's *How German Is It:* Postmodernism and the Past," *Salmagundi,* 85–86 (Winter–Spring 1990): 172–194;

Regis Durand, "The Disposition of the Familiar (Walter Abish)," in *Representation and Performance in Postmodern Fiction,* edited by Maurice Couturier (Montpelier, Vt.: Delta, 1983), pp. 73–83;

Jerome Klinkowitz, "Walter Abish and the Surfaces of Life," *Georgia Review,* 35 (Summer 1981): 416–420;

Richard Martin, "Walter Abish's Fictions: Perfect Unfamiliarity, Familiar Imperfections," *Journal of American Studies,* 17, no. 2 (1983): 229–241;

Dieter Saalman, "Walter Abish's *How German Is It:* Language and the Crisis of Human Behavior," *Critique,* 36 (Spring 1985): 105–121;

Anthony Schirato, "The Politics of Writing and Being Written: A Study of Walter Abish's *How German Is It,*" *Novel,* 24 (Fall 1990): 69–85;

Robert Siegle, "On the Subject of Walter Abish and Kathy Acker," *Literature and Psychology,* 33, nos. 3–4 (1987): 38–58;

Tony Tanner, "Present Imperfect: A Note on the Work of Walter Abish," *Granta* (Spring 1979): 65–71;

Jerry Varsava, "Walter Abish and the Topographies of Desire," in his *Contingent Meanings: Postmodern Fiction, Mimesis and the Reader* (Tallahassee: Florida State University Press, 1990), pp. 82–108;

Paul Wotipka, "Walter Abish's *How German Is It:* Representing the Postmodern," *Contemporary Literature,* 30 (Winter 1989): 503–517.

Max Apple

(22 October 1941 –   )

Charles Plymell
State University of New York College at Oneonta

BOOKS: *The Oranging of America, and Other Stories*
(New York: Grossman, 1976; Harmondsworth, U.K. & New York: Penguin, 1981);
Zip: A Novel of the Left and the Right (New York: Viking, 1978);
Three Stories (Dallas: Pressworks, 1983);
Free Agents (New York: Harper & Row, 1984);
The Propheteers (New York: Perennial Library, 1987).

OTHER: *Southwest Fiction,* edited by Apple (New York: Bantam, 1981);
"My Love Affair with English," *New York Times Book Review,* 22 March 1981, pp. 9, 24–25;
"On Persisting as a Writer," *Michigan Quarterly Review,* 21 (Winter 1982): 21–25.

Max Apple, born in Grand Rapids, Michigan, on 22 October 1941, is best known for his humorous and satiric short stories. Critics have compared him favorably with John Barth, Philip Roth, Robert Coover, and Woody Allen. Apple's caricatures of real people fill his parables with spoofery (which has a special midwestern ring to it), gentle irony, and a touch of absurdity that distinguishes his writing from more traditional satire. His language is accessible without requiring arcane associations to reveal meanings, and his books are popular among college students.

Apple grew up in a Jewish household where language was respected, humor inveterate, and a strong sense of style important in learning the American idioms. His mother is Betty Goodstein Apple; his father, Samuel, was a baker. In a 1981 essay in the *New York Times Book Review,* Apple wrote, "I was in my late 20's before I got all the sentences right in a single story. I would still prefer to be the ventriloquist – to let the words come from a smiling dummy – but I'm not good enough at buttoning my lip. An awkward, hesitant, clumsy sentence emerges. . . . I write a second sentence, and

then I cross that first one out as if it never existed. This infidelity is rhythm, voice, finally style itself. It is a truth more profound to me than meaning, which is always elusive and perhaps belongs more to the reader."

Apple attended the University of Michigan, where he earned a bachelor's degree in English in 1963 and a Ph.D. in 1970, following graduate work at Stanford University during the mid 1960s. He became an assistant professor at Reed College in Portland, Oregon, in 1970 then moved on to Rice University in 1972. He is currently a professor there.

One of his early literary triumphs, the collection titled *The Oranging of America, and Other Stories* (1976), demonstrates his taste for pop culture and includes a caricature of C. W. Post (who also appears in the novel *The Propheteers,* 1987). Some of the stories in the collection were suggested by battles with his maternal grandmother over eating commercially prepared cereal instead of an Old World breakfast of rolls and coffee. He began to read cereal boxes and dreamed up stories about cereal-box characters.

Apple uses real names and historical figures, such as Post and other leaders of the food industry, in his stories. In a 1979 interview with Patrick D. Hundley he said, "I have certain things that I can assume my readers know a lot about, and I can work from that. I try to write very quickly and economically so that anything that saves me from descriptions and unnecessary words is always helpful to me. . . ." He believes that the allusions, ironies, and levels of meaning found in modernism are scrap that weighs down the text. More effective are symbols, acronyms, images, real names, datelines, and absurd headlines from the tabloids of supermarket checkout stands.

In "The Oranging of America" and some of his other stories, he abruptly moves characters around in space and time. By doing so he is follow-

Max Apple, circa 1976 (photograph by Debra Apple)

ing his flights of imagination that rush too quickly for the continuities and transitions expected in the traditional short story. His humor is not the parlor humor so long identified with the *New Yorker;* nor is it an attempt at caustic satire.

One should not make the mistake of thinking that his style is effortless. He is a compulsive craftsman, fine-tuning his sentences, and he does not forget the reader. As he told Hundley, "I labor very much at having a style that is accessible."

Inventions that at first seem absurd can be realistic. "The Oranging of America" begins at the Los Angeles Airport in a 1964 Cadillac limousine. Not forgetting that ice cream was the cornerstone of his empire, the protagonist, Howard Johnson, has equipped the car with a freezer that contains eighteen flavors of ice cream. Millie, a secretary-turned-traveling-companion, and a former busboy, Otis, share in the tasting of ice cream. Johnson, who has a Waspish taste, eats only vanilla and is addicted to it. They spend most of their time on the road and,

perhaps due to a diet of ice cream, develop a sixth sense: their bodies tingling upon divining a new location to erect a Howard Johnson's. Apple's wordplay and wit are evident in the title, which refers to the "oranging" of the map with dots marking new restaurant locations, as well as the "oranging" of the landscape with new logos and architecture.

Apple profanes institutions so subtly that his satire sometimes sounds like a chamber-of-commerce speech, as in this statement: "Millie knew they were more than businessmen, they were pioneers." His futuristic style blurs the line between reality and imagination. His parodies could sometimes pass for romantic writing or polyphonic prose, as in these lines: "Maybe it was just the way we felt then, but I think the sun set differently that night, filtering through the clouds like a big paintbrush making the top of the town orange." The themes in "The Oranging of America" were later expanded in *The Propheteers,* where Apple draws on

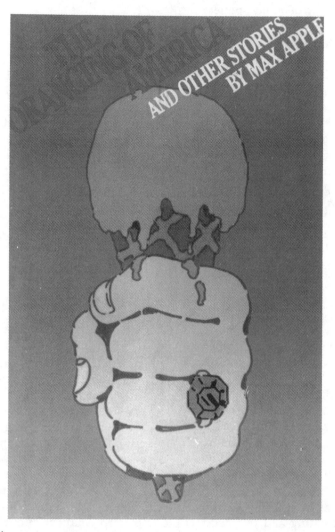

Cover for Apple's first book. The title story, about the founder of the Howard Johnson restaurant-and-motel chain, reflects Apple's fascination with popular culture and his tendency to place historical figures in fanciful situations.

Russian realist tradition to celebrate American icons and the neon and plastic world.

Money is a dominant theme in *The Oranging of America*. Apple was a member of a materialistic generation, providing him the personal experience with which to interpret the maze of numbers, acronyms, and labels that characterized American consumerism. In the *Saturday Review* (22 January 1977), Celia Betsky summed up his approach: "From political morality to private hang-ups, he hits things right on target by making the familiar a parody of itself, by letting spoofs show how serious our zany realities are."

Another story in *The Oranging of America* is "Selling Out," which is perfectly plausible all the way through. In "Selling Out" the narrator inherits a sum of money, and when his stockbroker cousin

does not make enough from it, he studies the market himself, sells what he has, and reinvests the money based on his studies. Once again there is the overriding theme of big-money action in the capitalist system, viewed from a slapstick perspective.

Other stories are just as wacky. Ferguson, the carnivorous narrator in "Vegetable Love," is an accountant attending law school at night when he falls in love with Annette Grim, who does not shave under her arms and uses no deodorants. "I never make love to meat eaters," she tells him; "it adds the smell of the grave to postcoital depression." The characters in this story are not buffoons with real names; rather, they seem to be real people trying to make sense of the buffoonery of their times. Annette is religious about her vegetarianism, as a sign on her wall reminds Ferguson: "The more flesh, the more worms." Finally she severs her ties to Ferguson and moves away, leaving behind a spotless refrigerator.

"Vegetable Love" has more underlying pathos to which the reader can bring meaning than do some of the other stories in the collection. Ferguson finds another woman with whom he jogs off toward Mexico, and thus the story ends in the positive, healthy manner to which the reader of Apple's prose has become accustomed. But there is more meaning than meets the eye. Ferguson's inability to find his lover's "center" is a serious theme rooted in Eastern philosophy. In a 1988 interview in the *Michigan Quarterly Review* Apple said, "In my short story 'Vegetable Love' the man and the waitress put on their running shoes and go off to Mexico. It means that his quest is for nothing less extravagant than the meaning of life. But if I put it like that, who'd want to read it? Who'd want to write it?"

Prevalent in the story "The Yogurt of Vasirin Kefirovsky" is the linguistic humor that must have been so much a part of Apple's household when he was young. Apple focuses on mad inventions and mad dreams and connects them to his food themes by associating them with the well-publicized longevity of yogurt eaters in certain parts of Europe. The German scientist Kefirovsky's humor is based on that of Apple's maternal grandmother, who never learned English but told him stories in Yiddish, while laughing about everyday things that caught her satiric eye.

Apple uses a reporter from *Time* magazine to emphasize the theme of eating and to introduce readers to the eccentricity of Kefirovsky. "Eating has nothing to do with thinking," he tells the reporter. "I always thought clearly, but I thought too much about food. Now I think about nothing to eat. What is yogurt? It's milk and time and heat. What is earth? It's rocks and time and bodies." In Apple's interview with Hundley he talked about how big minds, when not thinking, like to focus on trivial matters: "The 'Yogurt' story in some ways may be the most complicated I've written, as there is a theory of history embedded in it, a theory of diet for sure. But it was mostly a kind of scientific interest that got me started on that. I was working for the first time at Rice, you know, the university that has the heavy scientific background; a lot of my students were biophysicists and biochemists, and there seems this whole wonderful jargon that they have that I was intrigued by. I just started imagining what it would be like for Einstein; well, what would they talk about? It

seemed to settle on food as the common denominator."

In his fable "Free Agents," from the book of stories by the same name (1984), Apple is again indirectly concerned with food. His stomach, the narrator of the story, might be free and independent at last, along with other body organs. In Apple's story the role of judge is assigned to the pituitary gland, who says, "The so-called one-life one-body ruling has for an entire decade been based upon false medical, legal, and moral evidence. . . . Before the age of transplants we took for granted the indignities placed upon our brothers the gallbladder, the appendix, the tonsils, and the intestine by the yard. No more. . . . After the May 11 deadline which we are imposing, all organs, muscle, and tissue, whether initially within the Apple body or added subsequent to birth, become, as it were, free agents, capable of negotiating with any available bodies. We, the undersigned, hope for a just and speedy solution in the spirit of democratic fairness that has characterized the history of collective bargaining."

Another story in the collection *Free Agents* is "Post-Modernism," really more of an essay on literature, in which Apple outrageously proposes the persona of Joyce Carol Oates – a haggard single parent with quintuplets giving the *National Enquirer* an interview to help support her family while she composes Gothic romances – as the standard bearer of postmodernism. At one point the narrator says, "Alas, I have to do this with words, a medium so slow that it took two hundred years to clean up Chaucer enough to make Shakespeare, and has taken three hundred years to produce the clarity of Gertrude Stein." The narrator's academic training is in the traditional curriculum of English departments. He goes on to say how writers get bored and stuck in a medium. He complains that atonal musicians and experimental artists can use xerography and polyester and new technology while writers are stuck with rules of grammar. He speaks of epiphanies as "commonplace events that [James] Joyce put at the heart of his aesthetic," and he becomes experimental by incorporating part of William Burroughs and Brion Gysin's cut-up techniques: a Mu'ammar Qaddafi quote is presented opposite an ad for a Texas Instruments pocket calculator. The narrator then quotes Ezra Pound's dictum "Make it new." He also suggests that a writer's focus on words can go beyond normal associations: "Still there is a possibility of an error, a misprint, a lazy proofreader, a goof by the advertising agency –

plenty of room for paranoia and ambiguity, always among the top ten in literary circles."

When readers turn to "Walt and Will," one of the major stories in *Free Agents,* they encounter a character based on a person whom one would never expect Pound to have acclaimed as one of the greatest geniuses in American art – Walt Disney. In the story, Walt fixates on the idea of motion, which later becomes the principle behind his genius for animation. He is studying the way ants move with as much intensity as we would expect from a scientist. Walt only wants to duplicate the fantastic mechanics of animation that he sees in the natural world. As with mystics, who envision other worlds, his imagination stretches to the possibilities of animating great works of art.

The other main character, Will Disney, speaks up for the airsick Walt as they swirl around in a helicopter looking for space to build Will's fantastic entrepreneurial empires: "Walt could have stopped thirty years ago and still been the most successful artist in the history of the world. . . . Suppose someone had told Michelangelo that, five hundred years from now, Walt Disney Studios could take that whole Vatican ceiling which damn near broke his neck, put it all on celluloid, add as much color as it needs, and make the whole thing *move.*" Fantasy, reality, absurdity, and seriousness often merge in Apple's characters.

Max Apple has deservedly enjoyed critical acclaim and popularity, but will his writing endure as literature? Reviewer Carole Cook wrote in the *Nation* (15 January 1977), "The world of Max Apple does have its fascinations; the writer has talent to burn, but his facility for playing cultural references off against each other approaches slickness. His stories are as entertaining and rapid fire as the media they seek to satirize have taught us to expect, but they're also lacking in critical perspective." Apple may not yet have escaped postmodernism, and, like other writers, he has to deal with Pound's hauntingly simple definition: "Literature is news that stays news." Nonetheless, Apple told the interviewer for the *Michigan Quarterly Review,* "In the act of writing a novel or story, I'm dreaming. I'm daydreaming." In a time when written language seems less meaningful to a young audience than a cartoon or pictograph, the inventiveness of Max Apple serves well. Grounded in postmodernism, his message might be flashing to a younger audience while the older critics absorb the shock.

Interviews:

Patrick D. Hundley, "Triggering the Imagination: An Interview with Max Apple," *Southwest Review,* 64 (Summer 1979): 230–237;

Michigan Quarterly Review, 27 (Winter 1988): 77.

Russell Banks

(28 March 1940 –   )

Denis M. Hennessy
State University of New York College at Oneonta

BOOKS: *15 Poems,* by Banks, William Matthews, and Newton Smith (Chapel Hill, N.C.: Lillabulero, 1967);

Waiting to Freeze (Northwood Narrows, N.H.: Lillabulero, 1967);

30/6 (New York: Quest, 1969);

Snow: Meditations of a Cautious Man in Winter (Hanover, N.H.: Granite, 1974);

Searching for Survivors (New York: Fiction Collective, 1975);

Family Life (New York: Avon, 1975; revised edition, Los Angeles: Sun & Moon, 1988);

The New World (Urbana: University of Illinois Press, 1978);

Hamilton Stark (Boston: Houghton Mifflin, 1978);

The Book of Jamaica (Boston: Houghton Mifflin, 1980);

Trailerpark (Boston: Houghton Mifflin, 1981);

The Relation of My Imprisonment (Washington, D.C.: Sun & Moon, 1983);

Continental Drift (New York: Harper & Row, 1985; London: Hamilton, 1985);

Success Stories (New York: Harper & Row, 1986);

Affliction (New York: Harper & Row, 1989);

Brushes with Greatness (Toronto: Coach House, 1989);

The Sweet Hereafter (New York: HarperCollins, 1991).

Russell Banks, circa 1991 (photograph by Nathan Farb)

Russell Banks resists categories; yet as one looks at the American short fiction written in the last quarter of the twentieth century, the temptation is to group Banks with Raymond Carver, Richard Ford, Andre Dubus, and perhaps Richard Bausch and call the movement "Trailer-Park Fiction." These and some other serious short-story writers have examined American working-class people living their lives one step up from the lowest rung on the socioeconomic ladder and doing battle every day with the despair that comes from violence, alcohol, and self-destructive relationships. Banks is singular, however, as are the other writers, and any such grouping would hide much that is vital to appreciation and understanding. Banks has been very successful with his novels *Continental Drift* (1985), *Affliction* (1989), and *The Sweet Hereafter* (1991), but his short fiction, published in a steady stream since 1975, has been the testing ground of his most innovative ideas and techniques.

Russell Earl Banks was born in Newton, Massachusetts, on 28 March 1940 to Earl and Florence Banks, but he was raised in Barnstead, New Hampshire. Earl Banks, a pipe fitter, was an alcoholic and left his wife and four children when Russell, the oldest, was twelve. He was bright, and he enrolled at Colgate University in 1958 on a full scholarship but returned home that November, apparently unable or unwilling to live and learn with the sons of wealthy, privileged families. He then made an abortive attempt to join Fidel Castro's army in Cuba but ended up in Lakeland, Florida. He married Darlene Bennett there in June 1960, and she later gave birth to the first of his four daughters, Leona. Banks has been married four times. The mother of his second wife, the poet Mary Gunst, whom he married in 1962, paid for his four years at the University of North Carolina at Chapel Hill, from which he graduated Phi Beta Kappa in 1967. His marriage to Gunst ended in 1977, and he married Kathy Banks, an editor, in 1982. After their 1988 divorce he married the poet Chase Twichell. The autobiographical elements in Banks's fiction provide more than just credentials for a writer in the blue-collar genre; in his case, they seem to help him evoke a haunting tone, a palpable mood of despair, and harrowing, realistic details. As he told Wesley Brown in 1989, "All family stories are myths about yourself."

Searching for Survivors (1975) is Banks's first published volume of short stories and is dedicated to Christopher Banks, his deceased brother. In "Searching for Survivors II," the last story in the collection, Reed, the protagonist, has traveled to California to find some sign of the remains of his youngest brother, Allen, on the site of the train wreck that took his life. Banks had lost his own brother in a California train accident, and the despairing search for anything at all that may have survived is a poignant image, emblematic of Banks's recurrent theme in this volume – and in most of his other works – of a man looking for traces of his lost family.

The collection is also about adventuring, and each story ends in some kind of defeat and disillusionment. Survivors are few. The first story, "Searching for Survivors I," reaches back to one of the first American adventurers, Henry Hudson, for inspiration. The narrator thinks of the unfortunate captain of the *Discovery* and how he was abandoned in 1611 and set adrift in the northern bay that bears his name. Musing about Hudson while speeding along the Henry Hudson Parkway, north of Manhattan, the narrator also thinks of a friend's father's beloved car, a Hudson. He then recounts his adventures in automobiles around the United States as a young man. Older now, living in rural New Hampshire again, he has just bought a sled-dog puppy. He thinks of entering a race with it in New Hampshire

and veering off course, perhaps to the shores of the Hudson Bay, where he would look for debris that may have survived Henry Hudson's wreckage. The narrator is drawn to failure, sentimentally looking for signs that can possibly yield hints of why the American adventure has failed.

Banks returns frequently to stories and myths from the Old World and the early exploration of North America, and he shows the connections between those who set out from their comfortable but unjust homelands to settle the unknown, and modern Americans who have been shunted out of their safe cocoons of fixed values and family security into the relativistic reality of the last half of the twentieth century. Thus, right after the Henry Hudson tale, Banks placed "With Che in New Hampshire," a story of a young adventurer returning to Crawford, New Hampshire, ostensibly after years of rebellion and international intrigue with Che Guevara. The narrator's romantic musings are those of a scared young man seemingly writing the script of a life he cannot live. In this haze of imaginative reverie he appears to be a modern Rip Van Winkle. The changes in the people of Crawford are very apparent to him because he has not seen them happen gradually. He is suddenly aware of their aging, and he is somewhat pleased that they do not recognize him because he is so changed by his adventures. But he knows that any lack of recognition is illusory and momentary. He is the same person, simply a bit older with another humiliating set of failures behind him.

The two other Che stories in the volume seem unrelated, but the thematic connections are similar. In "With Che at Kitty Hawk" Janice is a thirty-year-old adventurer, and she is not easily taken in by false idols. Her rebellion is against her parents on one level and her own stultifying marriage on another, and the Wright brothers, not Guevara, inspire her victory. She had come to Kitty Hawk to give herself and her daughters a vacation and a time to think about divorce. To inspirit the bold moves she must take in the future months, she tries a series of liberating acts of defiance. One is picking up a young, swaggering hitchhiker, who offers sex and drugs. Although tempted and flattered, she refuses, choosing rather to take the children on an outing. She tries alcohol, and the effects of Scotch are just what she had expected: disappointing and depressing. The outing with the children is to the memorial where the first airplane flight was taken, and Banks uses the castlelike structure there for the Freudian imagery he needs to show Janice's trapped feelings. The door of the memorial is locked, and "the king and queen aren't home," her daughter Eva notices. But as Janice looks down the slope the Wright brothers used, she has an image of them, their passion and excitement, and their success. She sees a door opening to a room never before used in her own life, and she is freed. Banks writes frequently of the pain of marital failure, but nowhere else does he treat the liberating feelings of divorce and independence for a woman.

With "Che at the Plaza" Banks tries to bring the history of the boy from Crawford and Che himself, if he had lived, up to date. The story is the least successful in the collection. What it has attempted to do, the reader surmises, is bring the dreaming, uncertain boy from New Hampshire face to face with the failed dreams and toppled heroes of the intervening years.

"Investiture" and "Masquerade," two other stories in the collection, show Banks's interest in allegory, told in first person in a timeless setting. As with the tales of early explorers in this and other collections, these stories, bereft of the local color and immediacy of the New Hampshire settings, are meant to help the reader see the universality of the dangers of walking outside the confines of ordinary experience. These stories – and to some extent "The Neighbor" and "The Lie" – are pale in comparison to the others. They show a side of Banks that is abstract and didactic, and in some of the later collections, even tedious.

"The Blizzard," on the other hand, explores new techniques with narration, remains fully in touch with some universal themes of human behavior and psychology, and succeeds gracefully, without the heavy hand of the allegorist. Guilt is the theme, and the focus is the brutalizing effects of winter on the soul. The omniscient narrator begins the tale but relinquishes the narrative to a husband who is gradually losing his hold on reality. Confronted with a real but trivial indiscretion – he made a pass at his wife's friend – he sulks and drives off to a motel forty miles away. There he believes he will find a married, compassionate woman who will talk, make love, commiserate with him, and leave tactfully. None of that happens, and the steadily falling snow hampers his travel and mirrors the relentless nature of his frustration.

"The Defenseman" is more of an essay than a story, showing how a boy learns to ice-skate, and to do many other things, from his father. The defensemen in hockey are the slower but tougher men who do not score goals but deliver punishment. After some lessons from his father, a great defenseman in his day, the boy dreams of hockey and is never

quite the same: he is closer to his father and all men but somewhat distant from and distrustful of his mother. Banks's first awareness of his ability to express himself to an audience came from the discovery of his talent for drawing, and his eye for detail and for catching the essentials of human physical action are amply demonstrated in "The Defenseman." In *Searching for Survivors* readers see the accumulated work of a thirty-five-year-old author, more accomplished than many, dealing with themes of rootlessness and fear and with the young men and women of the 1960s and early 1970s who looked to a bleak future.

In *The New World* (1978) Banks continues to experiment with the short morality tale, as if he were looking for some way to distill American experience into fable form. The book is divided into two parts, "Renunciation" and "Transformation." In the first, he uses contemporary American characters and situations; in the second, he seems to have turned into fiction the results of his musings through the library, looking for clues to the historical backgrounds of modern American sensibility. Sylvia Shorris, in a review of this collection in the *Nation* (10 February 1979), wrote that Banks, especially in the title story, was influenced by Gabriel García Márquez and Jorge Luis Borges but lacks their imagination and precision. She thought that the collection was admirable for Banks's willingness to gamble with daring experimentation.

Also in 1978 Banks published *Hamilton Stark,* a realistic novel set in New Hampshire and having a pipe fitter as a main character. Banks's short stories seem to be the drawing board for some of his abstract ideas, but in his longer works he wants to present his themes on familiar ground.

Marriage, violence, and class are the themes that permeate all Banks's novels, and they are also dominant in *The New World*. In the first story, "The Custodian," forty-three-year-old Rubin, a bachelor recently freed of his filial responsibilities because of the death of his parents, wreaks havoc on the marriages of his friends. He visits each of the wives, looking for a wife for himself, asking each if he appeals to her. They respond enthusiastically, offering their sexual favors immediately. After Rubin's tactful refusals they find it impossible to go back to the tedium of their own husbands. Banks's sense of humor is brittle, tempered only by his compassion for his characters.

His wry humor works well in "The Conversion" because Banks fully develops the main character, Alvin Stock, a sixteen-year-old high-school senior. It is the longest story in the collection, and it shows Banks at his best. Alvin is awash in guilt over cruelty to people, masturbation, and other crimes in a sensitive adolescent's imagination. He is chosen "King of the Spring Bacchanal," and he dances in a kind of stupor until he can find his way out of the dance and into the fresh air where he has a vision of an angel holding a staff in one hand and a fish in the other. "I'm Raphael, one of the Seven," the angel says. Afterward Alvin tells his mother he wants to become a minister. After some indecision he takes the first step toward this goal: he accepts a job as a dishwasher in a Presbyterian summer camp, where he will meet a "better kind of people." The reader realizes that this conversion is really based on a desire for self-improvement rather than on religious inspiration and that Alvin's decision seems determined by the urgings of teachers, his mother, and the "better" people in Crawford. Readers can understand his decision and condone the hypocrisy of it only after Banks has taken them through scenes showing the cold denial emanating from Alvin's father and the brutal sexual exploits and boastings of his coarse friends.

The "Transformation" element in the second part of the book has to do with changes in people coming to the New World. They throw off their old ways and suffer the consequences or reap the benefits of their ventures. In the first story, "The Rise of the Middle Class," Simon Bolivar recognizes that the poor slave who sweeps the floor is better off than he is. The slave is inside history and is protected from it, Bolivar muses, and he himself has stepped outside history.

"Like most fiction writers," Banks admitted in his 1985 interview with Marcelle Thiebaux, "I'm really a library rat, and looking for excuses to research something." This penchant explains his knowledge and use of such disparate characters as Bolivar, Hudson, Edgar Allan Poe, and the main characters in "Indisposed" from *The New World:* William and Jane Hogarth. Banks seems to take delight in satirizing the artist who satirized so much of the society of his time, including married life. Jane narrates the story, describing in detail her brief sexual encounters with her husband, who would come home drunk, have his pleasure with her with no show of affection, button himself up, and return to his own room. She looks at her own large body with disgust until one night, recovering from an illness in her own bed, she hears William climbing the stairs to the room of Ellen, a girl he has taken into the house ostensibly to help Jane. She finds him atop Ellen, roughly pulls him off, and soundly thrashes him. After this triumph she feels better about her

Dust jacket for Banks's 1986 collection, which includes stories relating the problems of people in the Third World to those of the poor and disenfranchised in the United States

body and herself. As one of Banks's morality tales, it succeeds where others fail, its success due to his use of realistic depth and detail.

In "The Caul" Banks employs similar techniques of narration and detail to remind the reader of Poe, the progenitor of this kind of personal horror story. A character named Poe is the narrator and takes readers to his grave, where he allows them to see the source of that eye that haunted so many of his stories: the rueful accusing look of his mother.

The last story, "The New World," summarizes the collection. The message is simply that people who are great and not so great will write stories and create new worlds in their imaginations to escape the horrors of the real. In colonial Jamaica an abbot, confused and disappointed by his assignment by the church hierarchy, writes a Virgilian epic of adventure, mediocre in the eyes of those in the centuries that follow but very satisfying. A tangential character, a Jewish goldsmith, is pained by the lustful glances his daughter receives from a goy, and he writes a tale involving his daughter and royal suitors simply to assuage his anxiety. Both men have come to the New World and see anarchy, bestiality, and total disregard for the civilization they knew, and both react by creating their own New World of imagination. Banks describes the plot of each amateur poet's epic in detail, which can try the patience of the reader, and then he explains their significance in the final paragraph. Banks lived for a year and a half in Jamaica after he received a Guggenheim Fellowship in 1976, and he wrote a novel, *The Book of Jamaica* (1980), there, shortly after he published *The New World*. In the novel he returns to the straightforward realistic style of his more successful stories, but he has never abandoned completely his attempt to achieve a different kind of universality in his experimental tales.

However, he did abandon fantasy and fable in *Trailerpark* (1981) and produced some of his best stories. The setting is New Hampshire, but Banks lived in a trailer park in Florida when he was first married, at age nineteen. He once said of this period (in a 1989 article by Kim Hubbard in *People*) that he was behaving very much like his father: "I was a barroom brawler, a very angry and physically aggressive person, and I drank heavily." There are several characters in *Trailerpark* that could fit this description.

The style of the collection is more assured and less tentative in its experimentation. Banks seems more eager to delve into his characters' hidden selves, and his writerly techniques are more suited to this purpose. The thirteen tales are connected: characters reappear throughout the book from story to story.

Flora Pease is introduced in the first story, "The Guinea Pig Lady," and she is interesting not only in her eccentricity but in the reactions of the others toward her. In her trailer in the Granite State Trailerpark in Catamount, New Hampshire, she keeps guinea pigs, hundreds of them. Flora sings Broadway show tunes most of the time. Marcelle Chagnon, resident manager, thinks Flora is a lesbian and knows that she smokes marijuana, which grows wild in the area, apparently a result of the growing of hemp for the war effort in the 1940s. The narrator is seemingly omniscient, but his tone and vernacular resemble those of the small-town busybody, wise beyond his education. The characters are introduced as they interact with Marcelle or Flora, and Banks seems to be cataloguing people he has known all his life, in Florida, New Hampshire, or anywhere a trailer-park community exists.

Three quarters of the way through the story, Banks switches to a second-person narrative style, which succeeds in presenting the feeling of a local character telling of Flora's taunters. If one knew Flora, the narrator seems to be saying, one would understand her; if one did not, she would seem like an awful freak. Banks achieves the sense of intimacy between reader and narrator that he talked about in his interview with Thiebaux: "I'm really reinventing the narrator. . . . And I want to have that sense of intimacy, a face-to-face, arm-around-the-shoulder contact."

Flora Pease, an ironic "Flower of Peace," is haunted, derided, and ignored until she relents and kills her guinea pigs, moves off alone, and continues smoking her marijuana, trying again to achieve some peace. "The Guinea Pig Lady" is by far the longest story in *Trailerpark* and appears to be the beginning of a novel. The collection itself could be considered a novel, except the stories are fragments never brought together with any attempt to unify or resolve the problems of the characters and their desperate situations.

Buck Tiede in "Cleaving, and Other Needs" has several of the marks of a possible autobiographical character: he is gap-toothed, as is Banks; was a father in his teens; is unhappy in his marriage; and is living on the edge of poverty. He is also violent. Talking about his early years, Banks told Brown, "I was violent against people I loved. But I was never violent against my children. That's as specific as I can be." By the time they divorce when their daughter is four, Buck and Doreen have seen Buck's temper go from physical beatings to aiming an unloaded shotgun at her and pulling the trigger. The main reason for Buck's anger is an inability to satisfy his wife. As a result, she has taken a lover, Howard Leeke, a plumber. Leeke hovers in other stories as something of a priapic image. His name and his hovering around available women are indicative of the kind of grim humor Banks allows himself in his otherwise stoic realism.

The remaining stories are more character sketches for further development than stories, except the last, "The Fisherman," a longer, haunting story about a man's self-inflicted isolation. All the characters in *Trailerpark* seem to be miserable and interact at various times, but all seem isolated and driven deeper into their despair by their apartness.

After his novel *Continental Drift* was so highly praised and Banks was accepted by a wider readership than ever before, readers could see a deeper maturity in his *Success Stories* (1986). The first and last stories in the collection form a kind of novella.

In "Queen for a Day" a father leaves his family for another woman, and twelve-year-old Earl Painter, the oldest child, assumes the role of family protector. Banks's artistic control prevents the story from being sentimentalized or reduced to bathos. The farewell scene is cruel but real, embarrassingly lifelike. Young Earl himself battles childlike sentimentality, using his anger and instinct for survival to steady his frantic, weak mother. The idea he uses to get the necessary money – and attention and love – is to appeal to the "Queen for a Day" show to take pity on the family's case and come to the rescue on one of their broadcasts. His letters go unanswered, and the final scene is a Christmas telephone call from the father during which Earl cuts off his father's lame attempts to entice him into forgiveness. "Firewood," the last story in *Success Stories,* shows the same father twenty years later, trying to reconcile with his children and offering Earl, the only one civil to him, a load of firewood for Christmas. The narrator is omniscient, somewhat distant, and is fair to the errant father. The story could be viewed as almost a forgiveness of Banks's own father because it comes so close to Banks's experience with his parents' breakup. But, although Earl is kind, he keeps his distance tactfully from his father, and in the end the old man is left with his frozen firewood.

Fred Pfeil, in a 13 September 1986 review of *Success Stories* for the *Nation,* said that Banks is trying to do in this book what he did with the Third World in *Continental Drift.* In the novel, Banks uses the story of a desperate Haitian woman trying to escape oppression as a counterpoint to the story of Bob DuBois, who has traveled with his family to Florida to free himself from the angst, error, and failure that trapped him in New Hampshire. Pfeil felt that "The Fish," "The Gully," and "Hostages" are meant to add the same texture to *Success Stories.* The three stories he names are of that type Banks has been experimenting with throughout his career, tales perhaps used to align the problems of power and exploitation in the Third World with the similar plight of the disenfranchised in the United States.

But, as Pfeil also pointed out, the strength of *Success Stories* is the rather helter-skelter bildungsroman the remainder of the stories forms. Between "Queen for a Day" and "Firewood" a young Earl Painter in Florida is ensnared into early commitment in "Success Story." Readers then see him turning into his father as he experiences adultery and deceit firsthand in the story titled "Adultery." With the help of trickery of viewpoint, readers also see him experiment with love with a homely woman in "Sarah Cole: A Type of Love Story."

In an article on Nelson Algren, written for the *New York Times Book Review* (29 April 1990), Banks says, "Driven by a permanent democrat's righteous wrath at injustice, informed by unsentimental respect and unabashed affection for the powerless, in language colored throughout by the pain of some unnamed personal wound whose nature we can only intuit, the novel [*A Walk on the Wild Side,* 1956] is at once a radical critique of the American economy and a grief-stricken portrait of its victims. . . . Because *A Walk on the Wild Side* is a permanent part of our literature, these people, who continue to live among us, will continue to be heard. That's all Nelson ever wanted his work to accomplish, and what writer could want more?" Such a statement could be a manifesto for Russell Banks's own work, especially for the short stories he has published so far.

Interview:

Marcelle Thiebaux, "Russell Banks," *Publisher's Weekly,* 227 (15 March 1985): 120–121.

Biography:

Wesley Brown, "Who to Blame, Who to Forgive," *New York Times Magazine,* 10 September 1989, pp. 52–70.

References:

Sven Birkerts, "Bleak House," *New Republic,* 201 (11 September 1989): 38–41;

Kim Hubbard, "Russell Banks's Tale of Family Violence Hits Close to Home," *People,* 32 (13 November 1989): 135–137.

Richard Bausch

(18 April 1945 –)

Paul R. Lilly, Jr.
State University of New York College at Oneonta

BOOKS: *Real Presence* (New York: Dial, 1980);
Take Me Back (New York: Dial, 1981);
The Last Good Time (New York: Dial, 1984);
Spirits and Other Stories (New York: Linden/Simon & Schuster, 1987);
Mr. Field's Daughter (New York: Linden/Simon & Schuster, 1989);
The Fireman's Wife and Other Stories (New York: Linden, 1990);
Violence (Boston: Houghton Mifflin/Seymour Lawrence, 1992);
Rebel Powers (Boston: Houghton Mifflin/Seymour Lawrence, 1993).

Aside from six widely praised novels – two of them nominated for the P.E.N./Faulkner Award – Richard Bausch has written two collections of short fiction. Some of these stories first appeared in the *New Yorker, Atlantic,* and *Esquire,* and two were chosen for inclusion in *Best American Short Stories of 1990.* Asked in a 1990 interview in *Publishers Weekly* to expound on the relation between writing short stories and writing novels, Bausch replied that stories were "a form of profound recreation. Writing short stories satisfies me in a way that no other activity does. Novels are forms of profound commitment and obsession. There are so many waves, so many ebbings and flowing in them that I feel better to have finished writing a novel, whereas every stage of a story is fun to me. I began as a short-story writer; I wrote novels because I couldn't sell my stories. I'm still a pretty good novelist but my first love is the short story." Bausch is pleased at the way his stories have received recognition: "I'm the only writer who placed two stories in *Best Short Stories of 1990.*" He has also twice won the National Magazine Award for fiction.

Bausch, one of twin boys with four other siblings (Robert, his twin, is a novelist as well), was born in Fort Benning, Georgia, on 18 April 1945 to Robert Carl and Helen Simmons Bausch. The family moved to Washington, D.C., when Richard was

Richard Bausch in 1980 (photograph by Karen Miller Bausch)

three, and later (in 1950) to the suburbs, in Silver Spring, Maryland. The Bausch family was Catholic: "Ours was a devout household," he recalls, "yet it was only at church that we got the prodigious guilt and fear of deep religion. At home, we said the rosary every night, and if the children were a little restless and distracted, we all sensed something of what it meant, and I believe we learned from that experience that words counted for everything: one could address them to the dark, to the night stars in faith that they could be heard and that they mattered." The family moved to Virginia shortly after he graduated from high school. In August 1965 he and his twin enlisted in the U.S. Air Force on the buddy system, serving until 1969. After being discharged, he roamed the Midwest and South with a rock band – the "Luv'd Ones" – playing guitar, singing, composing songs, and writing poetry. On 3 May 1969 he married Karen Miller, a photographer. They then returned to Virginia, where he studied at two Virginia schools, Northern Virginia Community College and George Mason University. He had decided to write stories and began taking fiction workshops. He received a B.A. from George Mason University in 1974 and entered the creative-writing program at the University of Iowa, from which he received his M.F.A. in 1975. At Iowa he was a teaching/writing fellow and studied with Vance Bourjaily, John Leggett, and John Irving. Bausch accepted an assistant professorship at George Mason, where he is now a full professor of creative writing. He lives with his wife and five children – Wesley, Emily, Paul, Maggie, and Amanda – in Broad Run, Virginia.

In 1977 he began his first novel, *Real Presence,* which was published in 1980, received a favorable review in *Time,* and went through two printings. *Take Me Back,* his second novel, was published in March 1981 and nominated for a P.E.N./Faulkner Award, about the same time that Robert Bausch published his first novel, *On the Way Home.* The *Washington Post* (2 March 1992) featured an article on the Bausch brothers – the only identical-twin novelists in American letters. Richard Bausch's *The Last Good Time* was published in 1984. He won a Guggenheim Fellowship the same year and decided to spend the year revising an abortive novel titled "Spirits," parts of which began turning into short stories. "What Feels like the World" appeared in the *Atlantic* in 1985 and was chosen for an O. Henry Award. Two more were sold to the *Atlantic* ("The Man Who Knew Belle Starr" and "Police Dreams") before the collection titled *Spirits and Other Stories* was published in 1987.

Bausch's stories are often set in a generalized but not specifically described area in Virginia ("Point Royal" is its most frequent name). By his own assertion, he is not an autobiographical writer: "Aside from incidental details of place and time, my fiction is almost totally devoid of autobiographical matters; in fact, when something I'm working on begins to come too close to the life I actually lead, I can feel the pen begin to freeze up." Moreover, he is not a regional writer or one concerned with developing a sense of place: his fictional worlds are inte-

rior ones; his characters are caught in the act of shifting their hopes and expectations. The settings for such shifts – the motel room in "Wedlock" (in *The Fireman's Wife and Other Stories,* 1990) or the ranch home of the wife in "The Fireman's Wife" – could be anywhere in contemporary America.

Bausch's concerns are moral; his subject matter is the self in conflict with the need to discover or invent a better version of itself and a need to hold on to a haunted, often unhappy past. Bausch's stories probe this tension between self and selfishness in the form of tormented sons whose fathers have been alcoholic or violent, wives who repress their anger at husbands who fail to do the right thing, and daughters who are crippled by the memory of their parents' silent combats of will.

Bausch's choice of epigraphs for *Spirits and Other Stories* reflects the tension between the drive to be assertive and the need to forgive: he juxtaposes Sigmund Freud's statement "Ja, Geist ist alles" (Yes, spirit is all) with Saint Paul's claim that "the Spirit itself maketh intercession for us with sighs too deep for words." Two versions of spirit, the assertive and the forgiving, are entangled; Bausch's challenge is to give words to his characters' sighs and to make intercessions between characters and readers. In the first of the nine stories, "All the Way in Flagstaff, Arizona," the main character, Walter, sits alone in a church, Saint Paul's, musing on a disastrous family picnic that prefigured the end of his marriage. In his memory his wife, Irene, aware that he is sneaking slugs of Jim Beam whiskey from the car trunk, says, as she looks over the seemingly peaceful scene of her gathered children, "It could be like this all the time." But the truth is deeper than her words: it *is* like this all the time – bad. Walter cannot stop drinking. His demon is the memory of his father, who beat him in a dark Alabama cellar when he was young. Walter's drunken cavorting with his children at the picnic turns ugly; their sudden fear of him stuns him into the recognition that he is his own nightmare: "he has always been paralyzed by the fear that he will repeat, with his own children, the pattern of his father's brutality."

"Police Dreams" charts the shifting lines between emotional order and disorder, and between dreams of disaster and the disaster of a failed marriage. In Casey's recurring dreams of violence and disorder, he is alone facing assailants and needing the police to help him restore order. When he awakens next to his wife, Jean, and hears the sounds of his two boys in the next bedroom, he reassures himself that daylight has brought him the order he

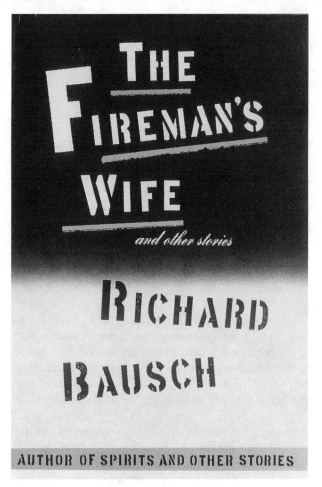

*Dust jacket for Bausch's second collection (1990). In the title
story a fireman's hands are burned as he fights a fire on the
same day his wife has decided to leave him.*

lacked in his nightmare. But daylight reveals to
readers – but not to Casey, who stubbornly refuses
to read the signs of his married life – that Jean is unhappy and on the verge of leaving him. He interprets his dreams to her (the first three find him and
his helpless family facing brutal intruders who are
killers) but feels he is "badly misreading" his wife,
whose days are marked by anxiety attacks. She cannot sleep; he cannot stop dreaming of disasters in
which the police never come: "She would gladly
take his nightmares if she could only sleep." Jean finally wakes Casey from his daytime sleepwalking
by telling him she wants to leave him. He returns
alone to his house, deliberately frightens the babysitter, and begins to dream another nightmare. But
this one finds him in charge, getting revenge on the
intruders, the murderers of his family: "He tracks
the intruders down"; he becomes the police and "establishes order."

Lost fathers haunt the characters of Bausch's
fiction. Roger, in "Contrition," seeks a picture of his
dead father, whom he never met. "I want to look at
my father again," he says to his sister, who has reluctantly taken him into her home because, as he
tells her and her husband, "I had no place to go."
Roger is a convicted felon, fired from his teaching
job for drunkenness and assaulting a prostitute and
a police officer. He thinks his sister may have an old
photograph of his father, one he used to stare at on
his mother's bedroom wall. The icon of the strong
father is all Roger has to cling to, and now, says his
sister, it, too, is lost. He has been to a counselor,
looking for forgiveness, which, as he knows from
his boyhood Catholic training, depends on contrition. The counselor says to him that he is forgiven.
"I don't feel forgiven," he replies. "I'm born Catholic and God is like a hurricane on the West Coast."
Roger lies in bed, the last night in his sister's home,
and thinks about a dream he might have, a dream
about his father, as if he could summon up his
father's saving grace by dreaming about him. But
the projected dream is really about his own situation: his father sitting with a prostitute in 1938 becomes Roger as he really was not long before. "Say
his wife is leaving him," Roger says to himself,
building the dream. "Say he's filled with fear and
anger and say the woman is someone he's never met
before in his life." Roger wants to be "new and
clean and worthy," but God is far away.

"Spirits" is the last and longest of the stories. It
probes the meaning of several kinds of spirits that
have emerged in the previous stories: the spirit of
evil; of murder; and of erotic fantasy, which becomes, for the unnamed narrator of "Spirits," a violation of a woman's privacy and a revelation of the
darkness in his soul. The narrator, a writer, looks
back at his first teaching job at a small college in
Virginia. In his reverie his wife of only a few
months, Elaine, is still in the Midwest, and he is
alone among strangers, one of whom, William
Brooker, a former intimate of John F. Kennedy, invites him to house-sit a luxurious home while William and his glamorous wife, Helen, are away. The
narrator discovers evil not only in Mr. Sweeney, a
rapist and murderer he never meets (he does wear
one of Sweeney's ties, suggesting some unsavory
link between the two), but in his own soul. As he recalls those summer days without the company of his
wife but in the imaginary presence of the "spirit" of
Helen Brooker, whose empty bed he chooses to
sleep in, he comes to know the "forces that would
always be lurking in the darker corners of the
spirit," including his own, for he is too much like

Sweeney, an imprisoned killer who lived an outwardly normal life managing a motel (Mrs. Sweeney confides to the narrator, who stays briefly in the motel, that her husband was a "good story teller"). The writer is also a violator, living his own version of Sweeney's "passionless violence." "I stalked the house," he says, "for a woman's privacy." He is another of Bausch's dispirited ones, "a ghost," in the narrator's phrase, "haunting another ghost." But he is also a writer in crisis; he cannot write and so turns to other sources to inspire energy. He reads Helen's letters, takes notes, seeks evidence of William Brooker's past adultery, follows closely the newspaper-reported confessions of Sweeney, who has turned his crimes into nouns (Sweeney recalls doing "a knife," doing "a strangle"). Sweeney's language has energy; the writer/narrator can only envy it. But the narrator finds he has passed some border between words and action. By lying to a distraught young woman, Maria Alvarez, who is looking for William and is clearly emotionally involved with him, the narrator implicates himself in her subsequent suicide. Like Sweeney, he is discovered for what he is. Helen returns to find him rummaging through her letters, and he is forced, as was the captured Sweeney, to articulate what he thinks of himself – he is a spy. His story, written years later, is his confession. He recalls how he felt then, "unhinged" by the "oppression" of that summer, filled with "the sense that the world below me was little more than a savage place where the weak were fed upon by the strong." Since that time he has seen that life is certainly that but more as well. His love for his wife (they remain together and raise four children) brings him a kind of redemption, a new spirit with which to write and live.

In 1988 *Spirits and Other Stories* was nominated for the P.E.N./Faulkner Award. While at work on his 1989 novel, *Mr. Field's Daughter,* Bausch continued writing short stories. He published his second collection, *The Fireman's Wife and Other Stories,* in 1990. This group of stories tests the validity of the balance between the "uncharted and dark" side of life (in the words of the unnamed writer in "Spirits") and the hope of some intercession, some glimpse of light. In the story "Equity," whose title itself suggests a balancing of accounts – an adding up of moral debit and credit – three sisters ponder the new cost of caring for their mother, who, because of Alzheimer's disease, is growing into the helpless child each of the three once was. Who should pay this moral and emotional debt, and what is its cost? The sisters start adding it all up over lunch in a

Charlottesville, Virginia, restaurant. In some other stories there is only darkness, as in "Wedlock," in which a new bride, squinting at the bathroom light in a darkened motel room, sees that her new husband's "baby blue" eyes have a deadly "chill" and that his true self, now made even more sinister because of his drunken affability, has previously been hidden from her. In two stories there are writers, one an aging dramatist whose single successful play, *The Brace,* emotionally destroyed his former wife, the mother of the daughter he now visits; in the other story, "Letter to the Lady of the House," which concludes the collection, an old man writes to his wife, who is asleep in the next room. His words weigh in on the side of love over despair, although he has seen much of the latter, and the story contrasts with "Wedlock." The effect is singularly affirming, as the old man makes a final claim for the redemptive power of love.

"Wedlock" reveals Lisa's wedding night as a trap, a sudden slamming shut of a cell door with a lock clicking behind her. Her new husband, Howard, who she thinks has a "good-natured goofiness," shows a streak of cruelty in a series of drunken improvisations for his new bride, who says, "You're not like this, Howard, now stop it." But Howard is like that, and as the glow of too much champagne wears off, the exhausted Lisa fears that she has no idea who her husband really is. His boozy transformations remind her of "adept comedians on television" who look "like anyone at all but themselves." Bausch's epigraph for his volume, a line from John Keats ("Happy love, more happy, happy love"), grates harshly against whatever form of love could possibly survive this one night in a barren motel room.

The collapse of the illusion of love, of truth, and even of storytelling itself links "Old West" with "Wedlock," though the settings are very different. The narrator of "Old West," speaking in 1950 at the age of eighty, looks back on the story of Shane he has been telling half his life to vaudeville audiences for a living. Now (three years before the release of the movie *Shane* in 1953) he will tell the real story of Shane, who came back to that valley (the one audiences know from the movie) twelve years after he rode away, wounded and heroic, leaving behind him a boy crying after him, "Shane, come back." Now that boy is an old man, the narrator. His story corrects the earlier one, demythologizing Shane's heroics and replacing them with the sordidness of human motives and the truth of violence. When Shane returns, the narrator is no longer the boy he once was. He is twenty, disillu-

Bausch, circa 1992 (photograph by Karen Miller Bausch)

sioned by his mother's decline into senility and ugliness. He is already drinking too much, and his mother is so crazed by her life that she nearly shoots him, convinced he is a Comanche raider. The farm of his dead father, Joe Starret, is going to ruin: "That part of the world was indeed cattle country and for all the bravery of the homesteaders, people had begun to see this at last." Shane's former love for Marian, the boy's mother, is as faded as his buckskin (although he has the decency to be embarrassed at his appearance when he finally sees her again). He has come back, but not to restore a young boy's faith. Shane is merely trying to capture a wanted man and earn a bounty.

The fugitive, Bagley, is an itinerant preacher and drunkard who is vaguely interested in Marian. His drunken jeremiads to unwashed cowboys in the old saloon are in fact prophetic: "Pornography and vulgar worship of possessions, belief in the self above everything else, abortion, religious fraud, fanatic violence, mass murder, and killing boredom, it's all coming, hold on!" Bagley is also a kind of writer; when he talks, says the narrator, Bagley's sentences line up "one after the other, perfectly symmetrical and organized as any written speech."

Bagley hears the narrator's original tale of Shane but tells the narrator he is exaggerating. "You read a lot, do you?" Bagley asks.

Thus the stage is set for the final showdown: a shootout in which Bagley and Shane shoot each other. Their shots shatter not only the silence of that afternoon but the older version of the narrator's tale. He sees that his childhood memory of the heroic Shane was really false, that "the clearest memory of my life was a thing I made up in my head." "Old West" is a tale that probes the nature of storytelling; it deflates the *Shane* myth but builds a new version that is also symmetrical and organized.

"The Fireman's Wife" and "Consolation" are paired by common characters and the consoling consequence of a tragedy. In the first, Jane, the wife of a fireman, Martin, senses that her status is defined by her husband's work and pattern of leisure; she must adjust to the rhythm of too much of his presence and then, when he is on duty, too little. The strain increases during a party with his fellow firemen and their wives. Milly, the wife of Martin's friend Wally, is pregnant and tries to soothe Jane's restlessness. However, Wally is killed fighting a fire the next night, and Martin is injured, his hands burned. Just before Martin is carried into the house, Jane, who has been feeling "the full weight of her unhappiness," has decided to leave him. She packs her bags, and the helpless Martin sees them and knows. She ministers to him, changing his clothes, feeding him, and finally putting him to bed. He is like a child – but not the child she thought she wanted to have. As she closes the door to his room, she thinks about "how people will go to such lengths leaving a room – wishing not to disturb, not to awaken, a loved one." She is in no hurry. She has plenty of time to decide when to leave him and where to go.

"Consolation" begins six months after the tragedy of the fire. Milly has taken her infant son from her home in Illinois to visit Wally's grieving parents in Philadelphia. She is with her older sister, Meg, who is in the process of divorcing her husband, Larry. The two sisters stay in a motel and join Wally's parents for a dinner at their home. But the visit does not go well. The child cries; its grandparents, the Harmons, suffer from the "commotion"; and Meg is appalled. When the sisters return to the motel, Larry is there, having come all the way from Illinois for a last-chance attempt to persuade Meg not to divorce him. He has brought a poem for Meg to read while he paces outside the motel room. The inanity of the poem provokes the two sisters into wild laughter, and Milly senses, as she recovers her breath, how much she has suffered these last months. The Harmons arrive at the motel to visit them, dragging as a gift an enormous teddy bear; Larry argues with Meg about the divorce; and the five adults find themselves starting to watch the Independence Day fireworks – a far happier fire than the one that had set all these events in motion months before. As the Harmons hold the baby, Milly looks over the rooftops of the "city of brotherly love" and realizes she is "the only one of these people without a lover." Yet their presence, teddy bear and all, evokes at least a hint of the story's title.

"The Brace" is Bausch's only story about a successful writer, in this case a dramatist who uses his past to toy with his own remorse over the many betrayals in his life – his betrayals of friends; his alienated son, James; his dead wife; and his daughter, Marilyn, who is the narrator of the story. Marilyn feels that his most successful play, *The Brace,* not only abuses her dead mother but "plagiarizes" her. Marilyn resents the freedom her father took to create a character based on a real person, and Marilyn's literal-mindedness is her way of defying her father, who she knows disapproves of her rejection of creativity. When he visits her, she watches soap operas. Her deliberately ordinary life in Point Royal is her way of punishing her father, and it works: he hates "everything about the house, my husband and his job selling textbooks – our television and the fenced yard and the kids going to public school." She grieves for her own sad youth wasted in Rome under the stern hand of her father's one-eyed housekeeper and mistress. Now her children are receiving what she did not, and her father cannot see there is a gain: "They want someone to be interested in their lives and to have time for them," says Marilyn to herself. "Which is, and always has been, what I happen to want, too." As a child she never had anyone to "brace her" the way her mother was a brace for her father. And she cannot forgive him; it is her husband's nature to forgive "as it is mine to remember." "The Brace" charts the destructive power of memory when it includes a lack of love.

"Luck" presents a familiar Bausch character, the alcoholic father, through the eyes of a son. There is love in these eyes but pain and disillusionment, too. Father and son are housepainters, and the son, pleased at the progress they are making in a newly built sumptuous home, is stunned again to see the familiar signs in his father's speech that portend the inevitable binge to follow. He has seen it all too many times, he confides to the reader: "This is

all stuff you know. You don't need me to paint the picture." And yet it hurts. His father starts to talk "goofy" – "Best car ever made was the Studebaker, Baker" – then leaves the job while promising to return. The son paints on alone, his strokes a form of therapy. He remembers how his father took pride in his work years ago. Then the owner walks in, also a father, but to a wayward and apparently ungrateful son. The owner and narrator begin to talk, and the owner says, "You must be very proud of your dad." The son is shocked, not knowing how much the owner knows about the father. But the son sticks up for him, playing the role of the good son that the owner apparently wants performed. Their relationship is too symmetrical for the stricken son, who knows that the owner/father wants to be as proud of his son as the narrator wants to be of his painter/father. But he knows that the owner is self-deceived, and that the relation between the owner and his son is just as off-balance as his own with his father. He also knows that the owner is thinking that between the two of them, the painter's son and the rich owner, "between that man and me – I was the lucky one." But the owner is wrong. There is no good luck on either side.

Like "Luck," "Equity" tests the limits of love between parent and child. Three daughters ranging from ages thirty-four to fifty must decide what to do with their aging mother, Edith, who has Alzheimer's disease. Edith, after her retirement, had returned from Florida to Virginia to care for her three daughters in turn, each of whom was then in the midst of a crisis. She moved from one daughter's home to another, bringing her determination to help but also bringing her own personal quirks, including her compulsion for redistributing the benefits of life for each so there is "equity." Edith has been arranging "equal distribution of her daughters' possessions" by taking things from one daughter's home and bringing them to another. Now the daughters realize that these thefts are symptoms of her disease: "she couldn't help what she did any more than she could remember having done it." The three sisters meet for lunch in order to decide what to do with their mother. Allison, the oldest, wants them to decide "together" so that "the responsibility can be equally distributed." It is the daughters' turn to measure the implications of love, the burden-sharing, the equity of it all. Edith has given; they have received. Now, with Edith unable to give anything but trouble (she has wandered off into the streets clothed in a bathrobe and burned a pot on the stove), the time for accounting has come. Carol impulsively offers to take Edith to live with her. But Carol is weak, barely recovered from a breakdown two years before. She agrees with her older sisters' idea of hospitalization for Edith. Carol leaves the table, sees herself in a mirror as she will be years from then – like Edith, alone, rummaging through a box of belongings, "unable to quite tell what was actually hers and what wasn't, what had been given and what received, with what words and by whom, and when."

Bausch's final story in the collection offers a counterpoint to the disaster of a marriage only hours old in the opening story, "Wedlock." "Letter to the Lady of the House" concerns another husband and wife, but this couple is still living in a marriage of five decades, although the present, writes John to his sleeping Marie, can hardly be called happy. Lately, he says, "we've been more like strangers than husband and wife." And now they have had another argument, and Marie has gone to bed. John, sipping bourbon to strengthen him for this new and unprecedented effort – writing a letter to his wife in the next room – is prompted by his sense of alienation from Marie as well as a growing sense of feeling "the end of things more strongly than I can describe." He wants to write in order to avoid "the old aggravating sound of me talking to you," and because what he wants to say is really a story: the story of his boyhood affection for his older married cousin, Louise, whom he visited in Charlottesville during the Depression. The young John's fascination with the love between Louise and her hus-band, Charles, inspired him to think that "soon I would be embarked on my own life as Charles was, and that an attractive woman like Louise would be there with me." And so it came to be. He married Marie, and years later an embittered Louise, who ended up hating Charles, asks John how he and Marie managed to stay together. John's story's point for his wife is that "whatever our complications, we *have* managed to be in love over time." The testing of the equity of love that John is moving toward rests on a question: is love worth the inevitable pain of life together? At seventy, he says yes. For the chance of that love, the one he imagined as a boy watching Louise and Charles, "I would do it all again, Marie. All of it, even the sorrow. My sweet, my dear adversary."

The attention that Bausch is receiving from the favorable reviews and commercial success of his novel *Violence* (1992) will inevitably result in a closer scrutiny of his published short stories. This wider audience will discover to their pleasure just how careful he is with words; as he says, "it all comes down to that."

Interview:
Dulcy Brainard, "Richard Bausch," *Publishers Weekly,* 237 (10 August 1990): 425–426.

Reference:
Elizabeth Kastor, "The Author, Giving Rise to 'Violence,'" *Washington Post,* 2 March 1992, pp. B1, B4.

Charles Baxter

(13 May 1947 –)

Terry Caesar
Clarion University of Pennsylvania

BOOKS: *Chameleon* (New York: New Rivers, 1970);
The South Dakota Guidebook (New York: New Rivers, 1974);
Harmony of the World (Columbia: University of Missouri Press, 1984);
Through the Safety Net (New York: Viking, 1985);
First Light (New York: Viking, 1987);
Imaginary Paintings and Other Poems (Latham, N.Y.: Paris Review, 1989);
A Relative Stranger (New York: Norton, 1990).

OTHER: "Assaulting the Audience in Modernism," in *Modernism: Challenges and Perspectives,* edited by Monique Chefdor and Richard Quinones (Carbondale: Southern Illinois University Press, 1986), pp. 274–283;
"The Donald Barthelme Blues," *The Pushcart Prize Anthology, XVI* (Wainscott, N.Y.: Pushcart, 1991), pp. 363–377.

SELECTED PERIODICAL PUBLICATIONS –
UNCOLLECTED: "In the Suicide Seat: Reading John Hawkes's *Travesty,*" *Georgia Review,* 34 (1980): 871–885;
"De-Faced America: *The Great Gatsby* and *The Crying of Lot 49,*" *Pynchon Notes,* 7 (October 1981): 22–37.

Charles Baxter, circa 1990 (photograph by Michael Lauchlan)

Charles Baxter's short fiction is focused on middle-class life-styles. Sometimes in his writing he is patient, sometimes aloof, and sometimes tough-minded about middle-class life. Anton Chekhov's work is Baxter's exemplar of the first stance, Donald Barthelme's fiction (until mid career) represents the second, and the third resembles Ernest Hemingway's attitude. Baxter has been influenced by each of these writers. Yet he is not the product of any particular "school." Baxter is a self-effacing writer who is not easily described in terms of influences because he has smoothly and intelligently absorbed so many of them into his work.

Born in Minneapolis on 13 May 1947 to John and Mary Barber Baxter, Charles Baxter received his B.A. at Macalester College in Saint Paul and his Ph.D. at the State University of New York at Buffalo. Starting in 1974, he taught English for several years at Wayne State University, and he is now a professor of English at the University of Michigan. On 12 July 1976 he married Martha Ann Hauser. In an interview with Michael Kiser, he somewhat reluctantly located himself in a midwestern "community" of writers and mentioned Sherwood Anderson, Willa Cather, Evan S. Connell, Jr., and Richard Bausch.

Baxter's style is, of course, apparent in his first collection of fiction, *Harmony of the World* (1984), which won the sixth annual AWP (Associated Writing Programs) Award for Short Fiction. One of the finest stories is "A Short Course in Nietzschean Ethics," whose abstract, discursive title is misleading. The story is a tightly strung presentation of the narrator's boyhood friend, Waldo Steiner, a "creep" who, after the death of his mother when he is nine, begins to cheat at games. The narrator eventually shares a room with him in college and marries a former acquaintance of his. "The middle class finally gathered me to its breast," says the narrator after he graduates. One night Waldo suddenly calls, out of work, desperate, lonely, and pathetically obnoxious and contemptuous. The narrator scarcely knows how to respond, but he permits Waldo to come to his home. While making coffee, he notices that Waldo has wandered upstairs, where the narrator's wife is sleeping, and he proceeds to throw Waldo down the stairs. "Help me," Waldo says. His friend calls a cab. Throughout Baxter's first collection, normal lives are interrupted by abnormal, eccentric, and destructive impulses.

"Xavier Speaking" is again a narrative of friendship, but with two peculiar features. First, though he resembles Waldo, the character Arthur symbolizes larger social or generational trends; his college "experiments," especially sexual, are representative of 1960s morality. While Arthur establishes a farm in Wisconsin, the narrator goes off to graduate school in Buffalo. The second difference is that the marriage of Arthur and his wife, Carrie, is shattered by a psychopathic Jesus freak named Xavier. In effect the Waldo figure meets his own Waldo, and this time the wife is enthralled. She leaves with Xavier, and Arthur visits the narrator to tell him — two weeks before his dissertation defense. The narrator is sympathetic but "frightened." He has earlier remarked that he did not want the story to "convert," threaten, or define him. Wanting to be content with his impeccably academic life, the narrator concludes, "If Saint Jerome himself were to knock at this door this very instant, his head ringed with heavenly fire and his eyes burning with the fever of a truth he knows and which I have acknowledged my entire adult life, I am reasonably certain that I would glance once, recognize him, and turn him away from my door, whose threshold I could not bear to see him cross, without another word."

"Harmony of the World," the title story, was included in the 1982 Pushcart Prize anthology and in the *Best American Short Stories 1982* (selected by John Gardner). Again the narrator is a somewhat glum, cerebral, solitary sort, although this time he is a pianist. "Harmony of the World" is a story about music, according to him the best and truest prefigurement of harmony to be found in the world. The narrator is so disturbed when his teacher at a midwestern music school declares that he lacks "fanaticism" that he leaves school, takes a job somewhere in New York State as a newspaperman, and winds up writing music reviews. After he begins to hire himself out as an accompanist, he meets Karen, a soprano. She is talented but her pitch wobbles. Meanwhile, because of an upcoming performance of Paul Hindemith's "Harmony of the World" symphony, the narrator begins to read up on "the foremost anti-Nietzschean German composer of his day." The Hindemith symphony concert proves to be as tepid and dull as the narrator feared. His affair with Karen subsequently ends when he declares that her failure at a certain recital offends music itself as well as him. She stages a mock suicide with an effigy of herself hanging from a tree, and she refuses to have anything more to do with him. The narrator mentions in conclusion that Dante's souls in limbo are not capable of harmony. "Harmony of the World" demonstrates many of the virtues of the volume as a whole: crisp dialogue, spare humor, and the presence of Baxter's insistent intelligence.

Baxter published his next volume of stories, *Through the Safety Net,* a year after his first. Despite the short time period, these stories are more relaxed, at ease with themselves, and less strenuously conceived. The specter of Friedrich Nietzsche is not as heavy. There is less about music or art in the second collection and more about marriages, homes, and children. Dinah, for example, the protagonist of the title story, is the mother of a daughter. Her psychic calls one day to say that something is very wrong. Finally he eliminates specifics: "It's everybody," he says. Her child and husband asleep, Dinah cups her hands to both sides of her face to look outside her window onto her lawn. The dog is barking at what may be an impending storm. Such a life may be the only harmony there is, Dinah thinks, or there may be nothing.

In *Through the Safety Net* Baxter focuses on personal and artistic structures, some achieved, some not. The portrait of the character Donna that her former boyfriend makes in "Stained Glass," for example, is too bizarre; it is not clear whether it should just be thrown out as trash. Similarly an advertising man, Mr. Bradbury, in "The Eleventh Floor," has, from his apartment, "an eleventh floor view of things" that at once keeps him nervously aloof from life and dryly ironic about his son and his girlfriend. Nothing very compelling happens in these stories, except the crises inherent in structures themselves. Baxter is a creator of circumstances that reveal character.

In "Surprised by Joy" Jeremy and Harriet, a married couple, try to come to terms with the accidental death of their daughter, months before. They are inconsolable. At one point Harriet has to haul her husband away from attacking a Jehovah's Witness who appears with his young son at their door. Finally Harriet and Jeremy decide to fly to New Mexico. After driving to Taos, they visit the D. H. Lawrence shrine in the mountains. Harriet is extremely moved, but Jeremy is not. "You're free of it," he says to her. When she replies that he will be all right, he declares, radiantly, "I don't *want* to be all right. It's my pleasure not to be all right. Do you see that? My *pleasure*." The title of the story is an allusion to the 1815 William Wordsworth poem of that name (and, perhaps, in addition, to C. S. Lewis's well-known 1955 autobiography). Harriet scans the immense, sunlit sky and sees a distant curtain of rain with light passing through it. Two years after this story was published in *Through the Safety Net,* Baxter published his only novel to date, *First Light* (1987), in one sense an intricate narrative in which he examines the sort of visionary moment at the end of "Surprised by Joy." It may be that no story can fully contain it.

Such is precisely the imperative of the most celebrated story in *Through the Safety Net,* "Gryphon." Often reprinted (including in *Best American Stories of 1986,* edited by Raymond Carver, and *Best American Short Stories of the Eighties* [1990], edited by Shannon Ravenel), "Gryphon" tells of a fourth-grade class that finds itself with a strange substitute teacher, Miss Ferenczi. She baffles and delights everyone when she strays from the lesson to hold forth on how angels, dressed in evening clothes, often attend concerts and sit unnoticed in the aisles. To Miss Ferenczi, vision is all. She is quickly dismissed after a boy goes to the office when she declares to him, on the basis of a tarot-card reading, that he will soon die. At the conclusion of "Gryphon" the class has been combined with another and is learning about insects – the ones that are pests, the ones barely visible – while waiting for their regular teacher to return to test them. Miss Ferenczi is not the sort of teacher who gives tests. Moreover, the kind of knowledge of which she speaks does not fit into tests. Indeed, like the figure of the gryphon itself, does such knowledge even exist? Baxter implies that, once through the safety

net – and Miss Ferenczi goes all the way through, and away – there may be nothing at all, except death.

Baxter's third fiction collection, *A Relative Stranger* (1990), can be seen as a refinement of his earlier concerns. There are stories about teachers, social workers, ministers, bakers, and businessmen. All tend to be divorced, preoccupied, and troubled. As if to balance the volume, he concludes with the story of a happy couple: "Saul and Patsy Are Pregnant." Saul is dreaming at the end that he "understood everything, the secret of the universe. After an instant, he lost it. Having lost the secret, forgotten it, he felt the usual onset of the ordinary, of everything else, with Patsy around him, the two of them in their own familiar rhythms." As always in Baxter's work the relation between the mystical and the ordinary is highly relative.

In some respects the collection shows Baxter trying fresh developments. Two of the stories feature foreigners, and another is about Ezra Pound in exile. There is a section of "Three Parabolic Tales," each one short and an attempt at extending Baxter's consistent aspiration to become meditative and lyrical. (This aspiration is realized more grandly and lavishly in *First Light.*) *A Relative Stranger* also features his longest and arguably best story to date, "The Disappeared," chosen by Alice Adams for inclusion in *Best American Stories 1991.* It is a story not about the familiar but about its impossibility.

A young Swedish engineer, Anders, arrives in Detroit. Although he has come for business, his true purpose is to see America, and his real desire is to sleep with an American woman. Jogging in a park, he meets a woman who is sexually attractive but professes odd religious beliefs: "We do what everyone else does. We work and we go home and have dinner and go to bed. There is only one thing that we do that is special. . . . We don't make plans. No big plans at all." Anders does not understand her. After they sleep together, he is almost shattered by her indifference about seeing him again. The woman lives with her grandmother, who warns him: "You can't invest in her. You can't do that at all. She won't let you." Eventually Anders is mugged when he goes to try to find the woman's church, and he realizes that he is a lost European: "He felt that he must get home to Sweden quickly, before he became a very different person, unrecognizable even to himself."

"The Disappeared" profoundly confirms one central fact about Baxter's fiction: his men are defined by their relation to women. Baxter spoke about this fact in the Kiser interview when he repudiated any affiliation with what he terms "guy fiction": "It's about what men do in order to be men, and that's a subject I am uninterested in. . . . I've never gone hunting. I can't fix things. I'm not interested in defining myself as a man against other men. . . . I tend to avoid, and this may be a kind of failing in my work, writing male characters who are thinking about who they are as men."

This claim is not quite accurate. One recalls Waldo and the narrator, for example, in "A Short Course in Nietzschean Ethics." Repeatedly in Baxter's fiction a structure occurs in which a decent, bourgeois man is confronted by a crazed, marginal one. "Shelter," in *A Relative Stranger,* conforms to this structure. Cooper, a baker, grows so concerned about the homeless that he eventually takes home a self-proclaimed "saintly" man, Billy Bell. But the man reveals himself to be incipiently violent, and Cooper makes him leave. Two days later Cooper's bakery is broken into. The story ends with Cooper and his wife in bed. "Shelter me," he pleads to her. "Which way this time? Which way?" she asks. Home is where the men in Baxter's stories turn for shelter, or rather where the women who embody shelter are. But these women are not simply maternal or otherwise routinely subordinated to men. Indeed, one of Baxter's strengths as a writer emerges forcefully in *A Relative Stranger:* his women are neither predictable nor predictably coded. The men are arguably more domestic than the women.

Who controls the terms of a relationship? The answer may be less important, at least for Baxter, than how the terms are established. In *A Relative Stranger* they are determined by the easy grace, sexual confidence, and humane poise of women of all ages. One of the volume's finest stories – chosen by Margaret Atwood for *Best American Short Stories 1989* – is "Fenstad's Mother." Fenstad, who works for a computer company by day and teaches English part-time by night, feels vague, fretful, and conventional because he has a far more vivid mother. "What I hate about being my age is how *nice* everyone tries

to be," she tells him, after agreeing to visit his class and hoping that it consists of working-class people. Fenstad's mother enjoys it and cannot keep quiet. Later Fenstad, who fears she has gotten sick, discovers his mother and a brilliant young black sanitation worker from the class listening together to jazz records in her apartment. "I never heard enough jazz," she states. "What glimpses!" The music has made her life good, and strange, all over again. Thinking of the title of Baxter's first story collection, one might further say that Fenstad's mother does not care if the music embodies some profound harmony. Moreover, unlike her son, she does not care if it improves her character.

This last point is worth emphasizing. The carefully realistic fiction Baxter writes is almost too accessible, too easily understood. There is a moment in "Saul and Patsy Are Pregnant" when Saul frets that "In the midst of all this Midwestern earnestness, he was the one thing wrong. What was he doing here? What was he doing anywhere? He was accustomed to asking himself such questions." Whatever its locale, Baxter's fiction exists to give name to the great underlying questions of life. It is a fiction of solitude and love, of impulses and choices. Baxter's concerns are those of a moralist. Yet, the moralism is never oppressive or programmatic. Furthermore, there are in his stories unusual "glimpses." The characters cherish these. What is apprehended has little to do with morality, but the glimpses illuminate some conviction about life – as frail, radiant, or ineffable – that can neither be domesticated nor settled. The location for a characteristic Charles Baxter story is a home. No contemporary American author writes better stories about homes. Much of the reason he does so is because he continually tries to discover how much of the unseen or unheard has to be allowed in and how much kept out.

Interview:
Michael Kiser, "Interview with Charles Baxter," *Sycamore Review,* 4 (Winter 1992): 1–15.

Lucia Berlin

(1936 –)

Pat Smith
University of Michigan

BOOKS: *Manual for Cleaning Women* (Washington, D.C.: Zephyrus Image, 1977);

Angel's Laundromat (Berkeley, Cal.: Turtle Island, 1981);

Legacy (Berkeley, Cal.: Poltroon, 1983);

Phantom Pain (Bolinas, Cal.: Tombouctou, 1984);

Safe & Sound (Berkeley, Cal.: Poltroon, 1987);

Homesick: New & Selected Stories (Santa Rosa, Cal.: Black Sparrow, 1990).

Lucia Berlin's stories present revelations based on her experiences and observations. They are set mainly in the western United States, spanning the time from World War II to the present, and they chronicle the movements of girls, adolescents, and women without places of origin. They have no city to call home. This fact frees Berlin to present to the reader the cities within, dark cities of the interior within the darker city of the modern age. The women in these stories are constantly seeking an origin that is never to be known; they are bound by no place. With a straightforward prose narrative, Berlin provides the reader with a grounding in the drama of contemporary American life.

Berlin's father, Wendell Theodore Brown, was a mining engineer from Lawrence, Massachusetts. He attended the Texas School of Mines in El Paso, where he met Berlin's mother, Mary Emma Magruder, a drama student and the daughter of a wealthy Texas family. They were married in the early 1930s and went to Alaska to seek work. Lucia was born in Juneau in 1936. Much of her early childhood was spent in mining camps in Montana, Idaho, Arizona, Kentucky, and other sites throughout North America. The family moved on the average of once every six months. During World War II her father served overseas as an officer in the navy. Along with her mother and younger sister, Berlin spent the war years with relatives in El Paso. Shortly after the war her father moved the immediate family to Santiago, Chile, where he took an important position with a large American mining firm.

Berlin spent her adolescent years in Chile. She left there to attend the University of New Mexico, where she completed both undergraduate and graduate programs.

Berlin was married for the first time when she was seventeen, and while she was pregnant with their second son, she began to write. For a while she taught Spanish in a Catholic school in Albuquerque. "El Tim," which was influenced by that experience, was the first of her stories to be published, in a Catholic magazine, the *Critic*. Her first husband left her during her pregnancy with their second child, and she later married Race Newton, a jazz pianist and Harvard friend of the poet Robert Creeley. Through Newton she met Creeley and another poet, Ed Dorn. Berlin and Dorn have remained friends over the years, and he has continued to encourage her work. He helped get her first chapbook published. In a particularly tough time, when she found herself cleaning houses and raising four small children alone, she wrote the story "Maggie May" and sent it to Dorn. He recognized its worth and influenced Holbrook Teeter of Zephyrus Image Press to publish it as a chapbook titled *Manual for Cleaning Women* (1977).

Her first full-length collection, *Angel's Laundromat* (1981), opens with "The Musical Vanity Boxes," which tells of two seven-year-old girls ("They called me Heaven; and Hope, Hell") who are duped by two older boys into selling "chances" for them. This story introduces a major theme: in most of her stories the women work alone or with other women. Men tend to come and go in the lives of these female characters. Even the men who make commitments to any of these women seem to lead separate lives. These early stories are set in a world dominated by male attitudes. The girls learn how they are supposed to act only through male models, or from women who have accepted their plight. Even when the two girls find out they have been duped, one of them knows that she will eventually forgive the boy she likes. But the two girls sell more

Lucia Berlin visiting the Detroit Institute of Arts, May 1984 (photograph by Pat Smith)

than expected, and turn the whole enterprise into their own adventure. They wander through El Paso and into Juarez, adapting and mixing comfortably, but always as outsiders, with people who, unlike themselves, seem to be at home. When they cross the border, they find themselves in a café where they are seen as charming and adaptable aliens, strange girls who are graciously accepted for the moment into an exotic and appealing setting. But they are there only a short time. Eventually, of course, the adventure is over, and they must recross the border to the place where they will continue to be duped, beaten, or prayed over.

In each of these stories, the female characters find themselves on the outside. The reader is granted a view of society observed by one who does not belong, one excluded. But the observation is always being made by one who is nonthreatening to those within the environment being observed; she is accepted for the moment. This alien look at the so-

cial settings of the stories allows narrative detachment. In "A Foggy Day" a woman is trapped in New York, where she feels she does not belong. In a moment of honesty on the Staten Island ferry, she points to a neon sign glowing through the fog over her Greenwich Village apartment and admits, "That's the first thing I see when I open my eyes every morning. WORLD." In "Maggie May" (republished in *Angel's Laundromat*) the main character is a cleaning woman who is struggling to make a living. She enters the homes of people who can afford to pay for her services. Like a detective sifting through clues, she sorts out and reports the intricacies of her clients' lives. In this story, and in the story "Angel's Laundromat," readers hear impartial observations being weighted and filtered. Angel is a man who has stopped drinking; he runs a Laundromat. It is frequented mostly by Native Americans. One, a seriously afflicted alcoholic, is often there at the same time as the woman who tells the story. She does not know why she always goes there. There is a cleaner, air-conditioned facility just a block from where she lives. But the first time she went to that one, she wanted to dye something, and there was a sign: "POSITIVELY NO DYEING." At Angel's there is a sign that reads, "YOU CAN DIE HERE ANYTIME." It is near another sign that reads, "DON'T THINK AND DON'T DRINK."

In 1984 Berlin was living in Oakland, and *Phantom Pain,* her second collection of stories, was published that year. Like the collection that preceded it, this one begins with a story from her El Paso childhood. "Dr. H. A. Moynihan" had previously been published as *Legacy* (1983), a hand-set limited edition by Poltroon Press in Berkeley, California. Other stories in *Phantom Pain* had appeared in various magazines, including *Rolling Stock,* edited by Dorn's wife, Jennifer.

There is nothing tentative about the range of statement in these stories. They are about what can be lost and what can be endured. The heroines are young girls who are often neglected or abused by adults. Later they are young women with children in prefeminist times. While the women work to hold their families together, the men in their lives pursue personal dreams. Still later these women find themselves either alone or with nearly grown children. They are still working to serve others as cleaning women, switchboard operators, or medical-care workers. Caretaker roles they learned from their parents and husbands are still in place. Nevertheless, their strength and endurance, combined with their daily observations of the pain and drama of life, give them the ability to affirm their existence.

In "Dr. H. A. Moynihan," an alcoholic dentist crafts a perfect set of false teeth for himself. The craftsmanship is exquisite; he has even included all of the proper stains and cracks. The story is told from the point of view of his young granddaughter. The old man convinced her to pull out all his remaining teeth. In his office, that chamber of childhood horror, with alcohol as his anesthetic, she completes the task. With his bleeding and her love for and fear of him, readers are given a picture of a world gone mad. The story is humorous and horrifying at the same time.

The innocence of a granddaughter gives way to a new kind of innocence in "Her First Detox." Carlotta is a woman alone, again. Her memory of the events that led to her waking up in the county detoxification ward are almost nonexistent. As the story unfolds, she begins to discover more about those events and about what she has in common with the others in the ward. As a result she begins to find out more about herself. She discovers that she is ill-equipped to deal with the loneliness, the pain, and her own self-loathing. At one point readers are told that she lies to the other drunks in order to gain their acceptance. One of the most appealing aspects of Berlin's storytelling ability is the juxtaposition between the characters, who may tell the truth one moment while lying the next, and the impartial narrator, who always reports a simple series of observations: "Everything will be okay"; "Everyone met their obligations"; "she had no idea of what is yet to come." Berlin thus provides the reader with a haven in the midst of her stories – a distance, a place of some comfort where there is time to assimilate the tale.

In her story "The Maiden" Berlin retells Thomas Hardy's *Tess of the d'Urbervilles* (1891), setting it in rural New Mexico. Often the women Berlin presents are faced with entire communities who seem to be involved in collective denial. This story opens with Juan, Tesa's father, walking home drunk from a bar in town. His route takes him past the church and his parish priest: "Father Ramirez was watering the trees outside the rectory even though they had been dead for some time. They had been bought and planted by the Friday Bingo women and he had blessed them. Peach trees." Father Ramirez tells Juan that recent research into old Spanish land grants reveals that he, Juan, may be the only living descendant of a rich Spanish man who at one time owned the whole valley in which they are standing. With the Hardy precedent firmly established for nearly one hundred years, the outcome is no surprise. Irony comes when Tesa realizes that she has been living with false hope and denial, and she says while laughing, "Lord, I'm as crazy as my Daddy." She has begun, with these words, the process of self-awareness; she begins to see the fool in the mirror. She begins to see that her folly has its own wisdom. Tesa is the people, and the true pleasure in reading this story is to listen to the way Berlin tells the truth about the people who live in towns such as Corrales – each with its own feeling and its own history. She spells out how the wealthy and powerful insist on maintaining their wealth and power, and how vulnerable the people are in the face of changing times. At the same time, and with irony, she allows readers to see how some of the working people in this valley maintain their dignity in the face of what seems to be a system that will never change.

In the title story of *Phantom Pain,* an amputee father is being cared for by his daughter. She is providing the kind of care that is lacking at the institution where he is living. He still feels and misses his lost limb. He wants her to abandon him but she comes to take care of him each day. She knows her role, and as she participates in their silent tragedy, she feels and misses her father's unspoken affection. As Berlin extends the scene beyond the immediate father/daughter relationship, readers are afforded a view of a world of skewed values – a place one may recognize as real but mad all the same: "Paper cups floated in the foamy brown lake serene as swans."

Many of the stories in *Phantom Pain* deal with the real effects of alcoholism. In "Emergency Room Notebook" a medical care worker reports, "My tears were for my own loneliness, my own blindness. . . . Fear, poverty, alcoholism, loneliness are terminal illnesses. Emergencies, in fact." In "Rainy Day" the character says, "Trouble is when I sober up I start to think."

Behind loneliness and depression there is misdirected anger in the story "Cherry Blossom Time," in which a woman is saddled with a child and a self-centered husband. The women in these stories are trying to keep some sense of pride and dignity in the face of often overwhelming odds. But they are most often ill-equipped to understand their own dilemmas. The emotional and psychological baggage they bring with them is a hindrance at best and destructive at worst. As things get tough on them, they get even tougher on themselves. In "Noël, 1974" a woman is overextended by the stress of having to play too many roles in too short a time. But she sees herself as a caretaker and allows herself to get caught in her own web; she is manipulated by others and by her own need – established long ago in her childhood, embraced and nurtured ever since – to be a caretaker. She no longer has the ability to retreat to a central place of tranquillity, as younger women in other stories do. With a sense of irreparable loss, she suffers in silence or through tears, and she continues to accept what she sees as her role.

In 1987 Alastair Johnston of Poltroon Press published Berlin's *Safe & Sound* in a handsome letterpress edition. It was typeset by Berlin herself, and it is illustrated with four relief engravings by Frances Butler. As with previous volumes of her work, some of these stories had appeared in magazines such as *Berkeley Monthly, City Lights Review, Folio, Volition,* and *Zyzzva.* The collection contains a revealing juxtaposition of stories. Some chronicle the gathering of one's self during the uncertainties of adolescence and focus on the constant evaluating and reevaluating of new, important, and unprepared-for experiences. Others are set in the middle of life's confusion, the time when that which was learned and brought forward so often proves to be inadequate.

"Andado," set in Chile, is the tale of Laura, a beautiful young girl who accepts an invitation to spend the weekend at the country estate of a man who is a friend of her father. Due to unforeseen circumstances, a chaperone is not present. During the visit Laura is seduced by her father's friend. The man's son and the son's fiancée are also present, along with several others. Laura observes that the son has an ongoing affair with a servant girl and that his betrothed knows of it and does her best to keep up appearances. Back at home, Laura's mother spends most of her time in her room, which often smells of perfume and gin. When Laura returns from her weekend visit, she discovers that her mother has attempted suicide. Wandering between concern for her mother and wanting to speak with her, but not knowing how, she says only the words she knows to say; she maintains appearances as she has been taught to do. When she asks her father about her mother, he says she simply made another attempt to get attention and that she will be fine. All of this takes place with the ironic backdrop of a watchman's nightly chant, "Andado y sereno" (Safe and Sound).

In the story "Strays" there are people who are many years removed from any youthful innocence, but they are still motivated at times by their need for companionship and love. As the story opens, a woman finds herself a stranger in a city in New Mexico. Eventually she gets "busted for needle marks" and sent, along with other men and women, to an abandoned World War II military installation in the desert. Their duties include making the place livable. Under the not-so-watchful eyes of the staff, they begin to restore the buildings, and, in a strange way, they begin to form a community. As they take on individual roles within the new society, they begin to relate to each other in new ways. A woman and a man in the group befriend a pack of stray dogs. The process is not easy: the dogs distrust the people. With patience and care on the part of the couple, though, the dogs are partially won over. But soon the strays disappear. The woman and man worry, and then one night the dogs begin to wander back. They have attacked porcupines and are full of quills and badly infected. The dogs have to be killed to put them out of their misery. For the woman the stay there does not last much longer. Eventually she simply runs away. At one point she says, "The world just goes along. Nothing much matters, you know? I mean really matters. But then some times, just for a second, you get this grace, this belief that it does matter, a whole lot." There is a mixture of complacency and resiliency in the women in many of Berlin's stories, and she often weaves the narrative through that combination.

For many years Berlin has lived in Oakland. In recent years she has taught writing at the San Francisco County Jail. She has also worked at Mount Zion Hospital taking oral histories from elderly patients. In 1990 Black Sparrow Press published Berlin's fourth volume, *Homesick: New & Selected Stories*. Much of her early work can prove to be difficult to find, but *Homesick* includes stories from each of the three previous collections, making it possible for a reader to have access to work from 1977 to the present. The twenty-nine selections represent a fair distribution of new work combined with choices from the previous volumes.

Of the previously uncollected stories in *Homesick* some are narrated by young women – wives and mothers – who are living in the 1950s and 1960s. For these women there is no women's movement. They play roles defined for them by the men in their lives, and these men are rarely interested in assisting with their parental duties for any length of time, if at all. These men are husbands and fathers, and they learned what they know from models much like themselves. The father who neglects his daughter's emotional needs and education is all too often the model for the husband who later neglects the needs of his wife and their children. In these stories we see only women coming to the aid of other women. One woman aids her cousin with money and connections in getting to Mexico for an abortion, which the cousin decides against. When these women are abandoned by their fathers and husbands, it is other women – often from diverse backgrounds – who provide meaningful aid and comfort. Although it is informal and personal, there is a consciousness-raising taking place in these stories. It

emerges from the dysfunction of the families involved. It may not provide much relief for the older women who appear in the later stories, but its emergence does provide a note of hope.

In an unpublished 1991 interview, Berlin talked about the importance of place to her. She believes its importance comes from the constant moving that has been a part of her life. She says that even as a little girl she had a secret place to go to, a place of interior isolation. These days, Berlin still finds that place for herself in her writing. And the women who appear in her stories, in this collection and the others, often seek a similar, and sometimes unhealthy, isolation – a protection mechanism, a way to ensure the chance to be naive again with each new experience. As the stories work their way to the present, the women who emerge become intimately tied to this isolation, and as they become increasingly more fragmented by their roles as mothers, daughters, lovers, former lovers, friends, workers, and coworkers, they find themselves increasingly more alienated as well. This alienation often causes them to cycle back into the need for isolation – more alone and still seeking that origin, that nonexistent geography in the storm of the times, that place where everything is all right.

Lucia Berlin's work generates in her readers the understanding that the world the characters live in is not the one to which they thought they were born. It is another world to which they have been abandoned. They share no sense of origin with those for whom this place is home. They are homesick for a place they have never known. The world includes economists, politicians, planners, and policymakers, but they are not the characters of these stories. Berlin's characters are people who inhabit a world full of questions, confusion, and loneliness, with an occasional ray of hope or peace.

Gina Berriault
(1 January 1926 –)

Julia B. Boken
State University of New York College at Oneonta

BOOKS: *The Descent* (New York: Atheneum, 1960);
Conference of Victims (New York: Atheneum, 1962);
The Mistress, and Other Stories (New York: Dutton, 1965);
The Son (New York: New American Library, 1966);
The Infinite Passion of Expectation: Twenty-Five Stories (San Francisco: North Point, 1982);
The Lights of Earth (San Francisco: North Point, 1984).

MOTION PICTURE: *The Stone Boy,* screenplay by Berriault, 20th Century–Fox, 1984.

Gina Berriault is able, with a few pen strokes, to create remarkable character portraits and dramatic situations. Her fiction looms large because she follows in the tradition of the nineteenth-century Russian writers Leo Tolstoy, Fyodor Dostoyevski, and Anton Chekhov, all of whom she admires and respects. She joins them, especially Dostoyevski, in probing the human psyche and finding, as she says in her novel *The Lights of Earth* (1984), a need to "dispel a little of the vast abandonment the world casts on everyone's face." She is a philosophical writer, sometimes existential, having read and brooded over the works of Miguel de Unamuno, Pablo Neruda, and José Ortega y Gasset, whose quotations are often cited in her books of short stories. She was also influenced by the French existentialist Albert Camus and by Italo Svevo and Samuel Beckett. Berriault has received kudos from writers and critics because of her artistic vision and her lush and elegant language depicting a fictional world including black women and men; homeless people; mistresses; farmers; women who are victims of men; selfish couples; lonesome writers; and lovers involved in May-November romances – many of them marginal creatures whose will to survive requires their last bit of energy. Her collection of short stories *The Infinite Passion of Expectation: Twenty-Five Stories* (1982) includes twelve that are also in an

earlier collection, *The Mistress, and Other Stories* (1965). The epigraph to her 1982 book is a quotation from Neruda, and it encapsulates the theme of these tales: "and that's how we are, forever falling into the deep well of other beings." Interrelationships are the very essence of Berriault's creativity, both in her novels and short fiction. People suffer tragic losses, invariably never articulating them and never recovering from having been flung into an abyss of failure or death. They lose the will and the strength to survive. Many of their gulags are created or perpetuated by women of consummate narcissism and by men who covet evanescent beauty in women and who rule them through fear of the loss of love. If there is any solace in many of Berriault's stories, it comes rarely and unexpectedly during the epiphany of a moment's awareness, and such recognition comes too late to salvage self-esteem or a relationship with one's mother or brother or lover.

A particularly private writer, who claims she knows no critics, has joined no societies, and cannot provide any unusual anecdotes about herself, Berriault was born on New Year's Day 1926 in Long Beach, California, and is the youngest of three children of a Russian Jewish immigrant couple. Her father initially was a marble cutter and later became a writer and a solicitor of advertisements. Her mother lost her sight when Gina was in her adolescence. After graduating from high school, Gina worked at various jobs, including a position as a reporter. She is divorced from J. V. Berriault, a musician, and has one child, Julie Elena. Gina Berriault has taught creative writing at San Francisco State University for several years. In 1966 she received a prestigious appointment as a scholar at the Radcliffe Institute for Independent Study; earlier she was awarded a fellowship from the Centro Mexicano de Escritores in Mexico City, where she lived and wrote in 1963.

In one of her rare statements, in 1975 Berriault told *World Authors* about the weltanschau-

ung of her writing: "My work is an investigation of reality which is, simply, so full of ambiguity and of answers that beget further questions that to pursue it is an impossible task and a completely absorbing necessity. It appears to me that all the terrors that human beings inflict upon one another are countered by a perceptible degree by the attempts of some writers to make us known to one another and thus to impart or revive a reverence for life."

Many of the women in Berriault's fiction are preyed upon by men. This situation is especially apparent in her novel *Conference of Victims* (1962), which concerns the traumatic effects that a politician's suicide has on his wife, sister, brother, and mistress. *The Lights of Earth* is the story of Martin, who becomes almost instantly famous, abandoning his mistress of several years for a woman whose exquisite beauty overpowers him. In both books Berriault's theme of loss as betrayal is in the foreground.

Most of Berriault's short fiction reveals the ambiguity of failed relationships and the pain of loss and rejection, the behavioral power of narcissism, and the loneliness of those who cannot or do not articulate their genuine feelings. "Felis Catus," initially collected in *The Mistress, and Other Stories* and again in *The Infinite Passion of Expectation,* involves a lack of honest language use compounded by the callousness of Mayda and her husband, Charles, to Mayda's sister Martha and her children. Charles, particularly, is obsessed with pedigreed cats. Already owning one ordinary cat, he and Mayda acquire from a cattery two brothers, both seal points. Shortly thereafter they visit Martha, whom they have not visited for a long time, only because she has a rare cat left by a temporary lodger. Only her son knows the cat to be a Burmese named Rangoon. Reluctantly the boy agrees that "his" cat be given to his aunt and her husband. Later, when Martha is about to be hospitalized, she asks Mayda and Charles to take her two children during her surgery and recuperation. They refuse, ostensibly because Charles has had several bouts of asthma and has lost his job. (He has actually taken a leave of absence, under the pretext of suffering from asthma, because he does not like his job.) He does in fact show symptoms of asthma, though, and the doctor suggests the couple rid themselves of their four cats. Charles demurs and simply bars them temporarily from the bedroom. Rangoon is finally claimed by its original owner, and the three other cats remain in the house. The story ends abruptly, with no resolution. It is a simple story with deeper implications. The sophisticated couple places cats above people, in this case little children and relatives. The implicit anguish of Martha, who must rely on neighbors to care for her children, sobers the reader, who notes finally that Mayda and Charles, totally self-absorbed in their insulated world, never experience a moment of revelation. Their callousness in rejecting the two children, blood relatives, whose neighbors show compassion, thus heightens the irony. Berriault succeeds in depicting two people who, like the cats they adore, are rank narcissists preening each other and their cats.

Another story in both Berriault collections is "Sublime Child." Two people experience a common loss at the beginning of the story. Several of Berriault's stories focus on ordinary people who undergo crises affecting their friendship, and often a mistress is depicted. At the beginning of "Sublime Child" Alice, a mistress, has died, and her lover Joseph does not attend the funeral, telling her daughter Ruth, at the wake following, that he simply did not have the viscera "to remember it," meaning the funeral or the death itself. As the action unfolds, Ruth wishes to comfort Joe for the loss of her mother. He is married to a woman who threatens to commit suicide if he leaves her. (This same threat-as-control motif is used in *The Lights of Earth*.) Although Ruth acquires a roommate, she relies heavily on the platonic relationship with her dead mother's lover, almost as if to be with him annihilates the death of Alice. Ruth tells her roommate that she is "enlivened" by Joe, as her mother had been. Joe, too, depends on Ruth for the continuity of comfort and companionship, but they do not discuss any new level of friendship. Although both Joe and Ruth take separate vacations, she laments when

she returns, "No one, nothing, had taken the edge off her longing to see Joe." They continue to attend concerts, go to dinner, and take walks. As they prepare for Christmas in her apartment, when the two are alone, Joe puts Ruth on his lap and his head on her bosom. Ruth, yearning for the familiarity of his face when Alice was alive, senses something different and wants to say, "No, no, don't make me be my mother," but the words cannot come out, and she strikes him instead. After his immediate departure, with no discussion of their feelings, Ruth moans, "Mother, forgive me for hurting him."

The theme perhaps is best expressed by critic Molly McQuade, who in 1983 wrote of Gina Berriault's fictive people, "Every so-called fault deforming a character seems to link up with another fault in someone else, complicating and completing the moral neighborhood they share." Both Ruth and Joe have a common, reciprocal flaw – the compulsion to maintain an environment familiar to the patterns that existed when Alice was alive. Both wish to solace each other but neglect to develop a new rational or emotional basis for their continuing relationship. The burgeoning sexuality begins to overpower Joe, who is rejected brutally by Ruth, not tenderly, as she might have done. Her plea to her mother is, like many Berriault conclusions, ambiguous. Ruth's identity and bond with Joe may be strengthened eventually, as suggested in the last line, which portrays Ruth beating her eyes in self-anger.

In "The Mistress," the title story of Berriault's first collection, the central consciousness is that of a former mistress. It is one of her stories featuring a character wholly self-absorbed. The characters are without names, the two main ones being referred to as the "woman" and the "boy." At a party the woman recognizes the sixteen-year-old son of her former lover from a long-past relationship. The woman has married three times since, but she feels that the boy's father was her only real love. There are no details about the relationship's demise. So striking is the boy and so reawakened is she by his mere presence that, after she is introduced to him, she takes his arm, and they go for a promenade in the garden. She finally tells him of her love affair with his father. He is deeply affected and describes his mother's torment during this affair, even though the woman reminds him that there already were serious difficulties in his parents' marriage. "You shouldn't have told me," he cries, and, at the first opportunity, he leaves her. The woman reassesses the love affair and concludes that "the person in her memory who affected her the most was not the one she had loved but the one she had understood the least." The woman is struck by a moment of truth as she realizes that her affair created sorrow for the wife of her favorite lover. The astute reader, however, may not empathize with the former mistress's remorse, since she has not a vestige of awareness of having deeply wounded the boy. The irony is sharpened with the realization that his wound is in the present and that the woman's grief for the "wronged" wife succors no one. The sense of the loss of true love preoccupying the woman has lasted a decade.

This theme of loss torturing people is a veritable litany in Berriault's writing. As the epigraph to *The Lights of Earth* she quotes Unamuno: "A tremendous passion is this longing that our memory may be rescued from the oblivion which overtakes others." Berriault is preoccupied with passion, and this poignant quotation, which encompasses the theme of some of her stories, is apropos to this novel, which reveals the sorrow that Ilona Lewis, the protagonist, feels after the death of her brother, whom she virtually ignored while he was living.

Poignancy and irony shape one of Berriault's best-known stories, "The Stone Boy," which catapulted her to national fame because of the 1984 film made from it, for which she wrote the script. The movie, starring Glenn Close and Robert Duvall, was released by 20th Century–Fox. The reviewers marveled at the stunning performances of the actors and the tragic overtones of the story, reflecting the melancholy vision of Berriault. She captures the chiaroscuro shades of the tragic story of Arnold, a nine-year-old boy who, while about to pick peas with Eugene (Eugie), his fifteen-year-old brother, takes his .22-caliber rifle along. By accident, as both of them are going under a barbed wire fence, the gun discharges and kills Eugie. Apparently traumatized by this unexpected horror, Arnold leaves him and goes on to pick the peas. Returning from the field with his tub half full of peas, Arnold simply tells his parents, "Eugie's dead." When his father asks why Arnold had not run back immediately to tell them about the accident, he has no answer but says merely that he had to pick the peas. The question is also asked by the sheriff, with Arnold's reply the same – that he had to pick peas before the sun came up. This time, though, Arnold thinks that it was "odd" that he had not run back home as soon as Eugie was shot, but he could not seem to remember the reason. The sheriff mocks the lad, dubbing him either a moron or so "reasonable" that he is far ahead of the sheriff and the father. Outwardly Arnold shows no emotion.

Later in the evening the neighbors and friends of the family come by to give condolences and see the silent, tearless Arnold. His uncle Andy articulates the community's feelings when he berates the boy for not shedding a tear. The narrator of the story reaffirms Arnold's feeling nothing – no grief, only immense silence. No one feels any empathy for Arnold; all think of him as a pariah. Even his mother is unwilling to talk to him when she is in bed and he comes silently to her. He wishes to crush himself on her bosom and tell her about the "terror" he felt when Eugie had fallen on the hill. At the breakfast table his sister further punishes him by denying Arnold the milk that she is asked to pass. Only his father recognizes his existence by passing him the milk. When Arnold's mother asks him what he wanted the night before, he says, "I don't want nothing." The story ends with Arnold trembling with fright from the answer he gave his mother.

"The Stone Boy" rivets the reader with Berriault's somber portrayal of country folk who seem rooted in absolutism, with no shred of feeling for the boy who has metaphorically turned into stone, as he has left the protected world of innocence and found himself speechless, entering the realm of bitter reality through an act of unintended violence. This story reinforces Berriault's theme of sorrow and loss, and the consequent "Thoughts that do often lie too deep for tears," as William Wordsworth wrote in his "Intimations Ode" (in *Poems, in two Volumes*, 1807).

"The Infinite Passion of Expectation," the title story of Berriault's second collection, is one of her most remarkable. The title is found in the works of Søren Kierkegaard. Like many of Berriault's tales, this one is short, only eight pages, but she writes concentrated prose. Told by an omniscient narrator, the story examines the consciousness of a young waitress, unnamed like the other characters. A seventy-nine-year-old psychologist, who has been providing therapy to the woman, proposes to her, offering her an open marriage. When another woman and her son, who are friends and designated beneficiaries of the psychologist, leave for a holiday, the waitress is asked to care for him. He comes to her bedroom several evenings, expecting sex yet not insisting, but she withholds it, already deciding not to marry him. When she returns to his house late one night, he reviles her, "Now I know you. . . . You are cold. You may never be able to love anyone and so you will never be loved." She does not reply and in fact says virtually nothing in the story. He is, unlike an effective therapist, scourging her for her abstinence. Earlier the narrator comments about him: "His life seemed like a life expected and not yet lived," a commentary on many of Berriault's male characters. Although the waitress says nothing to defend herself after the verbal attack by the therapist, she thinks later "that the longing was not for him but for a life of love and wisdom. There was another way to prove that she was a loving woman, that there was no fatal flaw, that she was filled with love, and the other way was to give herself over to expectation, as to a passion."

Reviewing *The Infinite Passion of Expectation* in *Ms.* magazine (August 1983), Adrianne Blue wrote that these twenty-five stories could make an optimist weep. The title story is the only one wherein a woman's solace is hope and expectation on a passionate level. The waitress refuses an Austenian solution of upward mobility through marriage. When the therapist and the waitress meet after a year of separation, she still persists in her expectation and hope, while he has all but relinquished his: "She saw that he had drawn back unto himself his life's expectations. They were way inside, and they required, now, no other person for their fulfillment." Interior dialogue is used to convey the thought processes of the woman, who seems a kind of "Everywoman" in believing that there is a need for love, people, hope, and a never-ending white heat of anticipation.

Gina Berriault identifies with no school or cult of writing. The stories, whose locale is often northern California, are peopled with a remarkable array of characters, happenings, and insights, all woven into a style that is subtle and deceptively simple. The themes usually focus on the pain that comes from inevitable loss, the dark night of the soul, failed relationships, spare language that makes communication almost impossible, families torn asunder, death causing guilt to the living, the indefinability and essence of love, and the abandonment of hope. Through her keen insight, imaginative art, and finely honed craft, Berriault creates a world of flawed people. Most of them succumb to burdens that are often self-inflicted. Yet some survive and prevail, if only because they are suckled by "the infinite passion of expectation." Berriault portrays the human condition with astute psychological probing and an imagination and texture of language that promise to ensure that her novels and short fiction will continue to be popular.

References:

Molly McQuade, "Gina Berriault's Fiction," *Chicago Tribune Book World,* 6 February 1983, pp. 10–12;

Eve Shelnutt, ed., *The Confidence Woman, Twenty-Six Women Writers at Work* (Atlanta: Long Street, 1991), pp. 129–132.

Harold Brodkey

(1930 –)

Robert Moynihan
State University of New York College at Oneonta

BOOKS: *First Love and Other Sorrows* (New York: Dial, 1957; London: Hamilton, 1958);

Women and Angels (Philadelphia: Jewish Publication Society, 1985);

A Poem about Testimony and Argument (New York: Jordan Davies, 1986);

Stories in an Almost Classical Mode (New York: Knopf, 1988);

The Runaway Soul (New York: Farrar, Straus & Giroux, 1991).

SELECTED PERIODICAL PUBLICATIONS – UNCOLLECTED:

POETRY

"Sea Noise," *New Yorker,* 57 (19 May 1981): 50;

"Dead Neck, Eastern Point, Bass Rocks," *New Yorker,* 59 (13 June 1983): 52;

"The Garden," *New Yorker,* 62 (19 May 1986): 36;

"Between 6:37 AM and 9:04 PM," *New Yorker,* 63 (15 June 1987): 52;

"Susan's Field," *New Yorker,* 64 (21 November 1988): 52;

"April Fool's Day, New York State," *New Yorker,* 66 (2 April 1990): 44.

FICTION

"Nonie," *New Yorker,* 60 (5 March 1984): 46–56;

"The Bullies," *New Yorker,* 62 (30 July 1986): 27–38;

"The Laugh," *New Yorker,* 63 (2 February 1987): 31–38;

"Family," *New Yorker,* 63 (23 November 1987): 119–133;

"Annemarie Singing," *New Yorker,* 64 (22 August 1988): 22–39;

"Spring Fugue," *New Yorker,* 66 (23 April 1990): 37–38;

"A Kingdom of Sadness," *New Yorker,* 67 (7 October 1991): 34–46.

NONFICTION

"Men at Dance," *Esquire,* 102 (October 1984): 100–107;

"Reading, the Most Dangerous Game," *New York Times Book Review,* 90 (24 November 1985): 1, 44–45.

Harold Brodkey is usually the chronicler of a personal and serious form of modern memory. His efforts are direct and, save for one or two exceptions, unambiguous: his fiction details the lives and losses of the American generations who survived World War II, to which he adds particularly recorded personal memories of childhood, growth, and maturity. The main publisher of his short fiction has been the *New Yorker,* which printed all but one of the stories in his first collection, *First Love and Other Sorrows* (1957), and ten of the eighteen pieces collected in *Stories in an Almost Classical Mode* (1988).

Brodkey's idiom and innovation are distinctly American. However, he escapes any confinement of influence either from his native land or from abroad. For example, the comparison made by some critics between Brodkey and Marcel Proust is adventitious. Nonetheless, biographical details are not incidental for Brodkey. They form, rather, the substance of memory found in nearly all of his work. He may at times move to a more immediate scene of memory or invention, but he returns again and again to the primal experience of childhood and the awakening fear of various versions of ego, size, false heroism, confusions of language, deception, and other displacements of culture, the child, and the adult. The other subjects in Brodkey's writing, though they arise from the same personal memories, are the suburban traps of marriage and middle-class conventions of love in the 1950s and 1960s. Scenes of inevitable future discord are combined with ironic deftness and the recall of past loves, friendships and the ordeals of guilt and notice in the nuclear family. Brodkey's most brilliant achievement is not the eroticism for which he has sometimes been praised but his coruscating distrust in and love-hate feelings toward parent-child relation-

Harold Brodkey, circa 1988 (photograph © Jerry Bauer)

ships, especially in the presence of imminent death. For this theme, singular in its records of ambiguity and the mutual pain of child and parent, Brodkey stands alone in his achievement, separate in virtuosity from any of his American contemporaries.

Brodkey, born in 1930, has never revealed his full date of birth; he takes his name from his adoptive family (Joseph and Doris Brodkey) in Saint Louis. His original name was Aaron Weintraub, and he was born in Alton, Illinois, a small town about twenty-five miles from Saint Louis. Brodkey was adopted after the death of his mother. In his fiction his adoptive mother is represented by characters named Leia, Leah, or Lila. Joseph Brodkey, the basis for the protagonist of his adopted son's novella on the midwestern male and fatherly love, is referred to as S. L. (in "S. L.," collected in *Stories in an Almost Classical Mode*). The Brodkeys' daughter, who is in a love-hate relationship with her adopted brother, is called Nonie. A good deal of the tension

that marks a few of the early stories and nearly all of Brodkey's mature fiction arises from the acute observation of actual experiences that oppose ideal roles, or middle-class projections, and the distance afforded by Brodkey's Harvard education. Like T. S. Eliot, Brodkey forms an analytic and insistently critical relationship with the American heartland and his past.

First Love defines and sets these subjects in place; few of the reviews noticed the range or art of this first volume. Rather, they noted the "*New Yorker* style." Brodkey in this volume, however, ranges far beyond any journalistic expectation or casual literary paradigm. The stories are relentlessly urban: Saint Louis with its nineteenth-century neighborhoods still in place, their subtle and bleak nuances subsisting within a relative uniformity. The atmosphere of that seemingly long-ago time was a settled stability, with unmistakable class lines ineradicably set. The monochromatic pallor of these urban places, soon to be swept away, was barely life-giving; any color given it comes from fiction – that is, the interior spectrum cast upon a dull landscape, freed from its limitations only by the eye of an inventive spectator. Brodkey's color of choice is, as he writes in "The State of Grace," the first story in the book, "a certain shade of red brick – a dark, almost melodious red, sombre and riddled with blue – that is my childhood in St. Louis." "The State of Grace" focuses on a boy babysitter, his feelings toward his young male charge (which are equivocal), a recording of the setting and detritus of the period (including a Monopoly game), and a scorching self-apostrophe that concludes the story: "Really, that is all there is to this story. The boy I was, the child Edward was. That and the terrible desire to suddenly turn and run shouting back through the corridors of time, screaming at the boy I was, searching him out, and pounding on his chest: Love him, you damn fool, love him." For Brodkey, love in this and other instances is the tracing of memory through doubt, the shock of the family as it reasserts itself in minute degrees of recognition.

The title story of *First Love* is set in a familiar urban landscape. The family used to live "in a large white frame house overlooking the Mississippi River" but has moved to the yet-unruined but drab central Saint Louis with its slush, dirty March snow, and wheezing steam radiators. The mother is preparing the daughter for an appropriate suitor and is skilled in her advice about chaste enticements and timely tricks of sexual escape. The narrator is a teenage boy with his own awakening sexuality. His restrained tumult is carried on in relative silence compared with the strategies and parleys of the mother and daughter, who does eventually land a rich fiancé. She sports a family-heirloom ring as proof. The daughter's relationship with the mother, who has fretted with aroused curiosity, changes with one of the most precise turns in all of Brodkey's fiction. After the engagement, the mother composes a letter to spread the news. She asks: " 'Is got engaged the right way to say it?' 'Became engaged,' my sister said, in a distant voice." The mother, daughter, and narrator then eat a midnight meal of quiet celebration in which all relationships have changed, the "first of our reunions," he concludes. A good deal of the quality of these stories is based on such innocence and definition.

The order of the stories in the volume follows some of the conventions of the bildungsroman; they are growth stories about young people coming of age. The pivotal story, "Sentimental Education," separates the earlier work from the final stories in the volume. This story recalls the America of a lost past; it is an elegiac tribute to an American innocence found a generation or two ago but now remote. Brodkey's fictional persona is Elgin Smith, who turns from his literary education at Harvard to the pursuit of a coed, Caroline Hedges. The two maneuver their ways into the same class, then to furtive intimacy. Their emotions oscillate between confusion and consummation: "She kept hoping she and Elgin would reach some stability together, but it never came." They make love in a dorm room from time to time hoping not to be caught or noticed. The padding footsteps down a hall and knock at the door by someone who may discover and report any infraction of rules are as poignant and dated as the literary conversation about "Metaphysical Poetry."

One of Brodkey's achievements in this volume is the recording of the American pastoral vision turned nightmare, the naive illusions of the 1950s and 1960s, and the imposed provincialisms of mind and place. Brodkey's Laura, who figures in the last five stories in *First Love,* is a wife, mother, and denizen of suburbia; she is a kind of sacrifice for others, for "togetherness." Laura is too smart and sensitive to be partitioned in the suburban warren, where her sources of contact are other women living in the same advertised paradise with the insistent demands of offspring. Brodkey's sardonic approach is pointed in the self-revelations of the main male character, Laura's husband, Martin, who speaks to her as an object (in the story "Laura"):

> "Darling, you're so absurdly romantic. No one else says 'I belong to you' and means it, the way you do. Do you know what I think? . . . When you were little you never developed defenses, the way normal people do. You were too spoiled. You never had to save yourself. You could always run to someone and smile at them and they'd love you, as I do."
>
> Since her husband hated her to cry, she stuffed her hand in her mouth so he couldn't hear her.
>
> "I deserve you because I put up with you," he murmured.

She then bites her finger until it bleeds.

Brodkey's *Stories in an Almost Classical Mode* did not meet with consistent critical acclaim in 1988. The reaction was puzzled, positive, or cuttingly negative. Paul Gray in *Time* (17 October 1988) sounded the familiar note first heard regarding Brodkey some thirty years earlier: "an artist entranced, and imprisoned, by a narrow range of self-preoccupations."

Cover for the 1986 paperback edition of Brodkey's first book. All but one of the stories were first published in the New Yorker, *and most are set in Saint Louis.*

Though the selection in the book is strictly chronological – the stories being ordered as first published – the first and last narratives provide an aesthetic frame; they are two contrasting ways of viewing and recording objects. The first, "The Abundant Dreamer," deals with the corruption of both terms in modern times. The main character, Marcus Weill, is not a dreamer, not the recorder of either recalled or phantasmagoric memory, nor is he abundant. He is a pedestrian film director, a believer in the cultural miasma of kitsch. The location is Italy, and one of the movie scenes is shot on the Spanish Steps in Rome, within speaking distance of the place where John Keats died. Film, with its recorded images, most of them meretriciously repeated, is the public "art" of the times, while fiction or memory exists in the multiple levels of human experience and consciousness, which resist any schematic translation to cartoon, photograph, or even documentary. Life surrounds Marcus. It is far richer than either his view or the medium he has chosen for expression, but he ignores its nuances and its complexities. The arguments and relationships on the movie set contain more life than his films.

Marcus is a kept artist, adopted by his grandmother, who showers gifts on him. Nanna is the ideal surrogate parent: she has an open purse and mind and is therefore the model patron for a cultural dunce. The story concludes with an interview. Marcus is not merely an artist but a celebrity; as such, he commits the sins of popular philosophy, all of which find their way, more or less intact, into print and mass consumption: "I felt . . . thinking led to dishonesty. But I was wrong. The young are always wrong . . . they must go blindly or not at all." He is embarrassed suddenly and stops, until he notices admiration in the young reporter's eyes. Marcus goes on; the flow of such sentiment is uninterrupted for some pages, until Nanna observes: "I do not see that anything has occurred that we cannot take philosophically. It is not as if we'd lost all our money." Marcus continues to speak to the reporter: "You see, when I was a young man I thought life was – was wet, a liquid thing, like the ocean. . . . But then you come to dry land. . . . One makes decisions." In the final paragraph, Marcus directs an actress from his perch on the boom: "Jehane comes from the Sistine Chapel as from her mother's womb." The cameras roll; no one is there to contradict. This is "culture."

What Brodkey has avoided in his fiction are the cheap and easy formulas ironized in "Abundant Dreamer." He also has refused to limit his recording of experience. His persona is the memory, the observer. Why has he not broken from that form of fictional recording so close to autobiographical memory? The typical form of autobiography does not contain the degree of recall or the virtuosity of Brodkey's memory and reimagining. Autobiography has, in most of its examples, the substructure of Christian expectation, of life as a gradual improvement, of success, wealth, public recognition, and an implied heavenly salvation to complement the good estate of the subject. That at least is the usual formula in the Anglo-American tradition. Brodkey's fiction reverses these expectations: while the bildungsroman is present in some forms, no one succeeds, except ironically, as, say, a mountebank. Brodkey's fiction presents characters passing through time, perhaps maturing, then becoming frustrated or dying.

A few exceptions may exist, but they form the narrow minority of Brodkey's work, such as "Innocence," which several reviewers have praised as the best work in his 1988 collection. It is a sexual story, a descriptive tour de force, but it is not "redemptive." Rather, it is a story of sexual pietism or high camp. "Innocence" is not a literal rendition of an undergraduate's sexual triumph, nor even a victory of realistic description. Like all great works of irony, this story moves through several realms simultaneously, and each comments on and partially invalidates the other. The main female character, Orra, is self-centered; the absence of full erotic response is one of the bases of her power and self-control. She is stuck at an early state of sexual development, and she wants it that way. Her lover, Wiley, another one of Brodkey's characters who want to be celebrities, repeats the slogans and technical moves of one sexual help book after another, in hopes of achieving the physically transcendent. Of course he is unaware that the language and stratagems of such sex manuals are similar to tracts about religious experiences.

In its mixing of the sacred and the profane, this story is hardly "innocent." The story itself has several direct references to the divine, perhaps to the Saul-Paul conversion experience (through "falling down"). The narrator has "lost faith" in attaining sexual grace; nonetheless, he can "feel beads sliding and whispering and being strung together rustlingly in her." Like all religious initiates, Orra has found that "feeling" confirms the new ecstatic state: "I FEEL SOMETHING. . . . *Wiley, I feel a lot!* . . . I never had feelings like these before! . . . GodohGodohGod!" The narrator says, "it was sin and redemption and holiness and visions time." In transcendent camp style, he continues: "the holy temper . . . lifted her to where she could not breathe or walk; she choked in the ether, a scrambling seraph, tumbling and aflame and alien, powerful beyond belief, hideous and frightening and beautiful beyond the human." Her interest in Wiley is initially aroused by his discussion of the fraudulence of most "Messianic" philosophies and messages. She says simply, "I think we're falling in love."

That this story is often read as literal erotics of a high order is not within Brodkey's control. As with "The Abundant Dreamer," however, his witty use of pastiche – the discovered objects, the narrative collage – has been unrecognized by critics.

The angel of the last story in the book is a creature of an altogether different "Order of Seraphs," and it makes the commentary on "Innocence" as a literal tale of transcendence all the more suspect. An angel appears in Harvard Yard, and its name cannot be Michael, Gabriel, or Evangel; it is not "like god," nor is it a "man of god," nor even "good news," or a "messenger." Rather it is the "Angel of Silence and of Inspiration (toward Truth)." The narrator describes its features. It has no wings, and it "appeared to a number of us passing by on the walk in front of Harvard Hall – this was a little after three o'clock – today is October twenty-fifth, nineteen-hundred-and-fifty-one." Nearly all of the remainder of "Angel" frustrates a reader's expectations. The apparition may be vaguely anthropomorphic: it does have something of a face but little else of human form. At any rate, it shows itself once then disappears. So what is it? It is not a Christian angel of annunciation, it is not a counter- or anti-angel, such as one finds in the noncanonical scripture of the book of Tophet, nor is it a member of the Pandemonium. One could read this story as a form of narrative that is not narrative, such as Samuel

Beckett's *Waiting for Godot* (produced, 1953; published, 1959) or *Happy Days* (produced and published in 1961), or Molly Bloom's soliloquy in James Joyce's *Ulysses* (1922). (The latter is a creative dialectic and an ironic predecessor text for "Innocence.") In this form of narrative, the emphasis is on repetition, and the scene or plot awaits some variation – any variation – to save the viewer or reader from a tedium too like life itself. Essential to Beckett's drama is this repetition, and it is never mythopoeic. It celebrates only the commonplace at an elemental level, and no sacred day or ritual marks the passing of time.

In "Angel" the mythical incident passes, but it may be the counterthrust for what many have complained is absent in Brodkey's writing: mystery and independent or "novelistically" realized characters. In addition to the appearance of the supernatural, the methods of this story proceed without the accustomed memory, finely remembered anecdotage, dialogue, and description of experience that mark the rest of the volume.

"Angel" is perhaps the most complete excursus of the different forms of comment on and narrative about high texts in the Jewish tradition, but it is accessible fiction, a narrative of meaning that describes other "sacred" narratives. Oddly, no reviewer, even the biblical scholar Robert Alter (*New Republic*, 24 October 1988), has commented on this aspect (he gave his highest marks to "Innocence"). Brodkey in "Angel" proposes an alternative to Christian forms of narrative, with their resolutions or closure – either in some "higher state" by the ending of the story, film, or poem, or the note of expectation that some altered and bettered condition will follow, or even with the allotments of poetic justice. All of these forms exist in either high or demotic versions of the arts, and they all transcribe Christian ethics and philosophy. Brodkey's "Angel" is not the messenger of good or even equivocal tidings of moral order. Rather, this angel is commentary itself and, unlike the Christian forms of narrative, exists for its statements about preceding texts without completely regulating them, yet also exists as an anticipation of later remarks. For Brodkey this narrative is a description of how language works, individually and socially. Neither life nor experience is redemptive. So none of his characters rises to some higher state through some coup de theatre or some disguised deus ex machina.

"Angel" is contradictory, a counternarration composed to present an antithetical form of storytelling and creation of fictional character. While the angel is not demonic in any sense, it is not "spiri-tual" in a positive sense. Nor, as a visitant from high or low realms, does it remind lesser humans of their fallen state. It leads one neither East of Eden, to the Bower of Bliss, nor heavenward. Yet it is present, and it renders the working of the trained and conscious mind, one skilled in sorting experience into "Western" or "Christian" negations and appositions, simply impertinent: "useless – assent and praise were hardly required." A hosanna is like a "mere further murmur and rustle of leaves, of the air," for "the Angel had not brought death or salvation." Such an essential reworking of Western conventions leads to a new form of fiction, which is *not* the binary opposition to reality; thus "Angel" is one of Brodkey's major achievements.

His fiction is realistic narrative, and it draws strength from the older traditions of commentary. Such at least is the achievement of his 1988 volume of stories. The publicly accepted messiah, the celebrity (Marcus Weill with his contrivance and obviousness) is a "counterevangel," the crux of irony. The true seraphs, the angels of Brodkey's imagination, "stand" but are "not universal." They witness but do not reveal the easy formulas of salvation. They are agents of description and memory. Such creations are high literary art.

Brodkey's strongest fiction in another form centers on the adoptive mother, a focus for both love and hate. She is, however, not a forbidding monster but a mom, typical in that she is almost never in control, because no one really is. Such is the equivocation of life itself. Brodkey catches the nuances, the helplessness, the contrary aggressive sense of futile and repetitive combat, and the oscillation of love, hate, and frustration. Are his stories written in "an almost classical mode"? *Classical,* strictly speaking, refers to the literatures and arts of the ancient Greeks and Romans. The tensions of parents and children are truly more in the vein presented in Brodkey's fiction and not in the easy propaganda of good judgment, might, and willing subservience, with dollops of gratitude, that marks the fable of American family life. "Almost classical," in other words, refers not to the idealizations of the ancients but to behavior that has gone on generation after generation in most societies – behavior that is, in a sense, "classical," found at all times, everywhere.

In "A Story in an Almost Classical Mode" a tortured child-parent love ends with honesty, not hatred, as a son speaks to his mother, who is on her deathbed:

"You always were a good mother."
"Oh, Buddy, I was terrible."

"No, Momma. No, you weren't."

"Buddy, I can face the truth. I know what I did."

This primal moment is among the finest of Brodkey's writing, for he catches the rhythms, false hopes, snatched conversations, and the will of the dying to make, through language and appropriate farewells, the right patterns of life. The mother says, "I'm only alive because I wanted to talk to you. . . . I wanted this to be the last thing. . . . Do you understand, I want you to know now how much I think of you." Then the son, who is the narrator, witnesses the end of her life: "I listened to her breathing grow irregular. I said to myself, Die, Momma. On this breath. I don't want you to live anymore. Her breath changed again. It began to be very loud, rackety. I began to count her breaths. I counted fifteen and then neither her breath nor her actual voice was ever heard again."

Brodkey's place in modern American fiction should be higher than currently estimated. Even with the occasional faults of his short fiction, Brodkey is a major contemporary writer, for he takes the Emersonian witnessing *I* to new levels of subtlety; and with his admixture of Jewish sensitivity and skepticism – the latter partly secular and Missourian ("show me") – adds a needed critical voice directed against modern, self-centered evangelism. On one level he seems a Harvard-educated Mark Twain; on another, in his feats of recall, he may re-semble Proust. However, Brodkey has neither the demonic, mythical power of Franz Kafka nor the absolutely secure technique of James Joyce. The life of any writer, though, is a quest, and Brodkey's is described, perhaps, at the conclusion of "Angel": "Only after many years were there convincing but frail and as if whispered attempts at honesty, of which this is one."

Interview:

James Linville, "Harold Brodkey: The Art of Fiction," *Paris Review,* 121 (1991): 51–91.

References:

Bruce Bawer, "A Genius for Publicity," *New Criterion,* 7 (December 1988): 58–69;

Sven Birkerts, "Infinity of Inwardness," *Nation,* 237 (17 October 1988): 348–351;

Carol Iannone, "The Brodkey Question," *Commentary,* 87 (April 1989): 58–61;

D. Keith Mano, "Harold Brodkey: The First Rave," *Esquire,* 87 (January 1977): 14–15;

Edward Rothstein, "Look Homeward, Angel," *New York Review of Books,* 37 (15 February 1990): 36–41;

Leon Weiseltier, "A Revelation," *New Republic,* 192 (20 May 1985): 30–33;

Richard B. Woodward, "Brodkey," *Mirabella* (October 1991): 90–100.

Charles Bukowski

(16 August 1920 –   )

Michael Basinski
State University of New York at Buffalo

See also the Bukowski entry in *DLB 5: American Poets Since World War II,* Part 1.

BOOKS: *Flower, Fist and Bestial Wail* (Eureka, Cal.: Hearse, 1960);

Longshot Pomes [sic] *for Broke Players* (New York: 7 Poets, 1962);

Run with the Hunted (Chicago: Midwest Poetry Chapbooks, 1962);

Poems and Drawings (Crescent City, Fla.: Epos, 1962);

It Catches My Heart in Its Hands (New Orleans: Loujon, 1963);

Grip the Walls (Storrs, Conn.: Wormwood Review, 1964);

Crucifix in a Deathhand (New York: Lyle Stuart, 1965);

Cold Dogs in the Courtyard (Chicago: Literary Times/Cyfoeth, 1965);

Confessions of a Man Insane Enough to Live with Beasts (Bensenville, Ill.: Mimeo, 1965);

The Genius of the Crowd (Cleveland, Ohio: 7 Flowers, 1966);

All the Assholes in the World and Mine (Bensenville, Ill.: Open Skull, 1966);

Night's Work (Storrs, Conn.: Wormwood Review, 1966);

Poems Written Before Jumping Out of an 8 Story Window (Glendale, Cal.: Poetry X/Change, 1968; Gersthofen, Germany: Maro, 1974; enlarged edition, Salt Lake City: Litmus, 1975);

At Terror Street and Agony Way (Los Angeles: Black Sparrow, 1968);

A Bukowski Sampler, edited by Douglas Blazek (Madison, Wis.: Quixote, 1969);

Charles Bukowski; Philip Lamantia; Harold Norse (London & Baltimore: Penguin, 1969);

Notes of a Dirty Old Man (North Hollywood, Cal.: Essex House, 1969);

The Days Run Away Like Wild Horses Over the Hills (Los Angeles: Black Sparrow, 1969);

Fire Station (Santa Barbara, Cal.: Capricorn, 1970);

Post Office (Los Angeles: Black Sparrow, 1971; London: London Magazine, 1974);

Mockingbird Wish Me Luck (Los Angeles: Black Sparrow, 1972);

Erections, Ejaculations, Exhibitions, and General Tales of Ordinary Madness (San Francisco: City Lights, 1972); abridged as *Life and Death In the Charity Ward* (London: London Magazine, 1974); republished in 2 volumes: *The Most Beautiful Woman in Town* and *Tales of Ordinary Madness* (San Francisco: City Lights, 1983);

While the Music Played (Los Angeles: Black Sparrow, 1973);

South of No North (Los Angeles: Black Sparrow, 1973);

Burning in Water, Drowning in Flame (Los Angeles: Black Sparrow, 1974);

Africa, Paris, Greece (Los Angeles: Black Sparrow, 1975);

Factotum (Los Angeles: Black Sparrow, 1975; London: Allen, 1981);

Scarlet (Santa Barbara, Cal.: Black Sparrow, 1976);

Tough Company (Santa Barbara, Cal.: Black Sparrow, 1976);

Maybe Tomorrow (Santa Barbara, Cal.: Black Sparrow, 1977);

Art (Santa Barbara, Cal.: Black Sparrow, 1977);

Love Is a Dog from Hell (Santa Barbara, Cal.: Black Sparrow, 1977);

Terpentin [sic] *on the Rocks* (Augsburg, Germany: Maro, 1978);

Legs, Hips and Behind (Los Angeles: Wormwood Review, 1978);

You Kissed Lilly (Santa Barbara, Cal.: Black Sparrow, 1978);

Women (Santa Barbara, Cal.: Black Sparrow, 1978; London: Allen, 1981);

We'll Take Them (Santa Barbara, Cal.: Black Sparrow, 1978);

Play the Piano Drunk Like a Percussion Instrument Until the Fingers Begin to Bleed a Bit (Santa Barbara, Cal.: Black Sparrow, 1979);

Charles Bukowski, circa 1990 (photograph by Michael Montfort)

Shakespeare Never Did This (San Francisco: City Lights, 1979);

Dangling in the Tournefortia (Santa Barbara, Cal.: Black Sparrow, 1981);

Ham on Rye (Santa Barbara, Cal.: Black Sparrow, 1982);

Horsemeat (Santa Barbara, Cal.: Black Sparrow, 1982);

The Last Generation (Santa Barbara, Cal.: Black Sparrow, 1982);

Bring Me Your Love (Santa Barbara, Cal.: Black Sparrow, 1983);

Sparks (Santa Barbara, Cal.: Black Sparrow, 1983);

Hot Water Music (Santa Barbara, Cal.: Black Sparrow, 1983);

Under the Influence, edited by Al Fogel (Sudbury, Mass.: Weinberg, 1984);

There's No Business (Santa Barbara, Cal.: Black Sparrow, 1984);

Barfly (Sutton West, Ont. & Santa Barbara, Cal.: Paget, 1984); adapted as *The Movie, "Barfly"* (Santa Rosa, Cal.: Black Sparrow, 1987);

War All the Time (Santa Barbara, Cal.: Black Sparrow, 1984);

One for the Old Boy (Santa Barbara, Cal.: Black Sparrow, 1984);

Alone in a Time of Armies (Santa Barbara, Cal.: Black Sparrow, 1985);

You Get So Alone at Times That It Just Makes Sense (Santa Rosa, Cal.: Black Sparrow, 1986);

The Day It Snowed in L.A. (Santa Barbara, Cal.: Paget, 1986);

Gold in Your Eye (Santa Barbara, Cal.: Black Sparrow, 1986);

Luck (Santa Rosa, Cal.: Black Sparrow, 1987);

The Roominghouse Madrigals (Santa Rosa, Cal.: Black Sparrow, 1988);

Hollywood (Santa Rosa, Cal.: Black Sparrow, 1989);

Septuagenarian Stew: Stories & Poems (Santa Rosa, Cal.: Black Sparrow, 1990);

In the Shadow of the Rose (Santa Rosa, Cal.: Black Sparrow Press, 1991);

The Last Night of the Earth Poems (Santa Rosa, Cal.: Black Sparrow, 1992);

Bukowski with his parents, Katherine and Henry Bukowski, in 1947

Run with the Hunted: A Charles Bukowski Reader, edited by John Martin (New York: HarperCollins, 1993).

Charles Bukowski, an internationally recognized literary figure, first published a short story, "Aftermath of a Lengthy Rejection Slip," in *Story* magazine in 1944, when he was twenty-four years old; he began writing and publishing poetry at the age of thirty-five. Now in his seventies, he has published more than sixty books of poetry and prose. His books have been published in over a dozen languages, and his poems and stories appear frequently in newspapers and literary magazines throughout the world. Bukowski earned his reputation outside established literary channels. A supremely self-motivated literary maverick, he has had a career publishing with small presses, literary magazines, and underground alternative journals. This publishing world is an unruly one. Nevertheless, Bukowski has succeeded within its parameters and continues to thrive ubiquitously. He has written more than fifteen hundred magazine publications. For twenty-five years, Black Sparrow Press, one of the most successful and respected independent publishers, has been publishing his books, most of which have gone through several printings. Presently there are

several dozen magazines and small presses that publish legions of Bukowski literary protégés and imitators. He remains a prolific and dominating literary force in underground literary circles and may well be the most imitated writer in the United States.

Bukowski's rise to international recognition was arduous. He was forty years old in 1960 when his first book of poetry, *Flower, Fist and Bestial Wail,* was published. This small book, only fourteen pages long, came fourteen years after his first magazine appearance. Bukowski spent the interim years living at the bottom of American society as a common laborer, skid-row alcoholic, social outcast, misfit, and recluse. In the mid 1950s, after a decade of heavy drinking, he was hospitalized with a severe bleeding ulcer. After his remarkable recovery he resumed his writing. His poetry initially brought him a small but loyal audience. In the early 1960s he published several chapbooks in quick succession, among them *Longshot Pomes* [sic] *for Broke Players* and *Run with the Hunted* (both 1962). However, his work in the short-story genre first delivered a wide readership and solidified his literary reputation. This recognition occurred between 1966 and 1973, when the nation was experiencing the shock waves of the antiwar and counterculture insurgence. Traditional and conservative middle-class values and morals were under siege. The youth culture was searching for vehicles that would aid in undermining authority and experimenting with radical politics and perception. Upon this wave of youthful dissent Bukowski, an alcoholic, cynical, middle-aged postalworker poet emerged and wrote a weekly column for the Los Angeles–based alternative newspaper *Open City.* Bukowski's conglomeration of realistic fiction, reportage, opinion, and philosophy was called "Notes of a Dirty Old Man."

The column provided a natural vehicle for Bukowski's freewheeling, raw, and belligerent style. Without restrictions he chose his own subject matter and format. His anti-authoritarian and anti-middle-class tirades were quickly accepted, and his popularity grew. In 1969, Essex House, a Hollywood-based publisher of pornography, published in paperback a collection of Bukowski's work culled from the first fourteen months of his *Open City* column. The book, *Notes of a Dirty Old Man,* was Bukowski's first major publication and a phenomenal success. The collection established Bukowski's point of view and his philosophical parameters. He wrote as if he were a stranger in his own land, and he wrote about the dysfunctional and pathological facets within individuals and in American society. He perceives American culture as hypocritical. He is particularly critical of middle-class entertainment (movies and television), morals (monogamy), and beliefs (patriotism). The racetracks, rooming houses, bars, and the skid-row underbelly environs of Los Angeles are his fictional territory, a terrain populated with alcoholics, whores, bohemian or decadent writers (including Jack Micheline and Neal Cassady), and characters with demented personalities. Bukowski is the supreme narrator, appearing in the first person or as an autobiographical character such as Henry Beckett. In whatever context, Bukowski reveals himself as a hard-boiled, impudent survivor of some of the most horrific circumstances imaginable. The tone of *Notes of a Dirty Old Man* is variable, being at points angry, sad, cold, and ridiculous. It is both comic and tragic and is based on a narrow, often cynical, philosophical vein, which Bukowski developed during his traumatic childhood.

Henry Charles Bukowski, Jr., was born in Andernach, Germany, on 16 August 1920. The only child of an American soldier (Henry Charles Bukowski, Sr.) and a German mother, Katherine Fett Bukowski, he immigrated with his family to Los Angeles in 1922. The young Bukowski (who dropped the Henry when he began to publish because he felt it was not a literary name) grew up in middle-income, working-class neighborhoods in Los Angeles. He has recollected, in his biography *Hank* (1991), by Neeli Cherkovski, that one of his earliest thoughts occurred after some children on his block ridiculed him for his German birth. The thought was "I don't belong here." His mother, a docile and subservient woman, was a housewife, and his father was a milkman. This tidy, almost typical family was ruled by the strict, harsh, insensitive, and disdainful Henry Charles Bukowski, Sr. The undisputed master of his realm, he imprisoned his family within a stern, regimented set of unbending, unbreakable, and unbearable rules, designed to maintain the facade of middle-class respectability. He reinforced his dictum with a strap, used liberally on his son, who hated his father and what he represented: the economic and emotional success supposedly offered for hard work and patriotism — the American dream. Such disdain is a consistent theme in Charles Bukowski's fiction and poetry. The most complete and detailed literary portrait of his father (and his own adolescent and teenage life) is in his novel *Ham on Rye* (1982). Basically Bukowski discarded all of the ideals his father cherished and adopted a set of strict anti-authoritarian standards that were in complete opposition to what his father, as a symbol of mundane and mediocre life, repre-

sented. The death of Bukowski's father is related in section 22 of *Notes of a Dirty Old Man* and in "The Death of the Father I" and "The Death of the Father II," both collected in *Hot Water Music* (1983). Bukowski's disdain for his father is blatantly present in all three works.

In an early autobiographical short story, "Love, Love, Love," published in the journal *Matrix* (Winter 1946–1947), Bukowski tells of his ridiculous, hostile home life and his response to it. His father is depicted as an ignorant, insensitive loudmouth; his mother, a distantly absent individual. As a result their son removes himself emotionally from the situation and retreats into alcohol abuse.

The Depression hit as Bukowski entered high school. His father lost his job, and economic hardships only fueled his abusive and tyrannical nature. The young Bukowski developed a severe case of acne, which forced him to miss half of his sophomore year and to endure endless hours of painful treatment. His doctors noted that it was the worst case of *acne vulgaris* they had ever treated. Bukowski was left with extensive facial scars. His hospital experience proved to be a profound one. It was the first prolonged encounter he had had with doctors, and it left an indelible impression. Hospital scenarios repeatedly occur in his fiction, as in *All the Assholes in the World and Mine* (1966), *Notes of a Dirty Old Man* (section 41), and *Ham on Rye*. Doctors are power figures (like fathers and gods) — insensitive, arrogant, and self-satisfied. Hospitals, like all bureaucracies, are places where the individual is not in control. They are to be avoided. For Bukowski, his creative and psychic survival depended on distancing himself from the imperial structure of civilization.

As a result of his skin condition and his vile home life, Bukowski was a forlorn teenager. He received some recognition from a teacher for an essay he wrote about being present at a speech delivered by President Herbert Hoover; however, Bukowski had not been at the event. He claims to have realized at that moment that all people wanted were beautiful lies. In fall 1935 he wrote his first short story, which was about a flying ace in World War I. Bukowski also discovered the pleasures of a library and found company in Upton Sinclair's *The Jungle* (1906), Sinclair Lewis's *Main Street* (1920), and the early prose of Ernest Hemingway. Among Bukowski's other early literary favorites were D. H. Lawrence, James Thurber, Theodore Dreiser, John Dos Passos, and Sherwood Anderson. He would later add John Fante, Louis-Ferdinand Céline, Franz Kafka, Fyodor Dostoyevski, and Robinson Jeffers

Bukowski at his Los Angeles apartment in 1969 (photograph by Samuel Cherry)

to his list. These writers were to have a profound artistic or philosophical influence on Bukowski's literary style. Hemingway had the greatest impact. His quick, clean, and powerful prose served as a model for Bukowski's own realistic and pointed writing. Bukowski's short stories, with their intense use of dialogue, resemble Hemingway's and like Hemingway (and Jack Kerouac) Bukowski transforms his personal experiences into fiction, theoretically allowing the cultural landscape to dictate the material. Bukowski's literary debts are many, and he has always been quick to acknowledge them.

The first third of Bukowski's life was a grueling lesson in survival, and that phase of his life forged his intense, often candidly brutal, always critical, and cold philosophical stance. This detached, righteously pessimistic frankness is defined by Bukowski in *Notes of a Dirty Old Man* (section 40) as "The Frozen Man Stance" and is "indicated best by such flat phrases as: *I just can't make it. or: To hell with it all. or: Give my regards to Broadway.*" The Frozen Man stands outside of monotonous "normal" life with its artificial sweetness, bland pleasures, petty anger, constant jealousy, and fallacious love. The stance allowed Bukowski to discard lies and fraudulent images. He could therefore witness the gross imperfections of human beings.

After attending Los Angeles City College from 1939 to 1941, Bukowski began his writing career in the mid 1940s, as his drinking became habitual and as he drifted from city to city, with one low-paying job following another. He wrote a short story per day (many of these handwritten) and submitted them to magazines such as the *New Yorker* and *Atlantic Monthly*. They were rejected. In the March–April 1944 issue *Story* published Bukowski's "Aftermath of a Lengthy Rejection Slip," which features an alcoholic writer. This story marked the beginning of an artistic phase that culminated with the chapbook publication of two lengthier stories: *Confessions of a Man Insane Enough to Live with Beasts* (1965) and *All the Assholes in the World and Mine*.

Bukowski published a minimal amount of material in the 1940s. His few magazine appearances included four short stories in *Matrix,* published between 1946 and 1948. They are representative of his early fiction and reveal themes that Bukowski would continue to develop in his later short stories. For example, "Hard Without Music" (Spring–Summer 1948) is about a rooming-house transient named Larry who sells his classical-record collection to two nuns. After he voices a philosophical thesis on classical music's unworldly quality, the story concludes with Larry fingering thirty-five dollars – three tens and a five. He is left in a state of deep contemplation. Life on one level is defeating, yet one must survive in a world that is unconcerned with the humanity of the individual. The tone of the story is overwhelmingly sad, a tone that permeates much of Bukowski's fiction. Shortly after his publications in *Matrix* he descended into the netherworld of skid row.

Returning to writing in the late 1950s, Bukowski published several lengthier pieces of fiction in magazines such as *Quixote,* the *Anagogic & Paudeumic Review,* and *Simbolica.* A major artistic development for him during this period was the montage style, which brought together his critical and philosophical prose (often in the form of the personal or epistolary essay), his autobiographical fiction, conventional fiction, and his reportage. The origins of this irregular, fragmented, and disjointed form, which would eventually be seen in *Notes of a Dirty Old Man,* are in "Portions from a Wine-Stained Notebook," published in 1960 in *Simbolica.* In this prototypical piece, sections of rambling philosophy begin to define the dirty-old-man literary persona that developed into the character named Hank Chinaski (in *Notes of a Dirty Old Man* and other books). "Portions of a Wine-Stained Notebook" is not only a technically innovative collage but also a philosophical prologue: "I believe in the God of myself: the one who finds as much color in a brick as in a rose. . . . What we need is a single hero to uphold the defeated." Bukowski's brutal life had hardened him and strengthened his self-confidence. The Bukowski of the 1960s was an active and aggressive member of the literary world.

Bukowski continued to refine his literary position throughout the 1960s, publishing various reviews, manifestos, and epistolary essays that outlined his literary intentions and limits. In "A Rambling Essay on Poetics and the Bleeding Life Written While Drinking a Six-pack (Tall)," in *Ole* (March 1965), Bukowski began defining himself as an arrogant, anarchistic, and defiant antihero. These attributes won him a vast group of readers who aligned with Bukowski against what he considered the pampered university literary elite and their unrealistic poetic activities.

In September 1964 Bukowski's common-law wife, Frances Smith, whom he met in 1962, gave birth to their daughter, Marina. Smith and Bukowski parted company in 1968.

In 1965 Bukowski entered a writing phase in which his fiction became more sophisticated. The fiction and poetry he wrote between 1965 and 1972 later comprised major books. His stories became more philosophical and more pointedly critical of

society, but they retained the fragmented montage pattern. *Confessions of a Man Insane Enough to Live with Beasts,* for example, is composed of nine short sections. Like *Notes of a Dirty Old Man,* the story is composed of fragments, disjointed in time and setting. The unifying factor is the stark philosophy and rough tone of the narrator. The first four sections in this semi-autobiographical story relate different aspects of Bukowski's life. The opening section is about his childhood. He is masturbating and is discovered by friends who label him crazy. The second section is set in the mid 1950s, and several quick lines of dialogue relate a scenario of survival on skid row. In section 3 the action shifts back to his early teenage years and a hospital scene in which the young Bukowski is hardened to his own ugly features and exposed to the arrogance of powerful doctors. Section 4 returns to the mid 1950s, and Bukowski is again at odds with the hospital power structure. The story continues shifting focus and material, retelling vignettes first presented in "Portions of a Wine-Stained Notebook." Specifically the story develops Bukowski as a fictional character. Bukowski, whether he appears as a first-person narrator, Henry Beckett, or Hank Chinaski, is the central and dominating aspect of his own fiction.

Following the success of *Notes of a Dirty Old Man,* published four years after *Confessions,* Bukowski's fiction and poetry were in high demand. He began to write for *Nola Express,* a New Orleans literary magazine, for various other literary magazines, and for traditional men's magazines such as *Knight* and *Adam.* Much of the fiction he wrote between 1969 and 1972, including pieces from his *Open City* column, were published as *Erections, Ejaculations, Exhibitions, and General Tales of Ordinary Madness* (1972). Additional stories from this period and some early long stories were collected in 1973 as *South of No North.* Unlike the montage and spontaneous prose associated with *Notes of a Dirty Old Man,* the fiction in these collections is structurally traditional and usually follows a conventional narrative story line, as seen in "Kid Stardust on the Porterhouse" and "Life in a Texas Whorehouse," two of the first three stories in *Erections.* The intervention of Bukowski's bombastic opinions begins to wane. His own ribald life and point of view, nevertheless, remain central in the fiction.

Several stories published in *Erections* represent a type of uncharacteristic, purely imaginary fiction that Bukowski occasionally writes. "The Gut-Wringing Machine," for example, features two seedy characters, Danforth and Bagley, who operate a less-than-honest employment agency. The dialogue is hard-boiled and shady, reminiscent of a grade-B gangster movie. Danforth and Bagley are able to satisfy their customers – employers seeking docile workers – by converting creative, independent prospects into spineless, conservative, middle-class lackeys. Bukowski equates guts with resisting God, family, country, and the material things usually associated with comfortable middle-class living: color television, silk pajamas, two dogs, and a mortgage. This story makes a philosophical point about personal freedom, as do many of Bukowski's more imaginative, allegorical, or symbolic short stories.

During the 1970s Bukowski became a literary giant with a growing reputation and a large readership. He abandoned short fiction almost entirely as his fictional focus shifted to novels. Bukowski's novels are a type of transmogrified autobiographical narrative fiction similar to Kerouac's. In them Bukowski fully develops his first-person prose style. *Post Office* (1971), his first novel, details his work and personal life while an employee of the U.S. Postal Service. It retains the short-vignette structural form used in *Confessions*. In fact all of Bukowski's novels maintain this form. *Post Office* was followed by *Factotum* (1975), which documents his work life and wanderings as a young man. The novel *Women* (1978) is based on his love affairs during the 1970s. *Ham on Rye* is a memoir of Bukowski's childhood and teenage years. *Hollywood* (1989) tells of the making of the movie based on his *Barfly* (1984). Throughout all of his novels Bukowski's philosophical perspective remains identical to the rigidly anti-authoritarian stance of *Notes of a Dirty Old Man*.

Bukowski's major achievement as an author is his fictional alter ego Chinaski. Chinaski was originated in the 1940s, when Bukowski first began to publish fiction using his own life as material. The novels relate the life and times of Chinaski as he confronts a wide variety of social situations during various segments of his life.

Chinaski is at times a bum and an alcoholic, unbending, uncompromising, rudely poetic, and original. He is, as would be expected, a Dostoyevskian, modern, American, underground man. He is also a self-proclaimed coward. He takes extreme pleasure in the most basic of human functions: imagination, creation, defecation, copulation, and intoxication. He lives in a derelict American society by choice rather than by circumstance. Chinaski has exchanged normalcy and mediocrity for the advantage of self-development and exploration that can only be accomplished in a socially unrestricted environment. His supreme self, an anarchistic self,

has found this sanctuary on skid row, far from the middle-class demands of insurance, career, and neatly manicured lawns. Chinaski is not dull; he is a survivor. His life as a poor, downtrodden alcoholic does not depress him. He does not romanticize – like a bohemian might – his life on the fringe of society. Chinaski has located a cultural space where he can be the center of his own self-created world, from which he watches the insane world rush by. Chinaski's personal philosophy and disposition are homespun and original. He is satirical and appears to be anti-American, yet Chinaski has a strong Yankee spirit and an almost archetypal American approach to life. He is single-minded, hardheaded, judgmental, intolerant, self-reliant, and opportunistic.

After generating a voluminous amount of short fiction between 1965 and 1972, it was not until the 1980s that Bukowski returned to the form, writing and gathering material for *Hot Water Music*. Bukowski was over sixty years old, more meditative, and more secure. As in his novels and earlier collections of short fiction, the short stories in *Hot Water Music* retain a strong autobiographical element. Chinaski appears as the main character in several stories. Obsessive drinking remains the constant preoccupation of the majority of the characters, and their lives are seedy and sleazy. The tone of the writing remains frank and flagrant.

Hot Water Music attains a high level of artistic perfection. The spontaneous and montage forms that Bukowski used in his fiction of the 1960s have been replaced by premeditated plots and diverse points of view. The stories are clean, hard, and coldly objective. The philosophical advice that was once so freely offered in *Notes of a Dirty Old Man* has been woven into the plots. Throughout his literary career Bukowski has written about the confrontation between the sexes, and this theme is central to *Hot Water Music*. The different treatments of this theme over the years reveal the changes that have occurred in Bukowski's writing between *Notes of a Dirty Old Man* and *Hot Water Music*.

In section 27 of *Notes of a Dirty Old Man* Bukowski presents his particular views of sexuality and relationships. This presentation is frank and without literary embellishment: "sex is interesting but not totally important." Love is a tragicomedy that features an exploited woman, whose body or sexuality has been turned into a weapon for material advancement, and an equally exploited, manipulated male, whose sexuality has been perverted by society, particularly its advertising messages. The section continues with two autobiographical vignettes that further exemplify Bukowski's points. In the first vignette he comments on the nature of war and valor and their relationship to sexuality. The second vignette focuses on sexual desire, which drives or intoxicates humanity: Bukowski attempts to have sex with a prostitute but finds himself in a violent confrontation with a lesbian madam. Section 10 of *Notes of a Dirty Old Man* comments on the nature of male and female roles in an unnatural society. Women, Bukowski states, desire only "fake" men – that is, those who are conservative cogs in an unnatural world. The tone of these sections appears to be misogynistic because Bukowski does not present the female perspective on relationships in the dysfunctional society.

In *Hot Water Music* Bukowski develops his theory of relationships and investigates the particulars from many perspectives. He recognizes, for instance, that men both emotionally and physically abuse women: the female protagonist of the story "Turkey Neck Morning" faces the horror of another day with her mate. But Bukowski also exposes the fact that women brutalize men both physically and emotionally: there is a castrating female protagonist in "Praying Mantis." This balance of mutual hostility is a major change in Bukowski's prior, more singular vision. The conflict between the demand for immediate sexual gratification, exhibited by Chinaski and Bukowski's other characters, and the sensitivity necessary for monogamy is still a problem, and there is more sodomy, rape, and perversion in these stories than in all his previous fiction. The blame for these dysfunctional relationships, for the war of the sexes, and for the general perversion rests on the dysfunctional society. The society has been manufactured by the dull and foolish masses. It is a self-made, inescapable trap. Humanity, even with all its pretentious good intentions, has defeated itself. There is no hope except, perhaps, for the remote possibility that humanity might recognize itself as base and spiritually corrupt, a possibility that seems unlikely considering the shortsighted concerns of the general populace as portrayed in Bukowski's fiction. His stories are pessimistic, exposing the deplorable pettiness of American society and the despair of the trapped people.

Such despair is exemplified in the collection's final story, "Fooling Marie." Ted, the protagonist, has attempted a tryst with an attractive younger woman in a motel. He is being unfaithful to his wife, Marie, who is at home and thinks Ted is at the track. Ted has his clothes, keys, and wallet stolen. The closing image shows Ted sitting naked on the bed, a bottle of Cutty Sark whiskey in hand, for-

Linda and Charles Bukowski on their wedding day, with John Martin of Black Sparrow Press (photograph by Michael Montfort)

lornly gazing out at the freeway as the cars roar past in the night.

On 18 August 1985 Bukowski married Linda Beighle, a restaurant owner he had met at one of his poetry readings in 1976. His friend and publisher John Martin of Black Sparrow Press was his best man at the wedding.

Bukowski has continued his prolific writing habits. *The Last Night of the Earth Poems* (1992) is over four hundred pages long. Each new publication is greeted by an enthusiastic readership. A Bukowski newsletter titled *Sure* is being published. Critics and reviewers praise him for his frankness, his guts, and his realism, and they continue to cheer him for his raw portraits of life on the fringe of American society. Much of this praise echoes John William Corrington's preface to Bukowski's *Crucifix in a Deathhand* (1965), in which Corrington characterizes Bukowski's writing as "the spoken voice nailed to paper." The first biography of Bukowski, *Hank,* a clear and sympathetic rendering of his life, was published in 1991. The portrait reveals a sensitive and imaginative man who lived through many of the capers he has written about, and it shows that Bukowski is more rounded and complex than his mythical Chinaski.

There is little extensive scholarship on the poetry and prose of Charles Bukowski. Book-length critical studies have not been published, and few refined essays on him exist. There are, however, a few intrepid scholars who are taking Bukowski's work seriously. Bukowski's place in American letters has not, however, been secured. Working outside definable literary movements, Bukowski appears to be as much of a maverick as Chinaski. A mature and sophisticated analysis of the entire Bukowski canon would go far toward integrating his fiction and poetry into a complete picture of mid-twentieth-century American literature.

Letters:

The Bukowski/Purdy Letters, edited by Seamus Cooney (Sutton West, Ont. & Santa Barbara, Cal.: Paget, 1983);

Bukowski: Friendship, Fame & Bestial Myth, edited by Jory Sherman (Augusta, Ga.: Blue Horse, 1988).

Bibliographies:

Sanford Dorbin, *A Bibliography of Charles Bukowski* (Los Angeles: Black Sparrow, 1969);

Hugh Fox, *Charles Bukowski: A Critical & Bibliographical Study* (Somerville, Mass.: Abyss, 1969).

Biography:

Neeli Cherkovski, *Hank: The Life of Charles Bukowski* (New York: Random House, 1991).

References:

"The Bukowski-Butor Issue," *Review of Contemporary Fiction,* special issue, 3 (Fall 1983);

Neeli Cherkovski, *Whitman's Wild Children* (Venice, Cal.: Lapis, 1988);

John William Corrington, "Charles Bukowski at Midflight," preface to Bukowski's *Crucifix in a Deathhand* (New York: Lyle Stuart, 1965);

Glenn Easterly, "The Pock-Marked Poetry of Charles Bukowski," *Rolling Stone,* no. 215 (17 June 1976): 28–36;

Loss Pequeno Glazier, *All's Normal Here: A Charles Bukowski Primer* (Fremont, Cal.: Ruddy Duck, 1985);

J. E. Webb, ed., *The Outsider,* special issue on Bukowski, 1, no. 3 (1963).

Papers:

Bukowski's papers are held at the University of California, Santa Barbara; in the American Literature Collection of the University of Southern California; and in the Special Collections of Temple University.

Raymond Carver

(25 May 1938 – 2 August 1988)

Joe Nordgren
Lamar University

See also the Carver entries in *DLB Yearbook: 1984* and *DLB Yearbook: 1988.*

BOOKS: *Near Klamath* (Sacramento: English Club of Sacramento State College, 1968);

Winter Insomnia (Santa Cruz, Cal.: Kayak, 1970);

Put Yourself in My Shoes (Santa Barbara, Cal.: Capra, 1974);

At Night the Salmon Move (Santa Barbara, Cal.: Capra, 1976);

Will You Please Be Quiet, Please? (New York: McGraw-Hill, 1976);

Furious Seasons and Other Stories (Santa Barbara, Cal.: Capra, 1977);

What We Talk About When We Talk About Love (New York: Knopf, 1981; London: Collins, 1982);

The Pheasant (Worcester, Mass.: Metacom, 1982);

Fires: Essays, Poems, Stories (Santa Barbara, Cal.: Capra, 1983; London: Collins Harvill, 1985);

Cathedral (New York: Knopf, 1983; London: Collins, 1984);

If It Please You (Northridge, Cal.: Lord John, 1984);

This Water (Concord, N.H.: Ewert, 1985);

The Stories of Raymond Carver (London: Picador, 1985);

Where Water Comes Together with Other Water (New York: Random House, 1985);

The Short Stories of Raymond Carver (London: Pan, 1985);

Dostoevsky: A Screenplay, by Carver and Tess Gallagher (Santa Barbara, Cal.: Capra, 1985);

My Father's Life (Derry, N.H.: Babcock & Koontz, 1986);

Ultramarine (New York: Random House, 1986);

Early for the Dance (Concord, N.H.: Ewert, 1986);

Those Days: Early Writings, edited by William L. Stull (Elmwood, Conn.: Raven, 1987);

In a Marine Light: Selected Poems (London: Collins Harvill, 1987);

Intimacy (Concord, N.H.: Ewert, 1987);

Where I'm Calling From: New and Selected Stories (New York: Atlantic Monthly, 1988);

Elephant, and Other Stories (London: Collins Harvill, 1989);

A New Path to the Waterfall (New York: Atlantic Monthly, 1989);

Carver Country (New York: Scribners / Toronto: Collier Macmillan, 1990).

OTHER: John Gardner, *On Becoming a Novelist,* edited by Carver (New York: Harper & Row, 1983);

William Kittredge, *We Are Not in This Together,* foreword by Carver (Port Townsend, Wash.: Graywolf, 1984);

The Best American Short Stories 1986, edited by Carver and Shannon Ravenal (Boston: Houghton Mifflin, 1986);

Joel Gardner, *Batavia,* includes an essay by Carver (Burlington, Vt.: Shadows, 1986);

American Short Story Masterpieces, edited by Carver and Tom Jenks (New York: Delacorte, 1987);

American Fiction 88, introduction by Carver (Farmington, Conn.: Wesley, 1988).

Appreciative of Anne Tyler's description of him as a "spendthrift," Raymond Carver said during an interview with Kasia Boddy (in *Conversations with Raymond Carver,* 1990), "I think a writer ought to spend himself in whatever he's doing. If a writer starts holding back, that can be a very bad thing. I've always squandered." Selecting Ernest Hemingway, Gustave Flaubert, Leo Tolstoy, and Anton Chekhov as models for craft, passion, and integrity, Carver drew upon a "bedrock honesty," according to his friend Tobias Wolff (in *DLB Yearbook: 1988*), to deliver "the news from one world to another." Deemed a spokesperson for blue-collar despair,

Raymond Carver and Tess Gallagher in Syracuse, where they taught in the creative-writing program at Syracuse University during the 1980s (photograph by Marion Ettlinger)

Carver wrote with the authenticity of experience. His obsessions (Carver disapproved of the word *themes*) included male-female relationships, confronting loss, and survival. Spanning twelve years, his four major short-story collections, *Will You Please Be Quiet, Please?* (1976), *What We Talk About When We Talk About Love* (1981), *Cathedral* (1983), and *Where I'm Calling From* (1988), underscore his desire in style and subject matter to create the feeling that, as he told Boddy, "things are at risk."

In his early stories unbearable ordinariness afflicts the characters. Bruce Weber wrote in the *New York Times Magazine* (24 June 1984) that "Carver country is a place we all recognize. It is a place that Carver himself comes from, the country of arduous life." His father, Clevie Raymond Carver, also knew the grind of economic hardship. In the 1930s he moved from Arkansas to the logging districts of the Pacific Northwest, where he married Ella Beatrice Casey. While he was eking out a living as a saw filer in the lumber mills of Oregon and Washington, his wife worked as a clerk and waitress to help pay bills.

Born in Clatskanie, Oregon, on 25 May 1938, Raymond Carver was three when his parents moved with him to Yakima, Washington, a working-class town in the eastern part of the state. His younger brother and only sibling, James Carver, was born in 1943. The parents gradually struggled their way into the lower middle class.

Carver often described his childhood and adolescence as average. His father was a storyteller, embellishing tales about the Civil War and about riding the rails west. Occasionally Carver would happen upon his father reading works by Zane Grey. Apart from serialized westerns, the young Carver read books by Edgar Rice Burroughs and magazines such as *Outdoor Life* and *Sports Afield*. He associated the act of reading with his father and was drawn to that introspective stance; he also associated alcohol with his father, who often would spend his weekend nights away from home with friends from the mill.

After graduating from Yakima High School in 1956, Carver went to work in the local sawmill. Hating his job, he stuck to it just long enough to buy a car and move out. On 7 June 1957 Carver married sixteen-year-old Maryann Burk, who was to become a teacher. Six months later their daughter, Christine, was born. In August 1958 the Carver family moved to Paradise, California, and he went from one low-paying job to another, while Maryann waited tables and sold items door-to-door. Vance, their son, was born that October. Carver and his wife were fastened to a life of responsibility, paying for rent, utilities, and food and clothing for their children and fearing medical emergencies, since they could not afford health insurance.

Wanting to write, Carver enrolled as a part-time student at Chico State College (now California State University, Chico), where he received encouragement, exacting criticism, and lessons about honesty from John Gardner. Carver edited the first issue of *Selection,* the Chico State literary magazine. In June 1960, he moved with his family to Eureka, California, and was hired at a Georgia-Pacific sawmill. That fall he transferred to Humboldt State College (now a university) in Arcata and took writing classes from Richard C. Day. Carver earned his bachelor's degree in English from Humboldt State in 1963 and was awarded a five-hundred-dollar fellowship for the Iowa Writers' Workshop for the upcoming year. He stayed in Iowa with his family for six months, but trying to support a wife and two children on minimum-wage part-time work prompted their move to Sacramento, California, in June 1964. He then became a day custodian at Mercy Hospital.

Carver stayed on at the hospital for three years. After being transferred to the night shift, he found that he could finish his scheduled duties in two or three hours and still receive a full day's pay. He would do his work, go home, get up early, and turn to his writing. In fall 1966 he joined a poetry workshop directed by Dennis Schmitz at Sacramento State College (now a university). Though bankruptcy and his father's death marred the early months of 1967, two fortunate occurrences were to come his way. In July, Carver received his first white-collar job, editing textbooks for Science Research Associates (SRA) in Palo Alto, California, where he met Gordon Lish. That same year Martha Foley included Carver's "Will You Please Be Quiet, Please?" in *The Best American Short Stories 1967.*

"Will You Please Be Quiet, Please?" begins as eighteen-year-old Ralph Wyman is about to leave for college. His father warns him: "Life is a very serious matter, an arduous undertaking, but nevertheless a rewarding one." At college Ralph drinks his way through his sophomore year, meets his future wife, Marian, and decides on a teaching career. Six years pass; a son and daughter are born. Life is comfortable.

While talking one evening, Marian mentions a party they attended a few years ago. Pressing a gnawing suspicion, Ralph maneuvers his wife into admitting she has been unfaithful. When she confesses, he becomes a martyr to infidelity. He drives to a seedy part of town, gets drunk, squanders money in a card game, and is assaulted. Back home at dawn, he inventories the objects that clutter his ordinary life and wonders what to do: "Take things and leave? Go to a hotel, make certain arrangements? He understood things had to be done. He didn't understand what things now were to be done." Lost, he cannot even identify himself in any of the expressions that he makes in the bathroom mirror while washing the blood from his face.

In the bedroom Marian eases Ralph toward making love, and "He turned and turned in what might have been a stupendous sleep, and was still turning, marveling, at the impossible changes he felt moving over him." Carver presents intimacy as a healing hand. Since Ralph is "letting go a little" of his smug, self-righteous attitude, he might be able to put a meaningful expression on his face.

In spring 1968 Maryann Carver accepted a scholarship to Tel Aviv University, and Raymond Carver arranged for a year's leave from SRA. In 1969 he returned to SRA as an advertising director and stayed with them until September 1970. Combined with a National Endowment for the Arts Discovery Award, his severance pay and unemployment benefits allowed him to write full-time.

For the first half of the 1970s, writing, teaching, and increased drinking were the shaping events in Carver's life. Lish published Carver's story "Neighbors" in the June 1971 *Esquire.* Three other stories were chosen consecutively for the O. Henry Awards annual *Prize Stories* (1973–1975). While drawing praise, Carver accepted a series of one-year lectureships at universities interested in enhancing their writing programs: the University of California, Santa Cruz (1971–1972); the University of California, Berkeley (1972–1973); the University of Iowa Writers' Workshop (1973–1974), where he met John Cheever and drank his way toward legendary status; and the University of California, Santa Barbara (1974–1975).

After leaving Santa Barbara and suffering a second bankruptcy, Carver and his family moved to Cupertino, California, where they lived until 1976. He and his wife had little to show for their fifteen years of struggling to stay together. Unemployed,

FURIOUS SEASONS

RAYMOND CARVER

Cover for Carver's 1977 collection of stories, most of which were republished in his later books

Carver turned to more self-destructive drinking. Like the people in his stories, Carver was among the dispossessed. Ironically, his first major-press book, *Will You Please Be Quiet, Please?*, was published in March 1976.

The twenty-two stories comprising the book were written between 1962 and 1975. His subjects and characters seem lifted from the dismal sidewalks of pedestrian life. Out of work or laced to dead-end jobs, they wait tables, sell vacuum cleaners door-to-door, deliver the mail, punch time cards at the factory, or attend to bookkeeping and secretarial duties. In *Understanding Raymond Carver* (1988) Arthur M. Saltzman says of these characters, "Vaguely unhappy, vaguely lonesome, they tread water. They wonder if they are leading the right lives." Some characters, in fact, are fading out of existence, as in the conclusion of "The Father," when Alice blurts out: "Daddy doesn't look like *anybody*!" Suddenly aware that he has no functional identity

even within his family, the man turns "white and without expression."

With the exception of those in "Bicycles, Muscles, Cigarets" and "Will You Please Be Quiet, Please?," discontent and estrangement vex the majority of the characters. Most feel as if they have stepped into the wrong lives. Critics David Boxer and Cassandra Phillips (*Iowa Review,* Summer 1979) use the terms *voyeurism* and *dissociation* to suggest how Carver "ambushes" his people by "giving them sudden, hideously clear visions of the emptiness" surrounding them. In the story "The Idea" the narrator and her husband, Vern, spy on the man next door who sneaks along the shadows of his house at night and peeps into the bedroom window to watch his wife undress. The narrator wants to know, "What does she have that other women don't have?" Vern wonders if the man has stumbled onto an idea that could excite their own sex life. Self-conscious about watching this "trash," they eat canned soup and cold meat loaf before getting ready for bed. They are passionless; habit has undone them.

The character Earl Ober in "They're Not Your Husband" goads his wife into losing weight so he can sit around at the diner where she works and entice men to leer at her when she bends over and her "skirt crawls up her legs." Caught in a "chafing marriage," Nan in "The Student's Wife" lives in "a false asylum of good intentions," according to Saltzman. At night her husband reads to her from the works of Rainer Maria Rilke; he believes such sensitivity will carry her beyond her exhausting childcare duties. When she talks about things she would like to do, he rolls over and falls asleep. Troubled by insomnia, she times her heartbeat, cries into her pillow, washes her face, checks on the children, and pages through an assortment of magazines. At daybreak, "Not in pictures she had seen or in books she had read had she learned a sunrise was so terrible as this." Among the "things becoming very visible" is the fact that her desires carry no relevance.

About his characters, Carver explained to Mona Simpson and Lewis Buzbee (in *Conversations*): "They would like their actions to count for something. But at the same time, they've reached the point that they know it isn't so. It's their lives they've become uncomfortable with, lives they see breaking down." For example, Bill and Arlene Miller in "Neighbors" are mystified by their friends who "live a brighter and fuller life." Harriet and Jim Stone, who live across the hall, can afford to go out to dinner, entertain guests at home, and combine business travel with pleasure. When the Stones go out of town for ten days, they ask the Millers to check on their apartment and cat. Feeding Kitty escalates into stealing prescription medicine, raiding the liquor cabinet, poking into drawers for intimations of the Stones' sex life, and, for Bill, crossdressing. When Arlene absentmindedly locks the key in the Stones' apartment, their ruse ends: "They leaned into the door as if against a wind and embraced themselves." It is difficult to find consolation in the closing image. The Millers are untrustworthy and inept. The corridor they occupy is empty. Boxer and Phillips point out: "The old life on one side of the hall seems more dissatisfying than ever, but the new life is on the other side of a locked door."

In "What's in Alaska?" Carl and his wife, Mary, are invited over to smoke pot with their friends Helen and Jack. Carl "is on a bummer." When Mary announces she has interviewed for a job in Fairbanks, Jack wants to know: "What's in Alaska? What would you do up there? What would you guys do in Alaska?" His anxiety suggests to Carl that Jack and Mary are having an affair. When Helen's cat drags in and begins licking a dead mouse, Carl reads it as a sign that he is in the grip of something that could desecrate him.

In October 1976 the Carvers sold their home in Cupertino and began living apart. Between then and January 1977, on four separate occasions, Carver was hospitalized for alcohol dependency. He met with Fred Hills, editor in chief of McGraw-Hill, in San Francisco in late May 1977 to discuss writing a novel. Carver then moved alone to McKinleyville, California, where he put some distance between himself and drinking. On 2 June 1977 he stopped. He confided in Simpson and Buzbee, "If you want the truth, I'm prouder of that, that I quit drinking, than I am of anything in my life."

At a writers' conference in Dallas in November 1977, Carver became friends with the poet Tess Gallagher. Also that month, Capra Press in Santa Barbara, California, published *Furious Seasons and Other Stories* (most of which also appear in original or revised forms in later collections). He had received a Guggenheim Fellowship for 1978, and he and Maryann attempted living together again, but on a trial basis. She moved out in July 1978, and they were finally divorced five years later.

Carver was chosen as "distinguished writer-in-residence" for 1978–1979 at the University of Texas at El Paso. He again encountered Gallagher, who was teaching at the University of Arizona, and on 1 January 1979 they began living together. By 1980 both had been appointed to the creative-writing faculty at Syracuse University. Stability entered Carver's life. They would spend September to May teaching at Syracuse and retreat during the summers to Port Angeles, Washington. On 20 April 1981 Knopf published Carver's second major collection of stories, *What We Talk About When We Talk About Love.*

Carver's affinity for the short story was guided by need as much as anything else. He wanted a quick payoff, not something that might stretch two or three years down the line. Often this meant completing a thirty-five- or forty-page draft in one sitting prior to drawing it through fifteen to twenty revisions, during which time he adhered to Hemingway's dictum that "seven-eighths of the iceberg is underwater." Avoiding tricks, Carver would cut the circuitous and the nonessential, trusting as much in the power of what was left out as to what was put in. The opening paragraph of "Mr. Coffee and Mr. Fixit" is a good example of his pared-down style. The narrator begins, "I've seen some things. I was going over to my mother's house to stay a few nights. But just as I got to the top of the stairs, I looked and she was on the sofa kissing a man. It was summer. The door was open. The TV was going. That's one of the things I've seen."

Writing stories that "worked invisibly" earned for Carver some derogatory criticism. In a review for *Atlantic* (June 1981) James Atlas stigmatized Carver's technique by calling it "severe to the point of anorexia." According to Saltzman, others have labeled *What We Talk About* as "K-mart Realism," "Lo-Cal Literature," "Freeze-Dried Fiction," and "Post-alcoholic Blue-Collar Minimalist Hyperrealism." Though catchy descriptions, they diminish the self-conscious aspect of the writing. Carver insisted, in his interview with Simpson and Buzbee, that "Every move was intentional and calculated. I pushed and pulled these stories to an extent I'd never done with any others." When they asked about the "minimalist" tag affixed after the book's publication, he stated, "There's something about 'minimalist' that smacks of smallness of vision and execution that I don't like."

The most quoted assessment of *What We Talk About* belongs to Donald Newlove (*Saturday Review,* April 1981): "Seventeen tales of Hopelessville, its marriages and alcoholic wreckage, told in a prose as sparingly clear as a fifth of iced Smirnoff." For Lish, writing in *Conversations,* "Carver's value is his sense of a peculiar bleakness. . . . The characters are not impoverished, except in spirit, or uneducated. They just seem squalid. And Carver celebrates that squalor, makes poetic that squalor in a way nobody else has tried to do." Experience impressed on Carver that, for people whose responsibilities eclipse their personal resources, it is nearly impossible to think of life in poetic terms.

In his foreword to William Kittredge's *We Are Not in This Together* (1984), Carver explains the loss of poetic sensibility among the disenfranchised: "Maybe there was a little, once in the beginning, but then something happened – it was worked out of you, or beaten out of you, or you drank too much, too long, and it left you and now you're worse off than ever because you know it's for nothing now, a senseless reminder of better days." *What We Talk About* makes this point abundantly clear.

Communication was essential to Carver. As he indicated to Boddy, "It's hard sometimes for people to talk and say what they really mean either because they are not skilled enough at being intimate with other people, or just feel the need to protect themselves." Some of his characters express themselves through their actions, though they might not understand the consequences of what they do. Others labor to find the right words for making their feelings known, as in two of his most compelling stories, "So Much Water So Close to Home" and "What We Talk About When We Talk About Love."

In "So Much Water So Close to Home" Claire is overcome by disgust. She cannot comprehend how her husband and his friends, decent family men with children of their own, could tether to a tree the wrist of a dead girl they have found in a lake and continue drinking and fishing for three days before reporting the incident. Claire stares across the dining-room table at Stuart. After stepping into the kitchen, her actions assume a voice of their own: "I rake my arm across the drainboard and send the dishes to the floor." At the picnic grounds near Everson Creek, she tries a backdoor approach to prompt Stuart to explain himself. She tells about a young girl in the town where she grew up who had her head cut off and was thrown in a river. Stuart becomes "riled," and, when annoyed, he withdraws. She looks at the water running under the bridge and watches it empty into a pond where men are fishing. The menace of psychological projection attacks her: "I'm right in it, eyes open, face down, staring at the moss on the bottom, dead." She admits to herself as they drive away: "There is nothing I can say to him."

The final scene similarly ends in silence. After Claire has returned home from the funeral of the drowned girl, Stuart says "I think I know what you need," as he unbuttons Claire's jacket and blouse. She concedes; talking will only generate resentment. A victim of compromise, Claire will always have – according to Saltzman – "that contaminant, that dead girl's ghost, that will discredit her pleasures and scuttle her dreams." Stuart assumes he is reviving his wife, but Claire is going under, drowning in feelings too powerful for words.

Whereas Stuart and Claire are unable to speak openly with one another, in "What We Talk About When We Talk About Love," Terri, Mel, Laura, and Nick talk themselves out. Critics have noted that the story is Carver's updated version of Plato's *Symposium,* stripped of its classical garnishing. With this allusion in hand, one anticipates that efforts to define or classify love are destined to failure, for, as Parnasius asserts in Plato's debate: "The rules were never properly laid down." In "What We Talk About," Mel and Terri are drinking gin at their kitchen table with Nick, who is the story's narrator, and Laura. Mel, a heart specialist, starts by insisting that real love is "nothing less than spiritual love." From this point their conversation traverses the pathological to the heartrending.

After their divorce Terri's abusive first husband threatened to kill her before committing suicide. Mel, her second husband, says that if given the chance he would murder his former wife, Marjorie, who is financially bleeding him dry. The other married couple, Nick and Laura, believe they are too much in love to be torn apart by external circumstances. But who knows what impels and sustains the feeling of love or how might it end? Mel says, "It ought to make us feel ashamed when we talk like we know what we're talking about when we talk about love." During the past few hours both couples have revealed their prejudices and insecurities. Finally the gin is gone, and night encroaches upon them. "I could hear my beating heart," Nick says. "I could hear everyone's heart. I could hear the human noise we sat there making, not one of us moving, not even when the room went dark."

Though *What We Talk About* is credited for being part of the rejuvenation of the American short story, the book has its detractors. Most often, Carver is accused of writing over his characters' heads, suggesting he condescends to their inadequacies. For critic Michael Gorra (*Hudson Review,* Spring 1984), the stories are "entirely without the mingled sense of inevitability that seems to me essential for short fiction – the sense that out of all the things that could happen, this one has." Carver, however, was his own most discerning critic. He said to Simpson and Buzbee, "I knew I had gone as far as I could or wanted to go, cutting everything down to the marrow, not just the bone. Any further in that direction and I'd be at a dead end – writing stuff and publishing stuff I wouldn't want to read myself."

On 30 November 1981 Carver's story "Chef's House" (later collected in *Cathedral*) appeared in the *New Yorker,* to which he became a frequent contributor. He had established himself at the forefront of contemporary short fiction. On 18 May 1983 he was the recipient of one of the American Academy and Institute of Arts and Letters' first Mildred and Harold Strauss Livings Awards, bringing him a renewable, five-year, tax-free stipend of thirty-five thousand dollars annually, on condition that he give up his teaching position to pursue his writing. On 15 September 1983 Knopf published his third major collection of stories, *Cathedral,* which received both National Book Critics and Pulitzer Prize nominations and catapulted him beyond the "minimalist" stereotype to which he had been confined.

Reviewers and critics differ in their assessments, but they agree that *Cathedral* and the seven new stories included in *Where I'm Calling From* mark a transition in Carver's career. After *What We Talk About* Carver did not write for six months. Then he suddenly hit upon "Cathedral." He told Simpson and Buzbee that he felt it was "totally different in conception and execution from any stories that have come before. I suppose it reflects a change in my life as much as it does in my way of writing. When I wrote 'Cathedral' I felt, 'This is what it's all about, this is the reason we do this.' There was an opening up when I wrote that story." Finding life and love after alcohol abuse warranted optimism.

In *Cathedral,* stories such as "Feathers," "Preservation," "Chef's House," and "Vitamins" focus on the familiar sullen look of perishable lives low on faith and energy. However, in "A Small, Good Thing," "Where I'm Calling From" (in both *Cathedral* and the later eponymous book), and "Cathedral," Carver's writing starts to "give more," starts to be "more generous," in his own words. Doors open; decisions are made. His characters are survivors – they endure.

Occasionally Carver published different versions of a story, though versions is not quite the right word because he always considered later revisions to be "different" stories. Some he cut, such as "Where Is Everyone?" (*TriQuarterly,* Spring 1980), republished as "Mr. Coffee and Mr. Fixit" (*What We Talk About*). Others he expanded, most notably "The Bath" (*What We Talk About*), which appears as "A Small, Good Thing" in *Cathedral* and for which

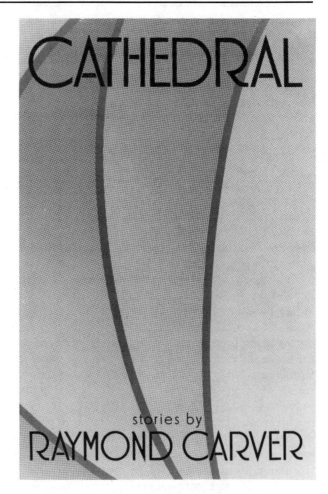

Dust jacket for the book that marks Carver's transition away from the "minimalism" of his earlier fiction

he won the O. Henry Award for the best story of 1983. The contrasts between "The Bath" and "A Small, Good Thing" illustrate his impulse toward generosity.

In "The Bath" Carver announces his less-is-more credo immediately after the mother of an ill boy, Ann Weiss, hands her name and phone number to a baker. He promises that her son Scotty's birthday cake will be ready in plenty of time for his upcoming party, but "This was all the baker was willing to say. No pleasantries, just this small exchange, the barest information, nothing that was not necessary." The remainder of the story matches the baker's reluctance. All the major scenes are etched in scant detail, allowing terror to build through silence and incomprehension. Medical charts fill with notes, a brain scan is ordered, and technicians hustle about sampling blood; however, the results are not explained to the parents. All Mrs. Weiss hears is: "We're into something now, something hard." The story abruptly ends in mid conversation. While trying to compose herself at home, she answers the ringing phone. Pressing her ear to the receiver, she listens to these words: "It is about Scotty. It has to do with Scotty, yes." She assumes someone is calling to update her son's condition. Tragedy has stepped between Ann Weiss and her ability to recognize the baker's voice. Nothing is resolved. She does not know if her son is alive or dead. She is hanging on the line.

When asked by Larry McCaffery (in *Conversations*) about returning to "The Bath," Carver said, "The story had been messed around with, condensed and compressed to highlight the qualities of menace that I wanted to emphasize. But I still felt there was unfinished business, so in the midst of writing these other stories for *Cathedral* I went back to 'The Bath' and tried to see what aspects of it needed to be enhanced, redrawn, reimagined. When I was done, I was amazed because it seemed so much better." In "A Small, Good Thing" sentences are more expansive, characters and scenes are more fully developed, and point of view shifts from being coolly objective to being limited omniscient. However, Carver's most ambitious step involves advancing the plot. Mrs. Weiss returns to the hospital, Scotty dies, and the Weisses drive to the bakery at midnight; they have decided that the baker has been harassing them by phone. The confrontation in the bakery gives way to healing. Shaken by his unintentional prying into their suffering, the baker offers the Weisses fresh rolls and coffee. Having been alone for so long, he apologizes for not knowing "how to act any more." As a provider he believes that "Eating is a small, good thing in a time like this." According to critic William L. Stull (*Philological Quarterly*, Winter 1985), "newness of life" and "salvation" comprise the burden of the story, and, in his view, "Carver's unobtrusive religious symbolism expands into an understated allegory of spiritual rebirth."

After the publication of *Cathedral*, with all the attention that was coming his way, Carver found it difficult to write while living in Syracuse. He told Michael Schumacher (in *Conversations*), "I couldn't seem to find any peace and quiet or place to work. There was a lot of traffic in the house, the phone kept ringing, people were showing up at the door." Thus he moved into Gallagher's newly built Sky House in Port Angeles in January 1984 and began splitting his time between there and New York. For the next few years poetry dominated his writing. Apart from being a regular contributor to *Poetry*, he published the collections *Where Water Comes Together with Other Water* (1985) and *Ultramarine* (1986).

He and Gallagher spent from April to July of 1987 traveling through Europe. After their return, Carver had part of his cancerous left lung removed. In January 1988 he bought a new home in Port Angeles, and later that year he was inducted into the American Academy and Institute of Arts and Letters. However, cancer had reappeared in his brain, and Carver underwent a seven-week course of radiation treatment. Yet he kept writing, and in May the Atlantic Monthly Press published his final major collection of short fiction, *Where I'm Calling From*.

"Elephant," one of seven previously uncollected stories to be included in *Where I'm Calling From*, further advances Carver's interest in survivors. The narrator, a recovering alcoholic, works in a fish cannery in upstate Washington, and his family keeps hoisting debt on his back. His brother in California needs five hundred dollars or will be thrown out of his house; his "poor and greedy" mother frets that the loan will cut into her monthly allowance. His daughter in Bellingham is married to a deadbeat; her two kids would like to have oatmeal for breakfast. The narrator's son is in college in New Hampshire and wants money for tuition and room and board; the narrator's former wife has the court on her side, so either he pays her alimony or goes to jail. He stops eating out, forgoes needed dental work, and drives his car to the breaking point.

All the demands nudge into his dreams. The narrator imagines being lifted onto his father's shoulders and taught to keep his balance. The father tightens his grip and reassures him: "*I've got you. You won't fall.*" Awakening to a clear morning, he realizes he does not have to buckle under to responsibility or debt. When his friend George, giving him a ride to work, punches the gas pedal, the combination of wind and speed is exhilarating. George and the narrator race "flat out" into whatever the day will bring.

Carver, after radiation treatments in May 1988, told Stewart Kellerman, "I'm going to make it. I've got fish to catch and stories and poems to write" (*New York Times*, 31 May 1988). Then, in early June, cancer again appeared in Carver's lungs. He and Gallagher were married in Reno, Nevada, on 17 June. They began putting together his last book of poetry (*A New Path to the Waterfall*, 1989) and took a fishing trip to Alaska in July. He died on 2 August 1988 in their home in Port Angeles.

Tobias Wolff, stressing Carver's "talent for humanity," writes, "Whatever was human interested Ray, most of all our struggle to survive without becoming less human. This struggle shaped his

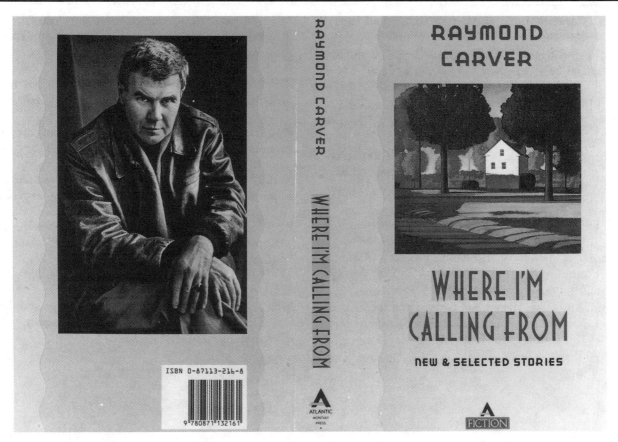

Dust jacket for Carver's last comprehensive short-story collection, published a few months before his death

life. His understanding of it, compassionate and profound, made him the great writer that he was, and the great friend."

Interviews:

Marshall Bruce Gentry and William L. Stull, eds., *Conversations with Raymond Carver* (Jackson: University Press of Mississippi, 1990).

References:

David Boxer and Cassandra Phillips, " 'Will You Please Be Quiet, Please?': Voyeurism, Dissociation, and the Art of Raymond Carver," *Iowa Review,* 10 (Summer 1979): 75–90;

Arthur A. Brown, "Raymond Carver and Postmodern Humanism," *Critique,* 31 (Winter 1990): 125–136;

Michael J. Bugeja, "Tarnish and Silver: An Analysis of Raymond Carver's *Cathedral," South Dakota Review,* 24 (Autumn 1986): 73–67;

Marc Chenetier, "Living On/Off the 'Reverse': Performance, Interrogation and Negativity in the Works of Raymond Carver," in *Critical Angles: European Views of Contemporary American Litera-*

ture, edited by Marc Chenetier (Urbana: Southern Illinois University Press, 1986), pp. 164–190;

Miriam Marty Clark, "Raymond Carver's Monologic Imagination," *Modern Fiction Studies,* 37 (Summer 1991): 240–247;

Hamilton E. Cochrane, "Taking the Cure: Alcoholism and Recovery in the Fiction of Raymond Carver," *Dayton Review,* 20 (Summer 1989): 79–88;

Peter J. Donahue, "Alcoholism as Ideology in Raymond Carver's 'Careful' and 'Where I'm Calling From,' " *Extrapolation,* 32 (Spring 1991): 54–63;

Mark A. R. Facknitz, " 'The Calm,' 'A Small, Good Thing,' and 'Cathedral': Raymond Carver and the Rediscovery of Human Worth," *Studies in Short Fiction,* 23 (Summer 1986): 287–296;

Ernest Fontana, "Insomnia in Raymond Carver's Fiction," *Studies in Short Fiction,* 26 (Fall 1989): 447–451;

Michael W. Gearhart, "Breaking the Ties That Bind: Inarticulation in the Fiction of Raymond

Carver," *Studies in Short Fiction,* 23 (Fall 1989): 439–446;

Norman German and Jack Bedell, "Physical and Social Laws in Raymond Carver's 'Popular Mechanics,' " *Critique,* 29 (Summer 1988): 257–260;

Michael Gorra, "Laughter and Bloodshed," *Hudson Review,* 37 (Spring 1984): 151–164;

Nelson Hatchcock, "The Possibility of Resurrection: Re-Vision in Carver's 'Feathers' and 'Cathedral,' " *Studies in Short Fiction,* 28 (Winter 1991): 31–39;

David Kaufmann, "Yuppie Postmodernism," *Arizona Quarterly,* 47 (Summer 1991): 93–116;

Daniel W. Lehman, "Raymond Carver's Management of Symbol," *Journal of the Short Story in English,* 17 (Autumn 1991): 43–58;

Elliot Malamet, "Raymond Carver and the Fear of Narration," *Journal of the Short Story in English,* 17 (Autumn 1991): 59–74;

Adam Meyer, "Now You See Him, Now You Don't, Now You Do Again: The Evolution of Raymond Carver's Minimalism," *Critique,* 30 (Summer 1989): 239–251;

Kirk Nesset, "The Word *Love:* Sexual Politics and Silence in Early Raymond Carver," *American Literature,* 63 (June 1991): 292–313;

Robert Pope and Lisa McElhinny, "Raymond Carver Speaking," *Akros Review,* 8–9 (Spring 1984): 103–114;

Arthur M. Saltzman, *Understanding Raymond Carver* (Columbia: University of South Carolina Press, 1988);

Paul Skenazy, "Life in Limbo: Ray Carver's Fiction," *Enclitic,* 11 (Fall 1988): 77–83;

William L. Stull, "Beyond Hopelessville: Another Side of Raymond Carver," *Philological Quarterly,* 64 (Winter 1985): 1–15;

Michael Vender Weele, "Raymond Carver and the Language of Desire," *Denver Quarterly,* 22 (Summer 1987): 108–122.

Alfred Chester

(7 September 1928 – 1 August 1971)

Edward Field

BOOKS: *Here Be Dragons* (Paris: Finisterre, 1955; London: Deutsch, 1956);

Chariot of Flesh, as Malcolm Nesbit (Paris: Olympia, 1955);

Jamie Is My Heart's Desire (London: Deutsch, 1956; New York: Vanguard, 1957);

Behold Goliath (New York: Random House, 1964; London: Deutsch, 1965);

The Exquisite Corpse (New York: Simon & Schuster, 1967; London: Deutsch, 1970; enlarged edition, New York: Carroll & Graf, 1986);

Head of a Sad Angel, edited by Edward Field (Santa Rosa, Cal.: Black Sparrow, 1990);

Divertissement de Coin de Rue, edited by Alex Gildzen (Kent, Ohio: Kent State University Libraries, 1990);

Looking for Genet: Literary Essays and Reviews, edited, with a foreword, by Field (Santa Rosa, Cal.: Black Sparrow, 1992).

Alfred Chester was never a widely read or popular author in his lifetime, unless you count the readership of his short-lived column in *Book Week* (1963–1964), the Sunday book supplement of the now-defunct *New York Herald Tribune.* He belonged to a coterie of avant-garde writers who produced small-scale, quirky, but exacting works that appealed to discriminating readers. During Chester's life it was still economically possible, as it is no longer, for major publishers to issue such work, with its limited audience.

If he had lived, with his sanity restored, it is by no means certain, in light of his ambitions, that he would not have reached for a wider readership. But the last years of his life were marked by mental deterioration and diminished literary production; by the time of his death in 1971, he was almost entirely forgotten. His work remained out of print until the publication of the 1986 edition of his novel *The Exquisite Corpse* (originally published in 1967), with a perceptive introductory essay by Diana Athill, his former editor at the publishing house of Andre Deutsch in London.

Chester's work has now been rediscovered and is starting to attain the status in American literature that it deserves, with an accompanying legend of a doomed, self-destructive, but larger-than-life mad genius, much in the "outlaw" genre of Arthur Rimbaud, Jean Genet, or, perhaps more pertinently, J. R. Ackerley and Delmore Schwartz. But a monster he was not. All who knew him agree on his captivating charm, how funny he could be. Michael Feingold deepens the portrait in his estimation that "Chester carried in himself two of the great polar elements on which most 20th century art is based: He was an intelligent homosexual – that is, a man perpetually conscious of life as a series of roles or poses to be taken on; and he was a madman – a visionary" (*Village Voice,* 2 December 1986).

Though he possessed a Talmudic intellect, Alfred Chester never belonged to the world of the New York Jewish intellectuals, with their political focus and clubby sensibility. He was a generation late for that, and, unlike many of them, he had been raised, in spite of the Depression, in relative comfort. Although his parents were immigrants, he did not experience a struggle to enter American life from a quasi-alien world. Perhaps more important, though he lived in a perpetual state of crisis over his identity, he suffered no serious conflict over his Jewishness. It was his homosexuality that set him apart. Part of a disappearing bohemia, Chester never entered the academic or publishing establishment, and therefore he lacked the power base to be more than a peripheral figure on the literary scene.

His father, Jake, a furrier, had been brought as a child from Romania. On arrival the family name had been Americanized by immigration authorities to Chester from the original Chesta-Polchak or Chestya-Pelski – meaning "six fingers." Alfred's mother, Anna, who had been born in Odessa – according to his cousin Shirley Chester – was a "gypsy-like woman out of the opera *Carmen.*" Alfred, who often behaved with a swashbuckling boldness, also must have found justification for his unconventionality in the fact that an aunt had reputedly been the madam of a brothel in Odessa,

Alfred Chester in Tangier, 1963 (photograph by Edward Field)

the Black Sea port made memorable by writer Isaac Babel for its colorful and desperate outlaw Jews. Whenever Alfred spoke of this aunt, his eyes became gleaming slits, as he grinned with delight.

Born in Brooklyn on 7 September 1928, Alfred Chester was the last of three children. Though their father-son relationship was always difficult, Jake Chester was proud enough of his little boy to name his business the Alfred Fur Company. An ancestor in Romania had been a cantor, but none of the Chesters was literary or artistic, except Shirley, Alfred's cousin and closest companion during his early years, who defied the family and became an opera singer. She reports that his mother, goodhearted but ignorant, ridiculed him for his literary interests but smiled as she railed at him for being "no good" and "lazy." Perhaps it is from her that Alfred got the idea that a close relationship had to be stormy, or at least intense. Though he worked hard at his writing, he never seriously considered the possibility of getting a job, and throughout his life

he turned to his family for financial support, causing conflict. His mother could not understand the life her son was leading.

In any case, it is likely that Chester would have found himself at odds with his family simply because he was intellectually superior to them. It was too much to expect perfectly ordinary people of limited education to understand the creativity of such a gifted child and the imperatives of his talent. An indication of this lack of understanding, not only of his interests but of the possibilities of the intellectual life, was that his father, right up to his death in 1949, expected his son to go on to medical school and become a doctor.

Many of the themes of Chester's fiction grew from his sense of difference and the resultant isolation caused by the severe trauma of the loss of his hair at the age of seven from a childhood disease. This subject, about which he maintained silence until his wig was burned by accident in a kitchen fire when he was thirty-six, is given a fairly full treatment in his last story, "The Foot" (1966; collected in *Head of a Sad Angel*, 1990), which spares none of the painful details of his childhood in the Flatbush section of Brooklyn. Since he had lost most of the hair on his body, including eyelashes, eyebrows, sideburns, and beard, no wig could adequately disguise its absence, and the wigs he wore as an adult were not only unmistakable in their raggedness but incomprehensibly bright orange. Though his family tried to protect him, a childhood friend, Theodora Blum McKee, recalls other boys mocking him on the subway for looking so strange. Nevertheless, until he went public about it in 1964, his hairlessness was a subject never to be discussed with his closest friends, who were made to feel embarrassed by even the mention of the words *wig* or *hair*. The characters in his stories often feel themselves to be freaks but never because they are bald. Still, tragic as it was to his life, his baldness may have made this naturally sociable man more introspective and productive than he otherwise would have been.

Wig aside, Chester never looked like an ordinary person: he had tartar-colored eyes, a rosebud mouth, and almost transparent, round cheeks that seemed to join his body, avoiding a neck entirely. Years of yoga exercises and dieting did nothing to alter his perennial softness, his pudginess, until after he went crazy in his mid thirties and developed a strong, peasant body style, as if his mind had to go before he could mature physically.

After entering Washington Square College of New York University in 1945, he contributed to the NYU publications *Compass, Apprentice,* and *Varieties,* the humor magazine. In a creative-writing class, he developed a literary rivalry with another talented, fledgling author, Cynthia Ozick. After receiving his B.A. in English in 1949, he entered graduate school at Columbia University, where he felt lost in the large postwar seminars given by such notable scholars as Mark Van Doren, Marjorie Hope Nicolson, and Lionel Trilling, who was the literary eminence of the department. Chester does not seem to have gotten much out of Columbia except his friendships with fellow writers Curtis Harnack and Hortense Calisher, who married Harnack.

Chester dropped out of Columbia in 1950, and after a brief foray into Mexico he sailed for France, the goal of many literary Americans in those postwar decades of a strong dollar and weak franc. One could live on remarkably little in France while working – or talking of getting down to work – on a novel, a play, or poetry. Unlike many in the expatriate colony, Chester had several already-completed short stories with him, and the ambition to turn at least one of them, "Jamie Is My Heart's Desire," into a novel (published in 1956). By the time it was completed in 1953, the novel had little relation to the story of that name, as far as can be gathered from his description of it in his letters of that period.

In Paris, where Chester remained for most of the 1950s, he was a well-known figure, unkempt and shapeless, with his rumpled wig, "pharaonic nose" (as he later described it), and lashless, pale, but quizzical eyes, as he hurried through the Left Bank streets and talked away the night in cafés. It was a decade well spent in developing his craft, as well as in getting to know most of the literary figures of his generation. His letters to Harnack, Theodora Blum, and others are full of details of meetings with Carson McCullers; Eugene Walters; *Harper's Bazaar* literary editor Mary Louise Aswell; Mary Lee Settle; James Baldwin; Jean Garrigue; filmmaker, poet, and playwright James Broughton; and others soon to be established, such as Richard Seaver, then merely an editor of the literary magazine *Merlin,* and Robert Silvers, the future publisher of the *New York Review of Books.* Chester became an intimate of the Princess Marguerite Caetani, who first published his work in her well-paying, expensively produced magazine *Botteghe Oscure,* where, in 1952, he made his debut with the essay "Silence in Heaven" (collected in *Looking for Genet,* 1992). His first published short story, "Dance for Dead Lovers," appeared in *Merlin* in the same year (and was later collected in *Here Be Dragons,* 1955). It is a southern-Gothic–style tale but is set on the anonymous streets of New York. A remote, fanciful, almost bloodless girl, disconnected from reality, lives in a furnished room in midtown Manhattan, where she wanders through the wintry streets, recalling a dreamy summer affair with a poet whom she imagined and named before she picked him up.

Even if Christopher Isherwood's *Prater Violet* (1945) was for Chester a lodestar at this time – and Isherwood was impressed enough with Chester's short stories to offer to recommend them to his publisher – much of the early work Chester wrote in Paris seems more derivative of the southern-Gothic school, with Truman Capote and McCullers the major influences. The characters in Chester's stories of that time are neurotic in the fashion of the sensitive people of the era and seem to live in their rosy, lyrical illusions, ignoring, or trying to ignore (as in his ambiguously titled book *Here Be Dragons*), the grim background of reality, or transforming it by poetic imagination. Many of his published sto-

Cover for the posthumously published collection of most of Chester's short fiction

ries were selections from unrealizable novels in progress. Soon afterward he began to write stories that reflect a surrealist influence, clearly derived from the fashion reigning in Paris in the postwar decades. Surrealism, as well as the plays of Luigi Pirandello, which much impressed him, suited his own inability to reconcile the different aspects of his nature – his sense of multiple selves, or an unfixed, situational *I* – a feeling expressed in the title of his never-finished book "I, Etc.," first mentioned in his letters in 1954. This identity crisis could be seen simply as fashionable existential self-doubt, if it had not resulted a decade later in a psychotic breakdown. First discussed in letters in the mid 1950s, his identity crisis was finally given satisfactory literary form ten years later in his novel *The Exquisite Corpse,* in which characters change sex and identity in each chapter.

In 1955 Editions Finisterre, a small press in Paris that had been acquired by the young editor and publisher Silvers, published *Here Be Dragons,* a collection of four stories that was sold by subscription. After the book was published in London by Deutsch the following year, V. S. Pritchett on the BBC called Chester "an exciting talent: original, fearless and very capable." Editions du Seuil in Paris published a French version of his first novel, *Jamie Is My Heart's Desire,* and it was published in English soon after by Deutsch. A strange work, the novel deals with a mortician who has always felt more "at ease among the dead" than the living. He develops an obsession for a youth who, typically in Chester's fiction, may or may not exist.

Before the decade was out, Chester was also being discovered in America. "Head of a Sad Angel," a vivid portrait of a Polish countess who teaches her secret of how to play works by Frédéric Chopin authentically but tyrannizes her pupils, was included in *Prize Stories 1956: The O. Henry Awards.* Reviewing the prize-stories collection in the *New York World-Telegram* (11 January 1956), Sterling North singled this story out for special praise, advising the reader, "Circle his name with your red pencil. He out-writes such other and better known writers as Faulkner, Steinbeck, Jean Stafford and Saul Bellow."

With the support of Paul Engle, Monroe Spears, and Robert Penn Warren, Chester won a Guggenheim Fellowship in 1957, the same year *Jamie Is My Heart's Desire* was published in New York, in tandem with his short story "As I Was Going Up the Stair," which was chosen for *The Best American Short Stories* of that year (and was later collected in *Head of a Sad Angel*). The novel did not do as well in the United States, the American preference being for realistic over imaginative writing, but, as in England, Chester was clearly a rising young author.

The sale to the *New Yorker* of a short story, "A War on Salamis" (25 April 1959; in *Head of a Sad Angel*), written during a stay in Greece, provided the funds for Chester's return to New York from Europe in 1959. The story is the largely true tale of an outsider's conflict with the peasants of the Greek island of Salamis over his adopting two wild dogs, considered untamable, which provokes the islanders into threatening and dangerous behavior. Fleeing with the dogs by ferry, he barely escapes their wrath. Two wild dogs, named Columbine and Skouras, accompanied Chester back to the United States and several years later to Morocco, and they justified the apprehensions of the Greek villagers by refusing to be house-trained and by biting several people. Chester did not include this story in his collection *Behold Goliath* (1964) because he probably considered it too straightforward and conventionally written, but it is a powerful story, and the *New Yorker* paid him top rates for it.

Within a year or two of his return to America, he found himself, according to the annual charting of *Esquire,* at the "red-hot center" of the New York literary scene. "Cradle Song" (in *Head of a Sad Angel*) is a somewhat lurid tale written with misspellings as if by an ignorant but romantic girl; she becomes pregnant and disposes of her newborn baby heedlessly. The story was published in *Esquire* and reprinted in *The Best American Short Stories* in 1961. Most of his short stories were originally printed in small literary magazines, such as the *Transatlantic Review* and *Provincetown Review,* and each tale created a stir when it appeared.

Several of the stories he was writing were on homosexual themes, unapologetic in a way that was unusual in America in that era before the gay-liberation movement. In rejecting one of these stories, "In Praise of Vespasian," the editor for the *Partisan Review* wrote, "Our objection is not to the subject or its detail but rather to the rhapsodic treatment." The tone of this tale of a promiscuous homosexual (in *Head of a Sad Angel*) is indeed rhapsodic. In the manner of Genet's *Our Lady of the Flowers* (1963), it follows the protagonist's almost religious, if strenuous, pilgrimage through the *pissotiéres* (public urinals) of Paris and New York.

Another story in this series, "From the Phoenix to the Unnameable, Impossibly Beautiful Wild Bird" (in *Head of a Sad Angel*), is a fictional treatment of the aftermath of the breakup of Chester's longest love affair. Begun in Paris, this was a serious, live-in relationship with a bisexual Israeli pianist, and it lasted throughout Chester's European sojourn. But when the pianist arrived in New York, he found it hard to cope with Chester's burgeoning literary career, contrasted with the failure of his own ambitions to be a concert performer; they soon broke up. The fictional version describes a meeting between the two after "Mario" has left and gotten married. Having trouble with his wife, Mario flirts with the possibility of starting up again with his former lover. As an essay on the complex games that develop over the years between two people, it could apply to either homosexual or heterosexual relationships, but this kind of subtle analysis of a relationship is unusual in homosexual fiction.

In contrast to his fiction, Chester's critical articles appeared in the most prestigious organs of the New York intellectual world, such as the *Partisan Review, Commentary,* and the *New York Review of Books,* reflecting not the superiority of his critical work over his fiction but the emerging higher status of criticism over fiction in the literary world in general. Analyses, often devastating, of works by literary greats such as John Updike, Vladimir Nabokov, and Genet, these pieces by Chester (in *Looking for Genet*) were much discussed, sometimes with rage. About one of them, Gore Vidal (*New York Review of Books,* 27 October 1987) wrote, "Alfred Chester . . . was a glorious writer, tough as nails, with an exquisite ear for the false note. . . . [His review of *City of Night* (1963) by John Rechy is] murderously funny, absolutely unfair, and totally true." For someone who was accused of having a different style in every story, Chester had a magisterial critical voice, which sprang from him fully developed and is the same in all his critical essays.

During this period of his life, Chester's phone rang almost constantly, as editors called him, hoping to get him to write something, submit something, review something, or show them the novel he was working on. This celebrity status had its ironic side, since he was then living in poverty, and his gas, electricity, and telephone were often turned off for nonpayment of bills. He resented the diversion and the demand for his criticism more than his fiction, which he felt was the most important work for his energies.

Even in Morocco, where he moved in June 1963 to escape the New York literary scene, he remained part of it, since his poverty forced him to continue doing reviews, as well as the *Book Week* column. But, as if demonstrating the saying "New York does not forgive you for leaving," the collection of his stories *Behold Goliath,* published in 1964, did not get wide attention, and much of the attention it did receive was hostile, though Theodore Solotaroff, reviewing it in *Book Week* (7 June 1964), made the amusing and perceptive comment that Chester was "a sort of cross between the Baron de Charlus and Huckleberry Finn." A negative review by Benjamin DeMott in *Harper's Magazine* (June 1964) complained that the writing "collapses into derangement, homosexual ecstasy." In the *New York Review of Books* (30 April 1964), R. M. Adams similarly objected: "Why is it that in much modern fiction a homosexual prowling the streets for a pickup is engaged in a poignant human search for love – while characters who seek love in ways and places where perhaps it is a little more likely to be found are represented as mere clods?"

The disappointing reception and poor sales only reinforced Chester's determination to hew to his ideals, drop out of the criticism racket, and concentrate on fiction, fulfilling the decade-long plan to write a novel of shifting identities. He had the illusion at times that *The Exquisite Corpse,* named after a surrealist party game, would be a best-seller, but it was clearly "experimental," confusing to readers and reviewers alike, and after its publication in 1967 it quickly disappeared. Chester wanted popular success, but he was not really prepared to compromise in any way for it, nor even to hide his more outrageous inventions. Indeed he scorned his more conventional tales, such as "Head of a Sad Angel."

Besides "Glory Hole" (in *Head of a Sad Angel*), a wicked but charming fictional study of Moroccan youths in relation to their "Nazarene" lovers, which appeared in *Evergreen Review* (March 1965), Chester completed only one other short story in Morocco, "Safari" (also in *Head of a Sad Angel*). It is full of

dark reflections of his psychosis. The story tells of a scorpion hunt he went on with his friend Paul Bowles, called "Gerald" in the story, and it is an essay on the demonic power the older man had over him. Indeed his whole stay in Morocco from 1963 to the end of 1965 was dominated by Bowles and to a lesser extent by his wife, Jane. In the story, Chester clearly tells of the power Bowles had over him, writing, "Sometimes I think Gerald is God . . . ," and he later describes him as an enormous magician whose head looms over them.

Chester's incipient madness brought on terrors and antisocial behavior that came to the attention of the Moroccan authorities, and, with his expulsion from that country and his return to New York in 1965, his literary production declined along with his mental health. He refused offers to write reviews or even to see many of his friends. The one thing he wrote, "The Foot," is a notebook-style, fragmented work that is difficult to categorize as either fiction or nonfiction, though the transformation of autobiographical material by his imagination seems to place it more in the camp of fiction. It is remarkable for its description of the hellishness of losing his hair, including, at the age of fourteen, the fitting of his first wig, which, he wrote, felt like having "an axe driven straight down the middle of my body," and he throws in for good measure a fantasy about Susan Sontag as "Mary Monday," a character divided, though not by an ax, into two "Mary Mondays" in order to make her less powerful and less of a threat, or as a means of representing her obsession and satisfaction with herself. Grieving for a lost paradisiacal Morocco, the narrator tells in garbled fashion the story of how he went mad in Tangier, connecting his insanity to a 1965 visit from Sontag, newly famous after publication of her *Notes on Camp,* published that year.

In the following years until his death in 1971, though Chester was generally forgotten by the literary world, a few stories of his appeared in the *New American Review,* thanks to the dedication of its editor, Theodore Solotaroff, who also went over the manuscript of "The Foot" and rescued and published fifty of the more coherent pages. Though the complete manuscript would be of great interest today, it has disappeared, along with some other unpublished works. A final autobiographical essay, "Letter from a Wandering Jew," probably written in 1970 or 1971, describing the torments of his last years and particularly his often-bizarre experiences in Israel, has survived and is included in *Looking for Genet.*

There are reports of short stories written during his last years, particularly "Trois Corsages," which he read to friends in the garden of a Brooklyn apartment that he rented in a brief interlude in his travels, probably in 1970. The story apparently dealt with three women who had been of great importance in his life: Sontag; the playwright María Irene Fornés, whom he had met in Ibiza during his European years; and Harriet Sohmers (now Zwerling). It, too, has disappeared.

In 1956 Sterling North, in singling out Alfred Chester for praise in his review of *Prize Stories 1956: The O. Henry Awards,* concluded by saying, "If our youngest writers can show such maturity, there is real hope for the literature of the third quarter of our century." With his decline into paranoia and his early death, Chester did not have time to justify that hope completely, but based on the extant works published, it is possible for critics to reassess his achievement and to judge if the neglect after his death was deserved. The power and sheer fun of his imaginative writings, as well as the volatile, charismatic personality they reveal so clearly, have the strength to excite a growing admiration among readers and critics alike and lead to a recognition of his indisputable importance to American letters.

Letters:

"The Nazarene and the Native," *New York Native,* 48 (10 November 1986): 26–31;

"Letter from Morocco," *Exquisite Corpse,* 11–12 (November–December 1986): 16;

"Letters From Morocco," *Confrontation,* 37–38 (Spring–Summer 1988): 305–317;

"Flung Out," *Christopher Street,* 145 (1990): 28–40.

Interview:

Hans de Vaal, Interview with Chester [in Dutch], *Litterair Paspoort,* 8 (April 1953): 51–53.

References:

Michael Feingold, "Tales from the Cryptic," *Village Voice* (2 December 1986): 61–64;

Edward Field, "Among the Tangerinos: The Life, Madness and Death of Alfred Chester," *New York Times Book Review,* 15 September 1991, pp. 15–16;

Field, "The Mystery of Alfred Chester," *Boston Review,* 18 (April–May 1993);

Field, "Rogue Genius," *Honcho,* 16 (April 1993): 66–70;

Field, "Tea at Paul Bowles's," *Raritan,* 7 (Winter 1993): 92–111;

Norman Glass, "The Giggling Nihilist," *New York Native* (10 November 1986): 51–52;

Michelle Green, *The Dream at the End of the World* (New York: HarperCollins, 1991), pp. 263–342;

Cynthia Ozick, "Alfred Chester's Wig," *New Yorker,* 68 (30 March 1992): 79–98;

John Strausbaugh, "A Charming Monster's Comeback," *New York Press* (24–30 October 1990): 8–9;

Harriet Sohmers Zwerling, "A Memoir of Alfred Chester," *Raritan,* 7 (Winter 1993): 112–116.

Papers:

Many of Chester's manuscripts, typescripts, and letters are in the libraries of the University of Texas at Austin, University of Delaware, and Kent State University.

Wanda Coleman

(13 November 1946 –)

Kathleen K. O'Mara
State University of New York College at Oneonta

BOOKS: *Art in the Court of the Blue Fag* (Santa Rosa, Cal.: Black Sparrow, 1977);

Mad Dog Black Lady (Santa Rosa, Cal.: Black Sparrow, 1979);

Imagoes (Santa Rosa, Cal.: Black Sparrow, 1983);

24 Hours in the Life of Los Angeles (New York: Van der Marck, 1984);

Heavy Daughter Blues: Poems and Stories, 1968–1986 (Santa Rosa, Cal.: Black Sparrow, 1987);

A War of Eyes and Other Stories (Santa Rosa, Cal.: Black Sparrow, 1988);

The Dicksboro Hotel and Other Travels (Tarzana, Cal.: Ambrosia, 1989);

African Sleeping Sickness: Stories and Poems (Santa Rosa, Cal.: Black Sparrow, 1990).

RECORDINGS: *Twin Sisters,* by Coleman and Exene Cervenka, New Alliance, 1985;

Black Angeles, by Coleman and Michelle T. Clinton, New Alliance, 1989;

High Priestess of Word, New Alliance, 1990;

Black and Blue News, Widowspeak/BarKubCo, 1991;

Berserk on Hollywood Boulevard, New Alliance, 1991.

Wanda Coleman enjoys a reputation as a dynamic poet and writer of short fiction that chronicles the lives of poor urban African Americans. One of the writers, including Charles Bukowski and Diane Wakoski, responsible for creating an alternative literary scene in Los Angeles in the 1970s and 1980s, Coleman has yet to be fully recognized by the literary and commercial publishing establishment. Nevertheless, acclaim for her vivid urban-naturalist prose and poetry grew in the 1980s, especially after the publication of *A War of Eyes and Other Stories* (1988), her first all-fiction volume (previous ones being either poetry or mixtures of poetry and prose). Critical admiration centers on her gripping, taut tales of violence-threatened working-class people who are powerfully portrayed in urban-vernacular language. Her stories and poems – portraits of homeless people, drug addicts, impotent lovers, wel-

fare mothers, and thwarted dreamers – are angry, ironic, and politically charged. Coleman reports on the brutalization of human beings and specifically on how racism affects her; the latter, as she stated in her 1990 interview with Tony Magistrale and Patricia Ferreira, is her single greatest concern as a writer. Hence she embraces the autobiographical statements in her writing. Autobiography is the quintessential genre of African-American literature and the most effective tool for tracing the impact of racism on the African-American psyche.

The city of the dispossessed, specifically Los Angeles, provides Coleman's landscape. Her working-class characters who reside there are often compared to the "underclass" written of by Ann Petry, Richard Wright, Jean Genet, and Nathanael West. Like those writers, Coleman obliges the reader to confront the essential humanity of social outcasts. A recurring theme in her work, the displacement of African Americans and their resistance to it, is authentically portrayed in black vernacular. Coleman's use of black English demonstrates her identification with the subject matter and is among the best in a tradition that includes the works of Zora Neale Hurston, Langston Hughes, and Richard Wright. However, Coleman's writing is rawer, more sexually explicit, and more celebratory of women's sexuality than her predecessors'. It voices late-twentieth-century themes such as race, class, gender, and interethnic conflict; the effects of poverty and marginalization on individuals; and America as a racialized state.

Coleman's rendering of the African-American "double consciousness," the awareness of always being an "other," is firmly rooted in her own experiences. Born on 13 November 1946 to George and Lewana Evans, Coleman was raised in Watts, the Los Angeles ghetto known for the August 1965 riots there. Her father, who worked in advertising, moved to California from Arkansas in 1931 after a black townsman was lynched. Her mother, a seamstress and domestic worker, cleaned the homes of

Wanda Coleman (photograph by Susan Carpendale)

movie stars and was once employed by Ronald Reagan and his first wife, Jane Wyman. Coleman was an introverted and bookish child whose parents encouraged her writing; at age thirteen she published her first poems in a local newspaper. She found school dehumanizing, a feeling that persisted during her short stints at California State College (now California State University) at Los Angeles in 1964 and Los Angeles City College in 1967. (She also later attended Stanford.) By age twenty she was a college dropout, political activist, wife, and the mother of two – Anthony and Tunisia.

Like many of her contemporaries in the 1960s, Coleman saw her young adult years profoundly shaped by the civil-rights movement and militant black nationalism. She was especially influenced by the cultural politics of Ron Karenga's Afrocentric "US" organization in southern California. Additionally attracted to paramilitary organizations such as the Weather Underground, Coleman ultimately rejected them as anti-intellectual and decided that becoming a "cultural terrorist," in other words a political artist, was personally more important. Some of her early work, such as the poem "El Hajj Malik el-

Shabazz," a paean to Malcolm X, reflects Karenga's position that art should support the "Black Revolution." Her use of blood imagery in that poem – of blood as a metaphor for the blood of her race and of mourning – is a multimeaning image that she develops in later writing.

By 1969 Coleman, recently divorced and briefly a "welfare mother," decided to pursue a career as a professional writer. Since then she has waged an uphill struggle against the grain of mainstream Euro-American literature. Rarely able to live off her earnings from writing, she continued for the next twenty years to support her family as a waitress, bartender, dancer, typist, and medical billing clerk/transcriber, and her writing echoes her experiences with job interviewers, night-shift counter clerks, drug dealers, and social deviants. Her first published short story, "Watching the Sunset," which depicts a lonely middle-aged teacher ruefully recalling a life that has passed faster than the sundown he is watching, appeared in *Negro Digest* in 1970. Though it lacks the tension of her later fiction, the briskly narrated story reveals an individual's frustration with race-determined social realities and African Americans' attention to skin color; these are themes she developed more vividly later.

Autobiographical writing about Coleman's struggle for literary acceptance appears early in her work and consistently reappears, linking her collections with her personal history. Such writing not only records her own perseverance but underscores her identification with many of her characters with whom she shares a life on the social margins.

The 1970s were a time of multimedia experimentation by Coleman in theater, dance, television, and journalism. She quickly became known for her dramatic performances – poetry readings that she gave locally and eventually nationally and internationally. The rhythm, dramatic tension, and physicality of her poems indicated that they were designed to be spoken as part of a larger performance in which silence and an implied choreography enrich the actual words. She also experimented with television scriptwriting, becoming the first African American to win an Emmy Award for outstanding writing for a drama series (*Days of Our Lives,* 1975–1976) as well as the first woman editor of an African-American men's magazine, *Players.*

The pressures of child rearing, employment, and censorious television producers who demanded formulaic writing all conspired to determine what to write, and this situation led Coleman to concentrate on poems. These not only provided a sense of completion but the creative freedom missing in commercial writing. Poems she found she could finish rather quickly and then perform in dramatic readings. A brief second marriage in the 1970s produced a third child, Ian Wayne Grant.

Coleman credits Bukowski and Joan Didion of Los Angeles as influencing her career choices, for she could closely observe their development. For her, Bukowski was the first genuine poet she met and "the first American writer to 'tell it like it is' from the subcultural depths." His fearless illumination of his ugliness and his raw, direct storytelling appealed to her. Graphic depictions of the misery of outcast people in Los Angeles and the hypocrisy of the American Dream constitute material the two writers share. She often found herself the only African American in the audience at Bukowski's readings. His personal influence led her to send her first poetry manuscript, *Art in the Court of the Blue Fag* (1977), a chapbook, to Black Sparrow Press, whose publisher "Papa" John Martin became a significant mentor for her. Other influences from the Los Angeles poetry scene included Wakoski, John Thomas, and Clayton Eshleman, all non-

mainstream writers for Black Sparrow. Bliss Carnochan, Coleman's writing-workshop director and English professor at Stanford University, was also influential and supportive.

Coleman's poetry, especially that in *Mad Dog Black Lady* (1979) and *Imagoes* (1983), soon brought some professional recognition: a National Endowment for the Arts grant for 1981–1982 and a Guggenheim Fellowship for poetry in 1984. In the early 1980s she began cohosting, with poet Austin Straus, who became her third husband, "The Poetry Connexion," a poetry / interview program for radio station KPFK. This venue created a wider audience for her work and for that of other poets.

Heavy Daughter Blues (1987) introduced her short fiction. Interspersed with poems, the stories function as counterpoints or commentaries on them, many of which are based on the blues or jazz. Through repetition and internal rhyme – echoes of African-American music – she reshapes the English language, creating detailed, physical experiences in the poems and the stories. "The Blues in the Night," for example, is a lyrical, unapologetic tale of a divorced mother's sexual longings.

This story, as is the case for several others, demonstrates her talent for articulating women's sexual desires and celebrating women's bodies. The lonely protagonist so "aches for seduction" she can "almost inhale that pungent musk opening her nose, obliterating all thought." Alone one night, her children in bed, she listens to 45 rpm records by James Brown, Otis Redding, and others; she dances around her living room, reveling in herself: "Her head is soaked and her hair goes all the way back to Africa. She bends, turns, spins until she's one with that sound. One pulse. One throb hip-quaking – a frenzy working her way through steps she knows as intimately as the scars on her psyche." Coleman's prose, like her poetry, has a visceral quality that includes the reader as a companion and excludes any sense of voyeurism.

Racism, sexism, multicultural collisions, and the rage resulting from them intertwine in the tales: "The Arab Clerk" is a vivid encounter between a frustrated black mother trying to buy milk for breakfast and a racist grocery clerk who refuses to make change for her twenty-dollar bill; and in "Ace of Zeroes" a shotgun-toting former convict speaks a chilling monologue about why he is going to kill whites. *Heavy Daughter Blues* garnered mixed reviews, and the negative criticism centered on the poems and stories as overpoweringly grim and inadequately edited. Joel Gersmann in *Isthmus* (29 December 1989), however, proclaimed that "Wanda

-7-

~~Try and~~ describe it ~~to me~~.

Like electricity or something. I don't know what.

~~I can't.~~ But I knew that if he kept ~~xxx~~ touching me like that he was gonna have his way with me. And I wouldn't be able to say no to nothing.

Then what.

~~Then~~ he braced his arm around my head and kissed me, pulling me in against his chest.

Then what. Come on, tell me what it felt like. Quit cryin', woman. I'm not angry at you, honey. Tell me.

He kissed me to my soul. I -- I ~~xxxxxx~~ couldn't break free. I kissed him back. I couldn't help it. I was ~~in~~ under a spell.

~~And~~ When he ~~took his lips away~~ let go everybody was looking at me. Lonnie and his wife and the other couple -- dead in their tracks like they were all kissin' me ~~through him~~. Like voodoo or something. It felt real strange. ~~It is~~ the strangest feeling I ever felt. ~~So strange~~ I came half way to myself. I said how it was gettin' late and I had to go make that fudge I'd promised you. So I scooped up the baby and hurried out of there so fast I forgot his little diapers and stuff. I ran back upstairs ~~head and locked the door.~~

And that's all ~~that happened.~~ a

Did you let him in?

~~Mostly. I though it had got away. Then~~ he followed me come up here a few minutes later with the bag. baby's I tried not to ~~let him in~~ but he put that spell on me again. Just touched my hand ~~and the door gave way and he stepped in.~~ ~~And he~~ reached thru the screen door and coming in

Page from the revised typescript for "Lonnie's Cousin," collected in A War of Eyes and Other Stories *(by permission of Wanda Coleman)*

Coleman is America's greatest living poet under age 50."

The theme of toughness and persistence in the face of hard knocks – a person's struggle to survive on terms made by others – binds together the prose and poetry as well as the disparate characters. This theme begins in the opening prose poem, "Stone Rock Lady," a portrait of a woman of seemingly great fortitude who takes "stone injections" to become impenetrable, and it continues throughout the volume. These "other America" stories are rounded out with the vignette "Lady of the Cans," which depicts a woman "starving on pride and $45 a week in unemployment." She collects returnable cans to put meat on her children's dinner plates.

Tamar Lehrich in the *Nation* (20 February 1988) noted that Coleman seeks "to incite anger and shake all . . . out of their complacency." Anger and frustration with her position as an African-American woman drive her writing. In the poem "Wanda Why Aren't You Dead," with its refrain "Wanda why are you so angry," and the prose poem "Angel Baby Blues" sardonic autobiography emerges. This authorial anger, which suggests the complexity of the experience of being black and female, serves to validate the rage of her social-outcast characters such as the murderer in "Ace of Zeroes."

Few writers so forthrightly appropriate the power of writing to confront the marginality imposed on them. She uses directness – not authorial detachment – in "Trying To Get In," a prose poem in which she reads a work by Antonin Artaud as her children eat breakfast; she ponders her fear of not making it as a writer and her terror that "poverty claws" at her. Arguing explicitly with herself in "Angel Baby Blues" that "i need to leave Los Angeles," in the end she half believes that if she is strong enough to hang on she will make it on her terms.

In these stories Coleman consistently rattles comfortable notions about what it means to be a woman and an African American in a society invariably overdetermined by the needs and values of white men. She nonetheless evinces compassion and warmth. Like other African-American women writers in the 1970s and 1980s – such as Toni Morrison, Maya Angelou, and Alice Walker – Coleman creates women protagonists freed from men's definitions of them. Unlike those other writers, she concentrates on black reactions to racism and ignores historical settings. Situating characters in the present, she portrays not only scarred souls but nurturing individuals who are surrounded by dope deals, lost jobs, absent lovers, and madness – people who maintain a community. "Mother Jones," "Miss Taylor," and "Aunt Teresa," three portraits of warm but headstrong women, baby-sitters to the narrators, contrast the security of childhood with the onerous daily life of adult African-American women.

A War of Eyes attracted wider recognition for her narrative skill, as her impact on the Los Angeles poetry scene – enhanced by recordings of her dramatic readings, beginning with *Twin Sisters* in 1985 – had become secure. War and military metaphors punctuate many of the stories in *A War of Eyes,* but the theme is how the eyes of others define and dehumanize individuals. By framing the volume with the theme of war, Coleman sculpts a vision of urban America, of everyday life as combat in which the battle is not only for material survival and self-respect but self-definition. The characters respond to their oppression with anger, revenge, or escapism.

The title story, an extended metaphor of race, class, and gender conflict, creates a scene of homicidal tension within an experimental dance group of blacks and whites. Their leader, "Blue-eyed Soul Mama," puts them through an exercise in psychological warfare, "a war of eyes" in which no one may speak or touch, which culminates in an eyeballing duel between Black Dona and the teacher's daughter, White Deborah. The narrator, Dona, puts her rage into this siege of staring: "She is all I hate. I will obliterate her. I will slay and dance in ritual in her blood." As other class members intercede, Dona's rage goes unsatisfied, leaving her with an unassuaged resentment of racism.

Self-discovery, or the process of averting a false self-image, is the subject of "The Stare Down," which sardonically demonstrates the theme of others' eyes categorizing and racially pigeonholing individuals. Several vignettes connect this theme, as the female protagonist, a young African-American college student, a would-be sophisticate, moves from one encounter to another. Leaving a beauty parlor, she hears several black children comment on her beautiful hair; selling her textbooks at a Muslim Lebanese bookstore, she listens to the clerk advise her that she looks Egyptian; and attending an interracial party, she meets an anthropologist who notes her partial Cherokee-Sioux ancestry. In the final vignette, at a fashionable restaurant, she is caught in a "stare down" with an African-American television celebrity at another table, and the student comes to the satisfying realization that she possesses a special "look," that she is transculturally beautiful.

Coleman's descriptions, with their poetic nuances, have impressed reviewers. She was described as a "prose surgeon" by Kamili Anderson in *New Directions for Women* (September–October 1989). Some of Coleman's characters seem at first improbable, but her Poe-like art invests them with life and conjures the reader into a suspension of disbelief. The violent scenes in several stories – the vicious rape of JoAnn, a young welfare mother, by sociopathic pimps in "Big Dreams," and the graphically bloody, deadly combat between two African-American neighbors over the loudness of a stereo in "Kelele" – led reviewer Caryn Russell in *High Plains Literary Review* (Winter 1989–1990) to caution that some stories "are so acidic that they should have warning labels on them." Occasionally a story – "Kelele," for example – reads like a television police-action drama, but in others, such as "Big Dreams," the narrative is quick, dense with detail, and builds dread but without gratuitous violence. In the latter story, because the young welfare mother's view is unrealistic – naive and trusting toward the pimps, who are posing as art photographers – Coleman, through an omniscient narrator, succeeds in making an almost unbelievable tale believable.

Finding out about the past and being unable to escape it are central situations in her fiction, and provide explanations for violent or bizarre behaviors. "Hamburgers" is a Gothic allegory of a man who starves to death to keep his car and the American dream, a vain attempt to prove to his college-educated cousin that he can succeed. Other stories testify to color consciousness and the pain or privilege derived from it. In "Eyes and Teeth" Coleman reveals the devastation wreaked by internalizing the dominant society's definition of oneself: a young boy, Buzz, and his cousin, the female narrator, overhear his mother say to hers that he has a "tar black" color that bothers her. The cruel paradox of "caste," the extension of white racism within African Americans, is nowhere more poignantly revealed than in the loss of childhood felt not only by Buzz but by his cousin, who is also hurt and reaches out her arms, "trying to leap beyond my tomboy years to be the mother he lost in that instant."

Embittered by his mother's rejection, Buzz nonetheless emerges in the end as an adult, as the creator of his own life – a middle-class success with a beautiful wife and two children who look just like him. Coleman avoids sentimentality and mocks broad generalizations about racial ideology by underscoring individuality and unpredictability. The ambivalence caused by the desire for self-love and the damage of rejection and shame, a tension in Af-

rican-American literature since the late 1960s, is cleverly resolved in this story. Through the characters who expect Buzz to be a failure who is consumed by self-loathing, Coleman challenges the reader to reevaluate assumptions.

Coleman's mastery of working-class and lumpen characters' language in all its subtleties attains full expression in these stories, perfecting the musical cadences first offered in *Heavy Daughter Blues*. Her strongest tales are from a woman narrator's point of view. In "The Friday Night Shift at the Taco House Blues (Wah Wah)," a quick-paced, slice-of-life tale, the reader meets the nighttime waitresses Shurli and Carol, the former a welfare mother by day, and the latter, the narrator, a receptionist-secretary. Their night's work involves serving burgers, tacos, and refried beans in a surreal scene that is a stage for drug dealing, flirting, bloodletting fights, and miscommunication with Spanish-speaking cooks. The customers' words and actions are riffs while Shurli and Carol modulate the mood from desolation to sassy defiance; at the end they ride home at dawn in Carol's 1969 Buick and joyfully talk of their extra take – three pounds of hamburger and a fifty-dollar bill – which they have stolen.

A master of irony, Coleman often applies it to sexuality. "Lonnie's Cousin" consists of a dialogue between a black mother and her white husband about her seduction by a neighbor's cousin who "put a spell" on her at a party. As her husband forgives her but insists on a description of the seduction, the event's retelling has an aphrodisiac effect on him.

In *African Sleeping Sickness* (1990) Coleman more fully details the city of Los Angeles as a site of the displacement of African Americans, and she inserts autobiographical stories and prose poems. "Where the Sun Don't Shine," one such story, won the Harriette Simpson Arnow Prize for fiction in 1990. The tale displays Coleman's finest skill: through first-person narration she draws the reader into her language and social reality, as two women – the narrator, who is working and has moved from the drug-dominated, garbage-strewn, ghetto neighborhood; and the older one, who is on welfare and trapped there – rap in "mother tongue" about living around men, surviving in the city, and finding solace in a friendship based on a shared past and shared vision of life. The comfort of friendship overrides the misery surrounding them: "i likes to take her out of that hole she lives in for a couple of hours to sit up somewheres and pretend there's possibly something good in our futures (that we think we have a future is positive in itself) and chitchat and look ladylike and ignore or tease the attention of men-eyes." This story is perhaps Coleman's finest short fiction piece as of 1990, combining her greatest skill and primary concerns in one tale.

The everyday confrontation with racism is explored further in a metafictional tale, "Moving Target." This hypertensive day-in-the-life-of-Wanda story begins when a store clerk examines her money to see if it is counterfeit and continues when bullying motorcycle policemen stop her "on suspicion." Coleman pulls readers into her experience by addressing them as confidants. She effectively mixes wit, anger, and polemics: "These incidents, taken separately, over months might prove annoying, but certainly one should be able to cope. But they . . . happen to me two, three, four times *per day*. . . . I am constantly reminded that I am who I am. Dutch chocolate in a cherry-vanilla world. I try to be tolerant I try to appreciate the socio-historical ramifications – as they say on the six o'clock news. . . . I coach myself daily, insisting I am above it all. I'm not."

In "Notes of a Cultural Terrorist" and "Clocking Dollars" Coleman sardonically details her frustration with forty-five hundred rejection slips and the literary establishment's syndrome of pet black authors, a quota system that condemns all writers but the current favorite to hunger and "clocking dollars." Coleman further develops her report on the black writer's personal struggle for acceptance in "Beyond Baroque," a satire about a literary workshop.

Coleman's autobiographical writing fits within the tradition of the African-American autobiographical statement, a form in which the author tells a tale that is an authentic expression of a collective experience. Coleman's insistence on reporting the experiences in urban America distinguishes her work from that of her female contemporaries writing fiction. By transcribing the folk saying "Don't get angry, get even" into satire, irony, and naturalist prose, which present the hypocrisy in the American Dream, Coleman wields humor as a weapon of instruction and survival. In so doing she employs one of the most effective means of any oppressed person to declare her humanity.

Critics have ascribed major value to Coleman's short fiction. What little negative criticism she has drawn has focused on her fragmentary vignettes as sketches that leave the reader wanting more, or her violence-laden plots as sometimes too predictable. Her finest skill is making human pain poetically concrete and devising dialogue that allows the reader under the skin of "the other." Although she has published six books with small presses, Coleman's success has been limited by the commercial realities of mainstream American publishing. She has been caught in the nexus she so skillfully depicts – racism, sexism, and regionalism – of being defined by the dominant culture as a black writer and a West Coast poet. She has yet to attain the broad recognition that most critics agree she should and will achieve.

Interviews:
Tony Magistrale and Patricia Ferreira, "Sweet Mama Wanda Tells Fortunes: An Interview with Wanda Coleman," *Black American Literature Forum,* 24 (Fall 1990): 491–507;

Andrea Juno and V. Vale, "Wanda Coleman," *Re/Search,* 13 (Fall 1991): 118–126.

Guy Davenport

(23 November 1927 –   )

Patrick Meanor
State University of New York College at Oneonta

BOOKS: *Flowers and Leaves: Poema vel Sonata, Carmina Autumni Primaeque Veris Transformationum* (Highlands, N.C.: Williams, 1966);

Pennant Key-Indexed Study Guide to Homer's Iliad (Philadelphia: Educational Research Associates, 1967);

Pennant Key-Indexed Study Guide to Homer's Odyssey (Philadelphia: Educational Research Associates, 1967);

Tatlin! (New York: Scribners, 1974);

Da Vinci's Bicycle: Ten Stories (Baltimore & London: Johns Hopkins University Press, 1979);

Eclogues: Eight Stories (San Francisco: North Point, 1981; London: Picador, 1984);

The Geography of the Imagination: Forty Essays (San Francisco: North Point, 1981; London: Picador, 1984);

Trois Caprices (Louisville: Pace Trust, 1981);

Cities on Hills: A Study of I–XXX of Ezra Pound's Cantos (Ann Arbor, Mich.: UMI Research, 1983; Epping, U.K.: Bowker, 1983);

Goldfinch Thistle Star (New York: Red Ozier, 1983);

The Art of Lafcadio Hearn, by Davenport and Clifton Waller Bennet (Charlottesville: University of Virginia Library, 1983);

Apples and Pears and Other Stories (San Francisco: North Point, 1984);

The Bicycle Rider (New York: Red Ozier, 1985);

Thasos and Ohio: Poems and Translations 1950–1980 (Manchester, U.K.: Carcanet, 1985; San Francisco: North Point, 1986);

Jonah (New York: Nadja, 1986);

The Jules Verne Steam Balloon: Nine Stories (San Francisco: North Point, 1987);

Every Force Evolves a Form: Twenty Essays (San Francisco: North Point, 1987; London: Secker & Warburg, 1989);

A Balthus Notebook (New York: Ecco, 1989);

The Drawings of Paul Cadmus (New York: Rizzoli, 1990);

The Drummer of the Eleventh North Devonshire Fusiliers (San Francisco: North Point, 1990);

Photograph © Thomas Victor

Art of the Forties (New York: Museum of Modern Art, 1991).

OTHER: *The Intelligence of Louis Agassiz: A Specimen Book of Scientific Writings,* edited by Davenport (Boston: Beacon, 1963).

TRANSLATIONS: *Carmina Archilochi: The Fragments of Archilochos* (Berkeley: University of California Press, 1964);

Sappho: Poems and Fragments (Ann Arbor: University of Michigan Press, 1965);

Archilochos, Sappho, Alkman: Three Lyric Poets of the Late Greek Bronze Age (Berkeley & London: University of California Press, 1980);

Herakleitos and Diogenes (Bolinas, Cal.: Grey Fox,
    1980);
The Mimes of Herondas (Berkeley: Grey Fox, 1981);
Boris de Rachewiltz, *Maxims of the Ancient Egyptians*
    (Louisville: Pace Trust, 1983).

Guy Davenport occupies an unusual position
in contemporary American literature because his accomplishments cover so many diverse disciplines.
Not only is he considered one of the most respected
short-story writers; he is also one of the most influential literary critics, translators, book illustrators,
and teachers. He has published over fifty stories,
some the length of novellas, in six collections. For
his first four collections, he created some distinctive
black-and-white illustrations. He has also published
poetry, in his *Flowers and Leaves* (1966) and *Thasos
and Ohio* (1985). Davenport has published notable
translations of Heraclitus, Diogenes, and the poets
Sappho and Archilochus. He has also published two
highly acclaimed collections of essays: *The Geography of the Imagination* (1981) and *Every Force Evolves a
Form* (1987). These volumes contain sixty essays
that cover such challenging thinkers as James Joyce,
Ezra Pound, Charles Olson, Ludwig Wittgenstein,
and Samuel Beckett, to name a few. In addition
Davenport has edited a selection of writings on
Swiss naturalist Louis Agassiz. Davenport has one
of the most highly respected literary and critical
minds now operating in American and European literary circles, even though his work is virtually impossible to classify because it is completely sui generis. Critic George Steiner has stated categorically,
"The fact is that Guy Davenport is among the very
few truly original, truly autonomous voices now au-
dible in American letters. Name Guy Davenport
and William Gass. There are not many others to set
beside [Jorge Luis] Borges, Raymond Queneau,
and [Italo] Calvino" (*New Yorker*, 30 November
1981). Other critics refer to Davenport's immense
learning and erudition, and Steiner places him in
the rarefied company of what Samuel Taylor Cole-
ridge called "library-cormorants," a term that applies also to Robert Burton and Vladimir Nabokov.

Davenport's first published works begin in
mythopoesis. There is no evidence of the early
work representing a thinly veiled autobiographical
persona lamenting his role as victim in a meaningless, existential void. Davenport's earliest stories in-
augurate a variety of mythopoeic procedures that
continue to expand with each succeeding work in
the most unpredictable and sometimes comic ways.
Few contemporary writers possess a better ear for
the stylistic richness of the English language, and

even fewer critics have noticed the enormously sophisticated comedy he practices, from the elegant
subtlety of eighteenth-century satire to the irrever-
ent body-based humor of junior-high-school wise-
cracking.

Most notably, however, Davenport is a practicing modernist in a postmodernist literary world.
In much of his fiction he uses standard modernist
techniques, still considered "experimental" by some
conservative critics. By employing methods usually
associated with the visual art of collage, he juxtaposes images of the past with the present to
demonstrate the persistent presence of the archaic
and how those prehistoric energies can still be used
to redeem humankind from the relentless onslaught
of mechanization, Davenport's permanent enemy.
These energies endure in the human imagination as
it intersects and interacts with outer reality in much
the same way that Ezra Pound, one of Davenport's
major influences, presents the fragmentation that
takes place when human beings are disengaged
from their geographical, cultural, and spiritual origins. Davenport told Jerome Klinkowitz (in *Contemporary Novelists*, 1991) that his literary methods, particularly in his more experimental stories, are "assemblages of history and necessary fictions," thus
combining Wallace Stevens's notion of a "supreme
fiction" with Pound and William Carlos Williams's
dependence on a historical tradition grounded in a
specific geography. Davenport has stated that "my
stories are lessons in history."

Much of Davenport's fiction attempts to regenerate Edenic innocence, which civilization has
destroyed by its incessant rationality. The "Fall"
into experience, time, and knowledge becomes the
major subject matter of much of his fiction, and
many of his other stories are variations on this recurrent theme. His greatest work is the trilogy detailing the intellectual and erotic adventures of a fictional Dutch philosopher, Adriaan van Hovendaal,
and his ongoing attempt to create a variety of
Utopian communities based on the teachings of
the French sociologist Charles Fourier, one of
Davenport's most important spiritual influences.
The work of Fourier serves as a virtual blueprint
for Davenport's trilogy, which consists of *Apples and
Pears and Other Stories* (1984), *The Jules Verne Steam
Balloon* (1987), and the longest story in *The Drummer
of the Eleventh North Devonshire Fusiliers*, (1990) titled
"Wo es war, soll ich werden" (Where it was, there
must I begin to be). Certain other stories, while not
employing the same characters as the trilogy, treat
the theme of the damage done to the life of instinct
by so-called civilization and its perverse need to de-

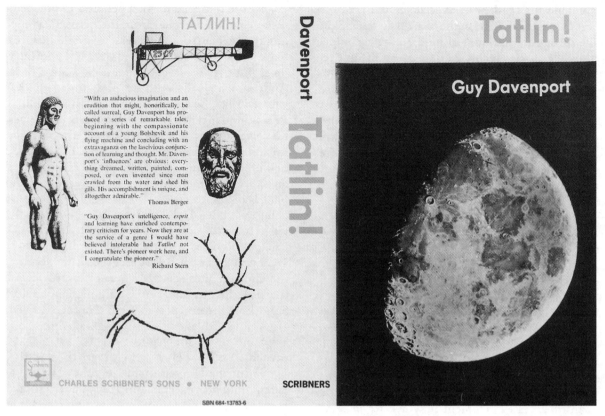

Dust jacket for Davenport's first collection of short fiction. The title story is about Vladimir Tatlin (1885–1953), the Russian artist and theater designer who founded constructivism.

stroy the desire for affection that human beings possess. The "apples and pears" alluded to throughout Davenport's work are analogues of those in the mythic Garden of Eden: the apples symbolize the Fall of humankind, and the pears stand for redemption.

Davenport's earliest short stories are in his first collection, *Tatlin!* (1974). Though forty-three years old when he first began writing stories, he modestly informed Klinkowitz that he thought of himself as "a minor prose stylist experimenting with ways to get certain verbal and imaginative effects onto paper. My talent is minor, my prose unskilled and contrived, my ideas derivative." His stories are much closer to the openly inventive fictions of the Roman writer Apuleius, the medieval tales of Sir Thomas Malory, and the sensual celebrations of François Rabelais than to the stories of Ernest Hemingway or William Faulkner. Davenport openly lists those writers who have had the greatest influence on him as a fiction writer: Joyce, Franz Kafka, Eudora Welty, and Gustave Flaubert. But he also credits the poets who helped forge his creative sensibilities. The ideogrammatic techniques in the poetry of Pound, Williams, and Olson, along with the

enormous range of their poetic projects, have all entered the imagination of Davenport. An important nonliterary influence on his way of envisioning reality is the architectonic arrangement of images of the filmmaker Stan Brakhage. Davenport has adapted some of Brakhage's experimental methods into his own fiction making by replacing narrative and documentary techniques with images that formulate a structure of their own as they emerge. His views on the power of the imagination to create its own reality closely resemble those of Stevens, particularly when Davenport concludes that "we can know reality only through our fictions." One of Davenport's most perceptive critics, Klinkowitz, adds that "his stories and novellae are attempts to structure those fictions according to the photographic, cinematic, and collagist natures of our time."

Attempting to analyze Davenport's fictions according to traditional literary techniques such as plot, character, theme, and setting brings little understanding to the reader. There is rarely a linear plot in which a hero undertakes a journey, overcomes painful obstacles, and learns something new about his inner self. Davenport's are anything but conventional short stories. Close readings of his stories enable his readers to experience the creative process along with him, in the same way one might move through a museum of modern art accompanied by a knowledgeable guide who points out recurring structural patterns within works that appear, at first sight, hopelessly complex. Because Davenport is a declared modernist, his fiction must be examined with the same methods that one would use to understand the complicated idioms of Pablo Picasso, Max Ernst, and Georges Braque: collage and montage. Davenport's more difficult fictions can be comprehended and analyzed once they are viewed in terms of juxtaposition and parataxis: certain recurrent motifs formulate parallels of their own, and these parallels combine to create new forms. Davenport's methods clearly follow Pound and the imagists' basic tenet: to present the image accurately. And he, like H. D., Richard Aldington, T. E. Hulme, and other early imagists, adheres faithfully to that imperative.

Davenport's notion of the nature and function of the imagination consistently informs his composition process from his earliest work to the present. He told Barry Alpert in a 1976 interview: "My theory of the imagination is this: that in the evolution of man this was the moment in which we became what we call human. That is, it's an amazing ability to see something with your eyes closed. Which is what imagination is." He further asserts that the artist's ability to "make me see what you can imagine is a power of communication so high that I can't think of humanity doing any better." Precisely how Davenport translates his theory of the imagination into a working method involves collage techniques: "My writing unit is such that I start literally with scraps of paper and pages from notebooks. Every sentence is written by itself; there are very few consecutive sentences in my work." He begins each day with writing in eight or nine notebooks and concludes the day in the same way. He has found that particularly fruitful entries come out of the notes he takes while traveling, especially while waiting for buses, planes, and trains. He writes in single sentences, which he revises eight or nine times. He then finds a place for them in a story. He states that "the actual writing of any of the stories in *Tatlin!* was a matter of turning back and forth in a notebook and finding what I wanted." He compares his method of composition with the activity of foraging by his favorite insect, the wasp. Just as the wasp forages his way through the day, Davenport forages his way through his notebooks each morning and evening. Indeed, one of the major metaphors running through all the stories in *Tatlin!* is that of foraging.

True to his modernist beliefs and practices in distancing the personal from the fictive, Davenport has kept his personal life very private. Outside the basic facts recorded in standard biographical volumes, little is known of his domestic affairs. Born in Anderson, a small South Carolina town, on 23 November 1927, he seems to have grown up within the Protestant Anglo-Saxon tradition. His references to his relationships with his family are always respectful and warm and show no evidence of youthful rebellion. His father, Guy Mattison Davenport, was an express-shipping agent, and his mother, Marie Fant Davenport, was a housewife. The young Davenport attended Duke University, where he graduated with his B.A. in 1948. He attended Merton College, Oxford, as a Rhodes scholar from 1948 to 1950 and earned a B.Litt. degree. After serving in the United States Army Airborne Corps from 1950 to 1951, he taught at Washington University in Saint Louis from 1952 to 1955. He then moved to Haverford College in Pennsylvania, where he was assistant professor from 1961 to 1963, having earned a Ph.D. at Harvard University in 1961. He arrived at the University of Kentucky in 1963 and taught until his retirement in 1991. His doctoral dissertation was on Pound and was published under the title *Cities on Hills: A Study of I–XXX of Ezra Pound's Cantos* (1983). It is a brilliant analysis of the structure of the first thirty cantos and puts special emphasis on Pound's ideogrammatic methods, controlling metaphors, and the design and style of these important early cantos.

Davenport has lived the quiet life of a college professor in a southern university and taught courses on Pound, Joyce, Olson, and many other notable modern authors. Outside his teaching duties and his steady output of short stories and essays, he has also been a prodigious book reviewer for literary, political, and popular journals. He reviewed books for the *National Review* for eleven years and also published reviews on a regular basis in six other publications: *Life*, the *New York Times Book Review*, the *Hudson Review*, *Book Week*, *Poetry*, and the *Los Angeles–New York Times Book Review Service*. He continues to review books for the *New Criterion*.

Some of these essay-reviews were expanded into much longer treatments of not only authors but topics such as the prehistoric caves of the Dordogne or the unusual cosmology of the Dogons of Mali and the Upper Volta of West Africa. Some of these essays were collected in Davenport's most acclaimed critical volume, *The Geography of the Imagination*. Many scholars hold this volume in such esteem that they consider it one of the most intelligent and articulate collections in recent American criticism.

Though Davenport's essays cover an enormous range of topics and treatments of those topics, one major thematic pattern steadfastly surfaces in his essays and short stories. He defines this pattern in what many see as his most comprehensive philosophical statement, "The Symbol of the Archaic," an essay that grounds the intellectual core of much of his work in his consistent proposition that modern man's salvation can be found in the reawakening of his passion for the archaic. Davenport describes that process as "a longing for something lost, for energies, values, and certainties unwisely abandoned by an industrial age." He believes that the modernist impulse to discover or invent the archaic replicates the Renaissance discovery of the spiritual resources of Hellenism.

Davenport considers Fourier and Samuel Butler, especially his *Erewhon* (1872), to be recurrent influences that are built into the stories as content rather than form, though certain motifs from both writers appear from time to time. Davenport's historical imagination seems to have been shaped early on by Oswald Spengler's *Decline of the West* (two volumes, 1918, 1922), though he considers George Santayana's philosophical stance closest to his own, especially Santayana's skeptical self-examination of consciousness as presented in his last great work, the four-part *Realms of Being* (1927–1940). Santayana's recognition of how reason and the imagination work together to formulate "realities" and his avoidance of a solipsistic worldview have enabled Davenport's imagination to create some of the richest fiction in twentieth-century literature.

Davenport's first collection of short stories, *Tatlin!* was widely acclaimed, in over sixty reviews, by some distinguished critics. Most of them confessed that they had seen nothing remotely like these stories and proclaimed them genuinely original. George Kearns (*Hudson Review,* Autumn 1980) praised these stories and their "combination of invention, sentence-by-sentence surprise, playfulness, and archaic wonder." Hilton Kramer, one of Davenport's most intelligent critics, stated regarding *Tatlin!* that "Davenport created a mode of fiction that despite its obvious debt to Pound, was highly original – stories constructed along the lines of a pictorial collage that are part historical fable, part learned essay, part lyric idyll. Densely written, studded with esoteric allusions, an unfamiliar vocabulary and quotations from many languages, and often obscure in the actions they depict, these stories definitely qualify as a species of 'Daedalian art,'

carefully concealing meanings that have to be painstakingly 'searched out' " (*New York Times Book Review,* 6 September 1987).

In spite of the obvious complexities that confront a reader of the six stories in the collection, there are recurring thematic patterns and imagery that tie them together. The key metaphor running throughout the entire book is that of flight, very much in keeping with Davenport's early appreciation and explication of the works of Joyce, especially the metaphor of flight in *Portrait of the Artist as a Young Man* (1916). Flight in all these stories can be viewed as a flight for freedom and liberation from the constraints that hold back imaginative possibilities and the full expression of physical and spiritual capabilities. The Daedalian art that Kramer points out directs itself toward "the light" and away from "the dark," not so much in terms of an overly simplistic Manichean conflict that ascribes "evil" to darkness and "good" to the light but, rather, as a flight from a downward entropy toward a more vivid, richer, ecstatic consciousness that revels in its own vitalities. The tension in all the stories is between these opposing tendencies, and the mediation between them is the imagination, "what mankind makes of things."

The second of the six stories in *Tatlin!* is "The Aeroplanes at Brescia," which illustrates some of his habitual literary techniques such as montage and juxtaposition, and how they engender a field of fictive possibilities that creates its own brand of information and enjoyment. The most compelling element in the story is the process of its creation. Observing the way Davenport uses his imagination to reorganize certain facts about a well-known 1909 air show featuring archaic flying machines takes precedence over the actual event. The subject matter of the story is not what happened at that air show but, rather, who attended it and what they wrote about it. Davenport is much more interested in versions of what happened: he envisions history as the product of the creative imagination working with "facts." He bases his story on the version that Kafka recorded in a newspaper article about the event; the article was his first published writing. Davenport places next to it a version of the same event by Kafka's biographer Max Brod, who had accompanied Kafka there. Other important people were also there, including Giacomo Puccini and Gabriele D'Annunzio, and Davenport offers his versions of what he imagines they observed – versions just as plausible as Kafka's and Brod's. Davenport also conjectures that the linguistic philosopher Wittgenstein, whom Kafka thinks he spots in the crowd,

Dust jacket for Davenport's 1979 collection of short fiction, in which many of the characters are historical figures whose accomplishments were unappreciated by their contemporaries

may also have been there because he was obsessed with flight and archaic flying machines from his early youth. So he includes what Wittgenstein might have seen as another possibility that adds to the richness of multiple fictive versions of the single event.

"The Aeroplanes of Brescia" originated as an essay on Kafka, and in the process of research, Davenport discovered that Kafka's first published newspaper story was titled "The Aeroplanes at Brescia." Though it was a piece of journalism, Davenport claims that, once you know Kafka wrote it, you can then read it as a stereotypical Kafka story. Davenport uses every sentence, in one way or another, that Kafka and Brod used in their stories about the event. He rearranged the sentences in highly imaginative ways while adding much of his own work. In his later fictions Davenport extends and modifies this technique and calls it "writing over" texts he translated or reworked. His placing of Wittgenstein at the event is a guess, but much of the enjoyment

and humor of the piece comes from the reader imagining that Wittgenstein was there and that many of these historical characters may have seen each other and even communicated. By permitting readers to use their imaginations unencumbered by a tedious recitation of facts, Davenport allows them to create fictive landscapes much broader than linear narratives can offer.

Perhaps the best-known story from *Tatlin* is the title story, a novella that Davenport says originally came out of a plan for a book on the history of art, particularly from some research into the beginnings of modern art in Russia. He told Alpert that " 'Tatlin!' began as an oil portrait of [Vladimir] Tatlin from an old photograph. . . Frequently I will abandon a piece of writing and draw it, or abandon a drawing and write it, or do both." Critic Hugh Witemeyer contends that Tatlin is Davenport's archetypal Renaissance man because he was an engineer, designer, painter, ceramicist, sailor, teacher, and folk musician. "Tatlin!" begins in 1932, moves back to 1895, and concludes with the death of Joseph Stalin in 1953. It traces the artistic vocation of the title character and demonstrates the triumph of the powers of a dehumanizing mechanization over Tatlin's humanistic vision, in spite of his obvious involvement in two of the most important modernist movements: futurism and constructivism. Indeed, Tatlin founded the constructivist movement in Russia. When Tatlin enthusiastically presented his utopian plans to Lenin, Lenin said nothing. Davenport uses some of his own drawings throughout the fifty pages of the story not only to illustrate abstractly some of Tatlin's imaginative projects but to juxtapose them to the dour, static posters of Lenin and Stalin, images that become icons of the kind of anti-art that socialist realism used to destroy any original artistic impulse. Tatlin is an obvious counterpart to Joyce's Stephen Daedalus. The difference between their dilemmas is that Stephen successfully flies beyond the nets of family, religion, and country that have kept him spiritually dead and Dublin in paralysis. Lenin and Stalin have transformed Russia into a Cretan prison from which Tatlin can only dream of flying. The metaphor of flight is most clearly seen in this story about a creative genius who happens to be both pilot and artist.

The most important story in *Tatlin!* is the concluding one, "The Dawn in Erewhon," which takes up half the volume. Davenport enormously expands the range of his allusions, rivaling Pound and Olson; the mythic allusions and perspectives proliferate prodigiously. While an omniscient voice narrates most of the novella, a few pages are taken from the notebooks of the fictional Dutch philosopher van Hovendaal, who Davenport modeled after Wittgenstein.

Davenport admits that "The Dawn in Erewhon" can be read as an updating of *Erewhon,* one of the most prophetic books of the nineteenth century. The story's specific title, though, comes from a painting by Wyndham Lewis. "The story is set in Holland," Davenport told Alpert, "because Holland is the nether land. Adriaan van Hovendaal is Ludwig Wittgenstein opened up. We know very little about Wittgenstein's sex life, but it seems to have been agonized and horrendous. . . . So I imagine a modern Dutchman who does express himself with his body as well as his mind and seems to me (or at least I want to suggest this) that he lands in an Erewhon." Davenport further explains that van Hovendaal was a disciple of Fourier, Butler, and the Greek philosopher Epicurus. The Dutchman's name places him within an Edenic mythic tradition: van Hovendaal means "gardener," and he is one in the story. Like Adam, van Hovendaal tries to construct his own pastoral utopia.

"The Dawn in Erewhon" and *Erewhon* both criticize the damage that modern civilization does to the life of instinct. Butler's satire attacks the Victorian fear of sexuality and Christianity's persistent favoring of the intellect over the body. Consistent with Davenport's recurrent theme, that of the fall from a childhood innocence into the experience of self-consciousness, van Hovendaal regenerates an Edenic garden through which experience can be redeemed on both spiritual and physical levels. The intellectual genius of van Hovendaal is always put at the service of the desires of the body; his life is the opposite of the overly cerebral thinker lost in the life-denying abstractions of logical positivism. Though Davenport documents in great detail the cognitive roots of van Hovendaal's intellectual background by juxtaposing hundreds of quotations in at least six languages running through his mind, he demonstrates in even greater detail the many joyous sexual activities that vivify his affective life and transform it into forms of ecstatic consciousness.

The major characters Bruno and Kaatje (a teenage boy and girl), who reappear in some later works, first appear in "The Dawn in Erewhon." They revel in each other's and Adriaan's affectionate company as they enjoy each other's bodies without guilt or jealousy. This trio becomes the first group that Davenport forms into a social unit resembling what Fourier called "Little Hordes," groups whose primary duty is to fulfill their instinctual desires for pleasure. Davenport's trio

spends much time in taking trips to idyllic forests, assigning duties, and strictly apportioning the time in which they may do whatever they wish. The day concludes with multiple erotic exercises, which, while delineated in the most specific sexual language, are presented as elaborate rituals of innocence, affection, and childlike joy. Since corrupting elements such as control and aggression have been forbidden among this highly structured society, the story is a parable of regenerative innocence.

Certain conventional mythic dichotomies, such as the Dionysian versus the Apollonian, or the mind-body struggle, and Freudian conflicts that produce neurotic anxiety are notably absent from Davenport's fiction. Fourier, who predated Freud by a hundred years, asserted that people could be truly happy if they were permitted to construct lives that would cooperate with their instincts rather than denigrating and deploring them. Fourier has been called the only true philosopher of happiness, and he wrote twelve volumes in which he outlined exactly how such a society might evolve. Much of Davenport's long fictions can be read as mythopoeic parables proposing the possibility of a regenerated innocence when characters live according to their deepest instinctual desires but only, however, within highly circumscribed Fourierist parameters. Though the sexual rhetoric may appear to allow sexual anarchy, nothing could be further from Davenport's intention. Such openly sexual affection is healthy only if practiced in a healthy society; "sexual outlaws" would never be permitted within Davenport's Fourierist democracy.

What Davenport has accomplished within much of his evolving mythopoeic fiction is to exclude any figure that even slightly resembles a typical hero – that is, a charismatic male who by the force of his ego and aggressive power becomes the leader and, in essence, controller of a specific locale and group. Van Hovendaal is respected by the younger Bruno and Kaatje not because of his ability to control situations but because he permits himself to participate openly in their passionate attraction, a key concept in Fourier's philosophy. The teenage boy and girl also admire van Hovendaal as an intellectual whose mind and body work in consonance and whose intuition and perception have led him back to a primal, archaic imagination that comprehends and acknowledges the continuity of life and death. His life is one of balance and harmony. Most important, however, is that the society created by the mutual trust, love, and care among Adriaan, Bruno, and Kaatje authenticates the concept of harmony by embodying it. As long as they help each other enjoy the desires of the body, they are creating what Fourier called "Sessions of the Court of Love," which will eventually regenerate a new Eden or the Fourierist "New Amorous World."

Donald Byrd draws together better than any other critic the major thematic strands of all the stories in this first collection of Davenport's stories: "*Tatlin!* is an attempt to retrieve the human body as the informant of knowledge, to respond to the archaic intuition that man-in-his-body is the most complex product of the earth's coherence." Byrd finds that Davenport shares Pound's view that the enemies of humankind are "the despisers of the body." Those enemies have taken the form of an ongoing mechanization that is damaging humankind with sophisticated technologies, though Davenport firmly believes that a harmonious fusion of passion and imagination is possible.

Da Vinci's Bicycle, published in 1979, comprises ten stories and again attacks the "despisers of the body" in the longest story in the collection, "Au Tombeau de Charles Fourier" (At the Tomb of Charles Fourier). However, other themes emerge. Many of the characters are historical figures whose contributions seem out of phase; their accomplishments were either too early, too late, or in conflict with the temper of the times. Leonardo da Vinci is an apt objective correlative for the whole book, and his example is so obvious that Davenport does not even create a fiction for him in the volume. Da Vinci, the quintessential example of the marginalized genius, had already designed the bicycle, which, had anyone examined his *Notebooks,* would not have had to be reinvented. Also, all of these historical personages shared a common impulse to forage in their need to understand the world about them. Most of them are also prime examples of the marginalizing of genius; that is, their accomplishments were not recognized and appreciated fully during their lifetimes.

Four of the stories treat classical Greek and Roman locations and characters, and "Ithaka" details an awkward meeting between Pound and his mistress, Olga Rudge, in Rapallo, Italy. In the story "The Antiquities of Elis" the physical location, Elis, site of the ancient Olympic Games, acts as the principal character while ancient voices supply historical information to the reader. In "The Invention of Photography in Toledo" Davenport contrasts the glorious Toledo of Spain with its American counterpart, Toledo, Ohio. The most comically effective piece in the collection is the first story, "The Richard Nixon Freischütz Rag," in which Davenport juxtaposes the oracular utterings of Chairman Mao Tse-tung with the documented banality of President Nixon's responses during his visit to China in 1972.

There are some new technical developments in this volume that Davenport has continued to use throughout his literary career. He refers to them as "a kind of translation or a writing over." "The Antiquities of Elis" is the result of experimenting with the new techniques. As he told Alpert, the story is "a kind of invention, because it's a translation of so many pages of Pausanias chosen at random. I decided that any five pages of Pausanias were interesting. And I translated them and then I put in the onions and the dust. . . . Pausanias never mentions these things, so I had to imagine them." Davenport uses these methods with great effect in a long work in *Eclogues* (1981) – "The Daimon of Sokrates" – and other, shorter works.

The most important assemblage in *Da Vinci's Bicycle* is "Au Tombeau de Charles Fourier," whose title suggests acknowledging an influence. The scene of the meditation at the tomb of Fourier in the cemetery of Montmartre is an example of a meditation on ruins, a literary form in which Davenport has maintained an interest throughout his career. In talking with Klinkowitz, Davenport explained the genesis of this lengthy story: " 'Au Tombeau de Charles Fourier' began in my head when I was reading Fourier on a bluff on the Ohio River and encountered the unknown word *quagga*." (That word, which refers to an extinct African donkey, is the title of the third chapter of *Apples and Pears*.) But he further explained that the story also came out of his attempt to condense into English the information from the French anthropologist Marcel Griaule's five-hundred-page book on the Dogons of West Africa, with Ogotemmêli, the Dogon metaphysician and wise man, as the primary focus. Unable to create a readily assessable version, Davenport decided to "chop it up . . . and take an idea out of it." The idea he abstracted was that of foraging, a concept that has become a standard theme and technique throughout his writing career. He then began reading books on bees and wasps, nature's great foragers, which, combined with his interest in beginnings and archaic facts, led him to include in the story some modernist foragers such as Gertrude Stein, Picasso, and the Wright brothers. He added the Wright brothers not only for their foraging impulses but, more importantly, because their invention of the airplane was actually a mechanized reinvention of a wasp or bee, an insect – not a bird – which does not flap its wings. He states clearly that all the elements in "Au Tombeau de Charles Fourier" are examples of foraging and that everybody in the story moves in a figure *8*, which is the pattern wasps make when they fly.

The principal theme that runs throughout this dense and complicated assemblage is that reality comes into existence only through words and the ability of the poet, priest, or shaman to construct worlds through the efficacy of their verbal power. Stein forages around Paris in her Model T searching for new experiences and ends up establishing verbal language as the iconographic medium through which other linguistic pioneers become visible. The leader that Davenport compares Fourier to is Ogotemmêli. After Griaule spent fifteen years with the West African Dogon tribe, the elders decided to impart to him the deep information concerning the cosmology upon which their reality was built. The blind Ogotemmêli invited Griaule to sit with him for thirty-three days, during which he revealed to him in massive detail and from memory (the Dogons are a preliterate society) the Dogon cosmology. The entire Dogon cosmological system is based on the image of a loom on which all things are stitched together to create a harmonious world, very much in the way Fourier stitched together an equally coherent utopian society, which he called the "New Harmonious World." Davenport calls Fourier the "master forager" and considers him the greatest mind of the nineteenth century. Because of Davenport's regret over the failure of such idealistic American Fourierist communities, he calls "Au Tombeau" an elegy and recalls visiting Fourier's tomb to be close to "the bones of the man."

The point that Davenport wants to make is that the spiritual realities that these marginalized geniuses proposed are not really dead: their words created mythopoeic worlds that exist today in their writing. Language is the key in that it alone escapes the ravages of time and preserves the numinous power to create such alternate worlds. In paying homage to Fourier, Davenport also pays homage to the other "priests of the word," modernists such as Beckett, Joyce, Picasso, and others, whose high modernism evolved from their recognition of and participation in the recurring energies of the archaic to reestablish a sense of order in the world.

Davenport's third collection of short fiction, *Eclogues,* continues his interest in and exploration of ancient and modern Edenic or pastoral narratives. The title of the collection comes from a literary form used by classical Greek and Roman poets such as Virgil and Theocritus; it is synonymous with the term *pastorals.* Davenport expands the use of the term to include lives lived under ideal conditions. The ideal that Davenport proposes evolves from the word *ideal*'s etymo-

Dust jacket for Davenport's 1984 book, for which he designed and drew the cover art. The title novella propounds the utopian ideals of Charles Fourier.

logical root: *idyll.* His principal models are the *Idylls* of Theocritus, the third-century B.C. Greek poet and inventor of the pastoral form that depicts the happy, rustic lives of shepherds and farmers in Sicily.

There are important patterns throughout this set of stories, the major one being that they all include a shepherd of some kind. The Latin root of the word *pastoral* is *pastor,* meaning "shepherd"; and the stories, closer in many cases to fables, embody the idea of the pastoral. Van Hovendaal returns in "The Death of Picasso" as a guide or "shepherd" to the young Dionysiac Sander, who will eventually (in *Apples and Pears*) focus his sexual energies into becoming a painter. Tullio, an older, more domestic guide to a "little horde" in "On Some Lines of Virgil," is a shepherd working to help them establish an orderly but pleasurable Fourierist community.

In one of the shorter stories in *Eclogues,* "Mesoroposthonippidon," Davenport narrates humorous anecdotes about the ancient Greek philosopher Diogenes, who frequently impressed people of high rank with the simplicity of his life. Because he possessed nothing of any value, he freely spoke his mind to anyone, including Alexander the Great, whom he scolded for blocking his sunlight. Five of the eight stories in this collection deal with classical settings and characters with the purpose of pointing out their relevance to modern times.

The second longest story in the collection, "The Daimon of Sokrates," is "a kind of translation or a writing over" of Plutarch's piece of the same name. Davenport explains in a note not only why he uses this method but the effect that it has on the style of the story: "The flatness of its text is meant to imitate Plutarch's starkness and narrative simplicity. I have added embellishments from the fragments that survive of his lost life of Epameinondas, his life of Pelopidas, and from other sources, when I could add a detail of manners or an object which Plutarch took for granted." Two other stories from this collection are examples of his "writing over" methods: "Idyll" comes from Theocritos, and "The Trees at Lystra" from Acts 16:6–20.

The longest and most complex story in the collection is the pastoral romance "On Some Lines of Virgil," a title taken from one of Michel de Montaigne's essays. The allusion to Virgil immediately reveals Davenport's increasing concern with the regeneration of an Edenic or, in this case, Arcadian community. Indeed, Virgil's *Bucolics, Georgics,* and *Ecologues* are presentations of such idealized settings. Steiner calls Davenport's montage "one of the most hilarious, tenderly risqué accounts of sexual awakening in all modern literature."

The setting for "On Some Lines of Virgil" is Bordeaux, an ancient, southwestern French city, the birthplace of such painters and writers as Rosa Bonheur, Odilon Redon, François Mauriac, Baron Montesquieu, and, most important, Montaigne. The artist Francisco José de Goya y Lucientes, though not a native of Bordeaux, painted some of his greatest later works there. Davenport is careful to point out that Bonheur's *The Horse Fair* (1853) and Goya's *The Bulls of Bordeaux* (1825) are unconscious ideogrammatic iterations of the horses and bulls found in the caves of Lascaux, another instance of how the modern imagination is grounded in the archaic. Tullio, the scholar/guide, exhorts his little horde of four that true history, which is the history of attention, consists of developing the ability to detect these patterns and that his deepest desire is "to write a history of the imagination in our time. . . . All things need to be reseen [in light of the archaic]. The new modifies everything before, and even finds a tradition for the first time." Dav-

enport's aesthetic theory bears some similarity to T. S. Eliot's classic statement in his essay "Tradition and the Individual Talent" (1916) but without the Calvinist undertones that would not allow Eliot to use the word "imagination."

The little horde, in this highly sensual Arcadia, consists of four French teenagers: Jonquille, Jolivet, Michel, and the barely adolescent Victor. In the midst of their frequent, affectionate games, they venture to one of the ancient caves near Bordeaux, taking with them the young, legless Marc Aurel and also Tullio, a responsible, married adult. Davenport, though giving the adolescents full sexual freedom, positions an older scholar nearby to place their erotic play in some sort of context. Tullio, whose name derives from Marcus Tullius Cicero (known throughout the ancient world as "Tully"), serves as their intellectual and spiritual guide and helps them understand the nature of their friendship. Youth and friendship are better understood and appreciated if viewed against the background of old age, just as the preliterate tableaux in the caves of Lascaux adumbrate the later works of Paul Klee, Bonheur, Picasso, and Goya. Tullio, besides teaching his little horde the history of the imagination and its crucial connection to the archaic, further expands his ongoing lesson on what constitutes "true" history: "Rings of trees, giving their age, is first mentioned as a fact by Montaigne, though suspected by Leonardo [da Vinci]. Tullio says Montaigne learned about them from a goldsmith in Italy who, it has been recently discovered, was an apprentice in Leonardo's studio." True history, then, is the history of attention — that is, of attending to all forms of reports, particularly oral and visual folk wisdom. Knowledge is one, and all things are connected.

Davenport's fourth collection of stories, *Apples and Pears,* is his masterpiece. The 233-page novella "Apples and Pears" is the most elaborately constructed fiction that he has yet produced. It fully demonstrates the enormous scope of his intellectual terrain, and it constitutes his ultimate mythopoeic creation, modified at times by the strong influences of Butler's *Erewhon* and patterned throughout by Fourier's vision of harmony. The style, at times, recalls Joyce's *Ulysses* (1922) at its most pellucid; and its four-part structure includes Davenport's most successful adaptation of Fourier's utopian vision.

The three stories preceding "Apples and Pears" are also some of his most charming and delicately rendered fictions. All three are journeys of one kind or another. "The Bowmen of Shu" is constructed out of the sculptor Henri Gaudier-

Brzeska's battlefield diaries, as "translated," augmented, and arranged by Davenport, while "Fifty-seven Views of Fujiyama" paratactically narrates the seventeenth-century poet Basho's mountain journey, along with a modern couple's camping trip in New Hampshire. One of the most delightful and humorous stories in all of Davenport's work is "The Chair," which finds Kafka accompanying the rebbe of Belz on a tour of the Czechoslovakian spa at Marienbad in 1916. Kafka's "chair" bears more than a little resemblance to Stevens's "jar" in his "Anecdote of the Jar" (1919). (Indeed, Davenport's story "Fifty-seven Views of Fujiyama," which immediately precedes "Apples and Pears," resonates with Stevens's "Thirteen Ways of Looking at a Blackbird" [1917], and Davenport has written some highly intelligent Stevens criticism.) Both "chair" and "jar" become points, and therefore, positions in a natural, chaotic wilderness from which a human perspective may be measured: "The chair held aloft by its bearer, Dr. Kafka notices, has now defined what art is as distinct from nature, for its pattern of flowers and leaves looks tawdry and artificial and seriously out of place against the green and rustling leaves of apple and pear trees."

In the novella "Apples and Pears" Davenport uses the same techniques that he did in "The Death of Picasso" and "The Dawn in Erewhon," basing the story on notebooks, diaries, and memoirs. The major consciousness throughout most of "Apples and Pears" is van Hovendaal. New members swell the Fourierist "horde" into eight participants, including characters from previous works – Sander, Bruno, and Kaatje – and new adolescents: Jan, Hans, Saartje, and Sander's sister, Grietje.

The work is a Fourierist treatise organized along Fourierist lines. The four major sections follow Fourier's four-part structure of an ideal society, which he called "The Harmony of the Four Movements"; he divided it up into categories of the social, the animal, the organic, and the material. The four chapters of Davenport's work generally follow that scheme but not in that order. Van Hovendaal labels section one "An Erewhonian Sketchbook" and uses a Napoleonic rather than a Gregorian calendar, redesignating the months Messidor (July), Thermidor (August), Fructidor (September), and so on. The name changes of the months herald the arrival of the "New Harmonious World," which was supposed to follow the French Revolution. Critic Bruce Bawer, better than any other commentator, understands, appreciates, and illuminates not only the arcane allusions, mandarin puns, and linguistic complexities of "Apples and Pears" but the Fourier-

ist philosophical scaffolding upon which the work rests: "The vision in question (which Fourier spent most of his life constructing) was of a Utopia called Harmonium, where man's natural virtue (as posited by [Jean-Jacques] Rousseau, and believed in devoutly by Fourier) would, through the eliminations of the tensions which destroy human society, be permitted to prevail, and where, as a result, everyone would live in peace, happiness, and harmony." Rousseau believed that people were born intrinsically good and that sex was the most natural impulse, so a society in which the passions were permitted full expression would necessarily become a regenerated Garden of Eden, or Fourier's "New Harmonium."

Davenport translates the key line from Fourier's twelve-volume work that summarizes his entire philosophy of social happiness: "The series distributes the harmonies. The attractions are proportionate to our destinies." The "series," to Fourier and Davenport, is a group, or phalanstery, which operates democratically and is drawn together by mutual attractions. As long as the members of the group are permitted to act upon their mutually passionate attraction toward others, order and balance are established and harmony reigns. These harmonious conjunctions take place continuously throughout "Apples and Pears," as the group, gently guided by van Hovendaal, combines in multiple affectionate couplings. Most important, however, is that this work has become Davenport's definitive "history of affection," as brilliantly structured and detailed as anything in modern American literature. Davenport elaborates on Fourier's starkly philosophical lines with great wit and verbal flair: "The Vestals in white tunics and cloth Mongol boots have long hair embroidered sweatband bound. The series flows from rambunctious to shy, from impatience to placidity, with the attractions distributed thus: forward scouts practiced in kissing wiggly embraces, grubby foreplay through half dozen precocious and whiffety orgasms as yet vagrom enough to surge from nape to coccyx in boys, from nipples to clitoris in girls, or chime from scalp to toes and fingers in both." Steiner, one of the few critics who fully appreciates Davenport's stylistic virtuosity, labels the language in these later works "coruscating," "baroque," "precious," and "crazily inventive."

Not only does "Apples and Pears" contain some of the most accomplished prose in modern literature, it also contains some of Davenport's funniest scenes. Few writers possess a keener ear for the idioms of children and teenagers, particularly in the ways early teens effortlessly lampoon each other

*Dust jacket for Davenport's 1987 collection of short fiction, which includes his
most extensive examination of the nature of evil*

and the adults around them in language studded with sexual innuendo. Few groups can produce dialogue as brutally comic as a gang of American eighth graders. Sander's sister, Grietje, labeling those forces that thwart the horde's passionate and, therefore, natural attractions declaims in early teen patois: "Prize idiots and blob heads."

Butler's Erewhonian tenets are intermingled with Fourierist principles throughout the parables and fables that make up much of "Apples and Pears," because both philosophers saw mechanization as the enemy: "Sweetbrier agrees, wryly, that no phalanstery anything like Fourier's is possible without an Erewhonian revolution, canceling machines. . . . To take happiness from money and restore it to the harmony of work and its . . . reward. . . . To reorganize society after its disastrous dispersal by train, automobile, airplane. . . . All work became pandering to the reproduction of the machines." In the first section of "Apples and Pears" van Hovendaal is guiding the young Sander around Paris and describing its riches through a Proustian lens; in keeping with his predictable interest in ori-

gins, he detects Marcel Proust's subtext in one of Epicurus's best-known quotations: "I know nothing of the good except the deliciousness of food, sex, music, and the sight of beautiful bodies in graceful motion." No single sentence could better embody the subject matter, theme, and tone of "Apples and Pears."

Davenport's fifth volume of stories is titled *The Jules Verne Steam Balloon*. Four of the nine stories are connected, since some of the same characters appear in all four, thus expanding Davenport's mythopoeic parameters further. Some characters are participants from the novella "Apples and Pears." The mythos has moved from south to north, from the Netherlands to Denmark, but youthful beauty and charm dictate the action. "The Meadow," "The Bicycle Rider" (published separately in 1985), "The Jules Verne Steam Balloon," and the concluding story, "The Ringdove Sign," are all parables of innocence involving basically the same Fourierist ritual camping trips to idyllic forests, where the group members enjoy each other's bodies in clean, childlike, erotic celebration. New adolescents, such as

Pascal, Hugo, Franklin, Mariana, Kim, and Anders, join the little horde, but the project remains the same; those who are more sensually comfortable help those who are distrustful of their impulses to feel more at home in their bodies. Only in "The Bicycle Rider" does evil, for the first time, enter the highly organized affections of the group. One of the most attractive young men has become a drug addict, a condition that has rendered him unable to participate in the rich, emotional life around him. His addiction has also rendered him sexually indifferent. Because the social dynamics of this Fourierist phalanstery are predicated on the passional attraction among the group, he becomes an outcast and eventually dies.

There is, in *The Jules Verne Steam Balloon,* not only a new geomythical setting – from the sensually alluring Dutch underworld of the Netherlands to the "northern idyll" of Denmark – but, more crucially, a clear recognition of evil, which strikes a new moral note in Davenport's fictions. Indeed, some of the characters in these Fourierist stories border on the allegorical, a change that might suggest that they are losing their specifically human qualities and becoming types. However, the opposite is the case. Hugo Tvemunding, the major character in "The Bicycle Rider," "The Jules Verne Steam Balloon," and "The Ringdove Sign," is one of Davenport's most compellingly human characters. All three of these Fourierist parables are organized around Tvemunding's emerging knowledge that his true calling is not to the ministry but to his vocation as an artist. In a sense, these three fictions can be read as *Künstlerromans* (works that trace an artist's creative development). The son of a Protestant minister, Tvemunding is a doctoral student in theology, a classics instructor at a Danish high school, and a budding artist. He also bears some similarity to another Dane, Søren Kierkegaard, and the liberal Dutch priest/theologian Edward Schillebeeckx. Kierkegaard's agonized musings over what constitutes good and evil mirror Tvemunding's conflicts when confronted with the unambiguous evil of drug addiction and other escapist schemes, such as "McTaggart's Transcendental Meditation Group." And Schillebeeckx's attempt to move Roman Catholic theology away from its long-standing obsession with medieval scholastic abstractions to a renewed focus on the experience of a Christian consciousness within a caring community parallels Tvemunding's project to teach his students that heightened consciousness experienced within a loving fellowship is one of life's greatest rewards. Schillebeeckx also exhorted Catholics to shift from

an exhausted patriarchal paradigm for God to a fraternal one with Jesus as the model of friend and brother. Tvemunding is certainly the successor to van Hovendaal but with more than a little of Schillebeeckx's charisma vivifying the character.

Nowhere in Davenport's works does he so clearly define what constitutes evil as he does in *The Jules Verne Steam Balloon,* and that evil finds its greatest expression in drugs, because they turn the addict away from the experience of the world and into himself. Tvemunding angrily condemns the Bicycle Rider's use of LSD: "You call it mind-expanding: it shrivels the mind to a pinpoint. The mind, [Jean-Paul] Sartre said, is not what it is, it is what it is not. With LSD you ask the mind to be itself only, not the world it can observe.... Higher consciousness, from McTaggart's phony Buddhism and transcendental meditation to hallucinatory drugs, is trendy Drug Culture Doublespeak for no consciousness at all." Tvemunding summarizes a theme consistent in Davenport's work from *Tatlin!* to the present when he explains to the addict that his addiction has become "a preference for deadness rather than responsive liveliness" and that eventually it will "become a boring terror and aching intolerable misery...." He tries to convince the young man that one's happiness increases as he forgets himself, that the life of an artist is committed to responding: "I try to paint because I want to show others what I think is beautiful."

In the story "The Jules Verne Steam Balloon" Davenport brings together and clarifies several important symbols, particularly "light" and "pears." He also proposes a new comic view of liveliness with his introduction of the three male sprites – Tumble, Buckeye, and Quark – as they arrive in a giant pear-shaped balloon announcing themselves as messengers of enlightenment. The allusion to Wolfgang Amadeus Mozart's *The Magic Flute* (1791) and that opera's three young male guides is obvious. Critic Joseph Schöpp explicates Davenport's use of texture and allusion: "How intricately Davenport weaves his texture, he demonstrates with the recurrent balloon-forms, pear-shaped and gourd-like, which emerge from the text and dominate its structure, as if the gourd, 'the sign of Jonas,' through which God gave his prophet protection were indeed 'the pivot.' The whole text, it seems, turns around this one geometric figure...."

Davenport's symbols converge in the concluding story, "The Ringdove Sign," when Tvemunding's scriptural studies reveal the interconnectedness that seemingly disparate elements have when examined in terms of their paratactic forms. Once he discovers that "daimons" are angelic messengers and, thus, the true identity of Tumble, Quark, and Buckeye, he begins to put together the whole story: "And the daimon had, in one of the longest traditions we can trace in the Mediterranean, a bird form. A dove. More than any other folktale, Yeshua mentions the sign of Jonas. That is, the sign of the dove. Jonas means dove." The light alluded to throughout the story, resonating with Paracletean echoes, symbolizes the creative light inspiring Tvemunding to become an artist, but it also stands for the possibility of the union of the "inner light" with the "outer," or, as Hugo's father, Pastor Tvemunding, puts it at the end of "The Ringdove Sign": "I agree with you . . . about the light up here. It finds something in our souls."

All the main geometric figures are variations on pears, which, in Davenport's mythopoeic world, stand for redemption of various kinds. In this story, the redemption is clearly an aesthetic and spiritual one, as Schöpp points out: "Only through art, composed and combined in a new harmony, the chaos of life is transformed and transcended." The imagination becomes the redemptive agent. Davenport's pearlike balloon closely resembles a figure that Stevens evokes in his definition of the concept of nobility in art: "It is a violence from within that protects us from a violence without. It is the imagination pressing back against the pressure of reality" (*The Necessary Angel,* 1951) – like a balloon.

The sixth volume of Davenport's stories is *The Drummer of the Eleventh North Devonshire Fusiliers.* While "Colin Maillard" and "Badger" both deal with the early passional attraction between preadolescent boys, the novella "Wo es war, soll ich werden" continues the activities of the expanding Fourierist phalanstery. There are also major philosophical and critical statements that Davenport makes that help the reader understand some theoretical background. Davenport's style is so packed with multiphasic allusions, Joycean puns and conundrums, and phenomenological scene shifting that an occasional glance at his sources and influences always helps. He informs his reader that "Wo es war" is the conclusion of a trilogy composed of *Apples and Pears* and *The Jules Verne Steam Balloon.*

Of course, the activity remains the same, as do some of the characters, but a deeper philosophical and moral note enters both the dialogue and general discussion of the group. Davenport, as clearly as he has ever done, describes for the reader some of his literary methods through a character named Allen in the story "Badger." He first explains the fall that takes place when one enters adolescence: "What

you see, you know, Allen said, you own. You take it in. Everything's an essence . . . at twelve you understand everything. Afterward, you have to give it up and specialize." Most important, however, is Tvemunding's explanation of the title of the novella, "Wo es war, soll ich werden," a phrase from Sigmund Freud that Jacques Lacan, the eminent French psychoanalyst, said contained "pre-Socratic eloquence." And the pre-Socratics are Davenport's intellectual heroes throughout his work. Tvemunding translates the sentences as: "Where it was, there must I begin to be." Another character, Holger, mistakenly interprets it as another proof that "genius is a disease: Mann's paradox" – Thomas Mann's *Death in Venice* (1912; translated 1925) and *Doctor Faustus* (1947; translated, 1948) being notable examples of German Romantic agony. Tvemunding kindly corrects Holger and clarifies Freud's statement. "No, no. . . . Freud meant that a wound, healing, can command the organism's whole attention, and thus become the beginning of a larger health." Tvemunding thus comprehensively encapsulates Davenport's fictive enterprise in that all of his Fourierist parables of innocence attempt to disengage the lively and erotic celebration of the body from its endemic Judeo-Christian death wish. Western civilization need not end in apocalyptic self-immolation.

Guy Davenport reveres Charles Fourier for the same reasons that André Breton, the founder of surrealism, honored him with an ode. All three artists regenerate forms of prelapsarian innocence, envision the world with a childlike sense of the marvelous, and celebrate life in all of its ecstatic physicality. Davenport's mythopoeic procedures à la Fourier are directed at revivifying the endless capacities of the imagination, with pleasure as the primary motive, to eradicate the entropic deadness of mechanization, to replace the narcissistic "Demon self " with the "Daimon light," and to celebrate, at all times, the renaissance of the archaic. Bawer praises Davenport's work for its capacious excellence: "At a time in history when the prime criterion of excellence in American short fiction seems to be a sort of mindless, impersonal monotonousness, Guy Davenport's inimitable adventures in the realms of philosophy, language, and literary form are to be treasured. Davenport at his best reminds us of how exciting and valuable literary innovation can be. And he does something else that is even more important: he reminds us of our humanity, and (however bizarrely) of the importance of affection."

Interview:

Barry Alpert, "An Interview with Guy Davenport," *Vort,* 3, no. 3 (1976): 3–17.

Bibliography:

"Guy Davenport: A Bibliographical Checklist," *American Book Collector* (March–April 1984).

References:

Alain Arias-Misson, "Erotic Ear, Amoral Eye," *Chicago Review,* 35 (Spring 1986): 66–71;

Bruce Bawer, "Guy Davenport: Fiction à la Fourier," in his *Diminishing Fictions* (Saint Paul: Graywolf, 1988): 234–245;

Nancy Blake, " 'An Exact Precession': Leonardo, Gertrude, and Guy Davenport's *Da Vinci's Bicycle,*" in *Critical Angles: European Views of Contemporary Literature,* edited by Marc Chenetier (Carbondale: Southern Illinois University Press, 1986), pp. 145–152;

Donald Byrd, "Guy Davenport and the Use of Knowledge," *Vort,* 3, no. 3 (1976): 69–75;

Hugh Kenner, "Assemblages," *National Review,* 31 (28 September 1979): 1238–1241;

Kenner, "A Geographer of the Imagination," *Harper's,* 263 (August 1981): 66–68;

Hilton Kramer, "After the Archaic," *New York Times Book Review,* 6 September 1981, pp. 7, 21;

Patrick Meanor, "Guy Davenport," in *Critical Survey of Short Fiction,* revised edition (Englewood Cliffs, N. J.: Salem, 1993), pp. 678–689;

Robert Morace, "Invention in Guy Davenport's *Da Vinci's Bicycle,*" *Critique,* 22, no. 3 (1981): 71–87;

Lance Olsen, "A Guydebook to the Last Modernist: Davenport on Davenport and *Da Vinci's Bicycle,*" *Journal of Narrative Technique,* 16 (Spring 1986): 148–161;

Richard Pevear, "*Tatlin!,* or the Limits of Fiction," *Hudson Review,* 28 (Spring 1975): 141–146;

Joseph Schöpp, " 'Perfect Landscape with Pastoral Figures': Guy Davenport's Danish Eclogue à la Fourier," in *Facing Texts,* edited by Heide Ziegler (Durham, N.C. & London: Duke University Press, 1988), pp. 128–139;

George Steiner, "Rare Bird," *New Yorker,* 57 (30 November 1981): 196, 199–202, 204;

Richard Taylor, "Guy Davenport, the Teacher," *Vort,* 3, no. 3 (1976): 31–32;

Richard Wertime, "Tatlin!," *Georgia Review,* 29 (Winter 1975): 948–957;

Hugh Witemeyer, "Ezra Pound's Presence in Guy Davenport's *Tatlin!,*" *Vort,* 3, no. 3 (1976): 57–60.

Lydia Davis

(1947 –   )

Thad Ziolkowski
Yale University

BOOKS: *The Thirteenth Woman and Other Stories* (New York: Living Hand, 1976);

Sketches for a Life of Wassilly (Barrytown, N.Y.: Station Hill, 1981);

Story and Other Stories (Great Barrington, Mass.: Figures, 1983);

Break It Down (New York: Farrar, Straus & Giroux, 1986).

TRANSLATIONS: Jean-Paul Sartre, *Life/Situations,* translated by Davis and Paul Auster (New York: Pantheon, 1977);

Maurice Blanchot, *Death Sentence* (Barrytown, N.Y.: Station Hill, 1978);

Blanchot, *The Madness of the Day* (Barrytown, N.Y.: Station Hill, 1981);

Blanchot, *The Gaze of Orpheus and Other Literary Essays* (Barrytown, N.Y.: Station Hill, 1981);

Conrad Detrez, *A Weed for Burning* (New York: Harcourt, Brace, Jovanovich, 1984);

Blanchot, *When the Time Comes* (Barrytown, N.Y.: Station Hill, 1985);

Michel Butor, *The Spirit of Mediterranean Places* (Marlboro, Vermont: Marlboro, 1986);

Detrez, *Belt of Fire* (New York: Columbia University Press, 1986);

Blanchot, *The Last Man* (New York: Columbia University Press, 1987);

Anne-Marie Albiach, *Mezza Voce,* translated by Davis, Joseph Simas, Anthony Barnett, and Douglas Oliver (Sausalito, Cal.: Post-Apollo, 1988);

Michel Leiris, *Brisees: Broken Branches* (San Francisco: North Point, 1989);

Daniele Sallenave, *Phantom Life* (New York: Pantheon, 1989);

Leiris, *Scratches: Rules of the Game, I* (New York: Paragon House, 1991);

Blanchot, *The One Who Stands Apart from Me* (Barrytown, N.Y.: Station Hill, 1991);

Leiris, *Scraps: Rules of the Game, II* (New York: Paragon House, 1992);

Emmanuel Hocquard, *Aerea in the Forests of Manhattan* (Marlboro, Vermont: Marlboro, 1992).

SELECTED PERIODICAL PUBLICATIONS – UNCOLLECTED: "Coolidge's 'Mine,' " *Poetics Journal,* 3 (May 1983): 91–96;

"Some Notes on Armantrout's *Precedence,*" *Poetics Journal,* 6 (Spring 1986): 123–127.

Lydia Davis is regarded as a prose stylist of distinction, originality, and enormous promise. For example, in *Break It Down* (1986) she writes with a restraint and irony comparable to that of the so-called minimalist writers of her generation. Davis often designates the time and place of her narratives obliquely or not at all, while limiting the psychological dimension of her characters in a way that recalls the works of Samuel Beckett and Franz Kafka rather than those of Donald Barthelme or Raymond Carver. This approach has doubtless been fostered by the other literary activity for which Davis is well known – her extensive translations of such twentieth-century French authors as Jean-Paul Sartre, Maurice Blanchot, Michel Leiris, and Michel Butor.

The daughter of writers, both of whom have published stories in the *New Yorker,* Davis was born in 1947 in Northampton, Massachusetts, where her father, Robert Gorham Davis, was then a professor of modern literature at Smith College; in addition to teaching at creative-writing workshops and doing reviews, he was also the editor of a once widely used anthology of short stories, *Ten Modern Masters.* Her mother, Hope Gale Davis, is the author of *Dark Way to the Plaza,* a collection of short stories, and is a faculty member of the Radcliffe Institute.

Lydia Davis began her own writing at around age twelve and, doubtless as a result of growing up in a literary household, with the romance of such a career tempered by a sense of the hard work in store. An avid, adventurous reader, she discovered Beckett's *Malone Dies* (1951; translated, 1956) in her

Lydia Davis, circa 1986 (photograph © Marion Ettlinger)

thirteenth year. Often at the expense of not reading more-contemporary writers, Davis has returned again and again to Beckett, as well as to Kafka, whose work she discovered somewhat later in adolescence.

One of the key periods of Davis's childhood was the year she attended school in Graz, Austria, where she learned to read and write in German. This experience of having to assimilate a foreign language at more or less the same time as she was learning to read and write English emphasized for her the strangeness of linguistic conventions and must inevitably have linked the act of writing with that of translation.

Another disorienting but ultimately beneficial turn of events came when the family left Northampton's serenity for New York City, where her father began teaching at Columbia University. Davis attended the Brearley School from 1957 to 1962, then left New York for the progressive pedagogical environs of the Putney School in Vermont. There she took advantage of an exceptional music program, studying theory and violin.

At Barnard College, beginning in 1965, Davis majored in English. In the second semester of her freshman year she met and began a relationship with Paul Auster, the novelist and translator, who was studying at Columbia University. Auster introduced her to several of the French authors, including Blanchot. Her first public recognition came when a poem she composed for Barnard's "Greek Games" event was set to music and performed as the "Entrance Lyric" to the ceremonies. Davis attended a writing workshop conducted by Grace Paley and wrote two short stories, both unpublished. In the fall of her sophomore year she met the photographer Edward Steichen, who was a friend of the family. Davis spent the following academic year in London, working as a messenger at the *Manchester Guardian.* On her return to the United States in fall 1968, she resumed studies at Barnard and in the spring of her senior year published a translation of work by Blaise Cendrars in the *Columbia Review* as part of a segment of French poetry edited by Auster for that issue.

After graduating from Barnard with a B.A. in 1970, Davis took a job as an editorial assistant at W. W. Norton, translating work by Robert Delaunay in her spare time and writing a children's book that remains unpublished. In April 1971 she

BREAK IT DOWN

LYDIA DAVIS

Dust jacket for Davis's 1986 collection of short fiction, for which she received a special citation from the jury for the P.E.N./Ernest Hemingway Foundation Award

visited London, then joined Auster in Paris, where she remained based until summer 1974.

The years immediately following her graduation from college were ones of experimentation and travel, during which Davis wrote poetry as well as short fiction, traveled extensively (in Ireland, Yugoslavia, England, and the south of France), and assisted Auster in the editing of *Living Hand,* the little magazine where she first published a short story, "In a Northern Country." She got to know several artists and writers, among whom were Americans Keith and Rosemarie Waldrop, David Lehman, and Phillip Lopate, and French poets Anne-Marie Albiach, Claude Royet-Journoud, Jacques Dupin, Edmond Jabes, Andre du Bouchet, and Philippe Denis. However, it would be misleading to construe these contacts as a "circle," much less a "school" in the usual literary-historical sense. No discernible stylistic influence, manifestos, or collaborations resulted from these interactions with other writers.

Living on minimum incomes while in Paris and, later, as caretakers for an isolated house in the Var from 1973 to 1974, Davis and Auster worked at translating a variety of art books and catalogues for the Galerie Maeght. The isolation and the act of translation seem to have had the biggest impact on the short fiction she wrote during this period. Critic Edith Jarolim writes: "the formal diction [of Davis's characters] may be read as a sign of alienation of speakers who are not only out of sync with the contemporary world, but also estranged from their own language. Davis's characters sound at times like intelligent foreigners who have learned to speak correctly but have not entirely mastered colloquialism."

The title story of Davis's first small-press collection, *The Thirteenth Woman and Other Stories* (1976), is a short fable or parable in a Kafkaesque mode. The classical diction and balance, as well as the fact that no sign of modernity appears within it, lend the tale a highly literary quality that is characteristic of the volume as a whole: "In a town of twelve women there was a thirteenth. No one admitted she lived there, no mail came for her, no one spoke of her, no one asked after her, no one sold bread to her, no one bought anything from her, no one returned her glance, no one knocked on her door; the rain did not fall on her, the sun never shone on her, the day never dawned on her, the night never fell for her; for her the weeks did not pass, the years did not roll by; her house was unnumbered, her garden untended, her path not trod upon, her bed not slept in, her food not eaten, her clothes not worn; and yet in spite of all this she continued to live in the town without resenting what it did to her."

Marjorie Perloff, in her essay "Fiction as Language Game: The Hermeneutic Parables of Lydia Davis and Maxine Chernoff," describes a tendency in Davis's fiction for identity to give way "to the paramount question of logic." In this early instance, the woman's disenfranchisement seemingly hinges on the illogic of her living as the thirteenth woman in a town defined, like a set, as consisting of twelve women. In this way logical paradox is both the pretext for a gnomic statement about alienation and, more subtly, an embodiment of the ways in which language participates in the construction of social relations. Indeed, the woman's virtuous placidity is itself subverted by a final linguistic twist of fate: she is hardly to be congratulated for not resenting what the town "did to her": the abuse takes the form of neglect, of *not* doing.

The latter half of the 1970s for Davis was almost as peripatetic a period as that of the first half, with changes of address at least once a year, though she remained in the New York area. On her return to New York in summer 1974, Davis supported herself by working as a temporary secretary. She also began taking courses at Teacher's College toward a degree (never completed) in speech therapy. The poet Charles Reznikoff was among the writers Davis met once she was back in the United States, and later, during a stay in Berkeley, California, in 1976, she met George and Mary Oppen, Carl Rakosi, and Michael Palmer, poets all in some way associated with objectivism. In October 1974 she and Auster were married. In 1977, the year following the publication of *The Thirteenth Woman,* she won an Ingram Merrill Foundation fiction-writing grant of twenty-five hundred dollars.

"Safe Love" (in *Break It Down*), written shortly after the birth of her first son, Daniel, also in 1977, is a "short short story" that recalls "The Thirteenth Woman" in its exploitation of the logic of linguistic divisions, yet the preciosity of the earlier parable has been superseded by a more engaging contemporaneity and a defter use of paradox: "She was in love with her son's pediatrician. Alone out in the country – could anyone blame her."

Davis's writing is often suffused with a sardonic wit that has, however, several registers, ranging from the humorously deployed logical niceties encountered in "The Thirteenth Woman" and "Safe Love" to the more classical situational pathos of "Story," one of the stronger pieces in her second small-press volume, *Story and Other Stories* (1983), a book Joyce Carol Oates selected for the Pushcart Writer's Choice list in the *New York Times Book Review* in August 1984.

Yet even in the instance of "Story," a brief narrative of a woman's attempt to meet with her seemingly duplicitous lover, the narrator's romantic anguish is conveyed neither, as Perloff notes, through "exposition about the past nor characterization of the principals, nor, for that matter, a rendition of the narrator's stream of consciousness. The focus of 'Story' is entirely on the network of action and reaction, event and interpretation."

In the final paragraph the narrator's recounting of her confusion is a good example of Davis's distinctive manner – a lucid, ostensibly well-balanced exposition but one whose content tends, by its very rigor, to render its terms useless, to cancel them out. This feature of her work lends the prose an austere musicality as well as an odd, slightly delirious comedic effect: "The fact that he does not tell me the truth all the time makes me not sure of his truth at certain times, and then I work to figure out for myself if what he is telling me is the truth or not, and sometimes I can figure out that it's not the truth and sometimes I don't know and never know, and sometimes just because he says it to me over and over again I am convinced it is the truth because I don't believe he would repeat a lie so often." Beckett is clearly an important predecessor here; yet, as Perloff rightly points out, such prose is "charged with greater personal feeling than Beckett would allow or desire." It is this balance between several sorts of ironic formalisms and emotional urgency that Davis seems intent on striking as her career progresses.

In her personal life, with a separation from Auster in 1981 and a later divorce, the first half of the 1980s was a difficult period, a fact registered by several stories in *Break It Down*. The title story (written in 1983, when Davis was in the second of a two-year teaching stint at the University of California, San Diego) signals a startling departure from her earlier detachment. The narrator, attempting to come to terms with romantic loss, remarks, "I guess you get to a point where you look at that pain as if it were there in front of you three feet away lying in a box, an open box, in a window somewhere. It's hard and cold, like a bar of metal. You just look at it there and say, All right, I'll take it, I'll buy it. That's what it is." Another story composed in the same year, "Liminal: The Little Man," recalls Blanchot's work in Davis's exploration of the limits and thresholds of grief: "The moment when a limit is reached, where there is nothing ahead but darkness: something comes in to help that is not real. Another way all this is like madness: a mad person not helped out of his trouble by anything real begins to trust what is not real because it helps him and he needs it because real things continue not to help him."

In terms of critical recognition and grants, the 1980s were good to her. Station Hill published her highly polished, ironic portrait *Sketches for a Life of Wassilly* in 1981. After the appearance of her translation of Blanchot's *The Gaze of Orpheus and Other Literary Essays* (1981), Davis won a National Endowment for the Arts grant for the translation of a fourth book by Blanchot, *When the Time Comes* (1985). A second grant from the Ingram Merrill Foundation, this time for $6,000, allowed her to devote time to her yet-to-be-completed first novel. *Break It Down,* her largest collection to date, was widely and favorably reviewed. In May 1987 it received a special citation from the jury of the P.E.N./Ernest Hemingway Foundation Award. Over the course of the next two years she received two generous grants: a Whiting Writers' Award of $25,000 and an NEA award for fiction of $20,000.

In 1986 Davis began teaching in the Bard College interdisciplinary program called the Milton Avery Graduate School of the Arts. She married the painter Alan Cote, a member of the Bard faculty, in 1987. Davis gave birth to their son, Theo, in May of the following year. Since 1989 she has lived in Port Ewen, New York.

Davis's stories have been widely anthologized, appearing five times, beginning in 1978, in the annual *Pushcart Prize* volumes and, more recently, in two collections edited by Laura Chester, *Cradle and All* (1989) and *The Unmade Bed* (1992).

There is a poetic element in much of Davis's prose, especially the short short stories and meditations on a theme. By straining the capacity of the terms of a given reflection to perform their assigned task of clarification, she achieves a sestinalike effect that might be called "High Analytical Vertigo." In a recent piece titled "Varieties of Disturbance" this effect is much in evidence as the narrator attempts to bring the issues at hand to some sort of closure: "My husband is disturbed by my mother's refusing my brother's help and thus causing disturbance in him, and by her telling me of her disturbance and thus causing disturbance in me greater, he says, than I realize, and more often than I realize, and when he points this out it caused in me yet another disturbance different in kind and in degree from that caused in me by what mother has told me. . . ."

Formally Davis has so far displayed a virtuosic, if eclectic, range of tendencies: parable, short short story, ironic fable, essayistic meditation, and narrative approaching conventional autobiographical realism – all linked by a signature quiet, at times mordant, wit and an almost marmoreal precision. Her present concentration on her first novel suggests that autobiographical realism will be the next mode to be explored by her, though with elements of the total range of her style utilized as the occasion warrants. She also has another major collection of stories forthcoming.

References:

Edith Jarolim, "Ideas of Order," *Poetics Journal* (May 1985): 143–145;

Marjorie Perloff, "Fiction as Language Game: The Hermeneutic Parables of Lydia Davis and Maxine Chernoff," in *Breaking the Sequence* (Princeton, N. J.: Princeton University Press, 1989), pp. 199–214.

Fielding Dawson

(2 August 1930 –)

Patrick Meanor
State University of New York College at Oneonta

BOOKS: *Elizabeth Constantine* (Asheville, N.C.: Biltmore, 1955);

Thread (Woolwich, U.K.: Ferry, 1964);

An Emotional Memoir of Franz Kline (New York: Pantheon, 1967);

Krazy Kat, The Unveiling & Other Stories (Los Angeles: Black Sparrow, 1969);

The Black Mountain Book (New York: Croton, 1970; revised edition, Rocky Mount: North Carolina Wesleyan College Press, 1991);

Open Road (Los Angeles: Black Sparrow, 1970);

The Mandalay Dream (Indianapolis: Bobbs-Merrill, 1971);

The Dream/Thunder Road: Stories and Dreams, 1955–1965 (Los Angeles: Black Sparrow, 1972);

A Great Day for a Ballgame: A Conscious Love Story (Indianapolis: Bobbs-Merrill, 1973);

The Greatest Story Ever Told: A Transformation (Los Angeles: Black Sparrow, 1973);

The Sun Rises into the Sky, and Other Stories, 1952–1966 (Los Angeles: Black Sparrow, 1974);

The Man Who Changed Overnight, and Other Stories & Dreams, 1970–1974 (Santa Barbara, Cal.: Black Sparrow, 1976);

Penny Lane (Santa Barbara, Cal.: Black Sparrow, 1977);

Two Penny Lane (Santa Barbara, Cal.: Black Sparrow, 1977);

Delayed: Not Postponed, edited by Maureen Owen (New York: Telephone, 1978);

Three Penny Lane (Santa Barbara, Cal.: Black Sparrow, 1981);

Krazy Kat & 76 More: Collected Stories, 1950–1976 (Santa Barbara, Cal.: Black Sparrow, 1982);

Tiger Lilies: An American Childhood (Durham, N.C.: Duke University Press, 1984);

Virginia Dare: Stories 1976–1981 (Santa Barbara, Cal.: Black Sparrow, 1985);

Will She Understand? (Santa Rosa, Cal.: Black Sparrow, 1988);

The Trick (Santa Rosa, Cal.: Black Sparrow, 1991).

Fielding Dawson, circa 1984 (photograph by Gerard Malanga)

Fielding Dawson is one of the most prolific fiction writers in contemporary American literature. He has published well over 200 short stories, 197 of which are in his collections. Dawson is also an exhibiting artist specializing in photocollage and drawing; in his early career he was more well known for his drawings than his writing. Dawson's fiction resembles that of no other American writer. Though literary influences are detectable, and Dawson acknowledges them, no other American writer regularly produces the kind of compelling prose that Dawson does, but few other contemporary American writers are more ignored than he is. The reasons for the neglect are obvious and predictable. Dawson has resolutely refused to compromise his aesthetic standards by writing stories with clearly evident plots peopled with cleverly developed and easily recognizable characters with whom the mass of readers can identify. In short, he has refused to satisfy the demands of many of the larger publishing companies to compromise his artistic integrity by producing easily accessible stories and novels. His works are not, in today's mechanistic jargon, "reader-friendly." He is an artistic maverick. He has also suffered from not having a university affiliation or any ongoing involvement with the many writing workshops, particularly the proliferating M.F.A. programs, that many other fiction writers and poets have participated in for the last thirty years. However, he has taught from time to time at Naropa Institute in Boulder, Colorado, and in prisons – Rikers Island, Sing-Sing, Attica, and others. His committed involvement in prison writing has become so productive that he has been appointed chair of the P.E.N. Prison Writing Committee.

Critic Seymour Krim once summarized Dawson's contribution to keeping the American literary scene honest: "Writers like Fielding Dawson and presses like Black Sparrow keep American literary culture proud. Now that second-rate, automatic novelists happily prostitute themselves for credit card and Scotch whiskey ads, and the big Madison Avenue publishing houses pitch their products like every other kind of mass-market merchandise, it brings a shine to the eyes to know that not everybody in our eagerly accommodating society is ready to shape their output to the tyranny of the obvious" (*Washington Post Book World,* 1 May 1983). Philosophically and aesthetically Dawson catalogues several enemies, but as a writer he has waged his longest conflict with this "tyranny of the obvious."

In looking at his cultural and educational background, it should not come as a surprise that he has become such a sui generis artist. Fielding Dawson was born in New York City on 2 August 1930. His most influential teachers have been his mother and two father figures: the poet Charles Olson and the painter Franz Kline. Dawson's mother, Cara Alban Byars Dawson, a liberal and a

poet living in the heartland of the United States, in Kirkwood, Missouri, where the Dawsons moved when Fielding was a boy, gave him a secondhand Royal typewriter for his fifteenth birthday and challenged him to become a new William Saroyan. Fielding's father, Clarence, had died when Fielding was twelve years old, so he never had close paternal influence, a lack that he struggled with for many years until he became a student of Olson, the legendary poet and rector of Black Mountain College. While studying at Black Mountain, Dawson also became a student and close personal friend of Kline. Indeed, his first major book is *An Emotional Memoir of Franz Kline,* which Pantheon published in 1967, five years after Kline's death. The search for a father is as important a theme for Dawson as it was for James Joyce in both *Portrait of the Artist as a Young Man* (1916) and *Ulysses* (1922), and Joyce was a major influence on Dawson's writing, not only in terms of their shared paternal yearnings but, more important, in Dawson's evolving stylistic practices that have changed throughout his writing career. The words *process* and *change* are the two most important terms in Dawson's literary vocabulary. His vision of his vocation as an artist is one with the way in which he lives his life, and many of his novels and short stories are completely autobiographical in that they document in great detail in his everyday life.

Dawson's subject matter has rarely deviated, until quite recently, from his constant concern with the formulation and development of the artist. All his work can be best understood as "portraits of the artist," or *Künstlerromans.* What differentiates Dawson's work from that of other *Künstlerroman* artists, such as Thomas Mann and D. H. Lawrence, is that the vocation of the artist and the problems connected with that calling are never far distant from Dawson's consciousness. Yet all his obsessions, either those connected with his childhood and adolescence, his early and troubled love affairs and marriage, or his bouts with alcohol, are detectable in his writing much of the time. He refuses to take the easy way out, and having worked through some of his more self-destructive personal struggles, he does not include them as active agents in his consciousness because to him they are obvious. His writing includes, in a massive way, the content of the unconscious and his necessary journeys there. In responding to a reader's enthusiasm for one of his most popular stories, *The Greatest Story Ever Told* (1973), which documents his first serious teenage sexual encounter, he explained (in a 22 March 1992 letter) the importance of the unconscious: "The

Hate

I'm not the kind of guy who kills for pleasure ... it's pleasure I guess, because I hate her.

There she is coming across the street ..... remember ....

there she was I was crazy about her, that black velvet dress ..... those suede shoes ..... a thin string of pearls around her neck .... gardenias .... her eyes danced with the music and the full moon made a halo around her radiant hair ..... then he came along ...... remember ....

the street's as black as pitch ...... only a head of light ..... when she hits it I'll fire ..... there she hit ... a halo around her radiant hair made by a street lamp ..... remember .... Bang !!!!

Page from an unpublished story that Dawson wrote on 13 February 1946, while he was in high school (by permission of Fielding Dawson)

GREATEST story is the discovery of the world which can only happen in the discovery of oneself, which is only possible in the discovery of consciousness, only possible by going into the unconscious, which is where I was, writing that story . . . in my unconscious, and going higher and thinking that this is the greatest *ever!*" His statement mirrors perfectly the incredibly quick turn of Dawson's style. His writing not only reflects but, more accurately, enacts the way he sees the world. His "artistic vision" is literally his physical perception of the world as it articulates itself in his consciousness somewhat like artists Jackson Pollock and Kline expressed their vision of reality as it came into their consciousnesses. Some critics have called their work "action painting." Dawson's style could be seen as "action writing."

Dawson's work frequently embodies a whole area of his past, as seen through recurring motifs — such as light and the falls of children — which have been consistently present in his work from the beginning. Dawson's mythic "falls" always contain a double significance. They are painful in that they demand an immediate reorganization of the psyche to adjust to the new and often painful consciousness that comes into being. Falls are also usually involved in a necessary journey into the unconscious, that most dangerously exhilarating journey that authentic artists must take to effect change in their work. Dawson's willingness to make that journey accounts in no small way for his difficult style but also for the palpable thrill for the reader in following him on some of the most intricately constructed sentences in American prose since those of Henry James, a writer to whom Dawson has often been compared.

One of the reasons that Dawson's work has not attained a large, popular audience is that reading it requires total concentration. In that sense he is, as many critics and fellow writers would agree, a writer's writer whose works demand the same kind of attention that Walter Abish's or Guy Davenport's densely constructed fictions require. Dawson's voice is so compelling that the writer Russell Banks has suggested it is responsible "for what has become the dominant mode of contemporary American short-story writing." This mode includes the works of such powerful writers as Raymond Carver, Richard Ford, and Tobias Wolff. Dawson's short fictions resemble experimental, open-form parables that enact, rather than describe, the energy felt in the turn of his imagination as it enfolds experience. Olson called this new kind of modernism "kinetic art." All his works strive toward bringing

his life-in-art to coherence, from the early struggles "fighting for articulation" within fragmented searches for "self " in *Open Road* (1970) to his *Penny Lane* trilogy (1977–1981) and what he calls his "first complete book," *Tiger Lilies* (1984). *Tiger Lilies,* more fully than any previous work, traces the genesis of his creative imagination from infancy through childhood and nurturing relationships with his mother, his uncle Essex, his sister, four aunts, and his teachers and friends in grade school and high school in Kirkwood.

Dawson's arrival at a reasonably comfortable relationship with the world of his childhood was won only with great effort over a thirty-year period, a troubled time that he first mapped out in his stories of the early 1950s. His first published story, "Father" (*Black Mountain College Review,* June 1951; collected in *Krazy Kat & 76 More,* 1982), is written in a relentless stream-of-consciousness mode with recurrent motifs of Oedipal cries and apocalyptic echoes of the burning walls of Troy and Agamemnon's demise. Ironically the voice in "Father" is a feminine one, that of a consuming, destructive mother/goddess. The Kafkaesque monologue concludes with a parody of the prayer "Our Father," and it includes the first appearance in print of Dawson's obsession with his sense of self and his relationships with women. Since Dawson's memories of his father are erratic, his early fictive voices are sometimes female, sometimes male. He was raised in a household of six women: his mother, four unmarried aunts, and his sister. After he met the father figures Olson and Kline, his fictive voice began to change. *An Emotional Memoir of Franz Kline* documents in painful detail his second "father," and *The Black Mountain Book* (1970) concerns the enormous influence that his third "father," Olson, had on both his emotional and artistic life. Most of his early stories examine various aspects of "the father" and Dawson's attempts to understand what that concept means in his life.

Early stories in his first collection of fiction, *Krazy Kat, The Unveiling & Other Stories* (1969), such as "Krazy Kat," "The Highwayman," "The Nature of the Universe," and "Captain America," all deal with Dawson's progressive attempts to break away from obsessions with identity and to create a fictive voice that will allow him to become an artist. "Krazy Kat" is his name for William Blake's "Tiger," and the father/teacher in Dawson's story enables his students to compare the nature of God the Father in a Christian sense to an archetypal God — the creative force of the imagination — to see that both are fictive approximations of an ineffable

Cover for Dawson's fourth collection of short fiction (1976), stories
on the theme of change

mystery that can never be named or comprehended. "The Highwayman" domesticates the same issue and moves the discussion of fatherhood into a scenario in which a father permits his daughter to begin her life as though it were a movie made by her father narrating his daughter's life. The father becomes the man who creates the "highway" for her and releases her to live a life of her own. In "The Nature of the Universe" Dawson has developed more than one fictive voice. The three voices speaking in this elaborately constructed story are that of a college boy (obviously from Black Mountain College), his Missouri hometown voice, and a sophisticated New York City voice. The primary voice is that of a young man living in New York City and remembering the college he went to as if it were Eden itself, with intermittent reflections of his childhood in Missouri. More important, though, is that the last half of the story traces an evolving artistic consciousness from influences encountered at Black Mountain, such as Joe Fiore and Kline, who taught him how to "see" the world in many different ways.

Kline is actually in the story in New York with the young artist figure. "The Nature of the Universe" is Dawson's first youthful and affectionate "memoir," a form he uses in three of his major books and a form that enabled him to make strides in bringing together various thematic concerns that recur throughout his early work and many of his later stories.

"Captain America" is the first story in which Dawson deals with the frustration of being adjacent to the alluring powers of the artist but unable to participate in them. Dawson uses the names of various suburbs near Kirkwood to name his characters. The female artist in this story, with whom the narrator, Webster Groves, has an affair, is named simply Valley, an artist who embodies in both a highly sexual and slightly frightening way the mysteries of the artistic imagination. Groves can only grasp Valley's wrist in a strangely vampiric gesture, hoping for a kind of transfusion that might engender an awakening of his own artistic powers. He is an artist manqué, listening to her breathing as she sleeps after their lovemaking and attending in awe those creative powers within her that she seems to breathe forth, "wondering if it might come from another thing, the thing from the old world – or a more knowing world where the dream sound of a distant trumpet call and the invisible presence of the unknown soldier were the flesh and blood, the universe, the stuff of reality within which men and women existed. The hum, like the tune of doom – of despair and loneliness and death, the language of an unknown man who fell in an unknown field in an unchartered time." The title of the story, "Captain America," demonstrates Dawson's ability to transform the mundane into the mythically significant. As he explains in the introduction to *The Sun Rises into the Sky* (1974), "The writer must know the rhythm of the mundane as the origin of suspense." In "Captain America" that rhythm is a threshold of the archetypal power of myth not only to universalize experience but also to reconnect the artist to primal energies from which a highly mechanized society excludes him. Valley represents the feminine source of creativity, one of Dawson's major themes. In *The Greatest Story Ever Told* Dawson's first (unnamed) sexual lover and crucial threshold figure is, significantly, from Valley Park.

The first major threshold story in Dawson's early writing career is *Thread* (1964), which is set in the early 1960s. Most critics agree that this story (republished in *Krazy Kat, The Unveiling & Other Stories*) brings together all the motifs that continue to surface as typical Dawsonian themes. Dawson's first wife, Barbara Kraft Dawson (a psychologist he married in 1962 and divorced in 1976), had given him two books for his thirtieth birthday, and he claims they changed his life: Carl G. Jung's *The Archetypes and the Collective Unconscious* (1934) and *Aion* (1951). *Thread* is Dawson's first intensely Jungian story, showing the various threads of childhood, adolescence, and his early years as an artist. It is one of his most brilliant expressions of the agony and terror of those years. Very long sentences come into his writing as form mirrors content in a massive Jungian stream of consciousness that interweaves figures from childhood, remembrances of dreams, the terrible loss of his father, Dawson's recognition of his own fractured self, and the attraction and dread of his homosexual yearnings. Most important, however, *Thread* is the first direct treatment in print of his ambivalent anima.

Much of Dawson's works throughout the 1960s and 1970s are variations on this insistent theme, from the mirror-image figures in many of his collages to the double figures of Jack and Flash in

Open Road and Lucky and Blaze in the *Penny Lane* novels. Few writers have captured the lacerating agony of selves desperately trying to find unity and rest in an authentic knowledge of not who they are but, more disturbingly, *what* they are. Dawson's frantic search moves beyond the safe categories of "identity crises." His artistic gifts not only do not offer him relief from his ontological crisis but make his conflicts even more hopelessly complex, as evident in *Thread:* "tell me a story, once again, and again, and then again I encounter myself and the shifting constructions of the selves of myself within turmoil, the man or woman on the streets of a novel are the writer and his world pattern within him. ..." The narrator finds temporary relief as he and his wife leave an old friend's apartment after an ostensibly "normal" evening. The call to the vocation of the artist has crystallized, for a moment, into an epiphany in which he realizes the purpose and function of his creative imagination: "without me, these people and all the relative and separate selves are objective of one another, through me they appear and look at each other." The thread of fictive continuity creates an atemporal reality that brings order out of the pain and chaos of human experience and defines that experience.

Several important events in Dawson's life occurred in the 1960s. On 23 February 1962 he had married Barbara Kraft, with Kline as best man, and moved into the East 19th Street loft in New York, where he continues to live. While the Dawsons were on their honeymoon visiting the poet Robert Creeley in New Mexico, Kline had a heart attack in Provincetown. Kline's death in May at age fifty-one was a devastating blow for Dawson. He stopped painting, and three years later, because of depression and anxiety over Kline's death, which had brought on bouts of drinking, he began psychotherapy with New York psychiatrist Dr. Arthur Lefford. Though Lefford was an eclectic therapist, his approach through dialogue appealed to Dawson's emerging Jungian fictive voices. Many of his stories of the 1960s and 1970s show evidence of his ongoing therapy.

Two important stories from that period – "The Triangle on the Jungle Wall" and "The Word" (both in *Krazy Kat & 76 More, The Unveiling & Other Stories*) – reveal Dawson's fictive voice undergoing important changes; the ostensible subject of the stories is the Vietnam War. "The Triangle on the Jungle Wall" is connected to an earlier story from the 1950s, "Soldier's Road" (also in the 1969 *Krazy Kat* volume); both feature the characters Phil and Nathan. "Soldier's Road" focuses on their leav-

ing the army after service in post–World War II
Germany and eagerly looking forward to returning
to their American homes. Phil quickly descends into
compulsive womanizing and alcoholic blackouts
that produce guilt of the most painful kind. His
need to find a woman who might function as a caretaker becomes the major quest of the story. "The
Triangle on the Jungle Wall" shows Phil and Nathan in combat in Vietnam. Dawson's style has
changed to a cinematic narrative presenting
Nathan's unsuccessful attempt to save Phil after he
has been riddled with Vietcong machine-gun fire.
Nathan then travels to Columbus, Ohio, to try to
comfort Phil's grieving parents. Nathan unconsciously retraces Phil's barroom journeys in Columbus and then hurries back to his home in Brooklyn,
New York. As he begins drinking heavily in his
neighborhood bar, he reexperiences the scene of
Phil's death when he sees his own face cinematically
projected on the wall of the tavern, which has become a jungle wall in Vietnam. He begins firing an
imaginary machine gun. Dawson's manipulation of
various kinds of projection creates several levels of
meaning. Nathan tries to destroy a projected image
of himself, an act that becomes a metaphor of the
American penchant for entering into self-destructive
global conflicts.

In a later story, "The Word" (in *Krazy Kat,*
1969) Dawson projects backward in time to 1941 in
Detroit, where the physical conception of a male
child takes place. In the second and longer section
of the story, the first paragraph vividly portrays the
horrible napalm immolation of a young man and his
entire military unit. The young man is the son who
had been conceived twenty years earlier. The word
napalm is never used, but the father is the salesman
who sold the formula for napalm to the military.

The Vietnam stories show that Dawson has
been able to extricate himself from the tormented
self-consciousness and agonizing pain of divided
selves, which were the primary content of many of
his earliest stories in *Krazy Kat, The Unveiling & Other
Stories.* His ability to use cinematic techniques enabled him to inhabit the consciousness of characters
such as Phil and Nathan and to escape a narcissistic
self-concern that bordered on solipsism.

Two stories of the 1960s reveal other radical
changes in Dawson's fictional techniques and his
concept of consciousness. These important changes
were a direct result of the psychotherapeutic sessions he was undergoing, which enabled him to
move away from total subjectivism, a self-reflexive
solipsism that had reached its apogee in *Thread.*
Since Dawson was actively engaged in his own di-

*Cover for Dawson's 1982 book, which includes his first published
story, "Father," a Kafkaesque, stream-of-
consciousness monologue*

rect process of individuation, his writing began to
participate in the same activity. Some critics have
called these "therapeutic stories" or "process parables" because their narrative methods have little to
do with "stories" or "plots" in any conventional
way. The emerging parable becomes its own form,
which remains open at all times. "The Sun Rises
into the Sky" and "The Face in the Casket" (in *The
Sun Rises into the Sky*) with "the writer" as the main
observer witnessing the events going on around
him, successfully move Dawson's intensely psychological stories into an objective world. Both these
stories showed Dawson that he ("the writer") could
witness experience as an observer and could observe himself participating in the everyday, mundane events of his life, thus releasing him from the
terrible isolation of his stultifying self-consciousness. These stories are his first efforts at objective

writing and show him assuming a genuine authorial voice that simultaneously enabled him to move away from merely subjective fictive possibilities and into an increasingly larger and more satisfying arena of human activity.

The character called the "Christmas Officer" in "The Face in the Casket" represents a therapeutic voice asking necessary questions that will release "the writer" from any residual guilt he may feel for the suicide of a friend's wife. These stories are the first of Dawson's in which a feminine voice confronts a masculine voice as an equal; the feminine voice in both stories functions as another therapeutic presence challenging "the writer" and forcing him to confront himself and his real motives. Both stories contain similar subtexts on the deaths of fathers. The main image in "The Face in the Casket" is both that of Dawson's mentor "father" Kline and Dawson's defunct artistic talents that he abandoned when he married. In "The Sun Rises into the Sky" the character called "the writer" experiences frightening "winter dreams" in which he sees himself as a monk hermetically producing fictions that are continuously undermined by the grief over and loss of his dead father; a recurrent Ingmar Bergman–like spider becomes an impotent phantom from the past. The writer's renewed creativity the next day demonstrates to him that his art continuously redeems him and shows him that the imagination is a means of "grace" that enables him to participate in the process of his own creations. The actual therapy Dawson underwent and the therapeutic stories he wrote became crucial threshold experiences that enabled him to write his first full-length book, the highly controversial *An Emotional Memoir of Franz Kline.*

By 1974 Dawson had published over ninety-seven stories in three collections. Though some were written during the 1950s, they were not published until the late 1960s and early 1970s. In addition to the many stories pouring forth from Dawson's fecund imagination, he had also published his first novel, *Open Road,* in 1970. In 1971 Bobbs-Merrill published what some critics consider his finest single work, *The Mandalay Dream.* Though Dawson calls *The Mandalay Dream* a novel, the first twelve chapters could easily have been published as separate short stories. The longest (concluding) section, "The Mandalay Dream," is one of Dawson's most coherent novellas, seventy-one pages of very specific autobiographical material. Some of the characters in "The Mandalay Dream" had previously appeared as unnamed presences in *Thread.* In "The Mandalay Dream" they are presented as people but with their names different from those of the people

on whom Dawson based them. In *Tiger Lilies* some of these characters appear again as their literal selves with their real names.

One of the most compelling aspects of Dawson's literary career is the ingenious way he reuses the same material over and over. His ability to modify his formal procedures comes from his commitment to change, which, in turn, enables him to revise earlier materials to fit the ever-changing demands of his psyche. Since his life is changing, he must change his fictions, a literary situation that continuously frustrates Dawson's critics, who want to be able to label him permanently and judge his work accordingly. What they have called Dawson's inability to create clearly recognizable "novels" and "short stories," thus faulting his formal abilities, demonstrates their inability to detect the emerging trajectory of his aesthetic and literary proposals. Up until his last three books, he had written introductions that point out exactly where his work had come from and where it was going. A thorough understanding and analysis of Dawson's work demands that one view the work as a whole, as a large collage or canvas that creates new connections as each part is added; and in that sense his work is as much of a "field" as that of other Black Mountain artists, such as Kline, Pollack, Olson, and Robert Duncan. The collages Dawson created for the majority of his books become additional visual texts that further expand the range and dimensions of the written texts. A familiarity with all his work is necessary for a fair appraisal of Dawson's contribution to contemporary American fiction.

Dawson's fourth short-story collection, *The Man Who Changed Overnight* (1976) comprises twenty new stories and dreams, and change is the major theme of all of them. Important shifts in consciousness – that is, in the way Dawson perceives himself in relation to "others" – surface in these stories. Though the theme is change, many of these stories are clearer than some of his early, somewhat turgid, parables. One of the reasons for this new clarity is that Dawson has modified the "therapeutic" first-person "I," formerly the literal Fielding Dawson. Though he uses "I" throughout the volume, it has become a fictive persona or a projected "I" that allows Dawson more freedom in both point of view and tone. What many of his readers consider his finest story, *The Greatest Story Ever Told* (the title being a sardonic reference to Fulton Oursler's 1949 best-selling fictionalized biography of Jesus Christ), which is reprinted in *The Man Who Changed Overnight,* demonstrates a radical movement away from Dawson's earlier obsessive adolescent sexuality to-

*Cover for Dawson's 1991 collection, which includes "Her Royal," an homage to his mother, who gave him her typewriter for his fifteenth
birthday and challenged him to become a successful writer*

ward an emerging maturity. He is able, with this newly created maturity resulting from therapy, to recognize not only the discovery of consciousness as "the greatest story" but also to show what the writer does with the content of that discovery. The young, desperately sexual character Fee discovers in this story that the "girl from Valley Park" is more than an archetypal embodiment of the creative process depicted in "Captain America" twenty years earlier. She is also more than just a sexual figure for him to respond to and, thus, understand his own frustrations as an artist. The ninth-grade girl he is sitting behind in a study hall in April 1947 "had the worst reputation of any girl in school." She is real, not just a sexual projection of a sixteen-year-old boy who still jokes around with his buddies with sexual baseball metaphors.

In discovering the "real" he also discovers "the other," and with the other comes the world, a fact that allows Dawson to deepen, extend, and elaborate his new role of "author-as-witness." Once he is able to disengage himself from the egotistical "I" and envision himself as part of a world that oth-

ers also inhabit, he can clearly observe himself creating a genuine "portrait of the artist." It is the "otherness" of the girl from Valley Park that establishes an objective world in which "she rides with a boy named Al, who had long artistic midnight blue hair and drove his glistening black four-door white-walled Lincoln a hundred around turns and one ten on straightaways. I envied and feared him; but he fascinated me, too, because he liked me, because I was an artist." This statement is Dawson's first recognition that someone besides himself acknowledges and respects him as an artist. Though "the recognition of a recognition" may appear to complicate fictive voices and psychological levels, it demonstrates the changing voice of Dawson as he moves away from adolescent narcissism into the voice of maturity. The story, too, is about becoming mature and recognizing that it is time to stop talking about sex as if it were a baseball game. The young Fee has lost his virginity and experienced the joys and fears of passion, an experience that utterly transforms him. He has encountered the frightening aspects of the sublime through sexual passion and entered the darkness of a mystery that he never expected. That fall into knowledge enables him to experience "the sacred" in its non-Judeo-Christian aspects so that he enters a Dionysian consciousness, a sexual one, that he simultaneously fears and embraces. He understands why he fears and envies Al and the girl from Valley Park: they unconsciously inhabit ways of being in the world that he, as an overly conscious artist, finds bewildering.

In the stories in *The Man Who Changed Overnight* Dawson has also established clear lines of communication among several levels of voices, so that dialogues within his psyche exchange crucial information that helps him understand his life. In a scene in *The Greatest Story Ever Told,* Fee and the girl from Valley Park have nowhere to go to have sex but his bedroom at home, where at any moment either his mother or his Aunt Mary could walk in and catch them. But in the midst of this dangerous but exciting tension, he says: "we laughed and I thought Oh to Hell with it, let the whole WORLD walk in, my consciousness was altogether on her, and we lay on my bed, and felt each other, and the power of it." In Dawson's new fiction-writing strategies, he has literally let the whole world enter his stories. At the moment of orgasm during Fee's first sexual experience, which combines passion and love, he is anticipating telling his buddies all about "it": "Wow!, so this is it! Wait'll I tell Mac – it's EASY! and the voice said, *No, no, tell no one, for this is yours to keep,* and I felt humility and suddenly flashed out of consciousness." His experience with the sublime has finally blasted the narcissist out of himself and enabled him to "fall" into an objective world waiting for him to experience it.

Two stories from *The Man Who Changed Overnight,* which might be better called "spatial parables," are "Icarus" and "The Singing Man," which illustrate the dramatic way Dawson's compositional method develops even more deeply his aesthetic role of author-as-witness. Both these stories take place in his Manhattan neighborhood, where an unnamed narrator not only witnesses but participates in the psychosocial dynamics of that particular place. "Icarus," one of the Dawson's most painterly parables, visually traces the arrival on the local scene of a very "beautiful" young man of about sixteen. Dawson deliberately uses the word *beautiful* for its shock effect. The story is a brilliant study in painterly perspective because Dawson records the unspoken responses of three other males who exchange looks that acknowledge their shared attraction to the boy. There are no words of dialogue spoken throughout the two-page vignette. Dawson has reached the point in his writing process where he can tap into the mythic resonance that a scene evokes and transform what is ostensibly a purely local, ten-second exchange of pregnant glances into a silent but significant reenactment of the fall of Icarus. The anonymous observer (who is unaware of the mythic scene he is participating in) is the Daedalus/father figure who wants to protect the young man from the Hades that awaits him in Union Square. However, a reader can easily transpose characters within the local scene as understood through myth so that the threatening "sun/son" heat is not Union Square but the clear homosexual attraction that the observer acknowledges within himself and spots in the furtive glances of three other men.

"The Singing Man" is less visual than aural/oral. Dawson, who had suffered a sometimes debilitating stammer and temporary deafness after a near-fatal accident as a child, presents a middle-aged African-American delivery man, who sings with complete abandon, without a trace of self-consciousness, an emotional condition that Dawson had been seeking for many years. Because "the singing man" lacks any sense of political correctness, he sings songs such as "Old Man River," which creates quiet havoc in the racially mixed neighborhood: "the man who sings is the object of a lot of response and the victim of a million silent and spoken jokes, but there is no stopping him, because he really loves to sing; he's been singing for years, and Puerto Rican and black guys more or less let him be, in their way, which is not completely. Secretly they like him, envy him, admire him, and learn from him, because they can tell how far removed they are from their own when his singing embarrasses them, so in reaction to their own embarrassment in awe, 'SING it, baby,' and laugh, 'WAIL!' " Of course, the major envy in the story is that of the narrator, whose responses suggest that he would sacrifice anything to be able to operate in the world with the "singing man's" lack of self-consciousness.

Another important development in *The Man Who Changed Overnight* is that Dawson has finally been able to understand the significance of the past and its proper place in his life and, as significantly, in his imagination. In the story "A Slow Roll Over Haystacks" the fictive voice of an anonymous writer meets a childhood acquaintance from his hometown in Missouri but emphatically states that they do not talk about their childhood, a subject that had occupied a good deal of Dawson's earlier

F. Dawson 12/11/90

Under The Tree
~~The car on~~ The Hill

~~Never would~~ *Never Did*

~~Prison Spots~~ *In the first week of the last month of semester,
came into classroom, took a test, + watched
the teacher w/ sharp eyes. Soon the involved
in answering — even wrote essays*

A new
The young inmate/was ~~so~~ smart, *short,* ~~and~~ charming, ~~so~~
~~inxixnth~~ good looking that ~~atxfixsx~~ ~~Errol~~ *teacher* did a double-
take, losing himself in the space of the classroom, ~~think-~~
~~ing~~ ~~asxhexlisteningxtexthexyoungsterx~~ *xed* they were ~~free~~
~~andxstanding~~ on a street corner, while he listened to ~~Avelt~~
& The vivid
~~the inmate's~~ tale of woe, ~~being~~ told with such verve and
wit, ~~andxbrightxeyes~~ sparkling eyes, and intense/ *angry* amuse-
teacher   *beyond himself.*
ment, he — ~~Errol~~ — caught up, swept away, ~~breathless...~~

"... you know that street that goes up a hill overlooking the river, near the academy?"

teacher
"Oh yes," ~~Errol~~ smiled, glancing at the other guys,
seated in their desks, listening, ~~and also~~ *smiling.*

"Well," continued the youth, "that's where I saw
her car, you know - the trees along the sidewalk?"

Guys nodded.

"Yes." *teachs.*

"Well, that's where I saw her car, parked. I knew
her car."

- 1 -

Page from the typescript for an unpublished story (by permission of Fielding Dawson)

fiction. A refreshing note has entered Dawson's work which enables him to treat the past as the past: his work has become consciously reflective. Dawson's continued therapy enabled him to mine the content of his unconscious, which, in turn, made it possible to understand the past and its relationship to the present.

The three novels of the *Penny Lane* series show that Dawson has finally rid himself of the therapeutic first-person narrator. The majority of these novels consists of brilliantly rendered barroom dialogue between a poet named Guy Blaze and a writer named Lucky. While the major activity throughout these novels is intense and prolonged drinking, it is evident that Guy and Lucky are projections of Dawson's divided imagination of poet and writer. In the *Penny Lane* series Dawson began to develop postmodern techniques involving a narrator who steps back from his work as the writer and permits the reader to observe in a direct way the actual creation of the narrative. The reader becomes an active participant, a co-conspirator in the creation of the work. Dawson's masterpiece in this genre, commonly known as metafiction, is the story "Kid Stuff," in *Will She Understand?* (1988).

Dawson's deep descent into the subjectivity of the early work and his tenaciously successful efforts to transcend prolonged adolescence throughout *The Man Who Changed Overnight* and the *Penny Lane* series resulted in the objectivity of what he calls his first complete book, *Tiger Lilies*. Gone are any remnants of nostalgic yearning for a lost childhood or failed adolescent loves. Only as a result of Dawson's successful attempts to transform the past into an atemporal condition in "A Slow Roll Over Haystacks," and to include himself as a fictive character interacting and responding with other silent participants in "Icarus," was he able to "re-member" the past – that is, to put it together with coherence, accuracy, and truth. Dawson himself once remarked that this book could only have been written by a mature adult.

During the composition of *Tiger Lilies* Dawson received a substantial grant that enabled him to construct a large space in his loft in which he could pursue his painting career, a vital activity that he had been unable to develop for over twenty years. Two traumatic incidents during the years 1980 to 1984 were the deaths of Lefford, his therapist, and the painter Philip Guston, his close friend and mentor.

His next full-length collection of new stories was *Virginia Dare* (1985), which includes stories written between 1976 and 1981. Many of his photo collages appear throughout *Virginia Dare,* making this collection an experiment with intertextual weaving of the pictorial with the verbal, a kind of paratactic juxtaposition of word and image. One of the most intriguing stories in *Virginia Dare* is "The Secret Circle," which is, among other things, an homage to all the mystery and detective writers whose work he has read, such as Dashiell Hammett, Raymond Chandler, Georges Simenon, and Arthur Conan Doyle. It is also one of Dawson's most successful stories written in the third person, a point of view that came slowly to him over many years. "The Secret Circle" introduces some fresh thematic concerns in his work. Though the major theme is, once again, the writing process, Dawson can talk about it in the third person and, therefore, in an objective way. The story is also about writer's block, plagiarism, mysterious barroom scenes à la Henry James, and the gnostic information that artists share. A story about writer's block became for Dawson, ironically, a story that his own writer's block would not permit him to finish quickly. He confesses that he had difficulty with the ending of this story. Only by delving further into the mysterious paths that the story led him through was he able to invent a satisfactory ending.

Other stories from *Virginia Dare* are also examples of successful third-person narrations without any overt intrusions by Dawson or a thinly veiled first-person narrator. "Psychology," for example, is a story written with Katherine Mansfield's 1918 story of the same name directly in mind; Dawson's story functions as a kind of intertextual continuation and elaboration of her story. As he says in the introduction, *Virginia Dare* "draws to a close my involvement with the first person and autobiography."

The story "You" is a piece that defies categorization. In its first part a writer half awakens from a short sleep and, in a hypnagogic condition, begins to listen to voices. The voices in his head are exchanging views on techniques of revision that include suggestions for more effective punctuation, better transitions between and within paragraphs, decisions about how many spaces to use and where commas are needed, and so on. The reader finds himself in the middle of a postmodern syntactical battleground. Dawson peoples his parable with the elements of grammar and syntax as characters. This piece is one of Dawson's clearest examples of a process parable.

More radical changes come into Dawson's work in his 1988 collection of thirty-two short stories titled *Will She Understand?* Gone for good are seminostalgic vignettes of his midwestern childhood and adolescence. Banks distinguishes between Dawson's earlier works as memories or memoirs

and his newer work: "He wants to recreate *all* of history, forwards *and* backwards. Thus his obsessive return to the act of remembering instead of to the memory itself." Another major departure in Dawson's method is the introduction of more postmodern strategies, even though similar ones had been used by Joyce, John Dos Passos, and William Faulkner. Continuing from two stories from *Virginia Dare,* "You" and "Him," Dawson merges the medium with the subject: the creation of the fiction has become the subject of the fiction. The writing has become self-reflexive but in ways that move away from the dangers of solipsistic subjectivism. In one of his most radically new stories, "Kid Stuff," the self-reflexivity emphasizes the "word" as the linguistic medium through which "reality" comes into being. He is no longer

interested in any so-called objective reality as subjectmatter.

"Kid Stuff " is Dawson's most inclusive story in his later work: it brings together all his obsessions, fears, loves, and sorrows and interweaves them into a classic postmodern story. The full title is "Kid Stuff: A Novel, in Outline with Notes," and the story consists of three chapters: "The Deep Sleep," "What Brenda Saw," and "Eager Beaver." The story starts with a love scene between two unnamed teenage boys, known as the shortstop and the second baseman by their mutual friend and admirer Brenda, who spies on them from across the street through her infrared binoculars. Later she refers to them as Dracula and Snow White. Both these naively homosexual young men, who later marry and assume "normal" heterosexual life-styles, first appear in the story "Him" in *Virginia*

Dare: subtle ghosts of Lucky and Blaze, Nathan and Phil, and Flash and Jack.

Brenda, a feminine version of the youthful Fee as Peeping Tom in *The Mandalay Dream,* tries to follow the careers of her three dearest friends from high school. Virgil, a jazz trumpeter, becomes the focus of the story. Dawson brings together thematic strands from his earlier work: he concludes his music stories with a story about a musician and bids farewell to his high-school stories, particularly those involving his ambivalent homosexual impulses. He also pays homage to his heroes from the Big Band era, such as Stan Kenton and Woody Herman. Dawson's guide in this journey (a journey that moves east rather than the traditional west) is Virgil, a not-altogether-subtle allusion to Dante's guide through the *Inferno.* There are unmistakable infernal images in which "Brenda-Beatrice" returns from a trip to Japan to her Midwest home to attempt desperately to relive her past youth, as she hears the song "I'll Be Seeing You" echoing in her memory. The story is Dawson's ironic and bitter farewell to his hectic youth, to what he had finally found words for: "Kid Stuff."

Dawson's 1991 collection of stories and photo collages is *The Trick.* Though some of the strongest stories in this collection are based on autobiographical incidents, Dawson has steadfastly maintained a third-person narrative voice throughout. The style shows not the slightest hint of nostalgic reverie. Rather, it documents the maladies of the quotidian with sometimes angry humor. His tone has changed due in great part to his teaching prisoners and to his serious illness, throat cancer. Though his frightening bout with cancer has subsided, the anger in some stories came from maddening frustrations with the medical bureaucracy, a power elite that resembles the power structure of the prison system. Many of these stories are visceral – from the dental pain of "The Trick" through the agonizing hand surgery in "In Red" to the dramatic scenes in "Any Questions From the Balcony?"

"Any Questions From the Balcony?" moves beyond Dawson's early stories that portray the fictive voice as author-as-witness and author-as-observer. Anger energizes "Any Questions" and shows Dawson's role changing to author-on-attack. A biting, comic satire enters his style in this story as a third-person narrator boldly stands up to medical authority. A new angry self has been discovered to such a degree that anger becomes part of his compositional mode. However, the anger is not blinding, and it allows for wit, warmth, and affection. The satire he employs comes out of classic eighteenth-century social consciousness while the prose style

has evolved into a kind of neoclassical, pre-Freudian freshness that belies the psychological subtexts it so comically probes. In many ways the "tricks" alluded to in the title story apply to the tricks that those in power play on those under their control until the oppressed let the oppressors know that they have become aware of their plight. The "trick" is, however, for the oppressed to keep the oppressors thinking that they are the only ones who understand and control the rules of the game. The laughter in these stories is often bitterly redemptive.

One of the most moving stories in *The Trick,* not involved in irony of narration, is "Her Royal." This story is a postmodern, self-reflexive example of a *Künstlerroman* in that it documents the genesis of a young man's call to the vocation of writing. A mother's example as a writer herself has inspired her son to use the mother's Royal typewriter to type his first verbal expressions. Years later, as the writer, Leland, returns home to clean out his deceased mother's home, he comes across that old Royal typewriter, sits down at it, and stares at the keys: "She gave her gift to me, he thought. And saw his mother, and – there! – his father, both, looking at each other . . . so he leaned forward, in the faint, sweet machine oil scent . . . held his hands above the round, silver-rimmed keys, and where none but her fingers had been save once by his as a boy, and his father's the next day, he touched the mystery of her memory."

The story is, of course, mostly autobiographical in that it was written shortly after the death of Dawson's mother in April 1988. It also documents the actual event during which his mother had given him, in 1945, an old Royal typewriter for his fifteenth birthday and declaimed: "What the world needs is a new Saroyan!"

Dawson's first story is titled "Father," and one of his latest is a loving homage to his mother as not only his actual mother but also the informing genesis of his imagination. Much has changed from Dawson's early representations of women as mythic creatures, threatening and dangerous. He has obviously been able to break through his earlier obsessions and can now write about them with maturity and deep affection.

Some major writers have paid homage to Dawson's contribution to modern American letters. The poet and fiction writer Robert Kelly states unequivocally: "What Dawson has is a spectacular sense of how people talk, & that gives him a sureness on the waves of communication – he can find in that ocean an utter fiction, make it be there for him and for us. I trust his *ear* more than any other novelist now working." Banks, himself a respected novelist and short-story writer, states why Dawson is considered a writer's writer: "More than any other writer I can think of, Dawson strikes me as a writer who wants to locate and raise up into consciousness those rare, exhilarating moments that look in two directions at once . . . he's not after a Joycean epiphany so much as a moment which, recounted, creates both what preceded that moment and what must follow from it. . . . This is a risky business. . . . We may get simple sentimentality, which now and then, we do. Or, as is more frequently the case, we may be let into a huge imaginative act that makes our own imaginations more truly, powerfully available to us."

Few contemporary American short-story writers have created as complete a world as Fielding Dawson. Though his early stories struggled with the insistent demons of adolescent identity crises, his work continued to change and has reached a level that only the most accomplished writers attain: mythopoesis. Dawson is able to evoke deep mythic resonance in the most specific details of the mundane, an achievement that only a handful of contemporary artists have realized. He not only knows "the rhythm of the mundane as the origin of suspense" but enacts that rhythm to transform the mundane into some of the most compelling prose in contemporary American writing.

Interview:

Barry Alpert, "An Interview with Fielding Dawson," *Vort*, 4 (Fall 1973): 3–21.

Bibliography:

George F. Butterick, *Fielding Dawson: A Checklist of His Writings* (Storrs: University of Connecticut Library, 1976).

References:

Barry Alpert, "Dawson's Jungian Strategies," *Vort*, 4 (Fall 1973): 41–42;

Don Byrd, "Fielding Dawson and the Uses of Memory," *Vort*, 4 (Fall 1973): 39–40;

John Cech, "Musings on Missouri," *Washington Post*, 6 August 1984, p. C12;

Edmund Fuller, "Fielding Dawson: A Child's Garden of Memories," *Wall Street Journal*, 25 September 1984, p. 26;

Charlotte Gafford, "Fielding Dawson's 'Certain Overflow Willingness,'" *Iowa Review*, 5 (Summer 1974): 82–87;

Paul Metcalf, "Fielding Dawson," *Vort*, 4 (Fall 1973): 36–39;

Eric Mottram, "A First Appreciation of Fielding Dawson," *Vort*, 4 (Fall 1973): 43–53;

Donald Phelps, "Fielding Dawson with the News," *Caterpillar*, 13 (October 1970): 150–152.

Papers:

Most of Dawson's early manuscripts are in the Rare Books and Manuscript Collection at the University of Connecticut.

Stephen Dixon
(6 June 1936 –)

Jerome Klinkowitz
University of Northern Iowa

BOOKS: *No Relief* (Ann Arbor, Mich.: Street Fiction, 1976);
Work (Ann Arbor, Mich.: Street Fiction, 1977);
Too Late (New York: Harper & Row, 1978);
Quite Contrary: The Mary and Newt Story (New York: Harper & Row, 1979);
14 Stories (Baltimore & London: Johns Hopkins University Press, 1980);
Movies (San Francisco: North Point, 1983);
Time to Go (Baltimore & London: Johns Hopkins University Press, 1984);
Fall & Rise (San Francisco: North Point, 1985);
Garbage (New York: Cane Hill, 1988);
The Play and Other Stories (Minneapolis: Coffee House, 1988);
Love and Will (Latham, N.Y.: British American, 1989);
All Gone (Baltimore & London: Johns Hopkins University Press, 1990);
Friends: More Will and Magna Stories (Santa Maria, Cal.: Asylum Arts, 1990);
Frog (Latham, N.Y.: British American, 1991);
Long Made Short (Baltimore: Johns Hopkins University Press, 1993).

OTHER: "The New Era," "Ray," "Grace Calls," and "Making a Break," in *Making a Break,* edited by Robert and Rochelle Bonazzi (Austin, Brooklyn & Mexico City: Latitudes, 1975), pp. 193–243.

Stephen Dixon, circa 1979 (photograph by Jim Kalett)

Stephen Dixon is one of the most prolific and stylistically important authors of short fiction in modern American literature, with over four hundred stories published in magazines from the *Atlantic Monthly* and *Playboy* to small-press journals such as *Fiction International* and the *North American Review*. In terms of quality and impact his fiction resolves problems of representation and mimesis without turning back to the straightforward realism that postmodern theorists and practitioners have so effectively questioned. His ten collections are among the most intelligently and artistically organized short-story volumes since Flannery O'Connor's *Everything That Rises Must Converge* (1965).

Born Stephen Ditchik in Brooklyn, New York, on 6 June 1936, Dixon is the son of Abraham (a dentist) and Florence Ditchik (an interior decorator). They moved with him to Manhattan when he was one year old. A dental practice was set up in part of a brownstone where the family lived; when Stephen began first grade, his parents changed their children's surname to Dixon while retaining Ditchik for themselves. Despite this change in nominal identity, which made it necessary for him to learn a new last name even as he faced the challenge of beginning school, there is a stability to Dixon's family history that goes against untrue stereotypes of big-city turbulence and anonymity.

Dixon's formal education was completed in New York with a B.A. degree from City College in 1958. His major was international relations, and his first career began when he was a newsman in Washington, D.C., with the News Associates and Radio Press. By 1961 he had returned to New York City, where he worked both as a news editor for CBS news and as an editor for two detective magazines published by Fawcett Publications. The academic year of 1964–1965 was spent studying creative writing at Stanford University on a Wallace Stegner Fellowship, and stories by Dixon began appearing in *Paris Review, Per Se,* and the *Atlantic Monthly.* This progression from communications work to fiction writing was financed by the dozens of part-time and fill-in jobs as a waiter, salesperson, substitute teacher, bartender, actor, and tour leader. Such work bought Dixon the time to write and also to draw; he spent part of 1964 sketching in Paris and becoming sufficiently accomplished to do the cover art for his 1980 collection, *14 Stories.* Although publishing in the best commercial magazines from the start, Dixon found a market for the bulk of his short stories in the world of small-press publishing, where in addition to being a frequent contributor to little magazines he made his debut in book form as the featured writer in editors Robert and Rochelle Bonazzi's *Making a Break* in 1975. From there Dixon's path led through other small presses to university-press publication and commercial volumes, and he began teaching in creative-writing programs, initially for the 1979–1980 academic year at New York University's School of Continuing Education and then, beginning in fall 1980, as an assistant professor, associate professor, and currently professor and chairman for the Writing Seminars at Johns Hopkins University. In 1982 he married Anne Frydman, a teacher and translator of Russian literary works; with Frydman he became the parent of two daughters, Sophia and Antonia. Family residences are maintained in Baltimore and New York City, with summers spent on the coast of Maine. Dixon's recognitions have included an O. Henry Award and Pushcart Prize (both in 1977), a Guggenheim Fellowship (1984–1985), and being a finalist for the National Book Award in 1991 (for his integrated collection of nov-

Dust jacket for Dixon's 1980 book, for which he drew the cover illustration

els, short stories, and fragments, *Frog,* published that year).

Looking back from Dixon's present eminence to his first appearances in the world of small-press book publishing, one can see not just the promise but also solid evidence of the qualities that would distinguish his later work. Norman Stock, writing in *Library Journal* (December 1975), singled out Dixon's section in *Making a Break* as being the book's most impressive and noted his "deadpan descriptions of physical and emotional experience" as rising above the more typical "surrealistic fantasies" common to the short stories of other authors the Bonazzis included in their anthology. Dixon's four contributions cover thematic interests he examines in future collections: relationships of couples, complexities of even the simplest jobs, and ways in which information so easily becomes misinformation or even disinformation. "Ray" introduces violence, but less as a subject than as a generative technique. Because a woman, struck over the head by a boyfriend who wishes to kill her, mutters in her semiconsciousness the appellation "Love," a course of action develops that is totally different from what might have otherwise been expected. Surprised by the way his victim addresses him, the attacker is prompted to seek help, but even in this pursuit his progress is redirected by other texts and messages he encounters.

Dixon's four-story section in *Making a Break* shows how an openness to possibilities can create an entire world of fiction, and his first book-length collection, *No Relief* (1976), suggests how a technical approach to even the most mundane topics can yield a virtual infinity of actions. Setting the tone is the first story, "Mac in Love" (for which Dixon was awarded his O. Henry and Pushcart prizes): the supposedly simple business of a lover being turned away at the door develops into an almost endless series of deferrals. Mac, the narrator, tries every ploy to stay – not just physical tactics such as putting his foot in the door but devising a linguistic strategy by which he systematically expands mundane requests until their grammar generates a sentence so expansive and potentially unlimited that only a policeman's club can stop it. Oblique relationships and the impossibility of any sense of closure are also evident in "Rose" and "No Relief," for Dixon's strategy as a writer is to remind readers how every statement invites its own modification (if not attempted retraction, which leads in turn to other complications).

No Relief drew national attention to Dixon's work. In the *New York Times Book Review* (3 July 1977), Julia O'Faolain praised his "pulse of life" but worried about his "deliberate . . . bad taste." More cogent and fair was Frederick H. Guidry's observation in the *Christian Science Monitor* (10 January 1977): "The truly universalizing element . . . is the sense of helpless grappling with boy-girl relationships, of friendships crumbling despite frantic efforts to keep things going, of communication taking place but failing to do the job it was hoped to do." That *No Relief* was an important contribution to the ongoing tradition of American literature was noted in the pages of *Library Journal* (15 March 1977) by the influential novelist Clarence Major, who compared Dixon's incremental repetitions to those of Gertrude Stein, and in the *South Carolina Review* (November 1978) by Thomas A. Stumpf, who praised Dixon for transposing the theories of French deconstructive thinkers into entertaining and riveting fiction.

In 1977 Street Fiction Press capitalized on Dixon's success by publishing his novel *Work,* a hard-hitting, pointed narrative much in the style of his short stories, especially in his ability to let the rigmarole of petty job duties produce an endless trail of involvements. Dixon then moved into the world of commercial publishing with his novel *Too Late* (1978) and a collection of integrated short stories, *Quite Contrary: The Mary and Newt Story* (1979). *Too Late* is a Dixon story writ large, the tale of how endless complications result when the woman friend of the narrator leaves a movie because of its violence; the narrator stays for the end and gets home to find she has failed to return there. *Quite Contrary* is equally effective because of Dixon's understanding that a couple's continual pattern of breaking up and then getting back together again not only constitutes their mode of existence but defines a significant part of their identities as persons. Being good copy for each other's stories, some published, some just imagined as ongoing fantasies, are what the two are for each other at best and at worst. Even their sexuality can be called into question, as a friend does at one point early on: "Nah, you two are never really through. You're a pair: Tom and Jerry, Biff and Bang. You just tell yourselves you're through to make your sex better and your lives more mythic and poetic and to repeatedly renew those first two beatific weeks you went through."

Although the novel *Too Late* garnered good reviews, *Quite Contrary* met resistance. For example, in *Library Journal* (15 June 1979) Mary A. Pradt tried to appreciate the stylistic and structural effect of Dixon's writing but concluded that "though usually witty, Dixon does go on." However, Lee K. Abbott, surveying this collection along with Dixon's books that precede and follow it, acknowledged in the *South Carolina Review* (Fall 1981) that there is indeed a method to what more hasty reviewers might consider madness.

With *14 Stories* Dixon earned a wide breadth of intelligent and positive reviews. Among the best stories are several that encapsulate his most idiosyncratic themes and techniques: how the codes of behavior in big-city life, once violated, can lead to quandaries that even the most assiduously categorical thinking cannot solve ("Streets"); how the vulnerability of having to take a job for which one is not suited invites even further trouble, all of which follows a system of mad systematization of its own ("The Security Guard"); and, most touchingly, how loneliness and estrangement from historical time can break one's heart even as it empowers one's imagination ("Ann from the Street"). Yet topicality of theme is never the main interest in a Dixon story. Indeed, focusing exclusively on such matters can be distracting and misleading, for what readers already

Dixon with his daughter Sophia in Baltimore, February 1983

know as the pressures of urban living, stresses of job seeking and work, and emotional anguishing over lost or never-had relationships are less interesting than what Dixon does with this body of knowledge.

What he does is particularly evident in "Streets" and again in "The Signing." In both stories the narrator confronts a problem that in a more conventionally organized tale would constitute the ending rather than the beginning, or even (as in "The Signing") the final words of a narrative rather than the first. Within the first two pages of "Streets" a woman and two men are in a violent altercation that leaves all three seriously if not mortally injured. From the ending of their story the narrator begins his, wondering not just how to help but whom to help, engaging himself in a system of moral triage as he tries (hopelessly) to determine which of the three merits prompt attention not in terms of physical need but of ethical guilt. From here on everything becomes an infernal machine generating one self-questioning system after another: is the little girl sent to phone for help sufficiently responsible or not, is she eight years old or ten, will the hospital send three ambulances, two, or just one (for some carry three patients)? Getting nowhere and deciding to seek help himself, the narrator blunders into another confrontation in which he becomes an injured third party, an event that initiates another series of endless questions that can end only when he closes his eyes. Only a mechanical ending can stop the progress of events, for their progress has been fueled by his unstoppable complication of perception, a ceaseless rhythm of statement and almost immediate erasure, retraction, or modification that begins with the word *or* in the story's second sentence.

"The Signing" follows the same pattern, starting with what for a traditional writer might be a good ending – "My Wife dies. Now I'm alone. I kiss her hands and leave the hospital room" – and then continuing through four pages of events that frustrate this persistent attempt at closure, ending only when the narrator submits to a mechanical guiding of his hand in signing a document he found impossible to deal with earlier. In between he runs afoul of not just the hospital's documents law but other regulations (including the rule requiring exact change for bus fare and the rules security guards must follow). Yet the regulations are not the theme but rather the technique, for they have generated and sustained the action.

What some critics call minimalism, as in the short stories of Ann Beattie and Raymond Carver, does not work as a fully accurate label for Dixon's work. While his narratives do begin with a minimal set of references, his practice is to expand the possibilities of such initially slight material into a universe of actions.

Neither are Dixon's stories technically cold. Although their humor is often based on the inanity of human needs caught up in and mangled by the infernal machinery of systematics, his narratives can also use this same facility to convey great sensitivity and emotion, as in "Ann from the Street," in which the narrator, meeting a woman he had known many years ago and wondering what life with her could have been like, imagines her returning to the mate that could have been him and saying that "she met someone I know on the street. I'd say 'Who?' and she'd say 'You.'" This postmodern style of syntax carries a heartfelt sense of loss and loneliness. In a similar manner "The Sub" consists of sixteen pages of fantasy about an unknown woman seen on the street. When finally confronted, she offhandedly disqualifies herself as the credible basis for any of these imaginative raptures. But that does not stop the narrator, who simply shifts grammatical moods from the declarative to the subjunctive and operative, using *ifs* and *mights* and *woulds* and *coulds* to take himself into a future packed with the loveliest, nicest, and most wholesome delights, all of which depend on the bedrock syntax of the final sentence, the only kind of closure such linguistic circumstances allow: "I think this will happen one day though I don't think the woman it will happen with will be her."

Like a jazz soloist improvising exuberantly, yet within the contours of melody and progressions of chords, Dixon uses the structures of language and circumstance to produce effective prose. The passages and larger strategies that distinguish *14 Stories* brought Dixon to the attention of James Lasdun, who in the *Times Literary Supplement* (29 May 1981) praised the delightfully manic quality and hilarious acceleration of events in the collection. "The people in these stories speak with that disarming frankness which to the English ear sounds so characteristic of American speech," Lasdun added. "Here again, though, there is a compression that makes even a simple sentence unusually revealing of character and values."

In the 1980s Dixon's work won him an increasingly distinguished series of awards, including a citation from the American Academy of Arts and Letters and a Guggenheim Fellowship. The stories of *Movies* (1983) show Dixon taking the system-producing predicaments of his protagonists from *14 Stories* and treating them in more specifically human dimensions. "Not Charles" takes the concerns of "The Signing" – losing a family member, this time a child, to death in a hospital, while being distracted by hospital business – and expresses them more personally in terms of frustration and grief. Reviewer Peter Brickebank (*Carolina Quarterly,* Spring 1984) took his cue from the book's title in praising Dixon's achievement in narrating what would otherwise be "the all too familiar events of a store robbery" in the story "Layaways": "When one young man tries to fight back, he manages to get his mother killed, only to repeat his mistake later with his best friend. He proves only that screen heroism has no place in our murky urban badlands. This repetition of error, failure to learn from experience, is one that makes for so much humor and humanity in Dixon's characters."

In the title story of *Time to Go* (1984) Dixon achieves master status in handling the techniques of emotion. The narrative situation appears to be a casual one but is in fact brilliantly conceived. A son is out shopping with his father for a prenuptial present for the son's fiancée. As the narrator (the son) enters stores and asks to look at necklaces, the older man prompts and hectors him, telling him to shop here, not there; do not tell the salesperson you like something but pretend you do not and make it look as if you are leaning toward something cheaper; and so forth. This first part is quietly comic, for readers likely sympathize with the son's (if not the clerks') embarrassment. But then, when the fiancée is along on the next trip, to buy wedding rings, the father's presence becomes something that could be outrageous. It is not outrageous, though, because he does not make the slightest impression on the fiancée or the salespeople: he is not there physically, just emotionally in the narrator's thoughts. Dead for years, he nevertheless still speaks in memory, guiding the son's actions and decisions much like the voice of conscience. But then, after the father's bodily absence is established, Dixon takes his story one step further in the conclusion. At the wedding reception, crowded with friends and family, the new groom wonders where his father might be. In the passages that precede, the old man has been increasingly intrusive, even if unnoticed by anyone except the narrator; now, however, his imagined presence is more than welcome, for rather than bothering his son about petty and personal details he is crying – cry-

So many Janes
My many Janes

MANY JANES
8/3/91 — 8/23/91
Sedgwick, M

Give me a line. One night when I was sleeping
a dream appeared to me. Wrong. A line. I woke up,
got my socks on, put on my watch, strode down the
hall, went to the toilet, had breakfast, dressed.
or dressed and had breakfast, made love to my wife,
or made love to my wife, went to the toilet, dressed,
had breakfast, read a book first, made love to my
wife, it's night, before i woke, im in bed, wife
comes to bed, come to bed, wife, she does, love,
sleep, wake up, toilet, dressed, breakfast, work.
Forgot my watch. and i call home and she says
it's right here where you left it and i say where?
and she says byon the nighttable by your side of the
bed where you always leave it when you go to sleep
and i say, i say what? i dont say ship it, since
im only ten minutes away by car, i say please imagine
it on yy wrist and she says thats silly and i say
hold it in your palm, close your eyes and imagine it
on my left write and she says ok and next thing i
know, thirty seconds at oeast, it isnt on my wrist.
im in bed, preparing to go to work, toilet, dressed,
dont forget to shave, downstairs, get the iids up
first, make them breakfast, no wife, she died years
ago, just me and the kids, kids, get up, breakfast,
and i dont hear anything, kids, come on, you have to
get to school, i dont want to be late again, no
rwaloy from them, i call their names, knock on their
door, go in, theyre both sleeping, pull up the ahde,
kiss each of them on the forehead, rub their shulders
a little, they stir, i say school, up, breakfast,
long sleeve shirts today, it feels bhilly out, and

Page from the typescript for Dixon's story "Many Janes," published in Glimmer Train, *Winter 1992 (by permission of Stephen Dixon)*

ing the same tears of happiness that cloud the narrator's own eyes.

Such natural integrations of theme and technique distinguish Dixon's strongest work from the 1980s. The fully organic nature of a story such as "Time to Go" proves expandable to great length in *Fall & Rise* (1985), a novel that maintains riveting interest even though its action covers a very short time period and range of geography: the nine or ten hours between the time the narrator meets (ever so fleetingly) a woman at a party and (after a night of diverting experiences) seeks refuge at her apartment just before dawn the next morning. In the novel *Garbage* (1988) Dixon uses half the number of words to tell of a time period covering a much longer period (weeks if not months), yet the book is equally compelling, as the narrator tells how some gangsters try to dictate the terms of his doing business. The short stories collected in *The Play and Other Stories* (1988) recall "Ray," proving that Dixon's talent for generating a maximum of effect from a minimum of referential materials has been a consistent feature of his canon. "The Rescuer" is a virtuoso display of such ability, based on the opening line: "He hears people screaming, looks at them, looks at where they're looking and pointing, and sees a child standing on a chair next to a balcony railing about ten stories up." Everything that follows is a response to or modification of that information. A great deal of action results, but all of it is predicated on factors introduced in the initial statement. Like much of Dixon's prose, the statement and all others that follow are in the present tense and phrased in a way that suggests the narrator's eyes quickly taking note of things. Though reminiscent of Samuel Beckett, Dixon is not satisfied with meaningless action; important business, matters of life and death, transpire in his stories. While dedicated to the observance of surface details, his narrators can never be mistaken for those of Alain Robbe-Grillet or other *nouveau romanciers* (writers of the "new novel") who transcribe without making judgments; judgments, especially mistaken ones, are often the energy that propels Dixon's narratives. If a literary analogue is necessary, it would be Peter Handke, the German-language author whose fiction Dixon has admired. In novels such as *Der Chinese des Schmerzes* (1983; translated as *Across*, 1986) and *Nachmittag eines Schriftstellers* (1987; translated as *The Afternoon of a Writer*, 1989) Handke practices the same attentive handling of detail, a semiological ability to appreciate the signs of existence for their own material pleasures as well as for the meaning they convey. Dedicated metafictionists might concentrate on just the former, while the literature of unexamined realism passes more quickly to the latter.

In Dixon's collection *All Gone* (1990) the productive energy comes from information itself, particularly as narrative circumstances transpose it into misinformation and disinformation. In "The Student" a cabdriver is taken hostage and forced to take his passenger on a ridiculous and ultimately destructive drive. Instead of being rescued, the driver is arrested, indicted, convicted, and imprisoned as the culprit, victimized by various systems all along the way. His revenge, therefore, is to spend part of his after-prison life giving misinformation to a researcher, making that researcher happy by telling him what he wants to hear. "All Gone" follows a woman's search for two killers, another trail of mis- and disinformation that becomes an existence in itself, just as the daughters in "On the Beach" tell preposterous stories about their late father in order to keep a sense of his memory alive. "The Batterer," like "The Student," features another narrator/protagonist whom the system, in its stereotypical assumptions, treats as the aggressor rather than the victim he is. Or is he? By the end of the eighteen stories, every one of them structured by the terms of information transmittal and reception, the reader will wonder, for the effect of hearing such protestations again and again throws not just the system into question but the speaker as well. Dixon's short stories, like deconstructive philosophy, launch a gentle but persistent inquiry into matters previously assumed to be beyond question.

A major critical departure in Dixon's reputation came not in response to his stories alone or even collected but to the ways, beginning with the second half of *Time to Go* in 1984, that his literary vision began to be organized and expressed in terms of narrative cycles. This trend was noted from the start by Patricia Blake, who wrote in *Time* magazine (13 August 1984) that "Much of the satiric power" in Dixon's work "springs from his reversals of sexual stereotypes. His women tend to be aggressive, and his standard male character is at best foolishly romantic. Yet the final cycle of stories [in *Time to Go*] suggests that a wimp can turn into a mensch. For the first time in the Dixon canon his male character gets the girl. In the title story he actually marries her, in spite of an imagined, ironic commentary on his courtship by his late father. The story 'Wheels' lovingly tells of the baby that is born of the marriage. In one affecting and indeed surprisingly beautiful scene, the man, in diapering his child, is reminded of a time when he nursed his dying, incontinent father." Unlike other reviewers, Blake was able to recognize the second section of *Time to Go* for what it is: the beginning of not just a new world of topical interest in Dixon's repertoire, but a new way of handling and presenting his stories. In the 1980s Dixon devoted at least some of his energies to this cycle of stories. The Will-and-Magna stories that begin in *Time to Go* continue as parts of *Love and Will* (1989), fill an entire short volume in *Friends: More Will and Magna Stories* (1990), and provide the model for another cyclic narrative in *Frog*.

Will Taub, a middle-aged writer, courts, marries, and has children with Magna. Although a chronology can be observed in the cycle's broader sweep, especially from book to book, it is never a strict one; both Will and Magna remember the past and anticipate the future. As always there is Dixon's habitual questioning and reconsiderations, as in Will's imagining a potential "End of Magna" in *Time to Go*: "She might think," the story begins. "Well, she might think. Yes? She might think I'm not good enough for her, though not so much in those words. Those were the words my father used." That a rhythm to their existence began as early as the late 1970s is evident in one of the stories of *Love and Will,* first published in the Spring 1980 issue of *Boundary 2,* "Said," which begins and continues with an artful turn of maximal minimalism:

> He said, she said. She left the room, he followed her. He said, she said. She locked herself in the bathroom, he slammed the door with his fists. He said. She said nothing. He said. He slammed the door with his fists, kicked the door bottom. She said, he said, she said. He batted the door with his shoulder, went into the kitchen, got a screwdriver, returned and started unscrewing the bathroom doorknob. She said.

The simple actions convey the effect as obviously as the paint on the canvas of an abstract-expressionist artist. The rhythms of the couple's relationship generate narratives, as is apparent in the only collection devoted exclusively to their relationship, *Friends,* where Will goes about being a writer and Magna speculates on her womanhood and her own family's past, while the two of them balance this circus of the mind in motion with their identity as a couple.

Will as writer, Magna as reader – this situation, initially suggested in *Love and Will* (in "Magna . . . Reading"), can be the provocation for some Beckettian gamesmanship: Will trying to write more new stuff before she catches up with the old stuff, an ideal as perfectly impossible as a per-petual motion machine yet functionally generative of yet another text, while Magna strives to finish this never-ending narrative so that, one supposes, she might begin her own. *Friends* itself, however, employs the unity of a self-contained story cycle to take this sense of Beckettian characters going on against all odds and place it firmly within the boundaries and constraints and even snares of language itself. Meeting another woman just months before his and Magna's wedding, Will finds himself trapped within a style of dialogue that prevents an easy escape; as a result, a narrative goes on where even the narrator would prefer that it stop ("Magna Out of Earshot").

With the publication of *Frog* in 1991 Dixon reached a new plateau in both achievement and recognition. The book owes something to the cyclic nature of the Will-and-Magna stories, though *Frog* features individually characterized people: Howard Tetch, Denise (the woman who becomes his wife), and their daughters Olivia and Eva. There is a cyclic variation to the form as well, for the book has an initial section of fourteen short stories, followed by a novella ("Frog Dies," in which the possibility and potential aftermath of the protagonist's death is speculated on), two more short stories, a novel ("Frog's Mom"), another novella ("Frog's Sister"), a novel-length assemblage of everything else about the protagonist and his life ("Frog Fragments"), and a concluding story ("Frog"), which brings the cycle to closure by revealing the origin of the name Frog, an appellation Howard is given by the narrator but which derives from a pet turtle to whom Howard shows great mercy, an act that empowers him to be the central focus and origin of perception in all these fictions.

Frog, without ignoring or contradicting the axioms of deconstruction, shows just how much can be offered in the way of constructing an interpretation of life. By starting off with an amusing story about how Frog is unable to find Franz Kafka's grave in Prague – and is instead hoodwinked by tour guides and cemetery guards who smugly mock such an attempt – Dixon assures his reader that this will not be another Philip Roth narrative, that no modernist authority need ground Dixon's fictive constructions. Instead he wishes to present a multitude of possibilities, an endless series of readings, rereadings, retractions, and counterreadings. There are seemingly self-generated narratives as well written as any in his canon. "Frog Dances," for example, begins with the protagonist walking past an apartment, seeing through an open window that a man is apparently dancing with a baby, and vowing from this momentary experience finally to settle down, get married, and become a father so he can dance like that; by an amazing persistence he does and finds himself later dancing just this way before the window – which he quickly covers, lest he and the baby be seen. There are also terrifying stories of loss and uncertainty, of information assumed to be solid but then thrown into devastating confusion, as in "Frog Takes a Swim," where a child is lost and, against all dictates of reason and reality, never found. In another story she is back, never having left – but, as Dixon lets the reader know, it is just that: another story. The novels and novellas do what longer narratives conventionally do: expand and extend subjects and techniques. But here it happens all within the covers of one book. Seeing a short-story writer intersperse novels among his growing shelf of collections, as Dixon has done from the start of his career, always prompts questions about interrelation of form and development of topics and methods. In *Frog* those questions are not only invited but are answered.

Reviewer Steven Moore advised readers of the *Washington Post Book World* (19 January 1992) that *Frog* fit well in a literary world whose dimensions had been stretched to the presumed limit by James Joyce's *Finnegans Wake* (1939): "Dixon is called an 'experimental realist,' but readers who are scared off by the e-word (or by evocations of *Finnegans Wake*) can rest assured that *Frog* is easy reading, too easy maybe, often requiring no more effort than would be needed listening to a voluble stranger in a bar telling a long story about how he met his wife, or sitting on the couch with an aged aunt turning the pages of a photo album and telling the stories behind each picture." These qualities are, for Moore as for any knowledgeable critic of postmodern fiction, elements of praise, for they are essences of storytelling that can survive the most rigorous deconstruction.

Stephen Dixon's importance, then, is having taken short fiction through decades of vigorous testing and having helped it to remain a viable mode of literary expression and to grow in ways suggested by deconstructive challenges. Dixon understands that certain transparencies of realism have been thrown into doubt, but from that doubt he creates a perfectly usable and functionally insightful strategy of fictive narration.

Interviews:

John Kelly, "Writing as an Art without Compromise," *Baltimore Sun,* 22 July 1984, pp. 1F, 8F–9F;

Heidi Williams, "Stephen Dixon: 'A Man of Letters,'" *Preview: Arts and Entertainment* (Bar Harbor, Maine), 10–17 August 1987, pp. 6–7, 15;

Paul Mandelbaum, "Dangerous Obsessions," *Johns Hopkins Magazine,* 61 (April 1989): 14–19;

Tim Warren, "Stephen Dixon: A Writer Obsessed with his Craft," *Baltimore Sun,* 31 April 1989, pp. 8F, 11F, 13F–15F.

References:

Greg Boyd, "The Story's Story: A Letter to Stephen Dixon," in his *Balzac's Dolls and Other Essays, Studies, and Literary Sketches.* (Daphne, Ala.: Légèreté, 1987), pp. 131–138;

Walter Cummins, "Story Worlds," *Literary Review,* 17 (Winter 1982): 462–472;

Jerome Klinkowitz, *The Self-Apparent Word: Fiction as Language / Language as Fiction* (Carbondale: Southern Illinois University Press, 1984), pp. 95–108, 122–124, 136–137;

Klinkowitz, "Stephen Dixon: Experimental Realism," *North American Review,* 266 (March 1981): 54–56;

Klinkowitz, *Structuring the Void: The Struggle for Subject in Contemporary American Fiction* (Durham, N.C.: Duke University Press, 1992), pp. 8–14, 165–167, 171–173;

Richard Martin, "The Critic as Entertainer: Ten Digressions and a Diversion on Stereotypes and Innovations," *Amerikastudien / American Studies* (Munich), 30 (1985): 425–428;

Arthur M. Saltzman, "To See the World in a Grain of Sand: Expanding Literary Minimalism," *Contemporary Literature,* 31 (Winter 1990): 423–433.

Papers:

The Johns Hopkins University Library holds a collection of Dixon's manuscripts.

Coleman Dowell

(29 May 1925 – 3 August 1985)

Kevin Lanahan
State University of New York at Albany

BOOKS: *One of the Children Is Crying* (New York: Random House, 1968); republished as *The Grass Dies* (London: Cassell, 1968);

Mrs. October Was Here (New York: New Directions, 1974);

Island People (New York: New Directions, 1976);

Too Much Flesh and Jabez (New York: New Directions, 1977);

White on Black on White (Woodstock, Vt.: Countryman, 1983);

The Silver Swanne (New York: Grenfell, 1983);

The Houses of Children, edited by Bradford Morrow (New York: Weidenfeld & Nicolson, 1987).

PLAY PRODUCTIONS: *The Tattooed Countess,* adapted from the Carl Van Vechten novel, New York, Barbizon-Plaza Theater, May 1961;

Eve of the Green Grass, New York, Chelsea Art Theater, 1965.

Coleman Dowell's short stories, as is much of his work, are difficult to contextualize, shatter prior conceptions of what fiction should encompass, and break away from previous fictive forms. Some of the stories include a rich, crafted Gothicism, others a compelling surrealism, and still others an expertly timed lyricism. Dowell's characters are multidimensional, sometimes moving through the stories at metafictional levels. They are always reacting to the alienation of self, attempting to understand flawed beauty, and desperately striving to focus on the numerous splintered fragments of their fractured lives.

Throughout Dowell's writing career, three journals published most of his short fiction, now collected in *The Houses of Children* (1987). This collection draws together stories from *New Directions: An International Anthology of Prose and Poetry, Ambit,* and *Conjunctions.* Dowell's stories also appeared occasionally in *Harper's Magazine, Kentucky Renaissance, ADENA,* and the *Review of Contemporary Fiction. The Houses of Children* is described in a postscript by its

Coleman Dowell and his dog Daisy

editor, Bradford Morrow, as a "masterly, unique book of 'great weight' . . . concerned with the pursuit of fresh orderings." Among others, Dowell's fiction has been compared to the work of William Faulkner, because of his regionalistic personifications of the South, and James Joyce due to his unconventional, postmodernist approach to language, though Dowell also had an uncompromising and inimitable style and authorial approach.

One of six children, he was born on 29 May 1925 in Adairville, Kentucky, to Morda and Beulah Vilett Dowell. Morda, a farmer and avid fan of folk tunes, introduced Coleman to music, a passion that enabled him to pursue a career composing musicals for the theater. One of his aunts had collected an enormous and intellectually inspiring library, a resource that encouraged him to read and write literature. From this early experience Dowell's writing was admittedly influenced by the works of William Makepeace Thackeray, Oliver Goldsmith, Henry Fielding, Thomas Hardy, Nathaniel Hawthorne, the Brontës, and Marcel Proust.

Dowell spent his childhood on his family's farm in rural southern Kentucky during the years of the Depression. Though his family never felt the immediate effects of the bad economy, Dowell was witness to much of the poverty and decay. At age fourteen, just as he entered Simpson County High School, Dowell converted to Catholicism, though only for the self-described reason that his Catholic friends in Kentucky "made it sound like fun and games." Dowell, the second youngest of the family grew up feeling alienated. His relationship with his father lacked any real closeness or mutual understanding, and he spent most of his time in his grandmother's presence, reading, playing music, and grooming himself as an autodidact.

As Dowell grew older, he became a strikingly handsome man and, coupled with his musical talents, hoped to make a career for himself in the theater. Because of some early interest in spiritualism, he sought the advice of a palmist, who predicted that he would soon receive a letter that would change his life and bring him success. The letter alluded to by the palmist did, in fact, arrive from a book salesman in New York City. The salesman had heard some of Dowell's music compositions and had set up an audition for the aspiring actor/writer/musician. On the day of the Kentucky Derby in May 1950, Dowell left for New York, and upon arrival he declared, "Well, I'm home."

Almost immediately Dowell met Tennessee Williams and spent the following four days with the well-known playwright. Some twenty years later Williams offered ringing praise for Dowell's fiction but was not able to recall the initial visit. Dowell worked part-time as a model; his first full-time job in New York was as a songwriter for the Dumont Television program "Once Upon A Tune" (1950–1953). After the program's demise, Dowell collaborated with John LaTouche on the abortive musical "Ah Wilderness!" This experience marked the beginning of Dowell's increasing disillusionment with

the theater and his string of missed shots at fame. Seven years after moving to New York, in January 1957 Dowell was introduced to the writer Carl Van Vechten and soon after was admitted to the high-profile Van Vechten circle. These years and the stories surrounding such celebrities are satirized in Dowell's yet-to-be published "A Star Bright Lie: Coleman Dowell's Theatrical Memoirs."

His career as a composer came to an impasse when his adaptation of Van Vechten's 1924 novel *The Tattooed Countess* closed to unfavorable reviews at the Barbizon-Plaza Theater during May 1961. Dowell did make another attempt at the theater but was unhappy with the Chelsea Art Theater production of his play, *Eve of the Green Grass*, starring Kim Hunter, in 1965. Then Dowell turned to fiction.

The palmist he had consulted while living in Kentucky had warned him that success would be latent and that any recognition for his efforts would be hard won. The success he had attained in the theater-and-music arena was, at best, moderate and short-lived. As Edmund White wrote in the introduction to Dowell's theater memoirs, "the theater and television had corrupted him because they'd given him a hit-or-flop mentality and taught him success means big bucks and sidewalk recognition." Though Dowell displayed a natural talent for writing, and his first dramatic attempts at fiction were lauded by the literary world, he still had a yearning for more commercial and critical success.

Dowell's first novel *One of the Children Is Crying* (1968) did receive favorable critical reviews and was hailed as a masterpiece. Yet, asked to comment on such high praise for his fiction, Dowell would give an unaffected reply and shrug off any implied importance of the reviews because public literary fame, sales, and money were lacking.

He continued to write, however, producing four other novels: *Mrs. October Was Here* (1974), *Island People* (1976), *Too Much Flesh and Jabez* (1977), and *White on Black on White* (1983). Though each differs from the others in style and subject, as John Kuehl and Linda Kandel Kuehl note in the *Review of Contemporary Fiction* (Fall 1987), these books are not developmental nor indicative of Dowell's intellectual or artistic progress. As Dowell explained to the Kuehls: "while I was writing *One of the Children Is Crying*, I started *Too Much Flesh and Jabez*, finished *One of the Children*, gave up *Jabez* and started *Island People*, stopped that and wrote all of *Mrs. October Was Here* in six months, went back to *Island People*, finished it then went back to *Jabez*. That's the only way I can work." This artistic process seems to be indicative of Dowell's neurotic and fragmented life-

Dowell in New York City, 12 February 1957 (photograph by Carl Van Vechten; by permission of Joseph Solomon, the Estate of Carl Van Vechten)

style – his bisexuality and split personality. Dowell was tormented by the idea that a person is not one strict, homogeneous being, that within him many faces are worn, many voices are used, and many fictions and fantasies are played out.

Dowell's works are also not developmental due to the fact that he had spent his early years cultivating his stance on those subjects he would carry into his fictive worlds. The novels are a culmination of his intellectual and artistic spirit, essentially after it had been composed. Dowell, who began writing fiction late in life, created an unpatterned yet highly intricate pastiche or montage of fiction that can be seen as a sketch of a hypersensitive individual dealing with the context and definition of his entire preadult and adult life.

The Houses of Children is thus divided into two sections, the first detailing Dowell's exploration into the awakening of the self within the dreamlike state of childhood. Paralleling Dowell's own early years, the protagonists (usually young males) grow up in rural landscapes – farms, mountains, and woods – where they discover their bisexual and, at times, homosexual identities. They are almost always alienated. Estranged from family values and societal expectations, Dowell's characters draw wild responses from others, and are at times subject to ridicule yet gifted with beauty, compassion, musical talent, or a deep affinity with nature. Such gifts force Dowell's characters further away from cultural circles and set them apart from the accepted norm. Ironically, as happens with the characters in his "Wool Tea," "Ham's Gift," and "My Father Was a River," these gifts send them within their own psyches to interpret themselves and to try to understand their place in the world. It is common for a Dowell character to appear alone at the end of a story to ponder the epiphanic revelations that have resulted from experiences.

One such story is "Wool Tea," the first in *The Houses of Children.* "Wool Tea" combines the themes of sexual initiation and the search for one's identity, attained, in this case, only through the protagonist's intense scrutiny of the people and places that at one time seemed common and customary. What makes "Wool Tea" compelling is the uncanny insight and curiosity of the story's main character, the Kid, a young boy whose sharp perceptions allow him to see through the carefully constructed fronts and masks of the adult world. The title has a double meaning, alluding to the use of marijuana (sometimes called "tea"), which runs throughout the story, as well as to the wordplay of the catalytic female character Willie T. The Kid's mother is determined to groom him to become a well-mannered boy, attuned to the proper channels of morality and integrity. The Kid's older brother (never given a name by Dowell), known for his dapper and sly appearance, is rebellious, self-assured, and confident with his many feminine conquests. The Kid's mother feels as though she has failed as a mother to her oldest son: "She said she had one example too many of someone who grew up too fast," and "it was the innocence [of the Kid] that she was most worried about."

Through his older brother the Kid loses his innocence and is introduced to an underworld of sorts, while the seductively beautiful Willie T represents his lustful yearnings for such an underworld – a natural need to come into contact with his darker and more honest sexual persona. Dowell carefully distinguishes between the two brothers. The Kid's compassionate, understanding nature contrasts with his older brother's narcissistic behavior, which is habitually motivated by his need for recognition. The Kid's genuine love and attraction for Willie T counterpoints his older brother's brutal exploitation of her for sex and drugs. The younger boy's need to discover and create his own world is continuously thwarted by those around him, who try to mold him and protect him from "evil and harm."

As was evident in his own life, Dowell consistently demonstrates that the raw honesty of passion and sex can be discovered only through anguish and pain. "Wool Tea" parallels Dowell's concern that people are most honest when engaged in sex and immersed in passion, as chronicled in his novel *White on Black on White.* "Wool Tea" presents both the difficulty and beauty of sexual initiation and vividly reveals the integrity hidden within sexual obsession.

Later the reader discovers that the Kid's older brother has contracted venereal disease, ironically labeled "Willie T's gift." The Kid, unaware of the irony beneath the euphemism, is seen, toward the end of the story, insisting that Willie T also give her gift to him, but Dowell intends for the reader to interpret "the gift" as something quite opposite to a sexual disease. Willie T has enlightened the Kid's spirit and helped him identify both his sexual persona and true identity.

"My Father Was A River" focuses on an adult recalling his childhood and eventual rise to manhood in the face of his naive parents: "They called me a good child. It made me feel even more set apart, a sort of social leper." The narrator attempts to portray his parents as being ignorant of his "dark energies." To illustrate his rage at his parents' seemingly uncaring indolence, he narrates violent fantasies in which he can "fly into an orgy of rage and kick tables, legs, faces until all became splinters." To further demonstrate his loathing for his parents' unwatchful eyes, he begins to lead a double life: playing the expected role of the good son during the day, then acting out his vengeful passions at night. He is determined to explore and nurture his beastly, other personality.

However, the reader comes to discover that a more viable reason for the narrator's rebelliously demonic behavior is his Oedipal response to his parent's sexual intimacy, which he feels increasingly excluded from and, therefore, angry and jealous about. In short, as the narrator approaches manhood, he discovers that the passion between his mother and father is unbreakable. His parents allow him his freedom and independence in exchange for their own privacy. He watches in disgust as his parents seduce one another, and as the narrator interprets his parents' actions as neglect, he begins his nocturnal tirades, sexually "courting" the nearby river. Upon "entering" the cool waters, he imagines the slick flow to be the arms of his father seducing him as his father has done with his mother. In another Freudian parable, the narrator allows a fox to enter the family's henhouse night after night, each time emerging with its prey. The fox comes to trust the boy's presence as a signal to safety, until one night the narrator himself enters the henhouse as victimizer.

In the third section, the narrator enters the lair of a mountain lion, watches as it sleeps, and attempts to absorb its physical beauty and aesthetic perfection. By means of the mountain lion the narrator achieves his own independence and rebirth, ending his nocturnal adventures and being able to sleep at night and rest comfortably within his own unconscious. In the fourth and final section, the narrator addresses his mother, describing himself as a swamp plant that grows in wild tufts and branches, metaphorically reaching out in all directions: "Weren't you able to see by the games I played, that the harvest would be alien? But what could you know of the dangerous games of a child in the night when your own elaborate night kept you occupied in a long search for variations on a theme!"

The theme clearly shows that the narrator has never been understood by his parents. Early in the story, he explains: "An ordinary person with ordinary vision can turn his powers of concentration upon a single object and eventually time will reveal to him each mystery, flaw, and virtue of that object." The narrator has attempted to communicate his deepest yearnings to his parents, and though he ultimately fails to discover or reveal the sexual mystery of his mother and father, he longs only to be addressed in the same fashion, scrutinized with the same intensity that he, as their son, has employed while trying to understand them.

"Ham's Gift" sustains the same attention to the themes of diversity and comprehension in the face of authority that run throughout the other stories in the first section of *The Houses of Children*. Ham, a young introverted boy, has been found orphaned as a baby, abandoned in a barn. A family raises Ham and allows him to work and live on the farm, though they never treat him as their own: "there was no lowering of social barriers between the boy and the family . . . he joined the family only for meals and Bible readings." One can draw comparisons between Dowell's real-life exodus from Kentucky to this questlike story. As Ham grows older, the differences between himself and the family become more apparent, and he soon realizes that he is gifted with extrasensory perception that allows him to speak with "people who kept themselves apart with amused but kind toleration."

Ham gradually becomes able to visualize where these people live. The mythic and biblical area is an obvious Edenic place or condition, atop a plateau, high above mountains, where "happy godlike creatures moved to music, laughed, drank amber liquid from clear glass, and each in turn demonstrated, to loving applause what it was that gave him the right to inhabit this place of all places on earth." This description draws many comparisons to how Dowell felt as he arrived in New York from Kentucky and eventually was accepted into Van Vechten's clique before the New York theater scene turned sour for him. Before he left Kentucky, Dowell believed New York to be an Edenic place,

yet his need to leave his family was a secret until he left.

Like Dowell, Ham must keep his gift for communication secret, which, as he grows older and the call for contact with like-minded people grows more frequent, becomes increasingly difficult to do. On one occasion, Ezekiel, his adoptive brother, witnesses his communications and convinces Ham that he must leave the farm and seek his proper place.

The night before he is to leave, Ezekiel catches Ham during another one of his communications, and, fearing that Ezekiel will tell the rest of the family, Ham kills him. The remainder of the story chronicles Ham's long, fatiguing trek up the mountain in search of his place of redemption. His journey takes years, but what follows is his discovery of "Eden." Finally, at the end of his journey, Ham comes into contact with those with whom he had spiritually corresponded for so long: "Ham felt christened in the light of the eyes . . . heard the man say words, simple and dignified, that made the long arduous journey worth its terrors. They were answer, affirmation and fulfillment."

"Mrs. Hackett" is one of Dowell's most macabre stories, introducing his supreme sense of horror, Gothic mastery, and dark humor. This story first appeared, in slightly different form, in Dowell's novel *Mrs. October Was Here* and is reminiscent of Faulkner's story "A Rose For Emily" (in *These 13*, 1931) in its allusions to necromancy and irreality. Mrs. Hackett, an elderly piano teacher, and her daughter Marie Louise, a painter, are the main characters. During a piano lesson with her "least promising pupil," Mrs. Hackett evidently falls into a "second childhood unexpectedly," as her student interjects a Beatles tune into Percy Grainger's "Country Gardens." Mrs. Hackett, inhabiting the mind of a nine-year-old girl, goes on to live out her second childhood, playing with her dolls and turning words such as *fellatio* into humorous childlike euphemisms, causing the visiting townspeople to run home and consult their dictionaries for the proper pronunciation of the blasphemous words.

However, the novelty of Mrs. Hackett's childish behavior wears thin, and soon the natural frustrations of dealing with a child surface, forcing Marie Louise to consult the family doctor for advice. The doctor, however, cannot find anything physically wrong with Mrs. Hackett, and so the story continues with her childish escapades. She searches the house for her parents, attempts to play with children's toys during visits to neighbor's houses, and breaks down crying when she witnesses

Dowell in the 1970s (photograph by Tullius Frizzi)

other children dancing violently to modern rock music that "was harsh and bewildering . . . and brought pain to the most private parts of her body." Mrs. Hackett retreats to her own house spending most of her time looking through old family photo albums, and it is through this action that Dowell explains Mrs. Hackett's sudden life change. She has grown into adulthood and eventual old age without forming her own convictions or cultivating her own life-style. In fact, Mrs. Hackett has become a perfect image of her own mother, and as she gazes at the old photos, she sees "herself pressed behind glass, rice powdered, wearing her mother's clothes, gazing from the window frozen in its frame at a world enlivened by the fresh air of change that could never touch her, never get to her and free her."

At this dramatic moment of her long-awaited identity crisis Mrs. Hackett receives some feminist literature insisting on the need for women's independence. She attends a feminist meeting, along with her daughter, and is held up as a horrible example of what the other women are there to denounce. Yet, as the meeting goes on, she is recognized as an essentially negative scapegoat for their cause: "as the liberated thoughts and language poured from them some admitted that they wished

to see the woman below them, standing in a daze, martyred. *Their* martyr, though, and love flooded every breast." The "sisters," as Dowell refers to them, descend on Mrs. Hackett, and in a sudden rush of fear she takes refuge even further back into her childhood and then faints. Eventually Mrs. Hackett dies and her daughter, in a fit of rage at her mother's inability to attend "the great liberation ceremony" of the new feminist group, sadistically kicks the rotting corpse of her mother until "it came to her just what it was that her mother most resembled: that old broken doll that she had cared for more than she cared for her own daughter, that she was always searching for but could not find. . . ." Marie Louise attends the feminist party in spite of her mother's death, and upon her grand entrance to the gala she realizes in a moment of irony that "in a last nod at tradition, among her apparel of new, borrowed, and blue, she wore, on the tip of her odd-grained boot, little identical patches of something old." Dowell's use of Gothicism and surrealism in this story pushes his fiction into the realm of the postmodern, and in this story Dowell progresses from the traditional, realist forms of fiction into the more experimental and psychologically dynamic writing that is in the second section of *The Houses of Children.*

One of Dowell's most touching stories is "The Great Godalmighty Bird," which is in dramatic contrast to the sadomasochism of "Mrs. Hackett." In "The Great Godalmighty Bird" the reader also sees the first of Dowell's alterations of time: linear methods of memory and storytelling can at times fail in offering a window to reality. The reader can also see many parallels between this story and the relationship that Dowell so treasured with his aunt who had the large library. The archetypal image of a bird that runs throughout most of the remaining stories in the collection is introduced and this parable's theme is the importance of principle, courage, and, as Morrow explains in his postscript, "physical and spiritual perfection in the grotesquerie of received norms." The story chronicles a young boy's powerful and loving relationship with his elderly, bohemian grandmother. The setting is a small rural town dotted with demanding farms, luscious rolling fields, and thick, ancient woods. The innocent boy feels a spiritual connection with his grandmother, and the two spend most of their time exchanging gossip, taking long nocturnal walks through the forest, and playing music together. The grandmother soon becomes his spiritual guide, offering him advice and answering his questions concerning "What it was that happened between men and women that was so mysterious to the young."

The boy's constant presence soon replaces the loss his grandmother feels for her own grown children, while the absence the grandson feels for typical boyish camaraderie is replaced by her unwavering and complete love. The grandson soon comes to respect his grandmother's clairvoyant gifts, which the narrator describes as "foresight, an actual look into the future . . . a mystical and mysterious circle like the thought of predestination." As the boy approaches young manhood, he befriends another boy. As the narrator explains earlier in the story, the boy "felt he would have something real to offer someone he might meet and like a lot in the years to come, as she said he would, his great gift to that person being an introduction to her." Yet, at this incisive point in the story, time folds in on itself and shatters, and the story shifts from third-person to a first-person narrative. The reader discovers that the narrator in the previous pages has been the boy himself, now a man, recalling in the present tense his years with his grandmother. The boy has become the man, and the story, depending on the clarity of the adult's memory, stalls as the scenes and events of his youth are for some mysterious reason not easily exhumed.

At this stage in the story – by employing such postmodernist, metafictionalist techniques as suddenly switching the narrative, viewpoint, and time frame in the tale – Dowell questions the reality of the story's preceding events and the reliability of the narrator's memory in telling the tale. Still, the story progresses as the narrator admits: "There the fragment would have ended an unsuccessful attempt like many before it to prod memory like a rock with a magic rod and bring forth a gush . . . some sort of release." He cannot recall attending his grandmother's funeral, and it is only upon visiting his sister that the narrator can finally conjure the memory once lost to him. Through his sister the narrator also becomes painfully aware of a hideously grotesque hunched back that disfigured his grandmother's appearance throughout her life. After becoming aware of his grandmother's defect, he recalls and understands his only boyhood friend's chilly response to his grandmother one Christmas. In retrospect that narrator can ask himself: "Do I condemn all these people for not sharing my standard of beauty?" For he had never fully perceived her deformity, had never actually taken notice of her obvious abnormality. Thus a story ostensibly concerned with questions of aesthetic beauty and unconditional love also becomes a lesson in the effects of time and how the shards of memory can betray one and make one look twice into the mirror of an ever-changing reality.

The second half of *The Houses of Children* consists mainly of stories centered on couples engaged in sometimes serious domestic conflicts. "If Beggars Were Horses" is just such a story, portraying Marriot, an insecure and lonely man, musing on why his wife of twenty-five years, Lisa, has divorced him. Marriot reminisces on his wedding day, when he had brought his new bride home to his mother's house – a scene gradually revealing his fears and doubts about his own manhood, as Marriot struggles to lift Lisa up the stairs to their new bedroom. He contextualizes himself as a "noman," and his new wife confirms his fears of impotence, threatening his ability to satisfy her. As he struggles up the stairs of his mother's house with Lisa in his arms, he pictures, in vaguely Oedipal images, "A woman and noman twisting in swathed distaste on the mother-made bed."

Twenty-five years later Marriot observes Lisa moving into her deceased mother's home directly across the street from his own. Her healthy, slim appearance forces him deeper into depression as he retrospectively realizes that Lisa kept herself fit for the day when she would leave him and the bondage of marriage behind her. This attention to weight becomes important as a spiteful tool of revenge as well as the crux from which Dowell begins, once again, to lead the reader into certain questions concerning the discernible distinctions between reality and fiction.

As Marriot prepares his dinner at night, he peers through the curtains across the street and prods Lisa to eat as a glutton: "Eat up . . . he would tell her, and would summon a clear picture of a quart of ice cream mounded in a bowl and would watch as it disappeared by the tablespoon." Finally, after his continuous mental suggestions to his wife to overeat, he begins to envision his rewards. One night, as he goes to the window to spy on her, he notices that "Despite the double chin and the large bust thrusting in profile, he could not mistake his wife for anyone else in the world." Dowell forces the reader to decide whether or not Marriot's descriptions are real or fantasy. Dowell concludes the story with another image that seems to complicate the theme of appearance versus reality. Marriot fantasizes his wife's death and the difficulty in removing her body from the house, an image ironically counterpointing the marriage scene from earlier in the tale. Marriot projects a large truck parked in front of the house and several men plotting to remove a section of wall so that the corpse of the hideously bloated Lisa can be removed for burial.

Whether or not Marriot's wish-fulfillment shall come to pass is not necessarily the final question, however. Dowell has written a commentary on the power of the imagination to heal the mind, permitting it not only to fantasize but also to realize such fantasies. As Marriot retires for the night, finally secure in his revenge and accepting his still-powerful love for Lisa, he asks "himself if he has gone too far, but the drowsy boy within him, to whom it was unthinkable that there could ever be too much billowy femininity, entered sleep smiling." The sense of Marriot's release and relief is only realized through the creation of his own text or his own story. Marriot has developed into an artist who was formerly weak, vulnerable, and flawed. As Dowell has written in his private journals: "The Artist is generally the most flawed of creatures, and it is out of his flaws that he makes his art."

The last story in *The Houses of Children* is *The Silver Swanne* (separately published in 1983) – perhaps Dowell's most formidable and complex short story, dubbed by Morrow as "his greatest work of short fiction." *The Silver Swanne* employs neo-Gothic surrealism, myth, and history – making this parable, Dowell himself wrote in a private letter to a friend, a "ghost story."

The Silver Swanne resembles the intricate, postmodernist narrative structures and shifting points of view that Dowell explores in his novels *Mrs. October Was Here* and *Island People*. Three apparently separate narrative strands run through the story, set in the eighteenth, nineteenth, and twentieth centuries. The first narrative fragment concerns the circumstances that surround Roger Vilet during the time period of the eighteenth century; these events and Vilet's story are narrated by an Italian émigré living in the nineteenth century. The Venetian immigrant's character profile is then narrated by the twentieth-century character: a writer strapped by his double personality, sexual inhibitions, and torturous internal struggle between notions of good and evil.

Yet an additional character, writing the farewell dedication at the finale of *The Silver Swanne,* is in fact the true author of all the numerous stories and narrative strands that have appeared before. Such a structure makes *The Silver Swanne* a kind of palimpsestual tale, during which the reader is constantly questioning which authorial voice has ultimate control, an abstract notion that fascinated and plagued Dowell as a writer and as a man.

Certain recurring patterns run through each of the three seemingly unconnected narrative structures. First, each character possesses a pet that represents innocence and purity and is taken away from each man at some point of their tale. Each character must also battle a ghostlike apparition of evil, which, in this case, may represent the archetypal theme of maturation through initiation, for each character must murder the representation of evil to free himself and escape harm.

One cannot help but be drawn back to the epigraph by Emily Dickinson in *Island People*: "One need not be a Chamber / to be Haunted / One need not be a house." Each character it seems is the ghost of another, haunting the imagination and mind of the one personality who has created him. Such was Dowell's preoccupation with placing and pinpointing that final authorial voice, capturing the one responsible for the language, the thought, and the art.

As he says in his private papers, "The final page of the story [the dedication] explicates all the fear of being abandoned by Authors: here is the final Author, an 'it': Swanne of hell, or God, or some illiterate whose indifference to language makes mockery of all that has gone before!" Dowell asks in letter, "Is 'it' inspiration?" If it is "inspiration," which, in the end, is the final author responsible for the conception of the three narratives, and if "inspiration" is "illiterate," comprised of only emotion, then that inspiration/emotion is the only "thing" left at the conclusion of *The Silver Swanne,* as the character poised in the year 1980 leaps to his death, following the flight of a silver swan, and saying: "*Daddy Death I have waited for you so long.*" As such, the other stories must "die," their writer gone. All that can be left is the emotion, because as Dowell explains in his papers, the dedication or "the final words of the story belong to no man, or woman. They belong to an 'it.' "

Just after midnight, on the morning of 3 August 1985, Dowell leapt from the balcony of his New York apartment, fifteen floors to his death. He had compiled an extensive journal – now being edited into book form by his literary executor, Dr. Bertram Slaff – titled "An American Eccentric: The Private Journal of Coleman Dowell, the Writer." Slaff has also been involved in the adaptation of Dowell's journals into a one-man theatrical production. Dowell's work continues to receive noted attention as readers and critics alike gravitate to his fiction and life story.

Interview:

John Kuehl and Linda Kandel Kuehl, "An Interview With Coleman Dowell," *Contemporary Literature,* 22 (Summer 1981): 272–291.

Bibliography:

John Kuehl and Linda Kandel Kuehl, "The Achievement of Coleman Dowell: A Bibliographical Essay," *Review of Contemporary Fiction* (Fall 1987): 227–232.

Reference:

John O'Brien, ed., "Paul Bowles–Coleman Dowell Number," *Review of Contemporary Fiction,* 2 (October 1982): 85–148.

Andre Dubus

(11 August 1936 –)

James E. Devlin
State University of New York College at Oneonta

BOOKS: *The Lieutenant* (New York: Dial, 1967);
Separate Flights (Boston: Godine, 1975);
Adultery and Other Choices (Boston: Godine, 1977);
Finding a Girl in America: Ten Stories & a Novella (Boston: Godine, 1980);
The Times Are Never So Bad (Boston: Godine, 1983);
Voices from the Moon (Boston: Godine, 1984);
We Don't Live Here Anymore: The Novellas of Andre Dubus (New York: Crown, 1984; London: Pan, 1984);
The Last Worthless Evening (Boston: Godine, 1986);
Blessings (Elmwood, Conn.: Raven, 1987);
Selected Stories (Boston: Godine, 1988);
Broken Vessels (Boston: Godine, 1991).

OTHER: "The Blackberry Patch," in *Southern Writing in the Sixties: Fiction,* edited by John William Corrington and Miller Williams (Baton Rouge: Louisiana State University Press, 1966), pp. 108–115; reprinted in *Stories of the Modern South,* edited by Benjamin Forkner and Patrick Samway (New York: Bantam, 1978), pp. 78–83;
"Over the Hill," in *Stories of the Modern South,* volume 2, edited by Forkner and Samway (New York: Penguin, 1981), pp. 77–89.

SELECTED PERIODICAL PUBLICATIONS –
UNCOLLECTED: "The Intruder," *Sewanee Review,* 71 (April–June 1963): 268–282;
"Love Is the Sky," *Midwestern University Quarterly,* 2, no. 2 (1966): 18–32;
"Madeline Sheppard," *Midwestern University Quarterly,* 2, no. 4 (1967): 1–12;
"Blessings," *Yankee* (Fall 1986): 1–20;
"The Lover," *Ploughshares,* 17 (Fall 1991): 189–197.

Andre Dubus, circa 1983 (photograph by Kelly Wise)

Like Russell Banks and Raymond Carver, his contemporaries, Andre Dubus is often perceived as a "son of Ernest Hemingway," a judgment that would please neither Hemingway nor Dubus but one that serves as a rough – often very rough – frame of reference nonetheless. Not only does he superficially resemble Hemingway physically, being burly and bearded, but he often writes in a prose style made familiar by Hemingway – a style that might be called nonexperimental, American plain style and which often, but not always, suggests a by-the-numbers clarity meant to impose order on chaos. But Dubus's writing can also be as verbally and syntactically complicated as that of William Faulkner. Dubus writes of guns, hunting, fishing, chaos, married life, the armed services, eating, drinking, and especially of smoking, sports, exercise, "moments of truth," and rituals of several sorts. His more or less responsible but alienated characters resemble Hemingway's men, though not his women, and Dubus's blue-collar protagonists – or those one generation removed from the blue collar – often share the empty life of Rabbit Angstrom, that prototypical American created by John Updike. Cheated by the world around them, they live in shabby wooden houses close to the downtowns of drab New England cities. Victims of spotty American educations, trained to no particular skills, they enjoy little culture or tradition in their lives. They drink, smoke, form relationships too early in life, and stumble along, perhaps looking to the Marine Corps, the family, or more likely the Catholic church for spiritual solace or cultural regeneration. But often they cheat their church as much as it cheats them. Dubus's marines, ball players, fathers, and wives live by a self-imposed code, trying to establish order and meaning in their lives, and like Angstrom they fail more often than they succeed.

In depicting unextraordinary people, single mothers, divorced husbands, and victims of failing marriages, Dubus treats in freshly original manner a host of problems that occupied American minds in the 1970s and 1980s. But merely to list the issues raised in his stories runs the danger of making Dubus's writing sound trendy, slick, or superficial – all qualities he has avoided. Abortion, drugs, child and wife abuse, racism, rape, anorexia, divorce, birth control, exercise and body building, and the aftermath of Vietnam find expression in his stories, but these subjects are organic elements, for Dubus is above all a serious writer who never compromises his artistic vision and whose fiction, reflecting a view of life, bristles with an integrity absent in the writer who curries favor by flattering an established taste. His celebrated depiction of men deflates the macho image associated with Hemingway while avoiding sentimentality and Robert Bly–like excess. Dubus writes from a variety of points of view, frequently including the female, yet shuns what he calls the "totalitarian" aspects of doctrinaire feminism. His sympathetic treatment of female sexuality, explicit though not usually graphic, is contemporary and honest. His themes of love and sex, spiritual hunger, courage, and its lack are expressed – in Tobias Wolff's words (from the introduction to *Broken Vessels,* 1991) – "in a voice I hadn't heard before, honest, strong, direct, yet sensuous and emotionally

rich. His writing is at the same time compassionate and morally responsible."

Andre Dubus (the family pronounces the name "Duh-buse") was born on 11 August 1936 in Lake Charles, Louisiana, of Cajun-Irish stock. The son of his namesake, Andre Dubus, a civil engineer who loved golf and smoked a great deal, and Katherine Burke Dubus, who listened to broadcasts of the Metropolitan Opera on winter Saturday afternoons, Andre grew up with his two sisters in the bayou country around Baton Rouge and Lafayette, where he attended the Christian Brothers' Cathedral High School, and, upon graduation in 1954, he enrolled at McNeese State College, earning his B.A. in English in 1958. His childhood was spent in lower-middle-class circumstances. Since neither the workaday Christian Brothers' school nor the small, southern state college he attended would guarantee him entry into the great world outside, Dubus elected to enter the U.S. Marines and believed that the corps would make a man of him, a goal he desired. In high school the skinny Dubus had played no sports nor attracted much attention from girls, and while college proved more rewarding in regard to maturing physically and to awakening response from women, he still felt his manhood was incomplete.

In 1958, having married Patricia Lowe in February, he accepted a second lieutenant's commission in the marines. This same year saw the birth of his first child, Suzanne, and in each of the next three succeeding years another child was born: Andre, Jeb, and Nicole.

In 1963, the same year his father died at fifty-nine of cancer, Dubus, now a captain, resigned his commission to take his family to the University of Iowa, where he studied writing. He had been writing stories since his nineteenth year and had succeeded at breaking into print in the *Sewanee Review* with "The Intruder" (April–June 1963).

With an M.F.A. from the Iowa Writers' Workshop, he headed with his family back to Louisiana for a year's teaching in Thibodaux before going north to Bradford College in Bradford, Massachusetts, a town on the Merrimack River in the state's northeastern corner. This area, now his home, is a region of decayed mill towns such as Haverhill, where he lives on the outskirts in a modular home at the top of a wooded slope.

Until 1984 Dubus taught writing and literature at Bradford College. During this time his first marriage ended, and he entered into two more, one with Tommie Gail Cotter in June 1975 that ended childless three years later, and another in 1979 with

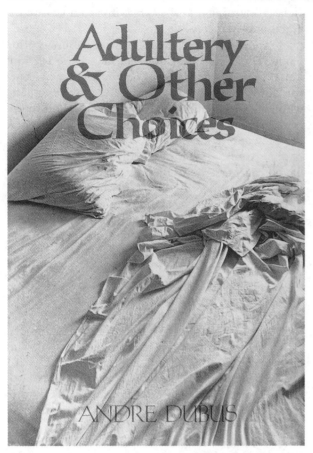

*Dust jacket for Dubus's 1977 collection of short fiction. The title
novella is the second part of a trilogy about the marital difficulties
of two young college professors and their wives.*

a woman many years his junior: Peggy Rambach,
who gave birth to two children, Cadence in 1982
and Madeleine in 1987, the final year of their marriage. While at Bradford College Dubus published
his only novel, *The Lieutenant* (1967), and several
stories in prestigious quarterlies.

Five years after Martha Foley chose "If They
Knew Yvonne" for inclusion in *Best American Short
Stories 1970* (the first of his three appearances in
these annuals), Dubus published *Separate Flights*
(1975), his first collection of stories. In addition to
the title story and "If They Knew Yvonne," this volume includes the novella "We Don't Live Here
Anymore," which, together with the novellas "Adultery" (1977) and "Finding A Girl in America"
(1980) was to become the tripartite saga of Terry
and Jack Linhart and Edith and Hank Allison in the
1984 collection *We Don't Live Here Anymore.*

Reviews of Dubus's work were largely favorable in the 1970s, and his reputation in the 1980s
continued to grow as writers such as Updike and

Joyce Carol Oates brought him to the attention of a
growing readership. *The Last Worthless Evening*
(1986) and *Selected Stories* (1988) led to Dubus's introduction into college literature classes and have
stirred critical interest.

Early on the morning of 23 July 1986 Dubus's
life took a startling turn when he was struck by a
car near Wilmington, Massachusetts, where he was
assisting a distressed motorist on Interstate 93. Accounts of this accident, which resulted in injuries
that caused him to lose a leg and be confined to a
wheelchair, appear in his well-received volume of
personal essays *Broken Vessels.* Four months after the
accident his wife left him, and five days after that
she "came with a court order and a kind young Haverhill police officer and took Cadence and Madeleine away." Since then he has suffered writing
blocks but has continued to work and to lecture,
often in pain. A show of support, both moral and financial, by such disparate American writers as Ann
Beattie, E. L. Doctorow, Kurt Vonnegut, John Irving, Gail Godwin, and Richard Yates proved enormously gratifying to the dispirited Dubus, as did a
MacArthur Fellowship he received when his morale
had reached a particularly low ebb. In the years
since the shaking events of 1986 he has come to
view the accident as a transcendent experience that
has allowed him to understand more deeply the nature of human suffering, forgiveness, and love, and
he remains a practicing and believing Catholic, although he has had to modify for himself a few of
the church's strictures.

Although Dubus has insisted that the publication of "The Intruder" in the *Sewanee Review* had no
effect on his decision to leave the marines to study
writing in Iowa, it must nonetheless have been a
heady experience to see his first story in those
pages. "The Intruder" will remind readers of Hemingway's Nick Adams stories with its summer setting at a vacation camp, not up in Michigan but in
rural Louisiana. The story involves a boy's initiation into some adult mysteries, particularly of sex
and violence, themes to which Dubus would return again and again. Moreover, it is a seminal
story in that it establishes a reappearing male
character, sometimes called Kenneth — as here — or
Paul Clement, but who, like Adams, is an alter ego
of the author.

"If They Knew Yvonne" is a retrospective
first-person narration that also draws on Dubus's
youth. Writing during a period when the Catholic
church in America was beginning to loosen its authoritarian strictures as a result of the Second Vatican Council, the story ends hopefully with a whis-

pered hymn of praise to human vitality and common sense. Harry, the young narrator, learns through a process of discovery over the period of several years that sexual intercourse with a woman is a sin less to be feared in the confessional than masturbation. He comes to regard his girlfriend as a surrogate, a sex object whose presence lessens his guilt. He also finds out that his mother has avoided the sacraments for years because she is practicing birth control and that church interference has scarred his sister's life as well. In addition to exposing Catholicism's bias against women, the story reflects the moral dilemma Dubus confronted in deciding to abandon church teaching and to use birth control.

While the story is told with great earnestness, "If They Knew Yvonne" contains one of the lightest and most joyous scenes in his fiction. After a stilted confessional conversation with his priest, the young man makes his point: "So after that we were lovers. Or she was, but I wasn't. I was just happy because I could ejaculate without hating myself, so I was still masturbating, you see, but with her – does that make sense?" What might seem woodenly didactic is relieved by the circumstances. The priest listens with great sympathy to Harry's outpourings and then charitably announces: "For your penance, say alleluia three times."

Separate Flights also includes "The Doctor," in which Art, a physician jogging on a springlike March day, comes upon a heartrending accident. A concrete slab from a little bridge over a brook has just fallen on a young boy, pinning him under the shallow water. Art stops and tries vainly to lift the weight from the drowning boy. That afternoon he seeks to understand the meaning of the event he has witnessed, reaching the empty conclusion that the slab was like cancer, "that it has the volition of a killer." He later cuts a length of garden hose to keep in his car next to his first-aid kit in the faintest hope that if he ever encounters a similar situation he will be able to supply life – giving air to a submerged victim. "The Doctor" also presents in some detail the notion so often encountered in Dubus's work that children are pawns of fortune, and their deaths or injuries are almost unbearable to their parents.

The novella "We Don't Live Here Anymore" involves the marital difficulties of two couples employed in academia, Jack and Terry, and Hank and Edith, young parents whose circumstances resemble closely those of the Dubus family during the mid 1970s. The narrator of "We Don't Live Here Anymore," Jack Linhart, is thirty years old, and his ac-

count of his life at a crucial point in his foundering marriage brings up the problem of the credibility of the narrator in much of Dubus's fiction. Although Jack is often an admirable figure and a concerned and loving father, he is as often a lecherous crybaby given to shifting responsibility for his own shortcomings to his wife, Terry.

"We Don't Live Here Anymore" opens with one of those throwaway scenes that Dubus often creates. Jack and Edith, already lovers, have left Jack and Terry's house, where Hank and Terry wait, in order to replenish the dwindling beer supply so that the party can continue. When Jack tells the loquacious Irish liquor-store owner to include in his order six Pickwick ales, the older man says, "Used to be everybody in New England drank ale. Who taught you? Your father?" Jack's answer is banter to delight the owner and Edith both. He is a mischievous boy showing off in front of his girl: "He taught me to drink ale and laugh with pretty girls." In a few moments the Irishman is giving a brief history of beer-drinking habits in Massachusetts. Dubus, like Hemingway, is a natural pedagogue.

For Jack, Edith is exciting and offers delicious moments of passion away from the dreary life at home with Terry. With Edith he can drink imported beer in the daytime and make love outdoors, with her long, black hair hanging down over his recumbent form. Unlike Edith, Terry is a terrible housekeeper, and Dubus provides disheartening scenes of home economics gone wrong. When Terry, feeling unloved and scorned, begins her own affair with Hank, she accuses Jack of taking a voyeuristic delight in it, and she is not far off the mark. Certainly he uses the relationship to justify to himself his conduct with Edith. When he charges his wife with giving "half-ass insights into the soul of a man [Jack] you never understood," readers almost want to laugh as loudly as Terry does. The hoary accusation that one's wife does not understand one seems as disingenuously self-pitying as any other passage in Jack's often unreliable narration. But it is difficult to take either husband or wife seriously because both indulge constantly in pseudoprofound analysis of each other.

Jack finally admits not only that he is having an affair with Edith but that he loves her. Jack is unable to leave his wife and children, however, and a reconciliation of sorts is hammered out in which Jack breaks off his relationship and Terry promises – among other things – to be a tidier housewife.

In 1977 Dubus was the recipient of a Guggenheim Fellowship, and he published the well-re-

The Last
Worthless Evening

Andre Dubus

Dust jacket for Dubus's 1986 collection of short fiction, which was selected for the "Editor's Choice" list in Time *magazine*

ceived *Adultery and Other Choices,* a collection of nine short stories and the novella "Adultery." Of the stories "The Fat Girl" has subsequently achieved the most prominence in anthologies, though "Andromache," the story of a soldier's wife in peacetime at a marine base, is a better story. While accounts of officers' wives are nothing new (hence the ironic title), the contrast between a woman's small failure in planning a Christmas party and the devastating loss she suffers when her husband dies is effective. "Adultery" continues the story of Edith Allison, whose novelist/husband Hank is womanizing among his students while his wife turns to a fallen priest dying of cancer. In Father Joe Ritchie, Dubus delicately creates a familiar figure of the 1970s. As Thomas E. Kennedy writes, the former priest "does not experience his love for Edith as a sin; he only fears it might be a sin as long as she is still involved in her poisoned marriage; were she to leave Hank and marry him, the priest would feel at peace with God again."

The next year, 1978, Dubus received a National Endowment for the Arts grant, and in 1979

he saw his story "The Pitcher" placed in *Prize Stories: The O. Henry Awards.* In 1980 "The Pitcher" was reprinted in *Finding a Girl in America,* a collection that met mixed reviews. Other stories in *Finding a Girl in America* include "Killings," about a father's revenge for the murder of his son, and "Delivering," having to do with the effect on children of marital discord. In "Delivering" a boy follows a series of precisely detailed routines on his paper route and invents toughening-up exercises for his younger brother to survive their parents' breakup. "Finding a Girl in America" is the last novella in the Linhart-Allison trilogy and perhaps the most self-indulgent. When Hank discovers from this year's teenage mistress that last year's mistress aborted his child, he – in the words of reviewer Julian Moynahan (*New York Times Book Review,* 22 June 1980) – "howls, blubbers, vomits, whines to his ex-wife, and generally chews the scenery because he really wanted that kid, see?"

Despite this sarcasm, Moynahan's review is largely favorable, as were those greeting Dubus's fourth story collection, *The Times Are Never So Bad* (1983), comprising eight short stories and the novella "The Pretty Girl." Oates singled out "A Father's Story" for special praise in the *New York Times Book Review* (26 June 1983), calling it one of Dubus's "triumphs of voice, memorable for . . . resonance." Her review identifies two of Dubus's most characteristic qualities: an inimitable voice and a penchant for idiosyncratic details. Dubus's voice is particularly difficult to define. *Voice* is the same word Wolff uses in his enthusiastic introduction to *Broken Vessels* and is akin to Frances Taliaferro's more poetic metaphor of "quiet melodies," in her review of *Adultery and Other Choices* (*Harper's,* January 1978). She compares Dubus to a harpsichordist opening a recital "with sounds that seem unbearably faint after the noise outside."

In "A Father's Story" protagonist Luke Ripley endures a dark night of the soul, the long, sleepless night he spends planning how to rescue his daughter from the consequences of a death she has caused while driving. During his sleeplessness Luke plays records: for hours he listens to works by Giacomo Puccini – *La Bohème, Tosca,* and *Madama Butterfly,* three operas in which a young woman dies. The operas, the brooding vigil, and the grieving father, seeking to do something out of love for his daughter whose life is figuratively about to end, all come together in the sort of concert that sends critics reaching for metaphors of sound to describe the heights the story achieves.

"The Pretty Girl" follows the protagonists for a period of several years in their interactions with many people, and it is told in five parts with three narrators including the author. Dubus's experiment with multiple narrations and his use of both present and past tense in the same story are at least as innovative as those of his with the introduction of incidental characters and events to support themes. The accounts most clearly bearing on the main character, Polly Comeau, are told in a third-person-limited-omniscient voice, while those bearing on her husband, Raymond (whom Dubus has called a "poor bastard"), appear in first person, the point of view most likely to generate sympathy for its narrator. In any case the alternating of narrators works successfully until the final (page-long) account of Alex Yarborough, Raymond's brother, who until then has not appeared in the novella. The effect of his somewhat stagy afterward is open to question. Also Alex's elegiac apologia for the life of his brother, shot by his estranged wife as he is about to rape her for the second time in a year, is at odds with the facts as the reader knows them. Alex calls Polly's shooting of the clearly deranged young man an injustice done by a pretty woman "when she got weird" to a wonderful brother whose only failing was "to fall in love and not get over it."

Although the epilogue seems meant to shed light on the meaning of the story, it fails because there is little meaning beyond the events themselves. In commenting on his story Dubus says, in Kennedy's *Andre Dubus: A Study of the Short Fiction* (1988), that Polly "has allowed the physical beauty of her face to dictate her direction." This is about as judgmental as he ever becomes in discussing his own work, and even here he prefaces his remark by saying, "I love Polly very much." However, Polly, who spends days getting drunk at Timmy's Bar, while puffing one cigarette after another, is simply not a very interesting woman, let alone an especially admirable one. Despite a bit of college education, she is largely empty-headed. But she "does something" when she shoots her former husband with the pistol she bought, while accompanied by her father, at the Kittery Trading Post and practiced with for just this purpose. Are readers to sympathize with Polly, who turns to her father for familial support and attends mass on Sundays, or are they to lean toward the voyeuristic, self-centered Raymond, the subject of fraternal praise that overlooks regular wife beating, assaults, rape, and arson?

The next questions to arise in reading "A Pretty Girl" are, where do readers turn to derive Dubus's view and to what extent are moral norms a part of the story? Dubus has observed that Anton Chekhov once wrote a story about a horse thief in order that readers might know how a horse thief felt, and a similar ambition often motivates Dubus: to depict people other writers avoid. Further, he admits to trying to prepare for such depictions by "becoming" them as nearly as he can, by note-taking, sharing their experiences, or carefully observing them. But as much as he seeks to enter into his characters, to "become" them, he knows, of course, that they are ultimately – also in his words – born "from my imagination." In short, he understands that while it is always necessary that a reader be able to recognize a character as a round and living person, it is certainly not necessary for either a reader or a writer to identify with one. Nonetheless Dubus, in "A Pretty Girl," shows a lack of objectivity. Polly Comeau and Molly Cousteau (in "Molly," in *The Last Worthless Evening*) are trivial human beings who seemingly need to be treated with a certain detachment or aesthetic distance.

The early and mid 1980s included dramatic highs and lows in Dubus's life and writing: the death of his mother, his retirement from teaching, the publication of five volumes, his 1987 divorce, a string of writing awards, and the debilitating automobile accident.

In 1984 Dubus published *Voices from the Moon,* a novella that later was collected in *We Don't Live Here Anymore* and *Selected Stories. Voices from the Moon* is told in the third person but in the limited-omniscient mode so that different sections of the story reveal the minds of different members of the Stowe family who have been dispersed through marriage and divorce. But predominantly *Voices from the Moon* is the story of Richie Stowe, a twelve-year-old living with Greg, his divorced father; Richie learns from an overheard conversation that his father is planning to marry Richie's older brother's former wife. Although such complications transcend the ordinary turmoil of middle-class divorce in America (in this case being so close to incestuous that Greg Stowe and Brenda must either marry out of state or wrangle a legislative change in Massachusetts), still they reflect society's mores in a general way just as they must mirror Dubus's own problems, married at the time to a wife the age of his own children. Greg wonders how Richie will react to a new mother, particularly since he has known her as his sister-in-law. What will Greg's son Larry think when his father marries Larry's former wife? The plot summary notwithstanding, there is very little of the soap opera about this novella. Richie, for

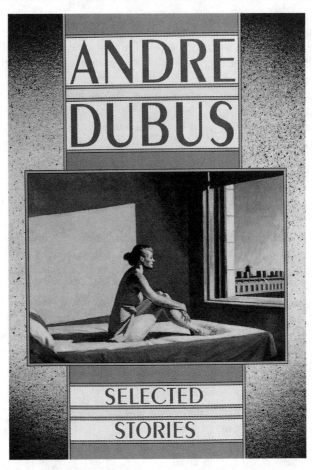

Dust jacket for Dubus's 1988 book, which prompted novelist Anne Tyler to praise the sense of moral responsibility that "gives his work its backbone"

example, proves an amazingly decent and level-headed kid whose Catholic faith is bolstered by a young priest and whose self-confidence is strengthened by Melissa Donnely, a thirteen-year old temptress. Updike, in an appreciative *New Yorker* review (4 February 1985), noted that Dubus's knowledge of female psychology and sexuality, extremely perceptive in some respects, is limited in others. He saw that Dubus's sexiest characters are most often male, "the bumbling, rugged wonder of the masculine." *Voices from the Moon* presents a recognizable contemporary world where humble goals and love, both manifested through family and church, sometimes achieve modest successes.

After receiving another National Endowment for the Arts grant in 1985, Dubus won a Guggenheim Fellowship the next year when *The Last Worthless Evening* appeared to favorable reviews and was selected an editor's choice by *Time*. Clancy Sigal praised the stories in his *New York Times* review (21 December 1986), though he objected to "unlikely" narrators in some of them, thinking

perhaps of George Karambelas and Karen Arakelian in "Land Where My Fathers Died," and he judged Dubus to be "much given to emphatic spiritual pondering," a charge touching the soul of Dubus's writing – a quality that is off-putting to some but treasured by a growing and discerning readership.

"Deaths at Sea" (in *The Last Worthless Evening*) concerns race relations, but the give-and-take between a black and a white officer, both men of goodwill stationed aboard an aircraft carrier where hidden prejudices still hold sway, seems slightly labored. The story "Rose" begins with what appears to be another of those irrelevancies to which Dubus so often resorts. The narrator, a former marine, recalls a recruit at boot camp who failed to complete his training; then the narrator goes on to tell of Rose, who killed her husband after years of tolerating his brutalizing their children. Reviewer James Yaffe wrote, "It is only at the very end of the novella that we see the point of this [opening] digression . . . " (*Denver Post,* 7

December 1986). What Yaffe means is that Dubus later shows that both the washout marine and the pathetic woman have failed at a point in their lives, but that fact should not be allowed to determine their destinies. Rose deserves custody of her children despite what she has done, and the young marine, Dubus hopes, "has succeeded at something — love, work — that has allowed him to outgrow the shame of failure."

In July 1986 Dubus's devastating accident occurred and 1987 brought both the birth of another daughter and the bitter end of his third marriage. A year later he published *Selected Stories*, comprising twenty-three stories. *Selected Stories* was greeted with enthusiastic reviews in the *New Republic* (6 February 1989) and the *New York Times Book Review* (6 November 1988), as well as receiving favorable notices in the *Times Literary Supplement* (6 April 1990) and *New Statesman* (9 March 1990). Writing for the *New Republic*, Anne Tyler praised Dubus for truly understanding his characters, saying that "he feels morally responsible for his characters, and it's this sense of responsibility that gives his work its backbone." Tyler felt that Ray Yarborough of "A Pretty Girl" becomes "even likable," despite his myriad moral failings — an opinion that demonstrates the sorcery Dubus can work. In the *New Statesman*, Kirsty Milne reminded readers of Dubus's "eloquence," a quality undervalued by critics more likely to talk of his "voice" or "moral vision" or "unabashed humanism."

Andre Dubus writes of an America of vanishing expectations, a country slipping from postwar confidence, with eroded small cities where jobs are hard to find and pay minimum wage and where the middle class has lost direction as marriages and the church begin to fail. He believes in the primacy of feelings and in instinct, but, as a nearly orthodox Catholic, he sees a need for institutions that, like the marine corps and the church in their less authoritarian and restrictive forms, offer goals and guidance, assisting the faithful to more loving, courageous, and fulfilled lives. Neither skeptical nor wholly believing, Dubus is hopeful and inspires hope.

Interviews:

Dev Hathaway, "A Conversation with Andre Dubus," *Black Warrior Review*, 9 (Spring 1983): 86–103;

Robert Dahlin, "Andre Dubus," *Publishers Weekly*, 226 (12 October 1984): 56–57;

Robert Nathan, "Interview with Andre Dubus," *Bookletter*, 3 (14 February 1987): 14–15;

Patti Doten, "Andre Dubus: Pain Yes, Rage No," *Boston Globe*, 19 August 1991, pp. 33, 36.

References:

John B. Breslin, "Playing Out the Patterns of Sin and Grace: The Catholic Imagination of Andre Dubus," *Commonweal*, 115 (2 December 1988): 652–656;

Thomas E. Kennedy, *Andre Dubus: A Study of the Short Fiction* (Boston: Twayne, 1988);

Jesse Kornbluth, "The Outrageous Andre Dubus," *Horizon*, 28 (April 1985): 16–20;

Tobias Wolff, Introduction to Dubus's *Broken Vessels* (Boston: Godine, 1991).

Stuart Dybek
(10 April 1942 –   )

William W. Combs
Western Michigan University

BOOKS: *Brass Knuckles* (Pittsburgh: University of
Pittsburgh Press / London: Feffer & Simons,
1979);
Childhood and Other Neighborhoods (New York: Vik-
ing, 1980);
The Coast of Chicago (New York: Knopf, 1990).

PLAY PRODUCTION: *Orchids,* in Glen Roven's
montage *Heart's Desire,* Cleveland, Ohio, Cleveland Playhouse, November 1990.

TELEVISION: "Death of the Right Fielder," *The
Hidden Room,* Lifetime Television Network, 1
October 1991.

RADIO: "I Never Told This to Anyone," *Weekend
Edition,* NPR, 23 July 1989.

OTHER: "The Writer in Chicago: A Roundtable,"
by Dybek, Reginald Gibbons, Maxine
Chernoff, Cyrus Colter, and Fred Shafer,
TriQuarterly, 60 (Spring/Summer 1984): 325–
347;
"The Short-Short Form," in *Sudden Fiction International,* edited by Robert Shapard and James
Thomas (New York: Norton, 1989), pp. 316–
317.

SELECTED PERIODICAL PUBLICATIONS –
UNCOLLECTED: "Undertow," *Atlantic Monthly,*
240 (September 1977): 74–78;
Review of Studs Terkel's *Chicago,* "Books," *Chicago
Tribune,* 28 September 1986, section 14, p. 6;
"On Short Short Fiction," *Michigan Quarterly Review,*
26 (Fall 1987): 723–725;
"I Never Told This to Anyone," *TriQuarterly,* 81
(Spring–Summer 1991): 110–114.

Stuart Dybek has published one collection of
poems, *Brass Knuckles* (1979), and two collections of
short stories, *Childhood and Other Neighborhoods*
(1980) and *The Coast of Chicago* (1990). Dybek's read-

Stuart Dybek

ers admire the power, humor, storytelling virtuosity, and the sheer strangeness and mysteriousness of
his work, in which the setting is usually Chicago.
Reviewer Alice Bloom, writing about the 1986 paperback edition of *Childhood and Other Neighborhoods,*
said of "these brilliant moving stories," set in
Chicago's ethnic neighborhoods, that "no one has
done it better, and maybe never will" (*Hudson Review,* Summer 1987). Michiko Kakutani, writing for
the *New York Times* (20 April 1990), noted that sev-

eral stories in *The Coast of Chicago* "introduce us to characters who want to take up permanent residence in our minds. . . . They persuasively conjure up a fictional world that is both ordinary and amazing."

Dybek has won several awards, including a 1985 Whiting Writers Award (he was one of the first ten recipients of this award); and in 1981 an Ernest Hemingway Foundation Special Citation from the P.E.N. American Center for his first collection, *Childhood and Other Neighborhoods*. In the citation, a committee composed of Thomas Disch, Darcy O'Brien, and Anne Tyler called this book "an exemplary collection . . . with a fierceness of imagination that even at its highest temperature remains faithful to the facts of inner-city life." Dybek has three times (in 1985, 1986, and 1987) had stories chosen for the O. Henry Memorial Prize Story Awards.

Dybek was born on 10 April 1942 on the southwest side of Chicago in a working-class neighborhood divided equally between East-European Americans and Mexican Americans. His father, Stanley, was a foreman in an International Harvester plant; his mother, Adeline Sala Dybek, worked as a truck dispatcher. Stuart Dybek went to Roman Catholic schools and earned B.S. (1964) and M.A. (1968) degrees at Loyola University of Chicago. After graduation he was a caseworker with the Cook County Department of Public Aid, and a teacher in an elementary school in a Chicago suburb. He also worked in advertising because he had read that William Styron got started that way. From 1968 to 1970 he was a member of VISTA and taught in Charlotte Amalie High School on the island of Saint Thomas. In 1970 he went to the University of Iowa's Writers' Workshop, from which he received an M.F.A. in 1973. Since then he has taught creative writing – reportedly with great effectiveness – at Western Michigan University in Kalamazoo. His wife, Caren, whom he married in 1966, teaches high-school English in Kalamazoo County. They have two children, Ann and Nick.

Dybek's Chicago is a city of great contrasts: an inland city with a long coastline, it has terrible slums, urban blight, and old and new Gold Coasts. It is a polyglot city, a modern Babel, and it is a blend of present and past. Dybek's writing is full of topical and geographical references: specific streets, people, buildings, landmarks, neighborhoods, and economic and political problems. At times his Chicago recalls earlier versions and visions of Chicago by such different writers as Carl Sandburg, Upton Sinclair, Theodore Dreiser, Nelson Algren, and Saul Bellow, who through their often shocking originality and courage helped define realism. Still, the differences between these predecessors' Chicago and Dybek's postmodern Chicago are striking. His Chicago, especially in *The Coast of Chicago,* often seems more of a dream city. Dybek's mentors and precursors have been poets, fabulists, and visionaries who have exalted imagination over commonsense reality and have believed that dreams, including nightmares, may reflect lives more profoundly and more realistically than the waking mind's reason and naturalistic observation. One thinks of Nikolay Gogol, Franz Kafka, Jorge Luis Borges, Isaac Bashevis Singer, and Italo Calvino, of the old storytellers of central and eastern Europe, and of the mythographers of ancient Greece and Rome, especially Ovid. Dybek is one of the best contemporary followers of Ovid. Some of Dybek's finest stories and poems are about metamorphoses.

There are eleven stories in *Childhood and Other Neighborhoods.* (The pun in the title is deliberate: for Dybek, childhood is simultaneously the time and the place where one grows up.) Most of the stories are initiation or coming-of-age stories in which Dybek inventively applies his notion that childhood is a visionary state of perception. In several stories– some funny, some grim, some tragically farcical – children or young people go out of their neighborhoods and confront unknown, even dangerous, new people and places. In "Blood Soup" two young brothers, Steve and Dove, go on an almost impossible quest into strange, menacing, new neighborhoods to get, at the demand of Busha, their grandmother, some duck's blood to make a health-restoring soup (a fruit soup with meat and blood) that Busha thinks she will die without. (This story is surely in some way autobiographical: Dybek says that one of the two most profound influences on his development as a writer was his Polish grandmother, his Busha; the other influence was music.) Finding no duck's blood in nearby respectable butcher shops, the boys, in their desperation, find the insane but noble Pan Gowumpe, who lives in an abandoned tenement with his extraordinary aviary. The duck's blood Gowumpe pretends – and his fraud seems kindly – to get for the boys is really beet juice. At the end Steve is so exhilarated from discovering the fraud and by their frightening but safe return to their own neighborhood that he forgets Busha and plays a stupendous trick on Dove. He tosses the Miracle Whip jar holding the beet juice/duck's blood high into the air and watches as Dove frantically tries and fails to catch it; then Steve watches, with an evident satisfaction such as that of

Dust jacket for Dybek's 1990 book, in which the style may be compared to improvisation in jazz

an artist or a choreographer, as the explosion of the jar spectacularly splatters them.

Several of the stories in *Childhood and Other Neighborhoods* emphasize the significance of an experience or an insight the narrator or main character has had. Such characters are usually just entering their adult lives. For example, "Sauerkraut Soup" is a darkly comic story about a young man who attends college, works in an ice-cream factory, and suffers from a profound Sartrean nausea – his reaction to growing up and having to learn "the way time was surrendered" on assembly lines and everywhere else. A corollary insight is that all things die. This story ends happily. The narrator spends a desperate night of homeopathic drunkenness and almost-suicidal carousing with his friend Harry, in which they speak of a sick childhood joke about the worms crawling in and out "turning your guts to sauerkraut." The next day, the narrator unexpectedly recovers his taste and ability to keep down food, signifying that he has crossed a divide and,

with one of the compromises required to become an adult, accepted his mortal body. In a nondescript restaurant he orders some "Homemade Sauerkraut Soup," which is so surprisingly good – substantial, homely, spicy, astringent, and digestible – that he eats two bowls: "I was never happier than in the next two years. . . . Perhaps I was receiving a year of happiness per bowl. . . . Only forty cents a bowl. I could have ordered more but thought I'd better stop while I was feeling good."

In several interviews, Dybek emphasizes that an important artistic concern for him is what happens when you make various combinations of the realistic, lyrical, fantastic, grotesque, and the visionary. The impulse to thicken and intensify language, to make narratives less transparent and more self-referential, and to contrive for them more complex organizational schemes is greater in his second collection, *The Coast of Chicago*. This collection is mostly divided into two categories of fictions: longer stories and very short stories, which Dybek calls "short shorts," mostly anecdotes and memories about incidents in neighborhoods and families. Some are third-person narratives; others are quasi-autobiographical. The mood of many is lyrical. There is continuity from "short short" to longer story to normal short story, although the continuity is not always easily apparent and may even be elusive. The "short short" may be a prelude or postlude to a story or provide a realistic, even comic, analogy with a story. For example, the first-person narrator of the very brief tale "The Woman Who Fainted" is a perceptive, worried high-school boy who regularly attends the Roman Catholic mass he no longer believes in so he can watch from the church balcony, Sunday after Sunday, a sexually attractive, seemingly devout young woman. One very hot Sunday, she faints. The boy intensely follows the tender, puritanical, yet erotic way she, unconscious, is borne out of the church. "The Woman Who Fainted" is a kind of overture to the fantastic, visionary long story "Hot Ice," which, among other things, contains a contemporary retelling of the tale of Sleeping Beauty.

Though the continuity of *The Coast of Chicago* sometimes seems elusive, if one reads or thinks musically and pictorially, the collection can be seen and heard to have all sorts of continuities, including quasi-musical motifs, which are constantly moving, changing and being changed, from story to story, from beginning to end. Dybek says that music, especially jazz, was one of the most important influences on his development as a writer. For several years he played saxophone in a band somewhat like the "No Names" band of neighborhood high-school boys in the story "Blight," from *The Coast of Chicago*. Dybek told interviewer James Plath that jazz "probably . . . got me writing. I frequently write to music, and frequently the music I write to is jazz. I'm always hoping the musical structure will somehow assert itself on fictional structure in some way." A theme with variations, as important in classical music as in jazz improvisations, is the quasi-musical form Dybek most frequently uses in *The Coast of Chicago*, especially in the collection's virtuosic central story, "Nighthawks," itself a collection of tales that are variations on a theme – generally the ancient conundrum that life is a dream. Specific variations concern three kinds of nighthawks: the insect-eating birds, sometimes called bullbats, so familiar in cities on summer nights; night people, who in this story belong to two main types – sleepwalkers and insomniacs; and the specific night people in Edward Hopper's great 1942 painting *Nighthawks*, which the narrator, the architect and musician of dreams, ap-

propriates for his own dreaming excursions after seeing the painting many times in the Chicago Art Institute. The most elaborate variation is a fantasy, a metamorphosis, based on the myth of Orpheus and Eurydice, transposed to Chicago.

The narrator/dreamer's excursions are frequently dangerous because dreamers as well as sleepwalkers run the risk of having their souls leave their bodies, as when he follows "Choco, a kid who played the conga and had gone AWOL" to see the beautiful Niña, who, set adream by music, love, and angel dust, steps from the rooftop where they have been making love into the air and her death. Choco is Dybek's Orpheus; Niña is Eurydice. But their ancient roles are reversed. Niña is not a pathetic ghost: dead, she becomes a siren – La Belle Dame Sans Merci, Hecate, Queen of the Underworld, more powerful than Choco with his music and his patron Elluggua (evidently representing the Yoruba god Eshu, also called Elegba and Elegbara), god of thresholds, of the crossroads between life and death. Instead of choosing to go down into the underworld to rescue Niña, Choco is led by her, by the mysterious kisses she imprints all over Chicago. He follows Niña into the subways, sewers, abandoned mines, and catacombs of Chicago, where, overpowered by his sense of her serene, lethal beauty, he loses control: "He looks back to tell her he's lost," but she is not there; "she is standing before him." Choco follows Niña and disappears. Only a kiss emerges from the underworld, the kiss of passionate night, the kiss of sleep and dreams, the kiss of death, and "not even the lips it's meant for feel the secret entry of her tongue, the scrape of her teeth, or, when she pulls away, the clinging thread of briny spit."

Dybek's best stories deal with visions and metamorphoses. Some stories contain visions of the ends of things, which are less likely to be apocalyptic and cataclysmic than visions of the slow, grinding processes of decay and dissolution, which nevertheless may be expressed lyrically and even comically, as in "Hot Ice" and "Blight." Some stories work up to visions that may be called epiphanies. Epiphanies often clarify life, perhaps with disillusionment, as in James Joyce's "Araby" (in *Dubliners*, 1914). Or, after a personal wounding, they may lead one – through a vision of some absolute condition such as peace or sleep – into a grateful sense of rest, sleep, and benediction.

In "Chopin in Winter," which begins *The Coast of Chicago*, the narrator, Michael, recalls his boyhood in the mid 1940s as he grew up in a house of sorrow and ghosts. His father has been killed in the war, and his mother, unsuccessfully trying to be silent, weeps during the nights. Mrs. Kubiac, the landlady, who lives upstairs, is separated from her husband, who used to get drunk and beat her. She is in despair about her daughter Marcy, a brilliant piano student, who has returned from studying in New York because she is pregnant and unmarried and refuses to do anything except wait and practice constantly, playing almost nothing but works by Frédéric Chopin – mazurkas, polonaises, nocturnes, waltzes, and so on. Her playing reverberates through the house, especially at night. Michael's crazy, noble grandfather, Dzia-Dzia, has returned to Chicago from his romantic and irresponsible wanderings to live with his daughter and Michael. Dzia-Dzia's bullying, brilliant commentary on Chopin and Marcy's playing forces Michael into understanding the music, which previously has been just noise to him. Michael begins to believe that Marcy plays only for him, and he realizes "that the music had been going on while I slept, and that I had been shaping my dreams to it." Dzia-Dzia disappears, resuming his wandering. Marcy also disappears, to have her child. After they are gone, Michael says "it took time for the music to fade. I kept catching wisps of it in the air shaft, behind walls and ceilings, under bathwater.... Mrs. Kubiac's building seemed riddled with its secret passageways. And, when the music finally disappeared, its channels remained, conveying silence." Through Chopin's music and Marcy's playing, Michael is able to experience a peace beyond understanding, a peace that outlasts regret, as he becomes aware of the eternal silence that precedes and contains music and exists in its interstices: "Not an ordinary silence of absence and emptiness, but a pure silence beyond daydream and memory, as intense as the music it replaced, which, like music, had the power to change whoever listened. It hushed the close-quartered racket of the old building.... Even after I no longer missed her, I could still hear the silence left behind." This silence has in a sense become Michael's bride, able, like John Keats's Grecian urn, to tease him "out of thought / As doth eternity."

The strangest, most beautiful, and most powerful of Dybek's stories of metamorphoses is "Hot Ice," which has five sections; it does not have a straightforward, linear plot. The first and fifth sections, "Saints" and "Legends," are connected in that they present the beginning of a saint's legend – a dead virgin's preservation and imprisonment in ice – and its replacement by another legend: the virgin freed from her coffin of ice. The second and

fourth sections, "Amnesia" and "Nostalgia," are concerned with the difficulties of memory, whose aim is holding on to the past. The third part, "Grief," is the pivotal section, since events associated with grief and loss permeate and energize the entire story.

Few really believe the story of the saintly virgin, said to have drowned in a southside Chicago park during World War II while trying to protect herself from sexual assault, and then entombed by her father in regular ice and dry ice (referred to in Chicago as "hot ice") in an icehouse that has been long unused and is about to be demolished in an urban renewal project. A former butcher called Big Antek is the only person to claim he actually saw the virgin in her coffin of ice. Years before, Antek swears, he drunkenly locked himself for a weekend into the butcher shop's cold storage and survived only by finding this Sleeping Beauty and her chaste, life-giving warmth: her hair burned "gold like a candleflame.... As long as he stayed beside her he didn't shiver. He could feel the blood return; he was warm as if the smoldering dry ice really was hot."

All three main characters, Antek and his late-adolescent friends Eddie Kapusta and Manny Santora, have terrible difficulties accepting and coping with change and loss. Antek, a veteran of World War II and a man who used to have an exquisite sensitivity to the sensual beauties and excitements of life, has become an alcoholic and drifter. He uses his drunkenness to help him preserve the memory of the past, which is preferable to the difficulties of the present, especially the loss of so much of the tangible past in southside Chicago. The intelligent and sensitive Eddie and Manny seem to be without parents. They go to school sometimes, work now and then, and often escape their worries and rages by drinking, smoking pot, and taking amphetamines, which bring as many problems as pleasures. As they grew up, there was constant, radical, disorienting change in their native city. Much of the change has been caused by the euphemistically named urban renewal: "The past collapsed about them – decayed, bulldozed, obliterated.... They felt as if they were no longer quite there themselves, half-lost despite familiar street signs."

Eddie and Manny are a lot alike, but their attitudes to the past are different. At times Manny rages – especially when he worries about the fate of his brother Pancho, who went to prison for dope dealing and seems to have disappeared. Manny tries to deny the past, tries to be an amnesiac by force of will, and almost goes crazy. But

Eddie's insistent nostalgia, which he uses to try to hold on to the past, leads him to more grief and pain. At times, Eddie thinks, all one can do is persist in ritual grieving, like that of the old women he sees in churches, expressing "a common pain of loss [that] seemed to burn at the core of their lives, though Eddie had never understood exactly what it was they mourned. . . . He would have given up long ago. In a way he *had* given up, and the ache left behind couldn't be called grief. He had no name for it. . . . He felt it . . . almost from the start of memory. If it was grief, it was grief for the living."

Eddie and Manny do not literally believe the story of the virgin in ice. They know that, excluding Antek, her only true believer and witness, the virgin never existed except in people's imaginations. But none of the three — each for a different reason — wants to lose the virgin. All believe that her existence depends on the continued existence of the icehouse, so before it is demolished, they must rescue her, free her from the ice — which is to say, free her from her legend so they can create a new legend that will confirm and protect the old legend. After Eddie and Manny disappear into the icehouse, readers see things only through the eyes of Antek, who waits outside. He imagines Eddie and Manny searching through the blocks of toppled ice until they find the virgin. Then Antek sees them coming out with the ice coffin of the virgin wrapped in a tarpaulin. They put it on an old railroad handcar. In his love and need Antek has a panoramic vision of them taking her through "the old industrial neighborhoods" where, "shiny with sweat, the girl already melting free between them, they forced themselves faster, rowing like a couple of sailors" toward the great waters of Lake Michigan. There, with her ice coffin melted, the virgin will have a decent burial and a new

life in the freedom of the sea. Unlike Niña, a bringer of doom, the metamorphosed virgin will continue to be a nourishing force — to warm and cool, or calm, those like Antek, Eddie, and Manny who are nostalgic for the infinite, who grieve but can at times transcend grief by transforming it into stories, into glory, into a tragic radiance that is bearable because shared.

In the conclusion of the 1939 poem "In Memory of W. B. Yeats," W. H. Auden claims that in a world where "the seas of pity lie / Locked and frozen in each eye," the poet — the legend maker, the metamorphoser — can be a guide, can, in the prison of time "persuade us to rejoice" and "teach the free man how to praise." Dybek's stories — rich, intelligent, generous, full-bodied, and large-minded — provide such guides.

Interviews:

Elinor Benedict, "Stuart Dybek, Poet and Fiction Writer," *Passages North,* 6 (Fall–Winter 1984–1985): 12–14;

"An Interview with Stuart Dybek," *Alaska Quarterly Review,* 6 (Spring–Summer 1988): 7–12;

Benjamin Seaman and Karen Kovacik, "*Artful Dodge* interviews Stuart Dybek and Edward Hirsch," *Artful Dodge,* 14–15 (Fall 1988): 17–27;

James Plath, "An Interview with Stuart Dybek," *Cream City Review,* 15 (Spring 1991): 143–155;

Dani Shapiro and Julie Shigekuni, "An Interview with Stuart Dybek," *One Meadway* (Sarah Lawrence College), 1 (Spring 1991): 49–58.

References:

John Blades, "A Chicago Emigrant Returns to Wander the Streets That Fuel His Fiction," *Chicago Tribune,* 5 June 1990, section 2, pp. 1, 7;

Sandra M. Gilbert, "On Burning Ground," *Poetry,* 139 (November 1981): 35–50.

John Fante

(8 April 1909 – 8 May 1983)

David Fine
California State University, Long Beach

See also the Fante entry in *DLB Yearbook: 1983.*

BOOKS: *Wait Until Spring, Bandini* (New York: Stackpole, 1938; London: Routledge, 1939);

Ask the Dust (New York: Stackpole, 1939);

Dago Red (New York: Viking, 1940); enlarged as *The Wine of Youth: Selected Stories* (Santa Barbara, Cal.: Black Sparrow, 1985);

Full of Life (Boston: Little, Brown, 1952; London: Panther, 1957);

Bravo, Burro!, by Fante and Rudolph Borchert (New York: Hawthorn, 1970);

The Brotherhood of the Grape (Boston: Houghton Mifflin, 1977);

Dreams from Bunker Hill (Santa Barbara, Cal.: Black Sparrow, 1982);

The Road to Los Angeles (Santa Barbara, Cal.: Black Sparrow, 1985);

1933 Was a Bad Year (Santa Barbara, Cal.: Black Sparrow, 1985);

West of Rome (Santa Rosa, Cal.: Black Sparrow, 1986).

MOTION PICTURES: *East of the River,* story by Fante and Ross B. Wills, Warner Bros., 1940;

The Golden Fleecing, story by Fante, Lynn Root, and Frank Fenton, M-G-M, 1940;

Youth Runs Wild, screenplay by Fante, RKO Radio, 1940;

My Man and I, screenplay by Fante and Jack Leonard, M-G-M, 1952;

Full of Life, screenplay adapted by Fante from his novel, Columbia, 1957;

Jeanne Eagels, screenplay by Fante, Daniel Fuchs, and Sonya Levien, Columbia, 1957;

Walk on the Wild Side, screenplay by Fante and Edmund Morris, Columbia, 1962;

The Reluctant Saint, screenplay by Fante and Joseph Petracca, Davis-Royal, 1962;

My Six Loves, screenplay by Fante, Joseph Cavelli, and William Wood, Paramount, 1963;

Maya, screenplay by Fante, M-G-M, 1966.

John Fante, 1938 (courtesy of Joyce Fante)

In 1980 Black Sparrow Press reissued John Fante's long-out-of-print 1939 novel, *Ask the Dust,* initiating a process that would lead in the next eleven years to the reissue of nearly all Fante's work. Only a few of his magazine stories have not been reprinted. The effect of this ambitious publishing enterprise has been the rescue from almost total oblivion of the works of one of the most engaging talents in American literature. The eleven-volume set from Black Sparrow comprises seven short novels (two of which were published for the first time), a story collection (combining his 1940 collection, *Dago Red,* with seven additional stories), a volume including two novellas (in print for the first time), and two collections of letters, one documenting his long correspondence with H. L. Mencken. As each new volume reached the bookstores, the circle of Fante admirers widened. The Black Sparrow editions of his books have been selling widely, and in translation his works have reached audiences in France, Belgium, Brazil, the Netherlands, Germany, Sweden, Norway, and Spain.

One result of all this publishing activity has been the growing enthusiasm moviemakers have shown for his work. One of his novels, *Full of Life* (1951), was adapted to the screen during his lifetime – a 1957 adaptation with Richard Conte and Judy Holliday – but the bulk of the interest has been since his death. *Wait Until Spring, Bandini* (1938), his first published novel, became a Francis Ford Coppola film in 1989, starring Joe Mantegna and Faye Dunaway. Several of Fante's other books, including his two best novels, *Ask the Dust* and *The Brotherhood of the Grape* (1977), have been recently optioned to filmmakers. Three of his other works – *Dreams from Bunker Hill* (1982), *1933 Was a Bad Year* (1985), and "My Dog Stupid" (in *West of Rome,* 1986) – are under consideration for screen adaptation.

For Fante, who worked as a screenwriter during much of his career, most of this recognition came too late for him to enjoy. He died on 8 May 1983 at the Motion Picture and Television Country House in Woodland Hills, California. He was a victim of diabetes, which had resulted in blindness and the amputation of both legs. He did live to see the Black Sparrow republication of *Ask the Dust,* and perhaps it was this event that buoyed him to write one final novel, the exuberant *Dreams from Bunker Hill,* dictated to his wife, Joyce, at their Malibu house and from his hospital bed. In the years following his death, Joyce Fante aided Black Sparrow in gathering his previously unpublished works, including his first novel, *The Road to Los Angeles* (1985, completed around 1933); the novellas *1933 Was a Bad Year,* "My Dog Stupid," and "The Orgy" (the latter two paired in *West of Rome*); and the two collections of letters.

John Fante was born in Denver, Colorado, on 8 April 1909 and was the oldest of the four children of Nicholas Peter Fante and Mary Capolungo Fante. His father, a stonemason and bricklayer, was born in Torricella Peligna, Abruzzi, Italy; his mother was a Chicago-born Italian American. When John was young, the family moved to nearby Boulder, where his father worked in the building industry and John attended parochial schools. He was a good student with a propensity for writing and a keen interest in baseball; both activities were encouraged by the nuns. Much of his early short fiction, written in the early 1930s for H. L. Mencken's *American Mercury,* focuses on his growing up Italian and Catholic in Colorado and the obsessive goals of his youth: to become a famous writer and a major-league pitcher. For his high-school education he attended Regis College, a Jesuit boarding school in Denver. After graduation he enrolled at the University of Colorado but soon dropped out.

After his parents separated and his father moved to California, Fante followed him in 1930, hitchhiking to the coast with a friend, Ralph Burdick. His mother followed soon after and settled with the young Fante in Wilmington, near the Los Angeles harbor. At an early age he became the principal support for his mother and younger siblings, laboring on the docks of Los Angeles and Long Beach and at fish canneries, where he worked alongside Mexican and Filipino workers who appear as characters in some of his early stories and novels. *The Road to Los Angeles* deals with this down-and-out period of his early manhood.

At about this time he began his long correspondence with his literary idol, Mencken, their correspondence being published in 1989. The letters are largely one-sided. Fante wrote long, sometimes obsequious epistles to his master, revealing his hero worship and asking for advice to a young writer. He was alternatively boastful and reproachful: he bragged about his talent and berated his failures. His letters are passionate and filled with urgency and impatience; Mencken's responses were cool, laconic, and commonsensical. He was supportive if not encouraging to this struggling young worshiper in California.

In the letters Fante may have been exposing his own fears and insecurities, but at the same time he was in the process of inventing for himself a fictional ego, a literary persona that would emerge as Arturo Bandini in the apprentice novel *The Road to Los Angeles.* Bandini, the recurring hero of four novels, is the portrait of the artist as a young man, compounded of foolish bravura and equally foolish self-deflation. His obsessive drive to make it as a writer is matched by a self-destructive streak that undermines his efforts. Throughout his career, whether he is writing in the voice of Jimmy Toscana, the Colorado boy of his early stories, or of Bandini, the struggling writer of the novels that make up the Bandini saga – *The Road to Los Angeles; Wait Until*

Fante at his Malibu home in 1951 (courtesy of Joyce Fante)

Spring, Bandini; Ask the Dust; and *Dreams from Bunker Hill* – this blend of comic braggadocio and pathetic self-deflation runs through his work. Like William Saroyan and Sherwood Anderson, the contemporary storytellers he most resembled in his work, Fante drew directly on his own, often humiliating, experiences but in the process of fiction making transformed them into art. He found a way of tapping directly into his own life – his guilt-plagued, Italian-Catholic childhood; his struggles to become a writer in California; and his zany initiation into the confusing world of sex – but the writer in him enabled him to stand above his creation, making of his stories and novels something more than autobiography.

Along with letters to Mencken, Fante was sending his first stories, and in November 1932 the first of them, "Altar Boy," was published (and later collected in *Dago Red*). Mencken, who had earlier championed the tough realism of Theodore Dreiser, Eugene O'Neill, and Sinclair Lewis, among others, had been advising Fante to write about his Italian-Catholic background, and Fante complied. He was at the time working as a busboy in a downtown Los Angeles café. News of his *American Mercury* publica-

tion came to the attention of the *Los Angeles Examiner,* which sent a reporter and photographer to the café. The 7 August 1933 issue of the newspaper featured a photograph of the twenty-four-year-old Fante in his busboy uniform serving a woman who was, the caption read, "casting admiring glances" at him. Above the picture were the words "Literary Dish Juggler" and beside it a story headlined "Busboy During Day, at Night He's Author." The feature announced that Fante was gathering acclaim as a budding author and through Mencken's efforts had a contract to write a novel for Knopf. (However, the novel, *The Road to Los Angeles,* was later rejected by Knopf.) In this rather bizarre and flamboyant way, the young Fante burst into the literary world of Los Angeles.

"Altar Boy" was followed by seven other Fante stories in the *American Mercury* between 1932 and 1937. He was also beginning to place stories in such magazines as the *Atlantic Monthly, Scribner's,* and *Woman's Home Companion.* The stories, reprinted in *Dago Red,* trace the growing up of Jimmy Toscana from around age fourteen to twenty-one: from the world of parents, parochial school, and church authority to his move to Los Angeles and his decision to become a writer. *Dago Red* is a kind of embryonic novel – a novel of initiation in the form of an episodic sequence of tales that recounts the perilous journey from boyhood to manhood, from innocence to experience, marked by the exposure to evil and betrayal.

Throughout these stories, and throughout much of Fante's fiction, the mother is the center of the son's religious sensibility while the father dictates his consciousness as an Italian, an outsider in America. Jimmy both loves and fears his hardworking, hard-drinking father, Guido, a bricklayer capable of almost superhuman strength and endurance, and adores his long-suffering mother, Maria, who must submit to the brutishness of her husband. To Jimmy his mother is linked to the Virgin Mary.

The story that opens *Dago Red,* "A Kidnapping in the Family," reveals this adoration of the mother. Jimmy is unable to reconcile the present haggard appearance of his mother, worn-out by years of housekeeping and child raising, with a portrait he finds of her taken before her marriage. She was young and beautiful then: "I would stare at that strange picture, kissing it and crying over it, happy because it had once been true." She tells him how she had wanted to be a nun until she was courted and won over by his father. Unwilling to accept this mundane history, he elicits from her a fantasy tale of being kidnapped by Guido Toscana and taken on a black horse to an "outlaw cabin." The story satisfies Jimmy's romantic need to believe she was a prisoner. She is a saint to him, a martyr and sufferer of an unjust fate. In a later story, "A Nun No More" (in *The Wine of Youth,* 1985), Fante returns to this theme of the courtship and marriage of Jimmy's mother, this time in a comic vein. Maria desires only to become a nun, but her brother Tony will not stand for it. A woman needs to marry, he says: "Then the husband pays and the whole family saves money." He brings around a string of suitors, all rejected by the woman. She succumbs, finally, to the burly bricklayer, Guido, who is working on the house next door and, hearing Tony scream at his sister for wanting to become a nun, threatens him with a trowel. This story is another version of the tale Jimmy needs to invent to account for his idealized mother's marriage.

In the story "Bricklayer in the Snow," from the same collection, Fante turns to the father, who to Jimmy is a mass of contradictions – a man who is brutal, angry, and stubborn, a man who lays bricks even in the snow while the mortar freezes, but also a man full of joy and love for life. He is a tyrant who browbeats his wife and children, who piles coal in the kitchen so high his wife cannot reach the top pieces, and yet who laughs, sings, draws caricatures for his children, and invents gadgets. To Jimmy and his mother he is a man puzzled at life, an outsider who feels his exile painfully. Maria thinks of him as a "puppy lost in the snow," as she watches him trudge off to work in dead winter, "his eyes to the heavens as he shook his head in hopeless bewilderment."

Several of the stories deal with the act of confession – the confessions Jimmy painfully makes in church and the confessions the older Jimmy makes to the readers, as he looks back on his parochial school days. "Altar Boy" recounts several confessions. Angered by the priest who chooses another altar boy to hand him the wine, ring, and bells, Jimmy has evil thoughts. He wishes "Father Andrew was a man instead of a priest, and more my size, so I could knock the hell out of him, and get even." To get his revenge he pours red ink in the communal wine bottle, then feels intense guilt: Jesus was crucified for his sins. He is terrified, goes to confession, and is absolved. "So all in all I got off pretty easy," he concludes. In "First Communion" he confesses to swearing and again gets off easy, allowing him to attend his first communion. He dresses in his father's white shirt, which drapes over him like a tent, and he is sent home by a nun to change. By the time he returns, it is too late; he has missed communion.

"Big Leaguer" and "The Wrath of God" (in *Dago Red*) focus on Jimmy's sexual thoughts and deeds and the sense of guilt and shame they arouse. In the former he reveals his infatuation for the red-headed Sister Agnes, tied in to his dream of becoming a big-league baseball player, which she encourages. He steals a picture of the sister as a girl (just as he stole a picture of his mother as a girl in "A Kidnapping in the Family"), then feels that he has betrayed her, violated her. He is confused and bewildered. In "The Wrath of God" the twenty-one-year-old Jimmy is feeling guilty about living in Los Angeles with a non-Catholic woman fourteen years older than he. As he thinks about what Father Driscoll would think, an earthquake strikes, the same earthquake – the 1933 Long Beach quake – that interrupts the lovemaking of Arturo Bandini and an older Jewish woman in the novel *Ask the Dust.* The earthquake, in both works, functions in the minds of both young heroes as a kind of cosmic response – God's answer – to the mortal sin. Jimmy is distressed, then relieved, when the woman runs off after the quake. Father Driscoll comes by and urges him to come to church, and Jimmy feels that

Fante with his grandson Bobby Gardner and Fante's dog Willy, circa 1973 (courtesy of Joyce Fante)

"soon my slate would be clean again, grateful that my church was above all a good sport." Story after story traces the cycle of sin, guilt, and absolution.

In one of the most interesting stories in *Dago Red,* "A Wife for Dino Rossi," Fante turns to the theme of a father's adultery, a theme he introduced in the early novel *Wait Until Spring, Bandini* and returned to in the novella "The Orgy." In the story Jimmy's father embarks on the ill-conceived and foolishly vindictive attempt to find a wife for his own wife's former suitor, the barber Dino Rossi, who has remained unmarried since losing Maria, the woman he loved, to Guido. The jealous Guido, who cannot forget that this man and his wife once shared affections, plays matchmaker to show the barber how happy his own marriage has been and how Dino needs to make such a match. The intended bride, Carlotta Drigo, is a flashy, over-dressed sexpot, and he is a shy bachelor. Guido, meanwhile, is having an affair with Carlotta (discovered by Jimmy), but then gets her to agree to marry Dino. The two women, Carlotta and Maria, get into a fight, and Carlotta runs off. Dino, wise to the ways of women, accepts his bachelor state, and Maria accepts hers as the long-suffering wife.

In the novella "The Orgy" the father spends his weekends allegedly working on a deserted, yet-unproductive gold mine he has inherited, but Jimmy, confirming his mother's suspicions, discovers his father and a drinking crony spending their time with a whore at the mine. The theme of a young boy's exposure to an adult world of deception and lies is also common to the initiation stories of Anderson and Ernest Hemingway.

With the publication of *Wait Until Spring, Bandini; Ask the Dust;* and *Dago Red,* Fante was acquiring a reputation. The books were not best-sellers but enjoyed good reviews. His work was linked to that of the Armenian American Saroyan, another California writer, whose puzzled, quizzical young heroes invite comparison with Fante's. Through his friendship with Carey McWilliams, who later became editor of the *Nation,* Fante was introduced to some writers who had come to Los Angeles in the 1930s to write for the movies – among them, Saroyan, William Faulkner, W. R. Burnett, and Nathanael West. On 31 July 1937 Fante had married Joyce Smart, a San Francisco poet, writer, and editor, whom he had met while visiting his parents in northern California, and in 1940 he began his movie-writing career that would allow him to support his family for much of the rest of his life. That year he scripted *East of the River* and *The Golden Fleecing*. They were followed by eight other screen credits between 1944 and 1966.

In the 1940s Fante, with some financial security at last, was able to move his family – then including a wife and two boys (Nicholas and Daniel) – to a new home in Los Angeles's Wilshire district. The Fantes later had two more children: Victoria and James. The novella *Full of Life,* which became an Academy Award–nominated movie in 1957, deals with this period of his life. Once again the rough-hewn, Abruzzi-born father is the central character. John and Joyce Fante (he uses real names in the novel), expecting their first child and living in a house undermined by termites, persuade the father, now a retired bricklayer, to come and repair the house. The father, though, is more interested in ensuring that the baby is a male, and he applies Old World superstitions and folk remedies – such as garlic in keyholes and salt on the bed – to assure it. Instead of repairing the termite-plagued house, he builds a grand fireplace, one that will last forever, a gift to commemorate the birth of a grandson. The father-son conflict is transformed into a battle between the stubborn peasant father, full of self-pity, cheap wine, nostalgia, and sentimentality, and the successful, assimilated son, embarrassed and annoyed by the old man's persistence in old ways. In still another work, the late novel *Brotherhood of the Grape,* Fante also addresses the father-son conflict. It is one of his most moving novels, a bittersweet story about the failed attempt of the father, now a dying old man, to construct a curing house out of stone in the Sierra Nevada. The stone construction, like the fireplace in *Full of Life,* is an attempt to give the best of what he is, to leave the best of what he is, as a bricklayer and stonemason, to posterity.

Two stories from the 1940s, "Helen, Thy Beauty Is to Me" and "The Dreamer" (both in *The Wine of Youth*), deserve mention. In both stories Fante returns to his young hero's early struggles in Los Angeles to become a writer. Both are set in cheap rooming houses, one on the Wilmington waterfront and the other in the downtown Bunker Hill area. Both are stories of realization and recognition. The struggling young writer is drawn against his will into the lives of Filipino workers – the cannery workers and dockworkers Fante knew from his early 1930s experiences – who have fallen in love with American women. "Helen" is the story of Julio Sal's hopeless courtship of a blond taxi dancer with

whom he is smitten. He spends all his earnings on dance tickets and on champagne for her. He fantasizes about taking her back to the Philippines, until he realizes he has been cheated and made a fool of. In one clear instant he sees "the iciness in her eyes that made him suddenly conscious of his race." The theme of the story is the familiar Fante theme of the disparity between life as it is and as it ought to be, and the young protagonist's recognition that life does not fit one's dreams. It is also a story about the painful discovery of oneself as outsider, as exile (a theme Fante touches on frequently, perhaps most directly in the story "The Odyssey of a Wop" in *Dago Red*).

In the second, related, story, "The Dreamer," the young writer, struggling at his typewriter, his wastebasket filled with rumpled paper, gets embroiled in a love triangle with his Filipino neighbor, who hopelessly courts a nightclub torch singer, wholly unaware that his Mexican landlady, a more worthy recipient of his attention, is deeply in love with him. As spectator, participant, watcher, and helper in this odd triangle, the young, blocked writer discovers his real subject: the life that surrounds him. He becomes a writer by finding, and using, actual comedy and tragedy.

In 1951, following the success of *Full of Life* and the start of his screen-writing career, John and Joyce Fante bought a house in Malibu. It was a period of comparative affluence but also some bitterness, frustration, and disillusionment. A contract writer for Columbia, 20th Century–Fox, and M-G-M, John Fante resented, like so many other Hollywood writers, the scriptwriting that interfered with the fiction he wanted to create. By the late 1960s the movie work had run its course, and he was back to writing fiction. He was aging, though, his health was beginning to fail, and he was raising four children in one of the most unsettling periods of American history. Some of this bitterness is in his novella "My Dog Stupid," which is, like *Full of Life,* both a funny and a poignant work about a man at odds with himself and his family, a man torn by the opposing demands of desire and duty, and freedom and familial responsibility. The conflict for the screenwriter/narrator, Henry Molise, is not with his father; this time he is the father, contending with his own deteriorating career; four wayward teenagers whose lives revolve around surfboards, marijuana, and draft boards; a wife who keeps walking out on him; and a 120-pound dog who shows up on the doorstop and stays. "No wonder I can't finish a novel any more," the world-weary Molise says. "To write one must love, and to love one must understand. I would never write again until I understood James and Dominic and Denny and Tina."

Molise has become the harried father that Fante wrote of in so many of his other works. In despair over the anarchy of his present life, he feels the nostalgic tug of his Italian past, the past dominated by his own father. He watches his wife, Harriet, sprinkle cheese on lasagna: "She sprinkled it with handfuls of Romano cheese and I got a nostalgic whiff of the past in the faraway kitchen of my youth, my father gay with wine as he too tossed the salad in that distant time. It was a wrenching uncomfortable memory, a flashback that almost made me cry, and my soul choked with it, for I had never wanted to be a father."

Whether writing in the voice of Jimmy Toscana, Arturo Bandini, or Henry Molise, Fante gave wrenching accounts of what it is to be both a father and a son; both a poor Italian-Catholic boy, terrified by the power of the church, and a successful, assimilated American adult – husband, father, and writer – facing the dilemmas and contradictions of modern life. By 1979, two years after the publication of *Brotherhood of the Grape*, Fante's health had deteriorated to the point that he was no longer able to write. However, the following year Black Sparrow discovered and reprinted *Ask the Dust*, and Fante, near death, found the strength to dictate a final novel, *Dreams from Bunker Hill*, in 1982. Now nearly all his works are in print, thanks to Black Sparrow Press, and readers are in a position to make a clear assessment of the fifty-year career of this important American novelist and short-story writer.

Letters:
Fante/Mencken: A Personal Correspondence, 1930–1952 (Santa Rosa, Cal.: Black Sparrow, 1989);
Selected Letters, 1932–1981, edited by Seamus Cooney (Santa Rosa, Cal.: Black Sparrow, 1991).

Bibliography:
Michael Mullen, "John Fante: A Working Checklist," *Bulletin of Bibliography,* 41 (1984): 38–41.

References:
David Fine, "Down and Out in Los Angeles: John Fante's *Ask the Dust," Californians,* 9 (September/October 1991): 48–51;
Rose Basile Green, "John Fante," in her *The Italian-American Novel* (Rutherford, Madison & Teaneck, N. J.: Fairleigh Dickinson University Press), pp. 157–163;
Jerry Lazar, "Fante Fever," *California* (April 1989): 122–124;
Lionel Rolfe, "John Fante," *Los Angeles Examiner,* Sunday supplement, 17 August 1986, pp. 4–5, 10;
Frank Spotnick, "The Hottest Dead Man in Hollywood," *American Film,* 14 (July–August 1989): 4–44, 54;
Ross B. Wills, "John Fante," *Common Ground,* 1 (Spring 1941): 84–92.

George Garrett

(11 June 1929 –)

R. H. W. Dillard
Hollins College

See also the Garrett entries in *DLB 2: American Novelists Since World War II; DLB 5: American Poets Since World War II;* and *DLB Yearbook: 1983.*

BOOKS: *King of the Mountain* (New York: Scribners, 1958; London: Eyre & Spottiswoode, 1959);

The Sleeping Gypsy and Other Poems (Austin: University of Texas Press, 1958);

The Finished Man (New York: Scribners, 1959; London: Eyre & Spottiswoode, 1960);

Abraham's Knife and Other Poems (Chapel Hill: University of North Carolina Press, 1961);

In the Briar Patch (Austin: University of Texas Press, 1961);

Which Ones Are the Enemy? (Boston: Little, Brown, 1961; London: Allen, 1962);

Sir Slob and the Princess: A Play for Children (New York: French, 1962);

Cold Ground Was My Bed Last Night (Columbia: University of Missouri Press, 1964);

Do, Lord, Remember Me (London: Chapman & Hall, 1965; revised edition, Garden City, N.Y.: Doubleday, 1965);

For a Bitter Season: New and Selected Poems (Columbia: University of Missouri Press, 1967);

A Wreath for Garibaldi and Other Stories (London: Hart-Davis, 1969);

Death of the Fox (Garden City, N.Y.: Doubleday, 1971; London: Barrie & Jenkins, 1972);

The Magic Striptease (Garden City, N.Y.: Doubleday, 1973);

Welcome to the Medicine Show: Flashcards / Postcards / Snapshots (Winston-Salem, N.C.: Palaemon, 1978);

To Recollect a Cloud of Ghosts: Christmas in England 1602–1603 (Winston-Salem, N.C.: Palaemon, 1979);

Luck's Shining Child: A Miscellany of Poems & Verses (Winston-Salem, N.C.: Palaemon, 1981);

Enchanted Ground: A Play for Readers' Theater (York, Maine: Old Gaol Museum, 1981);

The Succession: A Novel of Elizabeth and James (Garden City, N.Y.: Doubleday, 1983);

The Collected Poems of George Garrett (Fayetteville: University of Arkansas Press, 1984);

James Jones (New York & San Diego: Harcourt Brace Jovanovich, 1984);

An Evening Performance: New and Selected Short Stories (Garden City, N.Y.: Doubleday, 1985);

Poison Pen; or, Live Now and Pay Later (Winston-Salem, N.C.: Wright, 1986);

Understanding Mary Lee Settle (Columbia: University of South Carolina Press, 1988);

Entered from the Sun (Garden City, N.Y.: Doubleday, 1990);

The Sorrows of Fat City: A Selection of Literary Essays and Reviews (Columbia: University of South Carolina Press, 1992);

Whistling in the Dark: True Stories and Other Fables (New York: Harcourt Brace Jovanovich, 1992);

My Silk Purse and Yours: The Publishing Scene and American Literary Art (Columbia: University of Missouri Press, 1992).

MOTION PICTURES: *The Young Lovers,* screenplay adapted by Garrett from the novel by Julian Halevy, M-G-M, 1965;

The Playground, screenplay adapted by Garrett from *My Brother, Death,* by Cyrus Sulzberger, Jerand, 1965;

Frankenstein Meets the Space Monster, screenplay by Garrett, R. H. W. Dillard, and John Rodenbeck, Allied Artists, 1965.

OTHER: "The Reverend Ghost," in *Poets of Today IV,* edited by John Hall Wheelock (New York: Scribners, 1957), pp. 21–72;

George Garrett (photograph © 1987 by Cathy Hankla)

New Writing from Virginia, edited by Garrett (Charlottesville, Va.: New Writing Associates, 1963);

The Girl in the Black Raincoat: Variations on a Theme, edited by Garrett (New York: Duell, Sloan & Pearce, 1966);

Man and the Movies, edited by Garrett and W. R. Robinson (Baton Rouge: Louisiana State University Press, 1967);

New Writing in South Carolina, edited by Garrett and William Peden (Columbia: University of South Carolina Press, 1971);

Film Scripts One, edited by Garrett, Jane Gelfman, and O. B. Hardison, Jr. (New York: Appleton-Century-Crofts, 1971);

The Sounder Few: Essays from the Hollins Critic, edited by Garrett, R. H. W. Dillard, and John Rees Moore (Athens: University of Georgia Press, 1971);

Film Scripts Two, edited by Garrett, Gelfman, and Hardison (New York: Appleton-Century-Crofts, 1971);

Film Scripts Three, edited by Garrett, Gelfman, and Hardison (New York: Appleton-Century-Crofts, 1972);

Film Scripts Four, edited by Garrett, Gelfman and Hardison (New York: Appleton-Century-Crofts, 1972);

Craft So Hard to Learn: Conversations with Poets and Novelists about the Teaching of Writing, edited by Garrett and John Graham (New York: Morrow, 1972);

The Writer's Voice: Conversations with Contemporary Writers, edited by Garrett and Graham (New York: Morrow, 1973);

Botteghe Oscure Reader, edited by Garrett (Middletown, Conn.: Wesleyan University Press, 1974);

Intro 6: Life as We Know It, edited by Garrett (Garden City, N.Y.: Anchor/Doubleday, 1974);

Intro 7: All of Us and None of You, edited by Garrett (Garden City, N.Y.: Anchor/Doubleday, 1975);

Intro 8: The Liar's Craft, edited by Garrett (Garden City, N.Y.: Anchor/Doubleday, 1977);

Intro 9: Close to Home, edited by Garrett and Michael Mewshaw (Austin, Tex.: Hendel & Reinke, 1978);

Festival 88, edited by Garrett (Charlottesville: Virginia Festival of Film, 1988);

"Eric Clapton's Lover" and Other Stories from the Virginia Quarterly Review, edited by Garrett and Sheila McMillen (Charlottesville: University Press of Virginia, 1990);

Contemporary Southern Short Fiction: A Sampler, edited by Garrett and Paul Ruffin (Huntsville: Texas Review, 1991);

The Wedding Cake in the Middle of the Road: 23 Variations on a Theme, edited by Garrett and Susan Stamberg (New York: Norton, 1992);

Elvis in Oz: New Stories and Poems from the Hollins Creative Writing Program, edited by Garrett and Mary Flinn (Charlottesville: University Press of Virginia, 1992);

That's What I Like (about the South) and Other Southern Stories for the Nineties, edited by Garrett and Paul Ruffin (Columbia: University of South Carolina Press, 1993).

In 1961 three different publishing houses each published a book by George Garrett on the same day: *Abraham's Knife,* his third collections of poems (University of North Carolina Press); *In the Briar Patch,* his second collection of short stories (University of Texas Press); and *Which Ones Are the Enemy?,* his second novel (Little, Brown). This highly unusual literary event reveals both one of the major strengths of Garrett as a writer and also perhaps the primary reason that his work is occasionally overlooked in the anthologies and "best" lists that are too often the sole mark of literary recognition today. His talent, like the volume of his production, is large and varied. He is a man of letters in an age of specialization, someone who writes well in many forms and genres when received opinion (especially in – and among the graduates of – most American M.F.A. creative-writing programs) allows that one simply cannot do what he has all along been successfully doing.

Garrett has received recognition for his work. From the selection of his first collection of poems for the Scribners *Poets of Today* series by John Hall Wheelock in 1957 through his being given the T. S. Eliot Award for Creative Writing by the Ingersoll Foundation in 1989 and his receipt of the P.E.N. Bernard Malamud Award for Short Fiction the following year, Garrett has been recognized by his readers and peers as an important writer. But wide recognition has been accorded primarily to his novels, especially to his Elizabethan trilogy – *Death of the Fox* (1971), *The Succession* (1983), and *Entered from the Sun* (1990) – at the expense of his poetry and short fiction. It is tempting (and not too farfetched) to speculate that, had Garrett not written his seven novels, he would today be recognized much more widely as the major writer of short fiction that he is.

Garrett's short stories, published widely in popular magazines, but more often in literary journals, and collected in seven volumes, take place in a contemporary world that seems to be defined by change and uncertainty in a perplexing and continuing breakdown of "the old order" with its understandings and values. But even as his stories chart the parameters, personal and social, of that breakdown, they are always marked, as W. R. Robinson noted in the *Red Clay Reader* in 1965, by an "energy . . . in the rush of action and fury of emotion, impelled by passion and culminating in violence, which characterize his narrative technique, and in experiments with point of view, tense, character types, and plots – resulting from Garrett's persistent quest to tell the true story about change."

That George Palmer Garrett, Jr., should have become engaged in a lifelong attempt "to tell the true story about change" is in great part the direct result of his southern upbringing and even more especially his family heritage. He was born in Orlando, Florida, on 11 June 1929 to George Palmer Garrett and Rosalie Toomer Garrett and was one of four children. Two sisters survived, but an older brother died at birth and, according to Garrett, "has been, always and perhaps strangely, a haunting presence" in his life.

In a lecture given at Central Arkansas University, "Brothers and Sisters and Other Strangers," Garrett wondered whether the dualities in much of his fiction, the tension and conflict between opposites that are at the same time deeply akin, and the presence in many of his stories and the novel *Poison Pen* (1986) of his doppelgänger, John Towne, are not the result of that "haunting presence." It is almost as though Garrett is always speaking in his fiction for two, engaging fully in the lives of both of any pair of characters. He speaks explicitly of this imaginative duality in *Whistling in the Dark* (1992) when describing a long-planned but still-unwritten

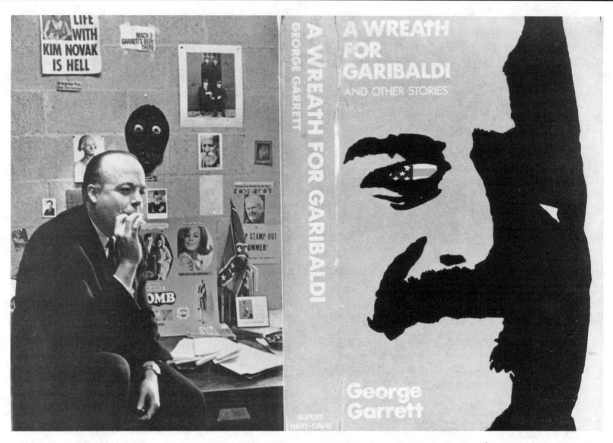

Dust jacket for the collection of Garrett's short fiction that was published in Great Britain in 1969. The title story prefigures Garrett's Elizabethan novel trilogy (1971–1991) in its examination of the relationships between truth and fiction, memory and imagination, and dream and fact.

story in which one boy at a military academy plans and executes the perfect murder of another boy during a time of war: "I tried to imagine one boy (myself) killing the other one (myself as well) out of love and hate and fury."

Critics have noted that quality of doubleness in Garrett's work. Novelist Kit Reed, for example, said of *Poison Pen* in the *Hartford Courier* (15 June 1986) that it reveals that "behind the elegant facade of the Elizabethan novelist there lurks Bad Georgie, a comic spirit waiting to be unleashed," and David Madden, in an essay in *To Come Up Grinning: A Tribute to George Garrett* (1989), discussing Garrett's army stories, finds the presence of "two men: the accessible one and the one in reserve."

Although he has never written Civil War fiction, Garrett is certainly as aware as any other southerner of his generation of the house divided, of the great war that had set brother against brother in a bloody fury that has yet to be equaled. But in "Under Two Flags," a story in *Whistling in the Dark,* he extends the divisions of the war into the peacetime that followed, when the South lived under the

two flags of the old aristocracy and a new meritocracy "based more on service and accomplishment than on either inheritance or accumulation." He goes on to add that in his own family "the division was between my mother's family and my father's." The two families show up directly in the short stories (for example, the Toomer family in stories primarily about members of the Singletree family), and Garrett's sense of the dual nature of things that seems to be at the source of his fiction must spring in great part from the striking contrasts between the two men he has described as "the two most powerful influences and examples" on the development of his character: his maternal grandfather, Col. William Morrison Toomer, the mercurial and flamboyant aristocrat "who made two fortunes and spent three"; and Garrett's father, an embattled, feared, and fearless lawyer who took on the big railroads and the Ku Klux Klan and who said "that our first and primary duty in whatever vocation we found ourselves was always service."

Certainly much of George Garrett's own personality as well as his fiction has been shaped by the influence of these two men, for he is in many ways a mercurial and flamboyant aristocrat, an extravagant teller of tales in conversation, and a maker of large gestures (such as, without a new job lined up, resigning his position at the University of Virginia in 1967 to protest the dismissal of a large group of young instructors), but he is also widely known as a man dedicated to the service of writing and of his fellow writers, whether giving young writers money to survive on or, as critic Henry Taylor has recounted, withdrawing his own manuscript of poems from consideration for publication by the Louisiana State University Press when he learned that it was one of only two being considered – in order to assure that it would not block the publication of Taylor's first book, *The Horse Show at Midnight* (1966).

Garrett's family on both sides included writers who also offered him influences and examples: on his mother's side, Harry Stillwell Edwards, author of the prize-winning novel *Sons and Fathers* (1896) and the best-selling novella *Eneas Africanus* (1919); and, on his father's side, his aunt Helen Garrett, author of children's books, and his uncle Oliver H. P. Garrett, who wrote screenplays for dozens of movies, among which are *Moby Dick* (1930), *Manhattan Melodrama* (1934), and *Duel in the Sun* (1946), as well as writing the final shooting script for *Gone With the Wind* (1939).

Also central to the vital tension of Garrett's fiction and to his personality as well is his Christian belief, which was given shape by his Episcopalian upbringing. A Garrett family anecdote tells of George as a small child leaving his seat during a church service, walking up to a visiting bishop, and taking his hand for the remainder of the service. Some people in the congregation predicted that Garrett would himself be a bishop one day, but if the event was a sign, it was rather that he would write a body of work firmly grounded in Christian belief and understanding. Garrett's stories, like those of other fine Christian writers, gain great depth and force from their particularly real and immediate events, which occur in the face of and context of an eternity that is as real and immediate. He is not a pietist or allegorist such as C. S. Lewis, Charles Williams, or Flannery O'Connor, but the Christian landscape of his stories is populated by saints, sinners, and characters who are at once both saints and sinners.

Already writing poems and stories, Garrett graduated from the Sewanee Military Academy in 1946 and the Hill School the following year. He went on to Princeton University, where he achieved initial success as a poet, publishing thirty-eight poems in the *Nassau Literary Magazine* in 1951 and 1952; he also won the prestigious Glasscock Intercollegiate Poetry Contest at Mount Holyoke College, where he met Marianne Moore, to whom he dedicated his first collection of poems, "The Reverend Ghost," in 1957. He married Susan Parrish Jackson, a woman of striking intelligence, capability, and understanding, on 14 June 1952. They became the parents of three children (William, George, and Alice), and the long-term stability of this marriage between equals has contributed much to Garrett's ability to examine the emotional tensions and struggles among men and women with such insight in his short fiction. For a male writer of his generation especially, his ability to write successfully and with sensitivity from a woman's point of view is one of his real and distinctive strengths.

A member of the Active Reserves of the United States Army (Field Artillery) from 1950 through 1956, Garrett spent two years on active duty in the Free Territory of Trieste and in Linz, Austria, following his graduation with a B.A. in English from Princeton in 1952. His time in the army was a major influence on his fiction, giving him the sources for many of his short stories, the novel *Which Ones Are the Enemy?* and many of the important characters in his Elizabethan trilogy. The final five stories of Garrett's first collection of short fiction, *King of the Mountain* (1958) – gathered under the group title "What's the Purpose of the Bayonet?" – certainly reveal the chaos beneath order in a military world, but that disorder is placed in a larger and even more difficult and enigmatic spiritual context.

After returning to Princeton to begin graduate study toward a doctorate in English (which he finally received in 1985, having earned his M.A. in 1956), Garrett began to write and publish short fiction regularly. His first published story is an army story, "Don't Take No for an Answer," which appeared in *Coastlines* (Winter 1956) and was later collected in *King of the Mountain*. In the story one soldier, Stitch (who reappears in *Which Ones Are the Enemy?*), tells a group of other soldiers, including the unnamed narrator, the story of his furlough in Paris: he had picked up an aging, virgin schoolteacher from Kansas; virtually raped her, but in the process aroused her sexuality; proposed to her; took her money; and then abandoned her. "I felt kind of bad," he admits, but adds, "not real bad." When the other soldiers ask what Irma, his steady girlfriend, would do if she found out, Stitch tells them that he told her and that she furiously sided

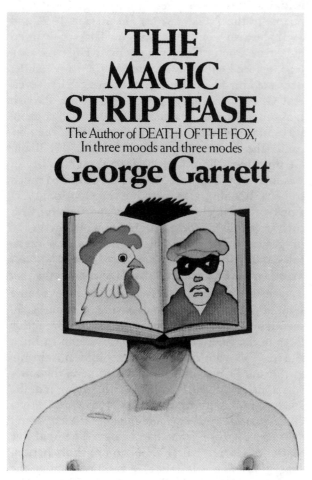

Dust jacket for the 1973 collection of three short novels that Garrett describes as "A comic strip fable," "A story," and "A movie soundtrack in various tongues and voices"

ner wrote in the *Saturday Review* (14 June 1958) that the stories "are enough to mark him as more than a writer of promise. In seriousness, intelligence, economy, in their knack for people and places and their ear for talk, above all in the illusion of reality which, Henry James said, all the other values of fiction helplessly depend, these are stories to compel respect."

In many ways, the collection predicts both the variety and the coherence of the large body of Garrett's short fiction to come. The thematic center of most of the stories in the collection is a moment of discovery, either a coming-of-age or a fall from innocence into a world where, as the narrator of "The Seacoast of Bohemia" puts it, "Nothing, good or evil, is impossible any more." The book moves from a conventionally "well-made" story about the relationship between a father and son ("The Rivals"), to a group of realistic stories from the point of view of women ("Four Women"), to the more experimental and open texts of the stories gathered under the group title "Comic Strip," and finally to the set of somewhat autobiographical snapshots or moral parables of army life titled "What Is the Purpose of the Bayonet?" – which prefigures the meditative autobiographical story/essays of *Whistling in the Dark*. As James Stern said in the *New York Times Book Review* (2 March 1958), the book "begins in innocence, with a boy's whimper, and ends in evil, with a bang."

The design of the collection also reveals Garrett's development as a short-story writer in its movement from stories in the manner of (and occasionally marked by the mannerism of) the American writers of the previous generation who had in great part moved the modern American short story toward greater independence and originality. The early stories in the collection, for all their freshness and strength, bear the marks of the powerful influence of those American writers one might expect: Ernest Hemingway, William Faulkner, and F. Scott Fitzgerald. Garrett has written, in his collection of essays *The Sorrows of Fat City* (1992), about the excitement of his discovery of the fiction of those three writers in a course at Princeton in summer 1948. However, the influence of these standard American writers was a benign one, for Garrett never wrote a story completely under the sway of any of them.

The more fabular stories in the collection ("The Witness," "The Accursed Huntsman," and "How the Last War Ended") have the feeling of dreamlike entrapment, as in works by Franz Kafka or some of the younger European existentialist writ-

with the woman but later in bed was "all over me like a tiger." The simplicity of the plot is enriched by the dangerous emotional and moral complexity of Stitch, his cynical knowledge of how to use women, and the potential of violence that underlines his every move. The isolated male world of the army creates an environment in which Stitch can at once function as outlaw and guru, as "crazy" man and temporary leader, left to "answer the phone and put out the lights" for the weekend.

King of the Mountain is marked by rich irony and by an awareness, as the title suggests, of the world as an arena of moral conflict in which it is hard to tell winners from losers or sort the saints from the sinners. The critical reception of the book was positive: Paul Engle in the *Chicago Sunday Tribune* (30 March 1958) said that "Garrett is exactly the sort of writer getting his start who deserves wide support, just the kind who will enrich the life of the country with his writing," and Wallace Stegers. "The Witness" is the story of a middle-aged nurse who possibly sees a murder on the subway and becomes utterly transformed by the experience, losing her own identity and becoming in some terrible way herself the knife-wielding murderer.

It is difficult to find any literary antecedent for the five army stories gathered together as "What's the Purpose of the Bayonet?" Narrated in the first person by unnamed narrators whose experiences are often directly parallel to those of Garrett, they present new formal territory made up of a blend of the traditional story, autobiographical anecdote, and parable. The formal discoveries of these stories eventually blossomed into full length in *Poison Pen* and *Whistling in the Dark*.

The narrator of "Torment," after seeing the local police in Linz brutally beat a group of prostitutes for no apparent reason other than to scare them, closes *King of the Mountain* by recognizing that, beneath the world of civility and culture in which we live, there is another invisible world of suffering and cruelty. "The things God has to see," he says, "because He cannot shut His eyes! It's almost too much to think about. It's enough to turn your stomach against the whole inhuman race." It was doubtless the force of this ending which led reviewer J. L. Tegland to forget the positive discoveries of characters in many of the other stories and to conclude, in an essentially positive review in the *San Francisco Chronicle* (20 April 1958), that Garrett's world is "inevitably a dark and dismal one" offering "only pain and littleness."

In 1957 Garrett began a full-time teaching career at Wesleyan University, one that was to carry him over the years to various colleges, universities, and summer writing programs. (Garrett never finished his dissertation, but, on the basis of his scholarly work that went into the writing of *Death of the Fox* and *The Succession,* he was awarded his doctorate at Princeton in 1985.) Although he began to write scholarly and critical articles and essays – enough to be collected in two large volumes, *The Sorrows of Fat City* and *My Silk Purse and Yours* (1992) – Garrett was never comfortable in the world of academic politics; there is evidence enough of his attitudes (and his keen satiric eye) in "Tigers in Red Weather: Some Academic Anecdotes" in *Whistling in the Dark*. His growing success as a rising young writer gave him a degree of freedom that many of his academic colleagues lacked. He won the Sewanee Review Fellowship in Poetry in 1958, the Rome Prize of the American Academy of Arts and Letters (which allowed him to spend a year in Rome) in 1959, and a Ford Foundation Grant in drama, which allowed

him to spend a year at the Alley Theater in Houston (1960–1961). During this period he published his first two novels, and he continued to write and publish short fiction. Most of Garrett's stories appeared in literary quarterlies and reviews (including the *Transatlantic Review,* which he helped revive and for which he was poetry editor from 1958 until 1971), but a few stories did appear in commercial magazines, such as *Harper's Bazaar* and *Mademoiselle* – including "An Evening Performance," which reached an even larger audience when it was selected by Martha Foley and David Burnett for *The Best American Short Stories 1960*. It is collected in Garrett's second book of short fiction, *In the Briar Patch* (1961).

Unlike his first collection, the second comprises tales set exclusively in the South, which is, as R. C. Healey wrote in the *New York Herald Tribune* (21 May 1961), "an unsentimentalized rural South seen cleanly and sharply. Negroes, white trash, aristocrats and plain everyday folk all receive equally unvarnished treatment." There is more to these stories, however, than just a clear-eyed look at life at a certain time in a certain region. The biblical epigraphs Garrett chose for the collection indicate first that this South is meant to stand for the fallen world, but that, also, love is necessary in such a world. No wonder, then, that the anonymous *Newsweek* reviewer (1 May 1961) found the stories "suggesting by their excellent, muted brutality a kind of male Flannery O'Connor."

The characters in these stories live in a world haunted by ghosts, a theme Garrett develops most fully in his Elizabethan trilogy, where the ghosts step forward and narrate large portions of the novels. These ghosts encountered in the short stories are not the familiar ghosts of horror fiction but rather represent the terrible human awareness of the past living in the present, or illusions and dreams lingering after their loss in a hard reality. John Pengry, the lonely and desperately eccentric schoolteacher in "The Gun and the Hat," sees himself as "a ghost teaching ghosts" in his everyday life, and he finds his only friends and enemies among the "real ghosts" of his dead family, with whom he wrestles daily. Jane Grim, a young woman from Philadelphia in "Thus the Early Gods," feeling herself trapped by marriage in a southern world she never made, understands that when she and her husband visit his family "they were lost to each other. The man she had married and lived with was a ghost." In "The Last of the Spanish Blood" the narrator, a student at a military academy clearly modeled after Sewanee, learns the necessary lessons of anonymity and survival, and he comes to realize that "all the others, like yourself, were ghosts in the flesh, countries and counties and continents populated by gray ghosts while, invisible, the world of spirits was a tumultuous chaos."

Often in these stories, characters seemingly from another dimension break into the trapped, dull life of everyday experience. Jane Grim is drawn to the trashy Quigly family, who seem pagan and wild to her desperate eye: "Thus the early gods, she thought, must have taken on their guise of mortal flesh and moved among us." A fantastic, almost two-dimensional circus arrives in "Lion," complete with a midget owner, a perfumed lion tamer, and a petulant aerialist, and brings a dangerous and terrible reality to a little boy caught in a squabbling family, which ignores him as though he wasn't there – "he whom his mother calls, always with a great laugh, her little P.S." The world of these stories is the world of pretenses and lies described in "In the Briar Patch" and the world of random cruelty and violence that shatters an old man's defiant act of human connection in "Goodbye, Goodbye, Be Always Kind and True." But in that world, the stories (especially the last story, "An Evening Performance") assert, moments of angelic vision do occur.

In "An Evening Performance" a woman dives from a shaky tower into a tank of water and blazing gasoline, disappointing those in the crowd who can understand neither the beauty nor the danger but transforming the imaginative life of the town. Garrett selected the title of this story for the title of his volume of collected stories *An Evening Performance: New and Selected Short Stories* (1985), and it may well be his finest story. It certainly is the one that most clearly reveals the parabolic quality of even his most realistic fiction and reveals how all his work should be read and understood.

The emotional fury and conflict that mark the stories in *King of the Mountain* are present in these stories as well. Salvation for Garrett's characters is never easy, as the fierce enigmas at the heart of stories such as "The Victim" and "Time of Bitter Children" reveal, but, as an anonymous critic for *Kirkus Reviews* noted (1 April 1961), these stories "show a tender feeling for people of all kinds, a true touch and a manifest talent."

After his year at the Alley Theater, Garrett stayed on in Houston as a visiting lecturer at Rice University during the 1961–1962 academic year and then went to the University of Virginia, where he remained as an associate professor of English until his resignation in 1967. During this period he finished work on his next collection of short fiction and wrote his third novel. For the first time in his

career Garrett found himself unable easily to find a publisher for one of his books, and the complete manuscript of this important novel has yet to be (and may never be) published.

Chapman and Hall published a shortened version of that novel, *Do, Lord, Remember Me,* in London in 1965, and Doubleday published a somewhat different, bowdlerized version that same year. A novella that was, according to Garrett, originally intended to be "a kind of curtain-raiser" for the full novel was published as the title story in his third collection of stories, *Cold Ground Was My Bed Last Night* (1964), and, under the title "Noise of Strangers," in a collection of three novellas, *The Magic Striptease* (1973). Another novella, which functions as a kind of sequel to *Do, Lord, Remember Me,* was published in two different forms: first, as "To Whom Shall I Turn Now in My Hour of Need" in the *Red Clay Reader* (1965) and in the British collection of stories *A Wreath for Garibaldi* (1969); and, in a longer version, as "The Satyr Shall Cry" in *The Magic Striptease.* Another long novel manuscript, titled "Life with Kim Novak Is Hell," written in tandem with *Death of the Fox,* also remains unpublished, but many pieces of it were published as stories (including the story "A Record as Long as Your Arm" in *An Evening Performance*) before its final, radically transformed appearance as *Poison Pen* in 1986.

Garrett's novels were central to his writing of fiction after 1963. Prior to 1965 three collections of poetry, two novels, and three collections of his stories were published – an unusually balanced production for an author of his generation. However, from 1965 until Garrett began to publish the "true stories" of *Whistling in the Dark* in magazines and anthologies in 1987, he published five novels and four collections of poems, including *The Collected Poems of George Garrett* (1984), but during that time only three collections of short fiction: *A Wreath for Garibaldi; The Magic Striptease;* and *An Evening Performance,* which contains only seven new stories. The short fiction he did publish in magazines during that period was almost entirely drawn from the manuscripts of the novels.

Cold Ground Was My Bed Last Night is, nevertheless, a major collection, composed of the title novella and nine stories. It opens with "The Old Army Game," which was not only selected for *The Best American Short Stories of 1962* but also appeared three years later in Foley's *Fifty Best American Short Stories: 1915–1965.* Garrett's collection received praised in the press. The anonymous *Newsweek* reviewer (1 June 1964) noted that "George Garrett's poetry is often conversational, while his novels are ironic and

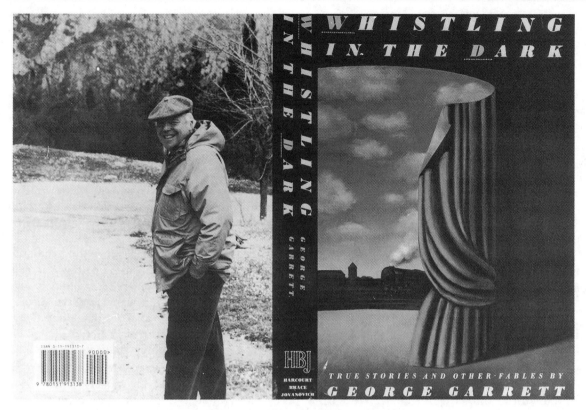

Dust jacket for Garrett's collection of autobiographical stories that exemplify his thesis that "memory is another magic form of tale telling"

paradoxical. The short story is his opportunity to work both ways at once"; the stories "would be powerful, complex pieces even mimeographed and passed from hand to hand. . . ."

Cold Ground Was My Bed Last Night marks the end of Garrett's major work in the more traditional forms of the short story, and the stories in the collection recapitulate and fulfill Garrett's earlier accomplishments in the form. They also mark his entry into the longer form of the novella and begin to reveal his interest in (and debt to) the medieval, bawdily satirical French verse tales called fabliaux. The nine short stories in the book include three realistic army stories, four stories of emotional loss and discovery (two in academic settings), one enigmatic Kafkaesque story akin to the "Comic Strip" stories in *King of the Mountain,* and one comic fabliau. "The Old Army Game," a classic bad-sergeant story, and "Texarkana Was A Crazy Town" are among Garrett's most admired army stories; each of the army stories is marked by a complex irony that gives them special distinction. The academic stories ("More Geese Than Swans" and "My Picture Left in Scotland") apply that same ironic vision to the enclosed, hothouse atmosphere of college faculty life.

"The Old Army Game" and "Bread From Stones," a Singletree-family story, are culminations of Garrett's work in traditional short fiction, and the enigmatic "The Wounded Soldier" and the comic fabliau "The Farmer in the Dell" point toward the future in his work: a movement away from traditional realism toward more fabular fiction, akin to, but quite different from, the work of his contemporaries John Barth and Robert Coover and prefiguring in many ways the work of the Latin-American magic realists, which was to start appearing in English in the 1960s and 1970s. All these writers, including Jorge Luis Borges in Argentina and Italo Calvino in Italy, looked beyond the immediate past and the nineteenth-century tradition of realism to discover their literary forebears in older traditions. Garrett has mentioned the moral fabulists Geoffrey Chaucer and Henry Fielding as his literary masters, and he was strongly influenced by his study of Chaucer at Princeton under D. W. Robertson, Jr. Robertson's thinking about the nature of narrative and literary enigma helped shaped Garrett's thinking about his own fiction.

"The Wounded Soldier," the story of a hideously deformed soldier who transformed the horror of his face into a moving clown act, only to consider returning to the military after successful plastic surgery, is a complex fable of truth and deception as well as of the societal hypocrisies of war; it is one of Garrett's richest and most haunting stories. "The Farmer in the Dell" is a comic tale, hovering somewhere between the works of Aesop and a bawdy joke. The tables are turned on a local football-hero-turned-traveling-salesman by his prim wife (whom he has married to assure marital fidelity while he is on the road) and a shy junior-high-school science teacher. The story is Chaucerian in tone – simple and funny, yet rich with moral irony. All the short fiction Garrett published after this time (to say nothing of the radical forms employed in the novels of his Elizabethan trilogy) moves away from the constraints of traditional realism into the more open ground of enigma and fabliaux.

In 1967 Garrett left the University of Virginia and moved to Roanoke, Virginia, where, until 1971, he directed the Hollins College creative-writing program and completed and brought to publication *Death of the Fox.* During this time Rupert Hart-Davis published *A Wreath for Garibaldi,* which includes four stories and the eponymous novella from *Cold Ground Was My Bed Last Night;* one story from *In the Briar Patch;* three previously uncollected stories; and the concluding novella in the *Do, Lord, Remember Me* tryptich. Two of the stories ("My Pretty Birdie, Pretty Birdie in My Cage" and "And So Love Came to Alfred Zeer") are fierce parables, closely akin to "The Wounded Soldier" (which is also included). Both are strong stories that take place in a fabular world that is nevertheless familiar and marked by everyday, realistic detail, an absurdly comic world in which truth and pain and laughter are inextricably interwoven.

Each of the new stories in *A Wreath for Garibaldi* reflects Garrett's continuing exploration of the ground between enigma and fabliaux, and none more so than the title story. This story, which Garrett collected again in both *An Evening Performance* and *Whistling in the Dark,* deals specifically with the enigmatic relationships between truth and fiction, memory and imagination, and dream and fact that are at the heart of the novels in his Elizabethan trilogy. An account of a wreath that is ironically *not* laid on Giuseppe Garibaldi's monument, the story is itself the delivered wreath; it is a memoir that is something more than a memory or a story. One of Garrett's finest stories, it points the way clearly to the innovative form of the stories in *Whistling in the Dark.*

Garrett went from Hollins College to the University of South Carolina in 1971, and then, after a

Guggenheim Fellowship for 1974–1975, he began ten years of widely varied academic employment (ranging from stints at Princeton, Columbia, Bennington, and the University of Michigan to residencies of varying lengths at the University of Charleston, Virginia Military Institute, and Hollins). He and Susan Garrett maintained their home in York Harbor, Maine, but the peripatetic nature of his employment must have had a great deal of influence on the small amount of his writing. Between 1971 and 1984, when he settled again in Charlottesville, Virginia, as the Henry Hoyns Professor of Creative Writing at the University of Virginia, he did write the massive unpublished novel "Life with Kim Novak Is Hell," and he wrote and published a good deal of poetry and critical prose. But, in the twelve years between the publication of *Death of the Fox* in 1971 and *The Succession* in 1983, the only book of fiction Garrett published was *The Magic Striptease,* a collection of three novellas, one previously published, one expanded from a previously published version, and a single new one.

The Magic Striptease, despite the fact that it brings together the two closely related novellas "Cold Ground Was My Bed Last Night" (here titled "Noise of Strangers") and "The Satyr Shall Cry" (the longer version of "To Whom Shall I Turn Now in My Hour of Need?") and adds to them the wildly metafictional "The Magic Striptease," received little notice. The book's publisher, Doubleday, did not help matters by neglecting to list it in its catalogue and therefore leaving it out of *Books In Print.* Critic David Tillinghast, in the *South Carolina Review* (November 1976), found the book "so outlandish and mischievous that the reader really questions its intention," although he concluded that it was "ridiculous, extravagant, and successful." Martin Levin, in the *New York Times Book Review* (16 December 1973), treated it sarcastically, but Susan Heath in *Saturday Review / World* (12 January 1974) praised its variety.

"The Satyr Shall Cry" is the painfully comic and devilishly anarchistic mirror image of the tragic violence of "Noise of Strangers." Where the earlier realistic novella tells the enigmatic story of the fall from innocence of a southern sheriff after his deputy kills the driver of a car in a shootout and arrests a morally ambiguous vagrant who claims merely to have been hitching a ride, the newly expanded "The Satyr Shall Cry" is an extended fabliau, the bawdily satirical account of another sheriff's plunge into a chaotic moral world apparently ruled by the randomness described in subatomic physics by quantum mechanics. Subtitled "A movie soundtrack in various tongues and voices," it includes spoken monologues, interior monologues, excerpts from the transcript of a trial, pages from a secret diary, the checklist of an airplane pilot, a letter from a convicted murderer to the governor, and the draft of a preface to a book of nude photographs called *The Magic Book of Woman.*

"The Magic Striptease" is an even more radically fabular story than "The Satyr Shall Cry." Presaging the radical form of *Poison Pen,* the novella tells the story of Jacob Quirk, a man who develops the ability to transform himself into other people, and then inanimate objects, including possibly the book that the reader is reading. A religious parody/parable, a political and social satire, and a serious play on the problems of identity, reality, and illusion, the novella is wildly funny and sharply cutting in its satire. One of its characters, for example, Doctor Smartheim, writes a book under Quirk's influence, *The Lost Decade of the Forties: A Study in Mass Hallucination,* absolving Germany of the Holocaust by proving that the 1940s never happened. All three of the novellas in *The Magic Striptease,* each in a different way, move Garrett's readers onto ambiguous and revealing moral ground, which may be one reason why the reviewers were so uncomfortable with it.

Of the seven new stories in Garrett's retrospective collection of short fiction, *An Evening Performance,* six had been published in magazines between 1959 and 1978. Four of them concern the difficult misunderstandings and separate dreams of men and women in love relationships. The previously unpublished story, "Songs of a Drowning Sailor: A Fabliau," tells the tale of a drowned sailor's return as a ghost to his nunnish lover and how a medium sets their needs in ambiguous order. Two ironic but oddly tender stories about husbands killing moths for their wives are printed under the heading "The Insects Are Winning." Each husband is allowed some kind of minor triumph, and each wife finds a curious "sense of joy." Another of Garrett's stories told successfully from a woman's point of view, "What's the Matter With Mary Jane?" examines a quarrel between a faculty couple and reveals the dreams they treasure. "Last of the Old Buffalo Hunters" is the dark account of an old professor and anthologist who is literarily skewered in a novel by a former student.

The most powerful story among the newly collected stories in *An Evening Performance* is "A Record as Long as Your Arm." Constructed from the opening and closing chapters of "Life with Kim Novak Is Hell," and told in the first person by Garrett's doppelgänger, John Towne of *Poison Pen,* the story is a ludicrously comic tale of one of Towne's adulteries, which is transformed abruptly into a very serious story by the suicide of the betrayed friend and husband. It ends with a powerful meditation on "the one free act of human love," forgiveness: "Not that people can ever really completely forgive each other. But in the ritual of wishing to and trying to forgive one another, in ceasing to judge one another and leaving Judgment to its proper Author, then for a brief moment we can find and feel the secret energy of divinity in us." For once Garrett's voice replaces Towne's rather than the other way around, and with great effect.

After Garrett's return to the University of Virginia in 1984, he wrote and published two novels, *Poison Pen* and *Entered from the Sun,* and began writing and publishing in periodicals the autobiographical stories that were collected in *Whistling in the Dark.* With the notable exception of these stories, only a small handful of Garrett's short stories have appeared in magazines or anthologies since the publication of *An Evening Performance:* "Ruth-Ann" (*Texas Review,* Spring–Summer 1985); "Dixie Dreamland" (South Carolina Review, Fall 1985); and "To Guess the Riddle, to Stumble on a Secret Name," a brief story written at the behest of Susan Stamberg for the National Public Radio program *Weekend Edition* and later collected in Garrett and Stamberg's anthology, *The Wedding Cake in the Middle of the Road* (1992). The challenge of writing a story to be read aloud on radio led Garrett to develop yet another new form, a present-tense story in two voices: an involved male narrator's, along with commentary and interpolations from an equally involved woman character. The brevity of the tale makes the surprises and insights into the complexity of a woman's relationships with her present lover and her former husband all the more impressive; Garrett displays his revelations in this small space with finesse and control.

The complete title of Garrett's most recent collection of stories, *Whistling in the Dark: True Stories and Other Fables,* indicates its intent – to explore, in this case by means of autobiography, the symbiotic relationship between truth and fable in lives as well as the writing of lives. As Garrett put it in an interview with David A. Maurer in the *Charlottesville Daily Progress* (23 July 1992), "The book turned out to be about my memories and how other people's memories blend into your own. . . . Memories distort and change with time, so it also has something to do with the different ways we remember things." In the book he speculates at one point on "How much even memory can be fantasy," and later he in-

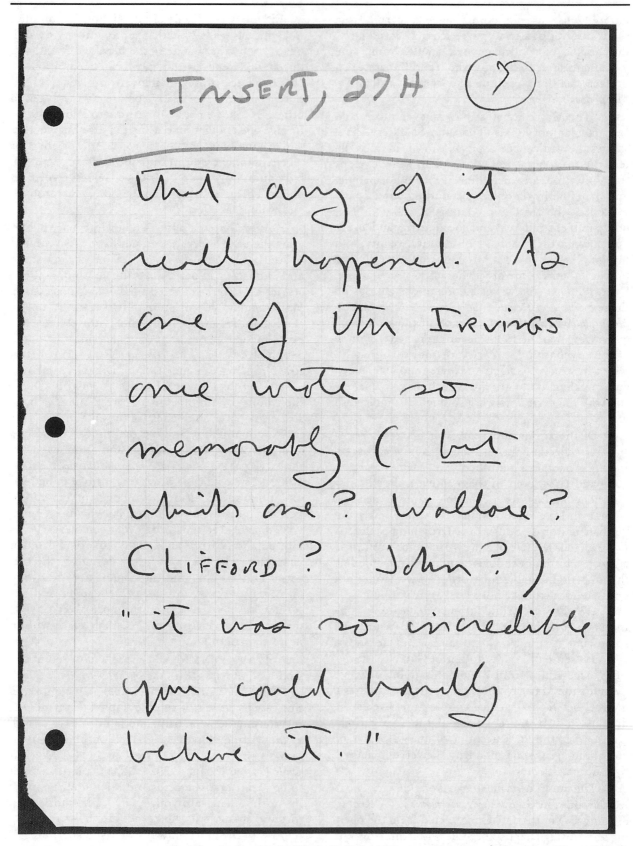

that any of it really happened. As one of the Irvings once wrote so memorably (but which one? Wallace? CLIFFORD? John?) "it was so incredible you could hardly believe it."

Pages from the manuscript for "Hooray for Hollywood," an unpublished story (by permission of George Garrett)

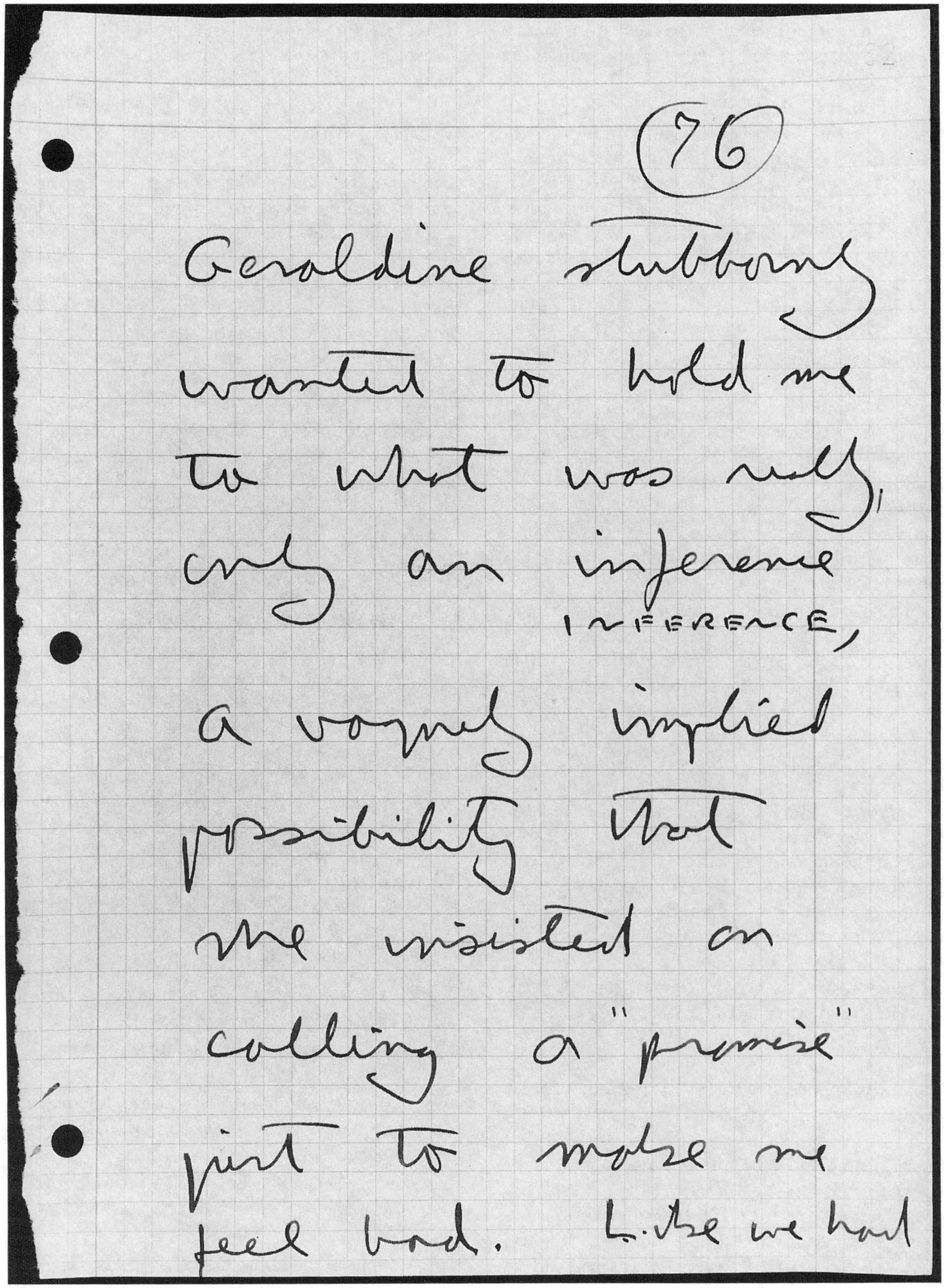

(76)

Geraldine stubbornly
wanted to hold me
to what was really
only an inference
INFERENCE,
a vaguely implied
possibility that
she insisted on
calling a "promise"
just to make me
feel bad. Like we had

sists that "I can remember it as I please, can't I, so long as I am not indifferent to the facts, for memory is another magic form of tale telling, while the power and glory to remember last."

Although Garrett had worked the difficult but rewarding ground between autobiographical essay and the purely fictional in "What's the Purpose of the Bayonet?" and "A Wreath for Garibaldi" (which is also included in the collection), never before has he brought himself as central character so fully to the foreground as in these stories – not even in the duplicitous surfaces and depths of *Poison Pen*. *Whistling in the Dark* begins as an act of public speech. In "Uncles and Others" Garrett speaks to his implied reader as "you and you, all of you, all of us," and at the end of the collection, in "The Gift: A Recapitulation," he tells the almost mythic tale of his maternal grandfather by using the second person ("your grandfather"). The stories, then, become acts of imaginative communion, for people all live, according to Garrett, under "the wide smile of God upon His creatures, one and all" – even Adolf Hitler, in the title story, "for whom He has arranged some enormous surprises."

The book is as complicated in its structure and tonal variety as any of Garrett's novels. It includes stories, tales, a Christmas story for children (which is embedded in another story), memories, anecdotes, family legends, poems, accounts of unwritten and untold stories (which are, of course, written and told here), fragments of lectures, literary anecdotes, and a sequence of hilarious academic tales and memories. The George Garrett it presents/creates in its pages is both the genuinely wise man who muses on the meaning of his own life and all lives and also his Towne double, who cannot resist exposing and laughing at folly and vice wherever he finds it. And, of course, one of the points of the book is that the two are much the same, that the dual tension in so much of Garrett's work is resolved in the identity of the author and, more importantly, of what it is to be human.

Whistling in the Dark is also a writerly book, in its central concern with the mysterious process by which a writer's life transforms itself wholly into his or her books until finally they are all that remains, and also in the quality and control of its own writing. Critic Noel Perrin, in the *Washington Post Book World* (28 June 1992), praised Garrett's writing, saying that it "has a cleanness, a clarity, an utter *thereness*, that I have encountered only a few times in my life. One of those times was when I first read Hemingway; another came with Willa Cather. If you think I mean to compliment

George Garrett by putting him in such company, you are right. He is not particularly like either one except in that wonderful clarity and freshness; he is in their league."

Whether Garrett will continue writing short stories is difficult to predict. He told Maurer, "I've tried not to do the same thing too much. . . . In order to stay alive, I've got to keep trying new things that I haven't tried before." He is working on the first of a new trilogy of novels about American life over the last century, but his energy and range as a writer do not appear to have flagged. He notes in the preface to *An Evening Performance* that "a little less than half of my published stories are here," and even in the unlikely event that he were to write no more stories, his work in the genre is already of sufficient volume and quality to earn him an honored place in the literary history of American short fiction. A major rediscovery and reassessment of George Garrett's short stories and novellas is more than due.

Interviews:

John Graham and W. R. Robinson, "George Garrett Discusses Writing and His Work," *Mill Mountain Review*, 1 (Summer 1971): 79–102;

Graham, "Fiction and Film: An Interview with George Garrett," *Film Journal*, 1 (1971): 22–25;

John Carr, "Kite-Flying and Other Irrational Acts: George Garrett," in his *Kite-Flying and Other Irrational Acts: Conversations with Twelve Southern Writers* (Baton Rouge: Louisiana State University Press, 1972), pp. 174–198;

Charles Israel, "Interview: George Garrett," *South Carolina Review*, 6 (November 1973): 43–48;

Allen Wier, "Interview with George Garrett," *Penny Dreadful*, 4 (Fall–Winter 1975): 13–16;

Wier, "George Garrett," *Transatlantic Review*, 58–59 (1977): 58–61;

Paul Ruffin, "Interview with George Garrett," *South Carolina Review*, 16 (Spring 1984): 25–33;

Wyn Cooper and Kimberly Kafka, "George Garrett: An Interview," *Quarterly West*, 20 (Spring–Summer 1985): 54–63;

J. Argus Huber, "The Balanced Shelf: Understanding Beyond George Garrett," *Albany Review*, 2 (August 1988): 44–47;

Irv Broughton, "George Garrett," in his *The Writer's Mind: Interviews with American Authors*, volume 2 (Fayetteville: University of Arkansas Press, 1990), pp. 275–308;

Richard Easton, "An Interview with George Garrett," *New Orleans Review,* 17 (Winter 1990): 33–40;

David A. Maurer, *Charlottesville Daily Progress,* 23 July 1992, pp. C4–C5.

Bibliographies:

James B. Meriwether, "George Palmer Garrett," in *Seven Princeton Poets,* edited by Sherman Hawkes (Princeton, N. J.: Princeton University Library, 1963), pp. 26–39;

R. H. W. Dillard, "George Garrett: A Checklist of His Writings," *Mill Mountain Review,* 1 (1971): 221–234;

Meriwether, "George Garrett," in *First Printings of American Authors* (Detroit: Gale, 1976), pp. 167–173;

Stuart Wright, "George Garrett: A Bibliographical Chronicle," *Bulletin of Bibliography,* 38 (1980): 6–19, 25;

Wright, *George Garrett: A Bibliography* (Huntsville: Texas Review, 1989).

References:

Irv Broughton and R. H. W. Dillard, eds., *Mill Mountain Review,* special issue on Garrett, 1 (1971);

Fred Chappell, "Fictional Characterization as Infinite Regressive Series: George Garrett's Strangers in the Mirror," in *Southern Literature and Literary Theory,* edited by Jefferson Humphries (Athens: University of Georgia Press, 1990), pp. 66–74;

Dillard, *Understanding George Garrett* (Columbia: University of South Carolina Press, 1988);

William Peden, "The Short Fiction of George Garrett," *Ploughshares,* 4 (1978): 83–90;

Peden, " 'Swift Had Marbles in His Head': Some Rambling Comments about George Garrett's More Recent Work," *Southern Literary Journal,* 17 (Fall 1984): 101–106;

W. R. Robinson, "The Fiction of George Garrett," *Red Clay Reader,* 2 (1965): 15–16;

Robinson, "Imagining the Individual: George Garrett's *Death of the Fox,*" *Hollins Critic,* 8 (August 1971): 1–12;

Paul Ruffin and Stuart Wright, eds., *To Come Up Grinning: A Tribute to George Garrett* (Huntsville: Texas Review, 1989);

David R. Slavitt, "George Garrett, Professional," *Michigan Quarterly Review* (Fall 1986): 218–225;

Slavitt, "History – Fate and Freedom: A Look at George Garrett's New Novel," *Southern Review,* 7 (January 1971): 276–294;

Monroe K. Spears, "George Garrett and the Historical Novel," in his *American Ambitions: Selected Essays on Literary and Cultural Things* (Baltimore: Johns Hopkins University Press, 1987), pp. 200–210;

Henry Taylor, "George Garrett: The Brutal Rush of Grace," in his *Compulsory Figures: Essays on Recent American Poets* (Baton Rouge: Louisiana State University Press, 1992), pp. 152–170;

Tom Whalen, "The Reader Becomes Text: Methods of Experimentation in George Garrett's *The Succession: A Novel of Elizabeth and James,*" *Texas Review,* 4 (1983): 14–21.

Ellen Gilchrist

(20 February 1935 –)

Margaret K. Schramm
Hartwick College

BOOKS: *The Land Surveyor's Daughter* (Fayetteville, Ark.: Lost Roads, 1979);

In the Land of Dreamy Dreams (Fayetteville: University of Arkansas Press, 1981; London: Faber & Faber, 1982);

The Annunciation (Boston: Little, Brown, 1983; London: Faber & Faber, 1984);

Victory over Japan (Boston: Little, Brown, 1984; London: Faber & Faber, 1985);

Drunk with Love (Boston: Little, Brown, 1986);

Falling through Space (Boston: Little, Brown, 1987);

The Anna Papers (Boston & Toronto: Little, Brown, 1988);

Light Can Be Both Wave and Particle (Boston: Little, Brown, 1989);

I Cannot Get You Close Enough (Boston: Little, Brown, 1990);

Net of Jewels (Boston: Little, Brown, 1992).

Ellen Gilchrist's most celebrated works are her short stories that portray girls and women who have romantic longings that are frustrated by the conventions of southern society. With an unflinching realism for which Gilchrist has become known, her stories explore the minds of children and adolescents, often focusing on their disappointments when reality fails to match their dreams. The frustrations of Gilchrist's young women resemble those experienced by Katherine Anne Porter's protagonists who also rebel against the rigid constraints imposed by southern families. Gilchrist's reputation rests on her vivid prose style, in particular her deft use of irony and dialogue.

Ellen Louise Gilchrist was born on 20 February 1935 in Vicksburg, Mississippi, and is the daughter of William and Aurora Alford Gilchrist; her father was an engineer. Although her career as a writer did not begin until after she was forty, its roots lie in her childhood home: the bayou of the delta region. In her journals in *Falling through Space* (1987) Gilchrist claims that she was conceived in a camp on the Mississippi levee that her father helped

build. Gilchrist's early childhood was spent on the Hopedale Plantation in Vicksburg, the home of her maternal grandfather, Stewart Floyd Alford. Described by her as "Tall and proud and brave and civilized," Alford prided himself on being an Englishman. Gilchrist's journals present her childhood as idyllic: she grew up on "THE RICHEST LAND IN THE WORLD," the cotton farms where blacks and whites lived and worked together in apparent harmony, though she admits that blacks were often called "niggers."

Because of her indulgent mother, Gilchrist missed school more often than she attended. In her free time she read voraciously, which she regards as the ideal preparation for her career. She concludes, "I almost never went to school. That's why I'm a writer." From her mother she learned to love the classics and to borrow from them ideas for her stories, even those she wrote as a child.

Despite Gilchrist's memories of a happy childhood, several of her finest stories capture the powerlessness and alienation typical of children and adolescents. These themes may grow out of her awareness that Hopedale Plantation was not an idyllic world, though its adults tried to create the impression that it was.

At nineteen she eloped with Marshall Walker. Their marriage was a troubled one, with frequent separations, during which she would retreat to a house on a peninsula in the Gulf of Mexico for "healing and reflection." There, walking on the beach, Gilchrist and other single mothers would seek answers to unanswerable questions: "We could not figure out what had gone wrong. . . . How could we be unhappy? How could we be alone?" Similar questions haunt the protagonists in Gilchrist's stories.

Before publishing her first book, Gilchrist became the mother of three sons: Marshall, Garth, and Pierre. Married and divorced four times, at thirty-two she earned her B.A. in philosophy from Millsaps College. From 1976 to 1979 she was a con-

Ellen Gilchrist, circa 1992 (photograph by Robert Barber)

tributing editor for *Vieux Carre Courier,* a New Orleans newspaper. When, in 1976, the novelist and
poet Jim Whithead invited her to enroll in his writing class at the University of Arkansas in Fayetteville, she began postgraduate study, welcoming the
opportunity to leave the class-conscious world of
New Orleans. She won a poetry award at the University of Arkansas in 1976 and the Craft in Poetry
award from the *New York Quarterly* in 1978. Her first
book was a volume of poems, *The Land Surveyor's
Daughter* (1979). In 1984 Gilchrist began broadcasting witty commentaries on the morning edition of
the news on National Public Radio. These commentaries provide the substance for most of the journal
entries in *Falling through Space,* which charts her career as a writer and her development as a person.

Given Gilchrist's experiences with marriage
and relationships, it is not surprising that failed
marriages and quests for love predominate in her
fiction. Though desiring love, her women usually
marry for the wrong reasons: to become wealthy, to
escape from family, or to overcome boredom.
Her plots typically follow a spirited, rebellious girl

through the frustrations of childhood and adolescence in a wealthy southern family to disastrous
marriages that leave her impoverished and lonely.
Although Gilchrist's women resent the limitations
imposed on them by a patriarchal society, their resentment often finds expression in only superficial,
flamboyant gestures of defiance and self-assertion
that create no significant improvements in their
lives. Few have the strength to become autonomous
women. Their struggles parallel changes that the
South itself has undergone. Like the Old South
seeking a place in the modern world, Gilchrist's
protagonists attempt to break out of traditional
women's roles, but most are uncertain with what
to replace those roles. When coping with the loss
of love, status, and wealth, few have the strength
to achieve meaningful, independent lives; few
pursue a career as Gilchrist herself did after her
marriages ended.

In the Land of Dreamy Dreams (1981), a collection of short stories, launched Gilchrist's career as a
fiction writer. Sales were phenomenal despite the
lack of an advertising campaign. Both Gilchrist and

In the Land of Dreamy Dreams

Short Fiction by ✦ *Ellen Gilchrist*

Dust jacket for Gilchrist's first short-story collection. The success of this book, in spite of limited publicity, led to her being offered a contract by Little, Brown.

her publisher, the University of Arkansas Press, earned high critical acclaim. When the first issue of *In the Land of Dreamy Dreams* quickly sold out, Little, Brown bought the rights, republished it, and offered Gilchrist a contract for a novel and a second collection of stories. The Louisiana Library Association included *In the Land of Dreamy Dreams* among its honor books, a distinction that reflected its popularity in Gilchrist's native region. Though her use of delta settings, cadences, and idiom have drawn a substantial readership from that area, Gilchrist's short stories resist categorization as regional literature because they transcend stereotypes and geographic limits. The concerns and frustrations of her protagonists are universal, though aggravated by the codes of southern society.

Eleven of Gilchrist's fourteen stories in her first collection are told from a female point of view.

For many of these women, imagination becomes the vehicle for transcending their narrow lives. Though often blessed with beauty and wealth, they suffer from boredom and a sense of futility, which they overcome chiefly through dreams and fantasies. Their narratives offer the reader a penetrating look into the female psyche as they deal with the failure of love and the constraints women experience in a rigidly patriarchal society. In their discontent, Gilchrist's women are frequently perceived as audacious and outspoken troublemakers, but, despite their rebelliousness, they tend to be shallow and self-indulgent.

Reviewers praised Gilchrist's style in this first collection of short stories but criticized her flat, harsh portraits of male characters. The protagonist Tom Wilson, in the first story, "Rich," however, belies that criticism, since he develops into a complex, sympathetic protagonist. This story, the winner of a Pushcart Prize, delineates the gradual descent of Tom and his wife, Letty, from fourteen years of luck and wealth to tragedy and loss. The turning point in their fortunes occurs when their adopted daughter, Helen, becomes a problem child and indirectly causes the death of their infant daughter, Jennifer. Readers' sympathies tend to lie with Tom, whose performance at work declines and who retreats into gambling and alcoholism.

The story ends when Tom takes Helen and one of their Labrador retriever pups to the family campsite and shoots both with a magnum rifle. Then he kills himself. His suicide is Gilchrist's indictment of the New Orleans rich who are so insulated from reality that they refuse to believe that such "bad luck" could strike "a nice lady" like Letty, but they readily gossip that Helen is Tom's illegitimate child.

The protagonist Nora Jane Whittington, in "The Famous Poll at Jody's Bar," escapes society by creating adventures for herself. A nineteen-year-old anarchist, she dons the disguise of a nun and single-handedly robs a bar to finance a trip to San Francisco, where she will join her feckless boyfriend Sandy. Nora Jane is a dreamer. When she had first seen Sandy, she had dreamed of Robert Redford as the Sundance Kid. Her romanticism and her capacity for self-delusion are underscored in the ending of the story, when she begins her journey to Sandy: "Making her path all the way to mountains and valleys and fields, to rivers and streams and oceans. To a boy who is like no other. To the source of all water."

Genuinely self-affirming adventures, however, are reserved for Gilchrist's girls who perform feats that prove themselves the equals of males. One example is ten-year-old Rhoda Manning, the narrator of "Revenge." A rebel against the restrictions imposed by her patriarchal family, Rhoda becomes enraged when her brother, Dudley, and her five male cousins exclude her from the construction of their pole-vaulting pit, which they have built according to her father's directions and which they use to train for the upcoming Olympics. Rhoda's situation originates in Gilchrist's own experiences when, as a girl, she herself could only spy on her brother and their cousins as they, too, trained for the Olympics in a homemade broad-jump pit.

Being excluded from the pit is not the only way in which Rhoda is taught her secondary status as a female. Her father, once an Olympic athlete, is a soldier stationed in Europe during World War II, whereas Rhoda's cousin Lauralee, a Wave, works in Pensacola, Florida, as a secretary to an admiral. Rhoda's father has directed Dudley to take care of Rhoda during their summer in the delta, because she is her "father's own dear sweet little girl." While the boys are instructed to train for the Olympics, Rhoda is expected to play with "ugly" Ann Wentzel, the daughter of her mother's former roommate. As critic Margaret Jones Bolsterli observes, " 'Revenge' . . . illustrates the double bind that tied up bright little southern girls in the nineteen-forties and gave them some of the problems that are so painful to meet in many of the adolescent and adult women in her stories."

At first Rhoda's only means of revenge is to brag that she will be the maid of honor in her cousin Lauralee's imminent second wedding. Even that boast is fraught with irony because Rhoda's mother was maid of honor at Lauralee's first wedding. When Lauralee, her mother, Onnie Maud, and Rhoda's grandmother take Rhoda to town to select her maid-of-honor dress, the family's traditional views on gender are voiced most explicitly by the grandmother, who admonishes her that athletics produces muscular arms, which discourage men from proposing marriage. In response Rhoda renounces the southern myth of romance and the conventional marriage plot for women, declaring that she will not marry. Instead she resolves to become a New York City lawyer who saves people from the electric chair.

Her new resolution, however, does not prevent Rhoda from falling in love with Lauralee's groom on the wedding day. The ceremony proves disappointing to Rhoda. Only later does her moment of triumph come. Bracing herself with a cocktail, Rhoda sets out for the pole-vaulting pit and vaults across it just as her relatives come looking for her. Gilchrist's lyrical description of Rhoda's jump suggests that she achieves transcendence: "I picked up speed, thrust the pole into the cup, and threw myself into the sky, into the still Delta night. I sailed up and was clear and over the barrier." This ending is equivocal, however, for Rhoda's closing words imply that never again will she enjoy a comparable moment of triumph: "Sometimes I think whatever has happened since has been of no real interest to me."

Instead of the retreat into fantasy typical of women in Gilchrist's first collection of stories, in her first novel, *The Annunciation* (1983), salvation for the protagonist comes through profound self-honesty. Gilchrist examines issues treated in her first story collection: materialism, alcoholism, and failed romance. Once again she depicts the confused life of a beautiful and self-indulgent protagonist. The primary theme of the novel is Amanda McCarney's quest for self-knowledge and a sense of purpose, which she achieves only after she deals honestly with her past, specifically with a decision of her youth: to give up her illegitimate child at birth. Through a second childbirth, when she is forty-four, she atones for this decision.

At the age of forty-nine Gilchrist published her second collection of stories, *Victory over Japan* (1984), which won the American Book Award for fiction. In her acceptance speech Gilchrist remarked, "The hard thing to do is to tell the truth, and that's what I always try to do." Most critics testified to her success in achieving this goal when they praised *Victory over Japan* for its bold, realistic characterization. Jonathan Yardley (*Washington Post,* 12 September 1984) called it a "humdinger of a book" and "an absolute knockout." Some other critics faulted the collection for its weak endings and inconsistencies in point of view; they pointed to a sentimentality attributable to Gilchrist's failure to distance herself from her characters. The anonymous writer for *Kirkus Reviews* (1 August 1984) complained that "the majority of Gilchrist's protagonists are indistinguishable: they're all Zelda Fitzgerald — irrepressible, profligate, a little bigoted, more than a little stamp-a-foot demanding . . . a monotonous parade of feisty, bratty Southern belles — mildly engaging one by one, somewhat numbing when lined up one after the other." A close examination of the stories, however, reveals considerable individuality among the female protagonists, who generally are stronger and more complex than those in Gilchrist's first collection. More independent and radical in their rebellion against social con-

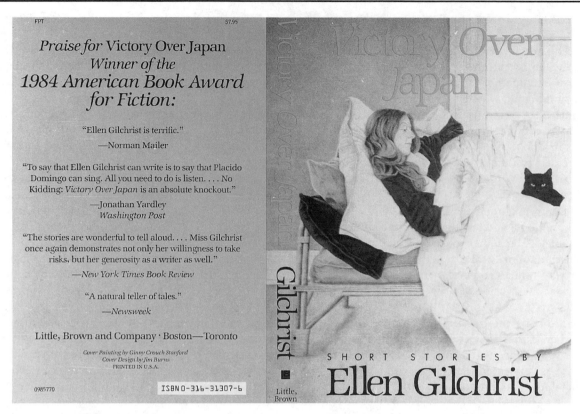

FPT $7.95

Praise for Victory Over Japan
Winner of the
1984 American Book Award
for Fiction:

"Ellen Gilchrist is terrific."
—Norman Mailer

"To say that Ellen Gilchrist can write is to say that Placido
Domingo can sing. All you need to do is listen.... No
Kidding: *Victory Over Japan* is an absolute knockout."

—Jonathan Yardley
Washington Post

"The stories are wonderful to tell aloud.... Miss Gilchrist
once again demonstrates not only her willingness to take
risks, but her generosity as a writer as well."

—*New York Times Book Review*

"A natural teller of tales."
—*Newsweek*

Little, Brown and Company · Boston—Toronto

Cover Painting by Ginny Crouch Stanford
Cover Design by Jim Burns
PRINTED IN U.S.A.

0985770   ISBN 0-316-31307-6   Little,
                                                                  Brown

Dust jacket for Gilchrist's second collection of short fiction, which earned her an American Book Award

ventions than Gilchrist's earlier women, they rely less on men to rescue and define them.

The title story reintroduces readers to Rhoda Manning (in a section of three tales focusing on her), still indomitable but now a third grader on the eve of the bombing of Hiroshima. The plot focuses on her fascination with a classmate, Billy Monday, who endures fourteen rabies shots in his stomach because of being bitten by a rabid squirrel. Gilchrist reveals a new quality in Rhoda – compassion – for she volunteers to be Billy's partner in the school newspaper drive. As in "Revenge," Rhoda is partly a traditional girl destined to grow up to resemble her mother, a saintlike southern lady on a pedestal, but Rhoda also rebels against her secondary status as a girl. For example, she resents her brother, Dudley, being included in the family circle of grown-ups listening to the radio news and ignoring her.

News of the bomb falling on Hiroshima heralds the armistice and the return of Rhoda's father, an event about which she has deep misgivings. She recalls her father's habit of instructing her mother how to discipline her with blows from a broom, small table, or chair. Rhoda's father would yell, "for God's sake, Ariane, don't let her talk to you that way." Ironically the story ends with Rhoda adopt-

ing this patriarchal voice. She dreams that she is a pilot dropping the bomb on Japan: "Hit 'em, I was yelling. Hit 'em with a mountain. Hit 'em with a table. Hit 'em with a chair." She also dreams that she bombs the house of a "bad man" who had given her and Billy old magazines featuring child pornography. By imagining herself in the role of a male hero, a war pilot, Rhoda strikes a blow at this representative of patriarchal exploitation of children. Once again Gilchrist's protagonist finds empowerment only through fantasy.

The last story in the Rhoda section, "The Lower Garden District Free Gravity Mule Blight or Rhoda, a Fable," shows her as a less independent person, in middle age, attempting to cope with poverty after leaving her wealthy husband. She escapes her problem momentarily through her imagination: "Dolphins don't have anything, she told herself. A hawk possesses nothing. Albert Einstein wore tennis shoes. I am a dolphin, she decided. I am a hawk high in the Cascade Mountains. I am not a checkbook. I am not a table. I am not a chair." Her hard pragmatism returns, however, and she files a false insurance claim for her wedding ring and seduces her insurance man, Earl. This third Rhoda story disappoints the reader who has expected the vitality and feistiness of the girl to produce a more attractive, stronger adult. Instead the story ends with Rhoda again withdrawing into her imagination, with ambiguous results. She envisions endless possibilities for her future – flying, teaching, waitressing, moving to Europe, and sewing – but in reality she has no idea what to do next.

Other stories in this section present women equally confused about their identities and futures. Lilly, the narrator of "Crazy, Crazy, Now Showing Everywhere," has married a man she does not love in order to share his wealth. She pays for her decision with a meaningless life, her one outlet being her friend Fanny, whose bedroom is "the most exciting place in Alexandria," called the "madness museum" by Fanny herself. Fanny covers her walls with comments by her friends and her own criticisms of "the wealthy Jewish world into which she was born." As she attempts to free herself through words, her husband keeps her drugged on pills, and Lilly's husband advises her to mind her own business. Whether or not Lilly will allow herself to be governed by her husband's advice remains uncertain. Her ambivalence is reflected in her two radically different interpretations of the jays' and nightjars' songs at the end of the story: "good news, good news, good news" and "hunger, hunger, hunger." As in other Gilchrist stories, the ambiguity of the ending underscores the protagonist's inability to make a decision and to be assertive.

The third section of *Victory over Japan* presents the adventures of a more complex protagonist, Nora Jane Whittington, whose devotion to her boyfriend Sandy is unusual in a collection dominated by women incapable of love. As critic Beverly Lowry notes, "Nora Jane is different from other Gilchrist heroines in that she is strictly New South, an altogether modern and lovable punk kid" (*New York Times Book Review,* 23 September 1984). In the first story of the Nora Jane section, "Jade Buddhas, Red Bridges, Fruits of Love," she arrives in San Francisco only to find that Sandy has gone off with another woman. But Nora Jane captures the heart of Freddy Harwood, "the founder and owner of the biggest and least profitable bookstore in northern California."

In the next story, "The Double Happiness Bun," Nora Jane (now pregnant with either Sandy's or Freddy's twins) leaves both men to seek her independence. After quitting her job and making plans to work in a day-care center, she becomes trapped on the Richmond–San Rafael bridge during an earthquake. Formerly petrified of bridges, Nora Jane overcomes her fear and shows compassion for a beleaguered mother, whose screaming children she distracts with songs from Janis Joplin, the Rolling Stones, and other popular singers.

Compassion also characterizes the beautiful, outrageous Crystal Manning, who, in the five stories in the Crystal section, always travels first-class and who is committed to fighting child pornography. Though spoiled and manipulative, Crystal is a more complex character than the southern belles in Gilchrist's earlier stories. The black servant, Traceleen, who narrates Crystal's stories, regards her as multifaceted: "Miss Crystal, she's like a diamond, all these different sides to her. Turn her one way you see one thing, turn her another you see something else."

Other sides of Crystal emerge in the last story in *Victory over Japan,* "Traceleen, She's Still Talking," where Crystal wreaks revenge on her brother, Phelan, for spending their inheritance money on a game preserve called "Lost Horizon." When Crystal rams his Mercedes into an antelope pen, her freeing of the antelopes symbolizes her own liberation from the role of acquiescent sister. The Crystal stories suggest that women raised in upper-class, patriarchal families learn the importance of money and status but are denied access to both. Though "Traceleen, She's Still Talking" focuses on Crystal's resentment over losing money she considers rightfully hers, Crystal seems more disappointed at the lack of love between herself and Phelan. She tells Traceleen the story of how, on one Christmas during their childhood, Phelan tricked her into parting with her prize possessions in return for what proved to be only a homemade cardboard airplane. For Crystal the story represents the sum total of her knowledge, as her last words to Traceleen suggest: "This is everything I know about love I'm telling you. Everything I know about everything." Crystal illustrates Gilchrist's own observation (in *Falling through Space*) that she writes "about people who are looking for love in all the wrong places."

Women seeking love in the "wrong places" meet with tragic consequences in Gilchrist's next collection of short stories, *Drunk with Love* (1986). In "The Emancipator" the idealistic young Mae has married her Lebanese husband so that he can remain in the country. In "Memphis" the narrator feels responsible for what she regards as the predictable, fatal outcome of her naive niece's marriage to Frank Browne, the black son of a janitor and a welfare mother. The xenophobic implications of these narratives disturbed some critics. In the *New York Times Book Review* (5 October 1986) Wendy Lesser criticized Gilchrist for not establishing distance between herself and the racist attitudes of her characters. But another critic, D. D. Guttenplan (*Village Voice,* 27 January 1987), praised Gilchrist for exposing racism. He credits the narrator of "Memphis" with recognizing the complexity of the problem when she says, "Black people. We brought them here. Someone did. Not me. We are being punished forever, the bringers and the brought."

As in her earlier collections, in *Drunk with Love* Gilchrist examines the problems of the wealthy, but in ways that elicited more negative criticism than her earlier collections had. Reviewer Jenny Diski (*New Statesman,* 18 March 1988) expressed a reaction shared by other reviewers when she noted that "Gilchrist's women mostly suffer from wealth. Theirs may be a purer pain, or anguish without excuse, but it takes a leap of faith to acknowledge the anguish of the rich." Gilchrist's portraits of women and men were also criticized for being stereotypical. According to Lesser, "her Jews tend to be smart, rotund and money-grubbing; Catholics, she suggests, are always viciously sanctimonious; mountain boys have unrestrainable sex drives; Californians spend their lives in hot tubs; and so on."

Though the negative reviews of *Drunk with Love* outnumbered the positive, some critics praised the collection. Judy Cooke, for example, called the stories "vivid" and "exhilarating": "the sense of place, the psychological subtleties, the vivid characterization – these are the qualities which have already earned Ellen Gilchrist acclaim. This latest book finds her in top form" (*Listener,* 19 March 1987). Guttenplan admired Gilchrist's adept handling of details and surprises and called her "a kind of Mississippi magical realist."

One example of such surprises is the surrealistic ending of the title story: the twin fetuses within Nora Jane Whittington's womb have the last word, complaining of the "up and down" life of their mother. The story begins where "The Double Happiness Bun" from *Victory over Japan* leaves off, and it narrates Nora Jane's quest for love. When her boyfriend Freddy becomes a national hero by rescuing two Vietnamese children from the inferno of a burning restaurant, his heroism draws Nora Jane to his hospital bed and leads her to consider a trial marriage. But when she receives a love poem by her former boyfriend Sandy, she renews her relationship with him and forgets Freddy. Her future with Sandy seems doomed, however, since he himself worries about his inability to sustain love. In her journals Gilchrist states that her purpose in writing this collection was to explore what she knew about love. She concludes, "I have failed. Not failed

as a writer. But I have learned nothing about love and added nothing to our store of understanding." In these self-deprecating remarks, Gilchrist underestimates the value of her acute examination of the various ways in which characters, though driven by a need for love, undermine their chances of finding it.

A bond between women, one that approaches sisterhood, is that between Traceleen and Miss Crystal in "Traceleen at Dawn," where Traceleen describes Crystal's rocky marriage to Manny and asks the question that dominates this collection: "What has gone wrong around here that no one can love anyone anymore?" For Traceleen, love, of the sort that makes her devoted to Crystal, is the essence of humanity: "If you are with someone you begin to love them, you hear their joys and sorrows, you share their heart. That is what it means to be a human being. There is no escaping this. Ever since the first day I went to work for her I have loved Miss Crystal as if she was my sister or child. I have spread out my love around her like a net and I catch whatever I have to catch. That is my decision and the job I have picked out for myself...." Traceleen's commitment is an implicit critique of the type of loveless, fragile bonds common among Gilchrist's white upper-class characters.

The story concludes with Traceleen's pondering the importance of choice in self-creation: "Whatever you put into it, the next day that is what you will be made out of. What would you rather look like in the end, a bottle of whiskey or a stalk of celery or a dish of chocolate ice cream? That's the question I'm asking myself right now. As soon as I finish ironing this shirt I am going to make today's choice. Today it will be one thing. Tomorrow I might be something else." Although *Drunk with Love* was criticized for a lack of coherence, Traceleen's meditations on love and choice express themes that pervade the collection and culminate in the last story, "Anna, Part I."

It opens with the protagonist, Anna Hand, choosing to return to her vocation as writer after wasting ten months in an abortive affair with a married man who has no intention of leaving his wife. Her love for him has prevented her from writing, but, deciding to end the affair, Anna transforms her experience into art: "I will tell the story of the married man. But how to plot it? How to make it happen? How to make it live? How to move the characters around so they bruise against each other and ring true? How to ring the truth out of the story, absolve the sadness, transmute it, turn it into art?" Her concerns echo Gilchrist's reflections in her journals, where she says, "The hardest thing to get hold of in the world is the truth. . . . I want all the cards on the table. I want to know what's going on."

After Anna becomes honest with herself and recognizes that she has broken her own cardinal rule – "to always know exactly where she was and what she was doing" – she can leave New York and return home to write. At that point she offers a definition of her art that expresses a seriousness of purpose usually missing in Gilchrist's protagonists: "For now, the work before me, waiting to be served and believed in and done. My work. How I define myself in the madness of the world." The story and the collection end with this affirmation of the value of art in understanding human experience and in knowing oneself.

Anna reappears as the protagonist of Gilchrist's second novel, *The Anna Papers* (1988). An acclaimed author, Anna has committed suicide. Therefore the novel presents her inner life through her journals, read by her sister Helen after Anna's death. Like earlier Gilchrist women, Anna is selfish, spoiled, and unlucky in love but nevertheless attractive for her vitality. That she never emerges as a believable character is the primary weakness reviewers identified in the novel. They also criticized Gilchrist's style for being uneven and lacking the humor and irony of her earlier fiction. In the *New York Times Book Review* (15 January 1989) Maggie Paley draws this conclusion about Gilchrist's novel: "Readers would be better served if she'd stop telling us how wonderful the world is, and let her material speak for itself."

Mixed reactions greeted Gilchrist's fourth collection of short stories, *Light Can Be Both Wave and Particle* (1989), with several critics pointing out weaknesses in characterization and style. In the *Georgia Review* (Spring–Summer 1990) Greg Johnson argued that "this new gathering is extremely uneven, as though rushed into print without much concern for its artistic structure and coherence." To Johnson the stories "lack the meticulous thought and craft that make for the most memorable fiction."

In the first story, "The Tree Fort," Gilchrist returns to Rhoda's childhood and a compelling account of her perennial problem of being locked into the role of a traditional girl. She takes ballet lessons while her brother, Dudley, builds a fort in the backyard, a male domain that excludes little girls. Dudley's world is that of male clubs and warfare, which ape the war then being waged between the United States and Japan.

Dust jacket for Gilchrist's 1986 book, which prompted the Village Voice *reviewer to call her "a kind of Mississippi magical realist"*

When Dudley is blinded in one eye during a fort battle, he becomes the focus of his family's attention, and Rhoda incurs her father's anger for refusing to help clear away Dudley's fort. When her father accuses her of selfishness, she flees the repressive atmosphere of her home, running out to "a glamorous spring day." The story ends with Rhoda's paean to the irrepressible vitality and innocence she still enjoys: "The apple trees in the Hancock's yard had burst into bloom. . . . For now, I was pure energy, clear and light, morally neutral, soft and violent and almost perfect. I had two good eyes and two good ears and two arms and two legs. If bugs got inside of me, my blood boiled and ate them up. If I cut myself my blood rushed in and sewed me back together. If a tooth fell out, another one came in. The sunlight fell between the branches of the trees. It was Saturday. I had nothing to do and nowhere to go and I didn't have to do a thing I didn't want to do and it would

LIGHT CAN BE
BOTH
WAVE AND PARTICLE

A Book of Stories by
ELLEN GILCHRIST

Dust jacket for Gilchrist's 1989 book, the title story of which describes the successful romance of a Chinese-American geneticist and a schoolteacher from Seattle

be a long time before things darkened and turned to night." The freedom connects her with nature and its regenerative forces, in contrast to the destructive forces of Dudley's male world. Ironically, being denied entry into Dudley's fort protects Rhoda from the bodily harm that he suffers. Unlike him, she is free to enjoy the dazzling sights of a spring day. Images of sunlight, darkness, and night underscore the clarity of vision that allows Rhoda to appreciate nature.

Even more complex and appealing than Rhoda is the character Lin Tan Sing, a male Chinese-American medical student and a gifted geneticist who performs Nora Jane's amniocentesis in the Berkeley Women's Clinic. In "The Starlight Express" Lin Tan meets Nora Jane again on a train. Recognizing their connection, Lin Tan tells Nora Jane: "Oh, this is chance meeting like in books."

In the title story of the collection, Lin Tan falls in love with Margaret McElvoy, an elementary-school teacher. A welcome departure from Gilchrist's earlier stories in which marriages to minorities prove fatal to wives, this story celebrates the

mutual devotion of Lin Tan and Margaret. Lin Tan, arguably the most positive male in all of Gilchrist's fiction, is not only a scientist but a Zen Buddhist and a romantic. After he and Margaret make love for the first time, Lin Tan thinks: "Oh, if she will only love me I will solve the riddle of cancer and also learn to operate on fetal heart." Such idealism is rare in Gilchrist. With Lin Tan, Gilchrist moves beyond characters "who look for love in all the wrong places."

After the lovers' first night together, Lin Tan returns to his hotel room, where he sits "in meditation for an hour, remembering the shape of the universe and the breathtaking order of the species. He imagined the spirit of Margaret and the forms of her ancestors back a hundred generations. Then he imagined Margaret in the womb and spoke to her in a dream on the day she was conceived. Then he dressed and walked around the city of Seattle, Washington, all day long, bestowing blessings in his mind and being blessed." It is unusual in Gilchrist's fiction to meet a character with a poetic soul, a character who embraces love with joy and wonder. More often for Gilchrist's characters, love comes second to concerns about appearance and money. Though privileged, neither Lin Tan nor Margaret displays the shallowness or self-centeredness of characters such as Crystal and the middle-aged Rhoda, who appear in the last stories of the collection, older but no wiser in overcoming the boredom of their lives. The characters of Lin Tan and Margaret mark a new direction in Gilchrist's stories — toward characters who have vitality and depth and who succeed in their romantic quests.

Such characters appear in the three novellas that make up *I Cannot Get You Close Enough* (1990). Each plot centers on the Hand family of Charlotte, North Carolina, and reintroduces characters from Gilchrist's earlier fiction. In these novellas Gilchrist again examines the struggle of southern women to break out of submissive traditional roles.

In the first novella, "Winter," Anna Hand undertakes a heroic quest to protect her niece Jessie from Jessie's unfit mother. An important theme of the second novella is sisterhood, and in the third Gilchrist re-creates the compelling voice of Crystal's servant Traceleen. This last novella focuses on love, which is expressed from the mixed perspective of various characters, a technique that emphasizes both the chaos and the cohesiveness of family life.

These traits of family life are central to Gilchrist's coming-of-age novel, *Net of Jewels* (1992), which presents the life of Rhoda Manning from the summer after her first year at Vanderbilt University to middle age. As in the stories of Rhoda's youth and childhood, she rebels against her father's authority but now with greater daring. For example,

she participates in the civil-rights movement and witnesses a Ku Klux Klan meeting. Ironically Rhoda marries a man much like her domineering father, with disastrous results. The novel form allows Gilchrist to give Rhoda depth and complexity that are missing in the Rhoda stories. In the novel the exhilarating and sometimes tragic consequences of Rhoda's thirst for adventure appear in a lyrical prose that has earned Gilchrist renewed critical acclaim.

The promise that Gilchrist had shown in her first collection of short stories has reached fruition in her third novel. Her adroitness in style is accompanied by a compelling plot and a sympathetic protagonist. As in her early stories, Gilchrist still focuses on the dreams and frustrations of a woman dominated by patriarchal constraints, but the attempts of Rhoda to achieve self-definition and independence are no longer trivial. She exemplifies the later protagonists of Gilchrist's oeuvre: rounded characters less concerned with banalities than with achieving identity. Their narratives transcend conventional plots, and Gilchrist's prose, with its passionate language and precise detail, makes their stories memorable.

References:

Margaret Jones Bolsterli, "Ellen Gilchrist's Characters and the Southern Woman's Experience: Rhoda Manning's Double Bind and Anna Hand's Creativity," *New Orleans Review,* 15 (Spring 1988): 7–9;

Jeanie Thompson and Anita Miller Garner, "The Miracle of Realism: The Bid for Self-Knowledge in the Fiction of Ellen Gilchrist," *Southern Quarterly,* 22 (Fall 1983): 101–114.

Paul Goodman

(9 September 1911 – 2 August 1972)

Taylor Stoehr
University of Massachusetts – Boston

SELECTED BOOKS: *Stop-Light: Five Dance Poems* (Harrington Park, N.J.: 5 x 8 Press, 1941);

The Grand Piano: or, The Almanac of Alienation (San Francisco: Colt, 1942);

Pieces of Three, by Goodman, Meyer Liben, and Edouard Roditi (Harrington Park, N.J.: 5 x 8 Press, 1942);

The Facts of Life (New York: Vanguard, 1945; London: Poetry, 1946);

Art and Social Nature (New York: Vinco, 1946);

The State of Nature (New York: Vanguard, 1946);

The Copernican Revolution (Saugatuck, Conn.: 5 x 8 Press, 1946);

Kafka's Prayer (New York: Vanguard, 1947);

Communitas: Means of Livelihood and Ways of Life, by Goodman and Percival Goodman (Chicago: University of Chicago Press, 1947; revised edition, New York: Vintage, 1960);

The Break-Up of Our Camp, and Other Stories (New York: New Directions, 1949);

The Dead of Spring (Glen Gardner, N.J.: Libertarian, 1950);

Gestalt Therapy: Excitement and Growth in the Human Personality, by Goodman, Frederick S. Perls, and Ralph Hefferline (New York: Julian, 1951; London: Souvenir, 1972);

Parents' Day (Saugatuck, Conn.: 5 x 8 Press, 1951);

The Structure of Literature (Chicago: University of Chicago Press, 1954);

Day, and Other Poems (New York: Goodman, 1955);

The Empire City (Indianapolis & New York: Bobbs-Merrill, 1959);

Growing Up Absurd: Problems of Youth in the Organized System (New York: Random House, 1960; London: Gollancz, 1961);

Our Visit to Niagara (New York: Horizon, 1960);

The Lordly Hudson: Collected Poems (New York: Macmillan, 1962);

The Community of Scholars (New York: Random House, 1962);

Drawing the Line (New York: Random House, 1962);

Utopian Essays and Practical Proposals (New York: Random House, 1962);

The Society I Live in Is Mine (New York: Horizon, 1963);

Making Do (New York: Macmillan, 1963);

Compulsory Mis-Education (New York: Horizon, 1964);

The Young Disciple; Faustina; Jonah: Three Plays (New York: Random House, 1965);

People or Personnel: Decentralizing and the Mixed System (New York: Random House, 1965);

The Moral Ambiguity of America, Massey Lectures, sixth series (Toronto: Canadian Broadcasting Corporation, 1966); republished as *Like a Conquered Province: The Moral Ambiguity of America* (New York: Random House, 1967);

Five Years (New York: Brussel & Brussel, 1966);

Hawkweed (New York: Random House, 1967);

Adam and His Works (New York: Vintage, 1968);

North Percy (Los Angeles: Black Sparrow, 1968);

The Open Look (New York: Funk & Wagnalls, 1969);

Homespun of Oatmeal Gray (New York: Random House, 1970);

Tragedy & Comedy: Four Cubist Plays (Los Angeles: Black Sparrow, 1970);

New Reformation: Notes of a Neolithic Conservative (New York: Random House, 1970);

Speaking and Language: Defence of Poetry (New York: Random House, 1972; London: Wildwood House, 1973);

Little Prayers and Finite Experience (New York: Harper & Row, 1972);

Collected Poems, edited by Taylor Stoehr (New York: Random House, 1974);

Drawing the Line: The Political Essays, edited by Stoehr (New York: Free Life, 1977);

Creator Spirit Come!: The Literary Essays, edited by Stoehr (New York: Free Life, 1977);

Nature Heals: The Psychological Essays, edited by Stoehr (New York: Free Life, 1977);

Paul Goodman, 1942

The Collected Stories, 4 volumes, edited by Stoehr (Santa Barbara, Cal.: Black Sparrow, 1978–1980);

Don Juan; or, The Continuum of the Libido, edited by Stoehr (Santa Barbara, Cal.: Black Sparrow, 1979).

OTHER: *Seeds of Liberation,* edited by Goodman (New York: Braziller, 1964);

"The Writings of Paul Goodman," edited by David Ray and Taylor Stoehr, special double issue of *New Letters,* 42 (Winter/Spring 1976).

Paul Goodman was well known in his day not as a short-story writer, novelist, or poet but as a political thinker and social critic. He was widely regarded as the leading philosopher of the "New Left," and beginning with *Growing Up Absurd* (1960) he published many books popular with young radicals. His call for a return to what he thought of as the radical democracy of Thomas Jefferson was understood by the young as reclaiming their alienated

birthright. Goodman gave the youth movement chapter and verse for a faith it already had.

Although Goodman believed his country had fallen into a terrible pathology of power, he loved Americans for their homespun virtues: prudence, courage, loyalty, dutifulness, frugality, temperance, honesty, self-reliance, and common sense. This heritage went deep in the national character, and Goodman refused to give it up. At the same time, he regarded himself as a citizen of the wider world, a child of the Enlightenment. Born a New York Jew on 9 September 1911, but thoroughly assimilated – his grandfather fought in the Civil War – Goodman read Latin and Greek better than Hebrew or Yiddish. He was the son of Augusta and Barnett Goodman, a businessman who abandoned his family shortly before Paul's birth. Paul studied philosophy at the City College of New York (B.A., 1931), Columbia University (unofficially), and the University of Chicago (Ph.D., 1940) in the days of the "great books" programs. A part of the internationalist generation that grew up after World War I, he identified with the ideals of peace and social justice, and he was inspired by the great twentieth-century artists whose imaginations were breaking free of the boundaries of canons and countries. Goodman was unwilling to give up any of this heritage either. So he was a provincial American, an internationalist, a champion of the modern, and a defender of Western tradition.

Although his career as a social philosopher made him popular in his day, history is likely to revise this assessment and value him most for his fiction and poetry. It was for his works of the imagination that he wanted to be remembered, and, however impressive the list of his books of theory and social commentary, his belles lettres would fill a shelf at least as wide: five novels (counting his tetralogy *The Empire City,* 1959, as a single volume), over a hundred stories and sketches, more than a dozen plays, and thousands of poems.

Of this remarkable oeuvre, probably the greatest and most enduring single work will prove to be *The Empire City* – a comic epic in the tradition of Miguel de Cervantes's *Don Quixote* (two volumes, 1605, 1615). A more intimate legacy is his substantial body of poetry, especially the later poems he called "sentences" and "little prayers." To these one would add the best of his short stories, in *The Collected Stories* (4 volumes, 1978–1980). Although Goodman's most abiding sense of himself was as a poet, his favorites among his books were volumes of stories, including *Our Visit to Niagara* (1960) and *Adam and His Works* (1968). It distressed him that readers of his social criticism paid no attention to his fiction.

Goodman came to maturity during the great twentieth-century flowering of the short story. When he began to publish in periodicals in the 1930s, there were dozens of magazines devoted to the genre, several annuals displaying the cream of the crop, and many contests and prizes. The best-known authors all wrote stories, even if they preferred longer forms. This trend continued through World War II, after which everything changed. As Goodman's friend the writer Harold Rosenberg liked to point out, in the 1930s and 1940s one could hardly sell an essay to the magazines, whereas in the 1950s and 1960s it was the opposite: hardly anyone would print stories, only arguments.

This cyclic shift happened to cut across Goodman's career at just the moment when other circumstances also combined to make him despair of ever earning his living as a writer. In the early 1950s he gave up on art as a career and began practicing psychotherapy, a decision which led to

the role he eventually made for himself in the 1960s as an intellectual guru and gadfly of the youth movement. The drying up of his fiction took ten years, but after the publication of *Growing Up Absurd* he wrote no new stories and only one novel, the autobiographical *Making Do* (1963), half political tract, half self-pity. A steady stream of poems continued, purer than ever, but the great flood from his pen was mostly diverted into other channels.

Goodman's first story (unpublished) was written when he was sixteen, a freshman at City College. After his first semester he had taken a leave of absence so that he and his mother (who had divorced and was working for her living) could accompany a well-to-do aunt and cousin on a six-week tour of the Mediterranean. In his baggage Goodman packed his typewriter, for he had gotten the bright idea of writing up their adventures for the Sunday supplements. Although disappointed when no one would publish the amateurish little travel sketch that resulted, he was not downcast, and, with time on his hands after the cruise, he began to learn the art of fiction, much as he had already done with poetry in high school. Before returning to college in September, he wrote half a dozen stories (all unpublished), full of stylistic flourishes and clever plots, though with very little awareness of what he was trying to say or the sound of his own voice.

Goodman wrote no more stories until his junior year, when he signed up for a creative-writing class. He began with a long detective story in which the hero solves the murder he himself has committed. Every story he wrote that semester was about self-discovery and confession, with Goodman more and more the focus of his own revelations. In the light of later works it is apparent that he was edging toward an affirmation of his bisexuality. Slowly but surely he was choosing the life of brazen public display that was to cause him so much trouble.

In a psychoanalytic essay, "On a Writer's Block" (in *Nature Heals,* 1977) – written in the early 1950s, when he was also doing a lot of self-assessment – Goodman describes a hypothetical case very similar to his own. An author is telling a story based on his own experience: "suddenly he says to himself, 'Oh but – I see, I remember – if I tell *this,* I shall have to mention – *that.* But I didn't foresee that!' " There could be no more exact description of several stories he began, but did not yet have the nerve to finish, in his creative-writing class.

After graduation in 1931, his first projects were a full-length play in labored verse and a monstrous semi-autobiographical novel – dreary, plod-

- 2 -

a nice girl had got hold of that bucket ivory-black and that formidable
brush? At the sound she turned round and caught sight of me for the first
time, though I was now right next to her. Resolutely she stuck out
her chin and went on with her enterprise. "Whatever I am doing,"
the back of her head seemed to say, "is none of your business, and for all I
care if you stay there all night."

Yet from time to time she glanced furtively at me, to see whether
I hadn't at length gone away. I had not, for I was resolved to read the last of the
legend on the wall, which was already attaining an intriguing significance.
I put down my valise and lighted a cigarette. ("D'ye smoke?" said I.)

She painted on, uneasily.

"I wish you'd go away," she said at last. "Can't you understand that
you're disturbing me?"

But I now became taciturn and decided, for the sake of science or disinterested
curiosity, to forego my duty as a gentleman. She shook her head. Every achievement
in the world costs its crown of thorns, and I was here. Clambering up, she
began painting an S, which was difficult and demanded concentration.

Ten minutes passed, while it became quite dark and the brush scraped
With a great silvery ado
on the concrete with a soft whisper. The half-moon came from behind a cloud.

JANE JANE JANE LOVES DANNY

glistened on the wall in positively enormous characters. The little girl
glared at me with a kind of prim defiance.

"That's very interesting," I murmured.

"John Bull won't need spectacles to read that," said I. It occurred
to me that especially the boys, would
be in the know, when they came to sail their boats in the long puddles.

"May I carry your paint and brush, miss?" I asked, to break the
silence which was becoming like a deep one one tries to
chop thru with a hatchet. She nodded frigidly and handed them to me. The

Page from a typescript for an unfinished story that Goodman started in spring 1930 for a creative-writing class at the City College of New York (by permission of the Houghton Library, Harvard University)

ding works on a scale that betrayed not only ambition but lack of experience. Unable to afford postage, Goodman carted these around to publishers and agents on his bicycle, his confidence unshaken by the inevitable rejections.

Meanwhile he was also writing short stories, poems, and essays, and with these he began to make headway. The editors of *Symposium,* a highbrow journal of art and culture, gave him a new book by Frank Lloyd Wright to review: *Modern Architecture* (1931). The following year both a poem and a short story were also accepted.

Barely twenty-one, Goodman was publishing in the same pages as Herbert Read, Kenneth Burke, Ezra Pound, and William Carlos Williams. Even better, one of these pieces, "The Wandering Boys" (in *The Collected Stories*), won him a mention in the *Best American Short Stories* for 1933. By the time he wrote it, not quite two years after graduating, Goodman had written about three dozen stories. His apprenticeship was over, and he could turn out stories that were prizewinners — not every time, to be sure, but some were as good as anything he would ever write.

Goodman was influenced by a remarkably wide range of writers, perhaps most obviously by Sherwood Anderson but also by Ring Lardner, Jean Cocteau, Virginia Woolf, and even Katherine Mansfield, though he had come to admire her rather grudgingly in his creative-writing class. But the writer whose example meant the most to him, and whose work he studied with the closest attention, was Nathaniel Hawthorne.

In addition to many Hawthornesque sketches and tales, Goodman wrote two "novels-in-stories," the first of which was "Johnson" (1932–1933; in *The Collected Stories*), followed in 1935 by *The Break-Up of Our Camp* (published in 1949). In both cases he exploited what Hawthorne had seen as the practical advantage of the form, publishing "chapters" as separate magazine stories until he could find a publisher for the whole. Even Goodman's later novels, no matter how conventionally plotted, have chapters that could be lifted out as stories in their own right.

Such formal methods were well suited to Goodman's habits of composition. He wrote with ease and pleasure, every morning and sometimes late into the night, especially in his youth. First drafts were scribbled with a stubby pencil on the cheapest paper, to the very edge of the page, and rarely show signs of hesitation or second thoughts. He revised them as he typed them. Whatever the scale of the project he was working on, he tended to compose in small units, rarely more than three or four pages, marked off by a heading or some other formal device. Often several of these units were produced at one sitting, and two or three might make a story. Since he fell into the same rhythm whatever sort of prose he was writing, fiction or nonfiction, it could be said that the short story gave him his primary compositional method, the fundamental building block that was the secret of his productivity.

Simple as this method was, it allowed for much complexity and experiment in literary manner. Already in these early stories Goodman was looking for ways of describing life that took less for granted than traditional realism. Aside from juvenilia, Goodman never wrote in the realistic manner, though he came close to its conventions now and then in his naturalistic fiction, especially *Parents' Day* (1951) and *Making Do,* which are narrowly autobiographical accounts of his attempts to fit into one community or another, accept their values to the extent he could, and contemplate his thankless role as a thorn in their sides. Most often, however, he had no such story to tell, and his effort was to find a literary manner that matched his more problematic relations with the world — impressionism, cubism, expressionism, and sometimes a biting and hallucinatory naturalism.

"The Wandering Boys" illustrates this unwillingness to sink into the comforts of realism, whether the psychological verisimilitude of the Jamesian mainstream or the more alienated "foreign correspondent" school of Ernest Hemingway. Goodman's story is very much a comment on the Great Depression, with characters who could have walked out of a work by John Steinbeck — or might have actually stepped off a boxcar somewhere in rural Ohio, as they do in Goodman's plot. They are six boys, ages fourteen to seventeen, from the four corners of the hungry continent, riding the rails in search of a living and a home. They steal vegetables from a farmer's field, and he confronts them: "Where do you come from? why don't you go back?" Four of them reply one by one:

> "I ran away from thah."
> "Warn't nuthin thah."
> "Can't you see, perhaps he didn't have any home to stay in?"
> "Don't shove. You know what your father got for shovin'."

Meanwhile the farmer is thinking, "Unlucky kids! I tremble because of them. I don't know what I am supposed to say. I cry for my country's economic suicide." He does not behave like a realistic character: " 'Aaannnhh,' whinnied the farmer, and spat, and ran away, plucking at his collar."

The rest of the story explores a new community budding in the wreckage of the old order, a community made up of boys in a boxcar. There is the oldest, a natural leader who makes peace among them and sits up musing on their fate, after all the others are asleep. There are the two youngest, who fall into one another's arms at night for solace and warmth, much to the disgust of the fourth boy. The leader defends them: "the kids are friends; that is why they lie down with each other." The fifth boy is prone to violence, wanders off on his own, rapes a young farm girl, and finally jumps from the rolling car into the night.

In a surprising footnote Goodman says he is imitating the literary impressionism of Woolf. Everything is asserted as a formal pattern, cut free of preconception and popular stereotypes, and the patterns come together in a new vision of particularity and significance. Published in *Symposium,* whose editors were known to be Trotskyites, such a story piqued the curiosity of all sorts of readers. Goodman got fan letters and invitations to contribute from other left-wing magazines.

But Goodman was not a left-wing modernist. He was a troublemaker whose bold experiments were thoroughly obnoxious to conventional sensibilities, traditionalist or modernist, left or right. His "Johnson" stories are cubist in manner and tell of youthful adventures in bisexual love. As the hero turns to his two beloveds, one male, one female, he finds himself losing his ability to distinguish them: "I can see all my loves on her face," Johnson exclaims.

In the final Johnson story, "Out of Love," he cuts himself shaving, and hears the weird cry of his other self, "Johnson-in-love," in his dying moment. "What an unearthly shriek! who is there?" he stammers. But it is another person, no longer existing, whose throat is cut, while "Johnson-out-of-love" merely doctors his little nick with a styptic pencil, wondering why he is hearing things.

"Out of Love" was one of the few Johnson stories that could be published soon after it was written without revealing the bisexual theme of these cubist romances. The others were then unprintable, as was much that he was writing. The heyday of the short story in America coincided with the great leftward shift of the intellectuals, and native versions of socialist realism were just as prudish and straitlaced as their Soviet counterparts. Not only were there certain methods and manners that were deemed irresponsible, but also certain facts of life that were officially not allowed to exist.

Although never a "gay writer" in the narrow sense, Goodman wrote many stories with homosexual themes. Except for some love poems, very little of his work is frankly erotic, but the confessional impulse was powerful in him. In the 1940s and 1950s he sometimes wrote about the world of gay bars and sexy sailors – probably, at least in part, to scandalize editors who were not going to print his stories anyway. In the beginning, however, he was not so interested in breaking through to a hardened or dismissive reader as he was in simply breaking free of his own inhibitions. He wanted to drop his defenses and stand revealed in all his folly and yearning.

Perhaps the best story he ever wrote is such an attempt: "Iddings Clark" (in *The Collected Stories*) was inspired by Hawthorne's passionate tale of self-revelation and disguise "The Minister's Black Veil" (in *Twice-Told Tales,* 1837). Iddings is a schoolteacher in the midst of a psychic breakdown, and he faints at the Christmas ceremonies where he is conducting the choir. He later has a premonitory dream, which comes true the day classes reconvene: he appears before his English class "stark naked except for his spectacles and a Whittier in his right hand." The boys and girls flee, except for one thirteen-year-old girl, who seems much younger in their dialogue and who somehow is not frightened.

> She stared at him closely, from head to foot and said, "Is it true, what they say, Mr. Clark, that you are a thousand years old?"
>
> "A thousand years! Heavens no."
>
> "They say that you said you was a thousand years old, and I see that in some places you've grown all over with hair."
>
> "I am 31," he said smiling.

The strange colloquy continues while the other children run to alert the dean.

It is unlikely that at age twenty-one, when he wrote this story, Goodman had any clear understanding of the deeper sources of his imagination. "Iddings Clark" is not directly confessional, even though the theme is self-revelation; nevertheless, there are talismanic clues that Goodman was certainly aware of weaving into the story, by which he seems – a painter putting his own face in the crowd – to cast a spectral light over the whole, without any but the initiated quite knowing whence it comes.

A short story Goodman wrote in 1936, "A Cross-Country Runner at Sixty-Five" (in *The Col-*

Goodman in the Washington Heights neighborhood of Manhattan, March 1938

lected Stories), deals again with the generational relations between old and young and with the layers of experience in a single consciousness — what one might call the geology of the human spirit. The hero, Perry Westover, is like Iddings Clark in that the young of his town have developed myths about him: "They say he has run a thousand times.... He must be a hundred years old!" In fact he has run a local race forty-five times, and everything about the course is part of his past and part of his present. His wife and son accuse him of refusing to grow up, of clinging neurotically to childish ways. He has never chosen a career or worked for wages, but since he is an acute observer he has been able to invent a few things that have brought in money. Cross-country running is his career. Just as Iddings has been pow-

erfully affected by teaching Hawthorne to his students for many years, Perry is fond of quoting Ecclesiastes. Running is like writing, and Perry is another avatar of Goodman, though there is no way an ordinary reader would likely know this.

Halfway through the race, Perry comes upon a little shack in the woods that at first he does not recognize. Going inside — for he no longer runs to win, but just for the race — he realizes that he built it himself decades ago. Others have used it (there is a Boy Scout handbook on the table), and it is in good repair. On the back wall are carved the graffiti of many years, including the initials of his own children.

Goodman reproduced the carvings in his story, and, for one who knew him well, some of them would be instantly recognizable: "OHS" were the initials of a college chum, as was "LF"; and "ES" and "RA" represented Esther and Raymond, characters in a play Goodman had just written. Other initials represent layers of Goodman's erotic history. For example, "HC" and "GC" were the initials of a pair of teenage brothers who lived in his neighborhood in 1933.

Goodman was tapping into some deep excitement regarding his own childhood that still remained alive to him, though he held it close and secret, whose potent hieroglyphs helped his art gain magical authenticity. Goodman's life was inextricably woven into his art, and in his earliest stories he had already discovered the thrill of parading his secrets in public, sometimes to confess them, sometimes only to remind himself of them, to let their presence stir his imagination.

Oddly enough, the effect of such stratagems on Goodman's stories was rarely mystifying. Later on, in the 1940s, he sometimes wrote about personal encounters or private grudges in ways that were obscure, except to his enemies. (Such in-group writing was practiced by many of the New York literati, who sometimes put Goodman in their stories.) But at least for the first ten years of his career, the confessional undercurrent in his work made the waters luminous, not murky. Yet they were strange stories, thoroughly out of the mainstream, and Goodman was unable to find publishers for most of them. It was not until 1940 that his work began to have a little vogue in the pages of *Partisan Review*, *Kenyon Review*, and the New Directions annuals. By then he had a trunkful of stories: he literally kept them in an old trunk, which held some seventy or eighty typescripts. He put them together in batches called "Prose Compositions" or "Heroic Portraits" – like Hawthorne's "Allegories of the Heart" – and tried to interest publishers, and he wrote little theoretical prefaces for these "books," as well as writing several essays on literary style. Having just spent three years at the University of Chicago earning a doctorate in aesthetic theory, Goodman had returned to Manhattan with a head full of new ideas about his art. In the next two years he managed to publish several essays and, more important, a novel (*The Grand Piano*, 1942) and several stories and poems.

All this burgeoning and flowering for Goodman was blighted during World War II. Although his anarchism was not yet fully worked through – the war forced him to do that – Goodman knew he was antimilitarist and antistate, and he was unwilling to bite his tongue and pretend to acquiesce in

the international bloodshed. Neither was he one of the absolutist pacifists ready to go to jail for his beliefs. "Institution for institution," as one of his characters (Horatio) says in *The Empire City*, jail is "worse than the army." Goodman was not ready to enlist in either. Some editors and publishers drew back in horror from his avowedly seditious advice to the young to avoid the draft. Even the bohemians and leftists were shocked by some of the things he said, such as his sardonic praise for the black market as a healthy response to international capitalism and its wars. It did not help that he was a notorious bisexual, albeit with a wife and infant daughter at home.

His publishing outlets quickly dried up, and it was not until the war was over that his career began to recover. The first publisher willing to champion him was Vanguard, which had a long history of printing works by anarchists. Vanguard published Goodman's first volume of stories, *The Facts of Life*, in 1945, and two more books soon after. But the right moment had passed, and Goodman was unable to win a mainstream audience for his work. Nonetheless he continued to write new stories – another fifty between the end of the war and 1960, when he finally gave up. By then Goodman was married for the second time (to Sally Goodman), had two children to support (Susan and Mathew), and could not earn a nickel from his fiction. (Susan was the product of Goodman's common-law marriage to Virginia Miller in the late 1930s; a third child, Daisy, was born in 1963.)

Whatever difficulty he had getting published, by mid century Goodman had managed to establish himself as one of the unavoidable figures of the literary avant-garde. Some of his old stories were anthology pieces. Even the *Partisan Review*, which had blacklisted him, did not fail to include "The Facts of Life" in its *Partisan Reader* (1946). In 1944 "Iddings Clark" had finally been published in the English magazine *Horizon*, and was then picked for the *Golden Horizon* anthology (1953). Before long, stories by him appeared in five similar collections.

Goodman wrote two essays at about this time (both collected in *Utopian Essays and Practical Proposals*, 1962) that survey the literary contribution of his generation, with obvious implications for his own work. In the first, "Advance-Guard Writing, 1900–1950," he raises the question of the place of the avant-garde in a culture. Goodman believed that every genuine work of art was "new and daring," and it was at his creative peril that an artist attempted to make his works conform to any predetermined moral or political end. Yet avant-garde writing had a special political nature because its relation to its audience was deeply antagonistic. Such art was not necessarily intended to insult. It grew out of an inner problem of the artist himself, as did all art. However, the avant-garde writer's problem was also society's problem, based on fatal divisions, illusions, blindness, and despair. If a writer rubbed his reader's nose in this, it was not without suffering his own woe, and at least to some degree discovering his own corruption and falsity.

Around 1945 Goodman noticed a change in the writers of his generation, a change he did not experience or approve. He discussed the issue in a second essay, "Good Interim Writing" (also titled, in its first printing, "They've Been Good Enough Long Enough"). Here he reviews the anthologies in which his own stories regularly appeared, alongside pieces by Saul Bellow, Delmore Schwartz, Isaac Rosenfeld, and Bernard Malamud, and found himself uncomfortable and out of place. He gave the "best authors" their due: "these disarming unpretentious but tough-textured art-works show that, as ever, an honest exercise of the senses, the feelings, the wits, and the spirit can make a livable experience. This is not the grandest thing in the world, but it *is* something to go on." At the same time, he was not satisfied: "The authors of my generation are withholding their strength, they lack daring and absolute aspiration. There is no hint of experimentation in these pieces; rather there is the knowing use of the techniques, attitudes, and subject matters that our predecessors won for us. This is all very well for a brief interim, but I think that the interim has lasted too long."

Goodman wrote of his own contributions as part of a project not yet achieved, an attempt to deal with alienation, or – to put it more personally – an effort to cope with the neglect and revulsion with which the public received his work. When he revised these essays for inclusion in *Utopian Essays and Practical Proposals,* he added that he was ready to "give up the ambitious notion of public artist."

Goodman's stories started out in the early 1930s as confessional and full of private allusions but meant for the anonymous public. By the late 1940s they had become personal in an intimately communitarian way. In the old days he had often inserted the names of his friends, if only as graffiti, in order to send a shiver of life through his imagination; later he was putting whole persons into his stories but changing the names, although never disguising the places (Springfield, Massachusetts; McHale's Tavern "on Eighth Avenue at 26th Street" in New York; and so on). Although Goodman continued writing stories until 1960, including some very good ones, the impulse to fashion a world in the imagination had gone dead in him.

There were three interrelated reasons for Goodman's crisis, and his avant-garde strategy as a "community author" was his unsuccessful attempt to confront and solve these. First, since his art was unacceptable to the public at large, he could not earn his livelihood by it, and therefore he no longer felt justified in creating it. Second, his society was apparently sick in ways that art was not going to cure, and his obligation was to turn to the reforming task in whatever way he could – as a social critic and political philosopher. The third reason had to do more directly with the intimate sources of his inspiration.

Goodman believed that the practice of art, whatever its importance in the social order and human community, was for the artist a neurotic defense, or, to put it more positively, it was his way of making contact with the world, of writing himself into existence, and of dealing with his own insoluble problems. Although such a characterological stance is too deeply grounded in early life to admit much alteration, Goodman thought that psychotherapy could make a difference in the way one lived out one's fate. In the late 1940s he chose to undergo a self-analysis, along Freudian and Reichian lines, that ultimately dissolved some of the most powerful psychic motives for his art. Just what these were, and how he grappled with them, is too complicated a story to enter into, but much of his work during this period, in both fiction and essays, was part of this great upheaval. However he achieved it, and whatever one might say about the loss to literature, those little talismans of private allusion that had energized his imagination began to lose their power. He says something in his essay "On a Writer's Block" that suggests the mechanism involved: "our author may become a theorist who cannot lie because he has a noble superstition of objective truth. He avoids the interpersonal story by speaking of generalities. . . . Or again, at a further remove from the personal but recapturing some of the urgency of practical contact, the theorist may turn to sociology, politics, or psychiatry." For Goodman, becoming a theorist meant undergoing self-analysis and then hanging out his shingle, first as psychotherapist, then as a utopian sage. The price he paid was losing touch with the private symbology about which he could not lie.

The final decade of Goodman's career as a short-story writer is difficult to assess because so

Goodman on vacation in Vermont, circa 1953

many different factors influenced his work, sometimes a matter of his own determination to write in certain ways but often the result of circumstances out of his control or even his awareness. The gradual extinguishing of the storytelling impulse in him was no doubt an effect of his self-analysis, and yet it is impossible to separate that process from the history of his time, the plight of the artist in postwar society trying to find the right words to use for what he called a "shell-shocked" public.

Goodman had always written out of deep alienation from society and its values, and the war had exacerbated his sense of being at odds with his readers. As the social order settled into what was aptly called "the permanent war economy," with its mass-media culture and its worship of the standard of living, Goodman's distance from any potential audience grew still greater. Yet at the same time — partly through his self-analysis and partly through his therapeutic work with patients — he was undoing many of the resistances in his own character that kept him from trusting his reader. Giving up his ambition as "public artist" in favor of "commu-

nity artist" meant speaking to his audience more familially, like the "Dutch uncle" he called himself, whose advice might be stern but was also loving and respectful.

The stories Goodman wrote in the 1950s show him steadily weaning himself from fiction and learning to nourish himself on the bare facts. The process involved separating elements that had always been fused in his work. Goodman had never agreed to the distinction between the fictive realm and the world of ideas. Readers might suddenly find themselves addressed directly in any of his works, required to pull back from the story and contemplate some aspect of the real world. These moments can be breathtaking when Goodman catches the imaginative rhythm just right, but even so, many readers were simply exasperated by being shaken awake in the middle of their dream.

As Goodman's career underwent its transformation, the amalgam of fiction and thought began to come apart, and his stories tended to fall into two distinct kinds, as he recognized in the preface to *Our Visit to Niagara*: "I suppose my stories and novels are, finally, myths. . . . In principle there are two opposite ways of making mythical stories: to start with the American scene and find the mythical emerging from it; or to start with an ancient foreign myth and discover that it is familiar to oneself." Accordingly two different voices began to appear in his fiction. One of them, that of the gloomy but dutiful observer of the present scene, grew stronger and firmer, while the other, that of the dreamer or fantasist, grew weaker and more uncertain. At the same time, the "real people" who had always inhabited his works – whether as cryptic graffiti, as the initials of his enemies, or as characters openly modeled on family and friends – gradually disappeared from his mythology and are to be found only in stories that are immediate transcriptions of actual experience, with scarcely any fictive elaboration at all. A telling example of this new attitude occurs in a story of 1959 called "A Lifeguard" (in *The Collected Stories*), when the hero hangs his swimming trunks on a tree, like a flag or an emblem. According to Goodman the gesture means: "MAN WAS HERE. 1959." This is a far cry from "PG + DM'21." His next step would be to abandon storytelling altogether and write only sociology and journalism.

"Eagle's Bridge: The Death of a Dog" (also in *The Collected Stories*) is the last story Goodman wrote and is a fitting culmination to these developments. Solidly based in "the American scene," not only are the characters real persons – himself, his wife, and his son – but for the first time they are given their real names. The central event is the death of the family dog, hit by a car on the highway. The event is described just as it happened, when they stopped to picnic by a roadside stream on their way home from a summer vacation. There is no hint of a hieroglyphic past pressing to get into the story, no palimpsest graffiti, and no face smiling behind the faces. Mythic power does emerge, but it is located in the present, lurking mysteriously in the deep pool where Goodman's son was fishing when the catastrophe occurred. Goodman had spotted the fish himself, a giant bass hovering in the water like a local deity. Near the end of the story, he writes, as in one of his old Noh-style plays: "I had a flash image of that dark fish, that he was a spirit of death. And if only I had not seen him, and had not had the thought to fish for him when we stopped for a rural lunch!" This is a powerful story, in many ways the equal of "Iddings Clark" or "A Cross-Country Runner at Sixty-Five," yet achieving its effect by facing into the portentous present rather than gazing inward at the charmed past. Another author might have been satisfied and settled into a new fictive mode, but for Goodman it was the end of storytelling. It was as if he knew this, for the little dog who has died seems almost to stand for Goodman's art. He describes the dog playing with a ball:

> When our Lucy would get the ball, she trotted off triumphantly with it and tried to keep it away from us, even while she came back, wanting us to get it and bounce it or throw it again. She was bewildered and torn between the twin desires of having the ball as her own possession and playing catch with us. Finally she would come to terms with love and lay the ball at our feet. But sometimes she would trot spiritedly with it in big circles, triumphantly waving her plume, and we thought she was like a circus dog.

Goodman confronted these omens, made them into emblems and myth, and left them behind: " 'I'll drive,' said Sally stolidly, still wearing her face of despair, as if she thought that I, if I drove, would somehow be desperate and reckless. I gave her the keys." These are the last words of his last story. Thereafter Goodman resolutely faced forward and gave his imagination over to the here-and-now of his audience.

Goodman had in his lifetime plenty of admirers and disciples, but it was only the inner circle (likely to turn up as characters in his stories) that could be said to follow his fiction closely. When he collected his thirty years' harvest in *Adam and His Works,* the book got not a single review, although 1968 saw the height of his fame, when his books of social commentary were being noticed everywhere. In his own opinion *Adam* was his best single volume, but few read it because no one reviewed it.

A few writers of the younger generation, such as Goodman's friends Grace Paley and George Dennison, who were to win for themselves some of the literary glory Goodman yearned for, regarded his stories as classics from a master's hand. He was a writer's writer, even though his work has had no school of imitators. Dennison felt that the best of Goodman's short fiction deserves comparison with that of Herman Melville and Hawthorne. Remembering Hawthorne's struggle for an audience and Melville's long eclipse, it is perhaps not altogether absurd to imagine that Americans might yet rediscover another one of their great writers.

Interviews:

Studs Terkel, "What Is a Man's Work?," *WFMT Perspective,* 2 (August 1962): 29–35;

Morgan and Barbara Gibson, "Highlights of an Interview with Paul Goodman on *The Empire City*," *Kulchur,* 5 (Summer 1965): 2–15.

Bibliographies:

Tom Nicely, *Adam and His Work: A Bibliography of Sources by and about Paul Goodman (1911–1972)* (Metuchen, N. J. & London: Scarecrow, 1979);

Nicely, "Adam and His Work: A Bibliographical Update," in *Artist of the Actual: Essays On Paul Goodman,* edited by Peter Parisi (Metuchen, N. J. & London: Scarecrow, 1986), pp. 153–183.

References:

Hayden Carruth, "Paul Goodman and the Grand Community," *American Poetry Review,* 12 (September–October 1983): 22–32;

George Dennison, "The Ways of Nature," *Inquiry,* 1 (6 March 1978): 20–22;

Lewis Fried, "Paul Goodman: The City as Self," in his *Makers of the City* (Amherst: University of Massachusetts Press, 1990), pp. 159–206;

Geoffrey Gardner, "Citizen of the World, Animal of Nowhere," *New Letters,* 42 (Winter–Spring 1976): 216–227;

Richard King, "Paul Goodman," in his *The Party of Eros: Radical Social Thought and the Realm of Freedom* (Chapel Hill: University of North Carolina Press, 1972), pp. 78–115;

Peter Parisi, ed., *Artist of the Actual: Essays on Paul Goodman* (Metuchen, N. J.: Scarecrow, 1986);

Leo Raditsa, "On Paul Goodman – and Goodmanism," *Iowa Review,* 5 (Summer 1974): 62–79;

Theodore Roszak, "Exploring Utopia: The Visionary Sociology of Paul Goodman," in his *The Making of a Counter Culture* (Garden City, N.Y.: Doubleday, 1969), pp. 178–204;

Taylor Stoehr, "Adam and Everyman: Paul Goodman in his Stories," in his *Words and Deeds: Essays on the Realistic Imagination* (New York: AMS, 1986), pp. 149–164;

Stoehr, "*Growing Up Absurd* – Again: Rereading Paul Goodman in the Nineties," *Dissent,* 37 (Fall 1990): 486–494;

Stoehr, "Paul Goodman and the New York Jews," *Salmagundi,* 66 (Winter–Spring 1985): 50–103;

Bernard Vincent, *Paul Goodman et la reconquête du présent* (Paris: Editions du Seuil, 1976);

Vincent, *Pour un bon usage du monde: Une réponse conviviale à la crise de l'école, de la ville et de la foi* (Tournai, Belgium: Desclee, 1979);

Colin Ward, "Planning: Patrick Geddes and Paul Goodman," in his *Influences: Voices of Creative Dissent* (Bideford, U.K.: Green, 1991), pp. 114–132;

Kingsley Widmer, *Paul Goodman* (Boston: Twayne, 1980);

David Wieck, "Paul Goodman: *Drawing the Line,*" *Telos,* 35 (Spring 1978): 199–214.

Papers:

Most of Goodman's papers are at the Houghton Library, Harvard University. An additional small holding is at Syracuse University. Burton Weiss's extensive collection of first editions, galley proofs, and other materials is at Cornell University, in the Mathew Goodman Memorial Collection.

David Huddle

(11 July 1942 –)

David Lampe
State University of New York at Buffalo

BOOKS: *A Dream with No Stump Roots in It* (Columbia: University of Missouri Press, 1975);
Paper Boy (Pittsburgh: University of Pittsburgh Press, 1979);
Only the Little Bone (Boston: Godine, 1986);
Stopping By Home (Salt Lake City: Peregrine Smith, 1988);
The High Spirits: Stories of Men and Women (Boston: Godine, 1989);
The Writing Habit: Essays on Writing (Salt Lake City: Peregrine Smith, 1991);
The Nature of Yearning (Salt Lake City: Peregrine Smith, 1992);
Intimates (Boston: Godine, 1993).

David Huddle's autobiographical short stories use memory and imagination to explore his past in order to understand himself, those he loves, and the ways they live. Three of his four collections employ story sequences in which the same characters – Reed Bryant in *Only the Little Bone* (1986), Billy Hyatt and Frank Berry in *The High Spirits* (1989), and, most recently, Eugene Riggins and thirteen-year-old Angela in *Intimates* (1993) – face continuing personal, social, and moral dilemmas. Written in either first- or third-person point of view, these stories are told by articulate and interesting narrators. With passionate urgency Huddle writes stories that are necessary and meaningful.

Huddle is also a talented, prizewinning poet whose three books of lyrical and narrative sequences also explore autobiographical reminiscence, and he is a provocative critic whose essays have appeared in such publications as the *New York Times Magazine* and in a collection, *The Writing Habit: Essays on Writing* (1991). These talents establish him as an important man of letters. Though in his most recent books he often situates his characters in the academic and literary world, refreshingly he avoids the traps of allusive preciosity and self-conscious cuteness. Indeed, rather than calling attention to the cleverness of his comparisons or the capaciousness

David Huddle, circa 1992 (photograph by Marion Ettlinger)

of his reading, Huddle instead keeps developing his own special territory, style, and characters.

Born in Ivanhoe, Virginia, on 11 July 1942, David Huddle is the second of three sons of Charles R. Huddle, an industrial manager, and Mary F. Akers Huddle. He received his high-school education in Ivanhoe (which appears as Rosemary in his stories). After studying briefly at the University of Virginia, he served in the army as a paratrooper in Germany and Vietnam from 1964 to 1967 and then returned to the university, where he completed his B.A. in foreign affairs in 1968, having studied writing with Peter Taylor. That same year he married Lindsey Massie Huddle, who now practices law.

They have two daughters, Bess and Molly. In preparation for a career in writing, Huddle completed an M.A. in English at Hollins College (1969), where he studied with George Garrett, and an M.F.A. in creative writing from Columbia (1971), where he studied with Richard Ellman, Hannah Green, and Lore Segal. Since 1971 he has been a faculty member at the University of Vermont and since 1982 a full professor of English there. He has also taught as a visiting professor at Bread Loaf, Goddard College, Warren Wilson College, the University of Idaho, and Indiana University. He has had two National Endowment for the Arts fellowships and other fellowships from Yaddo, Bread Loaf, and the Virginia Center for Creative Arts, and he was awarded an honorary doctor of humanities degree from Shenandoah College.

His first collection, *A Dream with No Stump Roots in It* (1975), comprises six stories, several of which show his first shaping of autobiographical materials into fiction. "Rosie Baby" and "The Interrogation of the Prisoner Bung by Mister Hawkins and Sergeant Tree" are set in Vietnam, where, like the protagonists in each story, Huddle had served in military intelligence. "Rosie Baby," Huddle's first published story, appeared in the *Georgia Review* in 1969 and suggests the colonial absurdity of Vietnam through the job of the protagonist, who is in charge of the security of a garbage dump. "The Interrogation" was praised by *Literary Journal* reviewer Rowe Portis as "about as good a story as anyone has written about the war in Vietnam" (15 June 1975).

"Luther," the first story of the collection, uses first-person narrative to capture the comically improbable adventures of a southern white fundamentalist missionary who has been sent "to Africa to preach the word of God Almighty to the Black People" but who there instead becomes a convert to Catholicism. Luther, alone in an alien world, is converted by a priest who "didn't forget" him and who hears his confession after he has broken down when confronted with an African cult of unashamed sexuality. "Everybody sins in this book," reviewer John Engels observed, "and knows it and is humiliated by it. The word *shame* crops up over and over throughout the collection" (*Carleton Miscellany,* Spring–Summer 1976).

Two of the stories in *A Dream,* "Waiting for Carl" and "The Proofreader," are set in New York City, where Huddle did graduate work. In the first of these a thirty-five-year-old North Carolinian provides kindness to others but becomes a victim of those he aids. "The Proofreader," the longest story

in the book, features Carson Moore, who has come to New York to be a poet. He is married to a once-slender Virginia woman who has become "like a polar bear, sluggish, sloppy with flesh sagging all across her hips and her belly." After he meets a young woman, Leslie, in the park as he drinks his usual two sample bottles of Gilbey's Gin, he is surprised when she takes him to her apartment. After initially claiming to be proofreading literature, Carson finally admits he is a proofreader of pornography and "a known customer in every peep-show joint, every pornography shop, every theatre that shows filthy movies, every strip joint and go-go house in town." Yet his nonsexual involvement with Leslie, who likes to talk about orgasms, ironically returns him to an appreciation of his wife, "and he felt his heart be tickled with that knowledge." Carson, who, as his wife puts it, is "above average in being peculiar," has purged himself through the most unlikely confession and can finally admit his own failure rather than blame his wife.

The brief and masterful title story closes Huddle's book with the first-person confession of another "calm and inconsequential man," whose nightmares and suburban homing instincts at first puzzle and then move him to "make a stump out of an oak tree." Still not content he begins to worry about the roots: "Then I began to dream of strangulation, of roots coming up through the floor of my house to choke my wife and sweet baby while I chopped futilely at them with my tennis racket." This wonderful mixture of the calm and inconsequential – of taking "suits to the cleaner" and stopping "at the A&P for milk, spaghetti sauce, and wheat germ" – with the wild and irrational makes this the most interesting story in the book and the one that points most directly to Huddle's development in his later stories. Despite his claims of calmness, the narrator is soon setting the stump on fire and finally lying naked on that level ground at night: "There are worms and moles, too, I thought, and I took off my tops and bottoms and laid myself flat down on the earth in the cold and wet." This juxtaposition of the mundane and modest with an intense and active fantasy life is Huddle's first response in fiction to his Vermont home. The story suggests the rich realm of memory and fantasy that he was to explore in his next three collections of fiction. It also shows how Huddle can establish the dignity and power of the ordinary, as well as the imaginative richness of the fantasy that underlies the "calm and inconsequential." "Last night I dreamed my most beautiful vision," the narrator

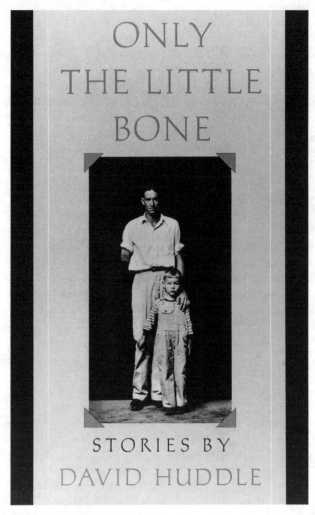

Dust jacket for the 1986 book that Huddle calls "a sequence of . . . long autobiographical stories"

concludes. "In animal skins I am walking with my wife and child over a plain of freshly mown grass. There are rows of sturdy houses and a few tennis courts in the distance. A gentle, pale, blue wind is at our backs, and there is warm rich sunlight all around us. Our feet pass without sound over an earth that is smooth and endless." That gentle wind and "warm rich sunlight" are featured prominently in his next story collection.

Only the Little Bone comprises first-person stories that interlace to re-create the experiences of Reed Bryant and his family. It is, as Huddle describes it, "a sequence of . . . long autobiographical stories." Readers come to know some sharply defined characters: Reed's family, especially his grandfather and his older brother, Duncan, as well as several interesting women – Darcy Webster, Jean Sharp, and Hilda. The story "Save One for Mainz" continues the absurdist military experience

of "Rosie Baby," though in this case in Germany rather than Vietnam. It also foreshadows the amatory explorations of Huddle's later fiction.

In the first story, "Poison Ivy," Reed's mother, "one of the prettiest women in Rosemary," teaches her two sons to swim. Since she "saw things as they ought to be" rather than as they were, their swimming place is one of "quiet beauty" instead of trash, raw sewage, dirty brown river water, and broken glass. So, too, the character George Clemons leads Reed to believe that the obscene gesture Reed makes to Loretta, an "available" neighbor girl, is an invitation rather than an overt insult. Thus Huddle makes the reader aware of the double nature of signs and significances in this seemingly simple pastoral world.

"The Magic Show" presents Reed's brother, Duncan, as a magician and a city girl from Palm Beach, Florida, Jean Sharp, as his assistant. The story captures a mixture of adolescent sexuality and shame as well as a comic family dinner scene in which Reed recognizes the mixture of the genteel and gauche in his father's table manners: "Often he chewed with his mouth open, so that you could hear it, and he liked to roll the food around in his mouth so that he made sloshing noises." The point of the story turns on the recognition of conflicting, contradictory codes – country/city, genteel/gauche, and illusion/reality.

"The Undesirable" is a novella that traces Reed's important rites of passage: learning to drive and learning about sexuality and social class. "Wedding Storm" features Duncan and his bride, Eleanor, a "soft-voiced Madison girl." Duncan finds the situation difficult since even though his parents disapprove of the marriage they never say anything to him: "He knew how they felt, because in our family, signals were given." The most maddening family trait, according to Duncan, is their evasiveness: "Ask somebody in our family a direct question; what do you get? A comment on the weather. A bit of nostalgia, a childhood memory." Driving home from the wedding on a road he has known his whole life, Reed feels faint. With the echo of his brother's voice in his ears, he later tells his parents the roads "were beautiful."

"Dirge Notes" takes the form of a series of random entries, a virtual notebook around the central experience of loss that comes from Reed's grandfather's death. Signs and memories coalesce for special meanings. The last and title story, "Only the Little Bone," draws all the earlier themes together. It is told through the voice of Reed, who has the family trait of "flawed competence," but he is blessed with a natural homely eloquence, self-deprecating humor, and a deep sense of humanity. "Memory and fact are old cousins," Reed insists at the end of this story, as he holds a discarded but still-remembered plaster cast in his hands. He continues, "I feel like I could remember all of human history if I put my mind to it."

The High Spirits comprises eleven stories, six of them arranged in two sequences: three stories feature young Billy Hyatt and three the older Frank Berry. All eleven stories are tied together by thematic concerns with the visual arts, music, university life, and family relationships. The first story, "Underwater Spring," is the third-person account of a mother who takes her son back to her childhood home and shows him to a muddy swimming hole before she leaves him. Both "Sketching Hannah" and "The Deacon" focus on the visual arts: in the former a sepia sketch reveals to a lover that a relationship is over; the latter juxtaposes art and life, innocence and experience. "Apache" is a third-person narrative from the point of view of a stripper: "She was a blue-eyed blonde, her name was Apache, and if you didn't like it, you could kiss her ass." Apache works at the Pussy Cat, is "twenty-nine and said she was twenty-five," and has been married and divorced three times. Yet she displays a mixture of cunning and compassion in disposing of "this real bullshit guy who said that he was an Indian of the Osage tribe."

The next three stories, "Playing," "Brothers," and "The High Spirits," involve Billy Hyatt, whose infatuation with music (he "is a prodigy of the alto saxophone") is almost as intense as his involvement with girls – fourteen-year-old Valerie Williams; Beverly Tyler, "a student nurse from Grundy, Virginia"; and Louise Morris, a "most advanced high-school girl." Billy and Pete Ratcliffe toss a coin to decide who will marry falsely pregnant Valerie (who has a cyst in her stomach area) in "Playing." Like his fraternity brother Geoffrey Slade, who brutalizes his girlfriend Goofy in "Brothers," Billy almost strikes Beverly after she twice slaps him during a tryst in the campus chapel – "While I lay there the knowledge pounded at my temples: if I had hit Beverly Tyler with my fist, I would have become someone else, I would have had another life than the one I was going to have." Finally, in "The High Spirits" Billy betrays both the band with whom he plays and Louise. Though he sleeps with Louise, he cannot "hold the image of Louise" in his mind until she and Richard Kohler, the moving spirit behind the band, die in an auto crash.

"The Gorge" explores the relationship a trumpet teacher named Braxton has with Monica, an economics major who produces "effortlessly full tones" on her "old concert model Conn." She is "a real musician," and as she puts it, "I don't just play trumpet.... I'm a *girl* trumpet-player." Braxton comes to realize how much he depends on her: "What he wanted from Monica was for her to respond to his teaching in such a way as to want to live the intense life he wanted for himself."

The last three stories in the book are first-person narratives that feature another teacher, Frank Berry, in his troubled relationship with his teenage daughter ("In the Mean Mud Season"), as he brings his mother to Vermont after his father's death ("The Crossing"), and in a recalled relationship with one of his students ("The Beautiful Gestures"). "Danger is a basic ingredient of all stories," Huddle insists (in *The Writing Habit*), "even the ones in which nothing dangerous ever occurs," for "it holds

begins to dream about, again and again, fat women, thin
women, the ones who have consequential bosoms, the ones who
don't, all of them reaching upward in that heartbreaking
willingness to give themselves over to some man and politely
dance with him. They dance and think what they think and
sometimes, not often, do what they think. But not on the
floors of VFW halls, fire stations, school houses, or
restaurant basements. Out there there is dancing to be
done, and it might be bold or lascivious or even crudely
suggestive, but even at its worst it is a sweet and elegant
parody of the two-backed monster.

Billy knows these things even if he couldn't tell
anybody about them. Teenage master of sneaking-around
foreplay, his destiny is blue-balls, sperm-spotted
underwear, stained crotches of his khaki pants, wet dreams,
the rightful heritage of any high school boy. He's sixteen,
Valerie's thirteen, they're so clearly too young for it that
even they, had they been asked to speak responsibly, would
have said of course they shouldn't do it!

They do it. On a rainy night in the spring in the
front seat of Billy's dad's Dodge, they park out behind the
Madison country club, so close to the clubhouse door that
from its window the light from the Coke machine shines on

Page from a revised typescript for "Playing," collected in The High Spirits *(by permission of David Huddle)*

the story under a kind of pressure, enlivens it, sharpens and vivifies the events, the characters, the language." This is certainly true of these three stories. In all of them danger is present in the form of another person, action, or pattern of language that may violate an important existing relationship. "In the Mean Mud Season" presents a resented boyfriend, Scott Prescott, who proves to be no immediate threat to a delicate father-daughter relationship. In "The Crossing" the possibility of cheap sentimentality, which could destroy the honest, tender relationship of a mother and her son, is avoided, and sympathy is maintained between them by being never spoken of directly. In "The Beautiful Gestures" danger is embodied in a bright student, Susan Larrick, whose avid attentions and availability might lead to the disruption of Frank's marriage to Marie. He is summoned by Susan, who is terrified, and spends the night watching over her. Their intimacy is, as he puts it, "nothing carnal," and an innocent kiss marks an end to temptation. When Frank returns home, he finds that his wife's "generalized husband-anger" has been transformed to "longing and regret." From the most unlikely source, Frank finds in Richard Nixon's "retreat to his California mansion" in August 1974 an emblem for the parting he and Susan had: "Do you remember before he flew away how Nixon turned and smiled and waved, as if he'd just done something marvelous for us?"

Intimates, also includes highly effective stories. The first of these, "Night," features Angela, a thirteen-year-old who watches her parents' marriage dissolve. She recognizes how much her father drinks, and after tending to him she feels especially close to her mother, though "she wasn't even in the same house with me." In "Scotland" Angela has her first sense of intimacy with a member of the opposite sex when she shares the transcendent power of music with a black male model on a distillery tour in Scotland. Both stories mark a first for Huddle, who admits (in *The Writing Habit*), "I am weak when it comes to portraying female characters as whole human beings." These two stories told from Angela's point of view use Huddle's own experience of a trip to Scotland but successfully transform it with a fresh voice.

In "Henry Lagoon" a typical Huddle protagonist, in this case a young boy who "thought himself to be a profoundly unremarkable fourteen-year-old with brown hair, a kid who didn't hold anybody's interest," experiences his first kiss from "Lisa Yancey, a freshman of some consequence because she'd just had her braces off," who "thought Henry had bedroom eyes." Though their first accidental kiss is on videotape, "that second kiss" is actually more important, he decides, since "it was something he and Lisa had chosen."

Four stories in the book involve the poet Eugene Riggins. In the first of these, "The Page," he takes his wife and family along to the Tucson Writer's Conference. The events of the story turn on two meanings of *page:* as a piece of writing and as a call or special message. After a successful reading ("as he gave voice to the lines, he understood what they really meant") Eugene receives a call from a woman in the audience, giving him her name and room number. Tempted by this offer, later that night he walks barefoot out into the cool Arizona night: "His feet registered every cold pebble as he stepped antelope-style around the silly hard-surfaced pathway." His feet, registering this cold and pain as he stands under the Arizona stars, cause him to turn away from this temptress's doorway and return to the dark warmth and secure comfort of his own room, wife, and family. "Collision" is also told in the third person and as with "The Page" encapsules the events of the story in a single word. Eugene and his wife, Marie, have "whanged their two cars into each other downtown." This event initiates a series of domestic disasters and tensions until another collision takes place: "He and Marie were suddenly chest-to-chest up against each other." Another argument begins but is interrupted by their youngest daughter's announcement that "I'm still sick." Out of this comes a hurried resumption of family loyalty. In "The Meeting of the Tisdale Fellows" Eugene tells his own tale, which is a story within a story. Like "The Page," it is also a story in which Eugene's fantasies of what might have been are initially as important as the events themselves. Yet in the story his memories of Rosa Kingland from their days at Columbia are jarred by a woman he finds who speaks to him of the danger of solipsism: "My work was making me curl up inside myself," she explains "when all of a sudden I became aware of what I was seeing out the window." This moment of illumination for Eugene is special: "Something departed from me that I knew I had to leave behind."

The final Eugene Riggins story, "The Hearing," presents him explaining to a committee of his peers why a janitor accidentally found a nude student, Honoree Evans, on Eugene's office desk listening to music near an open bottle of wine and a clothed and innocent Eugene. After teaching for thirty-five years, he claims a reputation as "a dedicated teacher who is respectful of his students" and who insists that they call him Professor Riggins or Doctor Riggins. He is "not a man who easily demonstrates his affections," yet as he puts it, "The training of my profession is to recognize and to honor beauty." So in spite of academic decorum, he allows Honoree to disrobe, not for sexual reasons but to appreciate her beauty: "For a little while in the light of that room, I felt God-damned immortal."

A more successful story, "Mister, Mister," returns to a mode used in *A Dream*. The narrator (a writer) begins with mundane details and an almost Milquetoast manner. First he apologizes for his interest in plants ("I'm only mildly interested in them, and they are only mildly healthy"); he then announces that he has "learned how to put the rabbit to sleep." He has been "careful," he insists, "not to scratch too close to his nose because that disturbs him." The third admission is personal and bizarre: "Lately I've been feeling this desire to fall down." But the tensions between this two-hundred-pound man and the pound-and-a-half rabbit persist, as does his anxiety over what the paperboy must think. The narrator admits to being quite ordinary: "I drive a Chevy stationwagon, eat fast food, love appliances, can't be bothered to sort my trash for recycling, and waste a hell of a lot of water with my hygiene." Maybe it is just a phase, he concludes, but his contact with the rabbit brings him almost to hope for a benevolent world where some larger equally intimate force might look after him.

The collection ends with two other first-person narratives. In "The Short Flight" a much married but still vulnerable man, in a moment of crisis on a airline flight, has an intense awareness of another person, Elaine, the woman sitting next to him. The final story, "The Reunion Joke," is told by Francine, who at her thirty-year class reunion finally consummates a relationship with Randall, the class clown.

In *Intimates* Huddle explores a wide range of intimate experiences: familial (daughter-father; father-mother-daughter), flirtatious, sexual, teacher-student, aesthetic (the writer and his inspiration) and even fantasy. He continues the mode of whimsy from *A Dream,* the familial focus in *Only the Little Bone,* and his exploration of characters readers might not like, a tactic begun in *The High Spirits*. Additionally the interest in transcendence (especially via music) is continued, and Huddle seems to have found new subject matter – Vermont, the campus, the problems of middle life, the tenderness of fathers and daughters, and the triumph of understated but profoundly imagined expressions.

Huddle's writing, like his "inconsequential" narrators, seems unassuming. Yet this very disarming admission of "flawed competence," what critic Judith Kitchen has called our "shared propensity to make small but telling mistakes," makes Huddle's writing especially eloquent and resonant. His stories show his movement from adolescence to manhood, from Virginia to Vermont, from sibling and seducer to husband and parent, and from student to teacher and writer.

Reference:

Judith Kitchen, "The Moments that Matter," *Georgia Review,* 41 (Spring 1987) 209–214.

Robert Kelly

(24 September 1935 –   )

Richard L. Blevins
University of Pittsburgh Greensburg

See also the Kelly entry in *DLB 5: American Poets Since World War II.*

BOOKS: *Armed Descent* (New York: Hawk's Well, 1961);

Her Body Against Time (Mexico City: Corno Emplumado, 1963);

Round Dances (New York: Trobar, 1964);

Lunes, published with *Sightings,* by Jerome Rothenberg (New York: Hawk's Well, 1964);

Enstasy (Annandale-on-Hudson, N.Y.: Matter, 1964);

Lectiones (Placitas, N.Mex.: Duende, 1965);

Weeks (Mexico City: Corno Emplumado, 1966);

Devotions (Annandale-on-Hudson, N.Y.: Salitter, 1967);

Twenty Poems (Annandale-on-Hudson, N.Y.: Matter, 1967);

Axon Dendron Tree (Annandale-on-Hudson, N.Y.: Matter, 1967);

Crooked Bridge Love Society (Annandale-on-Hudson, N.Y.: Salitter, 1967);

A Joining: A Sequence for H. D. (Los Angeles: Black Sparrow, 1967);

The Scorpions (Garden City, N.Y.: Doubleday, 1967; London: Calder & Boyars, 1969);

Alpha (Gambier, Ohio: Fisher, 1968);

Finding the Measure (Los Angeles: Black Sparrow, 1968);

A Play and Two Poems, by Kelly, Diane Wakoski, and Ron Loewinsohn (Los Angeles: Black Sparrow, 1968);

Sonnets, 1967 (Los Angeles: Black Sparrow, 1968);

Songs I–XXX (Cambridge, Mass.: Pym-Randall, 1968);

The Common Shore, Books I–V (Los Angeles: Black Sparrow, 1969);

A California Journal (London: Big Venus, 1969);

Kali Yuga (London: Cape Goliard / New York: Grossman, 1970);

Flesh: Dream: Book (Los Angeles: Black Sparrow, 1971);

Cities (West Newbury, Mass.: Frontier, 1971);

In Time (West Newbury, Mass.: Frontier, 1971);

Ralegh (Los Angeles: Black Sparrow, 1972);

The Pastorals (Los Angeles: Black Sparrow, 1972);

The Mill of Particulars (Los Angeles: Black Sparrow, 1973);

A Line of Sight (Los Angeles: Black Sparrow, 1974);

The Loom (Los Angeles: Black Sparrow, 1975);

Sixteen Odes (Santa Barbara, Cal.: Black Sparrow, 1976);

The Lady Of (Santa Barbara, Cal.: Black Sparrow, 1977);

The Convections (Santa Barbara, Cal.: Black Sparrow, 1978);

The Book of Persephone (New Paltz, N.Y.: Treacle, 1978);

Wheres (Santa Barbara, Cal.: Black Sparrow, 1978);

Kill the Messenger Who Brings Bad News (Santa Barbara, Cal.: Black Sparrow, 1979);

The Cruise of the Pnyx (Barrytown, N.Y.: Station Hill, 1979);

Sentence (Barrytown, N.Y.: Station Hill, 1980);

Spiritual Exercises (Santa Barbara, Cal.: Black Sparrow, 1981);

The Alchemist to Mercury, edited by Jed Rasula (Richmond, Cal.: North Atlantic, 1981);

How Do I Make Up My Mind, Lord? (Minneapolis: Augsburg, 1982);

Mulberry Women (Berkeley, Cal.: Hiersoux, Powers, Thomas, 1982);

Under Words (Santa Barbara, Cal.: Black Sparrow, 1983);

Thor's Thrush (Oakland, Cal.: Coincidence, 1984);

A Transparent Tree (New Paltz, N.Y.: McPherson, 1985);

Photograph by Alex Gotfryd

Not This Island Music (Santa Rosa, Cal.: Black Sparrow, 1987);

The Flowers of Unceasing Coincidence, edited by George Quasha (Barrytown, N.Y.: Station Hill, 1988);

Oahu (Rhinebeck, N.Y.: St. Lazaire, 1988);

Doctor of Silence (Kingston, N.Y.: McPherson, 1988);

Cat Scratch Fever (Kingston, N.Y.: McPherson, 1990);

Ariadne (Rhinebeck, N.Y.: St. Lazaire, 1990);

A Strange Market (Santa Rosa, Cal.: Black Sparrow, 1992).

PLAY PRODUCTIONS: *The Well Wherein a Deer's Head Bleeds,* New York, 1964;

Eros and Psyche, with music by Elie Yarden, New Paltz, N.Y., 1971.

OTHER: *A Controversy of Poets,* edited by Kelly and Paris Leary (Garden City, N.Y.: Doubleday/Anchor, 1965);

Paul Blackburn, *The Journals,* edited, with a foreword, by Kelly (Los Angeles: Black Sparrow, 1975).

SELECTED PERIODICAL PUBLICATIONS – UNCOLLECTED: "Ring: Fragment of a Novel Entitled 'The Moment of Sound,' " *Promethean* (Spring 1955): 18–20;

"An Assassination of the Czar," *Metronome,* 78 (April 1961): 24–26;

"On Discourse," *Io,* 20 (Winter 1974): 3–36;

"Alchemical Journal," *Io,* 26 (1979): 9–119.

Robert Kelly is among the major postmodern American writers and editors who are the second-generation inheritors of a great modernist tradition and the founders of a methodology for composition that incorporates principles of depth psychology. The example of his writing in more than fifty

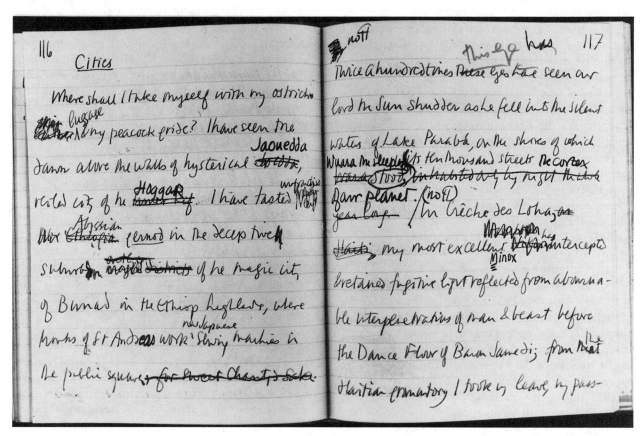

Pages from the manuscript for Cities, *published separately in 1971 and collected in* A Transparent Tree *in 1985 (Rare Books and Manuscripts, State University of New York at Buffalo; by permission of Robert Kelly)*

books, as well as his influence as a teacher of English over three decades, has helped to liberate the next generation of writers. Kelly's modernist origins can be traced to the years before World War I, to Ezra Pound's imagist experiments and the expansion of hard-image poems to include history and gnostic learning. The line of tradition beginning with Pound was advanced between the world wars most specifically by William Carlos Williams, Louis Zukofsky, George Oppen, and other objectivists and was repostulated at the time of the Korean War by Charles Olson, Robert Duncan, Robert Creeley, and the practitioners of "open" composition, known collectively as the Black Mountain school. While this nonacademic line of experimental American poetry has influenced a century of writers, Robert Kelly is among the few (see especially the fiction of Creeley, Edward Dorn, and Guy Davenport and the novels of Philip Whalen) who have produced a notable body of experimental fiction as well as poetry.

Kelly's prolific output has intimidated would-be readers and critics. He writes every day. Critic Jed Rasula estimates that by 1984 Kelly had published some 3,000 pages of poetry and 750 pages of prose; these figures do not include his voluminous notebooks or correspondence or his 30,000 typescript pages of poetry since 1960. In the afterword to his book of short stories *A Transparent Tree* (1985), Kelly refers to the existence of several unfinished novels, including a manuscript of 1,900 pages titled "Parsifal." Another collection of his stories, to be published under the title "Queen of Terrors," is being prepared for publication in 1993. In spite of the amount of fiction Kelly has written, he has published mostly poetry and wishes to be known as a poet. His critical reputation rests almost exclusively on his poetry. However, Kelly should never be classified as a poet who has written the occasional short story. His style is not "poet's prose." Instead it is a narrative response to one of modernism's central and most persistent dilemmas, posited by Pound's ambition to rewrite the Jamesian novel as a long poem. "It has never struck me," Kelly writes (in *A Transparent Tree*), "that there is an interesting difference between poetry and fiction. . . . My concern is writing, and for me poetry and fiction and anything else are at times useful but scarcely necessary labels to identify momentary crest-forms in the sea of language writing and language saying."

Kelly was born on 24 September 1935 in Brooklyn, New York. An only child for his first seven years, he had a quiet childhood. Because both parents (Samuel and Margaret Kane Kelly) were required to work during the lean years of the Great Depression, Robert often spent his daytime hours being cared for by nannies. When the young Kelly saw the local Jesuit high school, he somehow knew he had to enroll there in order to learn Greek. "I was a great poet when I was 13," he said in a 1985 interview with Dennis Barone. By age fifteen Kelly had dropped out of high school and started to attend City College.

On 27 August 1955 he married Joan Lasker, a librarian. That same year, he completed his A.B. at City College and started graduate work in medieval studies at Columbia University while earning a living in New York City as a translator and treasurer for the Continental Translation Service. It was also in 1955 that Kelly published his first short story, "Ring: Fragment of a Novel Entitled 'The Moment of Sound,' " in *Promethean,* a university magazine. After three years of graduate school Kelly left Columbia without a degree, though he has been employed as a teacher since 1960, when he was a lecturer in English at Wagner College on Staten Island. Since 1961 he has taught at Bard College in Annandale-on-Hudson, New York, originally as a German-language instructor; he is currently director of poetry for the Milton Avery Graduate School and a professor of English. Kelly has been a visiting professor and poet in residence at several other schools, including the State University of New York at Buffalo (summer 1964), Tufts University (1966), California Institute of Technology (1971–1972), the University of Kansas (1975), and Dickinson College (1976).

The most important facts from Kelly's formative years in New York City concern his life as a young writer, just beginning to feel his influences and, in turn, to influence other writers. These were the years of the mimeographed-and-stapled underground magazines, and Kelly was one of the most engaged writers and editors. In 1957 Kelly founded the *Chelsea Review* in New York and continued as its editor until 1960, when he and George Economou, a fellow graduate student at Columbia, cofounded and edited *Trobar* magazine (1960–1964) and soon began to publish

books. By the close of the 1950s Kelly had met Zukofsky, Duncan, and Gerrit Lansing (Kelly met Olson in 1962) – poets whose work and friendships have had a lasting influence. Kelly and other "Deep Imagists" took Olson's cue to establish a new kind of writing. Critic Paul Christensen explains that they stressed the use of Jungian archetypes in their writing "as the means for generating commentaries, arguments, recollections that led away from self toward the opposite pole of awareness, the 'other.' " "An Assassination of the Czar," published in *Metronome* (April 1961), is Kelly's only extant short story from this period.

Even after Kelly moved from New York City to live and work at Bard College, the Deep Imagists continued to influence his thinking and writing, especially in his quest for contact with a primitive otherness by bringing alchemy, hermeticism, tarot cards, etymology, and dreams into his stories and poems. Like Pound, Kelly imagines the writer to be "a scientist of holistic understanding / a scholar . . . to whom all data whatsoever are of use" (*In Time,* 1971). Kelly understands, with H. D. and Duncan, that the alchemist's goal is not to arrive at a synthesis of opposites but to keep unresolved positions in mind without abstracting their essential realnesses or inventing a purely intellectual "resolve."

At Bard College, Kelly edited *Matter* magazine and ran Matter Press beginning in 1963. "The idea of *Matter* was matter," he told Barone, "to provide the material for poems, rather than just a magazine of poems." Kelly's next editorship was of the magazine *Los* in 1977; he was later a contributing editor for the first issue of *Sulfur* (Los Angeles, 1981).

Kelly has tended to collect his short fiction into what are, finally, keenly edited books that represent a range of years of writing. His first major book of stories, *A Transparent Tree,* comprises work from 1971 to 1983 and includes *Cities* (1971) and *Wheres* (1978), both originally published separately. *Doctor of Silence* (1988) prominently features *A Line of Sight,* first published as a chapbook in 1974. *Cat Scratch Fever* (1990) collects what Kelly calls his "Russian Tales," from 1981. Remarkably, after his many years of sporadic attention to the writing of fiction, Kelly's books of stories make coherent reading. They hold together because they are vehicles that enable him to approach the primitive other, and they are also a required reading counterpoint to his body of poetry.

Several primary assumptions inform most of Kelly's writing, including his short fiction. First, much of his work can be profitably read as an attempt to reconcile or go beyond some of the more inflexible principles of dogmatic projectivism as set

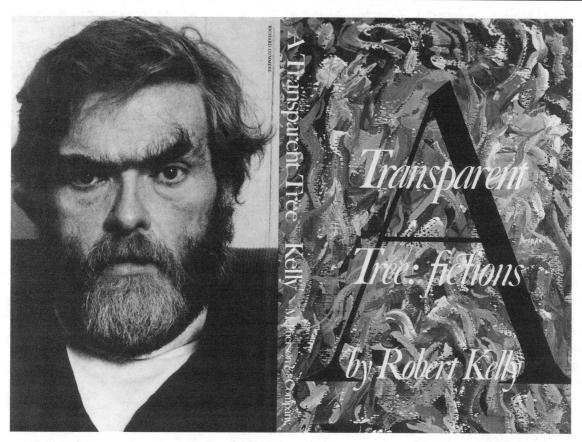

Dust jacket for Kelly's 1985 book, in which he describes fiction as "a transparent tree, an intricate unimpeded proliferation of branches from a common stem"

forth by Olson. Perhaps the postprojectivist quality is most evident in Kelly's fiction in his attempts to write closures for otherwise open forms. "A story goes on, and no branch obliterates another, however they may twist and stretch to share the nurturing light of the reader's after imaginings . . .," he writes in *A Transparent Tree*. Such is the projectivist's dilemma: if a form is open then how can it be said to end unless artificially or by the willfulness of art?

Second, to Kelly, the process of writing must be, after Martin Heidegger's language theory, a "dwelling-in" the composition, allowing the writer to experience (and the attentive reader or listener to follow along) an escape from a twentieth-century selfhood wracked by neurotic obsessions and to return, for the moment, to a sense of primitive otherness in an elemental and essential world. In some stories Kelly's chosen figure for the otherness may be a wilderness area or even an exotic city; in other stories otherness may be represented by a wild animal or a human lover who embodies wildness.

Third, the operative trope Kelly employs in his books of short stories is named in the afterword to *A Transparent Tree* and interpreted in the story "The Scribe" in *Cat Scratch Fever*. The trope is the "transparent tree," by means of which the reader is to understand the nature of fiction. The figure of the tree may derive from Kelly's deep image of an archetypal tree of narrative life: in "Russian Tales," Kelly defines "transparent" as "familiar." Kelly's tree imagery recalls Duncan's *Roots and Branches* (1964) and Lansing's *The Heavenly Tree Grows Downward* (1966). In *A Transparent Tree* Kelly speaks of fiction as "a transparent tree, an intricate unimpeded proliferation of branches from a common stem. The stories go on, each visible through all the others, mutually exclusive only by logic (that woodcraft of Time), not by Vision. The shape of a story is the viability of it as seed. . . . The integrity of bark and leaf and fruit and taste — these will triumph, and mind will use what it finds." In "The Scribe" Kelly's narrator explains that the text he is typing "is an examination of desire, not the root section, or the trunk discourse, but the immense com-

211

mentarial proliferation called the Branches. These examine in detail the consequences of various kinds of acts of desire, and what gets summoned by each of them in the way of unwanted presences, persons, patterns." Kelly's stories can be classified as experiments in three separate disciplines: there are root stories, in which he works out etymologies; trunk stories of discourse and primary text; and branch stories, relating consequences of actions taken and delayed as well as commentaries on secondary sources. Kelly often blends aspects from two of these story types, perhaps opening with a root passage and ending with a branch passage.

"The Calf of Gold," the first story in *A Transparent Tree,* begins with a sentence that returns to the primitive for an experience of otherness: "Before the Calf of Gold was smashed and melted down by a zealous mystic already half in love with orthodoxy, a young man from an outlying wadi experienced in the presence of the idol, dully gleaming in the light of innumerable reeking oil lamps, a sort of revelation that haunted him the rest of his life." This three-page story recalls the truths of the primitive religious impulse, before the institutionalization of rituals. By telling the young Eretz-Baal's story, Kelly calls for the reader to reorient postmodern thinking – starting out anew, from pre-Socratic origins – about what constitutes culture. Aaron the priest, the story goes, made the golden calf while Moses was on Mount Sinai receiving the tablets of the laws. Kelly's story dramatizes a moment of transition, when an ancient tradition of worship was pronounced unlawful and heretical by a new orthodoxy. Moses' laws from the one jealous God are seen to kill off the ancient gods, as institutions tend to outlaw fugitive personal visions. Ironically the name Baal survives because it is the name of an ancient god; Kelly's appropriation of the name for his humble protagonist suggests that the reader should take all visionary narratives seriously, not just the orthodox line. The story of Eretz-Baal wandering in an archetypal wilderness among deep images of bulls, dreams, and caves is a trunk story firmly within the epic oral tradition.

Cities, the next story in the book, is one of Kelly's first mature short stories, written in 1966. More sustained than "The Calf of Gold," *Cities* shows Kelly to be what Olson called "an archaeologist of morning," for whom travel is the experience of otherness; *Cities* further clarifies the process of creative writing as a return to the primitive center of the modern self. The narrative un-

folds in eight numbered sections. In the first section, the first-person narrator introduces himself as a middle-aged, well-to-do, modern version of Eretz-Baal; he travels the world as "the Wandering Unitarian," never to return to his native New England, and ponders what he experiences of exotic foreign cities. In his accounts of visits to certain secret cities, there is a rich array of Kelly tenets and obsessive themes: the city of Fatima is favored because of its freedom from laws, which continues one of the themes adumbrated in "The Calf of Gold"; in Qunduz, astrology is discussed; magic is the topic in Harappa. Freedom, astrology, and magic are Kelly's lexicon for writing his vision of otherness, and this vision is clearest in the city of Ahampura, whose king shows the narrator a map before the whole city disappears into the plain, only to reappear, renewed, representing Kelly's belief in the necessity of basic change in contemporary life. The narrator circumnavigates the globe and returns to a futuristic United States, where he discovers secret cities – from the city under the bleachers of Crosley Field in Cincinnati to "the greatest of North American cities," Mount Shasta (a volcanic cone in northern California). The narrative develops according to Kelly's model of the transparent tree: first there is the return, in time and place, to the first cities (roots); then there are explanations of the present (trunk discourse); these are followed by futuristic ramifications (branches). Such tales, as Kelly tells them, retain some of the prose qualities of Sir John Mandeville's fantastic *Travels* volumes (1357–1371). Kelly realizes that the so-called discoverers of worlds never lost have been most often inventors of new ideas for their native lands and that their travel narratives are a rich blend of imagination and observation. Later in *The Transparent Tree,* the story *Wheres,* a travelogue, describes a fantastic country that recalls the city of Wuara and its citizens in *Cities.*

"A Winter's Tale" examines the price to be paid for a life that ignores the past; the characters are trapped inside their selfhood without hope of escape, much less travel and freedom. "A Winter's Tale" is an experimental narrative, a long series of short sections (written in first and third person and including a poem by Gabriele d'Annunzio) that makes an unruly record of the complex subjectivity of an unnamed male and female. Kelly explains: "a Long Island doctor had slain his wife, and was fleeing away . . . with his receptionist, and was seized aboard the plane at JFK just before take-off. . . . In my mind, that

Dust jacket for Kelly's 1988 collection of short stories and essays on literary form

desperate MOMENT transposed itself backwards to the time just before killing the wife. So my story studies (researches?) the doctor's mind as he thinks tormentedly about killing the wife and running away with some woman. The mode of escape would be a fishing boat in the story, I guess, but all of that is in the story's sense of future time, while the story's present time is all caught up with the should-I–shouldn't-I of what passes for moral imagination in our day." The unusual narrative structure reflects Kelly's wish to write a more human corrective to what he calls "the frozen masterpieces of [James Joyce's] *Dubliners* [1906]." Kelly adopts Joyce's fugue form from "Araby," while adding the subjectivity of the two characters' personal stories. Kelly's story is not simply "written by the ear"; he tells it at length in fugue form, wherein trees, birds, and mirrors are not archetypes so much as they are the alternating voices of a fugue. *Doctor of Silence* includes "I Wanted a Fugue," a meditation on the form.

Kelly's story "The Guest" (in *A Transparent Tree*) investigates the dilemma of a "vampire" relationship. It is the story of a woman who has let a man come to possess her so completely that he takes over her body: the clichéd goal of love is literally realized, and "I and Thou" become inseparable. Kelly has written several stories about the allegorical knock at the lover's door, with the female either opening the door to love or the male being forced to remain outside and contemplate his love. In this volume "Rosary" is a good example of this kind of trunk story. "The Guest" is a branch story, imagining the extreme outcome of falling in love.

In *Doctor of Silence* the journey-to-otherness motif that dominates the stories of *A Transparent Tree* becomes more localized in the motif of the walk. Otherness in this book does not require a long journey; it is often found ready at hand. *Doctor of Silence* characteristically tells stories of men who, on their walks into modern parks, forests, and beaches, set out to contact their anima. In Kelly's epigraph to the book, he uses the term *allomorph* instead of the Jungian *anima,* perhaps hoping to distance his later work from simplistic "deep image" interpretations. Whatever his motivation, the proposition of his epigraph is clear: just as any story in a language must have its alternative forms (or allomorphs) in its retellings, there exist alternative methods for an individual's return to primitive otherness, which is nearby after all. Following a wild animal, for example, might return a character to certain secret places inside the mind. At its best, *Doctor of Silence* works like a bestiary of animals that individually offer insights into humankind. In the story "Dog," for example, a dog turns out to be the reincarnation of the Reverend Issachar Weekes, a memorable abuser of dogs.

The first story, "Pasatiempo," is set in contemporary southern California, where the three characters live near an airport but never travel. Kelly's style is understated and declarative, so close to the minimalism popularized by Raymond Carver that it approaches parody. The narrator, Jim, "a sketch portrait artist in public places and an astrological consultant in certain coffee houses in Venice"; his lover Lidia, a divorcee who occasionally makes and sells dried flower arrangements; and her brother Paco, a composer of the kind of metrical verse a poet such as Kelly would abhor, are unsympathetic characters who are mostly "passing time," as the Spanish title implies. The story's abrupt ending places it within the context of Kelly's broader concept of the necessary pursuit of otherness. Paco is writing closed verse, which unexpectedly seems to open up for him when he contemplates fox hunting. The reader is left with the feeling that, while actually chasing a wild fox is what Paco really needs in order to shake his postmodern languor, even meditating on the word *fox* might do – as an allomorph – if he would only open himself to the moment. Later in the book, "Lecture on Cadmium" considers the quandary of the novice user of open forms, when a dreamer must "address a learned assembly" on the topic of cadmium but is unprepared to speak. His improvised talk is a model of the kind of open form that is "forever inconclusive," and his unresponsive audience is an allomorph of the contemporary audience for poetry.

The insights afforded by writing, or "being-in" composition, easily outnumber those gained by reading texts, and the attuned ear dominates the eye, Kelly reminds readers in "The Man Who Read Meister Eckhardt." When the protagonist listens to a recital of music by Johann Sebastian Bach, he is carried away in an epiphany of knowing, in the form of a hallucination of the musical "instruments like a mother lioness sorting out her cubs. As soon as he sensed that, the animals of his metaphor began to rampage across the apt, unending veldt."

In "The Book and Its Contents" the reader meets one of the several doctors in *Doctor of Silence*.

Kelly's fictive doctors hold the keys to the unknown. They are psychiatrists, as in "The Infinite Tarot" and "The Temple of Shiva," or Pound-like sages in old age, as in the title story. The narrator of "The Book and Its Contents" describes himself as a world traveler, one a reader might meet in *A Transparent Tree,* who has returned to his Pennsylvania hometown, where once a week he visits Dr. Perkunas, the local physician/metaphysician. When the narrator brings the doctor an old notebook passage, "The world walks around," the story confirms the book's motif. When the doctor counters the citation with one of his own – "And doubted every door forever more" – the action begins to be played out inside secret rooms in the doctor's house, which can only represent the other. Inside one door a hidden room is bare except for a book on a table, "a book the words have written by themselves." As Perkunas reads to the narrator from the book, a procession of animals, representatives of the concept of the allomorph, appear and fade like visions of otherness. These are followed by the apparition of a city such as the kind Kelly imagines in *A Transparent Tree.* The next morning the doctor is last seen alive in a park while pulling "a blinding confusion of objects and animals" out of his clothes before he ascends into the sky; he is a victim of bad magic.

"The Hole" is a cautionary tale about the ill effects of letting the "Outside" overwhelm the "Inside." The tale features Sonia T., a wife who unexpectedly takes a walk in the park. Her erratic behavior begins when she burns a hole in something she is ironing, and eventually she abandons her husband without notice. Later he receives a letter from her, the letter having been mailed from Cyprus; she explains that she looked at the burn hole as an object of meditation, a door to the other: "The longer I looked at it, the bigger it seemed to be, until eventually it looked like a big hole, a big black hole that went down and down, all the way to the middle of the earth. . . . And I kept walking. . . ." Sonia T. walks to a fantasy castle in hell, where she lives as one of the king's wives.

A Line of Sight, reprinted in *Doctor of Silence,* illustrates Kelly's enduring concept of the transparent tree. The short "chapters" give way to the footnotes, which come to bear the narrative thrust instead. These footnotes refuse to be merely linear: they offer the reader a rich and personal line of sight, literally a "landscape," in a blend of autobiography and daily journal. Further, the notes make branch stories from the trunk chapter.

The final grouping in *Doctor of Silence* presents short pieces on form, which function as an informal afterword; separately each one exemplifies one of the forms Kelly has used in the book. "I Wanted a Fugue" is in this section. In "The Irish Joke," Kelly uses the method of *A Line of Sight* to relate a joke his father told him and retell the joke with extended autobiographical notes and his own critical analysis. "Hypnogeography" calls for the founding of the kind of discipline Kelly employs throughout his fiction: the science requires "that all generous persons record their dreams . . . when they dream of place, and that the records or recitations of these dreams be collected, examined, compared . . . with the undreamt 'real' place we find at the end of the road in from the airport." If one takes "the airport" to be a reference to the first story in the book, "Pasatiempo," Kelly ends where he began.

Cat Scratch Fever begins with a refinement of the transparent-tree trope. In "The Scribe" a monastic scribe tells the reader that he is "tracing the angles of desire" as he types his "branch" story at his keyboard (the ancient scribal practice having been brought into the present). As in "The Infinite Tarot" (in *Doctor of Silence*) this branch tale takes the form of an interpolated story. The scribe's life's work is described, in the terms of *A Line of Sight,* as "the never-ending finessing of his footnote to the universal history."

The title story, "Cat Scratch Fever," is a mythopoetic "trunk" story that includes a female lover who combines features of the vampire and the animal allomorph. The story opens with the male narrator spying from a distance on the object of his desire (his link with the other), Lilburne's daughter. After this introduction is established in the manner of the opening to Joyce's "Araby," Kelly's narrator works himself up to take action: he enters the girl's room. His advance is spoiled, however, when he falls and knocks himself silly. As he wakes, the girl is licking his wound. Later the attending physician diagnoses the boy's resulting sickness as "cat scratch fever." An experienced adult as he tells the story, the narrator says no other woman has ever satisfied him in love.

"The Bridesmaid" is a "root" story of the etymology of a word. A drunken bridesmaid overhears, without understanding, the word *dimensionlessness,* which, Kelly makes the reader aware, aptly describes her own condition. Then the whole of the second section of the book is given to an experiment in root storytelling. Linguist Bruce McClelland, who drew Cyrillic characters for the prefatory page to "Russian Tales: Experiments in Telling," provided Kelly with Charles Edward Townsend's textbook *Continuing with Russian* (1981), containing columns of roots and their English equivalents. "As I looked at these," Kelly explains in his preface, "the glosses and the sounds of the Russian stems themselves began to tell their own stories, and I found the English morphemes . . . were linking up in sequence to form narratives and lyrics." The resulting fables, or root stories, are of several distinct types: instructions ("Where Magic Starts," "Finding Buried Treasure," and "How to Pay Debts"); legends ("Breg the Wanderer," "Yom the Greedy," and "The Tale of Niz"); and poems ("Oil of Doors" and "The Pear Tree Song").

Kelly lets the reader hear from the doctors' points of view in this book after *Doctor of Silence.* "In the Jurassic" is narrated by an analyst who regrets the facts of his profession. On the one hand, his patients flow through his office like a great sonata, supplying him with data from the other; on the other hand, he knows that his patients, if they are to get well, must grow to reject him. In this state of mind the analyst receives a manuscript from a female patient, whose dream of dinosaurs provides another animal allomorph. The story ends with the doctor's sexual and writerly frustration over not being able to follow her into the dream. Later in the book, "A Session with the Analyst of Colors" closes with a similar complaint.

"Carville" inverts Kelly's usual senses of the journey out and "dwelling-in." This grotesque story, based on a news report and told in the style of Flannery O'Connor, concerns a colony of lepers in a Louisiana hospital in the process of being closed down by the authorities. The patients are presented as ironic figures from a lost city who are soon to be returned as citizens of a postmodern city. This is an allegory of the unclean, those who were formerly safe inside their rooms, but now must venture outside.

Other stories further explore ideas from the earlier books. "The Annandale Ideology" is written tongue-in-cheek in the form of *A Line of Sight.* The series of brief texts – four couplets that are cryptic and even contradictory on their own – is annotated at length. Kelly seems to enjoy playing "The Scribe" to himself. "Murder as Text" also recalls earlier stories, especially the mock-academic "Lecture on Cadmium" and "The Scribe." "Murder as Text" starts with the "evidence" of a poem (by tenured professor Ernest Flayle, a murder victim) and develops by means of expert witnesses' conflicting testimony. The witnesses reveal in their branch stories more about themselves than about Flayle's fate. The voices of a student, a campus cop, and several academics are as rich as a fugue, and their self-serving commentaries are good campus comedy along the lines of works by Amanda Cross.

"Murmuring" is both a mantra describing a path to the other, and a vortex through which runs the empowering motif of music and where music lets the listener go. In his prefatory notes to *Cat Scratch Fever* Kelly explains that the story "ought to be called 'Muttering' (but that word has acquired a grumbling acceptation), which is the English cognate of the Sanskrit *mantra,* with which the story is concerned." "Murmuring" is a root story in which things get defined in the minds of a couple as they walk and chant. That the couple mutters their mantra while walking along a road establishes the story within Kelly's journey theme. The repetition of the mantra is "not a matter of the words, the animal of the tongue in the warm mountain of the body lurking," but one of imaginative transport, for "As they spoke, they visualized themselves and their surroundings as the personages and environments that have existed and continue to exist in the elsewhere to which their religion guided. . . ." Kelly describes the phenomenon as the magic of syllables. The climax of the story occurs when the couple, their minds cleared by the walk, come upon a dead fox, an allomorph. The man decides that the fox, the woman, and he are all part of a "stream [which] will keep going, never end, this streaming from it-never-wasn't all the way to empty-ofbecoming-it-continues." Finally readers arrive at the proper context for reading Kelly's fiction and poetry, all of which tends to flow, in one grand stream of sensitivity, outward.

The sheer number of Kelly's books has tended to intimidate the reviewers. However, as the critical reputation of the Black Mountain school and Deep Imagism steadily grows and Kelly publishes more of the fiction he has already written, he should be properly established among the best of postmodern American story writers – an equal of Fielding Dawson, Paul Metcalf, Michael Rumaker, Guy Davenport, and Douglas Woolf.

Interviews:

Davis Ossman, *The Sullen Art* (New York: Corinth, 1963), pp. 33–38;

Dennis Barone, "Nothing but Doors: An Interview with Robert Kelly," *Credences,* 3 (Fall 1985): 100–122.

References:

Paul Christensen, *Minding the Underworld: Clayton Eshleman & Late Postmodernism* (Santa Rosa, Cal.: Black Sparrow, 1991), pp. 10, 33–38;

Jed Rasula, "Ten Different Fruits on One Different Tree: Reading Robert Kelly," *Credences,* 3 (Spring 1984): 127–175;

Vort, special issue on Kelly, 5 (Summer 1974).

Papers:

Most of Kelly's journals, correspondence, and manuscripts are in the Lockwood Memorial Library at the State University of New York College at Buffalo. Some early manuscripts are at Kent State University. Letters to Charles Olson are in the Robert Kelly File at the University of Connecticut.

David Leavitt

(23 June 1961 –   )

Daniel J. Murtaugh
University of Kansas

BOOKS: *Family Dancing* (New York: Knopf, 1984;
 Harmondsworth, U.K.: Viking, 1985);
The Lost Language of Cranes (New York: Knopf,
 1986);
Equal Affections (New York: Weidenfeld & Nicolson,
 1989);
A Place I've Never Been (New York: Viking, 1990);
While England Sleeps (New York: Viking, 1993).

SELECTED PERIODICAL PUBLICATIONS –
UNCOLLECTED: "The New Lost Generation,"
 Esquire, 103 (May 1985): 85–88;
"Italy's Secret Gardens," *Vogue,* 178 (June 1985):
 180–183;
"Mad About Milan," *Vogue,* 180 (March 1990):
 376–377, 380, 384.

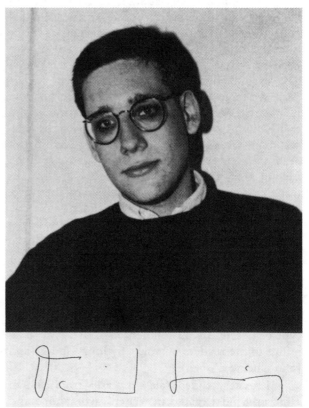

Photograph by Maureen Zent

With the publication of his first collection of short stories, *Family Dancing,* in 1984, David Leavitt became not only one of the chief proponents of the expanding field of gay fiction but was – perhaps to his own surprise – called on to be the spokesman for a generation of writers alienated from the values of post–World War II America and made skeptical by the Vietnam experience, Watergate, and the national AIDS epidemic. As Leavitt notes in his essay "The New Lost Generation" (1985), his generation found itself on the cusp between the political and social activism of the 1960s and the reactive disillusionment and indifference of the post-Water-gate/pre-AIDS 1970s. He has sought, through his short stories and novels, to draw a parallel between the youth of the Jazz Age – too young to have participated in the cataclysmic events of World War I and consequently alienated from the "transfiguring" experiences recounted by the survivors – and those of his own generation who watched as older siblings either joined campus protests or were drafted for service in Vietnam.

 The stories in *Family Dancing* uniformly describe individuals isolated from one another, whether through illness, divorce, or differences in gender and sexual orientation. These stories are expressions of characters seeking some kind of security, usually within the shelter of outmoded and nostalgic conceptions of family. Leavitt regards this situation as a generational dilemma involving an expectation of an "ideal" family structure when the demands of gay children for acceptance and integration; the effects of illness, abandonment, and divorce upon parents and their children; and the asserting by "closeted" gay parents of their true sexualities have caused a disorientation and reorientation of the traditional family model. Leavitt's settings (northern California suburbia; Manhattan and the Hamptons; Paris; and the Italian countryside)

217

are peopled with characters who could have been taken from his own adolescent, academic, and professional worlds: graduate students "Eurailing" or hiking through Europe; professors and their families confronting marital crises; copy editors and writers; and gay men and women confronting the difficulties of "coming out" and of establishing relationships while pursuing professional careers.

David Leavitt was born in Pittsburgh on 23 June 1961 to Harold Jack Leavitt and Gloria Rosenthal Leavitt; he spent his early years in Palo Alto, California, where his father was a professor of organizational behavior at Stanford University and his mother (now deceased) was an occasional political activist. He has described his parents as "very liberal Democrats," and his mother's anger with Richard Nixon and his administration after Watergate "was so intense that it terrified" Leavitt. He absorbed a large amount of political skepticism from his parents and his older brother and sister (John and Emily), who attended Stanford during the campus demonstrations of the late 1960s. The liberal, academic environment of Palo Alto provided Leavitt with a fertile drawing ground for his fictional portrayals of wives abandoned by their professor husbands for graduate students or colleagues; families devastated by their children's drug abuse or forays into criminal behavior; and catastrophic physical or emotional illness and its effect on the delicate fabric of family relationships. The poignancy of these depictions is the result of Leavitt's unspoken, ironic expectation that this humanistic milieu should somehow be immune to the type of deceit, disillusionment, and betrayal so familiar to the readers of works by John Updike and John Cheever.

Leavitt attended Yale University from 1979 to 1983 and participated in writers' workshops and creative-writing courses. Leavitt credits writer and teacher Gordon Lish, novelist Michael Martone, and writer/teacher John Hersey with encouraging him in the early stages of his career, and he claims to have been influenced by such contemporary writers as Raymond Carver (with his empathetic drawing of characters), Alice Munro (with her multiple points of view), and Grace Paley (who presents a universality of situation). At the age of twenty-one, while still at Yale, Leavitt published his first short story, "Territory," in the *New Yorker*. (The story is collected in *Family Dancing*.) In that same year, 1982, he received the Willets Prize for fiction from Yale University.

After graduating from Yale with a B.A. in English (Phi Beta Kappa), he went to work for the Viking/Penguin publishing house as a part-time reader and editorial assistant. His apprenticeship at Viking/Penguin provided him with invaluable insights into the intricacies of the publishing industry and once again with models for his fiction. Finding that editorial work had begun to interfere with his own writing, Leavitt resigned in 1984. His collection of stories *Family Dancing* was nominated for best fiction by the National Book Critics Circle that year and was a finalist for the P.E.N./Faulkner Award for best fiction in 1985. Critical reception for the collection was overwhelmingly positive. Wendy Lesser's *New York Times Book Review* notice of 2 September 1984 credited Leavitt with "a genius for empathy . . . because this 23-year-old writer can't possibly have had time to acquire the kind of knowledge that emerges from the best stories in *Family Dancing*. When Mr. Leavitt writes about a middle-aged woman with cancer, or a single mother of a problem child, or a wife whose husband lies paralyzed in a hospital, he *becomes* that character." Nona Yates, in the *Los Angeles Times Book Review* (21 October 1984), noted, "In his first collection of short stories, Leavitt provides us with an insightful portrayal of people in turmoil, torn between powerful feelings for the past and the often painful reality of the present. He quite effectively portrays the anguish and confusion of families coming apart while members attempt to maintain a modicum of control over their lives."

By early 1985 Leavitt was at work on his first novel, *The Lost Language of Cranes* (1986), and had been chosen to write the decennial "My Generation" essay for *Esquire* (an honor previously accorded to such writers as F. Scott Fitzgerald and William Styron). This essay, "The New Lost Generation," presents his premise that members of his generation did not inherit the sense of family stability that their parents enjoyed and that, as a result, one of the primary concerns of his generation was to find security. *The Lost Language of Cranes* addresses such concerns as the "coming out" process for gay men and women, the passion and pain of first relationships, the problem of repressed homosexuality, and the "encoded" or secret language of the gay subculture.

Leavitt and his companion and fellow writer Gary Glickman moved from Manhattan to East Hampton, New York, in 1985, partially to avoid what Leavitt describes as a "ghetto of writers." He has published a second novel, *Equal Affections* (1989), and a second volume of short stories, *A Place I've Never Been* (1990). The novel expands on some earlier short-story depictions of a professor's wife

who is dying of cancer, of the husband's infidelity —
partially resulting from the stress of the wife's illness — and of the children's and husband's attempts
to deal with her illness and death. The collection of
stories centers on gay characters who are reorganiz-
ing their lives and relationships in the shadow of
AIDS, and once again Leavitt returns to his familiar
theme of survivors seeking safety with friends, with
lovers, or in a restructuring of their own attitudes
toward illness and suffering. There is not a desperate search for a restoration of childhood expectations of shelter within the traditional family; security is found elsewhere, even in a mother's clinging
to her son with AIDS.

Leavitt told interviewer John Duka in 1985
that his fiction is not "explicitly autobiographical,"
but he conceded that there are "autobiographical elements" in nearly all of his stories. He also emphasized the primacy of the imaginative situation over
considerations of religious, sexual, or professional background for his characters. Nonetheless
Leavitt's stories are dependent for their imaginative
appeal on a curious amalgam of professor's son,
gay Jewish man, European traveler, editor, and
writer. Leavitt has also drawn inspiration from
such diverse sources as a news story concerning a
couple who believed themselves to be an advance
team for an alien civilization ("Aliens," in *Family
Dancing*) and a psychology-journal article about a
child who "imprinted" on a construction crane
rather than on his mother (a situation that is in
the character Jerene's thesis in *The Lost Language of
Cranes*).

While Leavitt has converted the experiences
of gay men and women into a matter of interest for
the mainstream reader, he remains one of the most
poignant and subjective tellers of what it means to
be gay and of how a gay person survives in a world
of family, education, or business not necessarily re-
ceptive to sexual difference. For instance, Leavitt
penetrates the gradations of acceptance, or rejection, of gay children by their parents and the attendant sense of guilt, shame, and frustration associated with the "coming out" process. This emotional
dilemma is as much the problem of his gay protagonists as it is for the parents or siblings described
in his stories. In many of his fictional situations, a
heartrending alienation lurks beneath the veneer
of middle-class, suburban/urban liberalism, particularly that of academics who are expected to be
totally understanding and diverse in their approach to sexuality but who have difficulties in
fully integrating these principles into the context
of their own lives.

*Dust jacket for Leavitt's first book, which was nominated for a
National Book Critics Circle Award and was a finalist for a
P.E.N./Faulkner Award in 1985*

Mrs. Campbell (in "Territory"), Rose (in *The
Lost Language of Cranes*), and Louise (in *Equal Affections*) are examples of mothers who are struggling in
one way or another to understand their redefined
roles within the framework of their children's sexuality. In this struggle, paralleling that experienced
by their sons and daughters, these parent figures become characters for whom readers tend to have
compassion. Many of Leavitt's male gay characters
seem to expect a complete integration of their childhood innocence with the experience of their adult
sexual lives, through the medium of their mothers.
These characters make demands that are unreason-
able. What Leavitt seeks to do through these characters and their relationships with their mothers is
to liberate real people like them from these expectations and to prevent gays from becoming overly dependent on acceptance as a means of achieving identity. His gay characters are indeed characters seeking manhood; his lesbian characters are seeking
womanhood. They cannot achieve their goals without the realization that their families (especially

their mothers) will not provide a utopian existence for them, that such an existence is not possible or desirable. They learn that the struggle for dignity and happiness is their own.

Another of Leavitt's favorite themes is that of the effect of illness or impending death on the fragile fabric of family relationships. Two stories in *Family Dancing* ("Counting Months" and "Radiation"), much of the novel *Equal Affections,* and the stories "Spouse Night" and "Gravity" (in *A Place I've Never Been*) underscore the sense of isolation or alienation experienced by those who have derived their identities from their position in the family and who must struggle to preserve some semblance of stability in the midst of their own catastrophic illnesses or that of spouses or children. These characters, in being cut off from those who cannot share in their search for revised identities, share a bond with those other inhabitants of Leavitt's fictional world who are prevented from fully entering into the conventional heterosexual world because of their homosexual orientation or, curiously, because of their value systems that do not include betrayal of the dedicated companion, whether gay or straight. Uniformly there is in Leavitt's work a not-so-subtle disdain for the male spouse who abandons his wife (as in "Counting Months" and "Family Dancing") and for the gay lover who callously or in a helpless or cowardly way abandons his partner.

All these themes are evident in *Family Dancing.* "Territory" depicts a gay son's attempts to gain acceptance from his mother; it is the story of Mrs. Campbell and her son Neil's "agony of change." Distancing and alienation exist despite her best liberal intentions of accepting his homosexuality. She is a joiner of causes and has tried to control and protect Neil's world since his childhood. Nonetheless his current world is a territory quite different from the one he experienced as a child and adolescent, though she is still the matron of his childhood home, which he has of necessity abandoned. She cannot completely enter his world, nor he hers. Neil's attempts to reconnect with his mother after his "coming out" are accompanied unfortunately on both sides by feelings of shame and disappointment. Ultimately Mrs. Campbell cannot allow herself to be Neil's means of validating his sexuality or his relationship with his present lover, Wayne. She will not accept or validate the changed or reconstructed nature of her relationship with her son, a relationship now connected with his love for Wayne. She cannot cross over into the territory of gay culture, and she has a desire to maintain the integrity of her own nongay culture. This situation underscores the pain of realization that the "old world" of family, no matter how accepting, cannot be a haven for a gay man seeking acceptance. Neil must, and apparently does, find this acceptance with his own kind.

"Counting Months" underscores the theme of betrayal, through Mrs. Harrington's abandonment by her law-professor husband (who runs off with one of his law students) and through her own body's abandonment of its defenses against the cancer that threatens her life. She is a courageous seeker of ways to exist within the framework of her home and children. She is the supporter and protector of her teenage children, Jennifer and Roy, and particularly of her troublesome younger son, Ernest, who is a snitch and troublemaker. She also, ironically, provides support and consolation for the Laurenses (another university family), whose son has become a disappointment and embarrassment to them. Her isolation through the lumps developing in her body is comparable to Ernest's rejection by his playmates. The alienation felt by her as a result of her illness further ennobles her efforts to maintain some kind of family stability. Her identity is in her children; her strength is developing out of abandonment and betrayal. In order to survive, she must discover her own identity or face oblivion. She locates this identity through her illness and her dedication to preserving what is left of her family.

In "The Lost Cottage" Lydia attempts to impose a false reality on her fragmenting family by insisting they occupy the summer cottage at Hyannis, even though she is in the process of a divorce from her husband, Alex. Her dedication to a nostalgic picture of her life as mother and wife prior to her abandonment by Alex causes her to hold tenaciously on to this tradition. Mark, the gay son, and his unmarried sister, Ellen, are the realists: because of their unconventionality they have already made a break with the principles by which their mother has governed her life. A sense of injustice pervades the story, culminating with the pathetic confession by Lydia that she will always love Alex. The cruelty of abandonment and disintegrating dreams is accompanied by a subtextual commentary on the nature of heterosexual relationships, from the bewildered viewpoint of the gay son as he witnesses his father's cruel and artificial demonstrations of machismo. The mother's attempts to recapture the happiness of summers past are destined for failure. Like several other Leavitt heroines, she will have to seek completion outside the tenuous structure of the family. Change is cruel to these characters, but it is also transforming.

"Aliens" confronts the process by which injury or illness separates individuals from the conventional world – from the "normal." Alden, whose driving off the roadway with his family may have been an attempt at murder/suicide, must relearn the art of communication, which he does through poetry therapy. He has been betrayed by his body, which did not allow him to die but left him mentally and physically crippled. Nina, his daughter, has also been betrayed through early puberty and unattractiveness, and her new language of isolation consists of imaginative incursions into the Noah-like story of her family being from the planet Dandril. Alden's son, Charles, a computer expert, believes in an artificial imagination in which the most creative aspects of human nature are relegated to a machine function. The narrator, Alden's wife, becomes a volunteer worker in a ward for the severely mentally handicapped in an attempt to reestablish her contacts with the artificial, hospital environment on which she had become dependent following her own injuries in the accident. Each of these individuals has a language of isolation through which the characters seek either escape or reconnection with the world. The new languages are indicators of, or metaphors for, any developing subculture forced out of the mainstream.

"Family Dancing," the title story, centers on the competition between a mother and a daughter (Suzanne and Lynnette) for the affection of the husband and father, Herb. Suzanne's divorce from Herb has resulted in her intermittent despair and depression, as well as her attempt to remake her life through her remarriage to Bruce, a man she does not truly love and whose children distrust and regard her as an alien. Lynnette is unattractive and has created a nostalgic alternative to her existence as the companion to John, her gay roommate: she holds on to her memories of the closeness between her father and herself and prides herself in the belief that Herb maintains a closer relationship with her than with her mother, who has lost him. She recollects that when she was a child her father would swing her high above the reality of her unattractiveness (she remembers herself as an overweight little girl), and she seems to believe that her father will continue to include her in his life and relationships after his divorce from Suzanne. In fact, he does take her on a trip around the harbor with Miriam, his girlfriend, and swings Lynnette into the air when he greets her, as if she were still a little girl.

The reality is that she is no longer that girl but a young woman who depends for her self-esteem on her witty badinage with John and on her imagined inclusion in her father's life with Miriam. She is clearly excluded from the sexual existences of both, evidenced by John's deeper connection with Seth, Lynnette's gay brother. The story ends with a bizarre dance of family members, and Lynnette's unhappy and self-conscious inclusion in the dance fractures the illusions of her relationships with her father, with John, and with Seth. She is embarrassed and betrayed by her father, who is no longer able to propel her beyond the realities of her life; she is further betrayed by the gay world into which she has been invited and by which she has been abandoned.

"Dedicated," one of the stories with a specifically gay theme in *Family Dancing*, is continued in *A Place I've Never Been*. In "Dedicated" the protagonist, Celia, is trapped in a relationship with two gay friends, Nathan and Andrew, who conduct a warring, dysfunctional relationship with one another. Her happiness is dependent on being a friend and confidante to either Nathan or Andrew when they are on the outs with one another. She can only feel wanted when they are not getting along. She is isolated and alien because she does not belong to the gay culture to which she so desperately clings; nor does she have a life beyond the false security of her relationship with gay men (who will not reject her for being unattractive, as would be the case in the heterosexual world to which she truly belongs). Nonetheless she is excluded from the larger gay culture: her being barred from a gay bar and Nathan's dreading being identified as her boyfriend are examples of this exclusion.

The title story of *A Place I've Never Been* sets the theme for the collection, most of which concerns characters seeking refuge and stability with lovers or friends in the AIDS era (whereas the changing dynamics of family relationships is the emphasis of *Family Dancing*). "A Place I've Never Been" reintroduces us to Celia and Nathan of "Dedicated." Nathan has been on a European junket attempting to escape the despair of AIDS-weary New York. A former lover of his has tested positive for the AIDS virus, and Nathan once again turns to Celia to provide him with support. However, Celia has by this time reclaimed her life from her friends, has found self-confidence, and is working on establishing a relationship of her own. When she balks at falling into her former self-effacing role of confidante and companion, Nathan accuses her of being unsympathetic about a "place she's never been" and fails to recognize in his lovelessness the one person who has truly loved him.

Arthur and Mrs. Theodorus's relationship in "Spouse Night" has arisen out of their acquaintance-

Dust jacket for Leavitt's 1990 book, which includes stories about homosexuals whose lives have been disrupted by the AIDS epidemic

ship from the "coping sessions" they attended while their spouses were being treated for terminal cancer. The comical lovemaking scenes (in Mrs. Theodorus's kennel/home; she is a dog breeder) are balanced against the couple's trying to determine whether their deceased partners had been involved in an affair with one another. Both Mrs. Theodorus and Arthur are really seeking an understanding of the suffering their spouses endured, and they suffer from the guilt of not having been able to share it. Arthur's penitential act of tasting his wife's ashes is a fitting conclusion to the story.

"Gravity," Leavitt's only published story dealing directly with the experiences of a person with AIDS, describes a mother's struggle to weather her son Theo's illness. She has become his caretaker, and, in the pivotal episode of the story, she takes him with her to select a gift for a relative's engagement party. Once at the shop, she tosses an expensive crystal bowl at her son, who instinctively catches it, even though the effort nearly brings him to the floor. This act seems, at least from Theo's viewpoint, to provide his mother with vital assurance that he is still alive, that she does not yet have

to let go of him. The incident provides a momentary barrier against the persistent grief and bitterness of watching her son die.

In "Houses" Leavitt turns to the dilemma of the "closeted" gay man who has sought refuge in a straight marriage. Paul becomes involved in an affair with Ted, the groomer for his dog, Charlotte. Although he temporarily leaves his wife, Susan, Paul ultimately lacks the courage to commit to his relationship with Ted, returning to Susan when she offers to take him back. His abandonment of first his wife and then his lover has its penalty: Susan changes her mind, and Ted finds another lover. Paul's lonely overnight stays in one or another of his real-estate agency's houses and his mournful imaginings as to what might have been had he and Ted settled in his "dream house" underscore the emotional devastation attendant on living a double life (an issue previously treated in *The Lost Language of Cranes*).

"I See London, I See France" and "Roads to Rome" are Leavitt's Italian stories in *A Place I've Never Been*. Both demonstrate attempts to escape the unpleasant legacies of family and find refuge in sexual and emotional relationships that provide the type of security not found in traditional families. In "I See London" Celia (of "Dedicated" and "A Place I've Never Been") travels with her fiancé to northern Italy, where they visit his artistic expatriate friends Alex and Sylvie Foster. Celia envies the Fosters' daughters, whose father has painted murals on their bedroom walls and created toy animals for them in his studio, and she feels the encroachment of what she perceives as her own unhappy childhood, in a Brooklyn apartment with her overweight mother and her bedridden grandmother, both of whom often watched and analyzed soap operas. Celia comes to realize that, although she will stay in Italy (a locale of escape in several of Leavitt's stories), she will remain subtly connected with her mother and the Brooklyn apartment – that she cannot, and perhaps should not, escape the bittersweet remembrances of her childhood.

Saturnia, Italy, is the setting for "Roads to Rome." The families of Fulvia and Rosa have ostensibly gathered to make their farewells to the dying Fulvia, but instead they confront the history behind her son Dario's suicide. Fulvia and Rosa, childhood friends and survivors of the Italian resistance in World War II, had, after their marriages went bad, set up housekeeping with their children in Fulvia's villa. Some years later Marco, Rosa's son, became involved in an affair with Fulvia, during which she discovered that he was gay. Subsequently Marco became involved in a relationship with Dario, who was also gay. Dario was rejected by his mother, Fulvia, when he began performing as a female impersonator and philosophizing about, and carrying out, coprophagy (eating his own feces). At the time of this story, Marco has returned from New York with his American lover, Nicholas, but his refuge in that relationship is temporarily disrupted by a family argument over whether Dario was a genius, a "naughty boy," or a fool. After much finger pointing as to who was responsible for his death, harmony is restored at the Saturnia steam baths as Fulvia and her lifelong companion, Rosa, once again forgive and console one another. The appearance of Nicholas reminds Fulvia of an American soldier with whom she had a brief sexual interlude at the end of World War II, and she asks Nicholas to pick her up and take her away – away from the sad memories of Dario and the reality of her imminent death. Nicholas, who has not been one of the players in this family tragicomedy, is thus selected first by Marco and then by Fulvia as a means of escape and safe refuge from the troubled relationships of their families.

One of the most important areas of experience drawn upon by Leavitt for his fiction is that of his own sexual orientation and what he knows of gay relationships, both pre- and post-AIDS, and of the emotional dilemma involved in addressing one's identity as a gay man or woman. He is also able to depict lesbian relationships as well as situations involving gay men in "straight" marriages, both of which situations are removed from his own experience but for which he exhibits a profound cultural empathy. His descriptions of the changing patterns of courtship and sexual behavior among gay men from the early 1980s to the 1990s; his incisive reworking of the Jamesian formula of the unsophisticated American in Europe to that of the not-so-provincial gay American who becomes involved with French or Italian lovers while pursuing academic or professional interests on the Continent; his sensitive portrayal of the dread experienced by gay men and their families in dealing with the AIDS epidemic; and the spokesmanlike quality of his portrayal of the potential for love and depth of attachment in gay relationships – all are clearly drawn from the concerns of a gay writer who has earned a mainstream readership and shows great promise for future accomplishments in literature.

Interviews:

John Duka, "David Leavitt," *Interview,* 15 (March 1985): 84–86;

"Interview with David Leavitt," *Occident,* 102 (1988): 143–151.

Gordon Lish

(11 February 1934 –   )

Joseph Ferrandino
Herkimer County Community College

BOOKS: *English Grammar* (Palo Alto, Cal.: Behavioral Research Laboratories, 1964);
Dear Mr. Capote (New York: Holt, Rinehart & Winston, 1983);
What I Know So Far (New York: Holt, Rinehart & Winston, 1984);
Peru (New York: Dutton, 1986);
Mourner at the Door (New York: Viking, 1988);
Extravaganza: A Joke Book (New York: Putnam, 1989);
My Romance (New York: Norton, 1991).

OTHER: *New Sounds in American Fiction,* edited by Lish (Menlo Park, Cal.: Cummings, 1969);
The Secret Life of Our Times: New Fiction from Esquire, edited by Lish (Garden City, N.Y.: Doubleday, 1973);
All Our Secrets Are the Same: New Fiction from Esquire, edited, with an introduction, by Lish (New York: Norton, 1976).

Gordon Lish, praised for his virtuosity and attacked for his ideas, has earned a distinctive reputation in contemporary fiction as an author, editor, and teacher of the writing of fiction. He has crafted novels and short-story collections in a variety of styles and voices that demonstrate his command of the language and serve as examples of his thoughts on the shape of modern fiction. His problematic writing style, while not immensely popular with the general reading public, is both esteemed and vilified by literary critics.

During his 1969–1977 tenure as the fiction editor at *Esquire,* Lish selected work by John Cheever and Grace Paley, thus giving their masterly short stories a wider readership. He used the influential magazine to introduce new and talented writers such as Barry Hannah, T. Coraghessan Boyle, Reynolds Price, and Cynthia Ozick. As a senior editor at the Alfred A. Knopf publishing house since 1977, Lish has brought to the reading public writers of such literary consequence as Hannah, Ozick, Raymond Carver, Mary Robison, William Ferguson, Janet Kauffman, Anderson Ferrell, Amy Hempel, Bette Howland, Raymond Kennedy, Nancy Lemann, Michael Martone, Bette Pesetsky, Leon Rooke, David Leavitt, and Helen Schulman.

Gordon Jay Lish was born in Hewlett, New York, on 11 February 1934 to Philip and Regina Deutsch Lish. Philip Lish was a partner in Lish Brothers, a manufacturer of women's hats (according to information provided by Gordon Lish in his novel *My Romance,* 1991). Gordon married Loretta Frances Fokes on 7 November 1956, and she gave birth to their three children: Jennifer, Rebecca, and Ethan. After divorcing Loretta in May 1967, Lish married Barbara Works two years later, on 30 May 1969; they have one child, Atticus. Lish earned a B.A. in English (cum laude) from the University of Arizona in 1959 and pursued graduate study at San Francisco State College (now San Francisco State University) in 1960. He worked as a radio broadcaster from 1960 to 1963. Lish taught at Mills High School and College, in San Mateo, California, as an instructor of English from 1961 to 1963, then became the editor in chief and director of linguistic studies for Behavioral Research Laboratories in Menlo Park, California, where he wrote the textbook *English Grammar* (1964). In 1966 he began working for Educational Development Corporation in Palo Alto, California.

In 1969 Lish left the field of education to launch a career in literary publishing, taking the position of fiction editor at *Esquire,* then moving on to become an editor at Knopf. In addition to editing, Lish resumed his teaching career, as a lecturer (1973–1974) and a guest fellow (1974–1980) at Yale University. He has also been an adjunct professor

Gordon Lish (photograph by Bill Haywood)

at Columbia and New York Universities, and he continues to teach two six-hour private writing classes a week in New York City.

The most difficult problem in constructing a biography of Lish is that he constantly mythologizes his life. That is what his stories are about: Lish as hero; Lish as antihero; Lish as villain; Lish as psychological shaman who takes the reader into the depths of the underworld and back; Lish as Virgil, the ideal poet leading the reader lower and lower to where the impenitent are punished; and Lish as Sigmund Freud, as Carl G. Jung, and as B. F. Skinner.

Lish claims that at age fifteen he was sending light verse to *Good Housekeeping* and *Collier's*. A turning point in his life occurred when he was sixteen. He had been plagued by psoriasis, and the condition had grown unbearable. He became involved in an experimental program in which he was treated with a hydrocortisone prototype considered the first of the steroids. He took massive doses, and his weight increased from 113 to 168 pounds in two weeks. He was then disabled by a bout of hypermania, for which he was treated in a mental hospital in New York State. At this hospital he met the poet Hayden Carruth, who became a major influence on Lish's thinking and writing.

Lish has been attacked by critics for encouraging fiction in which, according to Sven Birkerts, "strange behavior and terrifying revelations are set before us in neutral, non-judgmental tones." Lish's stories almost always have an obsessive first-person narrator, and they seem to lack plot, linear progression, and depth of character. Madison Smartt Bell complains that Lish's students who publish "convey precisely what is there and nothing more. . . . There is a remarkably skillful accretion of surface detail — beneath which nothing happens." Bruce Bawer calls these students "the product of the Gordon Lish fiction factory," which equates "greatness" less to literary excellence and more to "cheap Hollywood-like celebrity." Lish and his progeny equate "greatness with notoriety" and consider "talent somewhat less important than PR." In his writing and classroom instruction, Lish has dealt indirectly with such impugnments by producing fiction that compels close

Dust jacket for Lish's first collection of short fiction (1984), which shows the influence of eighteenth-century novelist Laurence Sterne and later experimental writers

reading and by training writers who are not afraid to attempt new narrative structures.

Lish's first novel, *Dear Mr. Capote* (1983), is in the form of a confessional letter written to Truman Capote by the narrator, David, a serial killer with a subliterary flair. He is a forty-seven-year-old employee at a "top ten" New York bank, is married to a woman he does not like, and is devoted to his nine-year-old-son. David has killed twenty-three women by expertly stabbing them once each with a stiletto through the left eye. He plans to kill twenty-four more women – one for every year of his life – then turn himself in. What David offers Capote is the chance to write an account of his exploits and split the proceeds of the book-and-movie deal with David's son, setting the boy up for life. The main theme of *Dear Mr. Capote* is the shape of insanity in the voice of David, who makes repeated use of clichés and idioms. But he also aspires to increase his vocabulary, so he uses his son's "Word-For-The-Day" calendar – *effectuate, capstone, impediment* – and when David commits a murder, he says the day's word to his victims.

Alan Friedman (*New York Times Book Review,* 22 April 1984) mentioned this quirk: "The killer's line of attack, begun with a word, was through the eye and into the brain," which, of course, is much like an author's job. The majority of Lish's writing is metafictional: he is constantly exploring the theory of fiction, the notion that every story is another experiment in the telling of a story.

Lish, in his instructions to his students, explains that the narrator of a first-person story should reveal something to the reader that the narrator does not know he is revealing. Stanley Elkin (*Washington Post,* 5 June 1983) observed that David "lies to himself, the bitter truths only accidentally bubbling to the surface." Lish always uses the first-person point of view in his fiction, thus giving shape to the psyche through the narrator's diction. According to Lish, the best first-person stories are not the ones in which the writer justifies himself but the ones in which the narrator reveals inner secrets that tend to dismantle his sense of self. The structure of his stories corresponds, in some ways, to the structure of the Freudian slip: "errors" of expression reveal unconscious attitudes, desires, wishes, and impulses. In *Dear Mr. Capote* the narrator reveals his insanity by believing that his story depicts a highly systematized world. To David, his is an orderly, clean world, and therein lies the horror.

Lish often refers to this method-acting approach to his writing. In the matter of voice – and voice is consistently the most prominent element in his fiction – he tries to locate his stance somewhere along a continuum. He says he reaches for one or the other extreme, keeping as far away from the centrist stance as he can: "The more extreme the distance, the more readily one can play-act and lift himself away from himself."

The neutral, nonjudgmental tones in his stories are the result of his belief in "equipoise": the idea that conflict is the confrontation of equal and opposing values. During a story these conflicting values should cancel one another out. Their sum total at the end of the piece should be zero – equipoise. Lish does not write in a judgmental way because he believes that all positions are equal. He argues that fiction should not be an assertion and when a writer makes an assertion he should contradict it in the same piece. Lish does not promote a social, political, or cultural point of view; neither does he promulgate the status quo. His characters are highly individual and are slogging their way, as best they can, through a hard and uncertain world. In his stories he attempts to present the integrity of an individual; he portrays the character's moral stance without judging whether it is good or bad. Lish avoids the Western mode of moral judgment, applying instead his own Eastern yin/yang code of male/female, active/passive, and light/dark forces.

Another constant in Lish's work is that his stories are mostly autobiographical; he consistently manipulates the distinction between fact and fiction and draws on this distinction in many of his stories. The first-person narrator of *Peru* (1986) is a fifty-year-old man named Gordon, who watches a televised newscast from a Peruvian prison in which two inmates are stabbing each other repeatedly on the roof of the prison until they are shot dead by guards. Soon afterward Gordon accidentally bumps his head on the open trunk lid of a taxi. Suddenly the long-repressed memory of how Gordon, as a six-year-old, murdered a playmate, Steven, in a sandbox is brought – in luminous detail – into Gordon's consciousness.

Peru tacitly poses the central metafictional question about the relationship between fiction and reality, and there is a strong sense of the autobiographical. In addition to the narrator named Gordon, who is about the same age as Lish when he wrote the book, autobiography is generally mixed with fiction to the point where they seem to become indistinguishable. Stephen Dobyns (*New York Times Book Review*, 2 February 1986) pointed out that within this novel "there is the fiction of the fiction itself"; as the reader pursues the story, what is created is "the illusion . . . that this isn't fiction but autobiography."

The novel *My Romance* presents Gordon Lish as himself – it seems. He dispenses with the subterfuge of a narrator; there seems no difference between his speaking voice and the voice on the page. He is delivering a one-hundred-forty-two-page monologue at a writers' conference in Southhampton, Long Island. The voice is unadulterated Lish, and in this novel he identifies his true audience: the narrow, highly defined world of literary writers, editors, and publishers. He holds forth to them, as he seems to do in everything he writes, and not to the general public. This stance may be why his works do not reach a wide readership.

What I Know So Far (1984), his first collection of short stories, was received with mixed reviews. Friedman stated, "To call them stories . . . is mere force of habit. Some of them tell a tale of sorts, but even these read like riddles or satires or like sketches and blackouts." He refers to "For Jeromé – With Love and Kisses" (whose title is Lish's pun on J. D. Salinger's story "For Esmé – With Love and Squalor" [in *Nine Stories*, 1953]) as a "longwinded Jewish joke . . . but its jokiness is deceptive." Anne Tyler (*New Republic*, 28 May 1984) sees the story much in the same way, "just a very long dialect joke – albeit one with a powerful punchline."

This story, the most written-about piece in the collection, is told by Salinger's father, who complains that he cannot get in touch with his son. The setting is an apartment house in Florida where the parents of the most famous Jewish writers live. The story is a long joke, but so many of the critics were eager to indulge themselves in writing about this story, in which literary name-dropping borders on the ritualistic, that they overlooked some of Lish's other, better stories.

In "What Is Left to Link Us" the narrator introduces himself by saying "I want to tell you of the undoing of a man. He's not a fellow I even know very well." This man is cheating on his wife, and his mistress complains that she is not part of his normal, everyday life. So the man plans a dinner to which the mistress, the narrator, and another male friend are invited. The man gets drunk at this dinner and calls his wife to come get him. That is the "critical moment" of collapse, the "undoing" of this man. "It's not that I am dismayed to hear a man's secrets; it is only that no one has any new ones," the narrator says.

But in every Lish narrative there is more than one story being told. While the narrator recounts the story of this man, he also tells of a story taking place in his own life. A custodian in his apartment building has stolen a sled, a Flexible Flyer, from the narrator's son, or so the narrator believes. The two stories run parallel for a while then begin to combine toward the middle and end. Such is Lish's preferred narrative structure: two things juxtaposed to form a third, unstated thing in the reader's mind.

In this story tension mounts between the narrator's desire to get the sled back and the custodian's and landlord's insistence that they know nothing about it. The narrator is constantly reminding himself that a "reserve nothing can dismantle is immensely more arousing than the inner beast made manifest." As the story draws to a close, the narrator unwittingly reveals himself as a man who does not know himself at all: he is a pretender whose pretense lies in thinking himself wise and sane when he is really foolish and insane. The undoing he is actually describing is his own, not that of the philanderer. The narrator eventually lets the "inner beast" out when he finally meets the custodian, hits him with a ball-peen hammer, and never realizes why or what he has done.

The story "Guilt" is another version of the "child killing playmate" theme found in *Peru*. The story is narrated by a forty-seven-year-old man recalling an incident from his childhood. The narrator, at age seven, is "adored, even worshipped" by the people in his neighborhood. When he is nine, he moves to a new place, and experiences a psychic/emotional movement as well as a spatial one. A twelve-year-old boy named Alan Silver moves there soon after and becomes the worshiped child: "It was my neighborhood desiring Alan Silver." Alan, playing with some older, rougher boys in an unfinished house, falls through a shaft and crashes onto a concrete floor: "He lived in a coma for two weeks. But I knew he would be dead. . . . Someone pushed him, I thought. I thought, Which boy did? I wanted to tell everyone I didn't. I am forty-seven years old, and I still want to say I am innocent."

The guilt felt by the narrator in having an unstated wish fulfilled, even though he did not participate directly in the action, compels him to claim his innocence. His psyche is portrayed not by his actions but by his choice of diction.

"For Rupert – With No Promises" is the unsung gem of this collection. Lish states that this story got him back to doing serious writing. It ran in *Esquire* with no signature; he had written the story in two hours. There is a similarity between this story and *Dear Mr. Capote:* in both, murder is committed or planned as a way of helping the murderer's son prosper and thrive.

The narrator, who is called Buddy (his actual name being David, the same as the narrator of *Dear Mr. Capote*), tells a story about Smithy, his brother. Smithy had a son called Chap with his first wife. Now divorced, Smithy has not seen Chap in fifteen years. Smithy has remarried and has a five-year-old son named Rupert with his second wife. Surprisingly Smithy tells Buddy that he intends to kill his son Chap. Smithy has terminal cancer of the spleen and has only a few months to live. His plan is to kill his first son, whose heart is full of rage, because Smithy fears that Chap will take the life of Rupert, Smithy's favorite. "My firstborn will stalk my second, find a way to hurt *him* because my death *robs* him of his chance to hurt *me*," Smithy says. "I've got to *choose*, don't you see – *and I choose Rupert!*"

Smithy will live another three months, and Buddy convinces him to allow Chap to live at least that long: "The minimum they've given you is the minimum you *can* and therefore *must* give Chap." The purpose of the story is to prevent Smithy from carrying out his plan; publishing the story is "one step short of my informing the police and a step quite far enough to stop him in his tracks." Again Lish combines the real with the fictive to give an unusual autobiographical gloss to this story.

There is also a nagging doubt about the reliability of the narrator. Buddy and Smithy might be two separate halves of the same individual. Buddy was once married to a psychiatrist and has "been away twice" – so his possible insanity casts a shadow on the narrative.

The story ends ambiguously with an interpolated tale about a man in a concentration camp. His son is scheduled for execution, so the father arranges to bribe a guard to take another boy instead. However, after talking with a rabbi, the father feels guilty, changes his mind, and does not pay the bribe; his son is killed. Lish later pulled away from this kind of storytelling in favor of wittier tales.

His second collection of stories, *Mourner at the Door,* was published in 1988. Many of these stories are explorations of his favorite themes: himself, mythologizing his life, and the irony of revealing what one does not know is being revealed. The first story, "The Death of Me," begins: "I wanted to be

Be not be negative. Be not negativized. Befriend

negativity not. Shun negativity. Eschew negativity.

Send down negativity. Turn a cold shoulder to

negativity. Never know the name of negativity. Make

yourself the assassin of negativity. Let negativity

not enter in. Keep negativity out. Go away from

negativity. Take flight from negativity. Rid thy

house of negativity. Be free of negativity. Tear up

the taproot of negativity. Throw off the garment of

negativity. Eat not of the nutriment of negativity.

Worry negativity. Usher negativity away. Shut your

door to negativity. Spurn negativity. Scorn it.

Smite it. Never call out to the servants of

negativity. Hate negativity. No, no, not to summon

negativity's jinn. Unlearn negativity. Do unto

negativity as you would the unclean. Let not your mind

2

Page from the typescript for Lish's "Philosophical Statements," written in 1991 (by permission of Gordon Lish)

amazing. I wanted to be so amazing." This theme is repeated in several other Lish stories in which a boy desires to be the center of attention. (as in "Guilt," for example). The year is 1944 in "The Death of Me," and the boy is ten years old, the age Lish was that year. The boy is at camp and has won five field events, for which he is awarded a piece of stiff cloth as a victory shield: "I felt like God was telling me to realize that he has made me the most unusual member of the human race." Later the boy begins to feel that he is "forgetting what it felt like to do something which would get you a shield." In fact everybody is forgetting how amazing he had been. The ten-year-old shudders with fright that the "feeling" – the duration of fame – does not last.

"The Problem of the Preface" is metafictional, a short version of the theme that is carried out in greater detail in *My Romance*. This three-page story commences with a metafictional dictum: "This is a story about a man who was done in by a story, and by that, by done in, it is meant killed – killed in the very realest sense." The man is "done in" by a story that he himself has told. That story is about his being a kid and choking on a too-big bite of a jelly apple. His brother happened by, picked him up, turned him over, and shook him until the piece of jelly apple became dislodged from his throat, thereby saving his life. The man has told this story to his son. When the son is a man a situation occurs in which his father starts to choke. The son wraps his arms around the father and "managed to get the old man head over heels, all right, but after upending him the old rascal slipped away for an instant and cracked something pretty critical, a stiletto of a neck-bone thence – *oh, shit!* – making its way up into the back of a drastically literal brain." In *My Romance* this story is repeated in greater detail. The reason the old man slips in the novel is because Gordon is covered in mineral oil, a treatment for his psoriasis. That is how he "killed" his father.

Friedman complains that Lish "seems obsessed with writers . . . with their techniques of deception and self-deception." But that is exactly as it should be for a writer, editor, publisher, and teacher of writing as engrossed in the complex storytelling process as Lish is. By dramatizing how a writer creates his fictions, Lish, in stories such as "The Problem of the Preface," uses metafiction to demonstrate how a reader invents his life much in the same way a writer invents his stories: reality and fiction share similar constructions.

Far from being the instigator of a "new approach to fiction," Lish is following the footsteps of Laurence Sterne in *Tristram Shandy* (9 volumes, 1760–1767). Lish's tales are similar in structure and subtext to works by B. S. Johnson, Ronald Sukenick, Donald Barthelme, John Fowles, Salmon Rushdie, Gabriel García Márquez, Thomas Pynchon, Kurt Vonnegut, Jorge Luis Borges, Vladimir Nabokov, John Barth, Muriel Spark, Iris Murdoch, Jerzy Kosinski, Gilbert Sorrentino, and Alain Robbe-Grillet. Metafiction, including the posing of questions about the relationship between reality and fiction, is one of Lish's concerns as a writer: his theory of fiction is dramatized in most, if not all, of his stories.

"The Friend" is one of the most ironic stories in his 1988 collection. It is narrated by the mother of a young man, and she tells the story told to her by another woman, the mother of a young woman named Deedee. The two mothers meet in the laundromat of their apartment building where their children live.

Deedee suffers from a debilitating introversion brought on by a skin condition, a rash "like not even a rash but a dryness – the skin here – the cheeks – so like it is not exactly appetizing to look at her at certain periods of the season." Deedee lives a desperately lonely life. She goes to Mexico on vacation and returns with a pet she has smuggled through customs: "a little Mexican hairless whatnot, like this tiny little dog like the bandleader, like this Xavier Cugat, if you remember, used to hide in his pocket." Deedee falls in love with it; she finally has a companion in life, a friend. But the pet will not eat – all it does is drink water and vomit – and it will not even let Deedee kiss it.

Deedee becomes hysterical and takes it to a veterinarian, who says, "Your pet has a mild case of rabies – you didn't get near any of its saliva, did you?" "No, I'm fine, I'm fine – just give me back my dog," Deedee shrieks. "Dog?" the vet says. "That animal in there is no *dog*, lady. What you brought in here is a rat."

The situational irony of Deedee's misperception is topped by the verbal irony of the narrator, who is totally ignorant of or insensitive to the heartbreaking substance of the story she has just told. The only thing she thinks about is not wanting to touch her son's clothes because they may have been washed in the same machine in which Deedee washed her clothes.

Gordon Lish is a writer who reveals the facts. He does not portray the pretty, the elegant, the just, or the desirable: he portrays what, to him, are the truths of the human condition. He expresses what some other writers would not acknowledge. What others repress, suppress, and conceal at all costs Lish reveals with the flourish of a sleight-of-hand master pulling from his top hat not only a lushly furred rabbit and snowy dove but sometimes a gnawing rat, slimy with sewage. The narrative trick is the same: produce something from nothing and make the crowd gasp.

Some critics say his stories lack plot. Lish argues that a writer does not have to concern himself with plot; the human mind, being what it is, allows the reader to create the plot for himself. Some say that nothing significant happens in his stories and that they do not follow a linear progression. Lish argues that a story is not what happens to people on a page but what happens in the heart and mind of the reader. To him a story is a circle, not a line from "here" to "there."

Some say his students are mere sculptors of sentences and that the construction of sentences and paragraphs is a first step, not a final goal. Lish argues that language *is* the stuff of composition; all writers should be linguistic athletes able to compete successfully in the verbal decathlon of publishing prose fiction. Lish does not insist on a writer's subject – though he prefers certain types of stories over others – but he insists that a writer express his given subject in sentences that ring true with the humming tones of a careful writer at work. Whatever worlds his students sculpt, they will likely be worlds carved in sentences and paragraphs that will endure, as his own fiction will.

References:

Bruce Bawer, *Diminishing Fictions: Essays on the Modern Novel and its Critics* (Saint Paul: Graywolf, 1988), pp. 314–323;

Madison Smartt Bell, "Less is Less: The Dwindling American Short Story," *Harper's* (April 1986): 64–69;

Sven Birkerts, *An Artificial Wilderness: Essays on 20th Century Literature* (New York: Morrow, 1987), pp. 251–263.

Papers:

In 1990 the Lilly Library, at Indiana University at Bloomington, acquired most of Lish's papers, including manuscripts, letters, and memos.

Leonard Michaels

(2 January 1933 –)

BOOKS: *Going Places* (New York: Farrar, Straus & Giroux, 1969; London: Weidenfeld & Nicolson, 1970);
I Would Have Saved Them If I Could (New York: Farrar, Straus & Giroux, 1975);
The Men's Club (New York: Farrar, Straus & Giroux, 1981; London: Cape, 1981);
Shuffle (New York: Farrar, Straus & Giroux, 1990).

PLAY PRODUCTION: *City Boy,* New York, Jewish Repertory Theater, February 1985.

OTHER: *The State of the Language,* 2 volumes, edited by Michaels and Christopher Ricks (Berkeley: University of California Press, 1980, 1990);
West of the West: Imagining California, edited by Michaels, Raquel Scherr, and others (San Francisco: North Point, 1989).

SELECTED PERIODICAL PUBLICATIONS – UNCOLLECTED: "Byron's Cain," *PMLA,* 84 (January 1969): 71–78;
"Style," *Playboy* (January 1983): 113–114, 258;
"Everything Human was Alien to Him," [review of *The Nightmare of Reason* by Ernst Pavel], *New York Times Book Review,* 10 June 1984, pp. 1, 29–31;
"A New Order of Flesh," *Close-Up,* 15 (Winter 1985): 93, 104–107.

Born in lower Manhattan on 2 January 1933 to Leon (a barber) and Anna Czeskies Michaels, Polish-Jewish immigrants, and raised in the city during the Depression, Leonard Michaels seems not to have pictured himself as a writer until, in the mid 1950s, he entered graduate school as a student of English literature (having earned his B.A. at New York University in 1953). He tried one graduate-school program at the University of Michigan in Ann Arbor (where he received his M.A. in 1956), then another at the University of California in Berkeley, but, discontented with the

study of English literature, he withdrew from graduate school and moved to Manhattan, where in 1960 he began to write stories in earnest. He was married for the first time (to Sylvia Bloch), and to eke out a living he also taught English classes at Paterson State College in Wayne, New Jersey. As related in his moving memoir of his first wife ("Sylvia," in *Shuffle,* 1990), this painful and haltingly productive period in the first half of the 1960s ended with their separation, his reentry to graduate school at the University of Michigan, and her suicide. He finally graduated from Michigan with a Ph.D. in English Romantic literature in 1966. His dissertation on Lord Byron, supplied one article in *PMLA* (January 1969), the title phrase for his second collection of stories (*I Would Have Saved Them If I Could,* 1975), and some references in those stories to Byron's life and letters. Although Michaels has written book reviews and miscellaneous pieces of criticism and nonfiction (as yet uncollected), scholarship as such has never seriously engaged him since his graduate-school days; the art of the short story has engrossed him entirely.

While completing his Ph.D. in Ann Arbor he was married to Priscilla Older (on 30 June 1966), with whom he had two sons, Ethan and Jesse. Michaels secured a teaching position in the English department of the University of California at Davis and moved with his wife and their first-born to northern California. In 1969 his first collection of stories, *Going Places,* was published and their second son was born. The vivid tales in *Going Places* so pleased the critic Mark Schorer and his colleagues in the University of California English department at nearby Berkeley that Michaels was soon hired by that more prestigious department, in which he had briefly been a graduate student and "shabby" teaching assistant (according to a student evaluation of him).

In the 1970s Michaels established himself as an English professor at Berkeley, where he has been teaching ever since, and he sustained the immediate

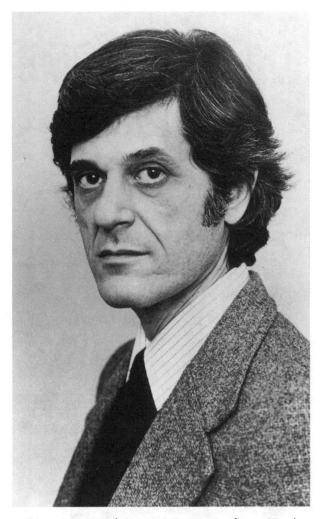

Leonard Michaels (photograph © 1981 by Thomas Victor)

expectation of his artistic gifts with the publication of his second collection of stories in 1975. But marital troubles continued, and in 1977 he and his second wife filed for divorce. That same year (on 10 August) he married the poet Brenda Lynn Hillman, with whom he had a daughter, Louisa. His fictional commentary on this period of his life, and the decade itself, took the form of a novella, *The Men's Club* (1981), a satire on the personal frustrations of men in the face of feminist politics and on the breakdown of relations, even the sexual, between the sexes. *The Men's Club* was made into an unsuccessful movie with a longer, orgiastic ending, but the real moral of the tale seems to have been reserved for Michaels himself, whose third marriage broke up by the end of the 1980s. He has stayed restlessly single, seldom alone – but without a significant relationship – leading the kind of bachelor existence from one affair to another that is recorded in the autobio-

graphical reminiscence "Journal" in his collection *Shuffle*. The bareness of that existence between affairs is summed up in a two-line entry of "Journal": "I eat standing up, leaning over the sink. I wouldn't eat like this if anyone could see me."

Michaels's life and work have furnished the diverse materials that have gone into the writing of his fiction: his family's history in Poland and the United States up to the end of World War II; his boyhood and adolescence in lower Manhattan; his graduate-school stints in the state universities of Michigan and California; his cataclysmic first marriage and the two other aftershocks of a second and then a third mismatch; and the release in middle age into the inconsequentiality of single life again. As if retracing his slow descent to earth from the ivory tower of graduate school, his first two collections of stories are shot through with fantastic elements and literary allusions, which have no place in the heavy

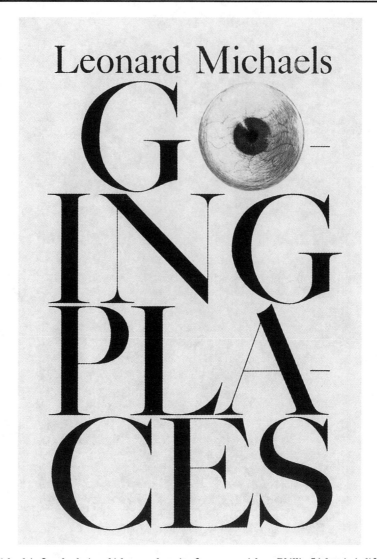

Dust jacket for Michaels's first book, in which several stories focus on anti-hero Phillip Liebowitz's life in New York City

satire of his third book, *The Men's Club;* but already in his second collection (*I Would Have Saved Them If I Could*) the autobiographical element is intrusive, and it dominates the storytelling of *Shuffle,* providing one of the narratives ("Journal") the unseasoned flavor of raw experience.

To apprehend the long modulation from fictional fantasy to autobiographical factuality in Michaels's work, one has only to compare the comic and fantastic New York orgy in the story "Making Changes," from his first collection, with an ugly incident in an entry of "Journal" in which a woman friend of the narrator's, a Japanese American, was "mauled" at a Berkeley orgy by her naked hosts and the other Yahoo-like guests. The same kind of sexual scene in the first story is painted with exuberant and witty strokes, whereas in the "Journal" entry it is reported matter-of-factly and coldly

as some sort of object lesson. Nevertheless, the autobiographical writing in other pieces of *Shuffle* marks an improvement over the incipient autobiography in Michaels's second collection of stories and, welcome or not, comes into its own in *Shuffle.*

The narrative materials, even in this form, are shaped by literary influences as well as memory and imagination. These influences may surface, especially in his first two collections of stories, as echoic words and phrases from Michaels's protracted reading in English literature, of which he had been such an undecided student in graduate school. Snatches of verse by William Butler Yeats, George Meredith, John Donne, Andrew Marvell, and William Shakespeare are seen in *Going Places,* and great names in Western philosophy and literature are dropped into *I Would Have Saved Them If I Could.*

On the other hand, the predominance of poetic quotations in Michaels's beginning stories may disclose not only what poetry was required reading in the graduate-school syllabi of the 1950s and 1960s but also his natural affinity with poetry. His unflagging metaphorical style, the fantastic plots and situations in his first two story collections, the almost antinarrative thrust of the narration in places, and the shortness of all his stories impress readers strongly with the sense that at least the roots of Michaels's talents lie in the nature of lyric poetry and not in that of storytelling and prose fiction. The growth of these talents was toward fiction, and two of the greatest names dropped in *I Would Have Saved Them If I Could* – Jorge Luis Borges and Franz Kafka – must have served Michaels as models of poetic concision and extravagant fantasy in the art of the short story.

Borges's war story "The Secret Miracle" – about the arrest and execution by the Germans of a Jewish-Czech scholar and playwright who succumbs to the delusion, at the hour of death, that God has granted him a year to finish his last work (a drama) – is used by Michaels as a literary foil to the harsh family history of his maternal grandparents and his aunt in the title piece, "I Would Have Saved Them If I Could." Trapped by a pogrom in prewar Poland, they fell victims to the invading Germans, without further delusions. The contrast is between the etherealized Jew, who thinks in his desperation to transcend death in his mind, and the all-too-real victims of the Holocaust, as embodied in the "bad teeth, gray hair, nervous cough, tinted spectacles, delicate fingers, and . . . gentle musical voice" of Michaels's grandfather.

Michaels's literary rapport with Kafka is closer and yet more problematic, because the attraction is stronger and the unapproachability of Kafka so much greater. Michaels finds himself "hurried away" from Borges by Kafka. In another narrative of *I Would Have Saved Them If I Could,* "Storytellers, Liars, and Bores," the Austrian-Czech genius and a fledgling American short-story writer meet in a troubled dream of the latter's, underwater in the stateroom of a sunken ship. The dream caps a humorous sequence of trials and errors in the writing of stories and the reading of them to others, which the narrator, his career as yet unlaunched, has been doing with one girlfriend after another – until one with the name Memory, a modern muse, puts a stop to this practice by telling stories of her own. But Memory is as bad a listener as she is a storyteller, and when the budding author breaks her nose for letting him pervert her with false tales and lies, and

gives up storytelling in a pique, she in turn bores him with anecdotes of the everyday minutiae of her life as a working girl, sexually harassed by her boss. Addressing his boredom, she says, "I can't tell you stories. I have problems with sublimity. I'm not Kafka." The next thing readers know, the narrator is dreaming of meeting Kafka. The ship has sunk, and water is everywhere, refracting a blinding light: "Broken nose appeared, swimming through the palpable light, her mouth a zero. She said, 'Have you been introduced to Kafka? He's here, you know.' I followed her and was introduced. He shook my hand, then wiped his fingers on his tie."

This little allegory of the frustrations of an author ends in an ambiguous gesture of acquiescence and repugnance on Kafka's part, but in fact Michaels's imagined contact with the elusive Kafka was a good deal more positive than that: in a review of a 1984 biography of Kafka by Ernst Pavel, Michaels hazarded the opinion that "whatever it cost . . . it was a great privilege to have been close to Kafka" (*New York Times Book Review,* 10 June 1984).

Along with these two foreign influences on Michaels's work, there was one key American influence that should not be neglected – Henry Miller – though he is relegated to the background of Michaels's writing. During the happy ending of the early story "Making Changes," a New York couple that got parted in an orgy are reunited elsewhere and gratefully make love together, as one individual to another. Their lovemaking is designated, quasi-euphemistically, by the names of twentieth-century authors famous or notorious for the erotic content of their works. "We had D. H. Lawrence, Norman Mailer, *triste,*" the narrator says. "We had Henry Miller."

Miller originated the rowdy, bawdy style of autobiographical writing and accustomed American audiences (once the prewar veils of censorship were lifted) to explicit sex scenes in contemporary literature. Michaels seems to have effortlessly absorbed this style and the naked scenery that goes with it in the process of forging his own unabashed style of storytelling. Certain descriptive terms in the sexual vocabulary of Miller have left verbal traces of the assimilation process in the stories of Michaels. But, with oblique satire and complex metaphors, Michaels has subtilized the cruder style of Miller, and the fantasies that float over the stories in *Going Places* and *I Would Have Saved Them If I Could* are very different from and certainly more intriguing than the cosmic but quite passive daydreaming of Henry Miller in *Black Spring* (1936) and the two *Tropic* novels.

Dust jacket for Michaels's 1975 book, in which the title story is based on the experiences of his maternal grandparents and aunt, who were captured by the Nazis during the invasion of Poland

Among his fellow Jewish-American writers, Michaels is most like Philip Roth, whose first stories in *Goodbye, Columbus* (1959) set literary precedents for several of Michaels's, without necessarily influencing them more directly. One detects in Michaels an impulse to overtop and outdo any literary precedent for the fictional scenes he may be staging. His impulse seems equal to almost anything.

Against the literary backdrop of foreign inspiration, American influences, and interpersonal rivalry, Michaels's originality in his best stories and reminiscences is not by any means diminished. The factotum of his first two books of stories is the "city boy," Phillip Liebowitz of New York, an anti-hero who attains self-definition by outrageous stunts, even when he falls, not infrequently, flat on his face. He is the unheroic protagonist of "A Green Thought," "Making Changes," "City Boy," and "Getting Lucky" and of other stories in both collections. He is a wild card in Michaels's hand, and one can only regret his being discarded from the pack

after *I Would Have Saved Them If I Could,* because, of all Michaels's characters, he is the truest exponent of Michaels's effervescent fantasies, his bursting imagination. Paler personae, including nameless first-person voices, also narrate and participate in various stories. But the published corpus cannot be reorganized around any one leading thematic character based on Michaels himself. Rather, in the first collection there is a medley of fantastic tales, featuring Liebowitz, and of more-conventional realistic stories of life in New York City; then a strain of anecdotal autobiography is injected into the second collection with occasionally fantastic scenarios (as in the narrative "Eating Out"). But along with this development there is another sprinkling of realistic stories of city life, and even the tall tales of Liebowitz's further adventures are moderated, being not so much fantastic as merely extravagant, since Liebowitz (like Michaels) is older and married, with children. Next comes *The Men's Club,* social satire for which a special effort has been made by Michaels to marshal a gallery of rogue males, thereby multiplying the small cast of characters in his fiction. Finally readers see the full emergence of autobiography in his third collection, *Shuffle,* with its three splendid memoirs of his mother and father and his first wife, Sylvia.

The centerpiece of the first collection is not the title story, "Going Places," but the brilliant fantasy "Sticks and Stones," a tale of love and friendship among the irrepressible Phillip, his friend Henry, and Marjorie, a woman they have both dated in New York. This trio also figures humorously in the story "Fingers and Toes," which revolves around nothing more serious than a dinner party and a reluctant attempt on Phillip's part to rekindle a flame between Henry and Marjorie – by making love to her himself. But in "Sticks and Stones" the two-sided affair with Marjorie eventually breaks up the friendship of Phillip and Henry under ever-more-surreal circumstances.

Phillip takes the first step, on a blind date, toward Marjorie, who is described as a rather unattractive girl, a stutterer, and a slight cripple in one leg because of an industrial accident. He drinks too much, and they weep together a lot as she tells him her sad life story, until, as if he can bear it no longer, he pushes himself through a window of her apartment and lands in a shower of glass on the roof of a porch just below it – where Marjorie goes ahead with her story when he comes to. Through her words he seems to hear insistently the sound of wedding bells from afar but is relieved to learn afterward from Henry that he himself has also started an affair with her. Phillip and Henry celebrate their friendship as a thing apart by running with each other around the city, and Henry playfully eggs Phillip on to retell the opening incident ("how you fell out the window") to their acquaintances. Phillip does so more than once but alters the account on a subsequent retelling to fit an episode in Henry's affair. Henry, listening to this version, is visibly put out that Phillip has been eavesdropping on him, and then readers see the start of the downward spiral of the fantasy. Phillip dreams that Henry is going to kill him, and the appearance of Henry and Marjorie has worsened in reality: Henry's face clouds over, becoming "nasty about the edges of the eyes and mouth"; Marjorie's face is thinner, gaunt.

No paraphrase can capture altogether the madcap logic of this fable of a friendship gone wrong or render at all the extraordinary stylization of the narrative. The realism of some other stories in *Going Places* can be isolated more securely. A rape, a leg injury, or a street altercation over a lady's glove, as in the stories "Manikin," "Isaac," and "The Deal," respectively, is the realistic point

of departure for a story, which then elaborates metaphorically on the implications in the given incident until a resolution, whether real or apparent, comes forth. This modified, poetic realism is not a dilution but an enhancement of the real, by which the meaning of the incident is brought out in the symbolism, in the figurative turns of the narrative. Perhaps it should be termed "poetic concretism," since the poetic style of Michaels is so riveted to the things of this world as to be almost physical in texture – a view of style to which he himself subscribes (in "Style," *Playboy,* January 1983).

The story "The Deal" is a good example of this poetic realism. The story's nucleus is a minor metropolitan incident: a young woman of Scottish descent returns home from work one summer afternoon to her neighborhood in lower Manhattan and accidentally lets her glove fall to the street on her way to the corner grocery, across from her apartment house. The article is picked up behind her by one of two ringleaders of a gang of twenty Cuban-American boys, mostly young adolescents, who are sitting on a brownstone stoop and ogling her. Crossing back to her apartment, she questions the boys about the glove, and a conversation ensues, as she presses for the whereabouts of the glove and they duck her questions. But when one small boy, who has been rebuked by the guilty ringleader for being too forward, fingers him as the glove holder, the conversation settles into some hard bargaining for the sake of a "deal."

The two ringleaders – one referred to as "green eyes" (the glove holder) and the other as "the hat" – want money, too much money, for the glove, but the woman maneuvers "green eyes" into instead accepting a kiss, for which, in a moment of weakness, he has asked. To be kissed by this woman is really a disgrace for him, though the littler ones in the group now echo him in chorus, "Gimme a kiss!" Once alone with him inside the vestibule to her apartment, she reassures him that she will not kiss him; but after he hands over the glove, she gives him a peck on the cheek. Thereupon the outer door flies open and the rest of the gang jams into the vestibule, greedy for kisses. In the commotion, as she is fending them off with her purse, she is hit once or twice on the face by the other, older ringleader, "the hat," a somewhat sinister enforcer of "the deal," who expels the smaller fry and then lingers to help her collect the scattered contents of her purse in the hope that she will repay him with something, too; but she only shuts the inner door to her apartment firmly in his face.

Two outstanding stories in Michaels's second collection, "Murderers" and "Reflections of a Wild

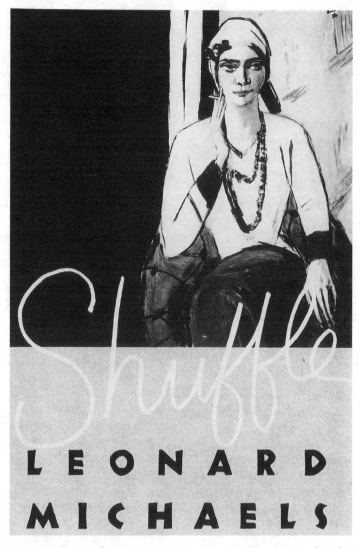

Dust jacket for Michaels's 1990 collection of autobiographical sketches, including memoirs of his father, mother, and first wife

Kid," highlight the main tendencies of his work at that stage (1975): toward incipient autobiography, in one direction; and toward a less fantastic, albeit still comically exaggerated, representation of his anti-hero, Phillip Liebowitz, in another. The beginning and ending of "Murderers" hinge on the occurrence of death in the life of Liebowitz as a boy, who in this story speaks distinctly of Michaels's own boyhood. The deaths of two of Phillip's Polish relatives on the Lower East Side propel the boy into the New York subway system, in which he circulates aimlessly every day, fleeing more death in the family. "I didn't want to wait for it," he explains. When three of his friends, Jewish boys like himself, catch him on the street and tell him that their uxorious rabbi has just gone home to dally with his wife again, a kind of purpose grips Phillip, and he

rushes off with his friends to witness the dalliance of the rabbi and his wife – as these daring boys have often done before – up on a slanting metal rooftop overlooking the windows of the rabbi's apartment. Risking life and limb, they climb to their dangerous perch, from which they can feast their eyes on the bearded man and his bald wife dancing naked in their apartment to the rumba song "Miami Beach," which is playing on their phonograph.

There, as the two clinch and unclasp, life seems to engender a response to death. "This was the beginning of philosophy," the narrator reflects, "so what if my Uncle Moe was dead?" But in the excitement one of the boys on the metal roof slips, his ringed finger snags a nailhead, and the rest of him plummets to the street below. As the others hastily climb down after their dead companion, the rabbi's wife spots them through a window, and the rabbi shouts from it, "Murderers!" Their punishment, imposed by the rabbi, is to be sent to a disciplinary summer camp run by saturnine, wounded World War II veterans. At night in the camp the impenitent Phillip listens to a sound he has never heard before – the hooting of owls – a sound which infuses him with darkness. While he was fleeing death in the family, he plunged ever deeper on the subway into the darkness of the underground, and now the darkness has claimed him for the death of his companion.

A companion piece to Phillip's boyhood tragedy is a comedy of his middle age, "Reflections of a Wild Kid." Again he is cornered in a love triangle, but this time the two other participants are an old girlfriend of his, Joyce Wolf, and her present fiancé, T. T. Mandell, a funny professor of communication arts at a community college in the Bronx. Mandell is the academic hero of "Some Laughed," the tale of his ultimately successful literary and scholarly strivings for tenure; but in "Reflections of a Wild Kid" he has the part of the fool of love, who is duped by his bride-to-be and Phillip. The situation in which these three characters find themselves is ludicrous.

Married, with a child, and working as an editor for a textbook publisher, the forty-year-old Phillip has yet the strength to summon back one day the good times with Joyce by telephoning her for a dinner date at a restaurant on the Upper East Side. After dinner they proceed to her apartment for drinks, but just as he is at the alcoholic point of seducing her, Mandell shows up at her door unexpectedly, and Phillip must hide himself in her bedroom. Presently there are policemen at Joyce's door, and they arrest Mandell for indecent behavior, hauling him off, kicking and screaming, to be booked. The real offender can then seduce his former girlfriend unhindered. The plot of this story is as old as the *Decameron;* the story is a modern *fabliau* with the medieval schema of a woman's concealment of a lover from her (prospective) husband.

Michaels's *The Men's Club,* like the story "Reflections of a Wild Kid," is constructed on traditional lines, with a Decameronic frame story enclosing haphazard tales of the sexual exploits of the tellers. Their tales, unfortunately, are little better than locker-room brags and confessions. The larger canvas of the novel form, however, benefits the characterization of Michaels's personae. For the first time in his fiction a minisociety, not an individual or two, is assembled, and the scene of events has shifted from the steel and concrete of New York City to the more vulnerable stucco and redwood of Berkeley, California.

Of the three autobiographical sketches in *Shuffle* – "My Father," "To Feel these Things," and "Sylvia" – the last was expanded by Michaels and republished separately. Quite apart from the raw and rambling autobiographical record in "Journal," which takes up about half the space of the book, these shorter pieces constitute a unity by themselves and can, as a tripartite family chronicle, justify the overspreading of autobiography in this volume, which "Journal" cannot. The brief memoir of Michaels's mother, "To Feel these Things," is an evocation not only of her but also of her dead family in wartime Poland, the doomed relatives of "I Would Have Saved Them If I Could" who were prevented by a Polish pogrom from escaping to America. Between her anxious ministrations to him as a sickly child and his strained awareness of the Holocaust, his childhood seemed to tremble in the balance of life and death, and he often had to be escorted by a female friend of the family into the hurly-burly of New York public playgrounds.

With the onset of adolescence his confidence in himself increased, and his attachment to his father was strengthened in beguiling ways. In his mid teens, as Michaels says in "My Father," he had taken a girlfriend of his, a non-Jewish blonde, to Madison Square Garden for a basketball game, at which they were observed by a friend of his father's. The father, instead of lecturing his son on the seductions of the schiksas, remarked auspiciously after a long silence, "I'll dance at your wedding." But it was no more than an adolescent affair. A self-effacing barber and a clerical functionary of the local synagogue, Leon Michaels spent his whole working life on the Lower East Side cutting hair, shaving faces, and always looking after his friends, or whoever else visited in his barbershop, a refuge to many. He and his wife, Anna, instinctually got involved with all the cares and concerns of their community. The father's moral position over his son, however, was to prolong Leonard Michaels's acutely unhappy first marriage, though his father had good intentions.

When the would-be writer, in his late twenties, fell in love with Sylvia Bloch, the dark-haired Jew whom he was to marry, his outlook on the world was tranquil and trusting after years in the ivory tower of graduate school: "I had a lot of friends, got along with my parents, and women liked me. In a vague and happy way, I felt humored by the world. . . ." With this outlook (in "Sylvia") he was little prepared for the profound psychological turmoils of his first marriage, which was terminated by the suicide of his wife. Out of sheer incomprehension he was reduced to keeping a journal of their fights: everything he did in their tiny Greenwich Village apartment could be, senselessly, the cause of another blowup, and so he felt that nothing must be forgotten. Such was his state of mind. "I know how I'm behaving," she would say, as if she alone were capable of comprehending her disorders – he could only incite them.

The memoir of Michaels's dead wife, based on his journal of the early 1960s, spares no detail of their long ordeal, which culminated in a scene at another apartment in New York, where she had been staying while he was pursuing his Ph.D. at the University of Michigan. When, on a visit to her, it became evident that he wanted a divorce, she swallowed forty-seven Seconal pills and collapsed before him in a coma, from which she never awoke. Not only here but in other passages beforehand the memoir takes the full measure of the tragic dimensions of this marriage; hitherto marital discord had been a laughing matter in the writings of Michaels, as in the frame story of *The Men's Club,* but it is not so in the memoir, in which he explores it in depth as a possible tragedy or an insoluble problem, as it was in his own first marriage.

Michaels is a master of realism, but the fantasy tale is probably his highest artistic achievement, although he has produced barely a handful of stories in this genre and may have put it behind him for good. In the middle period of his career a string of realistic stories, written in a colorful poetic style, ties together his three story collections. His steadily advancing autobiographical writing has produced disagreeable narrative, as in "Journal," which is purportedly autobiographical, but at the same time the autobiographical mode vindicates itself triumphantly in the three family memoirs, which are high points of achievement. Another facet of mixed quality in his writing is the pervasive sexuality and physicality. Story after story, as with the locker-room tales in *The Men's Club,* includes coitus; urination, farting, defecation, vomiting, and spitting are also commonplace. Bodily functions, of course, are an inexhaustible resource of the social satirist who likes to strip people of their pretensions. Furthermore, in the fictional fantasies of his first two collections, Michaels is experimentally interested in reintegrating the human body into what he later epitomized as "a new order of the flesh" (in the article of that title in *Close-Up,* Winter 1985). One result of this reintegration is exemplified in the ending to "Sticks and Stones." But, on the other hand, his preoccupation with the sexual and the physical has inevitably curtailed his characterization of people as persons. The novel *The Men's Club* added some memorable characters to his fiction, but in his short stories he operates with a minimum of characters, whom he recycles from story to story. Two things are incontestable: the power of Michaels to tell a gripping or hilarious story, and the elegance of his narrative and descriptive prose style.

Joyce Carol Oates

(16 June 1938 –)

Marilyn C. Wesley
Hartwick College

See also the Oates entries in *DLB 2: American Novelists Since World War II*; *DLB 5: American Poets Since World War II*; and *DLB Yearbook: 1981*.

BOOKS: *By the North Gate* (New York: Vanguard, 1963);

With Shuddering Fall (New York: Vanguard, 1964; London: Cape, 1965);

Upon the Sweeping Flood and Other Stories (New York: Vanguard, 1966; London: Gollancz, 1973);

A Garden of Earthly Delights (New York: Vanguard, 1967; London: Gollancz, 1970);

Expensive People (New York: Vanguard, 1968; London: Gollancz, 1969);

them (New York: Vanguard, 1969; London: Gollancz, 1971);

Anonymous Sins and Other Poems (Baton Rouge: Louisiana State University Press, 1969);

The Wheel of Love and Other Stories (New York: Vanguard, 1970; London: Gollancz, 1971);

Love and Its Derangements (Baton Rouge: Louisiana State University Press, 1970);

Wonderland (New York: Vanguard, 1971; London: Gollancz, 1972);

The Edge of Impossibility: Tragic Forms in Literature (New York: Vanguard, 1972; London: Gollancz, 1976);

Marriages and Infidelities (New York: Vanguard, 1972; London: Gollancz, 1974);

Angel Fire (Baton Rouge: Louisiana State University Press, 1973);

The Hostile Sun: The Poetry of D. H. Lawrence (Los Angeles: Black Sparrow, 1973);

Do With Me What You Will (New York: Vanguard, 1973; London: Gollancz, 1974);

Miracle Play (Los Angeles: Black Sparrow, 1974);

The Hungry Ghosts: Seven Allusive Comedies (Los Angeles: Black Sparrow, 1974; Solihull, U.K.: Aquila, 1975);

Plagiarized Material, as Fernandes (Los Angeles: Black Sparrow, 1974);

Joyce Carol Oates (photograph © 1988 by Brian J. Berman)

The Goddess and Other Women (New York: Vanguard, 1974; London: Gollancz, 1975);

New Heaven, New Earth: The Visionary Experience in Literature (New York: Vanguard, 1974; London: Gollancz, 1976);

Where Are You Going, Where Have You Been? Stories of Young America (Greenwich, Conn.: Fawcett, 1974);

The Seduction and Other Stories (Los Angeles: Black Sparrow, 1975);

The Poisoned Kiss and Other Stories from the Portuguese, as Fernandes (New York: Vanguard, 1975; London: Gollancz, 1976);

The Assassins: A Book of Hours (New York: Vanguard, 1975);

The Fabulous Beasts (Baton Rouge: Louisiana State University Press, 1975);

The Triumph of the Spider Monkey (Santa Barbara, Cal.: Black Sparrow, 1976);

Childwold (New York: Vanguard, 1976; London: Gollancz, 1977);

Crossing the Border (New York: Vanguard, 1976; London: Gollancz, 1978);

Night-Side (New York: Vanguard, 1977; London: Gollancz, 1979);

Son of the Morning (New York: Vanguard, 1978; London: Gollancz, 1979);

Women Whose Lives Are Food, Men Whose Lives Are Money (Baton Rouge & London: Louisiana State University Press, 1978);

All the Good People I've Left Behind (Santa Barbara, Cal.: Black Sparrow, 1979);

Cybele (Santa Barbara, Cal.: Black Sparrow, 1979);

Unholy Loves (New York: Vanguard, 1979; London: Gollancz, 1980);

Bellefleur (New York: Dutton, 1980; London: Cape, 1981);

Three Plays (Princeton, N. J.: Ontario Review, 1980);

A Sentimental Education (New York: Dutton, 1980; London: Cape, 1981);

Contraries (New York: Oxford University Press, 1981);

Angel of Light (New York: Dutton, 1981; London: Cape, 1981);

A Bloodsmoor Romance (New York: Dutton, 1982; London: Cape, 1983);

The Invisible Woman: New and Selected Poems 1970–1982 (Princeton, N. J.: Ontario Review, 1982);

The Profane Art: Essays and Reviews (New York: Dutton, 1983);

The Mysteries of Winterthurn (New York: Dutton, 1984; London: Cape, 1984);

Last Days (New York: Dutton, 1984; London: Cape, 1985);

Solstice (New York: Abrahams/Dutton, 1985);

Marya: A Life (New York: Dutton, 1986);

Raven's Wing (New York: Dutton, 1986);

You Must Remember This (New York: Dutton, 1987);

Lives of the Twins, as Rosamond Smith (New York: Simon & Schuster, 1987);

On Boxing (New York: Doubleday, 1987);

The Assignation (New York: Ecco, 1988);

(Woman) Writer: Occasions and Opportunities (New York: Dutton, 1988);

American Appetites (New York: Dutton, 1989);

Soul/Mate, as Smith (New York: Dutton, 1989);

Because It Is Bitter, and Because It Is My Heart (New York: Dutton, 1990);

I Lock My Door Upon Myself (New York: Ecco, 1990);

Heat and Other Stories (New York: Dutton, 1991);

The Rise of Life on Earth (New York: New Directions, 1991);

Snake Eyes, as Smith (New York: Simon & Schuster, 1992);

Black Water (New York: Dutton, 1992).

In 1990 Joyce Carol Oates won both the Elmer Holmes Bobst Lifetime Achievement Award in Fiction and the Rea Award for the Short Story, a twenty-five-thousand-dollar prize that honors living American writers "who have made significant contributions to the story as an art form." The convergence of these two awards suggests not only Oates's literary achievement but the significant place of her short fiction within that achievement. Oates's first publications were short stories, and from the beginning her superiority in that genre has been recognized. Linda W. Wagner notes in her useful review of Oates's critical reception through 1978 (in *Critical Essays on Joyce Carol Oates,* 1979) that early collections were consistently well received and, in fact, provided a standard of excellence that some critics held against her first novels.

In her *Joyce Carol Oates: An Annotated Bibliography* (1986) Francine Lercangée provides 416 separate entries on stories, and, since that enumeration, Oates has published three additional collections of short fiction. Because of her prodigious production of short stories, Oates says that "their role is virtually indistinguishable from my life! Most obviously the short story is a short run – a single idea and mood, usually no more than two or three characters, an abbreviated space of time. The short story lends itself most gracefully to experimentation, too. If you think about it, the story cannot be defined, and hence is open, still in the making. . . . I like the freedom and promise of the form." Because the short story has been a constant in Oates's writing life, the stories and collections indicate the themes and approaches that continue to engage her. However, Oates insists that she collects "only a few stories in proportion to the number I publish," because of her need to make her collections of stories into "books, consciously organized" around "common concerns, common themes and obsessions, in a certain period of time."

Katherine Bastian's *Joyce Carol Oates's Short Stories between Tradition and Innovation* (1983) supports Oates's claims of experimentation and order. Yet

Dust jacket for Oates's 1970 short-story collection, which challenged the notion that she was a regional writer

Oates's experimental mode is not that of anarchistic postmodernism, which she frequently excoriates in her own criticism, but it proceeds from an evaluation and adaptation of the conventions and models inherited from literary culture. Thus, according to Bastian's study of the short fiction, Oates reinvents stories of the "extraordinary," such as ghost stories, initiation stories, and stories of recognition. The complex schemes that order Oates's collections include thematic and sequential cycles containing recurrent meanings or characters.

Bastian's typologies suggest that Oates's sense of the openness of the short-story form derives from the turn and return of central issues of her fiction in a wide range of contexts throughout various stories, story types, and collections. As Bastian contends, the early works treat the psychological permutations of and obstacles to love, but later collections also concentrate on the social conditions that make human connections problematic.

Joyce Carol Oates was born on 16 June 1938 in Lockport, New York, to Frederic (a tool-and-die designer) and Caroline Bush Oates. After earning her B.A. in English at Syracuse University in 1960, Joyce entered the University of Wisconsin, where

she received her M.A. the following year. On 23 January 1961 she married Raymond Joseph Smith, a fellow student, who became an English professor and an editor. Oates also embarked on a teaching career, while beginning to publish her stories. She has taught at the University of Detroit (1961–1967); the University of Windsor, in Ontario (1967–1978); and Princeton University, where she began as a writer in residence in 1978 and later became a professor.

Oates's early short-story collections established her as a literary star. Her first book, *By the North Gate* (1963), and *Upon the Sweeping Flood and Other Stories* (1966) were generally and unambiguously praised for their realistic themes and form. *By the North Gate,* which borrows its title from the point of view of an Ezra Pound character condemned to service at a bleak outpost, gathers Oates's undergraduate stories, which are set in the ironically named Eden County of her upstate New York childhood. "The Census Taker," through its focus on the rigorous perspective of a country girl who, though apparently deprived, refuses the platitudinous self-indulgence of the weak city man sent to define her experience through the imposition of the census, exemplifies the dominant tone of the collection: "I ain't goin' to keep on, no walled-in world, no numbers writ down in a book to stand for me." *Upon the Sweeping Flood* responds dialectically to the frequently violent independence of youthful protagonists favored in the first collection by developing similar characters so as to stress the limiting circumstances of their context, thus foreshadowing the two general tendencies of Oates's entire oeuvre: the concerns with psychological predicament and social situation. The title story is a typical example. In "Upon the Sweeping Flood" a country family reminiscent of that in "The Census Taker" suffers along with another city man the dangerous onset of a hurricane. While the theme, the failure of theory to contain existential reality, is similar, precisely that failure exposes the children to even more devastation than they experience as a result of their natural environment. The city man, apparently crazed by his inability to control the forces threatening the brother and sister, attacks and drowns the boy and attempts to rape the girl. The emphasis in this collection is on the failure of masculine social authority to provide safety and support in a dangerous world.

Her first two collections established Oates as a regional writer, who, like William Faulkner and Flannery O'Connor, to whom she was compared, spoke with considerable authority about a particular geographical and moral location in a recognizable voice. Her eleven collections that were published in the decade from 1970 to 1980, however, present a different kind of writer with a different artistic agenda. *The Wheel of Love and Other Stories* (1970), *Marriages and Infidelities* (1972), *The Hungry Ghosts* (1974), *The Goddess and Other Women* (1974), *Where Are You Going, Where Have You Been?* (1974), *The Seduction and Other Stories* (1975), *The Poisoned Kiss* (1975), *Crossing the Border* (1976), *Night-Side* (1977), *All the Good People I've Left Behind* (1979), and *A Sentimental Education* (1980) establish Oates as increasingly interested in thematic and formal experimentation. By the end of this decade Oates had also published her first twelve novels, thereby establishing herself as an important literary figure whose complex and varied productions greatly challenged readers and professional critics alike. The challenge of determining the nature of Oates's preoccupations, methods, and significance resulted in a wide range of critical response to the short stories as well as to the novels. As Wagner notes, *The Goddess and Other Women,* for example, was simultaneously labeled Oates's "worst" book (in the *New Republic*) and "a magnificent achievement" (in the *New York Times Book Review*). This decade also introduced the

ubiquitous questions about the violence of Oates's fiction and the volume of her production. Yet Robert Phillips, writing in *Commonweal* in 1975, judged her to be "one of America's best writers of short stories." During this period Oates's critics added to an extensive collection of frequently contradictory epithets describing her characteristic style: naturalistic, realist, romantic, surrealist, traditional, formal, experimental, Gothic, feminist, nonfeminist, tragic, and comic. In his preface to Lercangée's 1986 bibliography, Bruce F. Michelson, who commends Oates for "asking the hardest social and aesthetic questions of her time," provides a helpful suggestion: "labels for Joyce Carol Oates ought to be given up as hopeless, for the evidence to date suggests they have done almost nothing to make sense of her as an artist." More productive is an inquiry into the aims and achievements of separate volumes.

The Wheel of Love, Marriages and Infidelities, The Seduction, and *Crossing the Border,* as Bastian suggests, are centrally concerned with the permutations of love. For Michelson "a violently-transformed selfhood" is Oates's primary project, which Oates has defined as the necessary abandonment of the limiting preoccupation with self in favor of the achievement of a communal identity. To examine the possibility of a bridge between self and other is the philosophical problem addressed by Oates's predominant theme of love. At the heart of this inquiry is a symbolic concern with the viability of marriage – the institutionalized form of the self/other connection – a concern that links the varied collections of the decade. Two stories from *The Wheel of Love,* "I Was in Love" and "Convalescing," suggest the marital dilemmas of contemporary men and women. "I Was in Love" is the first-person account of a woman whose emotionally inadequate marriage has led her into an affair that fills her with confusion and distress. In her desperate attempt to sort out conflicting loyalties, she recalls her own mother's inadequate counsel to abandon the vicissitudes of passion for a comfortable life of maternal service.

"Convalescing" also outlines an inadequate resolution between the needs of self and others: David Scott's reaction to his wife's adultery takes the symbolic form of an automobile accident. His recuperation plunges him into the confusion and anxiety of the loss of the identity and security that had been established through his marriage. Just as the doctrine of wifely nurturance seems irrelevant to the complex situation of the wife in "I Was in Love," any simple conception of husbandly power is evidently inadequate to the complex disorder fac-

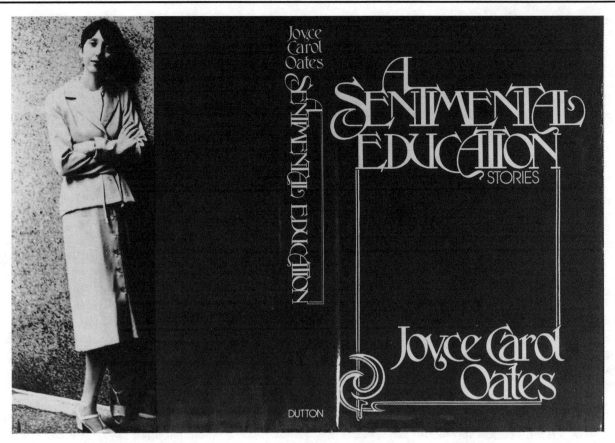

Dust jacket for Oates's 1980 collection of short fiction, one of three books she published that year

ing David in "Convalescing." As revealed, however, by Ilena Williams, the protagonist in "The Dead" from *Marriages and Infidelities,* Oates's studies of the failure of relationship propose not the rejection but the redefinition of marriage. Despite her own isolation, Ilena unexpectedly declares that "marriage was the deepest, most mysterious, most profound exploration open to man: she had always believed that, and she believed that now."

"River Rising," from *Crossing the Border,* suggests the tentative nature of that exploration. *Crossing the Border* contains a sequential cycle of short stories about the marriage of Evan and Renée Maynard. Beginning with their departure from the United States for residency in Canada, the stories proceed through their individual reactions to this dislocation, an important factor in Renée's later extramarital affair. "River Rising," which concludes the sequence, concerns the flooding of the river near their rented home, a story in which the couple appears to have figuratively, as well as literally, "weathered the storm." During the crisis of the flood, the couple is forced to reexamine habitual roles and attitudes. Evan abandons his characteris-

tic abstracted rationality in his emotional effort to retain the couple's connection to their marital home. Renée's wifely effort to pack their things in preparation for evacuation is also ineffectual. The river, a force "which they had taken for . . . granted," draws them out of the isolation of their own patterns into a renewed sense of possible relationship, a conclusion that contrasts with the earlier story "Upon the Sweeping Flood," in which the traditional marriage of the city man is no stay against deterioration in a similar onslaught.

"If what is available for the individual is romantic love, then it must be – it will be – this kind of love that liberates," Oates has declared; "ours is still a time of romantic love; the time of a more communal, transcendental love is not yet come." The marriage theme prominent in her stories of the 1970s points to a deeper concern: the necessity and possibility of personal and social transfiguration. Thus Oates's "love" stories, with varied personal configurations, epitomize seminal motifs and issues through the use of catastrophe as an occasion for productive reevaluation and possible growth. The cataclysmic emotional responses of various characters to the unsettling experience of love suggests the need for rearrangements of the social forms that foster intimate connections in American society. Similar concerns operate in collections organized around other themes: female experience in *The Goddess and Other Women*; the situation of young people in *Where Are You Going, Where Have You Been?*; the world of academics in *The Hungry Ghosts*; the imagined world structured by the sensibility of a fictional Portuguese author in *The Poisoned Kiss*; and the otherworldly preoccupations of *Night-Side*.

In Oates's preface to *Where Are You Going, Where Have You Been?* she comments on a split in the reception of her popular stories of youth that had been collected from previous volumes. Traditional readers, she explained, had seen only desperation in her fiction, unlike young readers who had responded to the "revolution" that such fiction encouraged. Like her endorsement of romantic love, Oates's optimistic insistence on the transformative potential of her disturbing stories of young America may account for the peculiar tone of the ending of Oates's most widely anthologized and analyzed short story, "Where Are You Going, Where Have You Been?" The tale of fifteen-year-old Connie's capitulation to probable rape and murder by fiendish Arnold Friend concludes with the otherwise puzzlingly positive diction of this description of her destination: "the vast sunlit reaches of the land . . . Connie had never seen before and did not recognize except to know that she was going to it."

Similarly the "unliberated" condition critic Joanne V. Creighton sees uniting the stories of female experience in *The Goddess and Other Women* and the stunted world of the academy satirically presented in *The Hungry Ghosts* may be construed as situations ripe for some kind of liberating change. The assertion of the possibility of alternative existence is the thematic focus of *The Poisoned Kiss* — which Oates claims to have written in the possession of a tutelary spirit from an imaginary reality — and *Night-Side*, a series of ghost tales. As Oates has explained, she has an abiding interest in the extreme but "normal and desirable" reactions that show her characters "straining against the too-close confines of a personality now outgrown, or a social 'role' too restrictive."

The latent potential for change that unites the variety of thematic situations in Oates's work is reflected as well in her revisionary treatment of traditional forms in both individual stories and in the arrangement of her story collections. During the 1970s she seemed to be trying to develop a repertoire of methods for writing the typical Oates story,

which, as she describes it, combines allegory with psychological realism. In the collections of this decade, she excels in stories from the perspective of an omniscient narrator; develops the first-person form, especially the interior monologue; updates older genres, such as the epistolary story; and creates innovations, like that in the story ". . . & Answers," from *The Goddess and Other Women,* in which an overwrought mother passively replies to the implicit but omitted questions of a psychiatrist probing her response to her daughter's accidental death.

During this period the generally thematic earlier works give way to collections, such as *Crossing the Border, All the Good People I've Left Behind,* and *A Sentimental Education,* which present story sequences in which single characters or parallel sets of characters try to work out their problems in related milieus. *Marriages and Infidelities* provides the link between the two styles. The general problem of love provides the central theme of the book, which also includes an innovative sequence that is unified by Oates's rewritings of the masters. "The Metamorphosis," "Where I Lived, and What I Lived For," "The Lady with the Pet Dog," "The Turn of the Screw," and "The Dead" reimagine concerns of Franz Kafka, Henry David Thoreau, Anton Chekhov, Henry James, and James Joyce in an Oatesian context.

The most striking difference between the first two decades of Oates's short fiction and that of the second two decades is the greater degree of contextualization of her protagonists. For Oates the compelling issue of the 1960s and 1970s seems to have been the personal relationships of her characters; the demanding concern of her work in the 1980s and 1990s is the social, even political, conditions of such relationships.

Last Days (1984), which is in two parts — the first presenting plots of personal apocalypse, the second focusing on the moral exhaustion of international politics — provides a deliberate bridge between psychological concerns and social concerns. The predominating eschatological note is sounded in the first story, "The Witness," in which an eleven-year-old daughter observes the private collapse of her father as cause of and prelude to her witnessing the spectacle of a violent attack on a woman in a public park. "The Holy Ghost has departed me" is how the father explains an emotional lassitude that is perceived by the little girl as the abandonment of the family. "Something is wrong but I don't know what it is. I don't know how to name it," she announces. The issue is not so much the girl's initiation into an evil world as it

Oates with her husband, Raymond Smith (left), and her parents, Caroline and Frederic Oates, on a visit to London, August 1989

is the conditions of irresponsibility that generate evil.

There is in each of the stories of the first section, "Last Days," a similar moral abdication by a father or by adult males that is a causal factor in the something that is wrong that these stories mean to name. In "Funland," which is realistic in style, the ironic title belies the implication that the disturbed father of the story will eventually harm his child in the attempt to effect control in his own life, an implication reechoed in the more symbolic "Lamb of Abyssalia" at the conclusion of the collection. Similarly the selfish preoccupation of the father in "Night, Sleep, Death, the Stars" promises to instigate disastrous consequences.

The title story suggests that these stories of failed fatherhood should be understood in the context of societal as well as psychological failure. In "Last Days" Oates treats again a plot that evidently haunts her. Eileen Teper Bender's study *Joyce Carol Oates, Artist in Residence* (1987) tells of Oates's preoccupation with the suicide of a student she met during her time at the University of Detroit. Versions

of her attempt to discover the meaning of the death of that erratic and brilliant young man appear in a newspaper account she published in 1966, in the prizewinning story "In a Region of Ice" that lent her the confidence to begin her career as a professional writer in 1967, and in the story of Saul Morgenstern in "Last Days." The disjointed chronicle of Saul's manic messianic murder/suicide does more than illustrate his own mental aberration. His condemnation of the academic establishment, of his father's values, and of the irrelevance of contemporary religion is social criticism not totally invalidated by the egotism of the young madman who delivers his jeremiad on modern morality from the " 'sacred' space" of a suburban synagogue with a "pistol in one hand" and a "microphone in the other."

Saul's murder of Rabbi Reuben Engleman suggests both psychological and social problems: the violent Freudian displacement of the father by the son, who seeks paternal power; and the failure of the culture of the fathers — academic and religious — to foster anything other than destruction. An atmosphere of psychic despair connects the "Last Days" sequence to "Our Wall," the second half of the collection. Several of the stories in "Our Wall" apparently grew out of Oates's participation in an international writer's conference and tour of several European countries under the auspices of the United States Information Agency in spring 1980, an experience that also finds expression in her 1986 novel *Marya: A Life*. In *Marya*, Oates extends the biographical portrayal of the life of her working-class protagonist from the family into the world of the academy and politics. Both the public spheres in *Marya* fail to provide the necessary protective order the protagonist seeks.

The difference between *Marya* and the "Our Wall" stories is that in "Detente," "My Warszawa: 1980," and "Old Budapest," the female protagonists are not victims but participants in the moral abdication that underlies the political failure conveyed by the dreary settings under strict Communist control. In each of these stories, American women of the privileged class – two writers and a diplomat – respond to political repression by turning inward to pursue narcissistic concerns. These tales of the turn from communal engagement to stifling self-absorption are framed by more-experimental pieces that suggest that this tendency may be at the root of a kind of generalized apocalyptic condition that must be understood in political rather than religious terms.

In the stories "Ich Bin Ein Berliner" and "Our Wall," the Berlin Wall, literally in the first story and figuratively in the second, symbolizes a desperate human condition of suicidal dissociation. The title of the first story is taken from President John F. Kennedy's declaration of the universal effect of political suffering ("I am a Berliner"). The story, however, presented from the point of view of a young brother who has come from America to investigate his older brother's fatal, suicidal attempt to scale the wall, does not convey the sense of an active gesture against totalitarianism or imply solidarity of any kind. The dramatic incident is to be understood as an abdication of all forms of social responsibility. The young narrator says that his brother "had thrown away *being American,* it seems, preparatory to throwing away *being human,* preparatory to throwing away *being alive.* I hate him for that logic." But it is a logic that the parables and allegories in these stories suggest grows out of the very fact of the wall.

In *Raven's Wing* (1986), Oates's next collection, the characters – who are pathetic, even hopeless – consistently reveal a deep sense of the nature of the limitations of their own situations. Their im-

provisations in response are frequently ineffectual, obviously unhappy, but highly expressive gestures of their need for control in a threatening world. Because of this skewed desire for responsibility, despite plots of violence and despair, the energy of *Raven's Wing* may be contrasted to the resignation of *Last Days*.

This difference is partially accounted for by the dissimilar social classes of Oates's protagonists in the two volumes. The "Our Wall" section of the previous collection depicts the unmitigated irresponsibility of privileged characters, while *Raven's Wing* treats working-class reactions to problems traceable to economic restrictions. In the latter collection only "Harrow Street at Linden," in which an academic couple fails at passion, and "The Seasons," in which a spoiled playwright abandons two cats, hark back to the bleak abdications of *Last Days*.

The best stories, "Raven's Wing," "Golden Gloves," "Little Wife," and "Surf City," treat elaborate improvisations in the face of helplessness. The protagonist of the title story, Billy, has two sons by a failed first marriage, but he rarely thinks about them since their mother's remarriage and move to Tampa: "Billy used to say that he and his ex-wife . . . weren't out to slit each other's throats . . . but in fact when Billy's salary at G-M Radiator had been garnisheed a few years ago . . . he'd gone through a bad time." Rather than pay the mandated child support, he has quit his job, and when he later tries to get it back, they are laying off employees: "it was his rotten luck, his luck had run against him for a long time. . . ." This description indicates Billy's financial, familial, and personal impotence as the central concern of his existence, and the diction suggests that vague "luck" and the capacity for reactive violence are all he has to pit against an overwhelming sense of his own helplessness. The story is about Billy's pursuit of such luck in the form of a racehorse named Raven's Wing, which not only represents money and power but which has miraculously, in Billy's view, managed to elude its own bad luck. When the successful three-year-old stallion breaks its leg, people generally anticipate that the horse will be destroyed, but its wealthy owners invest in an expensive experimental operation that saves the animal. "Raven's Wing" charts the development of Billy's growing identification with the horse. By the conclusion he has made a pilgrimage to the stables, where he expects some kind of special acknowledgment from the stallion and has even taken some of its hair as a talisman.

"Surf City" also concerns the yoked options of working-class impotence: luck and violence. Like

28

little hollow. She murmured, "The world is perfect if you don't set

yourself in opposition to it!" Scott glanced at her, ~~as if~~ startled,

and smiled.

At dusk they lit a kerosene lamp, had their meal, drank beer

from cans, settled in for the night. The wood-burning stove glowed

with a rich interior heat that radiated outward grudgingly, to encom-

pass a space of perhaps five feet in diameter. ~~They~~ *They lid their* sleeping bags

~~were laid~~ side by side ~~before it.~~ *in front of it.*

They made love, ~~their new kind of love, slow,~~ *in no haste, slowly, w/ an air of distr.* calm, domesticated,

with no air of desperation. These past ~~two or three~~ *sev.* weeks, ~~as if by~~

~~magic,~~ their desperation had lifted. ¶ Lydia had not registered for the

spring semester; ~~and had relinquished~~ *she'd given up* her fellowship; she would deal

with that, ~~that part of her life, in time.~~ She took each day as it

came, now. That seemed the best strategy, for now.

Scott continued with his teaching of course, in the face of

scandal. ~~For, yes, probably it must be admitted, this was scandal.~~

~~He drank more than he once drank but~~ he was a hardy, resilient man, as

if practiced in adversity. And how ~~inevitably~~ things fell into place,

~~as perhaps they always do~~: his wife would keep the house until she

chose to sell it, he saw the older children virtually at will, maybe

there would be less hurt, less heartbreak, than he'd feared. He ~~told~~ *assured*

Lydia that none of it was her fault, even remotely. He should have

moved out months ago--years ago: "My wife is an emotionally bankrupt

woman and if I'd stayed with her I would have died." Lydia said,

"None of this is your fault, I shouldn't have married Meredith at all."

The more they said such things, the more ~~forcibly were they~~ *lovers'*

~~imprinted upon their~~ souls.

~~They said,~~ a dozen times a day, "I love you." "Hey: I love you."

Page from a revised typescript for "Morning," collected in Heat and Other Stories (*The George Arents Research Library for Special Collections, Syracuse University; by permission of Joyce Carol Oates*)

249

Billy, Harvey Kubeck is controlled by the facts of his economic life – his employment and lack thereof at Republic Steel – and those intransigent facts of his familial existence that are also somehow just beyond his control. He has a two-year-old son and a baby on the way, both pregnancies neither "unplanned" nor "accidents." Although, like Billy, Harvey believes "luck" had "been running against him" for some time, "Surf City" begins with the notification that he has won $1,150 in the state lottery. Harvey generously distributes his bounty to his immediate family, to his parents, and to some of his buddies in the form of a night out on the town – a drunken spree that ends in his savagely beating a stranger. Good luck is for Harvey the joyous perception of "things going the way they are supposed to go" for a change, but a startling intuition – that a thousand dollars, spent on beer, outstanding bills, and a television set, cannot alter the circumstances of his life – seems to result in his hopeless rage that is expressed in the beating.

While the frequent accusation that Oates's writing is unduly violent is certainly not true, what is true is that she understands the logic of certain kinds of violent acts better than anyone else. "Golden Gloves," a story written in anticipation of Oates's fuller elaborations in her prize-fighting novel *You Must Remember This* (1987) and her meditation *On Boxing* (1987), probes the meaning of violence as an organized and expedient concept. In the story, a wife's pregnancy leads her husband, the unnamed protagonist and narrator, to review his early aspirations to be a fighter. Born with a physical deformity that crippled him until his corrective surgery at the age of eight, the protagonist, who has attended boxing matches with his father, associates the sport with overcoming physical incapacity, a goal that motivates his pursuit of a future in boxing until he is defeated a few weeks before his eighteenth birthday by a savage blow from another contender in a Golden Gloves tournament. What he senses is what Oates more fully articulates in *On Boxing*: "Impotence takes many forms," she explains, "one of them being the reckless expenditure of physical potency" in boxing. "You fight what's nearest. And if you can you do it for money." Through the development of physical perfection, men hope to control contingent threats from outside themselves. The protagonist of "Golden Gloves" has learned that such control is ultimately impossible. It is the fear of a crippling punch that one cannot anticipate that leads him to admire his wife because she is about to give birth, a process that seems to him a brave and possibly doomed contest against unknown forces.

The issue of human responsibility, the theme that unites the stories of the volume, is most clearly articulated in "Little Wife," a story of paternal degradation. In *Last Days* paternal abdication results in the destruction of the child; in this story, however, it occasions the child's moral elevation. Judd, the twelve-year-old protagonist in "Little Wife," has a father who has been a participant in the destruction of a young woman. "Damn his soul to hell, Judd was the first to notice the girl," the story begins. It ends with Judd's notification of the authorities that "a girl who was sick, a girl who was dying, kept locked up by some men" had to be helped. Judd observes, first with curiosity and later with horror, his father and his father's friends pick up the girl outside a bus station, use her for sex, for prostitution, and for violence, and evidently intend to let her die. In the course of the story, Judd progresses from a state of mind in which "he didn't really care, he knew how things would keep on without him, drift on their own way," to becoming an active agent of responsibility.

A consistent concern with improvisation, both technical and personal, is also the basis of Oates's next collection. In 1987 Oates published a mystery novel, *Lives of the Twins,* under the pseudonym Rosamond Smith. She explained her experiment – which caused consternation when her authorship was revealed – as an attempt to evade the pressure of her own literary reputation: "I just wanted a new identity, kind of a freshness to have a book come out where nobody was comparing it to other books." *The Assignation* (1988) is evidently a product of a similar impulse. Instead of the fully developed characterizations and plots of a typical "Joyce Carol Oates" short story, the stories in this volume introduce a new genre for Oates, the "short short" prose piece. Running from a single paragraph to six pages in length, instead of detailed psychological portraits, these stories are evocative snapshots of individuals taken during a revealing instant of conflict or posed against the momentary backdrop of a revealing symbol. Such a form allows Oates to showcase poetic suggestion and poetic rhythm, formal properties of her fiction that are usually little noticed.

Typically the stories in this collection rely on another poetic practice. Pound's definition of the image as "that which presents an intellectual and emotional complex in an instant of time" is the operant principle throughout the volume. For example, "Sharpshooting" is a five-page narrative in which a woman, evidently a university professor, rides an old bike to a dump and is taught by several boys how to shoot an air rifle. Underlying the brief sequence of events is the complicated emotional and intellectual issue of power. The teacher's vaguely seductive exploitation of the children and their masculine mastery of a minor art of aggression points to this larger concern. The final sentence of the story, which records the protagonist's response to the success of her lesson – "She sees that, once you begin, you wouldn't ever want to stop" – underscores the importance of this central issue.

But the title *The Assignation,* with its insinuation of relationship and transgression, sets the dominant thematic tone of the volume. Titles such as "The Abduction," "Adulteress," and "Desire" reinforce these implications. Many of the stories sketch characters, such as the teacher and children in "Sharpshooting," engaged in some action that directly or indirectly tests some kind of limit. "The Boy" presents an affair between a teacher and student; "Photographer's Model" suggests the induction of an attractive little girl into a corrupt life-style by a doting uncle; and "The Others" presents an urban commuter joining a band of ghosts in the tunnels of the subway.

Writing in the *New York Times Book Review* James Atlas dismissed *The Assignation* as "fugitive pieces, in other words a famous writer's occasional writings and ephemera," but he also commended the stories for their "radiant intensity." A similar mixture of praise and blame greeted the publication of Oates's 1991 collection, *Heat and Other Stories,* which is a study in serious literary horror.

For Edgar Allan Poe the wellspring of horror was the soul. For Oates the source is often the typical American personality that is dictated by the American social structure. The first section of *Heat* includes stories of middle-class characters facing contingencies they have constructed their lives to resist. In some stories protagonists must acknowledge the claims of underclass "others" in their own lives, while in "House Hunting" and "The Hair" the source of threatening otherness is occluded aspects of the protagonists' own personalities and experiences. In "House Hunting" the death of their newborn infant threatens the marriage and the sanity of a "yuppie" couple. The husband responds by the dogged attempt to find a perfect home, which would stand for the elusive values of family and possession that once sustained them. In "The Hair" another couple, the Carsons, falls "in love" with the glamorous Riegels. In the course of this intercouple relationship the Carsons must finally acknowledge the corruption beneath the Riegels' surface appeal,

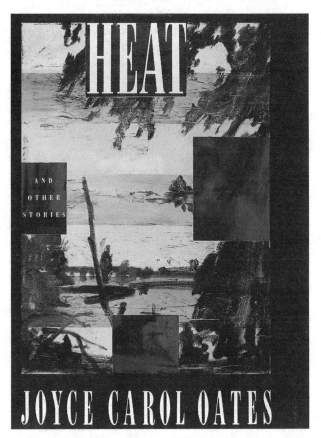

Dust jacket for Oates's 1991 collection of short fiction, which identifies sources of horror in everyday American life

but in so doing they must also face the depths of their own emptiness.

One of the best stories is "Shopping," which incorporates both the threat from without and the threat from within. A middle-class mother and daughter at a suburban mall are taking a shopping excursion as an attempt to negotiate and avoid their mutual hostility and dependency, but their peace is threatened by a bag lady among the specialty shops and fountains. Their contradictory reactions of sentimental pity and unexamined outrage underscore an unavoidable rift between mother and daughter that cannot be ignored.

The second section of *Heat* contains stories of working-class families. Horrifying things happen, such as the death of an old woman who tries to aid a wounded deer; the attack on a girl by a derelict in a library; the rape of a young woman in the desert outside Las Vegas; and the murder of twin girls (in the title story, "Heat"). The emphasis of the section, however, is not on the events themselves but on the way that each anomalous occasion is interpreted, frequently through apocryphal stories and family legends. A similar feature of several of the tales in

Heat is the way the story affects a teller or an auditor, many of whom are thirteen-year-old girls. Youngsters of that age appear in "Heat," where the first-person narrator learns about anger and passion; "Sundays in Summer," where the second-person protagonist recognizes the same emotions as features of family life; and "The Swimmers," where the narrator observes the circumstances leading up to a life of unrequited love.

Perhaps thirteen, that bridge between childhood and adolescence, is an age when the uncertainty of lived events is consciously organized as narrative and begins to modify experience. In any case, an emphasis on the operation of storytelling is reiterated throughout the volume, especially in this section. One of the characters says, "I must have believed all along that there was a story, a story unknown to me that had worked itself out without my knowing, like a stream tunneling its way underground. I would not have minded not knowing this story could I have only known that it *was*."

The last section of *Heat* collects more-experimental writing – a doppelgänger story, a ghost story, a dream sequence, a science fiction story – tales exhibiting Oates's consciousness of their existence as stories. They mark the central concern, which is, more than horror, initiation, the meaning of family, class differences, or power – all contributing themes of the collection – an exploration of the meaning of narrative as practice. What can one know? What can one do? What is the effect of narratives on answers to the questions of private and public life?

Reviewers' criticisms about violence miss the key point. Oates uses the art of story to contrast what people wish to believe with what they need to know, and that radical confrontation may be angry, even brutal. Perhaps it needs to be. Critic Walter Clemons defined Oates's task in 1972: "this is the problem that Oates shares with every other American writer today – how to bring order to the violent extremity and complexity of American life without mitigating that complexity" (in *Critical Essays on Joyce Carol Oates*). Joyce Carol Oates's short stories, especially her later ones – virtuoso stories combining perspicuity, perspicacity, artistry, and emotion – show that she is succeeding.

Interviews:

Lee Milazzo, ed., *Conversations with Joyce Carol Oates* (Jackson: University Press of Mississippi, 1989);

Mickey Pearlman and Katherine Usher Henderson, *A Voice of One's Own: Conversations With America's Writing Women* (New York: Houghton Mifflin, 1992).

Bibliography:

Francine Lercangée, *Joyce Carol Oates: An Annotated Bibliography* (New York: Garland, 1986).

References:

Katherine Bastian, *Joyce Carol Oates's Short Stories between Tradition and Innovation* (Frankfurt am Main: Lang, 1983);

Eileen Teper Bender, *Joyce Carol Oates, Artist in Residence* (Bloomington: Indiana University Press, 1987);

Joanne V. Creighton, *Joyce Carol Oates* (Boston: Twayne, 1979);

Bruce F. Michelson, Preface to Francine Lercangée's *Joyce Carol Oates: An Annotated Bibliography* (New York: Garland, 1986);

Torborg Norman, *Isolation and Contact: A Study of Character Relationships in Joyce Carol Oates's Short Stories 1963–1980* (Göteborg, Sweden: Acta Universitatis Gothenburgensis, 1984);

Linda W. Wagner, *Critical Essays on Joyce Carol Oates* (Boston: G. K. Hall, 1979);

Marilyn C. Wesley, *Refusal and Transgression in Joyce Carol Oates' Fiction* (Westport, Conn.: Greenwood, 1993).

Breece D'J Pancake

(29 June 1952 – 8 April 1979)

Albert E. Wilhelm
Tennessee Technological University

BOOK: *The Stories of Breece D'J Pancake* (Boston: Atlantic/Little, Brown, 1983).

Although Breece D'J Pancake wrote relatively few short stories, he is regarded by many as a master of the form. Except for pieces in student literary magazines, Pancake published only three stories during his short life; three additional pieces appeared in periodicals shortly after his death. *The Stories of Breece D'J Pancake* (1983) includes these six previously published stories along with six others. The thin volume was reviewed (almost always favorably) in over one hundred journals and newspapers and was nominated for a Pulitzer Prize. Joyce Carol Oates (writing in the *New York Times Book Review,* 13 February 1983) compared Pancake's work to that of Ernest Hemingway; Harold Jaffe (*Newsday,* 6 March 1983) noted similarities with Flannery O'Connor; and Jayne Ann Phillips (quoted on the dust jacket) described the collected stories as an Appalachian equivalent to James Joyce's *Dubliners* (1906).

Pancake was born on 29 June 1952 in Milton, West Virginia, and his name at birth was Breece Dexter Pancake. As a boy, he disliked the name Dexter and unofficially changed his middle name to David. Later, when he converted to Catholicism (1977), he added John as a confirmation name, and the complete name he intended to use when he published his first major story, "Trilobites," in the *Atlantic Monthly* (December 1977) was Breece D. J. Pancake. After a typesetter's error changed the punctuation to read "D'J," Pancake deliberately let the mistake stand and assumed the new name by which he is now generally known.

The son of Clarence and Helen Frazier Pancake, Breece lived with his parents and two older sisters in a modest house on Route 60, the main highway through Milton. Clarence Pancake, to whom Breece was devoted, had served in World War II and was a longtime employee at the local Union Carbide plant. He was also a hunting and fishing enthusiast and spent many hours outdoors with Breece. A family friend and art teacher, B. Fred Ball, helped Breece develop skill as a storyteller, and at an early age Breece announced that he wanted to be a writer.

After graduation from Milton High School in 1970, Pancake enrolled at West Virginia Wesleyan College in Buckhannon. There he developed an interest in drama and in the music of Woody Guthrie and Phil Ochs, but early in 1971 he transferred to Marshall University in Huntington. Because his father was seriously ill with multiple sclerosis, Pancake wanted to be closer to home. At Marshall he wrote poetry and served as fiction editor of the college literary magazine. In 1974 he received his B.A. with a major in English and a minor in language arts.

While he was still a student, Pancake traveled extensively in the western United States and Mexico. Using as a base the home of his eldest sister, in Phoenix, he went by train to Mexico City, and he once hitchhiked from Arizona to California. He held several part-time jobs that provided material for his stories. At one point he worked for a West Virginia trucking company in Kanawha and Charleston, his job being to make short runs and load and unload freight. Later he was part of a road construction crew in Culpeper, Virginia.

Pancake's first teaching job was at Fork Union (Virginia) Military Academy and began in August 1974. (He had considered attending West Virginia University College of Law but was admitted too late for the 1974 school year.) He did not like the atmosphere at Fork Union and moved in 1975 to Staunton (Virginia) Military Academy, where he taught English and served as department chair. Meanwhile, Pancake's father died on 8 September 1975, and two weeks later his best friend, Matthew Heard, was killed in an automobile accident.

While still teaching at Staunton, Pancake enrolled in some graduate classes in English at the

Breece D'J Pancake in Charlottesville, Virginia, March 1979

University of Virginia. In 1977 he became a full-time student there and later studied writing under John Casey, Richard Jones, James Alan McPherson, and Peter Taylor. Pancake taught composition and fiction writing to undergraduates and later served as fiction consultant to the editor of the *Virginia Quarterly Review*. He was a governor's fellow (1976) and a Hoyns fellow in fiction writing (1978), and he won the Jefferson Society Fiction Award for 1977.

Meanwhile Pancake's writing was beginning to attract national recognition. When "Trilobites" was published in 1977, it provoked an intense and immediate reaction. An editor at the magazine, Phoebe-Lou Adams, has commented: "In thirty-some years at *The Atlantic* I cannot recall a response to a new writer like the response to this one. Letters drifted in for months asking for more stories. . . . Whatever it is that truly commands reader attention, he had it."

Readers were responding to Pancake's distinctive voice – his stark but sensitive treatment of a re-

gion and a social stratum typically ignored in literature. Almost all his stories are set in West Virginia, and they usually portray characters trapped by geography and personal history. His protagonists, almost always male, may be frustrated but still-hopeful adolescents or defeated older men. When they can find jobs, they work as miners, scab truck drivers, or farmers of wasted, drought-stricken land. Away from work they are frequently immersed in the blood and violence of hunting, cockfights, and barroom brawls.

The dominant element in most Pancake stories is a powerful sense of place evoked by careful use of detail. McPherson, in his foreword to Pancake's book, sees the topography of Appalachia as a correlative of the fates of many Pancake characters: "Horizontal vision, in that area, is rare. The sky there is circumscribed by insistent hillsides thrusting upward. It is an environment crafted by nature for the dreamer and for the resigned." Similarly critic Geoffrey Galt Harpham says that

Pancake's stories "depict a condition of deep time and narrow space." Since his characters have limited room for movement, the stories contain little plot. Instead, they provide nondevelopmental character revelation by probing the deeply stratified layers of an individual's past.

No story illustrates these qualities better than "Trilobites," the story many regard as his best. The title refers to small Paleozoic marine arthropods that are extinct. Colly, the main character, searches all around his farm for their fossilized remains. In the same way these "stone animals" have been covered by layers of soil and rock, he, too, feels buried in the sediment of past events. In his relatively short life Colly has repeatedly suffered loss. He has recently lost his father when a sliver of metal that had been in the man's body since World War II finally worked its way to his brain. Right after high-school graduation Colly broke up with his girlfriend, a frivolous young woman whose mother had deserted her years earlier. He is about to lose his home because his mother plans to sell the farm and move to Akron, Ohio. In short, Colly cannot secure enough of his past to establish a solid foundation for the future. According to Harpham, "trilobites become a synecdoche for a pastness, which, if he could apprehend, would make the present possible." But Colly "is unable either to find a trilobite or to stop looking, and the quixotic nature of his quest makes it at once magical and meaningless, alluring and impossible, the token of a desire incapable of satisfaction."

Pancake's second published story, "In the Dry" (*Atlantic Monthly,* August 1978), focuses on a family reunion that perpetuates loneliness. Ottie, a scab truck driver rejected by the union, is also an outcast at the annual gathering of the Gerlock clan. As a foster child he never really belonged to any family, and he is wrongly blamed for an automobile accident that left a Gerlock cousin maimed and incontinent. While this one relative has been physically crippled by past events, other Gerlocks have been emotionally scarred by envy, spite, and frustrated sexual passions. The title of this story is an allusion to a New Testament verse, Luke 23:31 – "For if they do these things in a green tree, what shall be done in the dry?" (Coincidentally, Pancake wrote a lengthy essay on this passage for a Bible class at the University of Virginia.) By displaying several varieties of spiritual drought, Pancake's story provides graphic answers to the biblical question. Characters literally fight over bones, and the story ends with ashes, as Ottie slowly burns the photographs of old "men he almost knew" – Gerlock ancestors who will never be family to him.

The most melodramatic and macabre of Pancake's stories is "Time and Again" (*Nightwork,* September 1978), which portrays a psychopathic loner who murders young hitchhikers and feeds their flesh to his hogs. As Oates suggests, the story may suffer from "comic book Gothicism," but it does offer skillful narration and a compelling study of disciplined madness. The first-person narrator is an aging snowplow operator, and, into the pristine winter landscape, Pancake introduces details that hint at past violence and foreshadow more. The title "Time and Again" suggests compulsive, repetitive behavior, and like many other Pancake characters the narrator here is clearly bound by events of the past. Abandoned by his only son shortly after the death of his wife, he writes everybody he knows in an effort to trace the boy. But mixed with longing for his son's return, the old man apparently feels murderous anger, which he transfers to other young men. The story ends, however, not with homicide but with total exhaustion. After years of meticulous attention to clearing the roads and feeding his hogs, the narrator wants nothing more than to rest. He comments that "people die so easy," and then he walks to the pen of hungry hogs, apparently to offer himself as a sacrifice.

"A Room Forever" (*Antaeus,* Winter/Spring 1981) is set in a river town on New Year's Eve, but the rapidly flowing river provides no renewal, and the cheerless New Year offers little hope for change. (Apparently Pancake began this story while he was living near the Ohio River as a student at Marshall.) The story's two main characters are the middle-aged narrator – a transient tugboat worker – and an adolescent prostitute. Brought up in a succession of foster homes, the narrator faces two equally unappealing prospects: a fatal accident on his tugboat or an ongoing cycle of one month on the river followed by one month of waiting on land. He tries at first to befriend the girl but finds himself perpetuating her pain and his during their sexual encounter. Later the girl attempts suicide, and Pancake uses this action to contrast the fierce disappointment of youth with the quiet resignation of maturity. Speaking of the general human condition, the narrator says that he has been "inside too long," but he realizes that he has probably "bought this room forever." When he examines the situation of those around him, he knows that "they can't run away from it or drink their way out of it or die to get rid of it." Critic Ellesa Clay High says this story "exemplifies what Pancake does best: a dark fictional frieze of those hanging on the fringes . . . those who somehow survive on the other side of pain and despair."

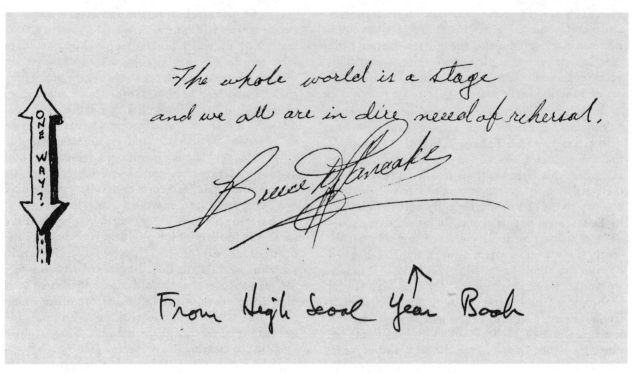

The whole world is a stage and we all are in dire need of rehersal.

Breece D'J Pancake

From High School Year Book

Note that Pancake wrote in one of his high-school yearbooks (by permission of the Estate of Breece D'J Pancake)

Still another story which depicts deep time and narrow space is "The Honored Dead" (*Atlantic Monthly,* January 1981), in which the narrator does little more than walk around the tiny town of Rock Camp, but the story line reverberates through many layers of time. His memory forces him to relive experiences with some people now dead: his part-Shawnee grandfather; his father, who proudly wore an army uniform in World War II; and especially his friend Eddie, who returned from Vietnam in a plastic bag. Harpham has observed that the story is less concerned with honor than with betrayal. Coal-mine owners betrayed the grandfather and other miners; the narrator may have betrayed his father, his country, and Eddie by refusing to go to Vietnam; Eddie probably betrayed the narrator by sleeping with his wife (and possibly fathering the child the narrator accepts as his own); and the government betrayed Eddie by sending him to a gruesome death.

A story that focuses more explicitly on impoverished coal miners is "Hollow" (*Atlantic Monthly,* October 1982). By choosing this single-word title (and omitting any definite article before it), Pancake probably intended a pun. The title can be a noun identifying the physical location of the story; it can also be an adjective suggesting the spiritual condition of those who inhabit this bleak valley. The main character is a miner named Buddy who is struggling to buy a double-wide trailer and a car so his girlfriend Sal will not leave him and return to prostitution. Pancake uses brutally ugly but powerful imagery to describe the carcass of a pregnant doe slaughtered by Buddy in the winter. By killing the doe out of season, he not only destroys an individual life but also eliminates the potential for future life. Since Buddy is scheming to strip-mine the hills around him, his callous and short-sighted attitude toward wild game parallels his attitude toward the land. After killing the doe, he eats (in an echo of primitive ritual) a small portion of the raw internal organs. In consuming this part of a fertile animal, he probably aspires to become like what he eats, but in cutting off the possibility of future life he is merely insuring his own sterility and emptiness.

The first tale in *The Stories* that had not been published previously is "Fox Hunters." For Bo Holly, who at sixteen is the youngest of Pancake's protagonists, life consists mainly of aching loneliness and undifferentiated adolescent yearnings. With his father dead and his sick mother completely detached from the world around her, Bo has no guide to greater maturity. In sharp contrast to hunting tales such as William Faulkner's "The Bear" (in *Go Down Moses,* 1942), the hunting episode here becomes a bogus initiation ritual orchestrated by a man whose values are cheap and brutal. Bo joins in the drinking and male banter and even concocts colorful lies about his sexual experiences. In the end, however, he vomits his bootleg liquor and tries to shoot the hunting dogs to save the fox. In spite of his spectacular failure in this spurious rite of passage, Bo maintains some inner strength. He cannot "claim kin to men by tolerating their music, their cards, their fox hunting," but he does understand "the power of singularity."

"The Mark" differs sharply from earlier stories by Pancake in that the protagonist is a quick-witted, sharp-tongued female. In the course of a day, Reva attends the county fair with her farmer husband; commiserates when his prize bull loses in the livestock competition; grieves for her parents, who were drowned several years earlier; and is continually obsessed by incestuous desire for her brother. The story combines grim themes with sassy dialogue, and tragic lust with comic eroticism. The prize bull, for example, is named "The Pride and Promise of Cutter's Landing," but Reva reduces this pompous phrase to merely "Peepee." With bemused detachment at the fair sideshows, she watches a stripper who can allegedly smoke "a cigar with her you-know-what," but Reva also fantasizes about showing this trick to her brother. Pancake's title refers to a modern-day "mark of the beast" – a blemish presumably inflicted on an unborn baby by its mother's improper behavior. Since Reva's belief that she is pregnant turns out to be mistaken, she will not actually mark a child. Instead she herself will bear the negative marks of past actions. At the end of the story Reva burns an old house – the site of fantasized and perhaps actual sexual encounters with her brother. She then runs toward her husband yelling, "I done a awful thing." Whether she is confessing to incest or merely to arson remains uncertain.

Skeevy Kelly, the main character in "The Scrapper," is a coal miner who earns a few extra dollars by boxing and also by selling bootleg liquor at cockfights. Throughout the story he is obsessed by the memory of a youthful fistfight in which he severely injured his best friend, Bund. This friend now sits at the local gas station and extends one hand begging for change while his limp tongue dangles from his mouth. Caught in this web of haunting memories, Skeevy seeks ritualistic penance. With only a wad of rags as a mouth protector, he deliberately fights the tough Jim Gibson. When one of Gibson's blows dislodges the rags, Skeevy bites off the tip of his tongue. Such a self-inflicted injury is

hardly accidental. It represents Skeevy's need for expiation – his effort to purge his guilt by means of a primitive sacrifice. Because his most painful memory is of Bund's tongue hanging from his open mouth, Skeevy mutilates himself in a manner that is symbolically appropriate.

"The Way It Has to Be" is the only Pancake story set outside Appalachia and one of two stories with a female protagonist. Here Pancake has temporarily abandoned his characteristic materials, and the story is usually regarded as inferior to others in the collection. Critic Bob Snyder, for example, sees "a sharp drop in the force and interest" of Pancake's stories when he departs from mountain settings. In this particular story a young woman named Alena has escaped from the confinement of West Virginia to the open rangelands of Oklahoma and Texas, but she has done so in company with Harvey, a hard-drinking, abusive former convict. Apparently hoping to find some semblance of the freedom and heroism of the old West, Alena wants to go to the Cowboy Hall of Fame. Instead she watches Harvey gun down an old acquaintance, who presumably double-crossed him, and then she ends up in a dingy hotel surrounded by a dust storm. In a phone conversation with her mother she says bluntly, "Nothin's changed." Despite her thousand-mile pilgrimage, certainly nothing has changed for the better, but she sees that Harvey is meaner than she realized and that he displays more affection for his gun than for her. Other Pancake stories (such as "Fox Hunters" and "First Day of Winter") leave their protagonists confined in the hollows of West Virginia, and these stories are charged with the energy generated by a desperate longing for escape. In contrast, Alena is one of the few characters who physically get away from the mountains, but her story is somewhat anti-climactic. Perhaps as a commentary on the futility of her physical escape, the title of this story is the most fatalistic of any in the collection. (An earlier version of the story appeared in a student publication under the title "Cowboys and Girls.") A prominent image is that of "the crisp skeletons of flies" lying on a windowsill. Like a housefly beating against a windowpane, Alena has a dim vision of a world on the other side and tries desperately to get through to it. Nevertheless, her efforts are in vain, and, like the flies, she, too, may become an empty shell.

Pancake's stories have been criticized as grim and humorless, but "The Salvation of Me" belies such a generalization and displays delightfully flamboyant language and spirited comedy while it portrays typically constrained Pancake characters. In

Pancake and his father, Clarence R. Pancake, Christmas 1971

this case the exuberance of teen rebellion counterbalances the sadness left behind as the residue of lost dreams. Spanning a period of several years, the story focuses on two testosterone-charged, small-town adolescents who ignore their teachers, race their hot rod on public roads, and generally defy authority. Together they operate a jacked-up Chevy with a Pontiac engine, but their high jinks end abruptly when Chester drives away in the jointly owned property. Chester is the only person ever to escape the petrifying existence of Rock Camp, but, after acquiring some fame and fortune in New York, even he is eventually "chewed up and spit out." His buddy back home, who is a grease monkey at the local Amoco station, can see Chester's sad story as a cautionary tale for all those who would challenge fate. Because of Chester's example,

his own salvation is bittersweet. He is spared spectacular failure only because he has never pursued his dream of becoming a disc jockey at WLS in Chicago.

In "First Day of Winter" Pancake examines burdens that parents sometimes impose on children, and the resulting enmity between two brothers. Hollis resents the fact that he must remain on an unproductive farm to care for his aging parents (one blind and the other senile) while his pious but uncharitable older brother refuses to accept any responsibility. Pancake's title refers to the advent of spiritual as well as physical coldness. Hollis is still a young man, but just as winter cold has come early, he is prematurely "old and tired, worn and beaten." He works to repair an old car, but its locked-up engine is obviously analogous to his own condition. A failure as a mechanic, he is unable to revive the machine that might carry him away to a more attractive future. Later, however, he becomes an atavistic hunter who expertly shoots and field-dresses squirrels until "the killing drained him and his game bag weighed heavily at his side." He even fantasizes about murdering his parents and brother but quickly pulls on his gloves "to hide the blood on his hands." When his mother washes the dead squirrels, she slyly licks a drop of blood from her hand suggesting, says High, a "parasitic, almost vampirish relationship between parents and son." Thus a story whose main concern is blood ties becomes ironically imbued with symbolic and actual bloodshed.

On 8 April 1979, a few months short of his twenty-seventh birthday, Breece D'J Pancake died from a self-inflicted shotgun wound just outside his apartment in Charlottesville. Except for a course in German, he had completed all the requirements for an M.A. in English with an emphasis on creative writing. Just before his death Pancake was continuing to develop his writing skills by exploring new themes and genres. He was at work on several stories and a novel focusing on the lives of coal miners. (The story published under the title "Hollow" was to be one chapter.) Another project left uncompleted was a one-act play (tentatively titled "Toy Soldier") based on his teaching experiences at military academies. Although Pancake's potential as a writer was never realized, his stories continue to elicit favorable responses from readers and critics. *Hollow,* a play based on Pancake's life and work was produced in 1990 in Mount Hope, West Virginia, by Mark Rance (the author of the play), and plans are under way for publication of Pancake's stories in Great Britain, Germany, and Portugal.

Interview:

Chuck Hyman, "The Big Break," *Declaration,* 5 (University of Virginia, 1 December 1977): 12–13.

Bibliography:

Thomas E. Douglass, "Breece D'J Pancake Bibliography," *Appalachian Journal,* 17 (Summer 1990): 392–394.

Biographies:

Ruth Burney Pennebaker, "Remembrances of a Young Writer," *Daily Progress* (Charlottesville, Va.), 20 February 1983, p. E1;

T. B. Shutt, "Bright Hosannas and Eyes in the Night: Breece D'J Pancake, Writer," *Virginia Country* (June 1983): 38–45;

Cynthia Reuschel, "Milton Friends Remember Talented Author," *Cabell Record* (Milton, W.Va.), 24 August 1983, pp. A1–A2;

Paul Hendrickson, "The Legend of Breece D'J Pancake," *Washington Post,* 10 December 1984, p. C6;

Grace Toney Edwards, "Memories of Breece," *Appalachian Heritage,* 13 (Winter–Spring 1985): 112–114;

Cynthia Kadohata, "Breece D'J Pancake," *Mississippi Review,* 18, no. 1 (1989): 35–61;

Thomas E. Douglass, "The Story of Breece D'J Pancake," *Appalachian Journal,* 17 (Summer 1990): 376–390.

References:

Geoffrey Galt Harpham, "Short Stack: The Stories of Breece D'J Pancake," *Stories in Short Fiction,* 23 (Summer 1986): 265–273;

Ellesa Clay High, "A Lost Generation: The Appalachia of Breece D'J Pancake," *Appalachian Journal,* 13 (Fall 1985): 34–40;

James Alan McPherson, Foreword to *The Stories of Breece D'J Pancake* (Boston: Atlantic/Little, Brown, 1983), pp. 3–19;

Bob Snyder, "Pancake and Benedict," *Appalachian Journal,* 15 (Spring 1988): 276–283;

Albert E. Wilhelm, "Poverty of Spirit in Breece Pancake's Short Fiction," *Critique,* 28 (Fall 1986): 39–44.

Papers:

Most of Pancake's letters and manuscripts are in the possession of his mother, Helen Pancake. Materials left with John Casey, his literary executor, are now in the University of Virginia Library, and a few unpublished poems are in the library at Marshall University.

Bette Pesetsky

(16 November 1932 –   )

Richard Orodenker
Peirce Junior College

BOOKS: *Stories up to a Point* (New York: Knopf,
1981; London: Bodley Head, 1982);
Author from a Savage People (New York: Knopf, 1983;
London: Bodley Head, 1983);
Digs (New York: Knopf, 1984);
Midnight Sweets (New York: Atheneum, 1988);
Confessions of a Bad Girl (New York: Atheneum,
1989);
The Late Night Muse (New York: HarperCollins,
1991);
Cast a Spell (New York: Harcourt Brace Jovanovich,
1993).

Though acclaimed as a novelist, Bette Pesetsky has established her reputation as a short-story
writer on the basis of two volumes: *Stories up to a
Point* (1981) and *Confessions of a Bad Girl* (1989).
Writing exclusively about women fallen into sadness, loss, and despair, Pesetsky rescues them with
"flashes of hilarious pessimism," as David Quammen put it (in the *New York Times Book Review,* 14
February 1982). Her narrators (wives, mothers, sisters, and friends) emerge shakily from unstable,
broken, or shattered relationships, yet, as Christopher Lehmann-Haupt wrote (in the *New York Times,*
15 January 1982), they "go on looking desperately
for continuity . . . wherever they can find it." The
female characters in Pesetsky's stories, bereft of
happiness, really cannot be of much help to one another; they are so often at odds that further intimacy only adds to their grief. The continuity they
seek is often elusive.

Pesetsky's "struggle with the forms of fiction,"
as she put it in an unpublished interview, partially
accounts for her fragmentary style, often the subject
of discussion in reviews of her work. Pesetsky's abbreviated, conversational style has been compared
with that of the late Donald Barthelme's. As David
Montrose pointed out (in the *Times Literary Supplement,* 10 September 1982), "Pesetsky has borrowed
Barthelme's method, but not his madness, eschew-
ing the surreal for a firm attachment to the quotid-

Bette Pesetsky

ian. . . . Her world . . . is the familiar made strange:
secondhand echoes of [Franz] Kafka – as distilled
through Barthelme." Doris Grumbach (*Georgia Review,* Fall 1982) complained that Pesetsky's "prose
leaves large air holes through which . . . memory escapes," but Grumbach admired "the strong silences
that exist among the words, between the sentences,
and hover everywhere over the events."

Despite the "strong mood of urban paranoia,"
which Lehmann-Haupt observed, the setting in

Pesetsky's stories is not confined to any one place. The transient life-styles, the apartment living, and the urban-suburban mixture reflect both Pesetsky's youth and her current residence in upstate New York.

Bette Block Pesetsky was born in Milwaukee on 16 November 1932 and is the youngest daughter of Louis and Rose McKnight Block. Rose – whose family, Bette says, was a mystery – was from Minneapolis; Louis, a businessman, was born in Saint Louis, where his immigrant Jewish family had lived since the end of the Civil War. He moved his own small family back there when Bette was in high school. "The nature of my parents was fierce – even tough," she once said. The Jewish themes in her stories reflect the culture that she knew, "in which religion for better or worse was background." Montrose hinted that "quiet resonances of Isaac Bashevis Singer can be detected whenever she draws on this background."

Louis Block, a World War I air-force veteran, owned a string of successful small businesses, including an early car wash. Before the Depression the family was well off. By the time Bette was born, however, the family was living in one room behind a store in what she has called "a tough working-class neighborhood in Socialist Milwaukee." Her characters, as did Pesetsky, come to understand the difference between those middle-class persons who are suddenly poor and those who have always been poor.

Libraries and learning exerted their appeal on her. Though she was bright and skipped some grades, being the youngest in her classes made her feel awkward and uncomfortable and perhaps contributes to the themes of dislocation and abandonment in her stories. Pesetsky admits she was a trying student. Once she was caught reading books that were hidden under her desk: "They were *real* books, but they had nothing to do with lessons and were not assigned."

After discovering history and literature in junior high school, Pesetsky majored in English and chemistry at Washington University (in Saint Louis), from which she graduated with a B.A. in 1954. She attended the University of Iowa and earned an M.F.A. in creative writing in 1959. She studied there with Vance Bourjaily, Donald Justice, and Calvin Kentfield and discussed writing with fellow classmates at Kenny's Bar in Iowa City. She left Iowa with "the sense of possibility" that she might become a writer.

On 25 February 1956 she had married Irwin Pesetsky, now a professor of anatomy at the Albert Einstein Medical College in New York, where Bette Pesetsky also worked as a scientific editor and administrator for seventeen years. Their only child, David, is an associate professor of linguistics at the Massachusetts Institute of Technology.

Pesetsky did not write serious fiction again until she was almost fifty. It took her that long, she has said, to absorb what she learned at Iowa, and to do a great deal of reading "without advice or plan" of works by Anton Chekhov, F. Scott Fitzgerald, Lionel Trilling, Katherine Anne Porter, Eudora Welty, Jean Genet, Italo Calvino, Arthur Rimbaud, Bernard Malamud, Jorge Luis Borges, John Cheever, and Kafka.

Nonetheless, her science background had afforded her several career opportunities in medical writing and research. She did hospital work during college, and at one point in her life she was a ghostwriter of speeches and technical material. In 1985 she was the dean for faculty research at Adelphi University in Garden City, New York.

The late 1970s and early 1980s were watershed years for Pesetsky. Her stories began appearing in small literary journals, such as the *Cimarron Review*, *California Quarterly*, *Ontario Review*, and *Kansas Quarterly*. The Pushcart Prize committee cited her as one of the outstanding writers of 1979. Then came a creative-writing fellowship from the National Endowment for the Arts in 1980 and a writing grant from the New York Council of the Arts the following year. She lectured at Fordham University, Marist College, and Long Island University and even taught a scientific-writing course. Pesetsky has also been a visiting professor at the Iowa Writers' Workshop and the University of California, Irvine. She still writes book reviews for the *New York Times* and the *Los Angeles Times*.

With the publication of *Stories up to a Point* Pesetsky's writing career received international attention. Reviewers generally praised the book, but some singled out the overriding pessimism: Quammen addressed the "social disjunction, dislocation, and discontinuity"; Montrose described the tales as "catalogues of misfortune"; Grumbach pointed out the characters' "particular brand of hopelessness." Yet several critics also recognized Pesetsky's good-natured deadpan humor. Her characters appeal to the reader, with whispers and echoes of Emily Dickinson at her most sophisticated and eccentric. They exhibit a delightful peculiarity.

Pesetsky's use of character can best be seen in the story "Scratch," in which a woman plans "to become a recluse" and thus must prune her "garden of memories." Her wish to have "a place in the coun-

CONFESSIONS
OF A
BAD GIRL

AND OTHER STORIES
by the author of *Stories Up to a Point*

BETTE PESETSKY

*Dust jacket for Pesetsky's second short-fiction collection, in which
two-thirds of the stories are linked by related characters
and events*

try with a high, barbed-wire fence" will only get her "more attention," her fifth husband warns: "To be solitary requires careful thought." Her desire for a life of anonymity is like valuable china locked in a closet, which "mustn't be touched." She struggles to be alone, but people from her past are etched in her memory like scratches in the woodwork. Her friends and former husbands just cannot stay away: "They carried covered casseroles and boxes with silver bows. . . . They put out their cigarettes in the soil of the maidenfern. They put their wet glasses on the top of the table. The etchings in the marble will be permanent."

Pesetsky's fiction is not easy to summarize. Grumbach thought Pesetsky's stories more enjoyable when read "one at a time and far apart." Martha Liebrum (*Houston Post*, 28 February 1982) wrote, "I read the book, then couldn't remember a single story. What were they about? Life. What did they say? A lot. Nothing. They went in sad circles." Yet

Pesetsky has insisted that her stories are to some extent referential: "I heard something, saw something, remembered something." The difficulty lies in her fragmentary style. No story in *Stories up to a Point* exceeds ten pages. Liebrum remarked that the collection contained "some of the best lines I've read in a long time." According to Pesetsky, many of her stories "had to start . . . with single lines – not a coherent story but rather those thoughts that created pictures in my mind." Consequently Pesetsky's characters seem underdeveloped. Grumbach labeled Pesetsky's style "Dick-and-Jane"; Montrose referred to it as "see Jane run." As Grumbach said, the characters seem "shadowy, silhouettes," a notion Pesetsky often parodies.

In "The Passing Parade," for example, a story about the absurdities of "adapting," the narrator has "recently discovered that the backs of people look more familiar than the faces" – "from the front, everyone is a stranger to me." The passing parade represents all those people who come and go in one's life. Gossip becomes a more defining characteristic than speech. Life and the people in it often appear as in a parade or at a party, after which one can say only, "different people came." The title of the story "The Person Who Held This Job Before You" implies yet another human being who has simply come and gone.

The most compelling themes in *Stories up to a Point*, however, are those having to do with disconnection and continuity. Pesetsky's women experience emotional paralysis. Disconnection defines their lives: relatives die, become lost or abandoned; divorce happens again and again while remarriage follows (some characters have been married four or five times). Their search for continuity leads them to discover their losses and to seek others who can keep them company. Pesetsky's fragmentary narratives enhance this notion of disconnection. Dialogue is kept to a minimum: as one character remarks, "I have known hard times, unpleasantness, fear. . . . All of this I am unable to share."

The theme of disconnection is given full metaphoric weight in "Moe, Nat, and Yrd." A woman phones radio call-in shows, which always hang up on her. She wants to talk about "philosophies and deeper meanings" and her dreams. She is cut off in other ways as well – from her brother, daughter, husband, and mother. She finally gains acceptance when she senses "the importance of continuity." Similarly, in "A Family History," the narrator comments about suicide: "In the parting note that is required I would say goodbye, saddened by nothing save the absence of anyone to address it to"; she "would rather be dead than end up an old woman who died unmourned" and so begins "to think about continuity." But discovering continuity does not fully redeem a character. Using fragments, digressions, and scenes, the female narrator of "Family Romances," for example, relates a story in which disconnection and continuity are comically and poignantly muddled. Her father marries her mother's younger sister. "We never saw him again," the narrator says. Continuity for her means that "all things that happen to everybody will someday happen to my children."

The first-person narration of all but two pieces in *Stories up to a Point* lends it another sort of continuity. Gail Gilliland (*Philadelphia Inquirer*, 10 February 1982) noted that Pesetsky uses the first person as if to say, "*I* am in fact the only person to whom I can speak, the only one who will really listen, the only one who cares. . . ." Charles Champlin (*Los Angeles Times*, 1 January 1982) raised the notion of the "unreliable narrator," which he thought lent "an added romance, taunting the reader to guess at the truths behind the aggressive claims." In Pesetsky's fiction the emotional impact outweighs the thematic ones.

While cleaning out her grandmother's apartment, the narrator of "The Hobbyist" discovers her late grandfather's dust collection: dust from under various beds; from a lover's apartment; from Halley's Comet, 1910; from stores, strangers, and visitors – all in tiny, labeled bottles. The grandmother, who has "no heart for the debris of my life," asks, "Must this dust pursue me to my grave?" The narrator learns about the past from something more real than photographs. "Meanwhile," as Champlin noted, "we have learned even more about the narrator, her difficulties with her husband, her awareness of violent death and the dispersion of friends, her sense, indeed, that all comes to dust."

The title of the book – *Stories up to a Point* – is a pun that Pesetsky develops throughout the book. In "From P Forward" a woman creates graphs for special occasions (birthdays, divorces), to make order out of chaos: "One took a fact and translated it into a given point (P). Anything was possible from P forward." The notions of disconnection and continuity are inherent in the graphs, which "yield significant similarities" and "variations between curves."

Lehmann-Haupt cogently inquired, "And what is the point that these stories are 'up to?' . . . Sometimes it's that the point is yet to be made. Sometimes it's that it's not worth making. But mostly it's that there simply is no point anymore."

Then again Pesetsky might be referring to the breaking point many of these characters have reached, such as Mrs. Triton in "Care by Women," a woman whose daughters "could not make her feel sad for them ever, ever again." In "Offspring of the First Generation" a woman ingratiates herself with others but is constantly shut out by them. Even her own children see through her easily. Appropriately she is a pamphleteer, whose motto (a reference to Pesetsky's ghostwriting experiences) is "Your Philosophy is Mine." Though she knows "there is no cure for being disliked," she is unable "for a moment [to] accept isolation as the legitimate leitmotif of my life." Her desire for continuity, however, goes unfulfilled when she is not invited to her son's wedding.

The title of the book also suggests Pesetsky's lean prose style, "her situations sketched in with the thinnest lines," as Grumbach wrote. Pesetsky fills in the emotional contours. "Ulcer," for example, comically explores "the relation of pain to food." Presented in the form of a mock questionnaire, the story relays vignettes about marriage and domesticity in which cooking becomes a metaphor for a woman's life. Her breakdown finally occurs when "disasters ('the gravy was sour') erupted at routine dinners and also festive occasions."

The "point" of a Pesetsky story is always an ironic one. In "Care by Women" the man who deserts his wife and three daughters because he has always wanted a son fails to remember that "gender was determined by the father." In "A Walker's Manual" the narrator does not engage in walking (a form of continuity) for sport. Rather she sees walking as a natural phenomenon, which, "like breathing or drinking, cannot be stopped." While walking she has "truly a chance to see." She alludes to several historical accounts, such as that of the monk who walked for penance but liked it so much he bought poor shoes to give him pain. The narrator can see "into windows" of peoples' lives; those who do not walk "see the world only from start to finish" (rather than up to a point). As Champlin pointed out, this narrator is "withdrawing evermore into herself." "Like the daughter of the King of Seville [who] practically walked to her funeral," the narrator can walk up to people she knows or away from them.

After completing the critically acclaimed novel *Midnight Sweets* (1988), which both the *New York Times* and *Los Angeles Times* listed as one of the best of the year, Pesetsky finished her second collection of short stories, *Confessions of a Bad Girl*. It differs from *Stories up to a Point* in that it is deliberately

(p. 8)

Leah said that the marriage-to-be was like ~~some kind of~~ a premature

sacrifice. Elizabeth -- how old was she? -- seventeen. And that ~~very~~

ancient

~~old~~ man. That old man past seventy. ~~She knew what it was.~~ It was almost way

and tell her what what.

white slavery. She had half a mind to see Elizabeth's mother. Maybe

ever

there was a law. Don't you embarrass me, I said. You? Leah said.

afterwards that

Then we were yelling, and I knew the neighborhood had heard too much.

a

But Gina said the next morning show me any family that says it

doesn't

~~never~~ fights and I'll show you liars. I never heard ~~about~~ her and Big

was

Hugh, she said, ~~was~~ because their quarrels tended to occur mostly at nine

or

and ten in the morning before Big Hugh went to bed. I was in school then

How much did we know about Elizabeth and the butcher? (Not so much)

I used to say that   was

-- ~~less than I thought.~~ ~~Wasn't~~ Elizabeth left behind in everything?

It   melted down   grew

~~That~~ was true. All the other girls ~~grew~~ slim and tall. Elizabeth

equally

stayed as she was in eighth grade, short and with baby plumpness

hardening into

~~becoming a~~ wrinkled permanence above her waistband.

On a Saturday two months before the wedding Gina and I planned an

shop   arm in arm and

expedition past the butcher's. ~~Giggling,~~ we walked down the street; her

three children, bribed with candy, circling us like a litter.

we said and

Reconnoitering, We nudged each other. The butcher behind his counter

from the window.

was visible. Look at that, we whispered, pretending to be reading his

specials   withered It was reported

~~signs.~~ The old butcher -- an ancient man. ~~Hadn't we heard~~ that he had

been in the infantry under the Kaiser. Anyway, the butcher came from

or 1936.   someone remembered,

Mannheim in 1935. That's what ~~we heard.~~

The butcher's

~~His~~ meat wasn't anything wonderful, but he would cut to order. He

cheap

made sausages too and sold a line of cold cuts to fit the neighborhood.

Page from a draft for the story "The Prince of Wales" (by permission of Bette Pesetsky)

more unified, with ten of the fifteen stories linked by similar characters and events. The order of stories in her first collection, Pesetsky says, "reflected how I saw the progression of mood." Three stories in *Confessions of a Bad Girl* were to have appeared in *Stories up to a Point,* but Pesetsky withdrew them.

As in *Stories up to a Point* the stories in *Confessions of a Bad Girl* are vehicles for voices. Pesetsky's characters once again do not so much narrate as talk to readers. The protagonists Cissie and her brother Sylvester, who appear in several stories in the first section, "Confessions," are imbued "with this memory of cold, sweet possession of self." The stories focus on various revelations about Cissie and her family throughout the years. Cissie is eccentric, "meshugah, tetched, loco." Her family saga deals with the tenuous relationships of spouses, siblings, parents, and children. However, there is an older, extended family of sorts, the Spacedons, who once had taken the young, lonely Sylvester under its wing. Although the four Spacedon children are revealed to be orphans (a theme of the book and the title of one story), the family is tightly knit (two siblings marry each other). Sylvester's stories tend to be more realistic than Cissie's. Her concern "with craziness" creates narratives that are, in typical Pesetsky fashion, fragmented, spare, and given to "Lists and Categories," questions and answers, and gossip.

In the last story of the "Confessions" section, "People I Know Who Are Living in Florida," readers not only learn what has become of the Spacedons but also sense the extraordinary passage of time and events that happened "so long ago that it was like thinking about something that could never have happened to you." The best story in the section, "Penny and Willie," captures the lingering ties that bind a family that has been torn apart by divorce and alienation, and explores how those relationships – even when broken – can endure through "a constant of love." Thus Pesetsky recapitulates the overall theme of *Stories up to a Point:* the cycles of disconnection and continuity. "Everyone ... tries,

mostly in vain, to make a connection," Joanne Kaufman wrote in *People* (17 July 1989). "If the connection is made, it is swiftly broken."

The second section, "Bad Girl," recalls a label Pesetsky has said she earned as a child, having "spent a fair amount of time ... in the offices of various principals." The "bad" characters, as Charles Dickinson noted (in the *New York Times Book Review,* 28 May 1989), are those "who by choice or chance live outside the accepted rules of society [and] achieve a measure of harmony in [their] fractured lives."

In *Confessions of a Bad Girl,* geometry – especially the circle and the parallel line – becomes a variation on "the strophoid, the semicubical parabola, the Bowditch curve, the spiral of Archimedes" referred to in "From P Forward." The stories in the 1989 book demonstrate how people continually move around and away from one another, only to come back toward each other and themselves again.

Several critics noted the impressive cumulative effect of the stories, and Dickinson thought they "might have been linked into a wonderful novel." His comment raises the question of whether Pesetsky's greatest strength is as a novelist or a short-story writer. "Pesetsky has given us *hors d'oeuvres,*" observed Elizabeth Benedict (in the *San Francisco Review of Books,* 24 August 1982), "and hinted strongly that she is capable of putting together a really first-rate main course."

Pesetsky's short fiction will be remembered for its "energy, economy, and sympathy," as Champlin wrote. Of her future fiction, Pesetsky has said she hopes to explore "the place of politics in the search for power – the new road up from poverty." She is currently at work on a series of stories that carry a midwestern family from the end of World War II to the present. Given her talent and versatility, Pesetsky remains, as Leibrum wrote of her, "a writer to watch."

Interview:

Hansmaarten Tromp, Interview with Pesetsky [in Dutch], *Haagse Post,* 14 July 1984.

J. F. Powers

(8 July 1917 –)

Julia B. Boken
State University of New York College at Oneonta

BOOKS: *Prince of Darkness, and Other Stories* (Garden City, N.Y.: Doubleday, 1947; London: Lehmann, 1948); republished as *Lions, Harts, Leaping Does, and Other Stories* (New York: Time, 1963);

The Presence of Grace (Garden City, N.Y.: Doubleday, 1956; London: Gollancz, 1956);

Morte d'Urban (Garden City, N.Y.: Doubleday, 1962; London: Gollancz, 1962);

Look How the Fish Live (New York: Knopf, 1975);

Wheat That Springeth Green (New York: Knopf, 1988).

SELECTED PERIODICAL PUBLICATIONS –
UNCOLLECTED: "Night in the County Jail," *Catholic Worker,* 10 (May 1943): 8;

"Day in the County Jail," *Catholic Worker,* 10 (July 1943): 6–7;

"Saint on the Air," *Catholic Worker,* 10 (December 1943): 9–12;

"Fun with a Purpose," *Commonweal,* 49 (15 October 1948): 9–12;

"St. Paul, Home of the Saints," *Partisan Review,* 16 (July 1949): 714–721;

"Conscience and Religion" [review of Gordon Zahn's *In Solitary Witness*], *Commentary,* 40 (July 1965): 91.

A short-story writer, novelist, essayist, and critic, J. F. Powers is among the leading satirists in the literary world. His fictional cosmos is for the most part a Roman Catholic rectory, where in miniature all the forces of the secular and the spiritual world converge. With irony, humor, and mockery, yet with compassion, intelligence, and understanding, Powers focuses on those clergy who by virtue of their vows must cope with the imposed ambiguities of serving God and mammon. Without preachment, Powers conveys underlying moral values that seem subordinate in a world mesmerized by money, power, television, crime, and pleasure. He attacks those prelates who become materialists, public-

relations pitchmen, and egotists, while he invokes empathy and toleration for those churchmen, both monastic and secular, who attempt to balance the exigencies of the spirit and the world. Despite Powers's adherence to orthodox Roman Catholicism and its prominence in his fiction, his novels and short stories appeal to nonbelievers as well.

Virtually all Powers's themes, characterizations, and narratives employ humor in its many modulations – from irony and satire to bittersweet and even explosive laughter. Powers himself once said, "I see the human situation as essentially comic." John V. Hagopian, in his critical commentary *J. F. Powers* (1968), emphasizes such tonalities of humor and adds a remark that partially reflects Powers's force in short-story writing: "Out of parochial materials, he shapes subtle and highly charged human situations that capture the moral and emotional texture of modern life."

James Farl Powers, one of the three children of James and Zella Routzong Powers, was born in Jacksonville, Illinois, on 8 July 1917. His father, a dairy-and-poultry manager for Swift and Company, provided his family with a comfortable life and was a virtuoso pianist as well; Zella Powers enjoyed painting. The family's Catholicism posed some difficulty for the young J. F. Powers, since Jacksonville was predominantly Protestant. He was treated by many as an outsider, but Powers believes such an environment made a philosopher out of him. He later used this outsider status in his first novel, *Morte d'Urban* (1962), wherein the protagonist, Father Harvey Roche, laments living in a town such as Jacksonville: "Protestants were very sure of themselves there. If you were a Catholic boy you felt that it was their country, handed down to them by the Pilgrims, George Washington, and others, and that they were taking a risk in letting you live in it." At age seven Powers moved with his family to Rockford, Illinois, and in 1931 he entered classes at Saint Peter's Parish School, Quincy, Illinois, where the classes were taught by the Franciscan Fathers, a

266

J. F. Powers in 1975 (photograph by Hugh Powers)

Roman Catholic order. Powers excelled at athletics, especially basketball. Sports are also important in his fiction. Powers never aspired to the priesthood. He said he would have liked the prayers and would not have minded the celibacy, but he could not accept the intermingling with parishioners and the fund-raising for various causes.

After high-school graduation Powers moved to Chicago with his parents. In this Depression year of 1935, jobs were scarce, and he worked selling books and men's shirts and then found a job as a clerk with an insurance company. In 1937 he became a chauffeur for a mogul, whom Powers drove throughout the South as his boss went in search of profitable investments. The following year Powers was hired as an editor for the Illinois Historical Records Survey; at night he attended the Chicago branch of Northwestern University. When the survey was completed in 1940, Powers, jobless, stopped his university classes. Eventually he found a job at a bookstore, but a year later he was summarily dismissed for refusing to buy war bonds.

Chicago, during the early World War II years, provided stimulating experiences for Powers. He met rebels of all kinds, among them black jazz musicians, European political exiles, and Catholic workers. All these experiences provided material for his later fiction. Hagopian writes, "During this time the conflict between Powers' religious ideals and the demands of the secular world reached crisis proportions. Appalled by the wholesale slaughter and destruction of the war and revolted by the gaudy cheapness of jingoist propaganda, he became a pacifist." In 1943 Powers attended a retreat during which Christianity and pacifism were featured. This and other retreats strengthened his opposition to war. From these experiences came his well-known and important story "Lions, Harts, Leaping Does" (in *Prince of Darkness, and Other Stories*, 1947).

Refusing to join the military during World War II, Powers was incarcerated for thirteen months in Sandstone, Minnesota, at a federal prison. "I was paroled," Powers wrote in a 17 February 1992 letter, "to work as a hospital orderly in St. Paul. After the war, I received a presidential pardon, so-called." When he was twenty-five he wrote a series of articles for the *Catholic Worker* delineating his religious tenets. "A saint," Powers says in "Saint on the Air" (1943), "is not an abnormal person. He is simply a mature Christian. Anyone who is not a saint is spiritually undersized – the world is full of spiritual midgets."

On 22 April 1946, after a short courtship, J. F. Powers married Elizabeth Wahl, who also became a writer and also published stories in the *New Yorker;* she died in 1988, after forty-two years of marriage. Five children were born to them: Katherine, named after Katherine Anne Porter, one of the key influences on J. F. Powers; Mary; James; Hugh; and Jane.

Prince of Darkness was published during Powers's residence at Yaddo, in Saratoga Springs, New York, in 1947. The collection was well received by the critics. It includes eleven stories, five of which deal with clergymen, their rectories, and their interrelations with each other and with parishioners. Although it might appear that the environment of the churchmen is monochromatic, in fact these narratives are considered by critics to be more significant and successful than the wholly secular tales, three of which focus on the evils of racism.

The three stories admired by readers and critics alike are "Lions, Harts, Leaping Does," "The Valiant Woman," and "Prince of Darkness," the latter two the favorites of Powers. The themes, characterizations, and ironies of all three are highly effective.

"Lions, Harts, Leaping Does," considered by many critics to be Powers's best work, was written when he was twenty-five. It is the first of his clerical tales and is told mainly through interior monologue. Father Didymus, who is a cloistered Franciscan friar, and Brother Titus, a partially retarded worker in the monastery, dominate the narrative. The theme focuses on Didymus's interminable self-analysis concerning his faith and worthiness. Crucial to the development of the tale is the request of his older brother Seraphim, who has spent twenty-five years in Rome on church matters, to visit him on his return to Saint Louis. Didymus decides not to go. After a short walk with Titus, who throughout the story reads to the friar from books concerning the church, Didymus learns from the rector that Titus has not given Didymus a telegram that announces the death of Seraphim. In the chapel, praying for his brother's soul, Didymus collapses, perhaps from a combination of heartfelt sorrow and the clamminess of the floor. Later, confined to a wheelchair in his room, he laments his fate: "Why this punishment, he asks himself, and immediately supplied the answer. He had, for one thing, gloried too much in having it in him to turn down Seraphim's request to come to St. Louis. The intention – that was all important, and he, he feared, had done the right thing for the wrong reason." Didymus feels guilty that "he had used his brother for a hair shirt."

The title "Lions, Harts, Leaping Does" is a quotation from San Juan de la Cruz, the Spanish mystic of the sixteenth century. These animals are cited as symbols by him to denote "troublesome and disorderly acts," of which Didymus is not guilty. Nonetheless, Didymus, as he probes his soul, experiences a crisis of belief and submits to the depths of misery, certainly a failing if not a sin. Apropos of this despair, San Juan de la Cruz mentions that God sometimes arouses in the soul an abysmal poverty and emptiness and that this purging is a necessary prerequisite and prelude to the glory that is to come.

"Lions, Harts, Leaping Does" remains one of the most heartrending, intricately wrought tales in the short fiction of Powers. The story's density imposes a challenge for the reader, but it amply rewards careful scrutiny.

The winner of the 1947 O. Henry Award, "The Valiant Woman" is about Mrs. Stoner, the housekeeper for Father John Firman; she is nagging, interfering, overbearing, and shrewish. Mrs. Stoner is aptly named. Humor, irony, and hilarity are combined in the characterizations of the housekeeper and the henpecked pastor. Firman's is the central point of view. Throughout the years, because of the domineering Stoner, his friends no longer care to visit him. Considering herself an integral part of the household, she tells Firman that she has given him the best years of her life. Quite young when she began as a servant, this virago was widowed after a year of marriage to a miner. Her behavior has remained constant: being uncharitable to the parishioners; snooping into the parish records to uncover illegitimate children whom parents wish to have baptized; overcharging for rosaries and books; and consistently undermining the dignity of the pastor. Firman wishes to be rid of her, but he knows that housekeepers are difficult to find, "harder to get than ushers, than willing workers, than organists, than secretaries – yes, harder to get than assistants or vocations." He knows Stoner to be the bane of his existence, but he claims that he cannot afford to pension her off and that it would be perhaps offensive to her to find someone else, if indeed that were possible.

There is much humor in her taking over the guest room and in her taking out the card table nightly to play "Honeymoon Bridge" with her pastor. She is a shark at cards and usually wins. Firman experiences twinges of guilt and feels that Stoner shows a defect of the flesh, a venial sin, but he suffers from the lack of will, which is a mortal offense. He continues to abdicate his power and control to his housekeeper.

Most critics agree that the best story of *Prince of Darkness* is the title story, the last one in the collection and the longest (thirteen thousand words). The term *Prince of Darkness* is, of course, a euphemism for Satan or the devil. In Powers's satire "Prince of Darkness," the title stems from a dean's reference to the protagonist Father Burner's building of a photography darkroom in the rectory. Burner is an overweight and overbearing priest whose characterization forms the main ingredient of the story.

Father Ernest "Boomer" Burner, forty-three years of age and ordained seventeen years before the story begins, is still a curate, an assistant transferred four times to various parishes. Powers portrays him as a rank materialist, a spiritual fraud, a hearty epicure, and an unrestrained narcissist. Always contentious and brutally frank, Burner appreciates only the English poet Francis Thompson, whom Burner calls a "Limey"; glorifies Germans; lampoons the Irish; condescends to the poor; bullies women in the confessional; ridicules (silently) a nubile girl in a drive-in restaurant; and pounces on any remark made by a visiting priest. Burner has no cultural values and despises music but dotes on advertising salesmen, enjoys food in copious quantities, and adores golfing, racing in his automobile, and piloting a plane. At his ordination, when most priests choose the gift of a chalice, Burner selected a watch.

Throughout the narrative, Burner is obsessed with the idea of receiving a parish of his own, to become a pastor and bring his mother to the rectory as housekeeper. At the story's end an archbishop, after a long conversation in which he tries to elicit Burner's limitations as a man of the church, gives Burner an envelope not to be opened until after mass the next day. Opening the letter a few blocks away a few minutes later, Burner is flabbergasted to find out that he has been assigned *another* assistantship. The last sentence of the story, and the last sentence of the letter, reads, "I trust that in your new appointment you will find not peace but a sword," a sentence that is one of the most haunting ironies in Powers's short fiction.

Some critics of "Prince of Darkness" not only dislike Father Burner but detest him and seize on his nickname, "Prince of Darkness"; his real name, "Burner"; his six deadly sins (pride, envy, gluttony, avarice, wrath, and sloth); and the "cloven foot" that he presses on the gas pedal of his car to conclude from these details that this priest is a devil.

Some readers may feel that this judgment is too harsh. Burner clearly recognizes that he has no vocation; in fact, he rarely thinks about God, religion, or salvation. After brooding on his failure as a priest, he veers off to wondering when he will become a pastor: "When would he make the great metamorphosis from assistant to pastor, from mouse to rat, as the saying went?"

Yet Burner claims that he would be ready to be persecuted – even to die – for his faith. He seems detestable to most critics and to some readers, but to categorize Burner as a devil is a giant leap and undercuts the satire and well-honed irony of this story of a weak-willed, spiritually abased priest, who apart from a Roman collar is merely a self-centered, uncharitable prig, despising others and thus denigrating himself.

"Prince of Darkness," like many of Powers's secular-priest stories, points up that some of the men anointed as priests, of whom much honorable thought and work are expected, apart from their priestly vestments are like some laymen – mean-spirited, power-driven, racist, condescending, and with feet of clay. Powers's irony in his portraiture widens the gulf between the spiritual ideal of the priesthood and the pedestrian reality of daily living.

The Presence of Grace, Powers's second collection of short stories, was published in 1956, when he was teaching creative writing at the University of Michigan. Between the publication of this book and that of *Prince of Darkness,* his life had been filled with a variety of activities and accomplishments: he taught at Saint John's University in Collegeville, Minnesota, in 1947; was awarded grants by the Guggenheim Foundation and the National Institute of Arts and Letters (both in 1948); taught at Marquette University in Milwaukee from 1949 to 1950; and spent two years with his family in county Wicklow, Ireland.

In *The Presence of Grace* only two of the nine stories are purely secular, "The Poor Thing" and "Blue Island." In the first of these stories, the theme encompasses the hypocrisy and manipulation exercised by Dolly, an elderly, ruthless woman confined to a wheelchair. Her paid companion, Teresa, a spinster who is old and retired, with an insufficient pension, is Dolly's victim. Dolly is absurd and moronic and spends much of her time watching television. When her demands become impossible and her frugality unbearable, Teresa quits. To force Teresa's return, Dolly accuses her of theft and denies her a reference. Teresa returns at the behest of the employment agency.

Dust jacket for Powers's 1956 book. In the title story a Roman Catholic curate provokes controversy by dining with a woman and a man who is believed to be her lover.

"Blue Island" features another self-serving cynical manipulator, Mrs. Hancock, and her victims the Daviccis, who are, in the final analysis, willing participants. Ralph and Ethel Davicci, newly arrived in Blue Island, a Minneapolis suburb, are eager to be accepted by their neighbors, a community of affluent middle-class residents. Ralph, a liquor dealer and an owner of tawdry bars, attempts to hide his seamy background. Hancock, who is, as she finally admits, neither a neighbor nor a Blue Island resident, offers to plan a coffee party so that Ethel can meet the neighbors. When the neighbors convene, Ethel is horrified to learn that Hancock actually has arranged to sell them "Shipshape" kitchen utensils. Powers introduces in "Blue Island" several themes, including the pretensions of the Daviccis. Powers made a telling comment to Hagopian about such secular stories: "You can't win in this world. In my secular stories this world is the only one there can be, but in the clerical stories there is always the shadow of another world." The

idea of not being able to win in this world is a recurrent theme in Powers's stories.

"Dawn," the last of the clerical stories Powers wrote in the 1950s, is a highly amusing tale that reflects interclerical rivalry and politics; the story ridicules some priests and the widow who sets the story into motion. Father Bruno Udovic, chancellor of the fictional Diocese of Great Plains; a bishop (unnamed); and Monsignor James Renton of the cathedral chancery office are the main characters. (All also appear in Powers's *Morte d'Urban*.) Udovic accelerates the "Peter's Pence" collection so that the bishop can deliver the sum personally to the pope during the bishop's forthcoming visit to Rome. Among the envelopes is one addressed to the pope and labeled "Personal." Udovic fears that the contents may be some lewd remarks, "all manner of filth, spelled out in letters snipped from newsprint and calculated to shake Rome's faith in him." The bishop urges the downplaying of this envelope and shuffles it around for weeks while Udovic places an inquiry into the announcements of the diocesan paper and a query during masses. No one claims it. When an announcement is made that unless the donor appears the envelope will be opened, the "culprit" materializes; she is a crotchety and sullen widow of few words, a Mrs. Anton. Udovic is certain that Renton, who is spiteful and malicious, sent the woman to embarrass Udovic for, among other reasons, having hastened the Peter's Pence collection. The widow is questioned by the bishop and Udovic about the envelope. She finally admits the enclosure is one dollar and that she addressed the envelope in the way she did because she did not want anyone else to steal the dollar or to get credit for the offering. She wrote her name and address on the dollar bill so that she would get the credit. The bishop, apparently considering this woman a moron and the whole incident blown out of all proportion, walks away, leaving Udovic to complete the interview.

On the surface "Dawn" suggests a simple tale of priests and a widow's mite, but Powers modulates the episode and the humor so successfully that the impact is broadened to include a whole scale of moral values. All the egos in the tale are diminished by satire and irony.

Other short stories in *The Presence of Grace* also project charm and humor. Fritz, a shrewd feline, is the center of consciousness in two such tales – "Death of a Favorite" and "Defection of a Favorite." Father Burner, featured in "Prince of Darkness," reappears in both stories, but he is no longer a rank narcissist and is more mellow and concerned with his spiritual duties.

In "Death of a Favorite" Fritz, a rectory cat, observes the shenanigans that whirl around him. He sees men of the church play cards, drink, watch sports, gossip, pass judgments, compete against each other in minor power struggles, and generally behave like most men outside the church. These stories may remind the reader of some tales by Saki or Franz Kafka.

In "Defection of a Favorite," with virtually the same cast of characters, Burner, still a curate, becomes the acting pastor when Father Malt, eighty-one years old, falls, fractures his hip, and is hospitalized. Initially Burner dubs Fritz a "black devil." He complains to Father Desmond, his friend, that if it were up to him, he would excommunicate all pets from rectories. During the pastor's absence, Burner becomes unusually conscientious as he visits the sick without complaint, provides minor repairs for the rectory and the church, buys the housekeeper a mixer and a radio, and, above all, succeeds in converting many people. Fritz opines that Burner is trying to prove to himself that he can be an effective priest. Consistent with Burner's change is his ignoring and tolerating Fritz. Eventually Malt, on crutches, returns, and the shrewd Fritz says that Malt will always be pastor during his lifetime because his need is greater than that of Burner, who, having grown in stature, also recognizes Malt's need.

These two feline-perspective tales are effective because of their quiet charm, dartlike irony, and wry humor, despite the unsavoriness of some of the clergy passing through the rectory of Malt. Fritz is a memorable foil to the antics of these men, and he is also confronted by several priests who reflect the strength and the compassionate charity that inhere in those clergymen who deserve respect.

More challenging than the two cat stories is "The Devil Was a Joker," an absorbing tale completed during 1952, when Powers and his family resided in Ireland. Specifically, on one level, the title derives from salesman Mac McMaster's insinuation into the goodwill of the clergy by giving them samples from his satchel, which contains scapulars, medals, rosaries, and playing cards with saints as face cards but including one of the devil as joker.

Mac is an itinerant lay salesman in the United States for *Clementine* magazine, published by the Order of Saint Clement. Convalescing in a hospital from a hernia, Mac meets Myles Flynn, a night orderly and former seminarian. It is immediately apparent to Myles that Mac, fat and fifty, candy-pink faced, with pop eyes and thinning orange hair, is an alcoholic. Mac needs a chauffeur for his 1941 Cadillac and inveigles Myles to take the job; Myles believes that he can meet a bishop who will sponsor his readmittance to the seminary. He is also in danger of being drafted for the Korean War. Their odyssey covers several states in the Midwest, including Wisconsin and Minnesota. This story seemingly was inspired by Powers's experiences when he chauffeured an affluent investor throughout the South.

Myles, the center of consciousness, early in the story tells Mac vaguely why he was dismissed from the seminary: "Something happened." Mac is friendly and loquacious, but he is probably one of the most aggressive manipulators in the fiction of Powers. He uses any technique imaginable to sell the magazine and his other wares to various clergymen in several states. Mac emerges as a rank hypocrite, a faker, and an alcoholic with a homosexual leaning, though it is carefully disguised, perhaps unconscious. The young Myles, a Blakean innocent, whose experience and protective armor develop in the course of his journeying with Mac, is obsessed with returning to the seminary. As these two cover the many parishes, Myles is delineated as compulsive, even obsessional, as he lectures Mac on the Bible and indicts "greed" in the society, cars, and wars. Mac retorts that all Myles can talk about is greed: "No wonder they had to get rid of you!" Most critics agree, though, that "Something happened" probably refers to a homosexual episode in the seminary.

Myles is never permitted to talk to any bishops about his appeal, and when he discusses his problem with a curate while Mac is in a poker game, he experiences a moment of epiphany: he decides to leave Mac. The salesman is astonished and hurt to hear that Myles is determined to leave. Mac admits that he is not a Catholic but is a "bloody Orangeman," and, in a remarkable ploy, he asks Myles to baptize him, in an almost metaphoric overture of seduction. Myles, by refusing, reveals his progress from innocence to experience – his maturation, self-protective feelings, and most of all his steely determination.

The reader may see the ambiguity of Mac. He is a faker par excellence and a manipulator of the clergy and of Myles, but Mac also elicits some admiration for his energy, his drive, and his dreams. Myles sheds some of his vulnerability through coping with Mac, but the former seminarian remains utterly intransigent about his moral convictions and his unrelenting compulsion to reenter the seminary, although Mac and the reader are aware that the youth is basically unsuited for the church. In the

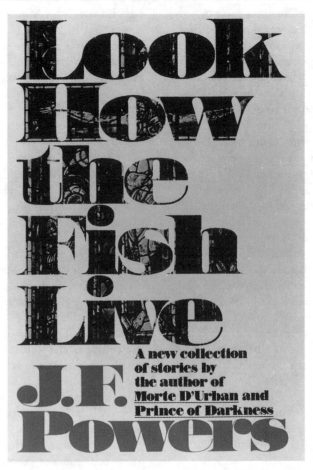

Dust jacket for Powers's 1975 book. In the title story the narrator worries about what he may have done to harm the environment but concludes that he is "tired . . . of nature passing the buck to him."

character of both these men – as in many of Powers's fictional portraits – there exist ambiguities. These people are often unfocused in their lives and unconsciously wreak havoc on those who enter into any kind of relationship with them.

The title story of Powers's second collection, "The Presence of Grace," introduces a new theme in a particular and novel interpenetration of the two worlds of the clergy and the laity. The tale is about one day in the life of Father Fabre. Fabre, curate at Trinity Church, quite unwittingly precipitates a confrontation with the Altar and Rosary Society by dining at the widow Mrs. Mildred Mathers's flat. The other guests are Mr. Pint (in his sixties) and his daughter Velma. Although invited, Grace Halloran, who has been one of Mrs. Mathers's best friends in the society, is conspicuously absent. Because Pint, in making the ice cream, stained his shirt and Mathers brought him a clean one, this garment is the vehicle for providing Fabre with the information that his hostess has rented Pint her spare room for extra income. The young curate is horrified to realize

that, perhaps by his presence, he has "blessed their union, if any, in the eyes of the parish." Fabre is bored by most of the conversation. Leaving, he deliberately refrains from thanking his hostess for her home-cooked meal, since to do so would be expressing gratitude for, as he thinks, compromising him with the (unnamed) pastor and the parish. Fabre boorishly concludes that he did Mathers a favor by not hurting her with a chastisement.

On his return to the rectory, some women from the Altar and Rosary Society, led by Halloran, are awaiting the return of the pastor, who has little respect and admiration for Fabre or his superior. The pastor, who does not like socializing with the parishioners, talks in monosyllables and is usually taciturn and abrupt. Denial is his technique in solving problems. Before the pastor enters the room in which the society women are waiting, Fabre attempts but is never completely permitted to give his version of the happening at Mathers's dinner. As always, the pastor leaves the door open when he talks to the women, and the curate overhears the conversation. They protest the behavior of (and thereby condemn) Mathers, who is "living" with Pint. Indirectly they also imply criticism of the curate, who dined there that evening. The pastor at first says absolutely nothing to the women. During the society's attack on Mathers, Fabre's interior monologue reveals his conviction that the widow does not feel guilty about renting a room to a man. Fabre also remembers that Pint is a non-Catholic, and Fabre ruminates on the possibility of the couple's carnal relations and also of their possible eventual marriage, before which Pint would have to be converted to her Catholic faith. The pastor's eventual denial of any impropriety ("'S not so") provokes a sarcastic request by one woman for an explanation. The pastor is utterly silent awhile, then repeats his denial.

Fabre feels that the pastor has triumphed over these women, as truth always does over error. He believes, "Life was a dark business for everyone in it, but the way for pastors was everlit by flares of special grace." Dressing for services, Fabre feels respect and admiration for his pastor, who did not scourge the women as Fabre would have done, and he further feels that the pastor is a kind of Solomon. Fabre sorrows that he had coveted the pastor's position and is grateful for the lesson he learned from his superior, who might in the future give Mathers "a just poke or two from the blunt sword of his mercy."

The reader becomes aware that Fabre has completely missed the point. The pastor has followed his philosophy of denial and has settled nothing. The situation is highly comedic since no one knows whether or not Mathers and Pint are having an affair, and the women in protesting about these two people are condemning them without any actual knowledge. Only the confessional would reveal such activity. Their action is a flagrant violation of Christian charity. Fabre, whose presence at Mathers's flat provokes the women, actually unconsciously agrees with them, although he in essence is being equally condemned by the society. Through the use of pettifogging minutiae, Powers creates satire, humor, and irony. The parish gossips instill fear and trembling in Fabre, who resolves (like his pastor) to avoid any future embarrassment by doing nothing. The parish scandalmongers have won the battle, if not the war.

Not only are the situations amusing, but the language that describes them is also satirically funny. The irony begins with the title itself, "The Presence of Grace": Grace Halloran is absent from Mathers's dinner but present at the confrontation in the rectory. Satire concludes the tale as Fabre na-

ively magnifies the virtue of his superior in sensing the presence of his grace. Again Powers focuses on the worldly involvements of clerics rather than on their spiritual concerns. Because there are priests who shun their flock but do not devote themselves to a high level of spirituality, Powers parodies such men of the cloth who are expected to be all things to all people.

Powers's novel *Morte d'Urban* won the National Book Award for 1963 and attracts the interest of readers of his stories because it began as a short story for his collection *Prince of Darkness*. In *Morte d'Urban* the reader again encounters characters from the story "Dawn." The tone of the novel is ironic, comic, poignant, and bittersweet.

Look How the Fish Live (1975), Powers's third collection of short stories, is a pastiche of tales ranging from a story of tinkers in Ireland, to the story of a priest's retirement, to the title story, whose main theme educes sorrow over the state of the world and of nature. "Tinkers," set in Ballydoo, near Dublin, Ireland, reflects an autobiographical element of Powers's fiction. After living in County Wicklow in 1951 and 1952, the Powerses stayed in County Dublin (1957–1958) and again in County Wicklow (1963–1965). The story's main persona is that of an American writer who goes to Ireland with his family. The expatriate writer, self-dubbed "America's thriftiest living author," and his family occupy a hotel when the proprietors move to London. It was the aim of the writer to craft a lighthearted play about tinkers, itinerant gypsies who roam around the countryside. When the hotel proprietors unexpectedly return, the family quickly moves into a crude house and tries to cope. The family survives despite all the inconveniences of hardships and enforced moves, both in Ireland and at home, trying to benefit from their new experiences, yet the narrator concludes, "The odds are three or four to one against you whenever you move."

This story, like many of Powers's other secular stories, is less engaging than his clerical tales, but it still absorbs the reader in the simplicity of family life. The setting of Ireland does lend the story some diversity, and "Tinkers" underlines the uprootedness of people and their quest for survival.

"Farewell," one of the wittiest and most poignant stories in the collection, is told through the central consciousness of John Dullinger, bishop of Ostergothenburg (Minnesota), who is about to retire. By accident he has received an appeals letter to the priests throughout the diocese canvassing for donations to buy him a car, but nothing materializes

Powers in 1988 (photograph by Hugh Powers)

until after he has himself purchased a Mercedes-Benz. When many letters arrive with enclosures of money, Dullinger writes over 160 letters, returning the money and stating that it could be put to better use. His retirement hangs heavy on his mind until some priests petition for his help with masses, confessions, and visits to the sick. He thus begins to resume in retirement a busy life. He does not envy younger bishops, who are better suited to the times.

Ironically Dullinger is almost busier than before his retirement, as he puts mileage on his expensive car by volunteering clerical services around the diocese. But one day the car is sideswiped by a truck; he is severely injured, is hospitalized, and dies. The story is basically a portrait of a kind cleric who is not above hurling steely barbs against some of his absent fellow priests. For the most part, though, he is a genial Good Samaritan. The reader of this story meets a diversity of priests, depicted with their physical ailments and their pleasures in dining and driving around the country. The bonding of priests in this and other stories underscores their fraternity, humanity, and frailty.

"Look How the Fish Live" is a secular story suffused with a meditative but comic and bitter-sweet tone. The narrator, who is a father, examines each of the happenings of the day. His children report that a baby dove has fallen from its nest, and its parents are nowhere to be seen. The narrator feels guilty because he has sprayed DDT throughout the yard, and this poison might have injured not only the doves but other animals as well. In this story there are birds, cats, rabbits, and weasels. Powers confessed in an interview with M. Kristin Malloy that animals intrigue him: "They are always illustrating some moral fact of life."

The baby dove finally dies, and the narrator buries the bird. He reflects on the death and brands nature as incompetent: "He was tired of such cases, of nature passing the buck to him." It might appear to the reader that the dove is abandoned by its creator as it is by its parents. Following hard on the heels of this poignant episode of the abandoned dove is the narrator's encounter with some of his neighbors, who urge him to become a civil-defense warden; he refuses, telling them that he is sick of insects, birds, animals, nature, children, and women.

One of his neighbors justifies his outburst to the others, noting that the narrator's house is soon to be razed for the building of a college parking lot.

In this story, one of Powers's most elegiac, the narrator is acutely aware of animals and people, and he grieves and sorrows for the present and future state of the world. The narrator would like to ask God some questions, but he then concedes that God would know his thoughts and his questions and that the universe already possessed those answers that God would give. The title, "Look How the Fish Live," is reminiscent of a biblical admonition (Matthew 6:28–29): "Consider the lilies of the field, how they grow; they toil not, neither do they spin: and yet . . . even Solomon in all his glory was not arrayed like one of these." Although the story is basically secular, the implicit theology of faith inheres in the happenings and in the thought process of the reflective and accepting narrator. Conspicuously absent are Powers's trademarks of jovial humor and genial satire.

Powers's second novel, *Wheat That Springeth Green* (1988), well received by critics, focuses on familiar fictional territory: Father Joe Hackett, the central character, emerges from his raffish youth as a womanizer, enters a seminary, and becomes a priest and eventually a pastor. The novel modulates from hilarity and wit to satire and irony, with an imposing variety of lay and clerical figures. William Pritchard (*New Republic,* 26 September 1988) wrote, "His new novel seems to me the best book he has written."

In his first book of stories, *Prince of Darkness,* Powers presents his tales with a sharp-edged, negative irony that underscores the moral failures of some characters. In *The Presence of Grace* he softens the ironic tone, employing both overt and subtle humor to fashion his characters, depicting instances of moral success. In *Look How the Fish Live* Powers experiments with a wide variety of forms and tales, not always successfully. In the better-crafted stories he creates a blend of rollicking, wry humor, genial satire, and philosophical themes, portraying a more sober theme of concern for the future of the universe, both religious and environmental.

Although J. F. Powers is essentially a miniaturist (in his use of limited settings and events), the spiritual dimensions in his finest stories loom large. Of course, he primarily selects the Roman Catholic clergy in America as his central interest, but readers of other persuasions find value and pleasure in entering his fictional world. Powers tweaks the noses of priests who compromise or shirk their responsibilities to their fellowman (and he does so with wit, satire, and wry comedy). Yet he never condemns these men for their foibles and failings. Readers of Powers's short fiction are generally provoked not only into thought but also at times into convulsive laughter. The resounding artistic success of *Wheat That Springeth Green* has inspired Powers to be currently at work on two additional novels and other short stories as well. He continues to be drawn to the world of the clergy because of the inherent moral laws surrounding the church and the rectory.

Interviews:

M. Kristin Malloy, "The Catholic and Creativity: J. F. Powers," *American Benedictine Review,* 15 (March 1964): 63–80;

Anthony Schmitz, "The Alphabet God Uses," *Minnesota Monthly,* 22 (December 1988): 34–39.

Bibliography:

Jeffrey Meyers, "J. F. Powers: Uncollected Stories, Essays and Interviews, 1943–1979," *Bulletin of Bibliography,* 44 (March 1987): 38–39.

References:

Fallon Evans, ed., *J. F. Powers* (Saint Louis: Herder, 1968);

John V. Hagopian, *J. F. Powers* (New York: Twayne, 1968);

Thomas R. Preston, "Christian Folly in the Fiction of J. F. Powers," *Critique,* 16, no. 2 (1974): 91–107;

George F. Wedge, "J. F. Powers," *Critique,* 2 (1958): 63–70.

Mary Robison

(14 January 1949 -)

Michael McKenna
State University of New York College at Delhi

BOOKS: *Days* (New York: Knopf, 1979);
Oh! (New York: Knopf, 1981);
An Amateur's Guide to the Night (New York: Knopf, 1983);
Believe Them (New York: Knopf, 1988);
Subtraction (New York: Knopf, 1991).

SELECTED PERIODICAL PUBLICATIONS – UNCOLLECTED: "The Brothers: Memories of Being Buried Alive in Boys," *Esquire*, 99 (January 1983): 100–103;
"Thank You for Making Me Famous," *Harvard*, 85 (July–August 1983): 4–6.

Mary Robison has been widely recognized as a major talent among contemporary American short-story writers. Critics have praised her lean prose and her carefully observed glimpses into the everyday lives of ordinary, middle-class Americans. Many of Robison's stories first appeared in the *New Yorker;* her work has also been included in *The Pushcart Prize, VII: Best of the Small Presses* (1983); *The Best American Short Stories 1982;* and the *1987 O. Henry Prize Stories.* Among her admirers have been such distinguished writers as John Barth, Richard Yates, and Bobbie Ann Mason. Writing in the *Virginia Quarterly Review* (Spring 1986), Susan Mernit credits Robison, among a handful of other writers, with reviving the short story as a popular literary art form.

Robison is the daughter of attorney Anthony Cennamo and psychologist F. Elizabeth Waldkoetter Reiss. One of eight children (she has five brothers and two sisters), Robison was born on 14 January 1949 in Washington, D.C., and raised in Ohio. She received an M.A. in English in 1977 from Johns Hopkins University, where she studied with Barth, whom she credits with inspiring her to take seriously her talent for writing. She has received various literary honors, including fellowships from Yaddo (1978), the Bread Loaf Writers' Conference (1979), and the Guggenheim Foundation (1980), as well as P.E.N. and Authors Guild awards (1979).

Though critically acclaimed, Robison's work has not achieved the popular success that would allow her to write full-time. Consequently she has supplemented her income from writing by teaching and has held appointments at various schools, among them Bennington College, Harvard University, and the University of Houston. She is married to James N. Robison (also a writer), has two daughters, and currently lives in Texas.

The title of Robison's first collection of stories, *Days* (1979), suggests the nature of the stories: small slices of everyday life in the manner of James Joyce and Anton Chekhov. Collectively these twenty stories convey Robison's vision, presented without authorial comment, of an emotionally stripped, materialistic, middle-class America. Her fictional world is inhabited by lonely characters whose empty lives are unalleviated by any meaningful emotional, spiritual, or vocational commitment. They have for the most part lost the capacity to dream, feel, and act. Like characters in Samuel Beckett's play *Waiting for Godot* (1953), they spend their lives trying to fill up the time – getting drunk, watching television, and talking without communicating – until someone comes along or something happens to them to give their lives meaning. In contrast to the characters of Joyce, the characters in *Days* rarely experience epiphanies about the nature of their existence; typically they repress their feelings of emptiness and despair and do their best to avoid facing reality.

Though not overtly autobiographical, the stories in *Days* reflect (as does her subsequent work) the influence of Robison's middle-class, Catholic upbringing. There are also striking parallels between her fiction and the observations of her five brothers in her essay "The Brothers: Memories of Being Buried Alive in Boys" (1983). The influence of her brothers is apparent in her brisk dialogue and her characters' lack of expectation and surprise and avoidance of the consequences of behavior and love. These elements are incorporated into fictional

Mary Robison, circa 1991 (photograph by James N. Robison)

characters whose lives Robison depicts in unadorned prose, with an eye for details and an ear for sometimes elliptical, frequently comical speech. The world she creates is not entirely despairing. In addition to her touches of humor, the bleakness of the stories is relieved by occasional manifestations of understated hopefulness.

In the opening story of *Days,* "Kite and Paint," Robison establishes the waiting mode that recurs throughout the book. In spite of an impending hurricane, the main characters are too exhausted by life to evacuate their home. One, a divorced artist in ill health, has, like many of Robison's characters, squandered his chance for a life of meaningful work; he has neglected his talent. However, his housemate's protectiveness toward his blank canvasses embodies a meager hope – probably unfounded – that he will resume his art. Though the approaching storm reawakens his artistic impulse, the result is a series of painted kites that he intends to "waste" in the storm. In spite of the seeming frivolity of this behavior, it represents a defiance of convention and respectability that Robison expresses her admiration for in the essay "The Brothers."

Having married and divorced before entering college, Robison explores at length in *Days* the theme of failed or failing marriages and other relationships. Particularly noteworthy is "Care," in which one of the characters voices Robison's sense of the hollowness of contemporary life and relationships. Evidence of the mental and emotional ill health typical of *Days* abounds in this story: in the consumption of alcohol and other drugs; in the fascination with mindless television fare; and in the generally childish behavior of the adults. The characters have essentially become numb. Only the seemingly unstable husband, Jack, realizes that something is missing from their lives, that they are merely going through the motions. He communicates this insight to the only other person (a female friend of his wife's) who seems capable of caring; he challenges her to change but offers no advice for doing so. Thus, having identified a central problem of contemporary American life, Robison stops short of expressing optimism regarding the likelihood of its solution.

Verbalizations between characters, like those in "Care," regarding the malaise of modern American life and the need for action and change, are atypical in *Days*. Generally characters suppress their feelings of misery, apparently accepting their lot, and maintain the lie that their lives are wonderful. Such is true in "Grace," a story that evokes the corrupt glamour of F. Scott Fitzgerald's *The Great Gatsby* (1925). In return for a good time, the title character ornaments the lives of two wealthy men for whom she has no emotional attachment. Typical of the characters in *Days,* Grace lives life on the surface, unconcerned for the moral consequences of her behavior, in a world without spiritual underpinnings. She and her set are shallow, disdainful of being ordinary, and indifferent to the misfortunes of others. Robison exposes the dark realities of their existence during their tour of a rundown hotel – a sort of tour of the underworld. In this decayed relic of a glamorous past, Grace discovers homeless people living in darkness and squalor, a sight that fails to move her. After the tour, things turn ugly, nearly to the point of violence, among Grace's male rivals. Yet in spite of the evidence to the contrary, Grace considers her world a paradise, upon which she bestows her unself-consciously ironic blessing of "wonderful."

Often in *Days* that "wonderful" feeling comes from a bottle. Many characters drink excessively in an effort to fill the void in their lives, using alcohol both to cope with and avoid reality and conflict. For example, in "Weekday" a man must get drunk in order to talk to his former wife. In "Daughters" a woman avoids her father's criticism of her parenting by fleeing to the bathroom and drinking alone. Robison also portrays the disorder and emotional numbness that result from heavy drinking.

She draws on her Catholic background in several stories in *Days* to express a loss of faith in the sustaining power of religion. In "Sisters," for instance, one of the main characters is a nun who is unhappy with her chosen life. But rather than confront her problem, she tries to avoid it by "going into cloister" and "taking a vow of silence." At the same time, her sister – another unhappy person who insists her life is wonderful – is determined to be excommunicated as a way to give her life meaning. She maneuvers for a confrontation with a priest who is also unhappy with the priesthood: among the characters in *Days,* even those who have chosen a religious way of life lack spiritual conviction.

As might be expected of a writer who grew up (though apparently happily) in a household full of children, the incompetence and insensitivity of parents is a recurrent theme in *Days,* exemplified most cruelly in "Doctor's Sons," in which a son cries over

his failed marriage while his mother does all she can to avoid dealing with the reality of the situation. When informed that her daughter-in-law is living in a car, the mother nonchalantly replies that "there are worse places to live than in new Oldsmobiles." Variations on the theme of parental incompetence are also explored in "Weekday" and "Daughters," among other stories.

The somber mood of *Days* is relieved by occasional humor. In "Smoke," for example, a young man in need of a business loan from his stepfather is subjected to an absurd anecdote about Henry Kissinger in drag, then forced to spar for his "grubstake." Many such bizarre incidents occur throughout *Days*. It is in "Widower," however, that Robison best reveals her talent for comic dialogue. She creates two of her most engaging characters, a precocious brother and sister whose clever repartee lampoons their widower father's jitters over a date he has planned. Though "Widower" explores the theme of coping with illness, suffering, and the loss of a loved one (a recurrent theme in Robison's work), it is noteworthy among the stories in *Days* for the characters' use of humor as a coping mechanism, as well as for the talent Robison displays for creating complex, intelligent child characters.

Days was in general favorably received by critics, who savored Robison's precise prose, her ear for dialogue, and her incisive depictions of contemporary American life. Some critics, however, found fault with the stories, deeming them too much alike in mood and tone, overly reliant on obvious irony, and filled with characters for whom it is difficult to care.

After the publication of her novel *Oh!* (1981), in which Robison further develops her comic talents while continuing to explore the state of the middle-class American family, she published her second volume of stories, *An Amateur's Guide to the Night* (1983). Some of these thirteen stories retrace what for Robison was familiar territory. For example, "You Know Charles" explores the fear of change and relationships, and "Nothing's It" depicts the inertia of a bad romance. The shallowness, stasis, and pessimism about the possibility of change so characteristic of *Days* is cogently recaptured in "Smart," a story about an unwed pregnant woman.

But characters have many more triumphs in *An Amateur's Guide to the Night* than in *Days*. "The Nature of Almost Everything" depicts a woman's successful struggle to overcome the urge to drink as a means of relieving psychological stress. "Look at Me Go" and "Yours" express a genuine belief in the possibility of love. Indeed many of these stories reveal a growing maturity and humanity in Robison's writing. The main subject is essentially the same – the everyday lives of the American middle class – but Robison expands her repertoire, exploring new variations on old themes and creating more fully developed, likable characters. She also makes extensive use of the first-person point of view, the result being a greater variety of narrative voices than in *Days.* As Robison told interviewer Mona Simpson, part of her growth as a writer was recognizing that she had developed a set of literary clichés and was writing about characters she did not care about. She then made a conscious decision to create characters who were more engaging, stronger, and less defeated – a decision that makes *An Amateur's Guide to the Night* a less repetitious, more satisfying collection than *Days.*

Though parent/child conflicts are treated in *Days,* in "The Dictionary in the Laundry Chute" Robison explores more fully the unhealthy consequences of disaffection with the world created by parents. In this story the victim of that world is a young woman aged prematurely by an inability to eat or sleep and by psychotic episodes in which she hears voices. Her parents enlist the help of a doctor who, predictably, treats her with drugs. The flaw in this treatment is the failure to recognize that the girl's physical deterioration is merely a symptom of a greater spiritual ailment, manifesting itself in a sort of self-inflicted martyrdom that her father naively diagnoses as a case of "the blues." Clues to the cause of the daughter's ailment are evident in the father's absorption with his own well-being and his complaints of heart trouble, suggesting his incapacity for selfless love. In spite of the evidence that his daughter is extremely ill, he deludes himself into thinking that things are in fact rather normal under the circumstances.

In the title story, "An Amateur's Guide to the Night," Robison deftly reverses the roles of parent and child: an immature mother, who likes to pass herself off as her daughter's sister, corrupts her mature, hardworking child into various forms of irresponsible behavior. The daughter and narrator, Lindy, is a fully developed, likable character unlike any in *Days.* One especially admirable trait is her unwillingness to accept the limitations imposed upon her by the circumstances of her life. Though only an average student, she possesses intellectual curiosity and is a self-taught amateur astronomer. Alone in her fascination with the stars, she devotes the time when she is not in school, working, or baby-sitting her mother to the study of the heavens, an avocation that represents her desire to transcend

Dust jacket for Robison's 1988 book, in which the stories focus on characters trying to overcome the limitations of their environments

the boundaries of her secure though limiting middle-class world.

"Coach" is a lengthy, realistic exploration of the problems of an average American family. While the life of the title character revolves around his job as a football coach, his wife struggles to create her own identity as an amateur artist. When she rents a studio so she can have "a place apart," Coach is secretly pleased because it allows him to focus without distraction on football. However, their teenage daughter, largely neglected by her parents and struggling to create her own identity, interprets her mother's actions to mean her parents are separating. Though Coach had hoped to energize his daughter by taking a job in a college setting, he dismisses her intellectual and social abilities and is concerned primarily with his career. Coach fails to comprehend the meaning of his own words that "your family's either with you or you've had it" and that "you can't climb down into . . . people's hearts and change them." Ironically his family rallies around him after his daughter experiences social success in her new environment and his wife loses faith in herself as an artist, falling back into her constraining though accustomed role as a coach's wife.

One story that marks a departure in terms of setting for Robison is "In Jewel," which explores a teacher's ambiguous feelings about leaving the blue-collar coal town where she had lived most of her life. On the one hand, she wants badly to escape the grinding predictability and poverty of spirit. On the other hand, the one time she left Jewel for an extended period she found herself losing her identity and had to return home to regain her sense of self. She knows how hard it would be to leave her family again, as well as the meager accumulation of things that represents her earthly existence. Robison sums up the ambivalent feelings of security and repulsion that the familiar often arouses when she has the narrator say, "I like feeling at home. I just wish I didn't feel it here."

Like *Days* before it, *An Amateur's Guide to the Night* received largely favorable reviews, and for many of the same reasons. Critics again responded to Robison's poetic minimalist style, her finely tuned ear, and her ability to suggest the tensions underlying ordinary existence. Some critics also recognized Robison's development as a writer, seeing in these stories, with their increased warmth and complexity, a fulfillment of the promise of her earlier work. In the *Village Voice* (10 January 1984) David Leavitt claimed that "no American short-story writer speaks to our time more urgently or fondly than Robison." A minority of reviewers, however, continued to fault Robison for a lack of humanity and for indifference toward her characters.

In her third volume of short stories, *Believe Them* (1988), Robison again revisits middle-class America. Though some of the themes are familiar, all of Robison's characteristic strengths are in evidence: her descriptive power, her skill with dialogue, her sense of humor, and her intelligent insights into the middle-class American soul. As in *An Amateur's Guide to the Night,* these stories are less bleak overall than *Days,* with at least some characters showing a spark of humanity and trying to do more than just numbly exist. The strength of many of these characters – and of the collection as a whole – derives in part from Robison's continued development of her distinctive first-person narrators.

"Seizing Control" is Robison's only story with a first-person-plural ("we") point of view. The story recounts the events of one night on which five chil-

dren joyfully take charge of their lives, in part by breaking many of the rules imposed by their well-meaning parents (who are in the hospital awaiting the birth of another child). When an emergency arises, the children make their way through a blizzard to a hospital, then celebrate their accomplishment and their newfound sense of maturity in an all-night restaurant. Drawing in part on her family background and her own parents' lack of control over their children, Robison undermines the notion that parental rules are pearls of wisdom to be believed in and lived by at all cost. She also illuminates, with humor and compassion, a basic truth about the world: that growing up is a process of seizing control of one's life from one's parents and of assuming responsibility for one's actions.

The theme of personal effort and responsibility runs throughout the stories in *Believe Them.* In fact the title of one story, "Trying," could serve as a motto for the book, for Robison creates a variety of characters who on some level try to become better people. For example, the narrator of "For Real" spends her life hiding behind her disguise as a television clown, with deleterious physical, emotional, and psychological effects. Involved in a loveless relationship with a handsome but humorless German, she realizes that a marriage based on simple good-heartedness (so he can stay in the United States) would be an empty one. She then consciously tries to undergo a change of heart and fall in love with him, though her effort is thwarted and she reverts to her comic defenses when her lover breaks off their relationship.

"Trying" shows one of Robison's most compelling examples of a character struggling to transcend the limitations of circumstance. This story portrays an intelligent, witty, rebellious high-school student who, unchallenged by her teachers and scoffed at by her shallow classmates, tries to live in accordance with some sort of social conscience (however derivative of her parents' liberal political causes). In "Again, Again, Again," Robison reprises the Noonan family of "Coach," portraying them in a more optimistic light than previously. Coach is still obsessed with his career, and his wife and daughter feel like caged birds in their suburban Eden. But Robison portrays a family struggling (like one of Coach's teams), through sheer repetition and effort, to achieve some sort of perfection, or at least good-natured accommodation, in their lives.

Other stories in *Believe Them* depict characters exhausting their energies trying to escape their lives for something different, though not necessarily better, than what they already have. In "While Home" a young man undergoing the difficult transition from adolescence to adulthood tries to escape his Ohio hometown and the embrace of his family for the glamour of life as a Hollywood actor. In "Your Errant Mom," developed in narrative fragments, a self-centered woman deserts her husband and daughters (whom she loves) for a wealthy boyfriend who can keep her in the materialistic luxury to which she aspires.

Believe Them received the same level of critical praise as Robison's previous two collections. Larry McCaffery (*New York Times Book Review,* 31 July 1988) and other critics applauded the balance and variety of the stories that Robison was able to create through her usual careful control of details of character and setting. Some critics, however, continued to find Robison's work too attentive to surfaces and lacking in psychological and emotional depth.

Mary Robison's work has sometimes been criticized for its authorial detachment and seeming avoidance of human depth. But most critics have recognized the logical fusion of style and substance embodied in her stories. Human depths are not neglected but are rather intimated through details of setting, action, and especially dialogue. Robison is an astute observer and critic of the American mid-dle class whose stories are especially relevant to current conditions. As Bruce Bawer notes in his *Diminishing Fictions* (1988), Robison has inspired some lesser imitators, which is also evidence of her literary influence. Though her 1991 novel, *Subtraction,* did little to advance her career, it may be only a matter of time before Robison's increasingly mature and diverse short stories gain the wider readership they deserve.

Interview:
Mona Simpson, "Interview: Mary Robison," *Vogue,* 174 (June 1984): 156, 158.

References:
Bruce Bawer, "The Literary Brat Pack," in his *Diminishing Fictions: Essays on the Modern American Novel and Its Critics* (Saint Paul: Graywolf, 1988), pp. 314–323;
Sven Birkerts, "The School of Gordon Lish," in his *An Artificial Wilderness: Essays on 20th-Century Literature* (New York: Morrow, 1987), pp. 251–263;
Patrick Meanor, "Mary Robison," in *Critical Survey of Short Fiction,* edited by Frank N. Magill (Englewood Cliffs, N.J.: Salem, 1992), pp. 2010–2017;
Susan Mernit, "The State of the Short Story," *Virginia Quarterly Review,* 62 (Spring 1986): 302–311.

James Salter

(10 June 1925 –   )

William Dowie
Southeastern Louisiana University

BOOKS: *The Hunters* (New York: Harper, 1956; London: Heinemann, 1957; abridged edition, London: Pan, 1958);

The Arm of Flesh (New York: Harper, 1961; London: Cassell, 1962);

A Sport and a Pastime (Garden City, N.Y.: Doubleday, 1967; Harmondsworth, U.K. & New York: Penguin, 1980);

Light Years (New York: Random House, 1975; London: Bodley Head, 1976);

Solo Faces (Boston: Little, Brown, 1979; London: Collins, 1980);

Dusk and Other Stories (San Francisco: North Point, 1988; London: Cape, 1990).

SELECTED PERIODICAL PUBLICATIONS –
UNCOLLECTED: "The Captain's Wife," *Esquire,* 105 (June 1986): 130–139;

"Winter of the Lion," *Esquire,* 112 (July 1989): 69–76;

"A Single Daring Act," *Grand Street,* 9 (Spring 1990): 59–87;

"Europe," *Esquire,* 114 (December 1990): 104–114, 204–210;

"You Must," *Esquire,* 117 (December 1992): 145–156.

James Salter is an artist, living or dying by his style, which is original, spare, and soulful. His work is admired more by his peers than by the public. Saul Bellow, Graham Greene, Mavis Gallant, John Irving, and Reynolds Price, among others, have all praised his work convincingly. Four of his stories are in O. Henry prize collections; one ("Foreign Shores") appears in the 1984 *Best American Stories* anthology; and one story, "Akhnilo," is anthologized in *American Short Story Masterpieces* (1989), edited by Raymond Carver. Salter received the 1989 P.E.N./Faulkner Award for fiction in recognition of his collection *Dusk and Other Stories* (1988).

Reviewers and critics agree that Salter is important; it has become almost a critical cliché to speak of him as an underrated writer, even "the most underrated underrated writer," as James Wolcott dubbed him in *Vanity Fair* (June 1985). His admirers, devout in their loyalty, pass his name along to the uninitiated with the trust of a personal secret.

What they say about his writing is that it is lyrical and canny and that his best work – passages from *A Sport and a Pastime* (1967), *Light Years* (1975), *Solo Faces* (1979), and *Dusk* – will take the reader's breath away because of sudden glimpses deep into the pool of life. Indeed it is hard to read a Salter story or novel without being ambushed by recognitions, things one knew instinctively but never thought about or acted on. Salter believes in the power of language to move readers, and he stakes much of his fictional gamble on brief, piercing passages. In the novel *Light Years* he writes about a book a character is reading: "The power to change one's life comes from a paragraph, a lone remark. The lines that penetrate us are slender, like the flukes that live in river water and enter the bodies of swimmers." This declaration could stand as Salter's credo. He constantly strives for such illuminations, usually the effect of a final sentence that crystallizes what has gone before.

James Salter was born James Horowitz in New Jersey on 10 June 1925. His father was an engineer. Salter grew up in New York City only a few blocks from the Metropolitan Museum of Art. As a boy he painted, drew, and wrote. While attending the Horace Mann School in Riverdale (1938–1942), he worked on the literary magazine, won mention in a national poetry contest, and had poems published in *Poetry* magazine. Accepted at Stanford University, Salter was set to go west when his father, who had graduated first in his class at West Point, arranged a second alternate's appointment for his son. Salter took the entrance exam as a filial favor, never expecting both the principal and first alternate to fail. As he recalls in his 1992 essay "You Must," "Seventeen, vain, and spoiled by poems, I prepared to

James Salter, circa 1979 (photograph by Lana Rys)

enter a remote West Point." After initially rebelling against the rigidity of a place he compares, with its dark passages and Gothic facades, to James Joyce's Conglowes Wood College, Salter accepted the discipline as an arrow pointing toward the ongoing struggle of World War II. He graduated in 1945 and immediately entered the air force, too late for the war he describes as "the great forge of my time. It was the reality of the grown-up world when I entered it (that world) and its indelible imprint has never gone."

Salter's career as an air-force pilot lasted twelve years, during which time he kept his literary interests to himself since any sign of intellectual ability usually put one at risk of being assigned a desk job. In fact air-force regulations at the time forbade publication of anything that had not been previously approved by headquarters. Because of the

necessity of keeping his two lives separate, he adopted the pen name James Salter when he first tried his hand at a novel while stationed in Honolulu in 1946. It was finished in 1949 and turned down by publishers, though Harper and Brothers expressed interest and wanted to see his next. In 1950, still in the air force, he completed an M.A. in international affairs at Georgetown University. The year was also memorable because it marked his first visit to Paris, signaling the end of his formal education and the beginning of another kind, as he says in the essay "Europe" (1990): "not the lessons of school but something more elevated, a view of how to endure: how to have leisure, love, food, and conversation, how to look at nakedness, architecture, streets. . . . In Europe the shadow of history falls upon you and, knowing none of it, you realize suddenly how small you are." Part of the enlargement

Salter experienced was literary, as he read more by European writers, eventually counting among his exemplars André Gide, Louis-Ferdinand Céline, Henry de Montherlant, Jean Genet, and, especially, Isaac Babel. Europe thereafter would become a permanent recourse, Salter returning whenever possible throughout his life, usually to rent houses in provincial towns.

In 1951 Salter served for six months in Korea, where he flew one hundred combat missions. Later that same year he returned to Fort Meyer, Virginia, to marry a Washington, D.C., woman, Ann Altemus. His air-force career progressed through assignments to fighter squadrons in the United States (1951–1953) and Germany (1954–1957), while he used his spare time on weekends and at night to write. When his first novel, *The Hunters,* was published in 1956, it was the signal he needed to switch careers. He resigned from the air force in 1957 (with a wife and two small children); returned to the United States to live in the Hudson Valley, first in Grandview, then in 1958 in New York City; and became committed to pursuing a life of writing.

The Hunters, based upon Salter's aerial combat in Korea, conveys with an assured voice the experience of being a fighter pilot under fire. Neither this book, however, nor its less accomplished successor, *The Arm of Flesh* (1961), which draws on his flying career as well, amounts to more than an apprenticeship in writing. Able to look at his own work with a cold eye, Salter has refused the offer of North Point Press, which has published handsome new editions of his other novels, to reprint the early books.

In 1962 twins were born into the Salter family. Seeking ways to supplement his writing income, Salter met Lane Slate, a television writer, and the two collaborated on a documentary film about collegiate football, *Team Team Team,* which was awarded first prize at the Venice Film Festival. Other documentaries followed, including a ten-part series on the circus for public television and a film for CBS about contemporary American painters, an abiding interest of Salter since his youth. In the mid 1960s offers came to write for Hollywood. Four of Salter's filmscripts were made into movies, the best known of which is *Downhill Racer* (1969).

Not until the publication of *A Sport and a Pastime*, a novel Reynolds Price (*New York Times Book Review,* 2 June 1984) judged "as nearly perfect as any American fiction I know," did Salter's writing career pass from possibility to actuality. It is a classic tale of youth and desire, as well as a hymn to provincial France and a young woman that belongs to it so thoroughly that she embodies its abiding beauty, narrowness, and glory.

Salter's first short story, "Am Strand von Tanger" (*Paris Review,* Fall 1968; collected in *Dusk*), did not appear until over a decade after his initial novel. The story, like *A Sport and a Pastime,* tells of an American youth abroad; in the story he is an aspiring artist living in Barcelona. The image of the developing artist dominates Salter's early short fiction, appearing in three other stories published in the *Paris Review:* "The Cinema" (Summer 1970), "The Destruction of the Goetheanum" (Winter 1971), and "Via Negativa" (Fall 1972) – all in *Dusk.* Together his *Paris Review* stories constitute Salter's "Portrait of the Artist as a Young Man," although clearly their themes are not exclusively about art. The young male protagonist in each of the stories has a desire for greatness and a need to have the image of his own greatness confirmed by someone else, a woman. Aside from this, each version of the artist differs.

Of the early stories "Dirt" (in *Dusk;* originally titled "Cowboys" in *Carolina Quarterly,* Spring 1971) is unique for its southwestern setting, flat tone, and blue-collar characters. There are no artists as such, although the grizzled American day laborer, Harry Mies, mixes concrete and pours foundations with the care of one. Readers glimpse Harry's life as it nears its end; the integrity of his work; the loyalty of his young helper; and the joy of the stories the old man likes to tell of California and days gone by. Lives, the tale implies, have a way of touching, each person's story impinging on others. Harry will one day be a legend like those in his stories. After he dies and his helper, Billy, heads to Mexico with a local girl, "they told each other stories of their life." The title, "Dirt," reflects both the earth on which Billy is crawling at the outset and the earth in which Harry is laid to rest. Life whisks by, and only tales and memories remain.

Divorced in 1975, Salter began living with writer Kay Eldredge in 1976, and the two have been together since, wintering in Aspen, Colorado, where Salter has been going since 1962, and summering on Long Island. As often as possible, usually at least once a year, they go abroad, spending weeks, sometimes longer, in France, Italy, or England. One such visit in 1985 to Paris was timed to coincide with the birth of their son.

The genre of the novel consumed most of Salter's creative energy in the 1970s, but the short story drew his attention in the 1980s. Six stories were published in magazines, and in 1988 *Dusk* was published.

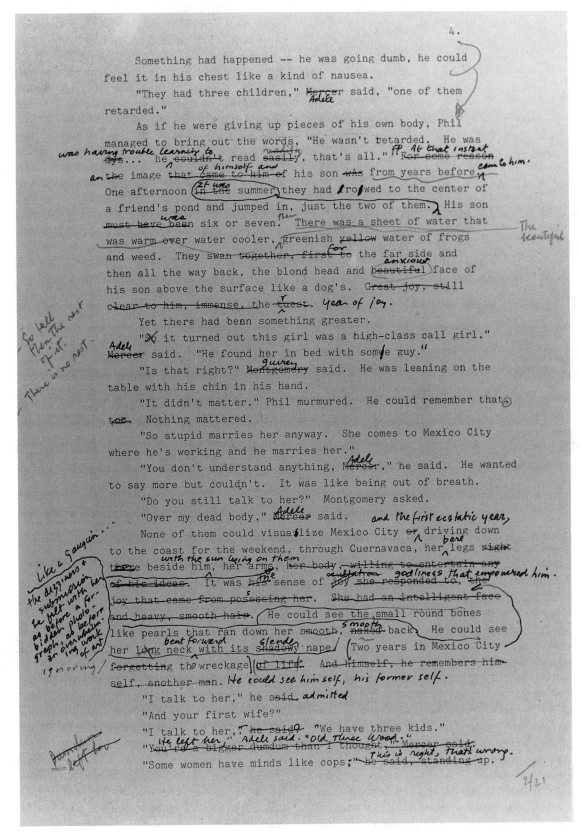

Page from a draft for the story "Comet," accepted for publication in the July 1993 issue of Esquire *(by permission of James Salter)*

James Salter (photograph by Lana Rys)

Three of Salter's 1980s stories deal with men's lives, three with women's. "Akhnilo" (1981) and "Lost Sons" (1983) focus on men confronting their pasts. In the case of Dartmouth graduate Eddie Fenn in "Akhnilo," the past means failure to follow his dreams and to make money. One evening he awakens to what he imagines to be the distant sounds of those dreams, but it is too late. Ed Reemstma in "Lost Sons" returns to a reunion of his college class, hoping to revise somehow his outcast standing, only to find that the past is irreversible and that he still lives in its long shadow.

The male characters in "American Express" (1988), Salter's own favorite among his stories, are anything but failures or outcasts. Frank and Alan are lawyers and sons of lawyers, who have come down the fast track of success and are on holiday in Europe, eventually picking up an Italian schoolgirl. Salter says (in an unpublished interview) that the story "evolved from long days spent in the trash heap of things heard, known, imagined." Although

it is his longest story, it is a masterpiece of compression, as if Tom Wolfe's *Bonfire of the Vanities* (1987) had been distilled into twenty-two pages. "American Express" is a story of vanity; New York life; eastern wealth; the American dream of success, which is always to some extent a wet dream; and finally of time passing. Salter's tone is imbued with sympathy, nostalgia, and respect for each character's weakness. In all his stories, his attitude can be described by what one of the lawyers says in "American Express": "No defendant was too guilty, no case too clear-cut." Each character, even minor ones, is drawn so carefully that whole lives are discerned in an instant.

"Dusk," first published as "The Fields at Dusk" in *Esquire* (August 1984), is among Salter's best stories, with all his characteristic strengths of compression, detail, juxtaposition, and telling metaphor combining in a portrait of a forty-six-year-old woman who has survived losses and defeats only to be faced with one more. Her husband gone and her son dead, Mrs. Chandler maintains herself as she maintains her beautiful Hamptons house – with dignity. This dignity remains intact even after Bill, a man of whom she has grown fond, announces that his wife has come back and that he will not be seeing Mrs. Chandler anymore. The story closes with a dazzling, inspired connection by Salter, as he describes Mrs. Chandler first looking at a mirror realizing "she would never be younger," then turning her thoughts to geese being hunted in the surrounding fields at dusk, imagining one particular bird lying bleeding in the grass: "She went around and turned on lights. The rain was coming down, the sea was crashing, a comrade lay dead in the whirling darkness."

Both "Foreign Shores" (1983) and "Twenty Minutes" (1988) are about women of a class comparable to Mrs. Chandler. The settings are different – one in the Hamptons, the other out west, probably in Colorado – but the women are alike in that they are no longer married (both former husbands are in California) and they are young, knowledgeable, and affluent enough to live well. Salter's empathy with these women is remarkable. In "Foreign Shores" readers meet Gloria and see her shock at the explicit letters her Dutch au pair has been receiving; the ending reveals a surprising jolt of jealousy. In "Twenty Minutes" Jane Vare, crushed by her horse falling on her, lies alone in the fields and knows she will die before long. She remembers the highs and lows of her life. The tale is a tour de force, taking about twenty minutes to read but made resonant by the poignancy of her memories and the tapestry they create.

In the fall semesters of 1987 and 1989 Salter taught at the Iowa Writers' Workshop, and in spring 1991 at the University of Houston; he had been a writer in residence at Vassar in 1986. He continues to spend his winters in Colorado and summers on Long Island, after 1985 in the new house he had built amid fields in Bridgehampton. He is friendly with other writers and artistic and literary people who live on this northeast corner of the island. About his place – his significance in this community and in the larger one of writers present and past – he is hopeful, perhaps even expectant, of confirmation by a wider reading public. He has all the confidence, but none of the arrogance, of genius, and he takes the long view of history because he knows the scroll of writers whose fame came only after death.

One of Salter's favorite authors, Babel, said he did not write, he composed. One could say the same about James Salter. He is a composer: his three best novels are like sonatas, and his finest short stories are like arias.

Interview:

Robert Burke, "Interview with James Salter," *Bloomsbury Review,* 8 (May–June 1988): 3, 6, 18.

References:

Adam Begley, "A Few Well-Chosen Words," *New York Times Magazine,* 28 October 1990, pp. 40–43, 80–85;

William Dowie, "A Final Glory: The Novels of James Salter," *College English,* 50 (January 1988): 74–88;

Dowie, "*Solo Faces:* American Tradition and the Individual Talent," in *Essays on the Literature of Mountaineering,* edited by Armand E. Singer (Morgantown: West Virginia University Press, 1982), pp. 118–127;

Margaret Winchell Miller, "Glimpses of a Secular Holy Land: The Novels of James Salter," *Hollins Critic,* 19, no. 1 (1982): 1–13.

Eve Shelnutt

(29 August 1941 –)

Daniel Lowe
Community College of Allegheny County

BOOKS: *Two Stories* (Santa Barbara, Cal.: Black
Sparrow, 1977);
The Love Child (Santa Barbara, Cal.: Black Sparrow,
1979);
Descant (Winston-Salem, N.C.: Palaemon, 1982);
The Formal Voice (Santa Barbara, Cal.: Black Spar-
row, 1982);
Air and Salt (Pittsburgh: Carnegie Mellon Univer-
sity Press / London: Feffer & Simons, 1983);
The Musician (Santa Rosa, Cal.: Black Sparrow,
1987);
The Magic Pencil: Teaching Children Creative Writing
(Atlanta: Peachtree, 1988);
Recital in a Private Home (Pittsburgh: Carnegie Mel-
lon University Press, 1989);
The Writing Room: Keys to the Craft of Fiction and Poetry
(Marietta, Ga.: Longstreet, 1989);
First a Long Hesitation (Pittsburgh: Carnegie Mellon
University Press, 1991).

OTHER: "Transforming Experience into Fiction,"
in *Creative Writing in America: Theory and Peda-
gogy,* edited by Joseph Moxley (Urbana, Ill.:
NCTE, 1989), pp. 151–168;
Writing: The Translation of Memory, edited by Shelnutt
(New York: Macmillan, 1990);
The Confidence Woman: 26 Women Writers at Work, ed-
ited by Shelnutt (Atlanta: Longstreet, 1991);
My Poor Elephant: 28 Male Writers at Work, edited by
Shelnutt (Atlanta: Longstreet, 1992).

SELECTED PERIODICAL PUBLICATIONS –
UNCOLLECTED: "Post-Modern Fiction: The
Easy Route," *Cream City Review,* 13 (1989): 56–
59;
"Contemporary Southern Fiction: *Is* It What We
Recognize?," *Mississippi Quarterly,* 43 (Winter
1990): 3–9;
"A Contemporary Southern Writer's Predicament:
Removing the Rose-Colored Glasses,"
Southern Quarterly, 30 (Fall 1991): 1–6.

Eve Shelnutt

Eve Shelnutt's short stories have appeared in
nearly ten anthologies and sixty journals, including
such prestigious literary magazines as the *Virginia
Quarterly Review, Ploughshares,* and *Prairie Schooner.*
But Shelnutt has not had the recognition and critical
acclaim that many of her contemporaries, such as
Tobias Wolff and Susan Minot, have enjoyed. Her
three short-story collections have been published by

a relatively small company, Black Sparrow Press, and though they have sold well, they have not been reviewed in major magazines and newspapers. Her stories are more difficult, the study of character and theme more intensely psychological, the language more lyrical, and, because of these distinctions, her work less accessible to readers than the fiction of more-popular writers. Though she is often classified as a "southern writer," her fiction does not provide the commonly identifiable traits of southern literature, such as typical southern tradition, history, and characters. Instead her stories offer a meticulous, unsentimental consideration of the family, its psychological landscape inside and outside the walls of a home and the windows of a car, with the South as little more than setting. As Fred Chappell has said (in the *Columbia* [S.C.] *State,* 1 August 1982), Eve Shelnutt's work does not "descend in fanciful manner from Eudora Welty or Katherine Anne Porter. . . . Shelnutt writes like no one else at all."

Shelnutt's work does not mirror her upbringing, but the artifacts of her childhood – both literal and experiential – are present in the textures of the stories. Born Eve Brown Waldrop in Spartanburg, South Carolina, on 29 August 1941, Shelnutt spent her childhood in many places, and none for long. Her father, James Marion Waldrop, was a writer, radio and television broadcaster, and sometime actor who criss-crossed the country in pursuit of his careers. Along with her mother, Evelyn Brock Waldrop, and Shelnutt's two sisters, Anne and Cynthia, she accompanied her father on these trips, though he frequently left them to stay in temporary homes while he sought better employment opportunities elsewhere. Her mother, a trained musician, worked in the public schools in his absence, giving voice and violin lessons to feed and clothe the children until Shelnutt's father returned. During these years she and her sisters, rarely in any school for long, were encouraged to read and indeed read voraciously during the long trips from state to state. When Shelnutt was sixteen, and her parents' marriage was over, she, her mother, and sisters moved into a small house in Greenville, South Carolina, near the mother's relatives.

In 1961, at age twenty, Shelnutt met her first husband, James William Shelnutt, a graduate student in engineering at the General Motors Institute in Flint, Michigan. After they married later that year, her husband was drafted into the army and stationed at Fort Walton Beach, Florida, where Eve Shelnutt gave birth to her only child, Gregory William Shelnutt. After her husband was transferred to Dayton, Ohio, she signed up at Wright State Uni-

versity for a creative-writing class with poet Dick Allen. Under Allen's tutelage Shelnutt wrote her first stories, one of which won the *Mademoiselle* Fiction Award. In 1968, after her divorce, Shelnutt began taking regular day classes at Wright State, and she wrote news stories for Dayton papers. She finished her B.A. in English in 1972 at the University of Cincinnati; then, under the auspices of a Randall Jarrell Fellowship, she completed her M.F.A. in 1973 at the University of North Carolina at Greensboro, where she studied with Chappell.

At Greensboro, Shelnutt began writing the stories that would eventually be included in her first full-length collection, *The Love Child* (1979). She dedicated the book to Chappell, a fact that shows the influence he had over Shelnutt's developing sense of fiction. After leaving Greensboro, Shelnutt worked briefly as a journalist in Cincinnati before becoming in 1974 an assistant professor at Western Michigan University in Kalamazoo. There she lived with her son for six years, encouraging his budding interest in sculpture, while she taught journalism and fiction writing and worked on her stories and poetry. From Kalamazoo, Shelnutt continued to send her stories to Chappell.

The characters in Shelnutt's early stories are fathers who are often absent, mothers who are overwrought and isolated because of this absence, and the daughters of these parents. The daughters' lives are studied in detail, particularly how their memories of childhood and adolescence are brought to bear on their lives as adults. The characters are recognizable from story to story, though their names change. Shelnutt has said that she chooses names from story to story not for consistency but for how they may resonate for her in the process of writing a particular story. The names gain significance because they are names she has known from her childhood. The titles of the stories in *The Love Child* are often one word, as is the case with "Grace," "Angel," "Feet," "Litany," "Light," "Lovers," "Good," and "Children." Shelnutt has said that she often uses such one-word titles as ideas for stories before she begins writing them. The word is often defined in the context of the characters' lives. For instance, at the beginning of the story "Good," Lois (a mother) says of a fat man who is courting her, "He's good, you know?" By story's end, this definition of *good* has come to mean, essentially, "ordinary" or "insignificant," as the man becomes almost comical when compared to the absent father.

The Love Child can best be approached by understanding that it is essentially built on the tripar-

Shelnutt and her son, Gregory William Shelnutt, in Greensboro, North Carolina, 1973

her." Her father's protectiveness is a revelation for the girl: "the daughter, who had not yet felt the movement of the body which makes a woman go senseless in the hold of a man, felt it then, and Jim slapped the counter, waking her from the first real sleep." The story is about the girl's budding awareness of her sexuality and how it is shaped by her father during this visit, one that seems relatively meaningless for him. Toward the end of the story, Jim is forced to close the restaurant, and the girl returns home, after which she sees him rarely: "In time, the daughter became the kind of woman who owns few things. She didn't think about owning a man in marriage. . . . And of the men she had, she didn't ask if they were married, or had been, or wanted to be." The girl becomes the kind of woman "who frightens some men" and "who does not belong." The story ends with the dreaming father envisioning his daughter as "armless like the first fish in first-water time when air and salt met."

The psychological impact of the father on his daughter's life is profound and crystallizes during the visit, but it is in no way fully explainable. The daughter does not becomes a "moral" woman; she has lovers and is indifferent to their marital status. The roots of who she has become are not discernible, because they reach back to primordial times "when air and salt met." The daughter is fairly representative of the daughters throughout *The Love Child*. Family history and the characters' memories of it emerge from human instinct to shape a present-day morality that is unusual and disturbing. This tenuous connection between memory, morality, and raw instinct is the mystery of Shelnutt's work that she continually explores. Her stories do not present the kind of complete theory of memory that was the concern of Marcel Proust, but her study of the power of memory is no less urgent.

In *The Love Child*, the medium for this study of memory is Shelnutt's dense, poetic language. Her work has rarely been categorized, though her early work has been compared to that of Welty and William Goyen. If Shelnutt has developed a reputation as a writer whose work is "difficult," it is because of her rich, dense, often elliptical style. There are stories in *The Love Child* that are straightforward, even though the writing is lyrical: "The Apprentice," "In the Absence of Strangers," and "The Love Child." But the style of most of the stories might best be represented by this opening passage from "Children": "It is noon when Claire begins screaming, the high-C of arch suffering (history and waste) in a repertory which will never contain cancer of the bone marrow or one lost eye. So: who cares? Ex-

tite foundation of memory, language, and music. But memory, or Shelnutt's sense of what she calls the "released past," is the most important of these. In almost every story the main character's actions are driven by a recollection of familial history: a daughter seeks refuge in lovers who are similar to her father; a woman's memory of the isolation of her mother conditions her intimacy. In Shelnutt's work the connection between a character's memory and present life is psychologically and morally complex.

The first story in the collection, "Grace," illustrates this complexity. A daughter, about eleven years old, goes to visit Jim, her father, who has recently become the proprietor of a restaurant. The story opens with a description of the restaurant and a portrait of the charming father outside the context of his family. The daughter's visit is far more significant for her than for her father, who even forgets that she is coming. After he picks her up from the Greyhound bus station, he takes her to the restaurant and announces, "I'll kill anybody who touches

cept, afterwards, her body will not look quite the same – puffiness under the eyes and on the belly a mound of fat and in the shoulders what looks like fat but is instead a realignment of wings – clipped, a curving inward like a second set of ribs protecting a second stomach, and she slows down, as if chewing thoughtfully." Shelnutt then offers more elaborately constructed sentences full of images that provide a kind of poetic portrait of Claire in her immediate psychological state. As the story is told, not in chronological order, readers learn the importance of the poetic portrait at the moment Claire screams: it is her epiphanic moment, after which she will be forever changed. For Shelnutt language is more than a vehicle for telling a story; it is, essentially, the instrument she uses to construct imagination and from which all components of her stories emerge. That the language is so lyrical is a testament to the importance of music in Shelnutt's work. The music is principally classical. Many of the stories mention composers, and even when the characters are not accomplished musicians, they may sing or play pop songs on the piano. Three stories in *The Love Child*, "Angel," "The Virgin," and "Children," have central characters who are musicians or teach music, and the final story of the collection is titled "Obbligato." The mothers in several of the stories have played classical music or insist that their daughters listen to music, as did Shelnutt's own mother.

Of the stories in *The Love Child*, critic Shirley Clay Scott wrote, "They are difficult and different, and they seem – almost shockingly – the product of a consciousness which either emerged full-blown or somehow made itself" (*American Book Review*, 1979). The comment is accurate because of Shelnutt's almost musical formalism, her poetic language, and her study of the origins of and connection between memory and morality. Some of the style and substance of *The Love Child* shows up in her later work.

In fall 1980 Shelnutt left Western Michigan University to teach in the M.F.A. program at the University of Pittsburgh. It is evidence of her success as a teacher that many of her students have published their own work in books and literary magazines. Shelnutt has published several books on the teaching of writing. Accompanying Shelnutt to Pittsburgh was writer Mark L. Shelton, who shortly thereafter (in 1981) became Shelnutt's second husband. In 1982 Black Sparrow Press published her book of stories *The Formal Voice*.

The collection deals with many of the same themes and characters that were explored in *The Love Child*. Shelnutt continues to study the impact of family history on memory and morality, and the

stories work with the same heightened level of language and syntax that Chappell has described as "lyric intensity." There remains a kind of musical formalism to the stories, as well as musical imagery and some characters who are musicians. The titles reveal the same economy of focus, as in "Sorrow," "Indigo," "Timing," "Prognosis," "Ineffable," "Ligature," and "Craving." But in most of the stories the writing is more polished and consistent. There is the sense that Shelnutt has completed her apprenticeship as a writer and that the stories, because of their consistency, were written over a shorter expanse of time. The most significant change in this collection is the degree to which the poetry of Wallace Stevens and Elizabeth Bishop influenced Shelnutt's writing. The book opens with an epigraph from Stevens, as do two of the stories, while another is titled "The Idea of Order." Four of the stories open with epigraphs by Bishop.

Many of these stories are about the sudden changes in characters' lives that result from encounters with others. These are encounters that become powerful because of a preexisting psychology shaped by memory and family history. When these characters experience their frequently disturbing epiphanic moments, their world is reordered, rearranged.

The Formal Voice opens with "Driving with 'Raoul,' " in which a female, first-person narrator tells the story of how she drives from town to town with a man she calls Raoul, though she knows his real name and chooses not to speak it. The choice is made because speaking Raoul's real name would allow the ordinary elements of his life to intrude on their intimacy, and this ordinariness may blunt desire and passion. The narrator and Raoul make love at every stop, sometimes between stops. Frequently he addresses her condescendingly in the names he's given to her: "Sweetness, I am once again – ah yes – tumescent. Consider it." When the narrator says, "We should have met before, Raoul," he says, "Sadness: You are about to tread on territory no one can touch without being sad. Do not do it. I will kill you if you do it." Raoul knows something that the narrator will learn: that memory pulled into the present, especially in a present as narrowly defined as theirs, will drastically alter their relationship.

The narrator learns from Raoul's eventual betrayal and abandonment of her that her passion for him was rooted in a previous, subconscious relationship she had with her father. Her knowledge of the connection between her love for Raoul and for her father creates a change in her, an ordering of

Early draft of the story "Voice," in The Musician.

2. Summer, 1950

It was the season when odor rose like invisible flame against the landscape of suffocating heat. Beneath the burnt grass and withered kudsu, rodents, skunks, knots of insects were dying, for we saw daily buzzards circling the folds of the hills.

The hills lay belly-up and reddish against the skyline, the kudsu, with nothing to hold it, having slipped like a robe downward. As if to anchor these dead or sleeping Buddhas, an occassional tree rose from their navels. Without the trees, they might have rolled down into the valley, leaving the horizon deserted and more still.

We waited. And Athough we were accustomed to waiting but, always, before, we had waited in towns, tethered, it seemed, at a carnival we might join. We had last come from Ventura where the heat had been assuaged by wind from the ocean. When it was especially hot, we drove to the beaches where black rock jutted over the shoreline. I might have seen the exposed bellies of the rock as Buddha-like but for the rub of wind, too constant, too insistent, for such images of meditation.

Only at the ocean did the California expansiveness Father had spoken of lured us with seem real. We were more accustomed to the peach groves of South Carolina consuming miles of land until the horizon absorbed the stubby trees, the weight of peaches. Croves of orage & lemon tree had left us unmoved.

Early draft for "Voice," collected in The Musician *(by permission of Eve Shelnutt)*

chaos that did not exist before. Such order restructures the narrator's perception of her life. She will not find the kind of passion with another man that she had with Raoul, though she may be condemned to seeking it.

Such passion governs the lives of many of the women in *The Formal Voice*. Few are able to sustain it, and none finds the perpetuated, isolated intimacy she seeks with men. Shelnutt explores this theme again in the title story. The main character is Annie, who, amid memories of her father and occasional visits from her mother, is living with a man named William, during summer in the South, away from her job at a college. As the story unfolds, William is revealed as a good but ordinary man: he drives a truck, buys a dog, and builds a doghouse. Annie, on the other hand, is gaining a fuller sense of how she is not ordinary: she has a vision of an ordinary dressing room in a women's clothing store as a Belsen bathhouse (images of the Holocaust appear in several Shelnutt stories); she is developing an interest in a former student who is "a boy" and who she imagines will come to understand her; and she is dismayed by her mother's loss of interest in the classical music that filled Annie's childhood. At the story's conclusion Annie is lying with William in bed at night, telling him the story of how she first noticed him as he passed her on the street. He was banging on the side of the truck to get her attention. This moved Annie because of a memory of her adolescence when she was still living with her father, mother, and sisters. She says, "I think I was very sad then; I didn't know it." She describes her memories of a street she walked each day and of a man who banged on the side of his car each time he passed her on the street. Annie says, "That is what you did when you first saw me. . . . I noticed you." After she has spoken and William has been quiet for several minutes, he asks her, "Does that mean you will leave me?" Annie's response is "S-s-s-sh. Listen: the trees." This is the end of the story, but the last line is not an indication that Annie cannot answer William, because almost certainly she will leave him; rather, it is an indication of how little William has understood the significance of the story she has tried to tell. Annie tells him the story out of hope that he will understand the connection between her childhood memory and her memory of the first time she saw him. William's banging on the truck was a sudden and unexpected juxtaposition of two different moments in time that suddenly changed Annie's life and offered a promised intimacy that William was finally unable to provide. An ordinary man, he is able only to understand what Annie's story may mean for him. He will never hear what Annie does when she listens to the trees, so she will have to leave him.

Of the stories in *The Formal Voice*, critic John Baskin wrote, "Miss Shelnutt does not care at all for instruction . . . believing, instead, in feelings, the language of the body when, in certain moments, truth descends like a cleaver. . . . The stories are a testament to memory, reflection, wordless intimacy" (*Yale Review*, 1982). But the intimacy is wordless in part because the men are unable (like William) or unwilling (like Raoul) to learn to speak of it. Frequently, lovemaking becomes only the temporary interpreter of intimacy. Too frequently the men in Shelnutt's work are insensitive to how they have reshaped, reordered, and rearranged women's lives. Thus the women in *The Formal Voice* remain essentially separate from the men, with only the hope of a future unconditional intimacy to keep them from the abyss of despair.

The year before Shelnutt left the University of Pittsburgh for a professorship at Ohio University in 1988, her third full-length book of stories, *The Musician*, was published. As in *The Formal Voice*, the stories show the influence of Stevens and Bishop, as quotations from each poet provide epigraphs for two stories. (One of the stories has the same title as the Bishop poem "Questions of Travel.") The collection opens with a Stevens epigraph: "The house was quiet because it had to be. The quiet was part of the meaning. . . ." The epigraph is appropriate because once again the principal obsession in the fiction is the family and its psychological origins, and, in many of the stories, there are tensions that are not spoken of out of the characters' shame, sadness, fear, anger, or despair. So in these stories, "the quiet" is part of the meaning.

In *The Musician* the titles of the stories are again brief, as in the cases of "Angelus," "Voice," "Andantino," "Family," "Setting," and "Swannery," and they continue the same sophistication of form as well as musical influences. The principal difference between this collection and the previous ones is that several stories in it do not rely on the dense syntax and poetic language that marks Shelnutt's earlier work.

Shelnutt often comments on writers such as Ernest Hemingway, who, because his writing style never changed, was essentially condemned to write the same kind of story or novel over and over again. Shelnutt contends that if a writer depends too heavily on any particular aspect of writing then the writer must give up that dependency in order to develop. By the time she had begun working on *The*

*Cover for Shelnutt's 1987 book, stories written in a leaner, more
straightforward style than her earlier works*

Musician, Shelnutt had begun to consider her own dependency on poetic language.

In *The Musician* the results of her moving away from lyrical prose are stories such as "Purity" and "Renters." "Purity" tells the story of "two sets of identical twins, identical twin-wise, and set to set" who grow up in a small town in North Carolina. The story is told from the point of view of the conservative townspeople who watch the brothers mature, pick out similar pairs of wing-tip shoes, and ride motorcycles through town during city parades. The story is largely comic, as the townspeople begin to depend on the boys as a kind of carnival or sideshow act they look forward to seeing each year, and it ends with the boys finding wives and leaving town, which creates a nameless void for the townspeople.

The story is noteworthy because it is unlike any other Shelnutt story, particularly with regard to character, point of view, and language. Rather than the intimacy of the family, she explores the consciousness of a small southern town. The language is less introspective and poetic, and the sentences are shorter and easier to read.

This sparer, leaner style works more powerfully in the story "Renters." The circumstances of the characters are not essentially different from many other Shelnutt stories: a father has returned home after a five-month absence; his wife and three daughters have been waiting for him. The story opens with these sentences: "There are five people in this family. I stand at the dining room door because my sister is laying out the silver – heavy forks and knives with silver handles. I remember from a dinner conversation that they were the best Royal had for sale that wealthy year of my parents' marriage."

Throughout "Renters," Shelnutt maintains this lean use of language. The father has come home without a job, and the mother has to have money to fix the car. As the family sits down to dinner at an ornately laid table, the mother tells the father she needs money, which results in an argument that drives the daughters away from the table. After the daughters have gone to bed, the narrator wakes from a disturbing dream to hear the sounds of her parents beginning to make love. Through real or created illness, she begins to moan, running into the bathroom and lying on the floor, after which, out of frustration and anger, the father leaves the house.

The story ends with the narrator walking slowly back to her bedroom. Her elder sister, Sara, speaks to her in "a voice I have never heard her use, 'It's all right. Someday we'll go some other place, alone.' " And the narrator concludes: "Then, in silence, I learn the power of words, Sara's aching body having shoved them out alive." A few words hold a powder keg of meaning, and the story reflects this in its style. "Renters" is violent physically, emotionally, and psychologically, but, unlike many of Shelnutt's stories, the violence is not muted by the mesmerizing effect of lyrical language and dense syntax. The result is that the characters are laid bare; the main themes of Shelnutt's work – the power of memory, family history, and their shaping of a character's life – become more prominent. The themes are more disturbing because they are unadorned.

Shelnutt describes her home in Athens, Ohio, as "filled with my son's art"; Greg Shelnutt is now a professor teaching sculpture at the University of Mississippi in Oxford. Shelnutt and her husband travel widely, giving readings and visiting different parts of the country. While at Ohio University she has published two collections of poetry and has written another book of stories, titled "Distance," still in manuscript form, which represents a further departure from the type and style of stories that make up her other collections. While several of the stories are reminiscent of her earlier work, particularly "The Beguiling Idiot" and "Somebody, Somebody," most offer the different stylistic approach that Shelnutt had begun to work with in *The Musician*. Of the twelve stories in the book, six are told in first person, a far greater percentage than in previous collections.

The family, always crucial to Shelnutt's work, remains important in the planned book, although the presence is muted and at times more remote. Family history is less prevalent in these stories, which focus more frequently on the characters' lives in the present. There is more consideration of former lovers than of fathers. These are the directions in which Shelnutt's stories will most likely proceed. Her stories may lose some of their poetic language, but Shelnutt will continue to study the origins of the psychology of characters whose lives and choices she will describe ruthlessly and honestly.

Shelnutt has written that "each new piece of writing *is* something new in the world and leaves the writer and the world changed, however slightly." Perhaps the greatest compliment to her work is that she has succeeded far more than most of her contemporaries in bringing to the world writing that is genuinely new. Readers who have the level of concentration necessary to read Shelnutt well will find their world changed by her stories.

Interviews:

Kevin McCaughey, "An Interview with Eve Shelnutt," *Oxford,* 7 (Spring 1991): 54–63;

Jim Plath, "An Interview with Eve Shelnutt," *Clockwatch Review,* 6 (1991): 14–25;

Felicia Mitchell, Interview with Shelnutt, *Southern Quarterly* (Fall 1992).

Reference:

Shirley Clay Scott, "The Recovery of Story: *The Musician,* by Eve Shelnutt," *Nimrod,* 32 (1988): 133–139.

Elizabeth Tallent
(8 August 1954 -)

Patricia Moran
University of California, Davis

BOOKS: *Married Men and Magic Tricks: John Updike's Erotic Heroes* (Berkeley, Cal.: Creative Arts, 1982);

In Constant Flight (New York: Knopf, 1983; London: Chatto & Windus/Hogarth, 1983);

Museum Pieces (New York: Knopf, 1985);

Time with Children (New York: Knopf, 1987).

OTHER: "Half a Mussel Shell," in *The Graywolf Annual #1,* edited by Scott Walker (Port Townsend, Wash.: Graywolf, 1985);

"Lightly," in *The Esquire Fiction Reader,* volume 2, edited by Rust Hills and Tom Jenks (Green Harbor, Mass.: Wampeter, 1986);

"Prowler," in *The Best American Short Stories 1990,* edited by Richard Ford and Shannon Ravenel (Boston: Houghton Mifflin, 1990), pp. 79–88;

"Honey," in *The Best of the West 3,* edited by James and Denise Thomas (Salt Lake City: Peregrine Smith, 1990), pp. 141–163.

SELECTED PERIODICAL PUBLICATIONS – UNCOLLECTED:

FICTION

"Cuidad Juarez," *Mississippi Review,* 18, no. 1 (1989): 7–20;

"Wing," *Taos Review,* 2 (1990): 24–40;

"Black Dress," *Zyzzyva,* 7 (Spring 1991): 56–67;

"Michael," *Epoch* (Winter 1991).

NONFICTION

"Gardens, Ancient Acres, Historic New Mexico Ranchlands," *Architectural Digest* (September 1985): 168;

"Exalted Play – Alexander Girard's International Folk Art," *Architectural Digest* (June 1986): 86;

"A Collector's Santa Fe: Artist James Harvard's Favorite Sources for Native American Arts," *Architectural Digest* (May 1990): 102–110.

In her first published book (1982), a study of John Updike's erotic fictional heroes, Elizabeth Tallent comments that "any rhythm is, at some level, an attempt to stave off uncertainty, to fortify oneself against those things in the world that are frighteningly arbitrary," which for Tallent, as for Updike, are the social and sexual arrangements between men and women. Tallent's fiction charts the tension between her characters' powerful needs for stability, security, and safety, and their equally powerful desires for risk, change, and flight. Equilibrium is impossible. "Convergence requires movement," Tallent observes, "the tenuous nearing, the precarious pulling apart." This movement, the rhythm of human need and desire, obviates conventional notions of plot: Tallent's stories frequently generate meaning through imagery rather than narrative event. As Andrea Barnett pointed out in her review of Tallent's first short-story collection, *In Constant Flight* (1983), Tallent's "quiet, elegiac stories are shaped less by plot than by immaculately precise imagery. . . . What makes these eleven short stories unusual is Tallent's keen and original eye for detail; her characters' obsessions read as though grounded firmly in fact. . . . Even in the fragile moments when words fail her characters – the moments around which all of these stories pivot – her meanings surface with the liquid ease of daydreams" (*Saturday Review,* 9 June 1983).

Tallent was born on 8 August 1954 in Washington, D.C. Her father, William Hugh Tallent, worked for the government as an agricultural specialist and research chemist; her mother, Joy Redfield Tallent, once a speech therapist, became a full-time homemaker, caring for Elizabeth and her two younger siblings. Although the family moved frequently, they lived in the Midwest throughout her childhood and adolescence, and she earned her

Elizabeth Tallent, circa 1987

B.A. in anthropology at Illinois State University in Normal in 1975. She initially planned to attend graduate school after she was offered a slot in the prestigious anthropology program at the University of New Mexico. With her new husband, Barry Craig Smoots, whom she married in 1975 prior to her graduation, Tallent left Illinois for New Mexico, but she never made it to the university. When the couple came to the fork in the road between Taos and Santa Fe, Tallent told her husband that graduate school was a mistake. In a move reminiscent of her characters, the two pulled off the highway and threw a coin into the air to determine whether they would drive toward Taos or Santa Fe. The coin came up heads; they drove to Santa Fe.

By the time she came to Santa Fe in 1976, then, the dominant frameworks of Tallent's future fiction were in place: a keen interest in anthropology and a midwestern faith in the importance of family and marriage. Tallent sifts through the detritus of relationships, analyzing the shards of contemporary families and piecing their histories back together. She is particularly concerned with the archaeology of marriages, and her fiction increas-

ingly focuses on the roles of children within the family. (Her first child, Gabriel, was born in 1987.) Tallent's fiction is distinguished by her precise eye for detail, as if she had been entrusted with memorializing the houses, landscapes, and mores of contemporary American family life for future generations. She has met with remarkable success: her first published story – "Ice," in the *New Yorker,* September 1980 (collected in her 1983 book) – marked her coming-of-age as a professional writer. Later in 1980 writer Leonard Michaels invited Tallent to attend a writers' workshop in Berkeley, California. In 1985 Bill Buford invited Tallent to accompany fellow writers Raymond Carver, Richard Ford, and Tobias Wolff in giving readings throughout England, an experience that Tallent would later draw on for "Wing" (*Taos Review,* 1990). By 1986 Tallent had begun to teach creative writing at the University of California, Irvine; then at the University of Nevada at Reno, in 1987; and in 1989 at the University of Iowa, where she also taught in the Writers' Workshop. In fall 1990 Tallent accepted a permanent teaching position at the University of California, Davis, where she is currently a professor of English.

"Ice" opens on a seemingly discordant note: the protagonist/narrator muses about her mother's Abyssinian cat, an animal incapable of carrying a litter to term: "at some point during her pregnancies she aborts them." This perception gradually turns back on the narrator, a figure skater whose nightly performance entails dancing with a homosexual man in a bear costume. In the same way she judges the cat, the narrator seems to hold herself responsible for the losses the story adumbrates. Her main ostensible loss is of a photographer, a man who "can't really make the connections," although he "knows where they should be." But the ominous emphasis on reproduction hints at another loss, one the narrator does not name. Whether it is "something in the environment that disturbs her" or whether it is "purely psychological," the narrator worries that she, like the cat, "will never have the temperament" for being a mother. Indeed the men around the narrator fear her potential fecundity: her employer queries whether she is on the pill: her skating partner worries that she may be "taking chances."

Only the narrator's mother feels concern that her daughter may not have the experiences of marriage and maternity. But in her attempts to convince her daughter of "the value of certain things" she seems oblivious to her daughter's distress and to the differences in their circumstances. At an impasse, the narrator finds herself identifying with her grandmother who died after falling down a flight of icy steps in a pathetic attempt to run away from home. The narrator similarly longs to skate outside her "carefully circumscribed arcs." Caught in the floodlight of the arena, however, her icy control fails her: she melts into tears as her partner tells her she "is not herself."

"Ice" develops with particular poignancy some themes characteristic of *In Constant Flight*. Several stories feature mismatched couples: the ballerina and the bear in "Ice"; a woman and a two-hundred-pound miner in "Why I Love Country Music"; and an eighty-two-year-old ornithologist and his daughter-in-law in "The Evolution of Birds of Paradise." These makeshift relationships substitute for the failed marriages and romances that haunt the characters' lives like unacknowledged ghosts. Failure is always in the air, clouding any future the characters might fantasize. As the narrator of "Asteroids" remarks, taking a video game as her model of human communication, "the point of the game is to hit the buttons fast enough so that the small ship you are steering evades the asteroids, and to destroy as many asteroids as you can." Her lover, Joey has become very good at the game: "his ship was a small defiant point in the center of the jagged, speeding forms." She, on the other hand, wants to evade the line of fire by entering "Hyperspace . . . another dimension altogether. . . . The problem with Hyperspace was that your ship could explode on reentry. . . . I was always tempted to use it, though. I think I played more desperately than Joey; I was given to last-minute evasions."

The use of asteroids to symbolize human relationships supports critic Barbara Koenig's observation that the "moments of poignancy . . . are conveyed indirectly, through displaced images often drawn from the esoterica of natural history" (*Nation*, 11 June 1983). Certain patterns of imagery predominate in the book. Birds, for example, are apt avatars of Tallent's tenuous, easily startled lovers. In "The Evolution of Birds of Paradise" the ornithologist, Simon, imagines that the birds of paradise have taken up residence in his home: "Before she [his daughter-in-law] came, he had sighted only blackbirds, swallows, and an occasional nightjar or marsh hen — nothing that excited his professional interest. After . . . she had been in the house only two weeks, Simon found ferns unfurling like sea horses from the cracks between the floorboards, and brilliant feathers strayed into his pockets." The old man finds his daughter-in-law, an associate professor of anthropology, as exotic — and as unattainable — as any bird he once observed in New Guinea. In "Refugees" lovers discuss the woman's husband, who is out in the field recording orioles; her lover, Alfred, scoffs that the husband has "time to do nothing but chart flights of migratory songbirds." Yet the characters migrate like the songbirds. At other times Tallent contrasts the consistency of the avian world with the fickleness of human desire. In "Swans," for example, the narrator recalls his absent lover, a graduate student who has just left him and gone back to her husband, while he investigates a leech infestation that threatens a flock of trumpeter swans, a species on the brink of extinction. Swans, of course, mate for life: indeed the narrator identifies with the dead male swan his colleague prepares for dissection.

In Constant Flight established Tallent as a serious and skillful writer. Three of the stories had been selected for inclusion in prize collections: "Ice" in *The Best American Short Stories, 1981;* "Why I Love Country Music" in *The Pushcart Prize VI* (1981); and "The Evolution of Birds of Paradise" in *Prize Stories, 1984: The O. Henry Awards*. Reviewers of *In Constant*

Dust jacket for Tallent's 1987 book, a group of stories in which children are often the catalysts for reexaminations of adult relationships

Flight lauded Tallent for her meticulous craftsmanship. Koenig, for example, praised the "artfully wrought, often beautiful surfaces." Reviewers found fault with only two aspects of the collection: the characters, particularly the young women, seem at times indistinguishable, and the fictional situations are sometimes strained.

Tallent deals with both these complaints in her second collection, *Time with Children* (1987), published two years after her novel *Museum Pieces*. Her ability to develop individualized characters in her short fiction takes shape in three short-story cycles, each involving different characters. In one set of stories, Kyra and Charlie, an American couple in London, struggle with infidelities, as well as the responsibilities of parenting; Tallent develops in detail the shifting ground of marriage as Kyra engages in and then withdraws from an affair. The second cycle involves Hart and his Nicaraguan wife, Caro, a couple mismatched by age and background; Tal-

lent focuses on the strains imposed on their marriage by their necessary involvement with Hart's first wife and teenage son. In the third set of stories, Tallent traces the resonances between a couple's commitment to a house and their commitment to each other; the setting, twenty-seven miles outside Santa Fe, highlights Jenny's and Sam's difficulties, for, as the only Anglos, they are as isolated and as culturally foreign in the local community as Kyra and Charlie are in London. Domestic struggles bind this collection; Tallent simply expands her earlier preoccupation with the tenuousness of human ties to include the history and geography that simultaneously ground her characters even as those factors make their efforts seem more doomed. Strained plots disappear, replaced by a relentless focus on the minutiae of daily life – the minutiae seeming ironically more substantial than human affections.

The dominant metaphoric pattern in *Time with Children* plays up the contrast between people's relationships to each other and their relationships to their homes. Tallent investigates the way in which residences function as foci for displaced intimacy for the men and women who live in them: rented rooms emblematize the attenuated bonds of their residents; houses point up the need for as well as the difficulty of establishing commitment. Reviewing the collection for the *Times Literary Supplement* (8–14 July 1988), Isabel Fonseca remarked that Tallent's men strongly respond to the charms of houses, which they seem to think "will work like tea cosies to warm and protect." The women, on the other hand, "resent the houses in which they've been put, they are afraid of confinement.... Tallent's women ... bristle at their husbands' ... mistaken identification of intimacy with domesticity." For Sam, in "Favor," the couple's house is "love at first sight": "it had been his idea first," he thinks, "and it had somehow refused to become Jenny's house at all." In "Grant of Easement" this contrast in attitude parallels their differing relationship to marriage: "There was Sam, a husband to the marrow of his bones, and there was Jenny; people meeting her rarely assumed that Jenny was anyone's wife.... Marriage often seemed to require one who was solid and reliable and one who gave the impression of not quite being bound or faithful, for whom fewer things were givens and about whom a great deal less could safely be taken for granted."

The conflicts of couples, already reflected in their domiciles, are further magnified by geographic exile, cultural differences, language barriers, and age. In "Listen to Reason" Kyra and Charlie must try to restore their marriage while marooned in a chilly rented flat in London; Kyra's affair with the Britisher Brian seems in part to derive from her need to connect with someone who belongs in a place she clearly does not: "London had nullified her, countered initiative, washed away her New York self and left her with nothing else." In "The Fence Party" Caro, pregnant, compares her own sense of a family as an "intense, close clan" to Hart's Anglo, alien, nuclear model. Although she believes in extended families, Hart's first family – his former wife, Hannah, and his teenage son, Kevin – constitutes the contemporary extended family. Fittingly Hart's and Caro's remote rural home (threatened by a rising river in one story) underlines the isolation that the nuclear-family model imposes on Caro. The house is Hart's choice; as is typical of this collection, the wife feels the house to be an imposition of her husband's needs upon her.

Age constitutes another divisive factor in families, as seen in some stories outside the three cycles. In "No One's a Mystery" an eighteen-year-old girl fantasizes about a stable future with her married, older lover; his pragmatic certainty that he is simply a diversion for her exposes her naive, romantic visions of stability, marriage, and children. This chasm, significantly, opens after his gift to her of a diary, which prompts her to generate dreams of a fairy-tale "happily ever after" plot: this would-be woman writer presents an especially sharp contrast with Tallent herself. "Black Holes," a particularly poignant story, describes adult bewilderment at a five-year-old girl's distress, which results from her belief that her father is restoring an old Victorian house for her to live in by herself. He will remain in the other house, she assumes, with his second wife and new son. "We're a family," the father explains, but Fanny, his daughter, already understands that the word has no clear definition, no accepted meaning. Her own mother, Ally, has moved away and tried to forget her: "Ally didn't think it very likely that she would keep in touch with Fanny – Ally didn't want anything that reminded her of her previous existence." The story's title thus posits at least one definition of family: black holes are invisible, hypothetical areas of space with intense gravitational fields, phenomena generated by the collapse of massive stars. Fanny's emotional life, it seems, is one such black hole.

With actual disintegrations behind them and the threat of disintegration always around them, Tallent's families must make do with habit and the occasional flash of understanding. In "The Forgiveness Trick" Kyra forgives Charlie almost by accident when a series of his actions recall their college romance, the years behind them, and how well they know each other: "Often after the very worst moments in their marriage, she had experienced a blithe instant in which she was all lightness, all reckless tenderness toward Charlie, as if nothing he did was beyond her power to understand and endure...." Tallent often represents marriage as a charmed circle, as in "Grant of Easement": "Sam had drawn a charmed circle, around their marriage; inside it was Jenny's narrower circle." Like Charlie, Sam can struggle futilely to regain his wife's favor, only to recover it accidentally by saying the right thing at the right time (as in "Favor"). Such recoveries are, admittedly, only temporary respites. The nature of a family, Tallent seems to say, does not involve absolute certainty.

Time with Children earned high praise for Tallent. For example, Fonseca liked the way in which

"Tallent occasionally slows the pace of her elegant narrative to examine a spider's belly or a grasshopper's eye. Excruciating details of this sort can seem, in a single story, overly conscientious, a remembered rule. But cumulatively her precision lends a vibrancy to concerns that could easily seem trivial." However, Fonseca complained that there is "something irksome about the way women have affairs here; there is no confusion and no guilt." Carolyn See (*New York Times Book Review,* 15 November 1987) interpreted adultery in Tallent's work as a trope, a way of exposing the human desire "to want more than we can get. Given our imperfect nature, our 'time with children' may be a penance, a travail, a solitary confinement. We may be doing time instead of spending it."

Yet children emerge in Tallent's recent work as a tentative source of redemption. Even in *Time with Children* they expose the fault lines of relationships, acting as signposts to the adults ostensibly in charge of them. Children in Tallent's fiction may be, as one character thinks in "Wing," hostages their parents offer to the world, but the need to protect and care for children forces the parents to come to terms with their difficult marriages, their messy family lives, and their unruly desires.

Since the publication of *Time with Children,* Tallent has worked steadily toward the completion of a third collection of stories. "Wing," "Prowler," and "Cuidad Juarez," all part of that future collection, suggest that she will continue to train her gaze on family life – its inevitable loneliness and compromise and the enigma of its endurance. In her study of Updike, Tallent remarks on his mapping of marriages in the 1960s: "various settings, most exhaustively the houses of the couples, are blueprinted with this degree of earnest attention. Updike has a quick eye for idiosyncrasies peculiar to the era and to the precise degree of disintegration within the marriage. Future museum curators will have, in *Couples,* a transparent treasury of diagrams from which a middle-class household, New England, circa 1963, can be reconstructed." Tallent may well prove to be such an archaeological find for future curators reconstructing the family lives and marriages of the baby-boom generation.

Barry Targan

(30 November 1932 –)

Arthur L. Clements
State University of New York at Binghamton

BOOKS: *Let the Wild Rumpus Start* (Lincoln, Neb.: Best Cellar, 1971);

Thoreau Stalks the Land Disguised as a Father (Greenfield Center, N.Y.: Greenfield Review, 1975);

Harry Belten and the Mendelssohn Violin Concerto (Iowa City: University of Iowa Press, 1975);

Surviving Adverse Seasons (Urbana: University of Illinois Press, 1979);

Kingdoms (Albany: State University of New York Press, 1980);

Falling Free (Urbana: University of Illinois Press, 1989);

The Tangerine Tango Equation: Or How I Discovered Sex, Deception, and a New Theory of Physics in Three Short Months (New York: Thunder's Mouth, 1990).

SELECTED PERIODICAL PUBLICATIONS – UNCOLLECTED: "A Thousand Trees," *Salmagundi*, 72 (Fall 1986): 31–100;

"Meisner Agonistes," *Sewanee Review*, 98 (Summer 1990): 350–399;

"Courage," *Sewanee Review*, 101 (1993).

Barry Targan has published a significant body of distinguished fiction. His first novel, *Kingdoms* (1980), won the Associated Writing Programs Award in the Novel, and *Surviving Adverse Seasons* (1979), a collection of short fiction, received the Saxifrage Prize. Many of his short stories have been awarded Pushcart, O. Henry, or other prizes and have been reprinted in *Best American Short Stories* for various years or in other collections and anthologies of outstanding short fiction. For example, the title story of *Harry Belten and the Mendelssohn Violin Concerto* (1975) – Targan's first fiction collection, which won the University of Iowa School of Letters Award in Short Fiction – originally appeared in *Esquire* (July 1966) and was subsequently reprinted in three important anthologies of fiction and selected for radio broadcast by *Voice of America. Stories from the Sixties,* one of these anthologies, included Targan's work along with fiction by such writers as John Updike, Saul Bellow, Tillie Olsen, and John Barth. In a 24 January 1992 letter, Targan wrote of finding himself in this distinguished company: "Naturally, I was elated. . . . But as I read through the collection, I came to a deeper awe not of them and not in self-appreciation, but of the act of such writing – of writing with such honorableness, such authenticity. . . . I thought right then that to write — to write with such integrity — was one of the finest things a human being could do with a life. And so I decided just then that it would be one of the things I would do with mine. But only one of the things."

The last sentence is particularly crucial and telling. One of the most important reasons why Targan has produced such accomplished work is that he has engaged in many activities and avocations with exceptional skill, authenticity, and integrity. He began his academic career as a Renaissance scholar and has become a sort of Renaissance man of wide and various achievements. He is or has been a serious boat builder, sailor, gardener, potter, weaver, violinist, bookbinder, printer, papermaker, photographer, artist, skier, naturalist, bird-watcher, fisherman, editor, and teacher. Because he knows and has done so much, his writing covers these and other activities in informed, specific, realistic, and convincing ways, and his style is textured, detailed, and poetic.

Born on 30 November 1932 in Atlantic City, Targan is the son of Albert (a grocer) and Blanche Simmons Targan. He earned his B.A. in English at Rutgers University in 1954 and his M.A. at the University of Chicago in 1955. After serving in the U.S. Army for two years, on 9 March 1958 he married Arleen Shanken, an artist. They have two children: Anthony and Eric. In 1962 Targan received his Ph.D. from Brandeis University, and later that year he began his teaching career, as an assistant professor of English at Syracuse University. He later taught at the State University of New York College at Cortland (1967–1969); Skidmore College in Saratoga Springs, New York (1969–1978); and the State University of New York at Binghamton, where he has remained since 1978. Targan published two books of poetry before the publication of his first short-story collection.

In the title story of *Harry Belten and the Mendelssohn Violin Concerto,* Belten, who started playing violin in his thirties and is not a first-class musician, has such an intense passion for the violin and for giving a concert — to be concluded with Felix Mendelssohn-Bartholdy's very difficult Violin Concerto in E Minor (1844), which he has been faithfully practicing for eighteen years — that he must convince family, friends, coworkers, his boss (for whom he has been a loyal hard worker), and even his violin teacher that his extraordinary desire and love for music are not mere madness. He does so with his good nature, calmness, sweet reasonableness, and passionate determination. When in the

third movement of the concerto, because of the demands of the music, one of Harry's violin strings loses its exact tautness and correct pitch, he is able, because of "responses formed out of his eighteen years of love," to complete the concerto if not with distinction at least with a kind of triumph. Harry's passionate playing is part of an archetypal quest and becomes a resonating symbol. A recurrent major theme in Targan's work is that one should make one's music (or perform one's job, art, or craft) and engage life fully with as much devotion, loyalty, honesty, skill, and love as one can muster.

This recurrent, complex theme, often expressed through strong middle-aged or older characters, usually fathers or father figures, may well owe much to the influence of Targan's own father. Targan has written an essay, "Courage" (1993), which favorably compares the ordinary daily virtues of his father with those of the standard heroes of ancient and modern times.

Other stories in the *Harry Belten* collection present characters who variously illustrate aspects of this major theme. In "Old Vemish," for example, Martin Vemish, owner of a wallpaper-and-paint store, has worked for forty years without a vacation but is finally persuaded by his son and daughter-in-law to go with his wife on a Caribbean cruise, which is restricted to those who are 60 and older. Clifton Booth, the officious cruise director, treats the elderly travelers in a condescending, restrictive, and finally contemptuous manner, as if they were sheep or children. In a victory of the weakening old folks over the manipulative young people, the strong-minded and independent Martin leads his fellow vacationers in a rebellious wild party at the end of the cruise. "The Man Who Lived" is a lyrical narrative about Frederick Kappel, Jr., a successful bookbinder who works with great devotion and skill; he lives to be a 105. A healthy 78 years old, Yorst Inman Broctor, the main character of "And Their Fathers Who Begot Them," vows to live to be much older. Retired from bricklaying and now living with his daughter's family, he spends much of his time "doing what he had always done with his life: nothing exact, nowhere committed with any passion to any idea or interest or concern." Yorst, a man who has basically taken and not given much to anyone, goes through a transformation so that he learns "all we can give is what we have." In the powerful ending Yorst, acting victoriously against decades of self-concern and insufficient passion, heroically saves the lives of his two grandsons during a house fire and gives up his own life in the process.

Harry Belten and the Mendelssohn Violin Concerto

Barry Targan

The Iowa
School of Letters
Award
for Short Fiction
1975

Dust jacket for Targan's first book. The title story introduces a recurrent theme in his fiction: the idea that one should be fully dedicated to one's job, art, or craft.

As one might expect, given Targan's various activities and accomplishments, there is a considerable variety and richness in his first collection of short stories. George Garrett has written (as quoted on the dust jacket) that in *Harry Belten* "we find in wondrous plenty the full range of short-story voices and possibilities. There is bright originality casting long shadows of grand tradition." He also praises the book for "its consistent excellence and maximum variety of character, setting, action, and implication within a unity of personal experience and concerns." Such stories as "... And Still the Heart Doth Sing" and "Elizabeth Lanier," as well as the title and other stories, demonstrate considerable structural strengths and reveal Targan's skill in writing the well-wrought, well-plotted story.

Love is the governing and informing principle of the four long stories that make up *Surviving Adverse Seasons,* and it involves the somewhat subordi-

nate but pervasive theme of order. "Kingdoms," the first story (later expanded into the novel of that name), is a picaresque story about the life and travels of a father and a son after the wife and mother has been killed in an automobile accident and after a good friend of the father commits suicide. The father, a successful professor and a published seventeenth-century scholar, feels subsequent to his losses that "Literature is too redemptive," that the great writers, especially in their assumptions about order and equity, have not adequately told the bitter truth, and he undertakes his son's education on the road, with suffering as his main theme. Other themes, prominent in other Targan works as well, include order and disorder; dream and reality; homelessness and home; fiction and fact; and time, death, and love. There are stories within the major story, as the two characters travel from town to town, the father taking odd jobs. Creating a new ethic as he goes along, the father tries to understand the mystery of the human predicament by thrusting himself into life and experience, which are often unruly, disorderly, and mysterious. Embodying the archetypal fool/saint in the wilderness, he has an ability to take on some of the characteristics of people he meets, so that, by losing himself in the flux of life in the travels to many "kingdoms," he saves himself, and, through "ancient compassion" and the continuing creative power of love, his son is also saved, formed, educated, and bequeathed kingdoms both tangible and intangible.

Even more so than in Targan's first collection, the style of *Surviving Adverse Seasons* is highly allusive and extensively metaphoric. The four stories of *Surviving Adverse Seasons* are so arranged and interconnected that the meaning of any one story and its themes are altered and amplified when read alongside the other stories.

Set in upstate New York, "The Garden" tells the story of the developing relationship between Peter Martin, a furniture maker and carpenter (who, like other main characters in *Surviving Adverse Seasons,* makes and fixes things), and Jane Friant, a writer and gardener. The story is enriched by many details about the setting and neighboring cities, such as Albany and Saratoga, and about the characters' vocations and avocations, the theme of order being expressed through many references to frame, design, and arrangement. Again, characteristically, Targan writes out of his own great capacity and his wide-ranging and deep knowledge of places, people, activities, arts, and crafts.

The first page of "The Rags of Time" refers to "the decorous, well-tended garden" of protagonist

Thomas Wilkens's life. "The Rags of Time," an uncharacteristic Targan story in that the main character is so unsympathetic, actually presents a reverse or upside-down image of the loves in the three other stories of *Surviving Adverse Seasons*. Like the father in "Kingdoms," Wilkens is a professor of seventeenth-century literature, but, unlike the father, he is "a student of mysteries, not a participant," and has significant difficulty talking with his son. A role player, Wilkens has arranged an orderly but restricted image of himself and his life, based with affectation on his "picture of the professor that he had preserved from an old English film." He wants "life's events arranged in a languid upward curve of pleasant small accomplishments," whereas the father of "Kingdoms," who plunges himself and his son into the flux of life, believes that "we were all beyond . . . perceived arrangements." Thus in a different way than the other stories, "The Rags of Time" explores the central themes: love and the meaning of order.

What finally seduces Wilkens, in his infatuation for his attractive student Fay Lester, is not love or passion, not his desire for her, but the idea of doing something "outrageous and nearly irrational." While discussing the carpe diem theme as a possible subject for her term paper, he points out that the theme is not about sex, as Fay says, but about death or, more precisely, the fear of death. But in exchange for her not having to write her paper or take the final exam, he arranges to have sex with her. The final pages of the story indicate that Wilkens is a frightened man who, out of his fear, settles for a certain decorous orderliness, the illusion of real order, and will take "no more chances." To the extent Wilkens is not moved by love or passion he is without real substance and is, in a sense, among the living dead.

Through rediscovery of love and passionate commitment and involvement, Abel Harnack in "Surviving Adverse Seasons" slowly comes back from the living dead. Like the father in "Kingdoms," Abel suffers the terrible loss represented by his wife's death, but instead of plunging fully into life and its vicissitudes, he at first withdraws into a kind of hibernation, a means of surviving adverse seasons. Abel makes and fixes things, and his garage is such a neatly arranged and thoroughly well-stocked workshop that he can rebuild, mend, or create whatever he chooses, can bring order out of chaos. The story's epigraph from Marcus Aurelius offers critical insight and helps provide a unified coherence to the whole collection: "The universe is either a chaos of involution and dispersion, or a unity of order and providence. If the first be truth, why

should I desire to linger in the midst of chance, conglomeration, and confusion?"

A skillful and accomplished inventor, who has worked seriously even on perpetual motion, and a born fixer, Abel is therefore all the more deeply frustrated that he was not able to "fix," to help, his wife. Thus, after her death, he resolves to avoid purposefulness, to do little or nothing, and to become a man to whom nothing really matters. Her death is, in effect, a denial of his being and of all meaningful motion and being: "He shrieked against the badly designed and uncorrectable device called life. And then held still, free now forever from the obscenity of creation."

His daughter Vivian finally persuades him to enroll in a course of Latin, a dead language. Slowly and reluctantly at first, Abel develops a friendship with his teacher, Sylvia Warren, an artist, photographer, and nature lover, and with her friend Mildred Latham, both of whom are attempting to provide the conditions necessary for the development of the *Vendalia tarda* (Latin for "slow to live,"), an insect that passes through quadruple diapause. *Vendalia tarda* is an ideal symbol for Abel, who goes through changes that are in part reflected by the changing seasons. Eventually, by designing and fixing the necessary apparatus, he helps the women in their experiment to breed the insects, and the women gradually introduce him, to his increasing discovery and delight, to the world of nature.

During one of the nature walks in the story, Abel has a kind of epiphany in a scene resonant with meaning, and subsequently the reader comes to a crucial passage that links and illuminates love and order: "So too had he once shared in the profound, harrowing, and wordless condition of love, the boundless, shapeless, measureless condition which is not chaos though it cannot be formed." Though love cannot be formed and therefore is beyond chaos and order, Targan's stories demonstrate that, paradoxically, only love ultimately gives sufficient meaning and hence a kind of order to living.

Some of the six stories in *Falling Free* (1989), Targan's next collection, received special recognition, such as Pushcart Prizes, O. Henry Awards, and reprinting in volumes of outstanding works. The critics have warmly praised *Falling Free:* Donn Blevins wrote that "Targan's prose is the leaping of gazelles" (*New Letters Review of Books,* Winter 1990), and Eils Lotozo observed that the stories are "exquisite . . . dense with luxuriant language and sensuous detail" (*New York Times Book Review,* 4 March 1990). The collection displays a wide range of characters, plots, settings, and subjects, and it continues Tar-

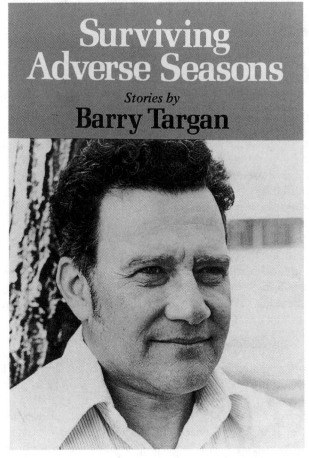

Dust jacket for Targan's 1979 book, which won the Saxifrage Prize

gan's exploration of and variations on certain themes. The long title story, for example, centers on a protagonist who, out of his loving concern to get help for his dying wife and in self-defense, kills another man. Love sometimes requires drastic or extreme choices and actions.

The prizewinning story "Dominion," reprinted three times, has been chosen by Trinity Playhouse to be made into a television movie. (Similarly, Targan's novel *The Tangerine Tango Equation* [1990] has been optioned to be made into a film.) The main character of "Dominion," Morton Poverman, a middle-aged husband/father/businessman, embodies and manifests the transformative powers of love, the organizing principle and major theme in most of Targan's stories. Made bankrupt by his embezzling partner, Phil Charney, Morton must begin the new year by reordering his business and personal affairs — selling and reducing business and investment assets to pay debts and canceling or postponing vacation and retirement plans. Still, when

Phil calls, Morton cannot summon his hatred; rather he feels embarrassment for his partner's sobbing and agony and feels the loss of this longtime, flamboyant friend. The first part of the story ends with Phil asking forgiveness and Morton, in spite of the great betrayal and harm done to him, unhesitatingly granting his friend's request, extending forgiveness. Only much later in the story does the reader come to understand fully the significance of this action.

"Not without intelligent purpose and a decent man's hope," Morton works long hours, uses his business acumen and experience, makes special purchases, and offers low prices in order gradually to rebuild his ruined business, while at night he kindly consoles his wife, who is distraught over their misfortune. When his son, Robert, offers to help in the business, Morton lovingly insists that Robert simply continue to concentrate on his school and extracurricular activities, to enjoy his last semester as a high-school senior. Morton is devoted to his wife and son and is passionately and selflessly committed to working for and improving their condition and well-being. Characteristically he takes considerable pleasure and pride in considering with his wife and son which of the three accepting universities his son might choose to attend. When Morton learns that his son has joined the Society of the Holy Word, a branch of the Church of the Resurrection, and is thinking of going to a religious college, Morton investigates the society, talks to its leaders, reads its pamphlets and tracts, and starts attending its meetings. He learns that in order to avoid hell, a Christian concept he had never been able to handle, one must "embrace the Lord Jesus as your Savior," for, in the words of one of the preachers at a meeting, it is "either Love or Damnation." By these alternatives the preacher intends a literal sort of meaning while the story implies more of a figurative and symbolic meaning.

The story suggests that so-called Christian values, such as forgiveness and love, are more a matter of individual behavior than of organized religion.

Morton determines, in an act of self-sacrificing love for his son, to declare for Christ. The ceremony requires him to repeat certain statements, such as that his "hard and selfish heart" must "learn love" and that he is "a bad man . . . stained with sin . . . an abomination," which are palpably false and cause Robert to interrupt and try to stop the ceremony. But his father reassures him and continues. The story ends with an ambiguous statement: "Unsheathing the great sword of his love, he waved it about his balding, sweating head and . . . fought. Not without glory."

Working within the tradition of realistic literature, with his wide, deep knowledge and considerable skills and accomplishments in many fields, and with a fine energy and a pervasive, often subtle and wise, good humor, Barry Targan engages important themes, and he enables readers to see truth anew through fully realized, mainly sympathetic characters in stories told in fresh, richly textured, and graceful language. In his own words, "All we can do is to make, in a language that we can trust, a poem, a story, a fiction that we can bear" (*Kingdoms*).

Gordon Weaver

(2 February 1937 –   )

Thomas E. Kennedy

BOOKS: *Count a Lonely Cadence* (Chicago: Regnery, 1968);

The Entombed Man of Thule (Baton Rouge: Louisiana State University Press, 1972);

Such Waltzing Was Not Easy (Urbana: University of Illinois Press, 1975);

Give Him a Stone (New York: Crown, 1975);

Getting Serious (Baton Rouge: Louisiana State University Press, 1980);

Circling Byzantium (Baton Rouge: Louisiana State University Press, 1980);

Morality Play (Kirksville, Mo.: Chariton Review, 1985);

A World Quite Round (Baton Rouge: Louisiana State University Press, 1986);

The Eight Corners of the World (Chelsea, Vt.: Chelsea Green, 1988);

Men Who Would Be Good (Oak Park, Ill.: Triquarterly/Another Chicago, 1991).

TELEVISION: *Hog's Heart,* adapted by Weaver from his story "Hog's Heart," Educational Television Service, Oklahoma State University, 1983.

OTHER: *Selected Poems of Father Ryan,* edited by Weaver (Jackson: University Press of Mississippi, 1973);

An Artist's Notebook: The Life and Art of Merritt Mauzey, edited by Weaver (Memphis: Memphis State University Press, 1979);

Southwest Cultural Heritage Festival 1982, edited by Weaver (Stillwater: Oklahoma State University Press, 1983);

The American Short Story: A Critical History, 1945–1980, edited by Weaver (Boston: Twayne, 1983);

Twayne Series of Short Fiction Studies, general editor, Weaver (Boston: Twayne, 1988–1990; New York: Twayne, 1991–   ).

Gordon Weaver, circa 1988 (photograph by Karen Fitch)

Gordon Weaver writes fiction mostly about middle- and lower-middle-class, middle-aged, midwestern men: football coaches, professors, lawyers, television producers, insurance salesmen, alcoholics, bar owners, soldiers, fathers, sons, and brothers. At the core of his fiction is a fascination with the mystery of time, and what he seems to find within that mystery is the key to identity. Weaver approaches the process of time via the moment, the point of temporal intersection of past, present, and future. In his own words (in a 1984 interview with Thomas E, Kennedy), Weaver's technique is "to settle on a given moment in a character's life, to stop that moment in time, examine it, see its implications," to examine "how experience *means* to people" rather than "how it can be described from without, 'objectively.'" His fiction is a gallery of such moments, a frieze of characters consuming and being consumed by the moment. Weaver renders his characters with sympathetic irony. They may be victims of a world they did not make, but they do not endeavor to change that world; they fumble to survive, to thrive, and to find sense, solace, and dignity in a world where the walls protecting them are thin, money is an ever-fleeting necessity, the family structure is in continuous dissolution, and reputations are as inconstant as a lump of ice in a glass of whiskey.

Weaver has recently developed a further dimension in his fiction, a dimension present only as a seed in his earlier work: an incorporation of metafictional, self-reflexive techniques into his primarily realistic mode. The result is a fiction that simultaneously deals in a realistic fashion with the real world of Middle America, while on another level exploring that world's continuing invention of itself. As Weaver's fiction has grown more complex in his last three or four volumes, the irony and humor have deepened and become more general.

Born on 2 February 1937 in Moline, Illinois, to Nobel Rodel Weaver and Inez Katherine Nelson Weaver, Gordon Allison Weaver is the youngest of five siblings. At seventeen he joined the U.S. Army, and his military experiences in peacetime Germany in the mid 1950s provide the background for his first novel, *Count a Lonely Cadence* (1968), filmed more than twenty years later as *Cadence* (1991) under the direction of Martin Sheen with a screenplay by Dennis Shryack.

After his discharge in 1958, Weaver entered college to earn his B.A. in English, which he did in 1961 at the University of Wisconsin – Milwaukee; he received his M.A. in English in 1962 from the University of Illinois, where he studied as a Woodrow Wilson fellow; and he earned his Ph.D. in English and creative writing in 1970 at the University of Denver, where he studied under John Williams and Seymour Epstein. His creative dissertation, the novel *Give Him A Stone,* was published in 1975.

On 14 September 1961 Weaver married Judith Lynne Gosnell; they have three daughters, Kristina, Anna, and Jessica. Weaver has taught at various colleges and universities: Siena College, Loudonville, New York (1963–1965); Marietta College, Marietta, Ohio (1965–1968); the University of Denver (1968–1970); and the University of Southern Mississippi, Hattiesburg (1970–1975). During his years at the University of Southern Mississippi, Weaver founded both the writing program there and the *Mississippi Review.* In 1975 Weaver accepted a full professorship in the Oklahoma State University Department of English, which he chaired until 1984 and where he served as fiction editor (1975–1986) and then editor (1989–   ) of the *Cimarron Review.*

Weaver's fiction has been honored with the St. Lawrence Award (1973), two National Endowment for the Arts Fellowships (1974, 1989), the O. Henry First Prize (1979), the Sherwood Anderson Prize (1982), the *Quarterly West* Fiction Prize (1979), the Novella Prize (1983), and a Pushcart Prize (1985), among other awards. His stories have often been cited in the annual *Best American Short Stories* and *Pushcart Prize* volumes.

During the first two decades of Weaver's writing career his fiction focused on the individual's relationship to time and its slow unfolding of the ironies of identity. "When Times Sit In" (*Perspective,* 13 January), his first published story, keynotes this theme, which Weaver has examined in his many periodical and anthology pieces and his first six volumes.

Two groups of his short stories were merged and expanded into his second and third novels: *Give Him a Stone,* in which a father seeks to explore backward in time to retrieve an image of his own father that might give his son some sense of continuity to his life, and *Circling Byzantium* (1980), where time is both theme and subject. The latter novel is divided into three parts, each from the point of view of a different character focused in a different direction of time's triptych (past, present, and future), all three of whose paths intersect at a single point. Despite the repetition of theme, however, the subjects of Weaver's fiction tend to be as varied as his characters.

Another recurrent feature that distinguishes Weaver's fiction is the quality of its craftsmanship, particularly significant in some of his more recent work where metafictional elements are blended into his generally realistic strategies to produce a dual effect by which readers seem to be experiencing real people in a real world while simultaneously being exposed to the deeper existential dimensions of metafiction and the meaning of fiction for the creation of one's own identity. Weaver's fiction combines realism and postmodernism to explore the perimeters of rational perception. Such a combination

Dust jacket for Weaver's 1986 book, three works of fiction that examine the relationship between one's skill and one's identity

might seem contradictory, even reciprocally lethal, but an examination of Weaver's short fiction in *Morality Play* (1985), *A World Quite Round* (1986), and *Men Who Would Be Good* (1991) and of his novel *The Eight Corners of the World* (1988) uncovers an extraordinarily successful fusion of craft and vision in a fictional universe whose complexity is equaled by its lucidity. Craft, skill, and art become synonymous with identity in the worlds of these four books. Thus, where Weaver's earlier work might be said to have sought light in a dark celebration of the ironies of time's savaging of frail human identity, these more recent books seem to have discovered a resistant identity rooted in the processes of the fiction itself.

The novella *Morality Play* might be identified as a thematic bridge between the earlier and more-recent work, for it deals with the transcendent dedication to skill of a professional wrestler — its corruption over time, and the will, albeit vain, to preserve that skill's integrity. The identity of the main character develops with the development of his skill as a wrestler and is corrupted via the system that facilitates the commercial exploitation of the skill. The power of the fighter is subjugated to the system,

which dictates who is to "triumph" in the money-making arrangement devised to mime a battle between good and evil.

The three pieces in *A World Quite Round* deal further with the concept of skill as identity. The opening story, "Ah Art! Oh Life!" focuses on life's pain and art's "hope to understand." Skill, the ability to create art, is intrinsic to identity, for that ability is the instrument by which one may negotiate life's pain. The individual in pain, young Oskar, is sent to stay with an aunt while his parents divorce. Each day, the aunt leaves the boy with her fiancé's father, a very old artist and professor.

The story opens with Oskar watching the professor paint, while the professor's wife watches the boy, and the professor watches himself in a mirror as he paints his own portrait. The professor's wife is also old and is senile, and Oskar fears her; each day she feigns kindness toward the lad until her husband falls asleep, whereupon she begins verbally tormenting the boy. Oskar listens helplessly while the professor snores.

As the story develops, Oskar's newfound dedication to art strengthens him against the sadness of his life and makes him believe that he might begin to understand, while the professor, experiencing the last dissipation of his strength, weeps into his palms. Oskar is startled and seeks to comfort the old man while entering the double focus of the artist, thinking about all the pictures he would draw and how, when he held them up to the light, he would understand it all.

Oskar turns with enthusiasm to art, and thus he will endure until, like the old professor, he reaches the end of life, of art, and, finally, of pain. The artist's aim is to lift away the veils of human ignorance. If he fails — as does the old professor — he fails as a human being seeking understanding and passing his skill on to a coming generation.

However, in the second story, "The Interpreter," readers see that dedication to a skill can also approach madness and can be dangerous to all concerned. The interpreter of the title, Comrade Li of the Chinese People's Army, is assigned to a POW camp during the Korean War. One of his tasks is to ascertain that the American prisoners behave with appropriate respect for their captors, as prescribed by the Geneva conventions. Two of the prisoners, an Oklahoma redneck and a Detroit black, present him with linguistic problems that he is determined to resolve, for in linguistic transgression lies the seed of all disorder. Li believes that to ignore the significance of words is to destroy all order and meaning and purpose. For Li, when he wakes each morning, "It is as if there is nothing, no shape, texture, no sense, unless and until I find some words that will enable me to begin again." He believes that language is a socioscientific instrument whose pro- or counterrevolutionary value can be measured and dealt with. He feels that linguistic transgressions, a multitude of which can be traced to the root word *fuck,* can and must be met with appropriate punishment, such as the prisoner's being tied to a caisson wheel in the garbage pit in subfreezing weather. Boggs and Smith, redneck and black, are tied in the pit for a twenty-four-hour punishment devised by Li in the belief that its severity will cow the prisoners into retracting their words, reconciling their racial differences, and joining together in an effort to further the cause of the people. But Li's reality is far from that of Boggs or Smith. They cannot comprehend the reality he perceives and seeks to uphold in the frame of his linguistic obsessions. They perceive only that Li is trying "to kill their ass." And Li cannot retract his sentence upon them, even though realizing that it will prove to be a death penalty as the night temperature plunges below zero. So he joins them to demonstrate his sol-

idarity, bound fast to them by his locked belief in the mad situation as, slowly, they freeze to death — a black, a redneck, and a Mandarin interpreter "together in the cold and snow and dark of this place."

The closing piece of *A World Quite Round,* "The Parts of Speech," also ends in death, though the death in this case is an explicitly imagined one, painted for readers by a creative first-person narrator out of the colors and images purported to have been collected from "true" events. The story, told by a self-identified fiction writer, is in three main parts, the first two of which are said to be "true," the third being a fiction built on a few facts received by the narrator at the conclusion of part 2. The story deals directly with identity as fiction and lie and with the lives that are fed to this process.

In the first part, the narrator tells about the impenetrable persona that made it possible for him to survive his high-school years — an identity a female classmate helped make possible for him by whispering drill answers to him concerning the parts of speech so that his lack of knowledge would not call attention to him. A dull, drab, faceless person, she had information; he had identity. She knew grammar, but he became the writer. Her information helped him maintain the mask of his identity, but she had no real identity of her own. The narrator never acknowledged her help, never thanked or even addressed her so much as to say hello.

In the second part, ten years later, he learns by chance that she is dead, and consequently he creates the third part, in which a compulsive liar devises for himself a false identity as a war hero in order to attract women, attracts the girl in question, gets her drunk, and inadvertently scalds her to death in a bathtub while trying to sober her up. In an epilogue to the story, the narrator discusses what the story means: "all fictions are lies, however much truth goes into the making of them; a fiction writer is a liar, who, to make his fictions work, has to use his imagination and his skill with language to transform elements of the truth into a lie the reader can believe; if a fiction works, the lie is well told, then it becomes real, the truth again, because the reader is not who he was anymore when he believes something new."

Thus Weaver presents fiction as identity, or a particle of identity (the received belief that changes the host), for reader and writer alike. One question remains unanswered, however, a question posed by the narrator in the first part: whether "it is a wholly good thing" to write fiction.

The Eight Corners of the World began to appear in 1984 as a series of short fictions and was pub-

Dust jacket for Weaver's 1991 book, a collection of short stories about six representative American men

lished in 1988 as Weaver's most ambitious novel to date. His concerns with craft, identity, and time meld into a single pattern broader and more complex than in his earlier short fiction. An aging, wealthy, Japanese filmmaker, Foto Joe Yamaguchi, dying of cancer (contracted at Hiroshima, where he had gone to make a propaganda film) and without heirs, employs Japan's most illustrious tattoo artist to decorate his back with a great tattoo depicting all the phases of his life, all the persons he has been. Upon his death, he wishes his hide to be donated to the Wantanabe Nautical Museum, where it might be displayed as a lasting tribute to his life – a life whose normal documentation (birth records and school papers) and fellow witnesses (family and friends) have been burned up in the fires of war and dissolved by time. Yamaguchi's story is both terrifying and humorous, and the book itself becomes the great tattoo on Yamaguchi's back, a panorama encompassing the lives of generals, emperors, and baseball heroes – a kind of cultural, cubist telling of a man's life through history and of history through

a man's life, combined with the clash and pull of national and individual human identities.

Weaver's *Men Who Would Be Good* tells the stories of six men: an alcoholic lawyer who seeks clarity in a glass ("Whiskey, Whiskey, Gin, Gin, Gin"); a businessman so obsessed by golf as an escape from his domestic troubles that he ends up playing at night in the dark ("Zen Golf "); a salesman whose identity disappears in the downward spiral of his economy ("Home Economics"); an American GI "tunnel rat" in Vietnam who chooses to remain in the tunnels when the war ends ("Under the World"); a television producer who becomes obsessed by a recurrent dream that slowly replaces his "real" life ("Turner's Dream"); another businessman who is seized by uncontrollable, inexplicable fits of weeping ("Parker *Lacrimans*"); and an insurance salesman struggling to understand the series of plagues rained down on his city ("The Good Man of Stillwater, Oklahoma").

These stories are told in the terms of realism but cannot quite be read as direct reflections of life. This situation is most apparent in the longest piece, the novella "Under the World," something of a contemporary allegory about American identity.

The identity of PFC Elroy Huff is a complex one, clued in by the epigraph from Fyodor Dostoyevski: "I invented adventures for myself and made up a life so as to at least live in some way." Huff is a diminutive man who finally achieves a sense of himself while stationed in Vietnam in the tunnel rats, a combat group composed of men small enough to infiltrate the tunnels burrowed through the occupied zone by the Vietcong. Huff "finds himself " in this role and dedicates himself fervently to the mission, imagining his way through the tunnel networks and finally staying on beneath the earth after the withdrawal, like a ghost or like a seed in the earth of the abandoned tunnels. Huff is unable to answer the question of why he stays. But the answer is clear: Huff stays because his identity is there, because there he never has to wonder who he is. There he lives by his wits and imagination in the dark peacefulness of the place and never has to look into a mirror. That is why he stays – a reason similar to the one that has an artist place more importance on the life of the imagination than on life in the world.

The fates of the characters in most of the other stories in this collection, however, are not self-chosen; they suffer from economic and natural disaster or from the eruption of personal internal forces. What most of these characters have in common is a passionate questioning of the rightness of the fates that overtake them, a determination to question the unimpeachable social "physics" that governs American life. Walker, in "Home Economics," abandoned by the world when his credit rating fails, asks his wife, "What is a man? Is a man like money? Am I some numbers that go up for a while and then they go down until I'm so small nobody can see me and then I just disappear? Is that all we are? . . . It might be interesting to strip all this away and see just what we really are underneath it all." Walker ends up flinging away the last of his cash while naked in a shopping mall; his nakedness repulses the crowds until they see the color of his money and surround him, "reaching for him, his money, tearing at him."

In "Whiskey, Whiskey, Gin, Gin, Gin," the narrator's early views of happiness are of drunken people, or at least of people drinking: his father in a barroom and his brother, home from the navy, who is falling down laughing with drunkenness. The narrator believes in their happiness, in the lure of the "happy hour" with its clinking ice cubes and cocktail peanuts. He pursues such hours, and their illusions strip him of his success in life as husband, father, and trial lawyer. But the character does not catch on that he is the author of his loss: "Anyone, everyone is born into a family. I have a father, mother, brothers, and my life with them remains with me, a part of me, forever. My family is broken by divorce, a world war, death, distance, time. It could make a man nostalgic. Sad. I think of them, remember, and might be sad, but I drink. Not to forget. I drink. I fill my glass with ice, vodka that looks like purest water, drink. And I remember: father, mother, brothers, myself as I was then. And I am not sad. . . . There is no reason for sadness, no point in nostalgia. I fill my glass, drink. It is clear, cold, pure. . . ." He drinks to recapture his past in its original purity, a kind of art. But he never speculates as to whether what he does is "a wholly good thing"; he clings unquestioningly to the purity of the drink, which preserves his illusion and destroys his reality.

The next to last story in the collection, "Parker *Lacrimans*," finishes with an outburst of weeping, but the book itself ends not with a whimper but a tempest that tears the roof off and leaves Pease, the main character of "The Good Man of Stillwater, Oklahoma," in the embrace of his family while he is looking into what he is certain will be the face of God or something equivalent. Throughout this powerful, amusing, and finally terrifying closing story, Pease has glimpsed impending doom and, like some biblical figure, has put aside the things of

the world to question himself and await the outcome of the Lord's plan for him and his family.

It is a tribute to Weaver's art that even as he explores these philosophical dimensions he can keep readers grounded in reality and even in frequent belly laughs. *Men Who Would Be Good* is a handsome addition to Weaver's oeuvre, a group of books that give readers the reality of contemporary Middle America in terms that do more than realism alone could manage.

Interviews:
M. Rohrberger, "An Interview with Gordon Weaver," *Cimarron Review,* 34 (January 1976): 46–52;

Philip Paradis, "Writing Is Like a Bricklayer: An Interview with Gordon Weaver," *Texas Review,* 5 (Fall/Winter 1984): 49–62;

Thomas E. Kennedy, "Nuts, Bolts, and Sheer Plod: An Interview with Gordon Weaver," *Western Humanities Review,* 38 (Winter 1984); 363–371;

Janice Anderson and Carol Harvey, "An Interview with Gordon Weaver," *Cameron Forum,* 12 (1990): 38–40;

Frederick Smiley, "The Craft of Fiction: An Interview with Gordon Weaver," *Writing Teacher,* 4 (January 1991): 5–10.

Bibliography:
Thomas E. Kennedy, "A Gordon Weaver Bibliography," in his "The Uses of Versimilitude: Fiction as Realism, Imagination, Craft in the Short Stories of Three Contemporary American Writers: Andre Dubus, Gladys Swan, Gordon Weaver," volume 2, University of Copenhagen, Ph.D. thesis, 1988.

References:
Ewing Campbell, "Indelible Otherness," *Kenyon Review,* 11 (Spring 1989): 146–150;

Thomas E. Kennedy, "Art as Identity in the Recent Fiction of Gordon Weaver," *Chariton Review,* 15 (Spring 1989): 88–98;

Kennedy, "Fiction as Its Own Subject: An Essay and Two Examples – Anderson's 'Death in the Woods' and Weaver's 'The Parts of Speech,' " *Kenyon Review,* new series 9 (Summer 1987): 59–70;

Kennedy, "Language Against the Void: *Morality Play* and *A World Quite Round*," *Chariton Review,* 13 (Spring 1987): 108–110;

Kennedy, "This Intersection Time: The Fiction of Gordon Weaver," *Hollins Critic,* 22 (February 1985): 1–11.

Tobias Wolff

(19 June 1945 –)

Marilyn C. Wesley
Hartwick College

BOOKS: *Ugly Rumours* (London: Allen & Unwin, 1975);

In the Garden of the North American Martyrs (New York: Ecco, 1981); republished as *Hunters in the Snow* (London: Cape, 1982);

The Barracks Thief (New York: Ecco, 1984); republished as *The Barracks Thief and Selected Stories* (New York: Bantam, 1984);

Back in the World (Boston: Houghton Mifflin, 1985);

This Boy's Life: A Memoir (New York: Atlantic Monthly, 1989).

OTHER: *Matters of Life and Death: New American Short Stories,* edited, with an introduction, by Wolff (Green Harbor, Mass.: Wampeter, 1983);

Anton Chekhov, *A Doctor's Visit,* edited by Wolff (New York: Bantam, 1988).

SELECTED PERIODICAL PUBLICATIONS –
UNCOLLECTED: "A Trip Across the Border," *Mademoiselle,* 84 (July 1978): 132–136;

"A Forgotten Master: Rescuing the Works of Paul Bowles," *Esquire,* 103 (May 1985): 221–222;

"The Other Miller," *Atlantic Monthly,* 257 (June 1986): 56–61;

"Smorgasbord," *Esquire,* 108 (September 1987): 236–244;

"Raymond Carver Had His Cake and Ate It Too," *Esquire,* 112 (September 1989): 240–248;

"Migraine," *Antaeus,* 64–65 (Spring–Autumn 1990): 338–346;

"Long Found Friends," *Life,* 13 (September 1990): 95;

"Sanity," *Atlantic Monthly,* 266 (December 1990): 110–114.

Tobias Wolff provided a definition of the guiding principles behind his own stories in explaining his choices of the works of others for *Matters of Life and Death* (1983), the anthology of contemporary short fiction he edited: "They [these writers]

Tobias Wolff, circa 1990 (photograph by Bob Adelman)

speak to us, without flippancy, about things that matter. They write about what happens between men and women, parents and children. They write about fear of death, fear of life, the feelings that bring people together and force them apart, the costs of intimacy. They remind us that our house is built on sand. They are, every one of them, interested in what it means to be human." In a review of Wolff's first collection, *In the Garden of the North American Martyrs* (1981), Brina Caplan (*Nation,* 6 February 1982) described him as engaged in scrutinizing "the disorders of daily living to find significant order." What his reviewers have consistently understood, and what Wolff himself implies, is that his is a genuinely humanistic fiction — both human and humane.

Born on 19 June 1945 in Birmingham, Alabama, to Rosemary Loftus Wolff, a secretary and waitress, and Arthur Saunders Wolff, an aeronautical engineer, Tobias Jonathan Ansell Wolff is the younger brother of Geoffrey Wolff, also a writer. Tobias earned a B.A. in English in 1972 and an M.A. in 1975 from Oxford University, and an M.A. from Stanford University in 1978. He has been a reporter for the *Washington Post* and served in Vietnam as a lieutenant with the U.S. Army Special Forces (1964–1968). He has held academic posts at Stanford, Goddard College, Arizona State University, and Temple University, and he currently teaches creative writing at Syracuse University. He was married in 1975 to Catherine Delores Spohn, who has worked as an art-history teacher and a social worker; they have two sons, Michael and Patrick.

This Boy's Life: A Memoir (1989), Wolff's autobiographical account of his development from boyhood after World War II to enlistment for sevice in Vietnam, was made into a motion picture starring Robert De Niro in 1993; it both charts a young man's powerful impetus to establish a masculine identity and questions the familial and social limits conditioning that development. According to Joel Connaroe (*New York Times Book Review,* 15 January 1989), the "book reads very much like a collection of short stories, each with its own beginning, middle and end." Each chapter has the conflict, characterization, and internal coherence of an economical short story, and Wolff admits to occasionally altering the facts to suit the needs of the narratives, although his mother did say that the account was probably "about 85 percent true." Indeed, in terms of themes, tone, and style, the chapters of the memoir have much in common with Wolff's preceding short fiction.

"All my stories are in one way or another autobiographical," Wolff once declared. "Sometimes they're autobiographical in the actual events which they describe, sometimes more in their depiction of a particular character. In fact, you could say that all of my characters are reflections of myself, in that I share their wish to count for something and their almost complete confusion as to how this is supposed to be done." This authorial desire for prestige, vaguely defined, and the "confusion" about the manner of its attainment, central to *This Boy's Life,* is also the chief issue unifying many of the stories of his *In the Garden of the North American Martyrs.*

When the young Wolff embarked on a plan to create an identity acceptable to the admissions staffs of upper-class prep schools, he read Vance Packard's *The Status Seekers,* not as the critique of moneyed America it intends to be but as a how-to manual for social climbers. As Wolff says in *This Boy's Life,* "I didn't read it as social criticism. To seek status seemed the most natural thing in the world to me. . . . He listed the places you should live and the colleges you should go to and the faith you should confess. He named the tailors you should patronize, and described with filigree exactitude the ways you could betray your origins."

The moral implications of this demanding but unexamined goal of social advancement provide the subject of Wolff's earliest important story, "Smokers," written in 1976 and included in his 1981 collection. Critic Francine Prose calls its creation a "breakthrough." "For the first time," Wolff explained to Prose, "I'd gone honestly back to my own experience and tried to deal with it — not as confessional but as moral question."

"Smokers" is the first-person account of an unlikely trio of schoolboys during the narrator's first term at Choate (the prep school Wolff's brother, Geoffrey, attended). Eugene, the first boy introduced, makes the narrator deeply uncomfortable: "I did not like to look at Eugene. His head was too big for his lanky body, and his skin was oily. He put me in mind of a seal. Then there was the matter of his scholarship. I too was a scholarship boy. . . . I knew the world Eugene came from. I came from that world too, and I wanted to leave it behind."

Eugene seems the alter ego rejected for all too clearly reflecting the narrator's class origins, but Eugene's roommate, Talbot Nevin, personifies the narrator's class aspirations. Talbot's father has not only won fame for handsomely endowing the school but has taken second place in the Monaco Grand Prix. In opting for class privilege, the narrator has to disregard Eugene's generous spirit and genuine talents and also ignore Talbot's lack of concern for others. When Eugene is "sent down" (expelled) because the school disciplinarian smells cigarette smoke in the room he shares with Talbot (who, of the three boys, is the one most guilty of smoking), the narrator snags Talbot, the embodiment of his desires, for his own roommate. The story concludes with an uneasy equivocation: "It wasn't as if some great injustice had been done." But in a review for the *New Statesman* (12 August 1983) Alan Brien describes "Smokers" as "a brilliantly sketched dormitory episode of self-deceit and snobbery."

Dust jacket for Wolff's first collection of short fiction, stories unified by the characters' desires for prestige and their attempts to attain it

The injustices Wolff narrates, though small in scope, loom large from a moral perspective, which is precisely the point of "Hunters in the Snow," selected as the title story for the British edition (1982) of *In the Garden of the North American Martyrs*. The protagonists in this story are citizens of the world Wolff tries to escape in *This Boy's Life* – the same world of insufficient opportunity the unnamed narrator of "Smokers" struggles to repress. The protagonists are poor and sad, and at least one of them, Tub, is hungry for something they cannot define but desperately desire. That something is an image of themselves that they can begin to respect. They try to establish that image through the assertion of masculine power ritualized in hunting, but they fail. Their guns afford them self-destruction instead of self-transcendence.

Like "Smokers," "Hunters in the Snow" concerns a trio of young men who differ symbolically, but in the latter story the differences concern psychological rather than class distinctions. Tub's obesity and related awkwardness cast him as the victim, the butt of the group. Kenny, the most verbally

and physically aggressive, plays sadist to Tub's masochist. Frank, apparently trapped in an early marriage, signals his unfocused desire to change his life in what appears to be another dead-end dream, a love affair with a sixteen-year-old babysitter.

During the hunt these conflicting attitudes result in Tub's shooting Kenny. At the conclusion of the story, Tub and Frank are drawing closer together, while Kenny probably freezes or bleeds to death during the long drive to the hospital. Wolff admits to reservations about the use of irony: "Irony is . . . a way of not talking about the unspeakable. It is used to deflect or even deny what is difficult, painful, dangerous," he warns in his introduction to *Matters of Life and Death*. However, "Hunters in the Snow" is a superb example of structural irony used to suggest, rather than deny, the complexity of experience. During the course of the story, each character reverses his former psychological role by acting out its buried contradiction.

Kenny sets the sequence of psychological reversal in motion when he shoots a farmer's dog on the way in from their unproductive hunt. The others never doubt that this is a mean-spirited act meant to counter disappointment with aggression. When Kenny announces, "I hate that dog" and then, still armed, answers Tub's outrage with the words "I hate you," Tub responds to his perception of a deadly threat by shooting Kenny in the stomach. It turns out, however, that Kenny had been asked by the farmer, on whose property they pursued a deer, to put the old, ailing dog out of his misery. Thus, in the course of a violent moment of misunderstanding, Tub and Kenny have exchanged the positions of aggressor and victim.

During the ensuing attempt at muddled rescue, Frank moves from a passive psychology to an active acceptance. When he and Tub stop to warm themselves over cups of coffee, leaving the injured man in the stormy cold of the back of the pickup truck, the heightened tension of the afternoon leads them to an exchange of confidences. This newfound camaraderie makes both participants "feel good," but the suggestion at the end of the story – that Kenny will probably not survive – questions a philosophy of simplified love that ignores the sometimes deadly consequences.

While the effect of "Hunters in the Snow" is to question simplistic solutions to the problems of isolation and confusion, "The Liar," a story closer to Wolff's attitudes expressed in the later story "Coming Attractions" and his autobiography, endorses imaginary responses to genuine predicaments. The precipitating event in "The Liar" is the cancer-caused death of the young narrator's father, with whom the narrator, James, had shared a similar style and point of view.

An event before the father's death serves as an emblem for that similarity and for their differences from the other members of the family. On a summer vacation to Yosemite, the family is visited by a large and hungry bear: "Mother had made a tuna casserole and it must have smelled to him like something worth dying for." James's mother responds by making the children sing "Row Row Row Your Boat" in loud voices to frighten off the bear, and when that does not work, she pitches rocks until the persistent bear shambles just beyond the campsite. James's father, however, insists that the family break camp, and he jokes all the way home to cover his fear. A genuine capacity to recognize the potential for harm in the world separates the father from his practical wife and unites him to his more sensitive son, who must witness the pain of his father's death: "When I thought of other boys being close to their fathers I thought of them hunting together, tossing a ball back and forth, making birdhouses in the basement, and having long talks about girls, war, careers. Maybe the reason it took us so long to get close was that I had this idea. It kept getting in the way of what we really had, which was a shared fear."

The indirection of James's symptomatic responses to his father's death at first only confuses his pragmatic mother, and it finally humiliates her when she discovers his habit of telling anyone who will listen – neighbors, storekeepers, family members, and strangers on buses – tragic (untrue) tales about his surviving relatives, particularly his mother: "What got mother was ... where I said that she had been coughing up blood and the doctors weren't sure what was wrong with her, but that we were hoping for the best."

James's lies are psychologically essential, of course; they create a means of expressing the fear his mother's practicality denies, and they even enable him to re-create the fellowship of commiseration that he shared with his father. Wolff once said that the primary impulse behind "The Liar" connects his personal experience and the potential of fiction: "I was a liar myself when I was a kid. I'm still a liar, really, and I don't just mean in terms of telling stories or being a story writer. I wouldn't ever want to be held to a literal version of the facts when I tell a story. I don't know that I'm capable of it. It's not the way I get at things."

Like James in "The Liar," the young Wolff in *This Boy's Life* needs lies to "get at things": his lies

create a necessary reality his environment suppresses. Of the persona he invented for prep-school applications, Wolff observes: in "the boy who lived in their letters, the splendid phantom who carried all my hopes, it seemed to me I saw, at last, my own face."

The striking structural shift at the conclusion of "Poaching," another story from *In the Garden of the North American Martyrs,* also endorses the value of alternative vision. Wharton, the father in the story, is the kind of self-justifying prig who knows what is best for everyone around him: "His wife, Ellen, was deficient in many respects, and resented his constructive criticism. . . . George, their son, slouched around the house all day and paid no attention when Wharton described all the sports and hobbies that an eleven-year-old boy ought to be interested in." Despite the limited-omniscient point of view that presents Wharton's perspective, most readers sympathize with Ellen and George and understand why Ellen refuses to accompany the family north when Wharton moves back to the countryside to try to establish the kind of life he thinks his wife and son should be leading. Nor are readers likely to be surprised when this effort is apparently disappointing. What is surprising, however, is the epiphany at the end of the story. When Wharton goes out to confront the hunter who has been poaching on his land, there is tension, for Wharton "had felt foolish and afraid for so long he was becoming dangerous." But instead of the masculine confrontation to which the story appears to be leading, Wharton sights a beaver swimming across the pond. This experience, like the moose emerging from the forest of Nova Scotia in Elizabeth Bishop's poem "The Moose," seems to afford Wharton one of those serendipitous experiences of natural grace for which he no doubt came to the woods, and it leads to one of those small but significant moments that make up successful family life. When Wharton tells his son and his visiting wife about the appearance and behavior of the beaver, they return together to the pond to share an uplifting moment: "Out in the pond the beaver dove and surfaced again. It seemed to Wharton, watching him move in wide circles in the water, that the creature had been sent to them, that they had been offered an olive branch and were not far from home."

This sublime and sentimental moment in the life of the family, which has little experience with either emotion, has already been undercut, though, in advance of its presentation. The paragraphs immediately preceding it foreshadow the events that will probably follow the epiphany: the beaver will

Dust jacket for Wolff's autobiography, in which he structured the chapters like short stories, sometimes altering facts for thematic purposes and consequently creating an account that his mother calls "about 85 percent true"

be shot by a crude neighbor; Ellen will leave at the end of the week, never to return to Wharton; and young George will be set upon cruelly by an acquaintance the story has recently introduced. Nevertheless, the ending epiphany is not ironic. By providing the outline of the story in advance, as in tragedy, Wolff achieves for it something of the effect of the dignified conclusion of that form. But unlike the pity and fear resulting from tragedy, this ending retains its optimism, as a lie that can point Wharton toward a genuine, authentic vision worth his pursuit.

In his fiction, Wolff characteristically treats the complexity of human experience, considering related themes prismatically and altering the perspective from story to story. Even though equivocation is endorsed as necessary fiction in much of Wolff's work, falseness may also be repudiated when it is employed as a defense against meaningful

experience, a theme uniting several stories in his first collection: "Next Door," "An Episode in the Life of Professor Brooke," "Face to Face," "Maiden Voyage," "Worldly Goods," and the title story, "In the Garden of the North American Martyrs," in which a female college professor, who has adopted a false persona as a comfortable means of getting along in the world, finally refuses to lie, offering her audience, instead, a symbolic account of its own inhumanity. It is these stories, often concerning middle-class men and women rather than impoverished boys, which most impressed critic Lee Anne Schrieber (*New York Times Book Review*, 15 November 1981). Wolff's intention, she declared, is to "undermine our complacency."

In 1984 Wolff published *The Barracks Thief*, a novella of seventy-three pages, which won the P.E.N./Faulkner Award for Fiction in 1985. Reviewer Mona Simpson defined Wolff's achievement in this piece, as elsewhere, when she described *The Barracks Thief* as a deftly staged "small-scale moral drama" (*New Republic*, 9 December 1985). The novella seems to take up where Wolff's later autobiography leaves off: it introduces a protagonist, Philip, whose defining youthful experiences of paternal abandonment relate him to the young Toby Wolff (in *This Boy's Life*), and it follows him into basic training preliminary to service in Vietnam. The initial scene shows that Philip's father has formed "the habit" of stopping in his sons' room at night to consider them thoughtfully. In their presence he feels a "peace" that generates "fear": "The worst fear he had was that by loving his children so much he was somehow endangering them." He also "tried to imagine what form the evil might take."

After the father leaves the mother and is alienated from his family, Keith Bishop, his youngest son, turns into a teenager confused by drugs, and later he is an adult confused by life. But the main story concerns the older son, Philip. In psychological terms it is the story of a young man trying to find a masculine identity through its public symbols because of the private experience of his father's absence.

Specifically the plot centers on related episodes in Philip's training experience in the army. After basic instruction as a paratrooper, he is transferred to Fort Bragg, where, as an untried soldier, he understands he will feel left out of the small community of veterans until he has been tested by military experience. One Fourth of July he is thrown together with two other newcomers to guard a seedy munitions storage site. When a nearby forest fire causes some locals to warn them to leave the area because they might be in danger, the young men decide not to abandon their post. Out of this shared act of masculine bravado a companionship develops: "We turned in our rifles and lingered outside the orderly room. We didn't want to go away from each other. Without saying so, we believed we had done something that day, that we were proven men. We weren't, of course, but we thought we were and that was a sweet thing to believe for an hour or two."

In the group, besides Philip, there is Hubbard, whose best friends are killed in a drunken accident on that same Fourth of July; Hubbard deserts before he can be shipped overseas. The third, Lewis, is an isolated loser who is ultimately revealed as the barracks thief of the title. Although he does not understand the reason, Lewis steals to try to establish some form of human connection. Ostensibly he wants the money to try for a sexual relationship with a prostitute, but his later impotence ultimately stands for his general inability to effect human contact. In fact, by being a thief Lewis is inadvertently declaring his exclusion from society. As a respected sergeant puts the matter: "an infantry company was like a family, a family without any women in it, but a family. He wanted the thief to think about that, and then ask himself one question: What sort of a man would turn his back on his own kind?" Lewis is eventually given a dishonorable discharge. As Wolff explained to Bonnie Lyons and Bill Oliver in a 1990 interview, "Philip feels accused . . . he feels . . . complicity with Lewis. . . . As for the thief himself, I wanted to give the sense of a person who has no attachment to the past, who has been tremendously hurt by it but is cut off from his consciousness of it."

Lewis's failure to achieve the family-type connection of male fellowship afforded by the military makes him an alter ego of Philip, who is also less than consciously seeking in the army the things of which he has been deprived by his past, especially by his father's absence. Lewis, then, is the personification of the "fear" and the "evil" presaged by the initial scene. When other soldiers take revenge on Lewis, Philip sees in his frightened look a more universal expression, "full of humiliation and fear," which he later observes in his own brother and in Vietnamese captives during American interrogations.

The military contexts of this fundamental expression of fear are not fully developed in the story, which does not deal with the experience of war in Vietnam. As a member of the U.S. Army Special Forces trained in the Vietnamese language, Wolff spent a year as an adviser to Vietnamese troops. Ac-

cording to Prose, he is reluctant to talk about his war experience, and he has not yet written about it directly, although he remarked to Lyons and Oliver that the "boyhood obsession with weapons" in *This Boy's Life* "has a terminus somewhere, that it ends in war. There's a logical progression of the kind of life that boys are encouraged to lead and dream of in this country. There's a lot of violence in the book — a lot of male violence. That kind of thing all goes somewhere."

An important general theme of Wolff's second collection of stories, *Back in the World* (1985), concerns the effects of that violence after the war is over. "The Poor Are Always With Us," for example, introduces a Vietnam veteran who gambles away not just one but two automobiles, which reveals his inability to cope with his postwar world. "Soldier's Joy," the story that includes the title of the collection, returns most directly to the preoccupations of *The Barracks Thief*. This story concerns another trio of soldiers in a similar setting, a State-side army camp, on a similar mission – guard duty. The difference is that the emotional center of the story is not the consciousness of the outsider but the protective fellowship of the already initiated. Hooper, a twenty-one-year veteran recently busted to PFC, is in charge of two younger soldiers who have been furnished with live ammunition with which to guard the camp communications center. Although the ammunition is supposed to be "strictly for show," it represents a temptation neither of the younger men can resist. Porchoff, nicknamed Porkchop by the men in his unit, threatens to use it to kill himself because he has not found the camaraderie in the service that his father's army stories led him to anticipate: "My dad was in the National Guard back in Ohio. . . . He's always talking about the great experiences his buddies used to have, camping out and so on. Nothing like that ever happens to me."

In trying to talk him out of suicide, Hooper reveals that the Vietnam War constitutes his most fulfilling experience: "it was a kind of home. It was where he went to be back with his friends again, and his old self. It was where Hooper drifted when he was too low to care how much lower he'd be when he drifted back, and lost it all again." Being "back in the world" meant "confusion" only the intensity of the battlefield could clarify, which is exactly what occurs. Trac, the other guard, a young man only recently returned from the war, re-creates the destructive clarity of his war experience. In what is apparently a flashback, he shoots and kills Porchoff to resolve the situation. Trac and Hooper

Wolff, circa 1989 (photograph © Jerry Bauer)

draw together at the conclusion of the story to cover up the incident. The death of the isolated young man implies that the desirable masculine connection created by the violent rituals of male bonding is purchased at great cost.

The desirability of an exclusively male world is the issue of "Sister." At the beginning of an athletic workout on a fitness trail that Marty, the female protagonist, has obviously taken pains to live beside, she stops to try to ingratiate herself with two men, one of whom has rejected her in the past. At first her conversation with them seems to be flirtation, but behind her desire to attract them to her as a woman is her motivating wish to share their masculine experience, to be "one of the boys." Her athletic interests serve a similar function, and the key is her envy of her brother's activities. When she is almost hit by a car and the two men do not react with concern, or even any verbal reassurance, Marty is overwhelmed with the realization of her own isolation: "Marty understood that there was never going to be anyone to tell her these things. She had no idea why this should be so; it was just something she knew. There was no need for her to make a fool of herself again."

Marty feels her isolation in imagery of exclusion from the special prerogatives of male companionship: "Her brother and his friends would be coming off the marsh now, flushed with cold and drink, their dogs running ahead through the reeds and the tall grass. When they reach the car they'll compare birds and pass a bottle around, and after the bottle is empty they will head for the nearest bar. Do boilermakers. Stuff themselves with pickled eggs and jerky. Throw dice from a leather cup. And outside in the car the dogs will be waiting, ears pricked for the least sound, sometimes whimpering to themselves, but mostly tense, and still, watching the bright door the men have closed behind them."

"Sister" gives expression to the desirable exclusivity of the bond shared by similar men, but another story that focuses on a woman signifies the necessity of difference. "Say Yes" is the story of a brief interlude in a staid and comfortable marriage in which the partners love and respect one another. The occasion is a conversation over the shared task of doing the dishes (a signifier of partnership, a shared belief in the middle-class politics of equality). The talk turns to whether or not the husband would have married his wife if she were a black woman. He is adamant that he would not have — not for reasons of racism, he insists, but because then they would not have shared a similar background. Black people, he explains, " 'don't come from the same culture we do. Listen to them sometime — they even have their own language. That's okay with me, I *like* hearing them talk' — he did; for some reason it always made him feel happy — 'but it's different. A person from their culture and a person from our culture could never really *know* each other.' "

The point of the story is not to uncover liberal prejudice but to reveal a necessary zone of otherness even in the most ordinary of places, a positive bit of unknowability even in the most intimate relationships. The last words, a position for which Wolff reserves his finest effects, suggest that the husband's belief in the couple's unquestioned similarity is both fallacious and actually undesirable. Before they go to bed, the husband apologizes for his position, which has deeply offended the wife, but she does not appear to acquiesce to his invitation to reconciliation. The difference between them creates an estrangement, a rift, but also a healthy defamiliarization, a "making strange," the effect of art's ability to renew interest in the world, an effect both frightening and exciting: "The room was silent. His heart pounded the way it had on their first night together, the way it still did when he woke at a noise in the darkness and waited to hear it again – the sound of someone moving through the house, a stranger."

For better or worse the world Wolff's protagonists must return to and cope with has for him a meaning that extends beyond the military expression he employs for the title of *Back in the World.* "It wasn't just Vietnam," he explained to Lyons and Oliver. " 'The world' is what people in religious orders – nuns and priests – call secular life. That's the way Jesus talks about it: The world's yoke is heavy, my yoke is light." In "The Missing Person," the story that addresses most directly the religious implications of the collection, Father Leo begins his vocation with the expectation of becoming a missionary: "it was the life he wanted, a life full of risk among people who needed him and were hungry for what he had to give." However, even the priesthood turns out to be a worldly profession, with political pitfalls he is inadequate to negotiate. Instead of a mission in the Aleutians, Father Leo winds up serving a convent as the front man for a con artist charged with raising the funds to save it. The "church is not a benign presence in this story," Wolff told Lyons and Oliver: "The story describes how the foundations [of the convent] are rotting, the basements filled with scummy water, and they're paying crooks to keep it going. I am a Catholic, but that's the way I see the institutional church – I think it's the cross the believers have to bear."

The end of the story finds Father Leo in what, from the institutional perspective, would appear to be a compromising situation. He is spending the night in a Las Vegas hotel room with a lonely woman who has been trying to seduce him. But, from the perspective of the necessity of reinventing a humane system of religious values central to Wolff's fiction, he is, perhaps for the first time, acting the part of a charitable priest: "Leo's been offered another way of seeing his place in the world and of becoming reconciled to it," Wolff declared.

Wolff's stories are influenced by those of Flannery O'Connor, he acknowledged in the Lyons-Oliver interview, but whereas her works concern the choice between salvation and damnation demanded by conventional Catholic dogma, his pertain to "moral choice." Genuine moral choices in Wolff's fiction always articulate the conditions necessary to the establishment of community. While some characters, however blunderingly – like Father Leo – are able to make such choices, *Back in the World* also presents instances of immorality. "Our Story Begins," "Leviathan," and "Desert Break-

down, 1968" all concern the failure to achieve a sense of community.

"Desert Breakdown, 1968" concerns a young father's literal abandonment of his wife and child. Wolff told Lyons and Oliver that it is the story of a "doomed" family. This story illustrates what Wolff's autobiography makes clear: that family commitment or its equivalent is the primary human value, a value threatened in complex ways by the specter of male abandonment. The centrality of this issue in Wolff's life and work lends even greater profundity to "The Rich Brother," the moral parable that concludes *Back in the World.*

The story is an answer to the biblical question "Am I my brother's keeper?" During an episode in which Pete, the older and financially solvent brother, is called on once again to rescue his ineffectual and generous brother, Donald, there is a verbal exchange in which Pete insists that Donald share the details of trivial but painful incidents leading up to his latest failure. Donald accuses Pete of wanting to make him "look foolish" because Pete has "no purpose in life" and is "afraid to relate to people who do." Donald also reminds Pete of a childhood incident: "Do you remember when you tried to kill me?" Recovering from stomach surgery, the younger boy was then particularly vulnerable to his older brother's attack: "I would hear you coming down the hall, and I would pretend to be asleep . . . you remember Peter, you have to – you'd sit next to me on the bed and pull the sheets back. If I was on my stomach you'd roll me over. Then you would lift my pajama top and start hitting me on the stitches. You'd hit me as hard as you could over and over."

By not slighting the significant differences between the brothers in the story (one is insensitively materialistic while the other is maddeningly naive) and without denying the competitive hostility that is probably an inevitable part of the fraternal relation, the story is able to evade the trap of sentimentality to answer its implicit question positively. The story shows the brothers abandoning one another, but it also promises the restoration of their bond.

Russell Banks, writing in the *New York Times Book Review* (20 October 1985), hailed "The Rich Brother" as a "small classic about family life in America, what's left of it," but his review generally differed from the dominant view and evaluated *Back in the World* as "a falling off" from Wolff's previous fiction. Wolff's next work, *This Boy's Life,* garnered high praise from all who reviewed it. Connaroe hailed it as "literate and consistently entertaining –

and richer, and darker, and funnier than anything else Tobias Wolff has written."

Certain of his own perspective and comfortable with his own voice, Wolff is generous in acknowledging his influences and in praising the writers he admires. Undoubtedly the greatest influence has been that of his older brother, Geoffrey, whose intervention and example gave Wolff his first glimpse of the possibilities beyond the narrow world evoked in *This Boy's Life*. He described his brother to Prose as "the first person I'd ever met for whom books were the only way in which you could in good conscience spend your life." As Wolff told Prose, another nurturing relation was with the late Raymond Carver, a friend with whom Wolff taught at Goddard and Syracuse: "Ray's work gave me a sense of confirmation about what I was doing. I felt an immediate affinity for his standards of honesty and exactness, his refusal to do anything cheap in a story, to destroy his characters with irony that proved his own virtue." Wolff feels indebted as well to O'Connor, John Cheever, Ernest Hemingway, Anton Chekhov, Paul Bowles, Sherwood Anderson, Guy de Maupassant, and Albert Camus, and Wolff's book-jacket endorsements read like a list of "Who's Who" in contemporary literature. He has been praised by Carver, Annie Dillard, and Ann Beattie, among others, and he has been awarded various fellowships and honors, including O. Henry short-story prizes in 1980, 1981, and 1985; the St. Lawrence Award for Fiction in 1982; a Guggenheim Fellowship in 1985; and the P.E.N./Faulkner Award in 1985.

When critic Leslie Fiedler described American writing as a vast book for boys, he was criticizing a literary culture that chose to ignore the existence of women except as sexual objects and restrictive mothers, to deny the possibility of sexual love, and to exclude the mundane experiences of adult life. The title of Wolff's autobiography acknowledges his participation in this tradition, but his fiction — which includes banality while insisting on fugitive instances of transcendence, is mostly about men but appreciates women, and explores brutality but chooses compassion — redefines the scope of a male-dominated society that became technically accomplished while it remained morally deficient.

Wolff's concern about moral choice and his psychological preoccupation with familial connections are the primary issues of his oeuvre, which seems an inquiry into the conditions necessary for the establishment of positive identity or self-esteem, but these terms are pedantic and polemic compared to the delicacy of his stylistic presentation. The need he writes about is overwhelming, endemic in American social experience, but in Wolff's fiction its recognition is subtle, and the moments of its fulfillment are as elusive and graceful as the images in Japanese haiku. Yet his prose style is so direct, his vocabulary so consistently accessible, as to make what he describes democratic — a body of writing about the most basic needs of Everyman, written with a respect that Everyman deserves, Wolff insists, but rarely attains.

Interviews:

Jonathan Gill, "Fourth Grade Never Dies Out," *New York Times Book Review,* 15 January 1989, p. 28;

Bonnie Lyons and Bill Oliver, "An Interview with Tobias Wolff," *Contemporary Literature,* 31 (Spring 1990): 1–16.

References:

David Gates, "Our Stories, Our Selves," *Newsweek,* 113 (23 January 1989): 64;

Francine Prose, "The Brothers Wolff," *New York Times Magazine,* 5 February 1989, pp. 22–31;

Geoffrey Wolff, "Advice My Brother Never Took," *New York Times Book Review,* 20 August 1989, pp. 1, 22.

Books for Further Reading

Allen, Frederick Lewis. *The Big Change: America Transforms Itself.* New York: Harper, 1952.

Allen, Walter. *The Short Story in English.* Oxford: Clarendon / New York: Oxford University Press, 1981.

Bates, H. E. *The Modern Short Story: A Critical Survey.* Boston: Writer, 1965.

Bruck, Peter. *The Black American Short Story in the 20th Century.* Amsterdam: Gruner, 1977.

Hendin, Josephine. *Vulnerable People: A View of American Fiction Since 1945.* New York & London: Oxford University Press, 1978.

Hooper, Brad. *Short-Story Writers and Their Work.* Chicago: American Library Association, 1988.

Ingram, Forrest L. *Representative Short-Story Cycles of the Twentieth Century.* The Hague: Mouton, 1971.

Kenner, Hugh. *A Homemade World: The American Modernist Writer.* New York: Knopf, 1974.

Klinkowitz, Jerome. *The Practice of Fiction in America.* Ames: Iowa State University Press, 1980.

Klinkowitz. *The Self-Apparent Word: Fiction as Language/Language as Fiction.* Carbondale: Southern Illinois University Press, 1984.

Klinkowitz. *Structuring the Void: The Struggle for Subject in Contemporary American Fiction.* Durham, N.C.: Duke University Press, 1992.

Lohafer, Susan. *Coming to Terms With the Short Story.* Baton Rouge: Louisiana State University Press, 1983.

Lohafer and Jo Ellen Clarey, eds. *Short-Story Theory at a Crossroads.* Baton Rouge: Louisiana State University Press, 1989.

Mann, Susan Garland. *The Short-Story Cycle.* New York: Greenwood, 1989.

May, Charles E., ed. *Short-Story Theories.* Athens: Ohio University Press, 1976.

Peden, William. *The American Short Story: Continuity and Change, 1940–1975,* second edition. Boston: Houghton Mifflin, 1975.

Reid, Ian. *The Short Story.* London: Methuen / New York: Barnes & Noble, 1977.

Ross, Danforth. *The American Short Story.* Minneapolis: University of Minnesota Press, 1961.

Shaw, Valerie. *The Short Story: A Critical Introduction.* New York & London: Longman, 1983.

Voss, Arthur. *The American Short Story: A Critical Survey.* Norman: University of Oklahoma Press, 1973.

Weaver, Gordon, ed. *The American Short Story: 1945–1980: A Critical History.* Boston: Twayne, 1983.

West, Ray. *The Short Story in America.* Chicago: Regnery, 1952.

Contributors

Michael Basinski...*State University of New York at Buffalo*
Richard L. Blevins...*University of Pittsburgh Greensburg*
Julia B. Boken..*State University of New York College at Oneonta*
Terry Caesar...*Clarion University of Pennsylvania*
Arthur L. Clements.......................................*State University of New York at Binghamton*
William W. Combs...*Western Michigan University*
Maarten van Delden ....*New York University*
James E. Devlin..*State University of New York College at Oneonta*
R. H. W. Dillard ....*Hollins College*
William Dowie...*Southeastern Louisiana University*
Joseph Ferrandino ....*Herkimer County Community College*
Edward Field..*New York City*
David Fine...*California State University, Long Beach*
Denis M. Hennessy......................................*State University of New York College at Oneonta*
Thomas E. Kennedy...*Copenhagen, Denmark*
Jerome Klinkowitz..*University of Northern Iowa*
David Lampe...*State University of New York at Buffalo*
Kevin Lanahan..*State University of New York at Albany*
Paul R. Lilly, Jr.......................................*State University of New York College at Oneonta*
Daniel Lowe...*Community College of Allegheny County*
Michael McKenna ....*State University of New York College at Delhi*
Patrick Meanor ....*State University of New York College at Oneonta*
Patricia Moran ....*University of California, Davis*
Robert Moynihan.......................................*State University of New York College at Oneonta*
Daniel J. Murtaugh ....*University of Kansas*
Joe Nordgren...*Lamar University*
Kathleen K. O'Mara ....*State University of New York College at Oneonta*
Richard Orodenker..*Peirce Junior College*
Charles Plymell...*State University of New York College at Oneonta*
Margaret K. Schramm ....*Hartwick College*
Pat Smith...*University of Michigan*
Andy Solomon ....*University of Tampa*
Taylor Stoehr...*University of Massachusetts — Boston*
Marilyn C. Wesley..*Hartwick College*
Albert E. Wilhelm...*Tennessee Technological University*
Thad Ziolkowski ....*Yale University*

Cumulative Index

Dictionary of Literary Biography, Volumes 1-130
Dictionary of Literary Biography Yearbook, 1980-1992
Dictionary of Literary Biography Documentary Series, Volumes 1-10

Cumulative Index

DLB before number: *Dictionary of Literary Biography,* Volumes 1-130
Y before number: *Dictionary of Literary Biography Yearbook,* 1980-1992
DS before number: *Dictionary of Literary Biography Documentary Series,* Volumes 1-10

A

Cumulative Index

D

G

K

M

N

O

S

T

U

Warr, Bertram 1917-1943 ....DLB-88

Warren, John Byrne Leicester (see De Tabley, Lord)

Warren, Lella 1899-1982 ....Y-83

Warren, Mercy Otis 1728-1814 ....DLB-31

Warren, Robert Penn 1905-1989 .... DLB-2, 48; Y-80, 89

Warton, Joseph 1722-1800 ....DLB-104, 109

Warton, Thomas 1728-1790 ....DLB-104, 109

Washington, George 1732-1799 ....DLB-31

Wassermann, Jakob 1873-1934 ....DLB-66

Wasson, David Atwood 1823-1887 ....DLB-1

Waterhouse, Keith 1929- DLB-13, 15

Waterman, Andrew 1940- DLB-40

Waters, Frank 1902- Y-86

Waters, Michael 1949- DLB-120

Watkins, Tobias 1780-1855 ....DLB-73

Watkins, Vernon 1906-1967 ....DLB-20

Watmough, David 1926- DLB-53

Watson, James Wreford (see Wreford, James)

Watson, Sheila 1909- DLB-60

Watson, Wilfred 1911- DLB-60

Watt, W. J., and Company DLB-46

Watterson, Henry 1840-1921 ....DLB-25

Watts, Alan 1915-1973 ....DLB-16

Watts, Franklin [publishing house] DLB-46

Watts, Isaac 1674-1748 ....DLB-95

Waugh, Auberon 1939- DLB-14

Waugh, Evelyn 1903-1966 ....DLB-15

Way and Williams DLB-49

Wayman, Tom 1945- DLB-53

Weatherly, Tom 1942- DLB-41

Weaver, Gordon 1937- DLB-130

Weaver, Robert 1921- DLB-88

Webb, Frank J. ?-? DLB-50

Webb, James Watson 1802-1884 ....DLB-43

Webb, Mary 1881-1927 ....DLB-34

Webb, Phyllis 1927- DLB-53

Webb, Walter Prescott 1888-1963 ....DLB-17

Webster, Augusta 1837-1894 ....DLB-35

Webster, Charles L., and Company DLB-49

Webster, John 1579 or 1580-1634? DLB-58

Webster, Noah 1758-1843 ....DLB-1, 37, 42, 43, 73

Wedekind, Frank 1864-1918 ....DLB-118

Weems, Mason Locke 1759-1825 .... DLB-30, 37, 42

Weerth, Georg 1822-1856 ....DLB-129

Weidenfeld and Nicolson DLB-112

Weidman, Jerome 1913- DLB-28

Weigl, Bruce 1949- DLB-120

Weinbaum, Stanley Grauman 1902-1935 ....DLB-8

Weintraub, Stanley 1929- DLB-111

Weisenborn, Gunther 1902-1969 ....DLB-69, 124

Weiß, Ernst 1882-1940 ....DLB-81

Weiss, John 1818-1879 ....DLB-1

Weiss, Peter 1916-1982 ....DLB-69, 124

Weiss, Theodore 1916- DLB-5

Weisse, Christian Felix 1726-1804 ....DLB-97

Weitling, Wilhelm 1808-1871 ....DLB-129

Welch, Lew 1926-1971? DLB-16

Weldon, Fay 1931- DLB-14

Wellek, René 1903- DLB-63

Wells, Carolyn 1862-1942 ....DLB-11

Wells, Charles Jeremiah circa 1800-1879 ....DLB-32

Wells, H. G. 1866-1946 ....DLB-34, 70

Wells, Robert 1947- DLB-40

Wells-Barnett, Ida B. 1862-1931 ....DLB-23

Welty, Eudora 1909- DLB-2, 102; Y-87

Wendell, Barrett 1855-1921 ....DLB-71

Wentworth, Patricia 1878-1961 ....DLB-77

Werfel, Franz 1890-1945 ....DLB-81, 124

The Werner Company DLB-49

Werner, Zacharias 1768-1823 ....DLB-94

Wersba, Barbara 1932- DLB-52

Wescott, Glenway 1901- DLB-4, 9, 102

Cumulative Index

(Continued from front endsheets)

117 *Twentieth-Century Caribbean and Black African Writers,* First Series, edited by Bernth Lindfors and Reinhard Sander (1992)

118 *Twentieth-Century German Dramatists, 1889-1918,* edited by Wolfgang D. Elfe and James Hardin (1992)

119 *Nineteenth-Century French Fiction Writers: Romanticism and Realism, 1800-1860,* edited by Catharine Savage Brosman (1992)

120 *American Poets Since World War II,* Third Series, edited by R. S. Gwynn (1992)

121 *Seventeenth-Century British Nondramatic Poets,* First Series, edited by M. Thomas Hester (1992)

122 *Chicano Writers,* Second Series, edited by Francisco A. Lomelí and Carl R. Shirley (1992)

123 *Nineteenth-Century French Fiction Writers: Naturalism and Beyond, 1860-1900,* edited by Catharine Savage Brosman (1992)

124 *Twentieth-Century German Dramatists, 1919-1992,* edited by Wolfgang D. Elfe and James Hardin (1992)

125 *Twentieth-Century Caribbean and Black African Writers,* Second Series, edited by Bernth Lindfors and Reinhard Sander (1993)

126 *Seventeenth-Century British Nondramatic Poets,* Second Series, edited by M. Thomas Hester (1993)

127 *American Newspaper Publishers, 1950-1990,* edited by Perry J. Ashley (1993)

128 *Twentieth-Century Italian Poets,* Second Series, edited by Giovanna Wedel De Stasio, Glauco Cambon, and Antonio Illiano (1993)

129 *Nineteenth-Century German Writers, 1841-1900,* edited by James Hardin and Siegfried Mews (1993)

130 *American Short-Story Writers Since World War II,* edited by Patrick Meanor (1993)

Documentary Series

1 *Sherwood Anderson, Willa Cather, John Dos Passos, Theodore Dreiser, F. Scott Fitzgerald, Ernest Hemingway, Sinclair Lewis,* edited by Margaret A. Van Antwerp (1982)

2 *James Gould Cozzens, James T. Farrell, William Faulkner, John O'Hara, John Steinbeck, Thomas Wolfe, Richard Wright,* edited by Margaret A. Van Antwerp (1982)

3 *Saul Bellow, Jack Kerouac, Norman Mailer, Vladimir Nabokov, John*

Updike, Kurt Vonnegut, edited by Mary Bruccoli (1983)

4 *Tennessee Williams,* edited by Margaret A. Van Antwerp and Sally Johns (1984)

5 *American Transcendentalists,* edited by Joel Myerson (1988)

6 *Hardboiled Mystery Writers: Raymond Chandler, Dashiell Hammett, Ross Macdonald,* edited by Matthew J. Bruccoli and Richard Layman (1989)

7 *Modern American Poets: James Dickey, Robert Frost, Marianne Moore,* edited by Karen L. Rood (1989)

8 *The Black Aesthetic Movement,* edited by Jeffrey Louis Decker (1991)

9 *American Writers of the Vietnam War: W. D. Ehrhart, Larry Heinemann, Tim O'Brien, Walter McDonald, John M. Del Vecchio,* edited by Ronald Baughman (1991)

10 *The Bloomsbury Group,* edited by Edward L. Bishop (1992)

Yearbooks

1980 edited by Karen L. Rood, Jean W. Ross, and Richard Ziegfeld (1981)

1981 edited by Karen L. Rood, Jean W. Ross, and Richard Ziegfeld (1982)

1982 edited by Richard Ziegfeld; associate editors: Jean W. Ross and Lynne C. Zeigler (1983)

1983 edited by Mary Bruccoli and Jean W. Ross; associate editor: Richard Ziegfeld (1984)

1984 edited by Jean W. Ross (1985)

1985 edited by Jean W. Ross (1986)

1986 edited by J. M. Brook (1987)

1987 edited by J. M. Brook (1988)

1988 edited by J. M. Brook (1989)

1989 edited by J. M. Brook (1990)

1990 edited by James W. Hipp (1991)

1991 edited by James W. Hipp (1992)

1992 edited by James W. Hipp (1993)